HEILONGJIANG

• Harbin

• Changchun

JILIN

• Vladivostok

Tumen

*Sea of
Japan*

HOKKAIDO

• Shenyang

LIAONING

NORTH
KOREA

• Pyongyang

Yalu

Liao

NEI MENGGU

• Hohhot

Yellow

• Datong

BEIJING

Beijing

Tianjin

TIANJIN

HEBEI

Bay of
Bohai

⊛ Seoul

SOUTH
KOREA

• Pusan

Sendai

HONSHU

Tokyo ⊛

• Nagoya

• Kyoto

• Osaka

JAPAN

• Taiyuan

SHANXI

Shijiazhuang

SHANDONG

Jinan

• Qufu

Fen

*Yellow
Sea*

KYUSHU

SHIKOKU

• Nagasaki

Luoyang

• Zhengzhou

HENAN

JIANGSU

• Xi'an

XI

Huai

ANHUI

Nanjing

Han

• Suizhou

• Hefei

Suzhou

Shanghai

SHANGHAI

Yangzi

Hankou

Lake
Tai

Hangzhou

• Ningbo

HUBEI

Fuchun

*East
China
Sea*

RYUKYU ISLANDS

Dongting
Lake

Poyang
Lake

ZHEJIANG

Yuan

• Nanchang

• Changsha

JIANGXI

Gan

Xiao

Xiang

HUNAN

• Fuzhou

FUJIAN

JANGXI

• Taipei

*PACIFIC
OCEAN*

TAIWAN

• Xiamen

GUANGDONG

Xi

• Guangzhou

• Xianggang

HONG KONG

nning

South China Sea

• Haikou

HAINAN

PHILIPPINES

┴┬┴	Modern Grand Canal
⌇⌇⌇	Great Wall
──	Province boundaries in China
▤	North China Plain
▓	Area of major loess deposits

Pre-Modern East Asia: To 1800

A Cultural, Social, and Political History
Second Edition

PATRICIA EBREY
University of Washington–Seattle

ANNE WALTHALL
University of California–Irvine

JAMES PALAIS
Late of University of Washington–Seattle

HOUGHTON MIFFLIN COMPANY
Boston   New York

Publisher: *Suzanne Jeans*
Senior Sponsoring Editor: *Nancy Blaine*
Senior Marketing Manager: *Katherine Bates*
Senior Developmental Editor: *Tonya Lobato*
Senior Project Editor: *Jane Lee*
Art and Design Manager: *Jill Haber*
Cover Design Director: *Tony Saizon*
Senior Photo Editor: *Jennifer Meyer Dare*
Composition Buyer: *Chuck Dutton*
New Title Project Manager: *James Lonergan*
Editorial Assistant: *Stacey Walker*
Marketing Associate: *Lauren Bussard*
Editorial Assistant: *Anne Finley*

Cover image: *Tang Dynasty (618–906 C.E.). Mendicant Friar.* Tang Dynasty, Mural from Dunhuang, Sinkiang Musée des Arts Asiatiques-Guimet, Paris, France/Erich Lessing/Art Resource, NY

Text credits appear after page 294.

Printed in the U.S.A.

Library of Congress Catalog Number: 2008926851

ISBN 13: 978-0-547-00539-3
ISBN 10: 0-547-00539-3

1 2 3 4 5 6 7 8 9-RRD-12 11 10 09 08

CONTENTS

MAPS AND FIGURES

PREFACE

There are many reasons to learn about East Asia. A fifth of the world's population lives there. Every day newspapers carry articles on the rapid transformations of the world economy that make China, Japan, and Korea a growing presence in our lives. Globalization means that not only are people crossing the Pacific in ever increasing numbers, but also that American popular culture draws from many sources in East Asia, from Korean martial arts to Japanese anime and Chinese films.

But why approach East Asia through its history, rather than, say, its economy or contemporary culture? Many reasons can be offered. One cannot gain an adequate understanding of modern phenomena without knowing the stages and processes that led up to them. Moreover, all of the countries of East Asia are strongly historically minded. To a much greater extent than in the United States, people know and identify with people and events of a thousand or more years ago. In all three countries, people still read for pleasure *The Three Kingdoms,* a novel written in fourteenth-century China about the leaders of three contending states in third-century China. Historical consciousness also underlies the strong sense of separate identities among the people of China, Korea, and Japan. The fact that time and again Korea was able to protect its independence despite the attempts of both China and Japan to conquer it is a central part of Korean identity today. Yet another reason to learn about East Asia in the past is its comparative value. As a region that developed nearly independently of the West, East Asia sheds light on the variety of ways human beings have found meaning, formed communities, and governed themselves, expanding our understanding of the human condition.

When the three authors of this volume were students themselves (in the 1960s and 1970s), the fullest and most up-to-date textbook on East Asia was the two-volume set published in 1960 and 1965 by Houghton Mifflin, *East Asia: The Great Tradition* and *East Asia: The Modern Transformation,* written by Edwin O. Reischauer, John K. Fairbank, and Albert M. Craig. Not only did we learn the basic political chronology from these books, but they introduced us to such central issues as the dynastic cycle, the interplay of the Chinese and "barbarians," the ways Korea and Japan adapted features of the Chinese model, the challenge posed by the West in the nineteenth century, and modern revolutionary movements. When it came time for us to develop our own research agendas, these books still cast a shadow as we pursued questions that they did not pose or delved more deeply into topics that they covered only superficially.

It was because we respected these books that we were willing to listen when Nancy Blaine of Houghton Mifflin approached us about doing a new history of East Asia for the current generation of students. We knew that the task would be daunting. Could we take into account the wealth of scholarship that had been published in the forty-odd years since the original *East Asia* books and yet produce the leaner, more visual book requested by students and teachers today? As we discussed how to meet these challenges, we came up with a plan for this book.

COMPARABLE COVERAGE OF KOREA

The growth of Korean studies over the last quarter-century now makes it possible to give Korea comparable coverage to China and Japan (we ended up giving China about 50 percent of the space, Japan 30 percent, and Korea 20 percent). We know that many teachers have been frustrated in their attempts to cover Korea in their East Asia courses for lack of suitable materials and hope that our efforts prove useful to both them and their students.

A BROAD FOCUS: CONNECTIONS CHAPTERS

A second key decision we made was to search for ways to keep in mind the larger whole as we told the separate stories of China, Korea, and Japan. Our solution was to periodically zoom out to look at the wider region from a global or world-historical perspective. Thus, after every few chapters we have inserted a mini-chapter on developments that link the societies of East Asia both to each other and to the larger global context. We have labeled these mini-chapters "Connections" because they put their emphasis on the many ways each society was connected to what went on outside it. For instance, the origins and spread of Buddhism are of great importance to all of the societies of East Asia, but much of the story can be told as a common story that connects East Asia with the rest of Asia. Similarly, many books write about World War II in East Asia in entirely different ways from in their China and Japan chapters. By stepping back and writing about the war from a more global perspective, we can help students see the larger picture.

BALANCED CULTURAL, SOCIAL, AND POLITICAL HISTORY

Even though the volume of scholarship on East Asia has increased manyfold since the original *East Asia* set was written, we decided to honor its example of striving for balanced coverage of the different strands of history. A basic political narrative is essential to give students a firm sense of chronology and to let them think about issues of change. Moreover, there is no denying that the creation of state structures has much to do with how people lived their lives. Even the fact that people think of themselves as "Chinese," "Korean," or "Japanese" is largely a by-product of political history.

We also believed that students should gain an understanding of the philosophies and religions of East Asia. Confucianism and Buddhism have both been of great importance throughout the region, but in very diverse ways, as the historical context has continually changed. Other elements of high culture also deserve coverage, such as the arts of poetry and calligraphy.

Yet we did not want to neglect topics in social, cultural, and economic history, where much of our own work has been concentrated. Even if the state is important to understanding how people lived, so were families, villages, and religious sects. We also wanted to bring in the results of scholarship on those who had been marginalized in the traditional histories, from laborers and minorities to women at all social levels.

A NARROW FOCUS: BIOGRAPHIES, DOCUMENTS, AND MATERIAL CULTURE

The danger of trying to cover so much is that we would have to stay at a high level of generalization. To keep our readers engaged and bring our story down to earth, we decided to devote three or four pages per chapter to closer looks at specific people, documents, and material objects.

Biographies

Most chapters have a one-page biography, often about someone who would not normally be mentioned in a history book. Although we found few truly ordinary people to write about for the earlier periods, we still ended up with a diverse set of individuals. The people sketched range from the most accomplished (such as the eminent Chinese poet Du Fu and the Korean admiral Yi Sunsin) to remarkably ordinary people (such as a woman whose job was to mind the neighborhood telephone). Three military men are portrayed; others were physicians, entrepreneurs, and founders of religious sects. We also have included some agitators and revolutionaries, and even a winning volleyball coach.

Documents

In our chapters we frequently cite short passages from primary sources, but we thought that students would also benefit from texts long enough for them to get a sense of the genre, the author's point of view, and the circumstances described. A few of those we have included were written by famous writers, such as Fukuzawa Yūkichi and Lu Xun. Some are excerpted from well-known pieces of literature, such as the play *The Peony Pavilion*. Others will be less familiar to teachers and students alike. Legal documents have been selected for what they reveal of ordinary people's lives. Religious texts of several sorts were chosen to help us see religion and popular beliefs in action. Many authors are utterly serious, complaining bitterly of war or corruption, for instance; others have well-developed senses of humor. All of the documents selected prompt active involvement and critical interpretation because they get readers to listen to the concerns of people of the past.

Material Culture

Texts are not our only sources for reconstructing the past; there is much to be discovered from material remains of many sorts. To give focus to this dimension of history, for each chapter we have selected one element of material culture to describe in some detail. These range from the most mundane—food, drink, clothing, houses, and means of transportation—to objects of art, including specific paintings, sculptures, or performing arts. Many of the objects discussed have economic significance—for example, fertilizers and the Grand Canal. Most of the features for the late nineteenth or twentieth century bring out ways material culture has changed along with so much else in modern times—from changes in the food people eat to new ways to amuse themselves.

THINKING LIKE A HISTORIAN

The "Documents" and "Material Culture" features challenge students to draw inferences from primary materials much the way historians do. Another way we have tried to help students learn to think like historians is to present history as a set of questions more than a set of answers. What historians are able to say about a period or topic depends not only on the sources available, but also the questions asked. To help students see this, we begin each chapter with a brief discussion of the sorts of questions that motivate contemporary historians to do research on the time period. Most of these questions have no easy answers; these are not questions students will be able to answer simply by reading the chapter. Rather they are real questions, ones interesting enough to motivate historians to sift through recalcitrant evidence in their efforts to find answers. The earliest chapter on Korea, for instance, poses the question of how the three states on the Korean peninsula were able to survive in the face of Chinese power. The chapter on early-nineteenth-century Japan points out that historians have studied the period for clues to the causes of the Meiji Restoration, wanting to know the relative weight to assign

to foreign pressure and domestic unrest. For the chapter dealing with China under the Nationalists, readers are told that the desire to explain the Communist victory in 1949 has motivated historians to ponder such questions as why May Fourth Liberalism lost its appeal and whether the economic politics of the Nationalists could have brought prosperity to China if Japan had not invaded. We hope that posing these questions at the beginning of each chapter will help readers see the significance of the topics and issues presented in the chapter.

USING THIS TEXT IN CLASS

East Asian history is commonly taught either as a one-term or one-year course. To fit both schedules, this text is available both as a single volume and divided chronologically. Since those who divide chronologically might prefer to break at the end either at 1600 or at 1800, the period 1600 to 1800 appears in both of the chronologically divided volumes.

Those who wish to supplement this text with other readings will find many suggestions on the website: **college.hmco.com/pic/ebrey2e**. Professors can also find art and photos from the text, downloadable for use in the classroom.

SECOND EDITION

Based on the advice and suggestions of teachers and students who used the first edition of this book, Anne Walthall and Patricia Ebrey revised it in the summer of 2007. Users seemed uniformly to like the features we had included—the Connections mini-chapters, the documents, biographies, and material culture features. Readers did, however, notice cases of uneven treatment, the inadvertent result of dividing responsibility for the chapters among the three authors.

For the first edition of this book, the three authors divided the work primarily by country of specialization, with Patricia Ebrey writing the parts on China, Anne Walthall those on Japan, and James Palais those on Korea. The Connections chapters we divided among ourselves chronologically, with Patricia Ebrey taking the early ones (on Prehistory, Buddhism, Cultural Contact Across Eurasia, and the Mongols), Anne Walthall taking the early modern and modern ones (on Europe Enters the Scene, Western Imperialism, and World War II), and James Palais doing the final one on East Asia in the Twenty-First Century.

Very sadly, James Palais fell ill during the preparation of the first edition and was not able to revise his chapters according to our original plan. He passed away shortly after the book was printed in summer 2006. At least he did·get to see the book in print, and he proudly showed it to visitors.

For this revision, Patricia Ebrey revised James Palais's chapters covering up to 1800 and Anne Walthall the remainder. In our revisions we made every effort to achieve greater consistency in emphasis and level of detail across the three countries. We hope that we have honored Jim's long commitment to the study of Korean history by making his work more accessible to a larger audience.

Making Comparisons

For the second edition, we have shortened the book a little, and we have added something new. To help students think about similarities and differences among the cultures of China, Korea, and Japan, we have added some explicit comparisons of specific elements in their cultures, including women's situations, Neo-Confucianism, popular religion, and food. Because the comparisons deal with long spans of time, they appear mostly in the second half of the book.

ACKNOWLEDGMENTS

Many people have contributed to the shaping of this book. The three authors have been teaching about the societies of East Asia for two or three decades, and the ways they approach their subjects owe much to questions from their students, conversations with their colleagues, and the outpouring of scholarship in their fields. As we worked on this text, we received much advice from others, from early suggestions of possible collaborators to critiques of our original proposal and reviews of the drafts of our chapters.

The reviewers' reports prompted us to rethink some generalizations, urged us not to weigh the book down with too much detail, and saved us from a number of embarrassing errors. We appreciate the time and attention the following reviewers gave to helping us produce a better book:

James Anderson, University of North Carolina at Greensboro; R. David Arkush, University of Iowa; Charles Armstrong, Columbia University; Craig N. Canning, College of William and Mary; Henry Chan, Minnesota State University; Alan Christy, University of California, SC; Sue Fawn Chung, University of Nevada, Las Vegas; Parks Coble, University of Nebraska; Anthony DeBlasi, University of Albany; Ronald G. Dimberg, University of Virginia; Franklin M. Doeringer, Lawrence University; Alexis Dudden, Connecticut College; Susan Fernsebner, Mary Washington College; Karl Friday, University of Georgia; James Gao, University of Maryland; Karl Gerth, University of South Carolina; Andrew Goble, University of Oregon; John B. Henderson, Louisiana State University; Jeff Hornibrook, SUNY Plattsburgh; William Johnston, Wesleyan University; Fujiya Kawashima, Bowling Green State University; Sun Joo Kim, Harvard University; Ari Daniel Levine, University of Georgia; Huaiyin Li, University of Missouri-Columbia; Angelene Naw, Judson College; Steve Phillips, Towson University; Jonathan Porter, University of New Mexico; Wesley Sasaki-Uemura, University of Utah; Edward Slack, Eastern Washington University; S. A. Thornton, Arizona State University; Constantine Vaporis, University of Maryland, BC; Lu Yan, University of New Hampshire; Ka-che Yip, University of Maryland, Baltimore County; Theodore Jun Yoo, University of Hawaii at Manoa.

We also are grateful for all the work put into this book by the editorial staff at Houghton Mifflin: Nancy Blaine originally convinced us to take on this job; Tonya Lobato handled editing; Linda Sykes secured the photos; Janet Theurer handled the design and the art program; and Jane Lee managed the production details.

CONVENTIONS

Throughout this book names are given in East Asian order, with family name preceding personal name. Thus Mao Zedong was from the Mao family, Ashikaga Takauji from the Ashikaga family, and Yi Sŏnggye from the Yi family.

Both Japanese and Korean have phonetic scripts (Japanese a syllabary, Korean an alphabet), though Japanese additionally makes extensive use of Chinese characters. There are standard ways to transcribe these scripts into our alphabet. Here we have used the Hepburn system for transcribing Japanese. For Korean, we have used the McCune-Reischauer system with a few modifications, primarily placing priority on pronunciation rather than orthography.

Chinese does not have a phonetic script. In this book the pinyin system of romanization has been adopted.

The basic vowels, *a, e, i, o,* and *u* in all three languages are pronounced as in Italian, German, and Spanish.

a as in f*a*ther
e as in *e*nd
i as the first *e* in *e*ve
o as in *o*ld (shorter in length and with less of the *ou* sound of English)
u as in r*u*de (shorter in length than English)

Diacritical marks over vowels change the pronunciations:

ŏ in Korean is like the *o* in r*o*t, except shorter in length than English
ŭ in Korean is something like the *oo* in f*oo*t

The macron over the *ō* or *ū* in Japanese indicates that the vowel is "long," taking twice as long to say, as though it were doubled. Macrons have been omitted from common place names well known without them, such as Tokyo and Kyoto.

ü in Chinese (used only after *l* or *n*) is like the German *ü*

The three languages are not so similar when one vowel follows another. In the case of Japanese, each vowel is pronounced as a separate syllable. In Chinese, they create a (one-syllable) diphthong (e.g., *mei,* which is pronounced like may). In Korean, two vowels also form diphthongs, but with some special pronunciations; *ae* is like the *a* in *a*dd; *oe* like the *ö* of German; and *ŭi* like the *uee* in q*uee*r.

Consonants for Japanese romanization are close enough to English to give readers little difficulty. In the case of Korean, voiced consonants (*j, g, b, d*) are like English. However, aspirated consonants (*ch', k', p', t'*) marked by a marked exhalation of air, and unaspirated consonants (*ch, k, p, t*) are like English but without any aspiration at all. In the Chinese case, divergence between how an English speaker would guess a pronunciation and how the word is actually pronounced is even greater. The most confusing consonants are listed below:

c   ts in tsar
z   dz in adze
zh j in jack
q   ch in chin
x   sh

In the case of Chinese, the romanization system does not convey tones, which are also an important element in pronunciation.

For both Chinese and Korean, other ways of romanizing the language are also widely used. The South Korean government has recently adopted a system of romanization referred to as the Revised Romanization system or the Ministry of Culture romanization system. It does not use apostrophes or diacritical marks. Comparisons of the two systems of romanization can be found at **http://www.eki .ee/wgrs/rom2_ko.pdf.**

In the case of Chinese, pinyin only became the standard system of romanization in recent decades. Some earlier spellings were based on dialects other than Mandarin (Peking, Canton, Sun Yat-sen). More often the Wade-Giles system of romanization was employed. From context, if nothing else, most readers have inferred that Mao Zedong is the same person whose name used to be spelled Mao Tse-tung, or that Wang Anshi is the pinyin form of Wang An-shih. Two older spellings have been retained in this book because they are so widely known (Sun Yatsen and Chiang Kaishek). Charts for converting pinyin to Wade-Giles and vice versa are widely available on the Internet, should anyone want verification of their guesses (see, for instance, **http://www.loc.gov/ catdir/pinyin/romcover.html**; **http://www.library.ucla .edu/libraries/eastasian/ctable2.htm**; or **http://oclccjk .lib.uci.edu/wgtopy.htm**).

PART ONE

The Foundations of East Asian Civilization in China

The Prehistory of East Asia

THINKING ABOUT THE WHOLE OF EAST ASIA before the invention of writing helps to remind us that East Asia has always been a part of Eurasia and did not develop in isolation. During the Pleistocene geological era (the last great Ice Age), plants and animals spread across Eurasia as far as Japan and then connected to the mainland. In later times, peoples, crops, and inventions traveled in many directions.

Early human beings *(Homo erectus)* appeared in East Asia over 1 million years ago, having gradually spread from Africa and West Asia during the Pleistocene. Peking Man, discovered in the 1920s, is one of the best-documented examples of *H. erectus*, with skeletal remains of some forty individuals found in a single cave complex. Peking Man could stand erect, hunt, make fire, and use chipped stones as tools. In recent decades, even earlier examples of *H. erectus* have been found in south China.

Modern human beings *(Homo sapiens)* appeared in East Asia around one hundred thousand years ago. The dominant theory in the West, supported by studies of the mitochondrial DNA of modern people, is that *H. sapiens* also spread out of Africa and displaced *H. erectus*, which became extinct. Chinese archaeologists have given more credence to the theory that *H. erectus* evolved into *H. sapiens* independently in many parts of the world, making Peking Man the ancestor of modern Chinese. They can point to similarities between Peking Man and modern Chinese, such as the shape of certain teeth.

During the period from 100,000 to 10,000 B.C.E., East Asia was home to numerous groups of Paleolithic hunters, gatherers, and fishermen. Many of these people were on the move, following the wild animals they hunted or searching for new environments to exploit. This was the period that saw the movement of people from northeast Asia to the Americas and also from south China and Southeast Asia to the Pacific and Australia.

During this long period, humans began to speak, and so the affinities of modern languages offer a rough clue to the spread of peoples in early times. In East Asia, three large language families can be identified. Korean and Japanese are related to each other and more distantly to other North Asian languages such as Turkic and Mongolian (the Ural-Altaic languages). Chinese has distant ties to Tibetan and Burman (the Sino-Tibetan-Burman languages). Many of the languages spoken by minorities in south China belong to a large group found widely in mainland and insular Southeast Asia (the Austro-Asiatic languages). Language affinities suggest at least three migratory routes through East Asia: from North Asia into Mongolia, Manchuria, Korea, and Japan; from China into Tibet and Southeast Asia; and from south China to both Southeast Asia and the islands of the Philippines and Indonesia. Other evidence suggests additional routes—for instance, from Southeast Asia and Micronesia to Japan.

All through Eurasia, much greater advance came after the end of the last Ice Age around 10,000 B.C.E. (see Map C1.1). Soon after this date, people in Japan began making pottery, some of the earliest in the world. Pottery is of great value for holding water and storing food. In China and Korea, the earliest pottery finds are somewhat later, but pottery was apparently in use by 6000 B.C.E. Throughout East Asia, early pottery was commonly imprinted on its surface to give it texture. In Japan this period is referred to as Jōmon and dated from about 10,000 to 300 B.C.E. The comparable period in Korea is called Chŭlmun and dated from about 8000 to 700 B.C.E. These cultures share many features. From shell mounds found in many places in both Korea and Japan, it is evident that sites were occupied for long periods, that shellfish were collected onshore, and that fish were caught from both rivers and the ocean. Other food sources were animals such as deer and wild boar, which were hunted. Dogs seem to have been domesticated and perhaps used as hunting animals.

China in the millennia after the last Ice Age followed more closely the pattern seen in western Eurasia involving

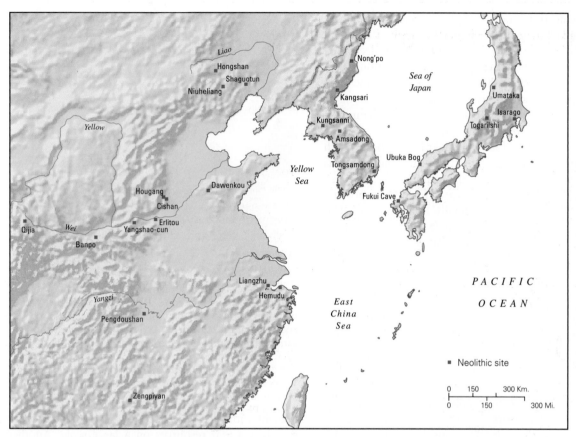

Map C1.1   Neolithic Sites in East Asia

crop agriculture, domestication of animals for food and work, pottery, textiles, and villages. Agriculture is a crucial change because cultivating crops allows denser and more permanent settlements. Because tending crops, weaving, and fashioning pots require different sorts of technical and social skills than do hunting and gathering, it is likely that skilled elders began to vie with hunters and warriors for leadership.

The dozen or more distinct Neolithic cultures that have been identified in China can be roughly divided by latitude into the southern rice zone and the northern millet zone and by longitude into the eastern jade zone and the western painted pottery zone. Dogs and pigs were found in both areas as early as 5000 B.C.E. By 3000 B.C.E. sheep and cattle had become important in the north, and water buffalo and cattle in the south.

Whether rice was independently domesticated in China or spread there from Southeast Asia is not yet certain. The earliest finds in China date to about 8000 B.C.E. At Hemudu, a site south of Shanghai and dating to about 5000 B.C.E., Neolithic villagers grew rice in wet fields and supplemented their diet with fish and water plants such as lotus and water chestnut. Hemudu villagers built wooden houses on piles, wove baskets, and made hoes, spears, mallets, paddles, and other tools of wood. They decorated their pottery and lacquered bowls with incised geometrical designs or pictures of birds, fish, or trees.

Millet, a crop domesticated in China, became the foundation of agriculture in north China. Nanzhuangtou, the earliest site found so far, is in southern Hebei and dates to about 8000 B.C.E. At Cishan, a site in Hebei dating to about 5500 B.C.E., millet was cut with stone sickles and stored in cord-marked pottery bowls, jars, and tripods (three-legged pots). Besides growing millet, the local people hunted deer and collected clams, snails, and turtles.

The east-west divide among Chinese Neolithic cultures in terms of expressive culture may well have had connections to less tangible elements of culture such as language and religion. In the west (Shaanxi and Gansu provinces especially), pottery decorated with painted geometrical designs was commonly produced from about 5000 to 3000 B.C.E. In the fully developed Yangshao style, grain jars were exuberantly painted in red and black with spirals, diamonds, and other geometrical patterns.

In the east, from Liaodong near Korea in the north to near Shanghai in the south, early pottery was rarely painted, but more elaborate forms appeared very early, with the finest wares formed on potters' wheels. Some had exceptionally thin walls polished to an almost metallic appearance. Many forms were constructed by adding parts, such as legs, spouts, handles, or lids. The many ewers and goblets found in eastern sites were probably used for rituals of feasting or sacrifice. Eastern cultures were also marked by progressively more elaborate burials.

At Dawenkou in Shandong (ca. 5000–2500 B.C.E.), not only were wooden coffins used, but even wooden burial chambers were occasionally constructed. The richest burials had over a hundred objects placed in them, including jade, stone, or pottery necklaces and bracelets. Some of the people buried there had their upper lateral incisors extracted, a practice Chinese authors in much later times considered "barbarian," and that is also seen in some Japanese sites.

Even more distinctive of the eastern Neolithic cultures is the use of jade. Because jade does not crack, shaping it requires slow grinding with abrasive sand. The most spectacular discoveries of Neolithic jades have been made in Liaodong near Korea (Hongshan culture, ca. 3500 B.C.E.) and south of Shanghai (Liangzhu culture, ca. 2500 B.C.E.)—areas that literate Chinese in ca. 500 B.C.E. considered barbarian. In the Hongshan culture area, jade was made into small sculptures of turtles, birds, and strange coiled "pig dragons." In the Liangzhu area, jade was fashioned into objects with no obvious utilitarian purpose and that are therefore considered ritual objects. Most common are disks and notched columns.

In China, the late Neolithic period (ca. 3000–2000 B.C.E.) was a time of increased contact and cultural borrowing between these regional cultures. Cooking tripods, for instance, spread west, while painted pottery spread east. This period must also have been one of increased conflict between communities, since people began building defensive walls around settlements out of rammed earth, some as large as 20 feet high and 30 feet thick. Enclosing a set-

Jade Plaque. This small plaque (6.2 by 8.3 cm, or 2.5 by 3.25 in) is incised to depict a human figure who merges into a monster mask. The lower part could be interpreted as his arms and legs, but at the same time resembles a monster mask with bulging eyes, prominent nostrils, and a large mouth. *(Zhejiang Provincial Institute of Archaeology/Cultural Relics Publishing House)*

tlement with such a wall required chiefs able to command men and resources on a large scale. Another sign of the increasing power of religious or military elites is human sacrifice, probably of captives. The earliest examples, dating to about 2000 B.C.E., involved human remains placed under the foundations of buildings. At about the same time, metal began to be used on a small scale for weapons. These trends in Neolithic sites on the north China plain link it closely to the early stages of the Bronze Age civilization there, discussed in Chapter 1.

For China, prehistory conventionally stops soon after 2000 B.C.E. It is true that in the Chinese subcontinent outside the core of Shang territories, subsistence technology continued in the Neolithic pattern for many more centuries. In Korea and Japan, the period before writing lasted longer, but during the first millennium B.C.E., technologies from China began to have an impact.

To understand the links between early China and its East Asian neighbors, we must briefly consider the wider Eurasian context, especially the northern steppe region. In terms of contemporary countries, the steppe extends from southern Russia past the Caspian and Aral seas, through the Central Asian republics, the northern reaches of China, and into

Mongolia and farther east. Horses were domesticated on the southern Russian steppe by about 4000 B.C.E. but spread only slowly to other regions. Chariots spread first, then riding on horseback. A fourteenth-century B.C.E. Hittite text on horsemanship discusses the training of chariot horses; within a century or so, chariots appeared in Shang China. The Scythians appeared as mounted archers in the tenth or ninth century B.C.E. East of them, the Karasuk, with a similar culture, dominated the region from western Mongolia into south Siberia. The Scythians and the Karasuk lived in felt tents, traveled in covered carts, and had bronze technology, including the bronze bit that made possible horseback riding. By the seventh century B.C.E. in the Altai region of Mongolia, there were two distinct groups of nomadic pastoralists: those who buried the dead under mounds and those who buried the dead in stone boxes. Their bronze implements, however, were much the same.

South of these groups on the steppe, but in contact with them, were pastoral-agricultural cultures in China's Northern Zone, stretching in terms of modern provinces from Gansu through northern Shaanxi, northern Shanxi, and northern Hebei, into Liaoning (southern Manchuria). During the late second millennium B.C.E., this zone was settled by a variety of cultures with distinct pottery and burial customs but bronze knives much like those of the steppe to the north. In the early first millennium B.C.E., warrior elites emerged in many of these cultures, and animal raising became more central to their economies, perhaps in response to a climate that was becoming colder and drier. From 600 to 300 B.C.E., evidence of horses becomes more and more common, as does riding astride. Some of these cultures adopted nomadic pastoralism, moving with their herds to new pastures. These cultures also adopted the art styles common on the steppe, such as bronze and gold animal plaques. They made increasing use of iron, which may have spread to them from the Central Asian steppe rather than from China, which was also beginning to use iron in this period. These Northern Zone cultures were in contact with the Chinese states, however, and early Chinese coins have been found at some sites.

The eastern end of this Northern Zone was directly north of Korea. Archaeologists have identified a culture there that lasted eight centuries, from the eleventh to the fourth centuries B.C.E., called Upper Xiajiadian culture. Finds include an ancient mine, along with distinctive bronze knives, helmets, mirrors, and horse fittings. The faces of the dead were covered with a cloth decorated with bronze buttons. During the next phase there was such a radical change in burial practices that archaeologists suspect that a different, and militarily superior, horse-riding group entered the area. This new group used both wooden and stone-cist coffins. A cist burial is one with a burial chamber built of stones to form a box, with a flagstone or similar large, flat stone to cover it. By the third century B.C.E., the cultures of the Northern Zone became increasingly homogeneous in material culture and rituals, with similar warrior elites and ornamental art.

These societies came into contact with people settled farther south in the Korean peninsula. As mentioned previously, after the end of the last Ice Age, the Korean peninsula was home to the fishing and foraging Chŭlmun (comb pattern pottery) peoples. By the middle of the first millennium B.C.E., a new culture, called Mumun (plain pottery), became established. Mumun sites, in contrast to the earlier Chŭlmun seaside ones, were on hillsides or hilltops. Grain production became more important, and metalworking was adopted. Bronze began to be used in Korea about 700 B.C.E. and iron by about 400 B.C.E. Mumun farmers grew barley, millet, sorghum, and short-grained rice, a mix of crops similar to north China. They heated their homes with flues under the floor, a practice that continued into modern times. Another distinctive feature of this culture, the use of stone-cist burials, links it to the Northern Zone. A fifth-century B.C.E. site in west-central Korea has a stone-cist burial, twenty-one pit buildings, red burnished pottery, a pottery kiln, a stone mold for casting bronze implements, whetstones for sharpening blades, bronze daggers and swords, and a bronze dagger of the type found farther north in the Northern Zone. Soon, however, Korea was producing its own distinctive metalwork, such as finely decorated mirrors. A new burial form also emerged: large above-ground stone vaults called dolmens.

The shift from Chŭlmun to Mumun probably reflects the same movement of people seen in southern Manchuria. Without textual evidence, however, it is impossible to decide whether the local Chŭlmun quickly adopted the superior technology of the Mumun people or whether the Mumun moved into the area in large numbers, gradually pushing out those who were already there. Some scholars speculate that the newcomers were the speakers of languages that were the ancestors of the Korean and Japanese languages.

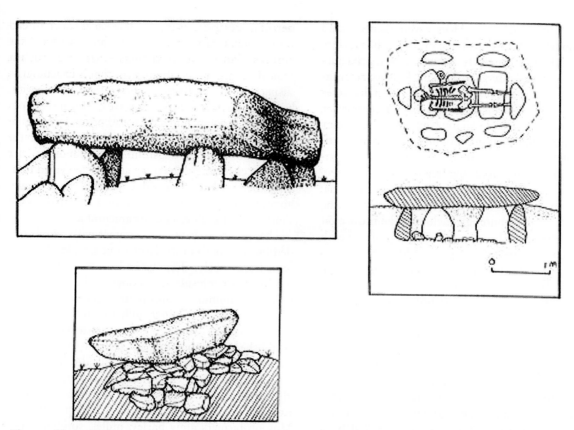

Figure C1.1   Dolmens. Burial structures capped with large stones, called dolmens, have been found in both the Korean peninsula and nearby parts of Japan. The two shown on the left were found in northern and southern Korea, respectively. The one on the right, which also shows the arrangement of the bones beneath the capstone, was found in Kyushu, across the Korean Strait.

Another important technology that made its way to Korea and Japan before writing was rice cultivation. Studies based on stone reaping knives suggest that rice spread north along the China seaboard, reaching Korea and Japan by about 300 B.C.E. In the case of Japan, rice seems to have been grown by the end of the Jōmon period but is more strongly associated with the next stage, called the Yayoi period. The Yayoi period is marked by distinctive pottery, found earliest in Kyushu, then spreading east through Honshu, though farther north more of the Jōmon style is retained in Yayoi pieces. Rice cultivation too was more thoroughly adopted in western Japan, with the marine-based way of life retaining more of its hold in northern Japan. Iron tools such as hoes and shovels also spread through Japan in this period, as did silk and associated spinning and weaving technology.

It is likely that the shift to Yayoi-style pottery and associated technologies was the result of an influx of people from Korea. Archaeologists have identified two distinct skeleton types in Yayoi period sites in western Japan, which they interpret as the indigenous Jōmon people and the new immigrants from Korea. The Jōmon type were shorter and more round-faced. The influx of the immigrants seems to have been greatest in Kyushu and western Honshu. Some scholars speculate that the Ainu, who survived into modern times only on the northern island of Hokkaido, are of relatively pure Jōmon stock.

Another sign that the influx of Yayoi people was not so great in eastern Japan is that bronze implements did not become important in the east, nor did easterners adopt the western Yayoi style of burying the whole body in a jar, a coffin, or a pit. Rather, in the east, reburial of the bones in a jar predominated. Because contact between southern Korea and western Japan continued through this period and because new technologies entered through this route, western Japan in this period was relatively more advanced than eastern Japan.

As we can see from this review of prehistory, contact among the societies of East Asia did not lead to identical developmental sequences. In China a millennium passed between the introduction of bronze technology and that of iron, in Korea only three centuries, and in Japan they were acquired together. In China the horse was first used to pull chariots, and it took five hundred or more years before soldiers were riding horses. In Korea and Japan, horses came with horse riders, and there was no chariot stage. Geography has much to do with the fact that Korea's direct neighbors frequently were not Chinese but nomadic pastoralists with distinctive cultures. Geography also dictates that passage from Korea to Japan was shorter and easier than crossing from China, giving Korea more direct influence on Japan than China had.

In Chapters 6 and 7, when we pick up the story of Korea and Japan again, it will be evident that as we move into the historical period, not only is the prehistoric period of continuing significance, but many of the same cultural processes continued to be at work.

China in the Bronze Age: The Shang and Western Zhou Dynasties (ca. 1500–771 B.C.E.)

China's Bronze Age began soon after 2000 B.C.E., and by 1200 B.C.E. there were bronze-based civilizations in several regions of China. The best known of these was centered on Anyang in north-central China, where the Shang Dynasty developed a complex state with writing and large settlements. The inscribed oracle bones found at Anyang confirm traditions about Shang rulers passed down in early texts.

In 1045 B.C.E. the Shang Dynasty was overthrown by an erstwhile ally-vassal, the state of Zhou. The early Zhou Dynasty is known not only from archaeological evidence, but also from transmitted texts, which provide the Zhou version of their righteous victory over the decadent Shang. The Zhou rulers sent out vassals to establish settlements in distant regions, creating a feudal-like system.

The issues that engage archaeologists, paleographers, and historians of China's Bronze Age remain the basic ones: Can we reconcile texts that talk of a sequence of dynasties with the archaeological evidence of distinct cultural centers? What were the consequences of the invention of writing? What can be inferred about Shang society and culture from surviving material artifacts such as bronze vessels? Is there any way to tell whether cultures outside the core regions of the Shang and Zhou spoke the same language or considered themselves part of the same culture? How significant in political and cultural terms was the transition from Shang to Zhou? Was anything significant learned from other parts of Eurasia in this period, or were all advances locally generated?

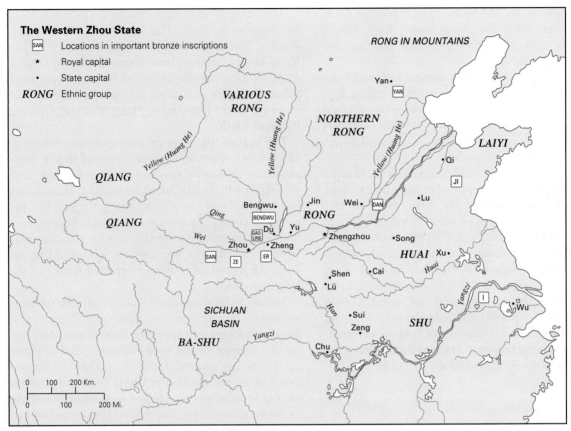

The Western Zhou State

- SAN — Locations in important bronze inscriptions
- ★ — Royal capital
- • — State capital
- *RONG* — Ethnic group

RONG IN MOUNTAINS

VARIOUS RONG

NORTHERN RONG

LAIYI

Yan • / YAN

Yellow (Huang He)

QIANG

QIANG

• Qi

JI

Bengwu • / BENGWU

Qing

Jin • Wei • / DAN

• Lu

Du • / GAO-LING

Yu

Wei

Zhou ★ / SAN / ZE

• Zheng / ER

★ Zhengzhou

• Song

HUAI Xu •

Huai

• Shen • Cai

• Lü

SICHUAN BASIN

Han

• Sui

Zeng

SHU

I

• Wu

Yangzi

BA-SHU

Yangzi

Chu

0   100   200 Km.

0   100   200 Mi.

Map 1.1 **Western Zhou China**

THE GEOGRAPHY OF THE CHINESE SUBCONTINENT

The term *China* as it is used in this book does not refer to the same geographical entity at all points in history. The historical China, also called China proper, was smaller than present-day China and changed in size over time. It can be thought of as the area settled by Chinese speakers or controlled by a Chinese state, or both. (To radically simplify complex issues of identity, references here to "the Chinese" can be taken to mean speakers of the Chinese language, a group that can also be referred to as the Han Chinese.) The contemporary People's Republic of China includes territories like Tibet, Inner Mongolia, Turkestan, and Manchuria that were the traditional homes of other peoples and were not incorporated into Chinese states until relatively late in their histories. In this book, to indicate the location of historically significant places within China, modern province names are used for convenience (see frontispiece map).

The geographical context in which Chinese civilization developed changed slowly over time: rivers and coastlines have shifted, forests have been cleared, and climates have warmed and cooled. The human geography has undergone even more extensive changes as the area occupied by speakers of Chinese has expanded and they have faced different neighbors.

China proper, by the nineteenth century about a thousand miles north to south and east to west, occupies much of the temperate zone of East Asia. The northern part, drained by the Yellow River, is colder, flatter, and more arid than the south. Rainfall in many northern areas is less than 20 inches a year, making it best suited to crops like wheat and millet. The dominant soil is loess—fine wind-driven earth that is fertile and easy to work even with primitive tools. Much of the loess soil ends up as silt in the Yellow River, causing the riverbed to rise over time.

Once people began to dike the river, it became flood prone, since when the dikes break, huge floods result. Drought is another perennial problem for farmers in the north.

The Yangzi River is the dominant feature of the warmer, wetter, and more lush south, a region well suited to rice cultivation and to growing two crops a year. The Yangzi and many of its tributaries are navigable, so boats were traditionally the preferred means of transportation in the south.

Mountains, deserts, and grasslands separated China proper from the sites of other early civilizations. Between China and India lay Tibet, with its vast mountain ranges and high plateaus. North of Tibet are great expanses of desert, where nothing grows except in rare oases, and north of them grasslands stretch from Ukraine to eastern Siberia. Until modern times, Chinese civilization did not spread into these Inner Asian regions because they were not suited to crop agriculture. The northern grasslands, where raising animals is a more productive use of land than is planting crops, was the heartland of China's traditional enemies, such as the Xiongnu and the Mongols.

THE SHANG DYNASTY
(CA. 1500–1045 B.C.E.)

China's Neolithic Age is discussed in **Connections: The Prehistory of East Asia**. China had agriculture from about 10,000 B.C.E.; by 4000 B.C.E. distinct regional cultures are evident; by 2500 B.C.E. settlements were sometimes walled, and burials give evidence of increasing social differentiation. It was from these roots that China's first civilization emerged soon after 2000 B.C.E.

Early Chinese texts refer to the first dynasty as the Xia Dynasty and give the names of its kings. The earliest Bronze Age sites may have some connection to Xia, but they contain no texts to prove or disprove this supposition. The Shang Dynasty, however, is documented in both excavated and transmitted texts, and no one today doubts that it existed. The key excavated texts are the oracle bone inscriptions found in and near the Shang settlement at Anyang, in modern Henan province. Although these inscribed cattle bones and turtle shells had been unearthed from time to time, it was only after 1898 that scholars connected them to Shang kings. Since then, rubbings of some forty-eight thousand bone fragments have been published, giving paleographers much to study.

According to tradition, Shang kings ruled from five successive cities. The best known is the last, Anyang, first excavated between 1928 and 1937. The Shang kings ruled there from approximately 1200 B.C.E. to 1045 B.C.E. At the center of Anyang were large palaces, temples, and altars that were constructed on rammed earth foundations (see **Material Culture: Rammed Earth**).

The Shang kings were military chieftains who regularly sent out armies of three thousand to five thousand men on campaigns, and when not at war they would go on hunts that lasted for months. Their armies fought rebellious vassals and foreign tribes, but the situation constantly changed as vassals became enemies and enemies accepted offers of alliance. War booty, especially the war captives who could be enslaved or sacrificed, was an important source of the king's revenue.

Bronze technology gave Shang warriors superior weapons: bronze-tipped spears and dagger-axes, used for hacking and stabbing. Bronze was also used for the fittings of the spoke-wheeled chariots that came into use around 1200 B.C.E. There is no evidence of animal traction in China before the chariot or of the use of wheels, spoked or solid disk, leading to the conclusion that the chariot was introduced to China by diffusion across Asia. Shang chariots were pulled by two or four horses and provided commanders with mobile stations from which they could supervise their troops; chariots also gave archers and soldiers armed with battle-axes increased mobility.

Shang power did not rest solely on military supremacy. The oracle bone texts show that the Shang king also acted as the high priest, the person best qualified to offer sacrifices to the royal ancestors and the high god, Di, who could command rain, thunder, and wind. The king also made offerings to an array of nature gods, such as the spirits of the sun and moon, the Yellow River, the winds of the four directions, and specific mountains.

Royal ancestors were viewed as able to intervene with the remote Di. They also could send curses, produce dreams, assist the king in battle, and more. The king addressed his ancestors in prayers and made offerings to them of millet wine, cattle, sheep, grain, and human victims. He discerned his ancestors' wishes and responses by interpreting the cracks made on heated cattle or turtle bones. King Wu Ding (ca. 1200 B.C.E.) had his diviner ask the high god Di or his ancestors about rain, the harvest, military expeditions, dreams, floods, tribute payments, sacrifices, and even a toothache.

MATERIAL CULTURE

Rammed Earth

From the late Neolithic period on, pounded or rammed earth was used in north China to build foundations and walls. In fact, in areas of loess soil, rammed earth is still used as a building material, primarily for the walls around houses and farmyards. The method used today begins with dumping loose soil into wooden frames, then pounding it into thin layers with wooden logs. At archaeological sites, the impressions of the pounders are often still visible on the top layer of the wall. Ancient rammed earth can be nearly as hard as concrete.

The most massive rammed earth structure of Shang date excavated so far is the wall surrounding the city of Zhengzhou (Henan province). It is about 1,800 meters on each side and about 9 meters tall. The base of the wall was as much as 20 meters thick. Chinese archaeologists have estimated that it contained 870,000 cubic meters of rammed earth, which would have required a labor force of ten thousand men working for eight years to dig the soil, transport it to the site, and pound it into a wall.

Earthen Walls. Walls are still constructed of rammed earth today. A frame of logs is built, the earth is pounded into place, and after it is dry, the frame is removed. *(Ronald G. Knapp)*

Shang palaces were undoubtedly splendid, but they were constructed of perishable material like wood, and nothing remains of them today. What has survived are the lavish underground tombs built for Shang kings and their consorts. The one royal tomb not to have been robbed before it was excavated was for Lady Hao, one of the many wives of King Wu Ding. Although it was one of the smaller royal tombs (about 13 by 18 feet at the mouth and about 25 feet deep) and not in the main royal cemetery, it was nonetheless filled with an extraordinary array of valuable goods. The hundreds of bronze objects in the tomb weighed 1.6 metric tons. About 60 of the bronze vessels had Lady Hao's name inscribed on them. The 130 weapons found in this tomb show that Lady Hao took an interest in military affairs. There were also 755 jade objects, 63 stone ones, and 564 made of bone. From inscribed bones found elsewhere at Anyang, we know that Lady Hao led several military campaigns, once with thirteen thousand troops against the Qiang tribes to the west. Some of the objects in her tomb appear to be tribute sent to Anyang from distant places. These include both bronze vessels from the south and knives and mirrors from the Northern Zone (occupied by non-Han peoples, discussed below).

In addition to objects of symbolic value or practical use, the Shang interred human beings, sometimes dozens of them, in royal tombs. Why did they do this? From oracle bone texts, it seems that captives not needed as slaves often ended up as sacrificial victims. Other people buried with the king had chosen their fate; that is, his spouses, retainers, or servants could decide to accompany him in death. Those who voluntarily followed their king to the grave generally had their own ornaments and might also have coffins and grave goods such as weapons. Early Shang graves rarely had more than three victims or followers accompanying the main occupant, but the practice grew over time. A late Shang king's tomb contained the remains of ninety followers plus seventy-four human sacrifices (not to mention the twelve horses and eleven dogs). Archaeologists often can identify sacrificial victims because they were decapitated or cut in two at the waist.

Human sacrifice was not confined to burials. Divination texts refer to ceremonies where from three to four hundred captives were sacrificed. In 1976, twelve hundred victims were found in 191 pits near the royal tombs, apparently representing successive sacrifices of a few dozen victims each. Animals were also frequently offered in sacrifice. Divinations proposed the sacrifice of one hundred, two hundred, or three hundred cattle, sheep, pigs, or dogs.

What about those in Shang society who were not buried in well-furnished tombs? The Shang nobility lived in large houses built on platforms of rammed earth. Those lower down on the social scale often lived in homes built partly below ground level, probably as a way to conserve heat.

In the urban centers, substantial numbers of craftsmen worked in stone, bone, bronze, and clay. Their workshops, concentrated in certain sections of the city, were often quite specialized. Some workshops specialized in hairpins, others in arrowheads, and others in ritual vessels. Another important product was silk made from the cocoons of the silkworm, which fed on the leaves of mulberry trees. Silk from Shang China has recently been discovered in an Egyptian tomb, evidence that its importance as an item of east-west trade began very early.

At the level of technology, the life of Shang farmers was not very different from that of their Neolithic ancestors. They lived in small, compact villages, surrounded by fields that they worked with stone tools. Millet continued to be the basic grain, but some new crops became common in Shang times, most notably wheat, which had spread from West Asia. Sheep, cattle, and pigs were all raised.

The primary difference between Shang farmers and their Neolithic predecessors is the huge gulf that separated them from the most powerful in their society. Shang rulers could command the labor of thousands of men for long periods of time. Huge work forces were mobilized to build the rammed earth city walls, dig the great tombs, open new lands, and fight in wars. Some scholars assume that those laboring for the king were slaves, perhaps acquired through warfare. Others speculate that these laborers also included conscripts called up as needed from among the serf-like farmers. Whatever the status of the workers, coercion, backed by violence, was an essential element of the Shang state.

Writing

The inscribed oracle bones demonstrate that writing was already a major element in Chinese culture by 1200 B.C.E. Writing must have been invented earlier, but the early stages of its development cannot be traced, probably because it was done on perishable materials like wood, bamboo, or silk.

What impact did writing have? Literacy is an ally of political control, facilitating communication across an expanding realm. From the oracle bones, we know that Shang kept records of enemy slain, booty taken, animals bagged in hunts, and other information, using lunar months and ten-day and sixty-day cycles to record dates.

Although only about 40 percent of the five thousand or so characters used on Shang divination texts have been deciphered, there is no longer any doubt that the language and the writing system of the Shang are directly ancestral to both the language and the writing systems of later Chinese. This script was logographic, like ancient Egyptian and Sumer-

Oracle Bone. The thousands of inscribed bones that survive from Shang sites are our best source for early Chinese writing. The questions they record were usually addressed to the king's ancestors. *(Institute of History and Philology. Academia Sinica/Laurie Platt Winfrey, Inc.)*

ian, meaning that each word was represented by a single graph (character). In the Chinese case, some of these graphs began as pictures, but other methods were adopted to represent the names of abstract concepts. Sometimes the graph for a different word was borrowed because the two words were pronounced alike. As in later times, sometimes two different graphs were combined; for instance, to represent different types of trees, the graph for tree could be combined with the graph for another word that sounded like the name of a kind of tree. More than half of the characters found on oracle bones combine components in these ways.

In western Eurasia, logographic scripts were eventually modified or replaced by phonetic scripts, but that never happened in China (though, because of changes in the spoken language, many words today are represented by two or three characters rather than a single one). Basic literacy requires knowing the characters for two or three thousand common words, and well-educated people learn a couple of thousand more. Because characters are composed of a few hundred components, this task is not as daunt-

ing as it may seem at first, but it still takes much longer than learning to read a phonetic script. Thus, because China retained its logographic writing system, it takes many years of study for a person to master reading and writing.

Why did China retain a logographic writing system even after encounters with phonetic systems? Although phonetic systems make learning to read easier, there are costs to abandoning a logographic system. Those who learned to read Chinese could communicate with a wider range of people than those who read scripts based on speech. Since Chinese characters remained recognizable after the passage of many centuries, despite phonological change, educated Chinese could read texts written centuries earlier without needing them to be translated. Moreover, as the Chinese language developed mutually unintelligible regional variants, readers of Chinese could read books and letters by contemporaries whose oral language they could not comprehend. Thus, the Chinese script played a large role in holding China together and fostering a sense of connection with the past.

For the history of East Asia, the Chinese script has a further significance. Korea, Japan, and Vietnam all began writing by adopting the Chinese script. For several centuries, reading and writing in these countries was done in a foreign language, Chinese. Since most available books had been written in Chinese, learning meant learning through a Chinese lens. In time, however, Chinese characters were used for their meaning or their sound to record the local languages. Those used for their meaning are much like Arabic numerals whose names are pronounced differently depending on the reader's language.

Metalworking

As in Egypt, Mesopotamia, and India, the development of more complex forms of social organization in Shang China coincided with the mastery of metalworking, specifically bronze. Beginning about 2000 B.C.E., people learned to prospect metals, remove them from their ores, and fashion them into tools or ornaments. The next stage, reached about 1500 B.C.E., involved large-scale production.

In Shang times, bronze was used more for ritual than for war. Most surviving Shang bronze objects are vessels such as cups, goblets, steamers, and cauldrons, which originally would have been used to hold food and wine offered to the ancestors or gods during sacrificial ceremonies. Both kings and nobles owned bronze vessels, but the kings had many more.

When compared to bronze objects made in other early societies, Chinese bronzes stand out for their quantity, their decoration, and the ways they were manufactured. Shang bronze making required a large labor force to mine, refine, and transport copper, tin, and lead ores and to produce and transport charcoal. To achieve the high degree of precision and standardization evident from surviving bronze vessels, there must have been considerable division of labor. Technically skilled artisans were needed to make clay models, construct ceramic piece molds, and assemble and finish each vessel. There also would have had to be managers overseeing the entire process. It has been estimated that two to three hundred craftsmen were needed to make the largest surviving Shang bronze vessel, which weighs 875 kilograms.

Scholars have not reached a consensus on the meaning of the decoration on Shang bronzes. In the art of ancient Egypt, Assyria, and Babylonia, images of domesticated plants and animals match our under-

Front View of a Shang Bronze Vessel. This rectangular covered vessel, about 10 inches (25 cm) tall, dates from the twelfth century B.C.E. At the base and the top register are opposed dragons. Between them are stylized mask (*taotie*) designs, with eyes, eyebrows, ears, horns, mouth, and front paws all floating free. The designs on the sides are compressed versions of the designs on the front. *(The Metropolitan Museum of Art, Purchase, Arthur M. Sackler Gift, 1974 [1974.268.2ab])*

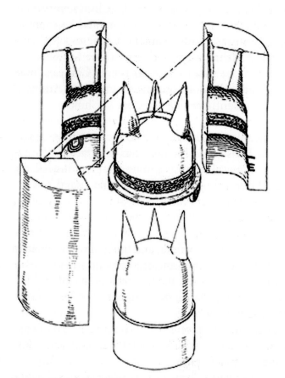

Figure 1.1   **Mold for Bronze Casting.** Shang bronze vessels were made with ceramic molds. After the molten bronze hardened, the pieces of the mold could be removed.

standing of the importance of agriculture in those societies, much as depictions of social hierarchy (kings, priests, scribes, and slaves) match our understandings of their social and political development. Why then did images of wild animals predominate in Shang China? The symbolic meaning of some animals is easy to guess. Cicadas, which spend years underground before emerging, probably evoked rebirth in the realm of ancestral spirits. Birds similarly suggest the idea of messengers who can reach realms in the sky. More problematic is the most common image, the stylized animal face called the *taotie*. To some it is a monster—a fearsome image that would scare away evil forces. Some hypothesize that it reflects masks used in rituals. Others associate it with animal sacrifices, totemism, or shamanism. Still others see these images as hardly more than designs. Scholars' inability to reach a consensus on something so basic as the meaning of the decoration on Shang bronzes reminds us of the huge gaps in our understanding of Shang culture.

DEVELOPMENTS OUTSIDE THE SHANG CORE

The Shang were constantly at war with other groups, tribes, or states, and the area in which the Shang king could safely travel was confined to northern Henan and western Shandong provinces. Key elements of their culture, however, such as their bronze technology, spread well beyond the area they controlled. In the middle Yangzi region, many bronzes have been found that share Shang technology but differ in design, some even using human faces in place of the *taotie*. Bells are particularly common in the Yangzi region, and at one site they were buried in groups in the side of a mountain. The profusion of objects in some tombs in Jiangxi province shows that the elites of this region were able to amass wealth on a scale similar to Shang elites. Their bronze vessels often have tigers on their handles, a style distinctive to the region. Whether this region should be considered a provincial version of Shang civilization or a different culture that borrowed extensively from Shang technology is still not certain. Without written documents like the divination texts of Anyang, there is no way to know if Chinese was the language used in this region.

As discussed in **Connections: The Prehistory of East Asia**, a more independent bronze culture existed north of the Shang core, where people grew millet and raised pigs, sheep, and cattle. Knives, axes, and mirrors are common finds there, but their bronze technology resembles that of Central Asia and Siberia more than the Shang core. Their practice of oracle bone divination, however, links them to Shang civilization. These finds could be evidence of the people who brought chariots to the Shang.

Another strong case for a distinct culture can be made for the civilization discovered at Sanxingdui in the western province of Sichuan. In 1986 two pits of Shang date were found, packed with objects never found in Shang sites, including elephant tusks and huge masks, some covered in gold foil (see the table). Both pits were filled in layers, with small objects on the bottom, then the larger ones, then the elephant tusks, then rammed earth. (See Color Plate 1.)

Contents of the Pits at Sanxingdui, ca. 1200 B.C.E.	
Pit 1	**Pit 2**
13 elephant tusks	67 elephant tusks
107 bronze rings	20 bronze masks
13 bronze heads	40 bronze heads
44 bronze dagger-axe blades	bronze statue
4 gold items	bronze trees
60 stone tools	4,600 cowrie shells
70 stone or jade blades	almost 500 small beads or
40 pottery vessels	tubes of jade, stone, or ivory
burned animal bones	burned animal bones

Why were these objects placed in the pits? Many of those in pit 1 had been burned before being deposited, and others had been purposely broken. Thus, one possibility is that these objects are the remnants of a huge sacrifice. Unlike major Shang sacrifices, however, there is no sign of human sacrifice. Some scholars speculate that the bronze figures of humans were being used to replace humans in a sacrificial ceremony. The heads most likely were originally attached to wood or clay statues and could have represented gods or ancestors. Thus, it is also possible that the statues with the bronze heads represented gods and that the local people had for some reason decided that those gods or their representations had to be burned and buried.

Further archaeological exploration has revealed that the pits lay within a large walled city nearly 2 kilometers square. Foundations of fifty or so buildings have been found, most rectangular but some round. Five other pits have been found, but they contained no bronze artifacts, only jade and stone ones. Perhaps because of flooding, the city was abandoned around 1000 B.C.E. No sites for later stages of this culture have been found, and there are no nearby sites from succeeding centuries that give evidence of comparable wealth. Perhaps whatever led to the abandonment of Sanxingdui also led to the collapse of the civilization.

The existence of sites like Sanxingdui has forced archaeologists to reconsider the political landscape during the centuries when the Shang ruled at Anyang. Shang rulers wished to see their own polity as the central one, but since we lack written records from sites of other cultures, there is no reason to assume that elites in other places had less self-centered notions of themselves.

THE WESTERN ZHOU DYNASTY (1045–771 B.C.E.)

Outside the Shang domains were the domains of allied and rival polities. To the west were the fierce Qiang, who probably spoke an early form of Tibetan. Between the Shang capital and the Qiang was a frontier state called Zhou, which shared most of the material culture of the Shang. In 1045 B.C.E., this state rose against the Shang and defeated it. The first part of the Zhou Dynasty is called the Western Zhou period (1045–771 B.C.E.) because its capital was in the west near modern Xi'an in Shaanxi province (to distinguish it from the Eastern Zhou, after the capital was moved near modern Luoyang in Henan province); see Map 1.1.

In early written traditions, three Zhou rulers are given credit for the Zhou conquest of the Shang. They are King Wen (*wen* means "cultured" or "lettered"), who expanded the Zhou domain; his son King Wu (*wu* means "martial"), who conquered the Shang; and Wu's brother, the duke of Zhou, who consolidated the conquest and served as regent for Wu's heir.

These rulers and their age are portrayed in the earliest transmitted text, the *Book of Documents* (see **Documents: The Announcement of Shao**). The speeches, pronouncements, and reports in this book depict the Zhou conquest as the victory of just and noble warriors, supported by Heaven, over the decadent Shang court led by an evil king. Bronze inscriptions provide another important source for the early Zhou period. Court scribes would prepare written documents on bamboo or wooden strips to specify appointments to offices or fiefs. Later, during a court ceremony, an official would read the document on behalf of the king. A copy of the document would be handed over to the grantee, who later had it reproduced in bronze so that it could be passed down in his family.

The early Zhou period did not mark an abrupt break with Shang culture, but some Shang practices declined. Divining by heating oracle bones became less common, as did sacrifices of human victims. Interring followers in tombs continued, though their numbers gradually declined.

The Mandate of Heaven

Like the Shang kings, the Zhou kings sacrificed to their ancestors, but they also sacrificed to the divine force called Sky or Heaven. The *Book of Documents* assumes a close relationship between Heaven and the king, who was called the "Son of Heaven." Heaven gives the king a mandate to rule only as long as he rules in the interests of the people. Because the theory of the Mandate of Heaven does not seem to have had any place in Shang cosmology, some scholars think it was elaborated by the early Zhou rulers as propaganda to win over the conquered subjects of the Shang. Whatever its origins, it remained a central feature of Chinese political ideology from the early Zhou period on.

The Zhou Political Structure

At the center of the Western Zhou political structure was the Zhou king, who was simultaneously ritual head of the royal lineage and supreme lord of the nobility. Rather than attempting to rule all their territories directly, the early Zhou rulers sent out relatives and trusted subordinates to establish walled garrisons in the conquered territories, creating a decentralized, quasi-feudal system. The king's authority was maintained by rituals of ancestor worship and court visits. For instance, in 806 B.C.E., a younger son of King You was made a duke and sent east to establish the state of Zheng in a swampy area that needed to be drained. This duke and his successors nevertheless spent much of their time at the Zhou court, serving as high ministers.

A Zhou vassal was generally able to pass his position on to a son, so that in time the domains became hereditary fiefs. By 800 B.C.E., there were about two hundred lords with domains large and small, of which only about twenty-five were large enough to matter much in interstate politics. Each lord appointed officers to serve him in ritual, administrative, or military capacities. These posts and their associated titles tended to become hereditary as well. Each domain thus came to have noble families with patrimonies in offices and associated lands.

Some Zhou bronzes record benefactions from the king and mention the services that had earned the king's favor. One inscription, for instance, recorded the rewards given to Yu for obeying the king's command to repel attacks of the Southern Huai barbarians. After his successful return, the king brought Yu into the ancestral temple and conferred on him two bronze ritual vessels, fifty strands of cowrie shells, and one hundred fields as reward for bringing back one hundred heads and forty manacled prisoners.

DOCUMENTS

The Announcement of Shao

Several texts in the Book of Documents *record speeches and pronouncements of the early Zhou rulers. Scholars used to distrust the early attributions of these texts, but with the discovery and study of more and more inscriptions on early Zhou bronzes, scholars now believe that many of them were in fact written in the first century of Zhou rule. The "Announcement of Shao" records a speech by the duke of Zhou or his brother, the duke of Shao, in which the duke explains the Mandate of Heaven to the newly subjugated people of Shang.*

Ah! August Heaven, High God, has changed his principal son and has revoked the Mandate of this great state of Shang. When a king receives the Mandate, without limit is the grace thereof, but also without limit is the anxiety of it. Ah! How can he fail to be reverently careful!

Heaven has rejected and ended the Mandate of this great state of Shang. Thus, although Shang has many former wise kings in Heaven, when their successor kings and successor people undertook their Mandate, in the end wise and good men lived in misery. Knowing that they must care for and sustain their wives and children, they then called out in anguish to Heaven and fled to places where they could not be caught. Ah! Heaven too grieved for the people of all the lands, wanting, with affection, in giving its Mandate to employ those who are deeply committed. The king should have reverent care of his virtue.

Look at the former peoples of ancient times, the Xia Heaven guided, indulged, and cherished them, so that they would strive to understand what Heaven favors, but by this time they have let their Mandate fall to the ground. Now look at the Shang; Heaven guided them, stayed near them, nourished them, so that they would strive to comprehend what Heaven favors; but now they have let their Mandate fall to the ground.

Now a young son succeeds to the throne; let him not, then, neglect the aged and experienced. Not only do they comprehend the virtue of our men of old—nay, more, they are sometimes able to comprehend counsels that come from Heaven.

Ah! Even though it be that the king is young, he is [Heaven's] principal son. Let him be grandly able to be in harmony with the little people. In the present time of grace, the king must not dare to be slow, but should be prudently apprehensive about what the people say. . . .

Those above and below being zealous and careful, let them say, "As we receive Heaven's Mandate, let it grandly be like the long years enjoyed by the Xia, and not fail of the years enjoyed by the Shang"—in order that [as one would wish] the king, through the little people, may receive Heaven's enduring Mandate.

Translated by David S. Nivison in *Sources of Chinese Tradition*, 2nd ed., comp. Wm. Theodore de Bary and Irene Bloom (New York: Columbia University Press, 1999), pp. 35–37, slightly modified.

The inscription concludes, "Yu dares in response to extol the Son of Heaven's beneficence, herewith making this offertory tureen; may Yu for 10,000 years have sons' sons and grandsons' grandsons eternally treasure and use it."

As in Shang times, there continued to be groups viewed as alien living in the same general region as the Zhou states as well as beyond the borders. Various groups of Yi ("eastern barbarians"), for instance, lived interspersed through the east, as did different groups of Rong ("northern barbarians") in the north and west. These groups spoke distinct languages, though they were not necessarily more primitive than the Zhou people in technology. Over the course of the nearly three centuries of Western Zhou rule, the Zhou kings drew many of these groups into the Zhou political

Chariot Burial. The type of chariot found in this Western Zhou burial pit, with large, many-spoked wheels, spread across Asia around 1100 B.C.E. *(Institute of Archaeology, Beijing)*

order by recognizing their chiefs as the lords of their domains. To participate in this order, they had to use the Chinese writing system for matters of state.

Ties of loyalty and kinship linking the Zhou vassals to the king weakened over time, and in 771 B.C.E. the Zhou king was killed by an alliance of Rong tribesmen and Zhou vassals. Zhou nobles fleeing this attack buried their bronze vessels, expecting to unearth them after they returned. One such hoard discovered in 1976 contained 103 vessels belonging to Earl Xing of Wei cast by several generations of his family. Instead of returning, however, the Zhou royal house and nobles moved east to the area of modern Luoyang, just south of the Yellow River in the heart of the central plains. Eastern Zhou never fully regained control over its vassals, and China entered a prolonged period without a strong central authority, which will be discussed in Chapter 2.

Western Zhou Society and Culture

Western Zhou society was highly aristocratic. Inherited ranks placed people in a hierarchy ranging from

the king, to the rulers of states with titles like duke and marquis, the hereditary great officials of these lords, and the lower ranks of the aristocracy called *shi*, men who could serve in either military or civil capacities. At the bottom were ordinary subjects. Patrilineal family ties were very important throughout this society, and at the upper reaches, at least, sacrifices to ancestors were one of the key rituals used to forge social ties.

Land in this system was held on feudal tenures, and the economy was a manorial one. When the Zhou king bestowed land on a relative or subordinate, he generally also gave him people to work it. These farmers were treated as serfs, obliged to provide food and labor for the lord, who was expected in turn to look after their welfare.

Glimpses of what life was like at various social levels in the early Zhou period can be found in the *Book of Poetry*, which contains the earliest Chinese songs and poems. Many of the folk songs are love songs. Others depict the farming life, which involved not merely cultivating crops like millet, hemp (for cloth), beans, and vegetables, but also hunting small animals and collecting grasses and rushes to make rope and baskets. The seasons set the pace for rural life, and poems contain many references to seasonal changes such as the appearance of grasshoppers and crickets.

The *Book of Poetry* also offers glimpses of court life and its ceremonies. Some have a critical edge. In the following stanza, the ancestors are rebuked for not providing aid to their descendants in distress:

> The drought has become so severe
> That it cannot be stopped.
> Glowing and burning,
> We have no place. The great mandate is about
>   at an end,
> Nothing to look ahead to or back upon.
> The host of dukes and past rulers
> Does not help us. As for father and mother and
>   the ancestors,
> How can they bear to treat us so?[1]

1. Ode 258, in Edward L. Shaughnessy, "Western Zhou History," in M. Loewe and E. Shaughnessy, eds., *The Cambridge History of Ancient China: From the Origins of Civilization to 221 B.C.* (New York: Cambridge University Press, 1999), p. 336.

Men and women had very different roles at court, and one poem shows that these differences were marked from birth:

> A male child is born.
> He is made to sleep on a bed.
> He is made to wear a skirt.
> He is made to play with a scepter.
> His crying is loud.
> His red knee-covers are august.
> He is the hall and household's lord and king.
> A female child is born.
> She is made to sleep on the floor.
> She is made to wear a wrap-cloth.
> She is made to play with pottery.
> She has no wrong and right.
> Only wine and food are for her to talk about.
> May she not send her father and mother any
>   troubles.[2]

SUMMARY

How different was China at the end of the Western Zhou period in 771 B.C.E. compared to China at the beginning of the Bronze Age in 2000 B.C.E.? Differences in technology were pervasive. At the beginning of this period, China was just beginning to fashion objects of metal; by the end, bronze workers had centuries of experience in casting all sorts of objects, and bronze was used not only for ritual vessels but also for helmets, swords, knives, axes, and other tools. Horses had been domesticated and trained to pull chariots. Writing had become a central feature in the life of the political elite, and a substantial body of literature was in circulation. Some elements of culture and organization had already undergone major transformations. Divination by oracle bones had largely disappeared, as had the practice of making offerings of human victims, except at the burial of rulers, where it continued somewhat sporadically. Previously alien groups were incorporated into the Zhou political order, and more and more of them participated in the culture associated with the Chinese written language. Thus, in all likelihood there were more people we can call Chinese by the end of this period.

---

2. Ode 189, in Paul Rakita Goldin, *The Culture of Sex in Ancient China* (Honolulu: University of Hawaii Press, 2002), p. 24.

Philosophers and Warring States During the Eastern Zhou Period (770–256 B.C.E.)

The foundations of Chinese thought were established in the five centuries that followed the transfer of the Zhou court to Luoyang in 770 B.C.E. In this period, the old Zhou fiefs came to function more and more like independent states linked to one another in a multistate system. Gradually, warfare between the states intensified, and social, political, and cultural change also quickened. By the third century B.C.E., only seven important states remained. Over the course of these centuries, hereditary ranks meant less and less, and rulers made more use of the *shi*, the lower ranks of the old aristocratic order. As the *shi* competed to offer advice to rulers, they advanced the art of argument and set in motion a tremendous intellectual flowering. China entered one of its most creative periods, when the ideas underlying the Confucian, Daoist, and Legalist traditions were developed.

Historians of ideas, warfare, and social and political change have all found the Eastern Zhou a fascinating period to study. Archaeological evidence remains fundamental to enlarging our understanding of this period and has been particularly valuable for showing the richness of the culture of the south, the region of the state of Chu. Few of the philosophical texts of this period were written by a single known author, so scholars have devoted much of their energy to distinguishing the earlier and later layers of texts. Knowing the importance of the strong, centralized state in later periods of Chinese history, historians have also drawn attention to the advances in statecraft of this period and the connections between the ideas articulated in the period and the social and political situation. Would comparable ideas have emerged if China had not been politically divided? How significant was the emergence of the *shi* to the intellectual history of this period? Is it more than coincidental that China's first intellectual flowering occurred in roughly the same centuries as that of ancient India, Greece, Persia, and Israel?

THE MULTISTATE SYSTEM OF THE EASTERN ZHOU

The Eastern Zhou Dynasty is conventionally divided into two periods named after books that recorded events of the time: the Spring and Autumn period, to 479 B.C.E., and the Warring States period after it. The history of the Eastern Zhou Dynasty is better documented than the history of the Western Zhou because of advances in the art of political narrative. For the Spring and Autumn period, the most important chronicle is the *Zuo zhuan*, a narrative covering the years 722 to 463 B.C.E., traditionally treated as a commentary to the much briefer *Spring and Autumn Annals*. For the Warring States period, *The Intrigues of the Warring States* presents lengthy narratives, arranged by state rather than chronologically. A third work, the *Discourses of the States*, also arranged by state, concentrates on speeches and covers both periods. The authorship and dating of all three of these works are uncertain, but at a minimum they contain Zhou material.

Although the Zhou kings were still considered the supreme monarchs, they no longer had the military might to force obedience. Sometimes supposed vassals would even attack the Zhou king. In this period, the ruler of one state would sometimes be recognized as the hegemon, the leader of the alliance of Zhou states (see **Biography: Guan Zhong**). These hegemons periodically called meetings of the allied states where rulers or leading ministers would swear to uphold the Zhou feudal structure. At a meeting in 657 B.C.E., the states swore not to dam irrigation waters, withhold sales of grain, replace heirs apparent, promote concubines to wives, or let women interfere in state affairs. The principal states of the early Warring States period are shown on Map 2.1.

Succession disputes were a common pretext for war between states. A ruler typically had concubines in addition to a wife and thus would have children by several women. In theory, succession went to the eldest son of the wife, then younger sons by her, and only in their absence, sons of concubines. In actual practice,

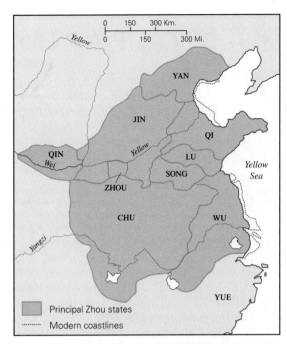

Map **2.1**   **Zhou States in the Sixth Century** B.C.E.

however, the ruler of a state or head of a powerful ministerial family could select a son of a concubine to be his heir if he wished. During his lifetime, this led to much scheming for favor among the various sons and their mothers and the common perception that women were incapable of taking a disinterested view of the larger good. Sons who felt unfairly excluded often journeyed to other states in search of allies. Since rulers regularly took their wives from the ruling families of other states, a contender could try the state that his mother or grandmother had come from or the states his sisters or aunts had married into. The rulers of these states were often happy to see someone indebted to them on the throne of a neighboring state and would lend armies to help oust rivals.

There were, of course, other reasons for warfare. States tried to maintain a balance of power and prevent any one state from becoming too strong. States on the periphery had the advantage, as they could expand outward. Thus, the four states to gain the most over the course of the Spring and Autumn period were Qin in the west, Jin in the north, Qi in the east, and Chu in the south. As Chu expanded from its base in the south, Qi organized other states to resist it. Sometimes the states in the middle, weary of being caught in the fighting between the larger powers, organized peace conferences.

BIOGRAPHY   Guan Zhong

By the time of Confucius the success of states was often credited more to the lord's astute advisers than to the lords themselves. To Confucius, the most praiseworthy political adviser was Guan Zhong (ca. 720–645 B.C.E.), the genius behind the rise of the state of Qi in eastern China.

The earliest historical sources that recount Guan Zhong's accomplishments are the commentaries compiled in the Warring States period to elaborate on the dry chronicle known as the *Spring and Autumn Annals*. The *Zuo zhuan*, for instance, tells us that in 660 B.C.E., Guan Zhong advised Duke Huan to aid the small state of Xing, then under attack by the non-Chinese Rong tribes: "The Rong and the Di are wolves who cannot be satiated. The Xia [Chinese] states are kin who should not be abandoned." In 652, it tells us, Guan Zhong urged the duke to maintain the respect of the other states by refusing the request for an alliance by a ruler's son who wished to depose his father. Because the duke regularly listened to Guan Zhong's sound advice, Qi brought the other states under its sway, and the duke came to be recognized as the first hegemon, or leader of the alliance of states.

Guan Zhong was also credited with strengthening the duke's internal administration. He encouraged the employment of officials on the basis of their moral character and ability rather than their birth. He introduced a system of drafting commoners for military service. In the history of China written by Sima Qian in about 100 B.C.E., Guan Zhong is also given credit for enriching Qi by promoting trade, issuing coins, and standardizing merchants' scales. He was credited with the statement that "when the granaries are full, the people will understand ritual and moderation. When they have enough food and clothing, they will understand honor and disgrace."

Sima Qian's biography of Guan Zhong emphasized his early poverty and the key role played by a friend, Bao Shuya, who recognized his worth. As young men, both Bao and Guan Zhong served brothers of the duke of Qi. When this duke was killed and a messy succession struggle followed, Bao's patron won out and became the next duke, while Guan Zhong's patron had to flee and in the end was killed. Bao, however, recommended Guan Zhong to the new duke, Duke Huan, and Guan Zhong took up a post under him.

In the *Analects*, one of Confucius's disciples thought this lack of loyalty to his first lord made Guan Zhong a man unworthy of respect: "When Duke Huan killed his brother Jiu, Guan Zhong was unable to die with Jiu but rather became chancellor to Duke Huan." Confucius disagreed: "Guan Zhong became chancellor to Duke Huan and made him hegemon among the lords, uniting and reforming all under heaven. The people, down to the present, continued to receive benefits from this. Were it not for Guan Zhong our hair would hang unbound and we would fold our robes on the left [that is, live as barbarians]" (*Analects* 14.18).

A book of the teachings associated with Guan Zhong, the *Guanzi*, was in circulation by the late Warring States period. Although today it is not thought to reflect the teachings of the historical Guan Zhong, the fact that later statecraft thinkers would borrow his name is an indication of his fame as a great statesman.

Another common reason for the hegemon to bring troops to the aid of a state was to help it fend off attack by various forces from beyond the Zhou world. But those labeled with the non-Chinese ethnic terms Di, Rong, or Yi were not always in a position of enmity to the Chinese states. For instance, Jin often enlisted Rong or Di polities to join it in fighting Qin. Moreover, some Rong and Di leaders were versed in Chinese literature. There was also intermarriage between the ruling class of Zhou states and the Rong and Di elites. Duke Wen of Jin's mother was a Rong, his wife a Di. The only written language in this world, however, was Chinese, which worked toward making Chinese the common language. In the south, the states of Wu and Yue emerged from outside the Zhou sphere but adopted Zhou cultural patterns; Yue, in fact, claimed to be descended from the Xia Dynasty, making it more ancient than the Zhou Dynasty.

Archaeological evidence confirms steady cultural exchange between Zhou and non-Zhou elements in this period. The rulers of the state of Zhongshan in the northeast were recognized as descended from White Di, who had been driven by other tribes from Shaanxi into Hebei in the sixth century. With help from the state of Wei, they established their own city there. Although Zhongshan was a very minor state, its rulers decided to call themselves kings when other states' rulers did. The tomb of King Cuo of Zhongshan, who died around 308 B.C.E., included inscribed bronzes that record historical events in typically Confucian language, full of stock phrases from the classics.

Rulers continued to be buried with followers in this period. Duke Mu of Qin had 177 people accompany him in death after he died in 621 B.C.E., and nearly a century later, in 537 B.C.E., Duke Jin was buried with 166. By this period, there were people who disapproved of the practice. In the state of Qin, the practice was outlawed in 383 B.C.E. Moreover, the sacrificing of war captives in ceremonies unrelated to burials no longer seems to have been practiced. Remnants of this practice could still be seen in the use of the blood of captives to consecrate newly cast war drums and the ritual of presenting captives at the ancestral temple or other altar.

WARFARE AND ITS CONSEQUENCES

The purpose and conduct of war changed dramatically in the Eastern Zhou period. In the Spring and Autumn period, a large army would have up to ten thousand soldiers, the chariot remained central to warfare, and states were ranked by how many hundreds of chariots they could deploy. A code of chivalrous conduct regulated warfare between the states. The two sides would agree on the time and place for a battle, and each would perform divination and sacrifices before initiating hostilities. One state would not attack another while it was in mourning for its ruler. Ruling houses were not wiped out so a successor could continue to sacrifice to their ancestors. Battle narratives in the *Zuo zhuan* give the impression that commanders cared as much about proving their honor as about winning. In 638 B.C.E., the duke of the small state of Song felt compelled to fight a much stronger state. Because his forces were greatly outnumbered, his minister of war urged him to attack the enemy while the enemy's forces were fording a river, but the duke refused. The *Zuo zhuan* reports that he explained his behavior this way: "The gentleman does not inflict a second wound, nor does he capture those

with gray hair. On campaigns the ancients did not obstruct those in a narrow pass. Even though I am but the remnant of a destroyed state, I will not drum an attack when the other side has not yet drawn up its ranks."[1] When combat was hedged with these ceremonial restrictions, war was less deadly—a wound ended the victim's combat status but not necessarily his life.

By the Warring States period, such niceties were being abandoned as advances in military technology changed the nature of warfare. Large, well-drilled infantry armies were becoming a potent military force, able to withstand and defeat chariot-led forces. By the late Warring States period, military obligations were nearly universal for men. By 300 B.C.E., states were sending out armies of a couple hundred thousand drafted foot soldiers, usually accompanied by horsemen. For Qin's campaign against Zhao in 260 B.C.E., it mobilized all men over age fifteen. Conscripts with a year or two of training would not have the martial skills of aristocratic warriors who trained for years and tested their skills in hunts. But infantry armies won out through standardization, organization, discipline, and sheer size.

Adding to the effectiveness of armies of drafted foot soldiers was the crossbow, invented in the southern state of Chu. The trigger of a crossbow is an intricate bronze mechanism that allowed a foot soldier to shoot farther than a horseman carrying a light bow. One text of the period claimed that a skilled soldier with a powerful crossbow and a sharp sword was the match for a hundred ordinary men. To defend against crossbows, soldiers began wearing armor and helmets. Most of the armor was made of leather strips tied with cords. Helmets were sometimes made of iron.

Although most soldiers were drafted peasants, it became common to select and train elite corps of crack troops. The elite troops in the state of Wei had to wear heavy armor and helmets, shoulder a crossbow and fifty arrows, strap a spear to their backs and a sword by their waists, carry three days' supply of food, and march about 50 kilometers in a single day. Those meeting this standard earned their household exemption from all taxes and labor service obligations.

---

1. Duke Xi, 22nd year. Translations cited by the traditional sections are by the author.

The development of infantry armies created the need for a new type of general, as rulers became less willing to let men lead troops merely because of aristocratic birth. Treatises on the art of war described the ideal general as a master of maneuver, illusion, and deception, ruthless in searching for the advantage that would lead to victory. He also had to be an organizer, able to integrate the efforts of the units under him.

Because cities were walled, attacks on them resulted in prolonged sieges, and generals were eager to try new ways to attack and defend walls. Portable ladders were brought to scale the walls. When attackers dug tunnels under the walls, defenders would use large bellows of the sort common in smelting iron to pump smoke into the tunnels and suffocate the attackers.

City walls were not the only defensive structure important to warfare of the period. States began building chains of watch stations and forts, often connecting them with long defensive walls. Permanent garrisons were left at strategic points to prevent the passage of armies. Barriers also allowed states to check those who entered or left their territories and to collect transit taxes from merchants.

The introduction of cavalry struck another blow at the chariot-riding aristocracy. Shooting bows and arrows from horseback was first perfected by non-Chinese peoples to the north of China proper, who at that time were making the transition to a nomadic pastoral economy. As the northern states expanded northward, absorbing non-Chinese communities of mixed shepherds and farmers, they came into direct contact with the horse riders of the steppe. In 307 B.C.E., the king of the northern state of Jin ordered his troops to adopt the nomads' trousers and practice mounted archery (see **Documents: The King of Zhao Persuades His Uncle to Wear Barbarian Dress**). Soon Zhao was using cavalry against other Chinese states, which then had to master the new technology to defend themselves. Larger infantry armies of one hundred thousand or two hundred thousand men would be supported by a few hundred mounted warriors. Cavalry were considered especially valuable for reconnaissance, pursuing fleeing soldiers, cutting supply lines, and pillaging the countryside. From this time on, acquiring and pasturing horses was a key component of Chinese military preparedness (see Color Plate 2).

As a result of all these developments in the art of war, conflicts came to be waged with greater intensity and on a much larger scale than ever before. Whereas Spring and Autumn period campaigns had lasted no longer than a season and battles no longer than a day or two, some campaigns in the Warring States period lasted for years, with separate armies operating independently on several fronts. Qin's defeat of Zhao in 260 B.C.E. came after a campaign that lasted three years and involved hundreds of thousands of soldiers on each side deadlocked across a front that stretched more than a hundred miles.

Because these developments in the art of war made commoners and craftsmen crucial, rulers of the warring states tried to find ways to increase their populations. To increase agricultural output, they brought new land into cultivation, drained marshes, and dug irrigation channels. By the sixth century B.C.E., some rulers were surveying their land and beginning to try to levy taxes on farmers. They wanted to undermine the power of lords over their serfs in order to get direct access to peasants' labor power. Serfdom thus gradually declined. Registering populations led to the extension of family names to commoners at an earlier date than anywhere else in the world.

The development of iron technology in the Zhou period also promoted economic expansion. Iron was cast from the beginning, unlike in the West, where iron was wrought long before it was cast. By the fifth century B.C.E., iron was being widely used for both farm tools and weapons. By the third century B.C.E., the largest smelters employed two hundred or more workmen.

The economic growth of the late Zhou period is evident in the appearance of cities all over north China. In addition to the thick earthen walls built around the palaces and ancestral temples of the ruler and other aristocrats, outer walls were added to protect the artisans, merchants, and farmers living in the surrounding area. Another sign of economic growth was the emergence of a new powerful group in society: rich people who had acquired their wealth through trade or industry rather than inheritance or political favor. Late Zhou texts frequently mention cross-regional trade in objects such as furs, copper, dyes, hemp, salt, and horses. To promote trade, rulers began casting coins, at first in the shape of miniature spades.

In the fourth century B.C.E., rulers of states started calling themselves kings, a step that amounted to announcing their intent to conquer all the other states. Rulers strengthened their control by dispatching their own officials rather than delegating authority to hereditary lesser lords. Rulers controlled these

DOCUMENTS

The King of Zhao Convinces His Uncle to Wear Barbarian Dress

The Intrigues of the Warring States is a collection of late Zhou historical anecdotes and fables about the political ploys adopted by the various competing states. The book, full of speeches by kings and court advisers, has been appreciated as a work of literature, even by those who were dismayed by its morality. In this passage, the king of Zhao has decided to adopt the trousers of the northern nomads, the Hu (also called Xiongnu), but he worried that others would make fun of him. He sent a messenger to ask his uncle, Gongzi Cheng, to join him in changing his dress. We begin here with the uncle's response.

[The uncle] Gongzi Cheng bowed twice: "I had, of course, heard of the king's Hu clothing but having been ill abed I had not yet gone to him to present my opinions. Since the king now sends me these orders, I must now make my clumsy gesture of loyalty.

"I have heard the Middle Kingdoms described as the home of all wisdom and learning, the place where all things needful of life are found, where saints and sages taught, where humanity and justice prevail, where the *Book of Poetry* and *Book of Documents and Canons of Ritual and Music* are used; a country where extraordinary skills and uncommon intelligence are given hearing, a land looked up to from afar, and a model of behavior for the barbarian. But now the king would discard all this and wear the habit of foreign regions. Let him think carefully, for he is changing the teachings of our ancients, turning from the ways of former times, going counter to the desires of his people, offending scholars, and ceasing to be part of the Middle Kingdoms."

When [the messenger] Wangsun Xie had reported, the king said merely, "I knew, of course, that he had been ill." Then, going in person to the home of Gongzi Cheng, the king urged his support: "Clothes exist to be useful and manners respond to conditions. Therefore the sage was guided by what was right and proper for each locality and encouraged behavior related to its conditions: always they sought to profit the people and strengthen their states," said the king. "To crop the hair, decorate the body, rub pigment into arms and fasten garments on the left side are the ways of the Ba and Yue [southern barbarians]. In the country of Daiwu the habit is to blacken teeth, scar cheeks, and wear caps of sheepskin stitched crudely with an awl. Their costumes and customs differ but each derives benefit from his own. . . .

"From Changshan to Dai and Shangdang, we border Yan and the Eastern Hu in the east, and Loufan, Qin, and Han in the west. Along this line we have not a single mounted archer. . . . I change our garments and mount archers to guard our borders with Yan, the Eastern Hu, Loufan, Qin, and Han. . . . With my men dressed as mounted archers I can today prepare for Shangdang nearby and exact vengeance upon Zhongshan at a distance."

Gongzi Cheng made deepest obeisance twice: "Such has been my stupidity that I had not even conceived of these arguments, your majesty. I had instead the temerity to mouth platitudes. But now that I too wish to carry out the hopes of Kings Jian and Xiang, the ambitions of our ancestral rulers, what choice have I but to make obeisance and obey your order?"

He was given the Hu garments.

Source: J. I. Crump, trans., *Chan-kuo Ts'e*, rev. ed. (Ann Arbor: University of Michigan Center for Chinese Studies, 1996), pp. 288–292, modified.

officials from a distance through the transmission of documents and could dismiss them if they proved unsatisfactory. For the *shi* (lower-level aristocrats), serving a ruler in this way offered new opportunities for advancement. There were plenty of *shi* eager for these opportunities because every time a state was destroyed, its old nobility sunk in status to *shi*. Although many *shi* did not have military skills by this period, they retained knightly values such as a sense of honor and an ideal of loyal service.

THE HUNDRED SCHOOLS OF THOUGHT

The late Zhou was a period when all sorts of ideas were proposed, debated, written down, and put to use, leading Chinese to refer to it as a period "when a hundred schools of thought bloomed." The political rivalry and constant warfare of the period helped rather than hindered intellectual creativity. Rulers turned to men of ideas for both solutions to the disorder around them and the prestige of attracting to their court wise and able men from across the land. Political strategists would travel from state to state, urging rulers to form alliances. Lively debate often resulted as strategists proposed policies and challengers critiqued them. Successful men of ideas attracted followers who took to recording their teachers' ideas on rolls of silk and tied together strips of wood or bamboo that functioned as books.

Historians of later periods, beginning with Sima Qian in about 100 B.C.E., grouped these thinkers into schools, using labels that have survived until today, such as Confucianism, Daoism, and Legalism, which may give the mistaken impression that people of the time thought in those terms. Even the books we have today are not identical to the books that first circulated, as the works of an author were added to, subtracted from, and rearranged after his death, usually by his followers. Scholars today try to distinguish the different layers of texts to analyze the development of ideas and emphasize the extensive interchange of ideas among diverse teachers and thinkers.

Confucius and the *Analects*

Confucius (whom early historians dated to 551–479 B.C.E.) was the first and most important of the men of ideas seeking to influence the rulers of the day. As a young man, Confucius served in the court of his home state of Lu without gaining much influence. After leaving Lu, he wandered through neighboring states with a small group of students, searching for a ruler who would follow his advice.

Confucius's ideas are known to us primarily through the sayings recorded by his disciples in the *Analects*. The thrust of his thought was ethical rather than theoretical or metaphysical. He talked repeatedly of an ideal age in the early Zhou, which he conceived of as a perfect society in which all people devoted themselves to fulfilling their roles: superiors looked after those dependent on them, inferiors devoted themselves to the service of their superiors, and parents and children, husbands and wives all wholeheartedly did what was expected of them.

Confucius saw much of value in family ties. He extolled filial piety, which to him encompassed reverent obedience of children toward their parents and performance of the expected rituals, such as mourning them when they died and making sacrifices to them afterward. If one's parents were about to make a major mistake, the filial child should try to dissuade them as tactfully as possible but should try not to anger them. The relationship between father and son was one of the five cardinal relations stressed by Confucius. The others were between ruler and subject, between husband and wife, between elder and younger brother, and between friends. Mutual obligations of a hierarchal sort underlay the first four of these relationships: the senior leads and protects, the junior supports and obeys. The exception was the relationship between friends, which was conceived in terms of mutual obligations between equals.

Confucian Virtues	
ren	humanity, benevolence
xiao	filial piety
yi	integrity, righteousness
zhong	loyalty, constancy
xin	honesty
jing	reverence, respect
li	propriety, ritual decorum

Confucius urged his followers to aspire to become true gentlemen (*junzi*, literally "son of a lord"), a term that he redefined to mean men of moral cultivation rather than men of noble birth. He contrasted gentlemen of integrity with petty men seeking personal gain. The gentleman, he said, "feels bad when his capabilities fall short of the task. He does not feel bad when people fail to recognize him" (15.18).

The Confucian gentleman should advise his ruler on the best way to govern. Much of the *Analects* consequently concerns how to govern well:

> *The Master said, "Lead the people by means of government policies and regulate them through punishments, and they will be evasive and have no sense of shame. Lead them by means of virtue and regulate them through rituals and they will have a sense of shame and moreover have standards." (2.3)*

To Confucius, the ultimate virtue was *ren*, a term that has been translated as humanity, perfect goodness, benevolence, human-heartedness, and nobility. A person of humanity cares about others and acts accordingly:

> *Zhonggong asked about humanity. The Master said, "When you go out, treat everyone as if you were welcoming a great guest. Employ people as though you were conducting a great sacrifice. Do not do unto others what you would not have them do unto you. Then neither in your country nor in your family will there be complaints against you." (12.2)*

Treating people as though they were guests and employing them as though participating in a great sacrifice were other ways of saying they should be treated according to *li* (ritual, manners, propriety, good form). In other passages as well, Confucius stressed the importance of disciplining one's behavior through adherence to ritual: "Respect without ritual is tiresome; caution without ritual is timidity; boldness without ritual is insubordination; straightforwardness without ritual is rudeness" (8.2). But ritual must not be empty form: "Ritual performed without reverence and mourning performed without grief are things I cannot bear" (3.26).

In the Confucian tradition, studying texts came to be valued over speculation, meditation, and mystical identification with deities. Confucius encouraged the men who came to study with him to master the poetry, rituals, and historical traditions that we know today as the Confucian classics. Many passages in the *Analects* reveal Confucius's confidence in the power of study:

> *The Master said, "I am not someone who was born wise. I am someone who loves the ancients and tries to learn from them." (7.19)*

> *The Master said, "I once spent a whole day without eating and a whole night without sleeping in order to think. It was of no use. It is better to study." (15.30)*

Confucius talked mostly about the social and political realms rather than the world of gods, ghosts, or ancestral spirits. Moreover, although he is portrayed as deeply committed to ritual, he was said to have performed sacrifices as though the spirits were present, leaving open the possibility that he was not convinced that ancestors or other spirits were actually aided by the offerings people made to them.

Mozi

Not long after Confucius died, his ideas were challenged by Mozi (ca. 480–390 B.C.E.), a man who came not from the aristocracy but from among the master craftsmen. He was, however, well read and, like Confucius, quoted from the *Book of Documents* and *Book of Poetry*. Unlike Confucius, however, he did not talk of the distinction between gentlemen and vulgar "petty men," but rather of "concern for everyone," sometimes translated as "universal love." He put forward the idea that conflict could be eliminated if everyone gave other people's families and other people's states the same concern he gave his own. Mozi contended that all people recognize the validity of this idea because if they have to leave their family in someone else's care, they choose someone who accepts this ideal. To counter the argument that impartiality is not easy to achieve, Mozi said the sage kings of old had practiced it, proving its feasibility. Mozi also argued strongly for the merit principle, asserting that rulers should choose their advisers on the basis of their ability, not their birth.

The book ascribed to Mozi (called *Mozi*) proposes that every idea be evaluated on the basis of its utility: does it benefit the people and the state? Using this standard, Mozi rejected many of the rituals emphasized by Confucius's followers, especially mourning parents for three years, which Mozi noted interrupts work, injures health, and thus impoverishes the people and weakens the state. Music, too, Mozi saw as a wasteful extravagance of no utility.

Mozi made a similar case against aggressive war, seeing no glory in expansion for its own sake. He pointed to the huge losses in weapons, horses, and human lives it causes. The capture of a city, he argued, is not worth the loss of thousands of men. But Mozi was for strong government and obedience toward superiors. He argued that disorder could be eliminated if everyone conformed his beliefs to those of his superior, the king conforming to Heaven.

Mozi had many followers over the next couple of centuries, and they organized themselves into tight groups. Because they saw offensive warfare as evil, these Mohists, as they are called, considered it their duty to come to the aid of cities under attack. They became experts in defending against sieges, teaching, for instance, that each soldier on the city walls should be held responsible for the two soldiers on his immediate left and right, a form of group responsibility later picked up by the Legalists.

After a few centuries, however, Mozi's school declined and eventually lost its distinct identity. Certain ideas, such as support for the merit principle and criticism of extravagance, were absorbed into Confucian thought in later centuries. Mencius, who lived a century after Mozi, borrowed his arguments against military aggression, and like him would often try to persuade rulers that they had not correctly identified where their advantage lay. Confucians, however, never accepted Mohist ideas about treating everyone equally, which they saw as unnatural, or of applying rigidly utilitarian tests to ritual and music, whose value they saw in very different terms.

Mencius

Among the followers of Confucius eager to defend his teachings against Mozi's attacks, Mencius stands out. We know of Mencius (ca. 370–ca. 300 B.C.E.) largely from the book that bears his name, which Mencius may have written in large part himself. Mencius came from the small and unimportant state of Zou, next to Confucius's home state of Lu. He was born too late to have studied with Confucius himself, but he quotes Confucius approvingly and was said to have studied Confucian teachings with a student of Confucius's grandson.

The first two of the seven parts of the *Mencius* record conversations that took place from 320 to 314 B.C.E. between Mencius and a king of Qi and two successive kings of Wei. The opening passage in the *Mencius* records one such encounter:

Mencius had an audience with King Hui of Liang [Wei]. The king said, "Sir, you did not consider a thousand li too far to come. You must have some ideas about how to benefit my state."

Mencius replied, "Why must Your Majesty use the word 'benefit'? All I am concerned with are the benevolent and the right. If Your Majesty says, 'How can I benefit my state?' your officials will say, 'How can I benefit my family,' and officers and common people will say, 'How can I benefit myself.' Once superiors and inferiors are competing for benefit, the state will be in danger." (1A.1)

Like Confucius, Mencius traveled around offering advice to rulers of various states. He tried repeatedly to convert them to the view that the ruler able to win over the people through benevolent government would succeed in unifying "all under Heaven." Mencius proposed concrete political and financial measures for easing tax burdens and otherwise improving the people's lot. He also tried to get rulers to give up seeking military victories. To seek military domination will backfire, he argued, for it will turn the world against you, whereas those who are benevolent will have no enemies.

Men willing to serve an unworthy ruler earned Mencius's contempt, especially when they worked hard to fill his coffers or expand his territory. He pointed out that Confucius broke off his relationship with his disciple Ran Qiu when he doubled the tax collection but did not do anything to reform the ruler's character.

Although the bulk of the *Mencius* concerns issues of governing, Mencius also discussed moral philosophy. He argued strongly, for instance, that human nature was fundamentally good, as everyone is born with the capacity to recognize what is right. He gave the example of the person who automatically grabs a baby about to fall into a well: "It would not be because he wanted to improve his relations with the child's parents, nor because he wanted a good reputation among his friends and neighbors, nor because he disliked hearing the child cry" (2A.6). Rather it was due to his inborn feelings of commiseration and sense of right and wrong.

Mencius quotes some conversations with a contemporary philosopher who disagreed with his interpretation of human nature:

Gaozi said, "Human nature is like whirling water. When an outlet is opened to the east, it flows east; when an outlet is opened to the west, it flows west. Human nature is no more inclined to good or bad than water is inclined to east or west."

Mencius responded, "Water, it is true, is not inclined to either east or west, but does it have no preference for high or low? Goodness is to human nature like flowing downward is to water. There are no people who are not good and no water that does not flow down. Still, water, if splashed, can go higher than your head; if forced, it can be brought up a hill. This isn't the nature of water; it is the specific circumstances. Although people can be made to be bad, their natures are not changed." (6A.2)

Sometimes Mencius related men's moral nature to Heaven. Heaven wants men to be moral and operates in history through men's choices. Heaven validates a ruler's authority through the people's acceptance of him. But Mencius did not think all rulers had been validated by Heaven; true kings tended to appear only about every five hundred years.

Xunzi

The *Xunzi* was written in large part by Xunzi (ca. 310–ca. 215 B.C.E.), who lived a half-century after Mencius and was Mencius's rival as an interpreter of Confucius's legacy. Xunzi explicitly opposed Mencius's view of human nature, arguing that people are born selfish and that it is only through education and ritual that they learn to put moral principle above their own interest. Much of what is desirable is not inborn, he said, but must be taught:

> *When a son yields to his father, or a younger brother yields to his elder brother, or when a son takes on the work for his father or a younger brother for his elder brother, their actions go against their natures and run counter to their feelings. And yet these are the way of the filial son and the principles of ritual and morality. (13)*

Neither Confucius nor Mencius had much actual political or administrative experience. By contrast, Xunzi worked for many years in the governments of several of the states. Not surprisingly, he showed more consideration than either Confucius or Mencius for the difficulties a ruler might face in trying to rule through ritual and virtue. He strongly supported the view, earlier articulated by Mozi, that the worthy should be promoted even if they were descendants of commoners. In response to a question on how to govern, Xunzi said the ruler should promote the worthy and capable, dismiss the incompetent, and punish the evil without bothering to try to reform them. Xunzi, like Mencius, supported the basic message of the Mandate of Heaven: "The ruler is the boat, the common people are the water. It is the

water that bears up the boat but also the water that capsizes it" (9).

Xunzi was a more rigorous thinker than his predecessors and developed the philosophical foundations of many ideas that Confucius or Mencius had merely outlined. Confucius, for instance, had declined to discuss gods, portents, and anomalies and had spoken of sacrificing as if the spirits were present. Xunzi went further and explicitly argued that Heaven does not intervene in human affairs. Praying to Heaven or to gods, he asserted, does not induce them to act. "Why does it rain after a prayer for rain? In my opinion, for no reason. It is the same as raining when you had not prayed" (17).

Although he did not think praying could bring rain or other benefits from Heaven, Xunzi did not propose abandoning traditional rituals. In contrast to Daoists and Mohists, who saw rituals as unnatural or extravagant, Xunzi saw in ritual an efficient way to attain order in society. Rulers and educated men should continue traditional ritual practices such as complex funeral protocols because the rites themselves have positive effects on performers and observers. Not only do they let people express feelings and satisfy desires in an orderly way, but by specifying graduated ways to perform the rites according to social rank, ritual traditions sustain the social hierarchy. Xunzi compared and contrasted ritual and music: music shapes people's emotions and creates feelings of solidarity, while ritual shapes people's sense of duty and creates social differentiation.

Daoism and the Laozi and Zhuangzi

Confucius and his followers believed in moral and political effort. They thought men of virtue should devote themselves to making the government work to the benefit of the people. Those who later came to be labeled Daoists disagreed. The authors of the *Laozi* and *Zhuangzi* thought striving to make things better generally makes them worse. They defended private life and wanted the rulers to leave the people alone. They sought to go beyond everyday concerns and let their minds wander freely. Rather than making human beings and human actions the center of concern, they focused on the larger scheme of things, the whole natural order identified as the Way or Dao.

Both the *Laozi* and the *Zhuangzi* date to the third century B.C.E. Master Lao, the putative author of the *Laozi*, may not be a historical figure, but the text ascribed to him has been of enduring importance.

A recurrent theme in this brief, aphoristic text is the mystical superiority of yielding over assertion and silence over words. "The Way that can be discussed is not the constant Way" (1). The highest good is like water: "Water benefits all creatures but does not compete. It occupies the places people disdain and thus comes near to the Way" (8).

Because purposeful action is counterproductive, the ruler should let people return to a natural state of ignorance and contentment:

> Do not honor the worthy,
> And the people will not compete.
> Do not value rare treasures,
> And the people will not steal.
> Do not display what others want,
> And the people will not have their hearts
>   confused.
> A sage governs this way:
> He empties people's minds and fills their bellies.
> He weakens their wills and strengthens their
>   bones.
> Keep the people always without knowledge
>   and without desires,
> For then the clever will not dare act.
> Engage in no action and order will prevail. (3)

In the philosophy of the *Laozi*, the people would be better off if they knew less, gave up tools, renounced writing, stopped envying their neighbors, and lost their desire to travel or wage war.

Zhuangzi (369–286 B.C.E.), the author of the book of the same name, was a historical figure who shared many of the central ideas of the *Laozi*, such as the usefulness of the useless and the relativity of ordinary distinctions. He was proud of his disinterest in politics. In one of his many anecdotes, he reported that the king of Chu once sent an envoy to invite him to take over the government of his realm. In response, Zhuangzi asked the envoy whether a tortoise that had been held as sacred for three thousand years would prefer to be dead with its bones venerated or alive with its tail dragging in the mud. When the envoy agreed that life was preferable, Zhuangzi told the envoy to leave, as he would rather drag his tail in the mud.

The *Zhuangzi* is filled with parables, flights of fancy, and fictional encounters between historical figures, including Confucius and his disciples. Yet the book also deals with serious issues, including death. Zhuangzi questioned whether we can be sure life is better than death. People fear what they do not know, the same way a captive girl will be terrified when she learns she is to become the king's concubine. Perhaps people will discover that death has as many delights as life in the palace. When a friend expressed shock that Zhuangzi was not weeping at his wife's death, Zhuangzi explained that he had at first, but then began thinking back to before she had life or form or vital energy. "In this confused amorphous realm, something changed and vital energy appeared; when the vital energy was changed, form appeared; with changes in form, life began. Now there is another change bringing death. This is like the progression of the four seasons of spring and fall, winter and summer" (18). Once he had realized this, he stopped sobbing.

Zhuangzi was similarly iconoclastic in his political ideas. In one parable, a wheelwright insolently tells a duke that books are useless since all they contain are the dregs of men long dead. The duke, insulted, threatened to execute him if he could not give an adequate explanation of his remark. The wheelwright then explained that he could feel in his hand how to chisel but could not describe it in words. "I cannot teach it to my son, and my son cannot learn it from me. So I have gone on for seventy years, growing old chiseling wheels. The men of old died in possession of what they could not transmit. So it follows that what you are reading are their dregs" (13). Zhuangzi here questions the validity of verbal reasoning and the sorts of knowledge conveyed in books.

The ideas of the *Laozi* and *Zhuangzi* can be seen as a response to Confucianism, a rejection of many of its basic premises. Nevertheless, over the course of Chinese history, many people felt the pull of both Confucian and Daoist ideas and studied the writings of both schools. Even Confucian scholars who devoted much of their life to public service might find that the teachings of Laozi or Zhuangzi helped them put their frustrations in perspective. Whereas Confucianism often seems sternly masculine, Daoism was more accepting of feminine principles (yin of the yin-yang pair) and even celebrated passivity and yielding. Those drawn to the arts were also often drawn to Daoism, with its validation of spontaneity and freedom. Rulers too saw merit in the Daoist notion of the ruler who can have great power simply by being himself without instituting anything.

Legalism

Over the course of the fourth and third centuries B.C.E., as one small state after another was destroyed, rulers, fearful that their state might be next, were ready to listen to political theorists who claimed expertise in the accumulation of power. These theorists, labeled Legalists because of their emphasis on the need for rigorous laws, argued that strong government depended not on the moral qualities of the ruler and his officials, as Confucians claimed, but on establishing effective laws and procedures.

In the fourth century B.C.E., the state of Qin, under the leadership of its chancellor, Lord Shang (d. 338 B.C.E.), adopted many Legalist policies. Instead of an aristocracy with inherited titles, social distinctions were based on military ranks determined by the objective criterion of the number of enemy heads cut off in battle. In place of the old fiefs, Qin divided the country into counties and appointed officials to administer them according to the laws decreed at court. To increase the population, migrants were recruited from other states with offers of land. To encourage farmers to work hard and improve their land, they were allowed to buy and sell it. Ordinary farmers were thus freed from serf-like obligations to the local nobility. Nevertheless, direct control by the state could be even more onerous, as taxes and labor service obligations were heavy.

In the third century B.C.E., Legalism found its greatest exponent in Han Feizi (d. 233 B.C.E.), who had studied with the Confucian master Xunzi but had little interest in Confucian virtues. Alarmed at the weakness of his own state of Han, Han Feizi wrote to warn rulers of the political pitfalls awaiting them. They had to be careful where they placed their trust, for "when the ruler trusts someone, he falls under that person's control" (17). This was true even of wives and concubines, who think of the interests of their sons. Given subordinates' propensities to pursue their own selfish interests, the ruler should keep them ignorant of his intentions and control them by manipulating competition among them. Warmth, affection, or candor should have no place in his relationships with others.

Han Feizi saw the Confucian notion that government could be based on virtue as naive. Even parents calculate their long-term advantage in favoring sons over daughters. One cannot expect rulers to be more selfless than parents. If rulers would make the laws and prohibitions clear and the rewards and punishments automatic, then the officials and common people would be easy to govern. Uniform laws get people to do things they would not otherwise be inclined to do, such as work hard and fight wars, which were essential to the goal of establishing hegemony over all the other states.

The laws of the Legalists were designed as much to constrain officials as to regulate the common people. The third-century B.C.E. tomb of a Qin official has yielded statutes detailing the rules for keeping accounts, supervising subordinates, managing penal labor, conducting investigations, and many other responsibilities. Those who violated these statutes were fined.

Legalism saw no value in intellectual debate or private opinion. The ruler should not allow others to undermine his laws by questioning them. Rulers of several states adopted some Legalist ideas, but only the state of Qin systematically followed them. The extraordinary but brief success Qin had with these policies is discussed in Chapter 3.

Yin and Yang

The thinkers and books discussed here had the greatest long-term impact on Chinese civilization, but the late Zhou "Hundred Schools of Thought" also included much else. There were logicians, hedonists, utopians, hermits, and agriculturalists who argued that no one should eat who does not farm. There were natural philosophers who drew lessons from their study of such fields as astronomy, medicine, music, and calendrical calculations. The concepts of yin and yang were particularly important to natural philosophy. Yin is the feminine, dark, receptive, yielding, negative, and weak; yang is the masculine, bright, assertive, creative, positive, and strong. Yin and yang are complementary poles rather than distinct entities or opposing forces. The movement of yin and yang accounts for the transition from day to night and from summer to winter. They are also involved in health and illness. The *Zuo zhuan* quotes Physician He on the six *qi* (vapors, forms of energy), which he defines as yin and yang, wind and rain, dark and bright. These six qi divide to make the four seasons, radiate to make the five colors and five sounds, and, when they go to excess, produce the six illnesses.

The Art of War

Another important strand of thought of this period concerns military strategy. Sunzi's *Art of War*, dating probably to the third century B.C.E., warns against bravado. Since warfare causes loss of life and property, it is better to win without expending resources. "One hundred victories in one hundred battles is not skillful; what is skillful is subjugating the opponent's army without battle" (Chap. 3). Great generals are not those who charge up hills against overwhelming odds but those who advance only after they know they can win. Heroism is a useless virtue that leads to needless deaths. Discipline, however, is essential, and Sunzi insisted that the entire army had to be trained to follow the orders of its commanders without questioning them. Spying on and manipulating the enemy are tactics worth learning, as is doing things the enemy will not anticipate. Often phrases in the *Art of War* echo the *Laozi*: "The form of the military is like water. Water in its movements avoids the high and hastens to the low. The military in its victory avoids the solid and strikes the empty. Thus water determines its movement in accordance with the earth. The military determines victory in accordance with the enemy."[2]

The World of Spirits

The development of rationalistic and naturalistic ways of thinking does not mean that people no longer took an interest in the world of spirits. The records of divination found in the tomb of an official who died in 316 B.C.E. show that illness was seen as the result of unsatisfied spirits or malevolent demons, best dealt with through exorcisms or sacrifices to the astral deity Taiyi (Grand One). Some texts give incantations that could be used to exorcise offending demons. There were also ceremonies that could offer protection from evil spirits. To escape trouble on a trip, travelers were encouraged to perform a ceremony at the threshold of the gate to the city. They would call on the sage-king Yu to clear the road for them, draw five lines on the ground, then pick up some of the soil by the lines, and put it in the folds of their robe by their bosom. Texts on these occult and magico-religious subjects that have been found in

excavation of late Warring States tombs have shown that traditions in these fields were transmitted in writing much as those of the philosophers were.

WARRING STATES LITERATURE AND ART: THE CASE OF CHU

All through the Eastern Zhou Dynasty, despite political division, peoples on the periphery of the Zhou world were drawn into it. This does not mean, however, that all cultural differences were eliminated. As discussed in Chapter 1, the bronzes found south of the Yangzi River during the Shang Dynasty employed the same technology used at Anyang yet often featured highly distinctive decoration. For the Zhou period, because of the much greater survival of texts and an abundance of archaeological finds, it is possible to trace how the south steadily became a more integral part of the Zhou world and yet maintained a distinctive style.

The dominant state in the south was Chu. From Western Zhou times on, Chu gradually expanded, absorbing fifty or more small states as it pushed its borders northward and eastward. In the Eastern Zhou period, Chu became one of the strongest and most innovative states. In 548 B.C.E. it conducted a survey of its population to assess tax and military duties. Chu also was the first to form counties (*xian*) out of newly annexed land and to dispatch officials to administer them (instead of conferring the land on hereditary lords). In 334 B.C.E. Chu conquered the state of Yue, gaining control of the Lower Yangzi region. By the third century, Chu was a full participant in the alliances designed to maintain a balance of power. This does not mean that those in the central regions no longer put it down as a primitive or barbarian region. Mencius chastised a man for following a teacher who came from Chu, saying, "I have heard of men using Chinese ways to transform the barbarians but not of being transformed by the barbarians" (*Mencius* 3A.4).

It has been estimated that 70 percent of known Eastern Zhou tombs are in the Chu area. Much more in the way of lacquer and silk survives from tombs in this region than elsewhere in China for this period—a function of the high water tables in many places—giving us a remarkably full picture of the material life of the elite of Chu. Flowing, curvilinear lines, sometimes incorporating birds, dragons, snakes, and other creatures, are found on embroi-

---

2. Translation by Kidder Smith in Wm. Theodore de Bary and Irene Bloom, eds., *Sources of Chinese Tradition*, rev. ed. (New York: Columbia University Press, 1999), p. 221.

MATERIAL CULTURE

Lacquer

Lacquer is made from the sap of a tree native to south and central China. When it is heated and purified, the sap makes a light, strong, smooth, and waterproof material that is highly resistant to decay. By Eastern Zhou times, craftsmen were using lacquer on furniture, coffins, bowls, cups, musical instruments, and sculpture. In most cases, many layers of lacquer were applied over a wooden core. Lacquer objects could be decorated with pictures or designs, using lacquer colored with pigments such as cinnabar for red and carbon for black. See also Color Plate 3.

Lacquer Cup. This six-inch-long cup was found in Tomb 1 at Mashan, Jiangling, Hubei province, and dates to the early third century B.C.E. It is decorated with images of two large birds in red, black, and yellow colors. *(Jingzhou Prefecture Museum, Hubei Province)*

dered silks, inlaid bronzes, and painted lacquer (see **Material Culture: Lacquer**).

One of the most interesting of the Chu tombs, excavated in 1986–1987 in Baoshan, Hubei province, was for an official who died in 316 B.C.E. The tomb had four chambers filled with ritual vessels, furniture, and other objects of daily life such as fans, mirrors, boxes, weapons and chariot fittings, and books. The books include reports by the local government, texts on divination, and an inventory of the tomb's contents. Although the calligraphy of the books is elegant, many of the characters are in obsolete forms that have not yet been deciphered.

The distinctiveness of Chu culture can also be seen in the masterpiece of Chu literature, the *Songs of Chu* (Chu ci). The fantastic poems in this work are worlds apart from the poems in the *Book of Poetry*. The principal poem in the collection, titled *Encountering Sorrows*, is the lament of Qu Yuan (ca. 340–278 B.C.E.), an anti-Qin minister who lost the favor of the Chu kings and was sent into exile. Distraught that his loyalty to his ruler was not appreciated, he finally threw himself into a river. In the poem, Qu Yuan describes his misfortunes, declares his virtue, maligns those who have defamed him, and goes on a cosmic quest for a lord worthy of his devotion. On that venture, he imagines himself wandering on the clouds and looking down on the earth. The structure of the almost four hundred lines of this lengthy poem corresponds to shamanic spirit quests in which the shaman declares his worth and goes to heaven to seek the god or goddess who spurned him. Several of the shorter poems in the *Songs of Chu* fall into this tradition as well. The one that follows is titled the "Lord of the Yellow River":

> With you I will roam to the river's nine channels,
> when blasts of wind rise driving waves across
>   stream,
> we will ride my coach of waters, its canopy, lotus,
> hitched to paired dragons, by basilisks flanked.
> I climbed Mount Kun-lun, I gazed all around,
> the heart flew aloft, it went sweeping off free.
> soon the sun was to set, I, transfixed, forgot
>   going,
> and then to the far shore I looked back with
>   care.
> My roofs are of fish scales, halls of the dragon,
> turrets of purple cowries, palaces of carmine—
> why is the holy one here, down in the water?

Bells of the Marquis of Yi. The tomb of a minor ruler who died in 433 B.C.E. contained 124 musical instruments, including drums, flutes, mouth organs, pan pipes, zithers, a set of 32 chime stones, and this 64-piece bell set. Five men using poles and mallets, and standing on either side of the set of bells, would have played the bells by hitting them from outside. *(Cultural Relics Publishing House)*

We will ride on white turtles, goldfish attend us,
with you I will roam by the river's isles,
where the current is rushing, there we'll go down.
You clasp your hands, journeying eastward;
you go with the Fairest to the southern shores
where the swell of the waves is coming to meet
  us,
and the schools of fishes, will send off my bride.[3]

SUMMARY

How did China change during the five centuries of the Eastern Zhou period? The Chinese world had grown by absorbing previously peripheral areas like Chu in the south and Zhongshan in the north. The economy had changed from one that was essentially manorial to one in which coinage was in use, trade was much more extensive, and iron was widely used for tools. The social structure had similarly been transformed from one in which membership in the elite depended almost entirely on birth to one in which there was considerable opportunity for advancement for talented *shi*. City-states had become territorial states, with rulers making use of officials to draw on the resources of their entire population. Conscription was nearly universal. Warfare was no longer hemmed in by notions of chivalry and as a consequence had become much more deadly. Intellectual discourse was much richer, with a great many texts in circulation that sought to persuade through argument and example. Distinct schools of thought had emerged. The writing of history had advanced, with much more in the way of extended narratives.

3. Stephen Owen, *An Anthology of Chinese Literature* (New York: Norton, 1996), p. 160.

3

The Founding of the Bureaucratic Empire: Qin-Han China (256 B.C.E.–200 C.E.)

Qin's battle-hardened armies destroyed the Zhou royal domain in 256 B.C.E. and the last of the independent states in 221 B.C.E., thus unifying the Chinese realm. Although Qin rule did not last long, the succeeding Han Dynasty retained its centralized bureaucratic monarchy. Both Qin and Han mobilized huge armies to confront the emergence of a powerful enemy to the north, the Xiongnu tribal confederation. In part to deal with the Xiongnu threat, the Han government extended its territories to the east, west, and south.

In contrast to the Qin government, which favored Legalism, the Han government preferred that its officials be learned in the Confucian classics. With these officials, the Han government proved remarkably successful in coordinating administrative control of a population of about 59 million people. Still, the imperial institution proved vulnerable to manipulation by the families of empresses and by palace eunuchs.

The Han Dynasty is the first of the five major dynasties that lasted more than two and a half centuries (Han, Tang, Song, Ming, and Qing), and scholars often look at the Han with these later dynasties in mind. The structure and operation of the government have been major concerns: What enabled Han to succeed where Qin had failed? What was the impact of the centralized state on ordinary people's lives? What were the consequences of the support the government gave to Confucianism? What type of Confucianism did the government support? Later dynasties had difficulties on their northern borders reminiscent of the Han-Xiongnu confrontation, drawing scholars' attention to this initial stage. Was conflict between China and its northern neighbors inevitable given the differences in the economies of the two regions, or could different policies have led to different outcomes? Did the Han Dynasty's great territorial expansion aid it in any way, or was it costly overextension?

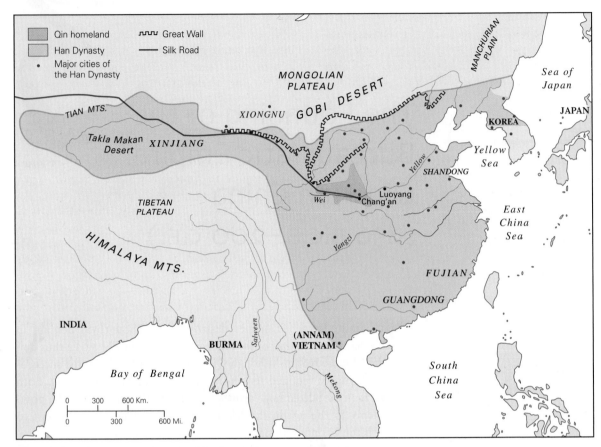

Map 3.1   The Han Empire at Its Maximum Extent, ca. 50 B.C.E.

THE QIN UNIFICATION (256–206 B.C.E.)

The year 221 B.C.E., one of the most important dates in Chinese history, marks the beginning of the Chinese empire. That year, the state of Qin, which had adopted Legalist policies, succeeded in defeating the last of its rivals, thus creating a unified China (see Map 3.1). As discussed in the last chapter, following the counsel of Legalist advisers, Qin had restructured itself in the fourth century B.C.E. The power of the old nobility and the patriarchal family were curtailed to create instead a direct relationship between the ruler and his subjects based on uniformly enforced laws and punishments, administered by officials appointed by the king.

One of the most influential men in Qin in the decades before the conquest was a rich merchant, Lü Buwei. That a merchant could use his wealth to gain political favor is evidence of the high social mobility

of the age. Lü was said to have decided that gaining control of a state offered more opportunities to grow rich than commerce did, and to have come up with a scheme to accomplish that by favoring a potential heir to the throne, then helping him succeed to it. Once Lü's protégé became king, Lü became chancellor. There followed a string of stunning victories over other states, allowing Qin to increase its territories steadily. This king died after only three years on the throne, and in 247 thirteen-year-old King Cheng came to the throne, with Lü as regent. One of the orders he issued was that common people who had amassed riches through their own enterprise be granted noble ranks. Those so honored included a man who traded silk for animals with the Rong barbarians and a widow who managed the family cinnabar mines.

Lü recruited scholars to come to Qin, where he put them to work on a book that would present a unified philosophy for the unified realm he envisioned. The resulting book, *The Annals of Mr. Lü*, combines cosmological correlative thinking with political philosophy from all the major schools. The ruler should be tranquil and unassertive, as *Laozi* had advised, but select wise ministers and trust their advice, an essentially Confucian attitude. The state should aid farmers, keep taxes low, and encourage merchants. Filial piety is extolled, as is learning.

After King Cheng began to rule on his own, he sent Lü Buwei away. Lü, seeing that he was losing favor, committed suicide. King Cheng's next chancellor was Li Si, a fully committed Legalist who, like Han Feizi, had studied under the Confucian scholar Xunzi. With Li Si's astute advice, Qin was able to reorganize each territory as it took it over. By 230 the tide of war had shifted in Qin's favor, and the final six states—Han, Zhao, Wei, Chu, Yan, and Qi—were defeated in rapid succession. All of a sudden Qin had to rule millions of people who had until then been desperately battling to avoid such a fate.

The First Emperor (r. 221–210 B.C.E.)

Once Qin ruled all of China, King Cheng decided that the title "king" was not grand enough and invented the title "emperor" (literarily, "august theocrat," *huangdi*), using words that linked him to the sage rulers of the mythical past. He called himself the First Emperor in anticipation of a long line of successors.

The First Emperor initiated a sweeping program of centralization that touched the lives of nearly everyone in China. To cripple the nobility of the defunct states, the First Emperor ordered nobles to leave their lands and move to the capital, Xianyang (near modern Xi'an). To administer the territory that had been seized, he dispatched officials whom he controlled through a mass of regulations, reporting requirements, and penalties for inadequate performance. These officials owed their power and positions entirely to the favor of the emperor and

Character					
Qi					
Chu					
Yan					
Han					
Zhao					
Wei					
Qin					
Translation	peace	horse	positive	level	city

Figure 3.1 **Standardizing the Writing System**

had no hereditary rights to their offices. To make it easier to administer all regions uniformly, writing systems were standardized, as were weights, measures, coinage, and even the axle lengths of carts. Private possession of arms was outlawed in order to make it more difficult for subjects to rebel. Thousands of miles of roads were built to enable Qin armies to move rapidly. Transportation was also improved by expanding canals linking rivers, making it possible to travel long distances by boat. Most of the labor on these projects came from farmers performing required labor service or convicts working off their sentences.

The First Emperor shared the Legalist suspicion of intellectual diversity. In 213 B.C.E., after Li Si complained that scholars used records of the past to denigrate the emperor's achievements and undermine popular support, the emperor ordered the collection and burning of all useless writings. The only works excepted were manuals on topics such as agriculture, medicine, and divination. As a result of this massive book burning, many ancient texts were lost.

The First Emperor's Tomb

The First Emperor started work on his tomb soon after he came to the throne. In 231 B.C.E., the area around the tomb was made a separate administrative district, and the people of the district were made responsible for the construction and maintenance of the imperial tomb. Twenty years later, thirty thousand families were resettled to the district, and several hundred thousand forced laborers were sent there as temporary workers.

In 1974, about a kilometer from the tomb, a pit was discovered filled with life-sized terra-cotta figures of soldiers. Since then, as archaeologists have probed the region around the First Emperor's tomb, they have found more and more pits filled with burial goods of one sort or another. Sometimes actual objects were used, in other cases replicas. One pit had two finely made half-size bronze chariots, each drawn by four bronze horses. In another pit were thirty-one rare birds and animals that had been buried alive in clay coffins laid in rows. Although these were real birds and animals (probably from the huge imperial hunting park), they are guarded by a terra-cotta warden. Actual horses were buried in other pits. In many cases, a small pit had a single horse and a terra-cotta groom. In one pit, however, were bones of three hundred horses. There is also a pit where more than a

hundred human skeletons have been found; according to inscribed shards, these were conscript and penal laborers who died on the job.

By far the most spectacular of the pits discovered in the vicinity of the First Emperor's tomb are the three that contain the terra-cotta army. Historians had no knowledge of this army, so its discovery was a complete surprise. Pit 1 has more than six thousand figures of warriors arrayed in columns, most of them infantry, but with some chariots near the front. Pit 2 has cavalry plus more infantry and chariots and may represent a guard unit. Pit 3 seems to be the command post, with fewer soldiers. The floor of these pits had been made of rammed earth covered by ceramic tiles (some 256,000 for pit 1). Wooden supports held up roof beams strong enough to keep the roofs from caving in from the weight of the earth above.

The soldiers were made of simple clay formed with molds. Although viewers often described the soldiers as individualized, in reality they were made of interchangeable parts. For instance, there were two basic forms for hands, with fingers straight or curved, but they could appear quite different depending on how they were attached to the sleeves and the angle at which the thumb was attached. Hand finishing—for instance, of the hair—could make figures seem more distinct as well. After the soldiers were molded, they were painted with lacquer, which both preserved them and made them seem more lifelike. These figures carried real weapons, such as spears, halberds, swords, and bows and arrows. The weapons were of high quality (some of the blades are still razor sharp) and were mass-produced in state factories. To ensure quality control, each weapon was inscribed with the names of the worker who made it and the person who supervised him. Each also had a serial number.

Why did the First Emperor want so many replicas of soldiers buried near him? For several centuries, there had been a trend in Chinese burial practice to bury representations rather than real objects in graves. To some extent, this could have been a cost-saving measure: if replicas were just as good as the real thing in the afterlife, why take so much wealth out of circulation by placing it underground? But possibly replicas were considered in some way superior because they caught the unchanging universal aspect of the thing, not one particular manifestation. It is perhaps hard to believe that a ceramic representation of a bronze ritual vessel could be as useful in the afterlife as a real bronze one, but one can imag-

The First Emperor's Army. The thousands of life-sized terra-cotta soldiers placed in pits near the First Emperor's tomb were originally painted in bright colors, and they held real bronze weapons. They testify both to the emperor's concern with the afterlife and the ability of his government to organize production on a large scale. *(Laurent Lecat/AKG-Images)*

ine that a ceramic guard, which will never decay, could be preferable to a mortal one.

The First Emperor's personal fears and beliefs undoubtedly also contributed to his decision to construct such an elaborate underground world. Three times assassins tried to kill him, and perhaps as a consequence he became obsessed with finding ways to avoid death. He sent a group of young men and women to search for Penglai, the famed isles of immortality in the Eastern Sea. He listened to seers and magicians who claimed to know other techniques for achieving immortality. Was his huge tomb a fallback plan—a way to reduce the sting of death if he couldn't escape it altogether?

Although the First Emperor filled the pits near his tomb with terra-cotta replicas of his minions, his successor saw to it that some human beings were buried there as well. According to Sima Qian, writing in about 100 B.C.E.:

The Second Emperor said, "Of the women in the harem of the former ruler, it would be unfitting to have those who bore no sons sent elsewhere." All were accordingly ordered to accompany the dead man, which resulted in the death of many women. After the interment had been completed, someone pointed out that the artisans and craftsmen who had built the tomb knew what was buried there, and if they should leak word of the treasures, it would be a serious affair. Therefore, after the articles had been placed in the tomb, the inner gate was closed off and the outer gate lowered, so that all the artisans and craftsmen were shut in the tomb and were unable to get out.[1]

---

1. Burton Watson, trans., *Records of the Grand Historian: Qin Dynasty* (New York: Columbia University Press, 1993), p. 65.

Presumably when the archaeologists excavate the tomb itself, they will find the bones not only of the First Emperor, but also of those who accompanied him in death.

Some twentieth-century Chinese historians have glorified the First Emperor as a bold conqueror who let no obstacle impede him, but the traditional evaluation of him was almost entirely negative. For centuries, Chinese historians castigated him as a monster: cruel, arbitrary, impetuous, suspicious, and superstitious.

Qin Law

The Qin was always thought to have had a particularly harsh legal system, but little was known about its exact provisions until 1975 when 625 bamboo strips inscribed with Qin laws and legal texts were found in a tomb in Hubei province. The tomb was for a man who served the Qin government as a prefectural official. Some of the texts reconstructed from the strips contain statutes related to management of government granaries and labor service. One book explains legal terminology in question-and-answer format.

The penalties imposed by Qin law were hard labor, physical mutilation, banishment, slavery, or death. Labor could last from one to six years. Mutilation included shaving the beard, shaving the head, branding the forehead, cutting off the nose or left foot, or castration. Death also came in several forms, the most severe of which was being torn apart by horse-drawn chariots. To make sure that criminals were caught and offenses reported, Qin set up mutual responsibility units of five households, whose members were required to inform on each other or suffer the same penalty as the criminal. For particularly heinous crimes, even distant relatives could be enslaved.

Penal labor was a common punishment. Those guilty of theft or homicide were sentenced to long terms, but even those sentenced to pay fines often had to work off their sentence with labor, credited at the rate of eight coins a day (six if one received food rations). Those who owned slaves, oxen, or horses could receive credit for the work they did, or they could hire others to work in their place. Men and women were treated differently. Men had heavier work assignments but received larger rations. A man could volunteer for service on the frontier for five years to redeem his mother or sister but not his father or brother.

Government officials had to take similar responsibility for the performance of their departments.

Every year in the tenth month, officials had to send in detailed reports to be used for the evaluation of their performance. If they did more or less than expected, they were punished by fines calculated in sets of armor and shields.

The Xiongnu and the Great Wall

As far back as written records allow us to see, the Chinese had shared the Chinese subcontinent with other ethnic groups. To the north were groups that the Shang and Zhou called Rong and Di. At that time, the economy of these northerners was similar to that of the Chinese settlements, with millet agriculture, animal husbandry, and hunting. Many of these groups were eventually incorporated into the northern Zhou states, which gradually expanded north. Over time, those not incorporated into China seem to have come to depend more and more on animal husbandry, perhaps because the climate grew colder or drier. They took to riding horses before the Chinese did, and by the seventh century B.C.E., many of these groups were making the move to nomadic pastoralism. Families lived in tents that could be taken down and moved north in summer and south in winter as they moved in search of fresh pasture. Herds were tended on horseback, and everyone learned to ride from a young age. Especially awesome from the Chinese perspective was the ability of nomad horsemen to shoot arrows while riding horseback. Their social organization was tribal, with family and clan units held together through loyalty to chiefs selected for their military prowess. At the end of the Zhou period, there were three main groups of nomads in the Northern Zone: the Eastern Hu in the east (northern Hebei-Liaoning region), the Xiongnu in the Ordos (northern Shaanxi-Shanxi), and the Yuezhi to the west.

In 215 B.C.E., one of Qin's most successful generals, Meng Tian, led a huge army (said variously to be one hundred thousand or three hundred thousand strong) to attack the Xiongnu and drive them out of the Ordos region. Once he had succeeded, he built forty-four roads to the region and fortified towns, projects that required tens of thousands of laborers. People sentenced to guard the borders were moved to settle the new fortified towns.

Another way Meng Tian helped secure the area was by deploying a reported three hundred thousand conscripted peasants and convict laborers to build the Great Wall. The Zhou states in the north had all built walls in particularly vulnerable places, and Meng Tian used these walls when possible, connecting them together. The histories do not offer many details on this project, other than saying that the resulting wall was "more than ten thousand *li* long," but "ten thousand" is not meant to be an exact number. It must have been an enormous job, however, as much of it was built by labor-intensive rammed-earth techniques. Moreover, the region was sparsely settled, and food for the workers had be to transported long distances to supply them. Much of the wall crossed mountains, adding to the difficulty of the construction. The Qin Great Wall was farther north than the Great Wall that can be seen today, which was built much later in the Ming Dynasty and was made of brick and stone rather than rammed earth.

The Great Wall did not prove an impassable barrier to the Xiongnu. During Qin times, the chief of the Xiongnu was Touman. The Xiongnu's failure to defend its territory against the Qin armies naturally weakened his authority, since Xiongnu chiefs were above all military leaders. Touman's own son Maodun soon challenged him. Maodun first trained his bodyguards to kill on command, executing anyone who failed to instantly obey his commands that they shoot his favorite horse and favorite concubine. When he was satisfied that they would do what he said, he ordered them to shoot his father and declared himself the Xiongnu chief.

During the next few years, Maodun led the Xiongnu to defeat both the Eastern Hu and the Yuezhi. Some of the Yuezhi simply moved west, but the Eastern Hu were incorporated into the Xiongnu tribal confederation. Maodun also campaigned north of the Gobi, uniting the tribes in modern Mongolia. His quick military victories made him a charismatic leader whom others wanted to follow. Some of the tribes he defeated were incorporated as tribute-paying vassals and others as slaves. By this time, the Qin Dynasty was falling apart, and Maodun was able to reclaim the Ordos region that Qin had taken from the Xiongnu only a few years earlier.

THE HAN DYNASTY (206 B.C.E.–220 C.E.)

The First Emperor died in 210 B.C.E. while traveling. He had trusted no one, and at this juncture no one proved trustworthy. The chief eunuch plotted with a younger son to send orders to the heir apparent and General Meng Tian to commit suicide. The younger son became the Second Emperor and had several of his brothers executed. The chief eunuch was elevated to chancellor after he got the Second Emperor to execute Li Si. By this time, the Qin state was unraveling. The Legalist institutions designed to concentrate power in the hands of the ruler made the stability of the government dependent on the strength and character of a single person.

In the ensuing uprisings, many of the rebels called for the restoration of the old states, but this was not what happened. The eventual victor was Liu Bang (known in history as Emperor Gao, r. 202–195 B.C.E.). The First Emperor of Qin was from the old Zhou aristocracy. Liu Bang, by contrast, was from a modest family of commoners, so his elevation to emperor is evidence of how thoroughly the Qin Dynasty had destroyed the old order.

Emperor Gao did not disband the centralized government created by Qin, but he did remove its most unpopular features. He set up his capital at Chang'an, not far from the old Qin capital. He eliminated some laws, cut taxes, and otherwise lessened the burdens on the people. After a century of almost constant war and huge labor mobilizations, China was given several decades to recover. Responding to the desire to restore the old order, Emperor Gao gave out large and nearly autonomous fiefs to his relatives and chief generals. Very soon he recognized that giving followers independent resources was a mistake, and he spent much of his reign eliminating the fief holders who were not relatives. After his death, the fiefs of imperial relatives were also gradually reduced in size.

Even before Emperor Gao had completed the consolidation of the empire, he came to realize the threat posed by the Xiongnu. In 200 B.C.E. the Xiongnu under Maodun attacked one of the recently appointed kings, who decided to go over to the Xiongnu. With his help, the Xiongnu then attacked the major city of Taiyuan. Emperor Gao personally led an army to retake the region, but his army suffered terribly from the cold. Maodun led a huge army of horsemen to surround the Han army. Given little choice, Emperor Gao agreed to make yearly gifts of silk, grain, and other foodstuffs to the Xiongnu. The Xiongnu considered this tribute, but the Han naturally preferred to consider it an expression of friendship.

After Emperor Gao's debacle, the early Han emperors had concentrated on pacifying the Xiongnu, supplying them not only with material goods but also with princesses as brides (which they hoped in time would lead to rulers with Chinese mothers). These policies were controversial, since critics thought they merely strengthened the enemy. Moreover, as they pointed out, no matter how much wealth the Han sent to the Xiongnu, they kept raiding the borders.

The Han emperor in theory was all powerful but in actuality depended on his chancellor and other high officials for information and advice. Nine ministries were established to handle matters ranging from state ritual to public works. Officials, graded by rank and salary, were appointed by the central government for their merit, not their birth, and were subject to dismissal, demotion, or transfer, much in the way Qin officials had been. Local officials— magistrates and grand administrators—had broad responsibilities: they collected taxes, judged lawsuits, commanded troops to suppress uprisings, undertook public works such as flood control, chose their own subordinates, and recommended local men to the central government for appointments. The main tax was a poll tax of 120 cash (coins) on adults (less for children). Adults also owed a month of labor service each year. Land tax, largely retained by the county and commandery governments, was set at the low rate of one-thirtieth of the harvest.

When Emperor Gao died, his heir was a child, and the empress dowager (the widow of the former emperor) took control until her death, fifteen years later. This Empress Lü is described in the histories as a vicious, spiteful person, and after her fall, her entire family was wiped out. For centuries to come, she would provide an example of the dangers of letting a woman take power, even if she was the mother of the emperor.

The Han emperor who had the greatest impact on Chinese culture and society was Emperor Wu, who came to the throne as a teenager in 141 B.C.E. and reigned for fifty-four years. Unafraid of innovation, Emperor Wu initiated many of the most significant developments in Han culture and government. He took an interest in the arts and patronized both music and poetry. Like many other men of his age, Emperor Wu was fascinated with omens, portents, spirits, immortals, and occult forces, yet he wanted his officials to study Confucian texts.

Emperor Wu expanded the empire through military means. To push the Xiongnu back, he sent several armies of one hundred thousand to three hundred thousand troops deep into Xiongnu terri-

tory. These costly campaigns were of limited value because the Xiongnu were a moving target: fighting nomads was not like attacking walled cities. If the Xiongnu did not want to fight the Chinese troops, they simply decamped. Moreover, it was very difficult for Chinese troops to carry enough food to stay long in Xiongnu territory. What they could do was consolidate the land the Xiongnu had vacated by the same methods Qin had used: building forts, appointing officials, and dispatching settlers.

To pay for his military campaigns, Emperor Wu took over the minting of coins, confiscated the land of nobles, sold offices and titles, and increased taxes on private businesses. A widespread suspicion of commerce—from both moral and political perspectives—made it easy to levy especially heavy assessments on merchants. Boats, carts, shops, and other facilities were made subject to property taxes. The worst blow to merchants, however, was the government's decision to enter into market competition with them by selling the commodities that had been collected as taxes. In 119 B.C.E., government monopolies were established on the production of

Xiongnu Gold Plaque. Xiongnu art shows connections to that of the scythians and other nomads of the steppe, especially in the use of animal designs. *(The Metropolitan Museum of Art, New York, Gift of J. Pierpont Morgan, 1917. Photo © The Metropolitan Museum of Art)*

iron, salt, and liquor, enterprises that previously had been sources of great profit for private entrepreneurs. Large-scale grain dealing also had been a profitable business, which the government now took over under the guise of stabilizing prices. Grain was to be bought where it was plentiful and its price low; it would either be stored in granaries until prices rose or transported to areas of scarcity. This policy was supposed to eliminate speculation in grain, provide more constant prices, and bring profit to the government.

The relative success of the Han form of government validated the imperial system, which drew from both Confucian rhetoric and Legalist bureaucratic methods. To put this another way, the Zhou notion of All-Under-Heaven ruled by the paramount Son of Heaven, an idea fully supported by Confucian thinkers, now had attached to it the structures of the centralized bureaucratic empire, indebted though these were to Legalist ideas.

Official Support for Confucianism

Emperor Wu was the first Han emperor to privilege Confucian scholars within the government. He listened to the Confucian scholar Dong Zhongshu, who gave him advice much like Li Si's to the First Emperor. "Because the various schools of thought differ," he said, "the people do not know what to honor," and he advised that "anything not encompassed by the Six Disciplines and the arts of Confucius be suppressed and not allowed to continue further, and evil and vain theories be stamped out."[2] Emperor Wu soon decreed that officials should be selected on the basis of Confucian virtues, and he established a national university to train officials in the Confucian classics.

The Han government's decision to recruit men trained in the Confucian classics marks the beginning of the Confucian scholar-official system, one of the most distinctive features of imperial China. Since one of the highest duties of the Confucian scholar was to admonish the ruler against misguided policies, officials whose educations imbued them with Confucian values did not comply automatically with the emperor's wishes. Still, emperors found employing

Confucian scholars as officials efficient; because of their ingrained sense of duty, they did not have to be supervised as closely as the Legalist model required. That did not mean that emperors took all aspects of the Confucian model of governing to heart themselves or always treated their Confucian officials with respect. Emperor Wu was so averse to criticism that he once had an official executed on the charge that a wry twist of his lips showed that he disapproved in his heart, and the emperor's temper led him to put five of his last seven chancellors to death.

Wang Mang

The Han practice of hereditary succession to the throne from father to son meant that the heir might be a young child. During the last decades of the first century B.C.E., several boys succeeded to the throne. Adult men of the imperial lineage did not serve as regents; they were regularly sent out of the capital to keep them from interfering in court politics. That left the mothers and grandmothers of the new rulers, along with the women's male relatives, as the main contenders for power during regencies. Wang Mang came to power as a relative of Empress Wang (d. 13 C.E.), who for forty years had been influential at court as the widow of one emperor, mother of a second, and grandmother of a third. After serving as regent for two infant emperors, Wang Mang deposed the second and declared himself emperor of the Xin (New) Dynasty (9 C.E.–23 C.E.).

Although he was condemned as a usurper, Wang Mang was a learned Confucian scholar who wished to implement policies described in the classics. He asserted state ownership of forests and swamps, built ritual halls, revived public granaries, outlawed slavery, limited private landholdings, and cut court expenses. Some of his policies, such as issuing new coins and nationalizing gold, led to economic turmoil. Matters were made worse when the Yellow River broke through its dikes and shifted course from north to south, driving millions of farmers from their homes as huge regions were flooded. Rebellion broke out, and in the ensuing warfare a Han imperial clansman succeeded in reestablishing the Han Dynasty. The capital was moved from Chang'an to Luoyang. As a consequence, the first half of the Han is called the Western or Former Han, and the second half is called the Eastern or Later Han (reminiscent of the Western and Eastern Zhou).

2. William Theodore de Bary and Irene Bloom, eds., *Sources of Chinese Tradition*, rev. ed. (New York: Columbia University Press, 1999), p. 311.

Palace Eunuchs

During the second century C.E., Han court politics deteriorated as the eunuchs (castrated men) who served as palace servants vied with relatives of the empresses for control of the court. For centuries, eunuchs had been a part of palace life, charged with managing the women's quarters. Eunuchs were in essence slaves; a common source seems to have been boys captured from the "southern barbarians." Court officials looked on palace eunuchs with contempt. Emperors who had grown up with them, however, often saw them as more reliable than officials since they had no outside base of power.

During the Eastern Han period, eunuchs were able to build a base of power within the palace, with the result that weak emperors became their captives rather than their masters. In 124 C.E., a group of eunuchs placed on the throne a child they could manipulate. They gained even more power after 159, when an emperor turned to them to help him oust a consort family faction. In 166 and 169, officials staged protests against eunuch power, but the eunuchs retaliated. In the purges that followed, the protestors were put in jail, banned from office, and even killed in a few cases.

INTELLECTUAL, LITERARY, AND RELIGIOUS CURRENTS

Perhaps stimulated by the Qin destruction of books, learning and literature of all sorts flourished in Han times. At the end of the Western Han period, the imperial library had some 596 titles, divided into six categories: classics, philosophy, poetry, military treatises, mathematics and natural science (including astronomy, the calendar, and divination), and medicine. Also important to the history of books in China is the development of paper. Over the course of the Han, various plant fibers were tested, and by the end of the period, paper that had a good, absorbent writing surface was produced. Books were much less cumbersome when written on rolls of paper than on strips of wood or bamboo.

Early in the Han period, a form of Daoism called Huang-Lao Daoism became particularly influential. *Huang* (yellow) refers to the Yellow Emperor and *Lao* to Laozi; both were treated as deities of vast powers. Emperor Wu was attracted to these teachings and tried to make contact with the world of gods and immortals through elaborate sacrifices. He marveled at stories of the paradise of the Queen Mother of the West and the exploits of the Yellow Emperor, who had taken his entire court with him when he ascended to the realm of the immortals. Emperor Wu inaugurated state cults to the Earth Queen in 114 B.C.E. and Grand Unity in 113. In 110 he traveled to Mount Tai to perform a sacrifice to heaven at the peak and a sacrifice to earth at the base. Although claims were made that these sacrifices were of ancient origin, in fact they were designed for him by court ritualists steeped in Huang-Lao ideas. Religious practices among ordinary people were influenced by Huang-Lao ideas, but also by a great variety of other ideas about spiritual beings and the forces of the cosmos (see **Documents: Lucky and Unlucky Days**).

Han Confucianism

Confucianism made a comeback during the Han Dynasty, but in a new form. Although Confucian texts had fed the First Emperor's bonfires, some dedicated scholars had hidden their books, and others could recite entire books from memory. The ancient books recovered in these ways came to be regarded as classics containing the wisdom of the past. Han scholars studied them with piety and attempted to make them more useful as sources of moral guidance by writing commentaries to them that explained archaic words and obscure passages. A Han Confucian scholar often specialized in a single classic and passed on to his disciples his understanding of each sentence in the work.

The Five Classics
Book of Changes
Book of Documents
Book of Poetry
Spring and Autumn Annals
Book of Rites

Perhaps inspired by the political unification of the realm, some Han Confucians attempted to develop comprehensive understandings of all phenomena. Their cosmological theories explained phenomena in terms of cyclical flows of yin and yang and the five phases (fire, water, earth, metal, and wood).

DOCUMENTS
Lucky and Unlucky Days

Some of our best evidence of common beliefs in Han China is found in the writings of critics such as Wang Chong (27–ca. 100 C.E.). Wang's lengthy Balanced Discourses *includes refutations of a wide range of beliefs and practices, from the idea that people could become immortals and fly high above the earth to the notion that ghosts could come back to harm people. In the passage here, he attempts to refute the idea that taking action on an unlucky day can cause people harm.*

People today commonly believe in evil influences They think that when people fall ill or die (or there are repeated calamities, executions, or humiliations), some offense has been committed. If inauspicious days and months are not avoided when starting a project, moving, sacrificing, burying, taking up office, or marrying, then the demons and spirits that one encounters at these ill-fated times will work their harm. Thus illness, disaster, legal penalties, death, even the extermination of a family are all thought to be brought about by not taking care to avoid ill-fated times. In truth, however, this is wild talk. . . .

Rulers anxious about their office and commoners concerned about their bodies believe in this theory and do not raise doubts. Thus when a ruler is about to embark on an enterprise, diviners throng his halls, and when ordinary people have work to be done, they inquire into the best time. As a consequence, deceptive books and false texts have appeared in large numbers. . . .

Rare are the diseases not caused by wind, moisture, or food and drink. After people have gone out in the wind or slept in a damp place, they spend money to find out which noxious influence [has attacked them]. When they overeat, they should practice abstinence, but if their illness does not improve, they say the noxious force has not been identified. If the person dies, they say the diviner was not careful. Among ordinary people, such talk is considered wisdom.

Among the 360 animals, man ranks first. Man is a living creature, but among the ten thousand creatures, man is the most intelligent. But he obtains his lifespan from Heaven and his *qi* from the origin in the same way as the other creatures. . . . It makes no sense that the misfortune caused by demons and spirits would fall on man alone, and not on other creatures. In man the minds of Heaven and Earth reach their highest development. Why do heavenly disasters strike the noblest creature and not the mean ones? . . .

If I commit a crime and am arrested by the magistrate and sentenced to punishment, no one says I did something wrong. Instead they say that someone in my family was negligent. If I have not been careful where I lodge or go overboard in food or drink, they do not say I have been immoderate, but that I have disregarded an unlucky time. When people die one after the other and dozens of coffins await burial, they do not say the air is contaminated but that the day of a burial was inauspicious. . . .

The city of Liyang one night was flooded and became a lake. Its residents cannot all have violated taboos on years and months. When Emperor Gao rose, Feng and Pei were recovered, but surely its residents had not all been careful in their choice of hours and days. When Xiang Yu attacked Xiangan, no one survived, but surely its residents had not all failed to pray. The army of Zhao was buried alive by Qin at Changping; 400,000 men died together at the same time. It is hardly likely that when they left home not one of them divined for a propitious time.

Source: Wang Chong, *Lunheng jiaoshi*, ed. Huang Hui (Taibei: Commercial Press, 1964), 24.1004–12. Translated by Patricia Ebrey.

Correspondences of the Five Phases					
	wood	fire	earth	metal	water
seasons	spring	summer		autumn	winter
directions	east	south	center	west	north
weather	wind	heat	thunder	cold	rain
colors	green	red	yellow	white	black
emotions	anger	joy	desire	sorrow	fear
organs	eyes	tongue	mouth	nose	ears

They saw the cosmos as fundamentally moral: natural disasters such as floods or earthquakes were portents indicating that the emperor had failed in his responsibility to maintain the proper balance in heaven and earth.

The emperor was of unique importance in this cosmology because he alone had the capacity to link the realms of heaven, earth, and man. The leading Han Confucian scholar Dong Zhongshu (195?–105 B.C.E.) wanted a ruler who would serve as high priest and fount of wisdom, who would be all-powerful but also deferential to learned scholars. Dong drew on ideas from earlier Confucian, Daoist, and Legalist texts to describe the ruler as the "pivot of all living things," who is "quiet and nonactive" yet "deliberates with his numerous worthies" and knows how to tell if they are loyal or treacherous.[3]

Sima Qian and the *Records of the Grand Historian*

History writing began early in China. In the early Zhou period, court chroniclers kept track of astronomical matters and advised rulers on the lessons of the past. Two of the Five Classics, the *Book of Documents* and the *Spring and Autumn Annals*, are historical works, the former a collection of documents and the latter a chronicle. By the Warring States period, not only did each of the states compile historical records, but citing examples from the past had become a common way to support an argument.

The art of history writing took a major step forward in the Han period. During Emperor Wu's reign, two historians, father and son, undertook to write a comprehensive history of the entire past.

Sima Tan (d. 110 B.C.E.) served as the court astronomer under Emperor Wu and had access to the government archives. His son Sima Qian (145–ca. 85 B.C.E.) carried on his work and brought it to completion.

Before Sima Qian was able to complete his history, he angered Emperor Wu by defending a general who had surrendered to the Xiongnu. As a consequence, he was sentenced to castration and service as a palace eunuch. This punishment was so humiliating that he was expected to choose the honorable alternative of suicide. Sima Qian explained in a letter to a friend why he decided to accept his humiliating sentence: he could not bear the thought that the history would not be completed. "I have compiled neglected knowledge of former times from all over the world; I have examined these for veracity and have given an account of the principles behind success and defeat, rise and fall." His ambitions were large: "I also wanted to fully explore the interaction between Heaven and Man, and to show the continuity of transformations of past and present."[4] Only by finishing the work could he make up for the dishonor he had suffered.

Like the Greek historians Herodotus and Thucydides, Sima Qian believed fervently in examining artifacts and documents, visiting the sites where history was made, and questioning people about events. He was also interested in China's geographical variations, local customs, and local history. As an official of the emperor, he had access to important people and documents and to the imperial library. He quoted documents when they were available, and in their absence he invented dialogues to bring events to life. The result of his efforts, ten

---

3. Ibid., pp. 298–299.

4. Stephen Owen, *An Anthology of Chinese Literature: Beginnings to 1911* (New York: Norton, 1996), p. 141.

years in the making, was a massive work of literary and historical genius, the 130-chapter *Records of the Grand Historian*.

The *Records* presents several perspectives on the past. A political narrative begins with the Yellow Emperor and continues through the Xia, Shang, and Zhou dynasties, down to Sima Qian's own day. It is supplemented by chronological charts with genealogical data and information on the organization of governments. Key institutions are given their own histories in topical chapters on state ritual, court music, the calendar, waterworks, finance, and other matters of concern to the government. Thirty chapters give the separate histories of the main ruling houses of the states of the Zhou period. Biographies of individuals take up more than half the book. Although many of those portrayed played important political or military roles, Sima Qian also singled out other notable men, including philosophers, poets, merchants, magicians, rebels, assassins, and foreign groups like the Xiongnu. At the end of each chapter of biographies Sima Qian offered his own comments. Sima Qian's experiences with Emperor Wu did not incline him to flatter rulers. Not only did he give ample evidence of Emperor Wu's arbitrariness and policy errors, but he also found many ways to draw attention to those whose merit went unrecognized in their day.

By writing so well, Sima Qian had a profound impact on Chinese conceptions of history and personal achievement. In the centuries that followed, the *Records of the Grand Historian* was read as much for the pleasure of the narrative as for historical data. The composite style, with political narratives supplemented by treatises and biographies, became standard for government-sponsored histories. Subsequent histories, however, usually covered only a single dynasty. The first of these, *History of the Former Han Dynasty*, was the work of three members of the Ban family in the first century C.E. (see **Biography: The Ban Family**).

Reeling and Weaving. Many Han tombs had scenes of daily life depicted on their walls. In this example, seated below a finely drawn tile roof are three women reeling, twisting, and weaving silk. The weaver is using a treadle-operated loom. *(National Museum of Chinese History, Beijing)*

BIOGRAPHY   The Ban Family

Ban Biao (3–54 C.E.), a successful official from a family with an envied library, had three highly accomplished children: his twin sons, the general Ban Chao (32–102) and the historian Ban Gu (32–92); and his daughter Ban Zhao (ca. 45–120).

After distinguishing himself as a junior officer in campaigns against the Xiongnu, Ban Chao was sent in 73 C.E. to the Western Regions to see about the possibility of restoring Chinese overlordship there, lost since Wang Mang's time. Ban Chao spent most of the next three decades in Central Asia. Through patient diplomacy and a show of force, he reestablished Chinese control over the oasis cities of Central Asia, and in 92 he was appointed protector general of the area.

Ban Gu was one of the most accomplished writers of his age, excelling in a distinctive literary form known as the rhapsody (*fu*). His "Rhapsody on the Two Capitals" is in the form of a dialogue between a guest from Chang'an and his host in Luoyang. It describes the palaces, spectacles, scenic spots, local products, and customs of the two great cities. Emperor Zhang (r. 76–88) was fond of literature and often had Ban Gu accompany him on hunts or travels. He also had him edit a record of the court debates he held on issues concerning the Confucian classics.

Ban Biao had been working on a history of the Western Han Dynasty when he died in 54. Ban Gu took over this project, modeling it on Sima Qian's *Records of the Grand Historian*. He added treatises on law, geography, and bibliography, the last a classified list of books in the imperial library.

Because of his connection to a general out of favor, Ban Gu was sent to prison in 92, where he soon died. At that time the *History of the Former Han Dynasty* was still incomplete. The emperor called on Ban Gu's widowed sister, Ban Zhao, to finish it. She came to the palace, where she not only worked on the history but also became a teacher of the women of the palace. According to the *History of the Later Han*, she taught them the classics, history, astronomy, and mathematics. In 106 an infant succeeded to the throne, and Empress Deng became regent. The empress frequently turned to Ban Zhao for advice on government policies.

Ban Zhao credited her own education to her learned father and cultured mother and became an advocate of the education of girls. In her *Admonitions for Women*, Ban Zhao objected that many families taught their sons to read but not their daughters. She did not claim daughters should have the same education; after all, "just as yin and yang differ, men and women have different characteristics." Women, she wrote, will do well if they cultivate the womanly virtues such as humility. "Humility means yielding and acting respectful, putting others first and oneself last, never mentioning one's own good deeds or denying one's own faults, enduring insults and bearing with mistreatment, all with due trepidation."[1] In subsequent centuries, Ban Zhao's *Admonitions* became one of the most commonly used texts for the education of girls.

---

[1]Patricia Buckley Ebrey, ed., *Chinese Civilization: A Sourcebook*, rev. ed. (New York: Free Press, 1993), p. 75.

CHINESE SOCIETY IN HAN TIMES

During the Western Han period, with the establishment of peace and the extension of the empire's frontiers, the Chinese population grew rapidly. The census of 2 C.E. recorded a population of 59 million, the earliest indication of the large size of China's population. These people shared status as subjects of the Han, but their daily lives varied enormously, depending on their social status and where they lived.

Common Farmers

The bulk of the population in Han times (and even into the twentieth century) was made up of farmers living in villages of a few dozen to a few hundred households. At the technical level, agriculture continued to make advances. The new and more effective plow introduced during the Han period was fitted with two plowshares, guided by a pair of handles, and was typically pulled by a pair of oxen. Farmers used fans to blow the chaff from kernels of grain, and they used either mortars and pestles or hand mills to grind grain into flour. Irrigation of farmland was aided by brick-faced wells and pumping devices ranging from a simple pole with an attached bucket and counterweight to a sophisticated machine worked by foot pedals. Because the Han Empire depended on free farmers to pay taxes and provide labor services, the government tried to keep farmers independent and productive. To fight peasant poverty, the government kept land taxes low, provided relief during famines, aided migration to areas where there was vacant land to be opened, and promoted agricultural advancements, such as planting two crops in alternate rows and planting a succession of carefully timed crops. Still, many farmers fell into debt and had to sell their land. Those who did not migrate in search of new opportunities usually became tenant farmers, often accepting quasi-servile status as the dependent of a magnate. Poverty also contributed to the supply of slaves, as men could sell their wives or children into slavery to pay debts.

Elite Groups

The old nobility of Zhou times did not survive Qin's destruction of the Zhou states and its determinedly anti-aristocratic policies. Still, Han historical sources are full of references to people who outranked ordinary farmers in wealth and power. Some of these gained power through proximity to the throne. Liang Ji, whose power derived from his position as father of the empress, was said to have had huge properties and mansions, to have forced commoners to become his slaves, to have used commoners doing labor service to work on his own properties, to have let his retainers extort property and favors, and so on. Members of the imperial clan and the adopted relatives of eunuchs could similarly take advantage of their positions to accumulate wealth and power.

Other groups whose great wealth outraged observers were merchants and manufacturers. Zhao Cuo in 178 B.C.E. complained that merchants suffered none of the hardships of farmers, got the best food and clothing, associated with the nobility, and had more power than officials. Sima Qian spoke of how great merchants commanded the services of the poor. If a merchant's wealth was ten times their own, they would behave humbly toward him. If it was a hundred times their own, they would fear him. If it was a thousand times their own, they would work for him. And if it was ten thousand times their own,

they would become his servants. Even those with noble titles, he added, depended on these rich merchants for loans.

Government officials had high standing in Han times, though rarely did they have the great wealth of the richest merchants or imperial relatives. In the Western Han, some men rose to high office from modest backgrounds. Kuang Heng, for instance, came from a farming family and hired himself out to get the money to study; he eventually became a respected classical scholar and high government official. Yet most of the time, those who could afford to get the education needed to become officials came from families of means, most often landholders.

Access to office was largely through recommendations. At the local level, the county magistrate or commandery grand administrators appointed their own subordinates from among the local educated elite. The grand administrators also made recommendations to the central government of men who were "filial and incorrupt," who then became eligible for higher office. Another route to office was to study with a well-known teacher. Patron-client ties were very important in linking members of the elite, especially in the Eastern Han, when former subordinates and students could be counted on to come to one's assistance in political conflicts.

At the local level, better-off families were expected to act as the leaders of their communities and offer assistance to their neighbors and relatives in need. In the second century C.E., leading families in communities often erected stones inscribed with accounts of their good works, such as building or repairing bridges or shrines. Tombs and funerary monuments of the Eastern Han offer further evidence of the self-perception of such families. By decorating funerary architecture with pictures of famous filial sons, dutiful women, or loyal ministers, they were portraying their families as steeped in Confucian traditions. Not all those with power at the local level were Confucian scholars, however. Han sources are full of complaints of the "great families" or "powerful men" of local communities who intimidated their neighbors and built up their property by taking advantage of families in debt.

During the course of the Han, the educated elite (called the *shi*, the same term used in Zhou times for the lower level of the aristocracy) came to see themselves as participants, even if indirectly, in national literary, scholarly, and political affairs. The agitation against the eunuchs and consort families in the second century C.E. helped strengthen these feelings. The persecution of the leaders of the movement protesting eunuch power, which took place between 166 and 184, created a large group of articulate, energetic, concerned men excluded from office. Their prestige showed that social honor was something the elite conferred on itself rather than something the government controlled through its appointment of men to office.

The Family

During Han times, both the administrative structure of the centralized state and the success of Confucianism helped shape the Chinese family system. Since Shang times, at least at the highest social levels, patrilineal ancestors had been a central feature of the family. By the time of the registration of the population in Qin and Han times, everyone had patrilineal family names. Han laws supported the authority of family heads over the other members of their families. The state preferred to deal only with the family head and recognized this person's right to represent the family. The family head was generally the senior male, but if a man died before his sons were grown, his widow would serve as family head until they were of age. Family members were also held responsible for each other; for serious crimes, relatives of a criminal were made slaves.

During the Zhou period, inheritance had favored the eldest son, who succeeded to both aristocratic titles and the responsibility to maintain ancestral rites. By Han times, primogeniture in ordinary families applied only to ancestral rites. Family property such as land was divided among all sons. Daughters did not get shares of the family property, though well-to-do families might provide a daughter with substantial goods as her dowry when she married. Because the family farm had to be divided every generation (at least when there was more than one son), a family with several sons risked rapid downward social mobility.

Marriages were arranged by family heads, generally with the bride joining the husband's family. Men could divorce their wives on any of seven grounds, which included barrenness, jealousy, and talkativeness, but could do so only if there was a family for her to return to. There were no grounds on which a woman could divorce her husband, but divorce by mutual agreement was possible.

The legal underpinnings of the family were closely connected to Confucian teachings. It was one of the Confucian ritual texts that first defined the seven grounds for divorce. Confucian ritual texts compiled in Han times also give elaborate descriptions of the proper deference that sons and daughters-in-law should show to parents. The *Book of Rites*, for instance, told daughters-in-law to rise at the cock's crow, wash and dress, and then call on their parents-in-law: "Getting to where they [the parents-in-law] are, with bated breath and gentle voice, they [the daughters-in-law] should ask if their clothes are too warm or too cold, whether they are ill or pained, or uncomfortable in any part; and if they be so, they should proceed reverently to stroke and scratch the place."[5] Male-female differentiation was much stressed in this book. For instance, in explaining why the man goes to fetch his bride in person, it says, "This is the same principle by which Heaven takes precedence over earth and rulers over their subjects."[6]

In Han times filial piety was extolled in both texts and art. Pictures of famous filial sons were used to decorate not only the walls of tombs but even everyday objects like boxes. The brief *Classic of Filial Piety* argued that at each level of society, sincere filial devotion leads people to perform their social duties conscientiously and prudently, creating peace and harmony. Stories circulated of exceptional sons who willingly sacrificed their own comfort to amuse their unreasonable parents.

Other Han texts addressed the virtues women should cultivate. The *Biographies of Exemplary Women*, compiled by Liu Xiang, told the stories of women from China's past who had given their husbands good advice, sacrificed themselves when forced to choose between their fathers and husbands, or performed other heroic deeds. It also contained cautionary tales about scheming, jealous, and manipulative women who brought destruction to all around them. Another notable text on women's education was written by the scholar Ban Zhao. Her *Admonitions for Women* urged girls to master the seven virtues appropriate to women: humility, resignation, subservience, self-abasement, obedience, cleanliness, and industry (see **Biography: The Ban Family**).

---

5. James Legge, trans., *Li Ki: Book of Rites* (Oxford: Oxford University Press, 1885), 1:450, modified.
6. Ibid., p. 440.

Ancient Worthies and Paragons of Virtue. A large basket found in a tomb in the Han colony of Lelang (North Korea) is decorated with ninety-four paintings of famous figures from the past, many labeled with their names. *(Central History Museum, Pyong-Yang, North Korea/McCune, Evelyn,* The Arts of Korea, an Illustrated History, *Charles E. Tuttle Company, Publishers, Rutland, VT, 1962)*

CENTRAL ASIA AND THE SILK ROAD

It was during the Han period that the Chinese first learned that theirs was not the only civilization with cities and writing, and also that these distant civilizations had been obtaining silk from China from merchants who traveled across Eurasia.

This discovery was made when Emperor Wu decided to send Zhang Qian as an envoy to look for the Yuezhi, a group that had moved west after defeat by the Xiongnu several decades earlier and which Emperor Wu hoped would return to fight the Xiongnu for him. Despite being captured by the Xiongnu and delayed several years, Zhang eventually reached Bactria, Parthia, and Ferghana (in the region of modern Afghanistan). However, the

Yuezhi, once found, had no interest in returning to help out the Han. In 115 B.C.E., Zhang was sent again, this time to look for another group, who proved just as unwilling to return. Zhang's travels, however, were not totally in vain. From his reports of these two trips, the Chinese learned firsthand of the countries of Central Asia and heard about the trade in silk with other countries farther out, such as Rome. In 104 and 102 B.C.E., a Han general led Chinese armies across the Pamir Mountains to subdue Ferghana. Recognition of Chinese overlordship followed, giving China control over the trade routes across Central Asia, commonly called the Silk Road (see Map 3.1). The city-states along this route did not resist the Chinese presence, since they could carry out the trade on which they depended more conveniently with Chinese garrisons to protect them. (See **Material Culture: Silk from the Silk Road.**)

Much of the trade was in the hands of Sogdian, Parthian, and Indian merchants who carried silk and other goods by caravans all the way to Rome. There was a market for both skeins of silk thread and for silk cloth woven in Chinese or Syrian workshops. Caravans returning to China carried gold, horses, and occasionally handicrafts of West Asian origin, such as glass beads and cups (see Color Plate 4). Through the trade along the Silk Road, the Chinese learned of new foodstuffs, including walnuts, pomegranates, sesame, and coriander, all of which came to be grown in China. This trade was largely carried by the two-humped Bactrian camel. With a heavy coat of hair to withstand the bitter cold of winter, each camel could carry about 500 pounds of cargo.

BORDERLANDS

During the Qin and Han periods, the Chinese empire was extended by both armies and by migrants. Emperor Wu sent armies not only into Central Asia but also into northern Korea, where military districts were established to flank the Xiongnu on their eastern border (see Chapter 6). Armies were also sent south, extending the frontiers into what is now northern Vietnam.

In the south, migrants in search of land to till often were the first to penetrate an area. They moved south along the rivers, displacing the indigenous populations, who retreated farther south or up into marginal hillsides. A comparison of the censuses of 2 and

MATERIAL CULTURE

Silk from the Silk Road

The Chinese product most in demand outside China was silk. The silkworm had been domesticated in China by the Shang period, and the excellence of Chinese silk technology in Zhou times is well documented through excavations of tombs. Silk is very strong and amazingly fine. A single silkworm can spin a filament 1,000 meters long but a minuscule 0.25 millimeters thick. Several of these filaments have to be twisted together to make the yarns used for weaving. Besides basic flat weaves and light gauzes, Chinese weavers also made patterned weaves, including multicolored ones that required the use of a draw loom to separate the warp threads.

Many fragments of Han period textiles have survived in the arid climate of Chinese Central Asia, at sites along the Silk Road. The piece illustrated here was excavated from tomb 8 at Niya, along the southern arm of the Silk Road. The weave is exceptionally fine, with 220 warp threads per centimeter. The five-color woven design shows clouds, birds, a single-horned beast, and a tiger along with Chinese characters. The inscription, which is the command of a Han emperor to a general leading troops to bring order

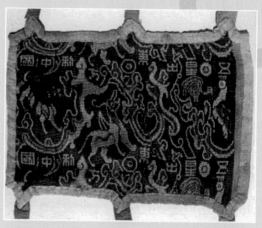

Silk Arm Cover. Excavated at Niya along the Silk Road, this small piece (12.5 by 18.5 cm) is finely woven in five colors: blue, green, red, yellow, and white (the colors of the five planets). *(Xinjian Institute of Archaeology)*

to the northwest frontier, reads: "The Five Planets appear in the east. This is very auspicious for China. The barbarians will be defeated."

---

140 C.E. shows that, between those dates, between 5 and 10 million people left the north China plain for the Yangzi Valley or places farther south.

The government fostered migration by building garrisons on the frontiers to protect settlers, merchants, and adventurers. Once enough settlers had arrived, the government created counties and sent officials to administer them and collect taxes. Often officials sent to the frontier counties tried to encourage the assimilation of the local population by setting up schools to train local young men in Chinese texts. The products of Chinese industry—iron tools, lacquerware, silks, and so on—were in demand and helped make Chinese merchants welcome.

Nevertheless, Chinese expansion often ran into active resistance. In the region of modern Yunnan, the Dian state was dominated by horse-riding aristocrats who made captured enemies into slaves. They drew wealth from trade conducted in both Chinese

coins and cowrie shells. Although the Dian did not have a written language, they were skilled metalworkers whose bronze drums often were decorated with images of people and animals. In 109 B.C.E., Emperor Wu sent an army that conquered Dian and made it a tributary state. Although the Dian repeatedly rebelled, the Han government was able to reestablish its overlordship each time.

The Case of Vietnam

To the north and west of China proper, there were natural boundaries to the Chinese way of life, as crop agriculture was not suited to the deserts, grasslands, and high mountains in those regions. The southern boundaries of China proper were not so clear and took centuries to become established. Crops that could be grown in modern Guangdong province could also be grown farther south, especially along the coast in what is today Vietnam. The rivers that are central to this region—both the Red River, which empties into the ocean near modern Hanoi, and the Mekong River, which empties near modern Saigon—start in the highlands of southwest China, and migrants following these rivers would end up in what is today Vietnam. Travel along the coast was also easy, even in early times.

Vietnam is today classed with the countries to its west as part of Southeast Asia, but its ties are at least as strong to China. The Vietnamese appear in Chinese sources as a people of south China called the Yue who gradually migrated farther south as the Chinese state expanded. In the Red River valley in northern Vietnam, they mixed with local people who had bronze technology, could kill elephants with poisoned bronze arrowheads, and knew how to irrigate their rice fields by using the tides that backed up the rivers.

The collapse of the Qin Dynasty in 206 B.C.E. had an impact on this area because a former Qin general, Zhao Tuo (Trieu Da in Vietnamese), finding himself in modern Guangdong province, set up his own kingdom of Nam Viet (Nan Yue in Chinese) that extended as far south as modern-day Da Nang. Trieu Da/Zhao Tuo called himself the Great Chief of the Southern Barbarians, incorporated local warriors into his army, encouraged the adoption of Chinese material culture, and supported intermarriage between Chinese settlers and the local population. Through these measures, he gained the support of the local people and was able to rule to the age of ninety-three, all the while resisting Han efforts to make him accept vassal status.

After almost a hundred years of diplomatic and military duels between the Han Dynasty and Nam Viet, Emperor Wu sent armies that conquered it in 111 B.C.E. As in Korea, Chinese political institutions were imposed, and Confucianism became the official ideology. The Chinese language was introduced as the medium of official and literary expression. The Chinese built roads, waterways, and harbors to facilitate communication within the region and to ensure that they maintained administrative and military control over it. Over time, Chinese art, architecture, and music had a powerful impact on their Vietnamese counterparts.

Chinese innovations that were beneficial to the Vietnamese were readily integrated into the indigenous culture, but the local elite were not reconciled to Chinese political domination. The most famous early revolt took place in 39 C.E., when two widows of local aristocrats, the Trung sisters, led an uprising against foreign rule. They gathered together the tribal chiefs and their armed followers, attacked and overwhelmed the Chinese strongholds, and had themselves proclaimed queens of an independent Vietnamese kingdom. Three years later, a powerful Chinese army reestablished Chinese rule.

China retained at least nominal control over northern Vietnam until the tenth century, and there were no real borders between China proper and Vietnam during this time. Many Chinese settled in the area, and the local elite became culturally dual, serving as brokers between the Chinese governors and the native people.

MAINTAINING THE EMPIRE

Maintaining the Han Empire's extended borders required a huge military investment. To man the northern defense stations along the Great Wall took about ten thousand men. Another fifty to sixty thousand soldier-farmers were moved to the frontiers to reduce the cost of transporting provisions to distant outposts. Drafted farmers from the interior did not make good cavalry troops, and as a consequence, a de facto professional army emerged on the frontiers, composed of Chinese from the northern reaches of the empire hired as mercenaries, reprieved convicts, and surrendered Xiongnu. In 31 C.E. the Han abolished universal military service, which it had inherited from the Warring States.

In the middle of the first century C.E., a succession struggle among the Xiongnu brought one of the rival claimants and his followers to the Chinese border seeking protection. These "Southern Xiongnu" were permitted to live in Chinese territory, primarily in the Ordos region in the great bend of the Yellow River. In 90 C.E., Chinese officials counted 237,300 Xiongnu living in China, of whom 50,170 were adult males able to serve in the army, and substantial numbers of other non-Han groups were also settled in Chinese territory. With the collapse of the Xiongnu confederation, a group from Manchuria, the Xianbei, rose to prominence and absorbed many Xiongnu into their tribal structure. The expeditionary armies of the Eastern Han included soldiers from all of these groups; in some campaigns, Han Chinese formed a tiny minority of the soldiers.

During the Han period, China developed a system of diplomacy to regulate contact with foreign powers. States and tribes beyond its borders sent envoys bearing gifts, which the Han emperor responded to with even more lavish gifts for them to bring back. Over the course of the dynasty, the Han government's outlay on these gifts was huge, perhaps as much as 10 percent of state revenue. In 25 B.C.E., for instance, the government gave tributary states twenty thousand rolls of silk cloth and about twenty thousand pounds of silk floss. But although the diplomacy system was a financial burden to the Chinese, it reduced the cost of defense and offered the Han imperial court confirmation that it was the center of the civilized world.

SUMMARY

What changed over the four centuries of the Han Dynasty? The area that could be called China was greatly expanded. Confucianism had become much more closely identified with the state and with the social elite. A canon of classics had been established, as well as a way of writing the history of a complex empire. The effects of the destruction of books by Qin had been largely overcome, and a great many books were in circulation. Paper was coming into common use. By 200 C.E., Chinese officials were much more knowledgeable about the military threats of China's northern neighbors and had much experience with all sorts of stratagems for dealing with them, such as setting up military colonies and recruiting auxiliary forces. China had knowledge of countries far to its west and knew that trade with them could be advantageous. Perhaps above all, by the end of the Han period, the centralized bureaucratic monarchy had proved that it could govern well; it could maintain peace and stability and allow the population to grow and thrive.

Buddhism in India and Its Spread Along the Silk Road

EAST ASIAN CIVILIZATION WAS NEVER completely isolated from the rest of Eurasia. Wheat and the chariot arrived in China from west Asia in Shang times. Animal art spread across the steppe in late Zhou times. Nevertheless, ancient China had less contact with other early centers of civilization, such as Mesopotamia, India, Egypt, and Greece, than they had with each other. India was geographically the closest of those civilizations, and therefore it is not surprising that it was the first to have a major impact on East Asia. The vehicle of its impact was one of its religions, Buddhism.

Early India differed from early China in a great many ways. Much farther south, most areas of the Indian subcontinent were warm all year. In the region of the Indus River, there had been an ancient literate civilization that was already in decline by 1800 B.C.E. The Aryans, in India by 1000 B.C.E. if not earlier, were Indo-European-speaking people who became the dominant group in north India. The culture of the early Aryans is known from the *Rigveda*, a collection of hymns, ritual texts, and philosophical texts composed between 1500 and 500 B.C.E., but transmitted orally for centuries. The *Rigveda* portrays the Aryans as warrior tribes who glorified military skill and heroism; loved to drink, hunt, race, and dance; and counted their wealth in cattle. It presents the struggle between the Aryans and indigenous peoples in religious terms: their chiefs were godlike heroes, their opponents irreligious savages.

Early Aryan society had distinguished between the warrior elite, the priests, ordinary tribesmen, and conquered subjects. These distinctions gradually evolved into the caste system. Society was conceived in terms of four hierarchical strata that did not eat with each other or marry each other: priests (Brahman), warriors or officials (Kshatriya), merchants and landowners (Vaishya), and workers (Shudra). The gods of the Aryans shared some features of the gods of other early Indo-European societies such as the Persians and the Greeks. The *Upanishads*, composed between 750 and 500 B.C.E., record speculations about the mystical meaning of sacrificial rites and about cosmological questions of man's relationship to the universe. They document a gradual shift from the mythical worldview of the early Vedic age to a deeply philosophical one. Associated with this shift was a movement toward asceticism. In search of a richer and more mystical faith, some men retreated to the forests.

Ancient Indian cosmology imagined endlessly repeating cycles. Central concepts were *samsara*, the transmigration of souls by a continual process of rebirth, and *karma*, the tally of good and bad deeds that determined the status of an individual's next life. Good deeds lead to better future lives, evil deeds to worse future lives—even to reincarnation as an animal. The wheel of life included human beings, animals, and even gods. Reward and punishment worked automatically; there was no all-knowing god who judged people and could be petitioned to forgive a sin, and each individual was responsible for his or her own destiny in a just and impartial world. The optimistic interpretation of samsara was that people could improve their lot in the next life by living righteously. The pessimistic view was that life is a treadmill, a relentless cycle of birth and death. Brahmanic mystics sought release from the wheel of life through realization that life in the world was actually an illusion.

The founder of Buddhism was Siddhartha Gautama (fl. ca. 500 B.C.E.), also called Shakyamuni ("sage of the Shakya tribe"), but best known as the Buddha ("enlightened one"). Our knowledge of his life is filtered through later Buddhist texts, which tell us that he was born the son of a ruler of one of the chiefdoms in the Himalayan foothills in what is now Nepal. Within the Indian caste system, he was in the warrior, not the priest (Brahman) caste. At age twenty-nine, unsatisfied with his life of comfort and troubled by the suffering he saw around him, he left home to become a wandering ascetic. He traveled south to the kingdom of Magadha, where he studied with yoga masters. Later he took up extreme asceticism. According to tradition, he reached enlightenment while meditating under a bo tree at Bodh Gaya. After several weeks of meditation, he preached his first sermon, urging a "middle way" between asceticism and worldly life. For the next forty-five years, the Buddha traveled through the Ganges Valley propounding his ideas, refuting his adversaries, making converts, and attracting followers.

In his first sermon, the Buddha outlined his main message, summed up in the Four Noble Truths and the Eightfold Path. The truths are as follows: (1) pain and suffering, frustration and anxiety are ugly but inescapable parts of human life; (2) suffering and anxiety are caused by human desires and attachments; (3) people can understand these weaknesses and triumph over them; and (4) this triumph is made possible by following a simple code of conduct, the Eightfold Path. The basic insight of Buddhism is thus psychological. The deepest human longings can never be satisfied, and even those things that seem to give pleasure cause anxiety because we are afraid of losing them. Attachment to people and things leads to sorrow at their loss.

The Buddha offered an optimistic message, however, because people can all set out on the Eightfold Path toward liberation. All they have to do is take steps such as recognizing the universality of suffering, deciding to free themselves from it, and choosing "right conduct," "right speech," "right livelihood," and "right endeavor." For instance, they should abstain from taking life and thus follow a vegetarian diet. The seventh step is "right awareness," constant contemplation of one's deeds and words, giving full thought to their importance and whether they lead to enlightenment. "Right contemplation," the last step, entails meditation on the impermanence of everything in the world. Those who achieve liberation are freed from the cycle of birth and death and enter the blissful state called *nirvana*.

Although he accepted the Indian idea of reincarnation, the Buddha denied the integrity of the individual self or soul. He saw human beings as a collection of parts, physical and mental. As long as the parts remain combined, that combination can be called "I." When that combination changes, as at death, the various parts remain in existence, ready

to become the building blocks of different combinations. According to Buddhist teaching, life is passed from person to person as a flame is passed from candle to candle.

The success of Buddhism was aided by the Buddha's teaching that everyone, noble and peasant, educated and ignorant, male and female, could follow the Eightfold Path. Within India this marked a challenge to the caste system, central to early Brahmanism and later Hinduism. Moreover, the Buddha was extraordinarily undogmatic. Convinced that each person must achieve enlightenment on his or her own, he emphasized that the path was important only because it led the traveler to enlightenment, not for its own sake. He compared religious practices to a raft, needed to get across a river but useless once on the far shore. Thus, there was no harm in honoring local gods or observing traditional ceremonies, as long as one kept in mind the ultimate goal of enlightenment.

In his lifetime, the Buddha formed a circle of disciples, primarily men but including some women as well. The Buddha's followers transmitted his teachings orally for several centuries until they were written down in the second or first century B.C.E. The form of monasticism that developed among the Buddhists was less strict than that of some other contemporary groups in India, such as the Jains. Buddhist monks moved about for eight months of the year (staying inside only during the rainy season) and consumed only one meal a day obtained by begging. Within a few centuries, Buddhist monks began to overlook the rule that they should travel. They set up permanent monasteries, generally on land donated by kings or other patrons. Orders of nuns also appeared, giving women the opportunity to seek truth in ways men had traditionally done. The main ritual that monks and nuns performed in their monastic establishments was the communal recitation of the sutras. Lay Buddhists could aid the spread of the Buddhist teachings by providing food for monks and support for their monasteries, and they could pursue their own spiritual progress by adopting practices such as abstaining from meat and alcohol.

Within India, the spread of Buddhism was greatly aided in the third century B.C.E. by King Ashoka. As a young prince, Ashoka served as governor of two prosperous provinces where Buddhism flourished. At the death of his father about 274 B.C.E., Ashoka rebelled against his older brother, the rightful king, and after four years of fighting succeeded in his bloody bid for the throne. In 261 B.C.E., early in his reign, Ashoka conquered Kalinga, on the east coast of India. Instead of exulting like a conqueror, however, Ashoka was consumed with remorse for all the deaths inflicted. In this mood, he embraced Buddhism.

Ashoka used the machinery of his empire to spread Buddhist teachings throughout India. He banned animal sacrifices, and, in place of hunting expeditions, he took pilgrimages. Two years after his conversion, he undertook a 256-day pilgrimage to all the holy sites of Buddhism, and on his return he began sending missionaries to all known countries. Buddhist tradition also credits him with erecting throughout India 84,000 stupas (Buddhist reliquary mounds), among which the ashes of the Buddha were distributed, beginning the association of Buddhism with monumental art and architecture. Also according to Buddhist tradition, Ashoka convened a great council of Buddhist monks at which the earliest canon of Buddhist texts was codified.

Under Ashoka, Buddhism began to spread to Central Asia. This continued under the Kushan empire (ca. 50–250 C.E.), especially under their greatest king, Kanishka I (ca. 100 C.E.). In this region, where the influence of Greek art was strong, artists began to depict the Buddha in human form. By this period, Buddhist communities were developing divergent traditions and came to stress different sutras. One of the most important of these, associated with the monk-philosopher Nagarjuna (ca. 150–250), is called Mahayana, or "Great Vehicle," because it is a more inclusive form of the religion. It drew on a set of discourses allegedly preached by the Buddha and kept hidden by his followers for centuries. One branch of Mahayana taught that reality is "empty" (that is, nothing exists independently of itself). Emptiness was seen as an absolute, underlying all phenomena, which are themselves transient and illusory. Another branch held that ultimate reality is consciousness, that everything is produced by the mind.

Just as important as the metaphysical literature of Mahayana Buddhism was its devotional side, influenced by the Iranian religions then prevalent in Central Asia. The Buddha became deified and was placed at the head of an expanding pantheon of other Buddhas and bodhisattvas (Buddhas-to-be who had stayed in the world to help others on the path to salvation). These Buddhas and bodhisattvas became objects of veneration, especially the Buddha Amitabha and the bodhisattva Avalokitesvara (Guanyin in Chinese,

Ghandaran Sculpture of the Bodhisattva Maitreya, ca. 100 C.E. In northwestern India and Afghanistan, Greek sculptural traditions influenced the portrayal of buddhas and bodhisattvas. *(Calcutta Museum, photo by Patricia Ebrey)*

Kannon in Japanese, Kwanŭm in Korean). With the growth of Mahayana, Buddhism became as much a religion for laypeople as for monks and nuns.

Buddhism remained an important religion in India until about 1200 C.E., but thereafter it declined, and the number of Buddhists in India today is small. Long before it declined in India, however, it spread to much of the rest of Asia. One route was east to Sri Lanka and most of Southeast Asia, including Indonesia. Another was northeast to Nepal and Tibet. More important for the history of East Asia, however, was the route northwest through Central Asia. During the first few centuries C.E., most of the city-states of Central Asia became centers of Buddhism, from Bamiyan, northwest of Kabul, to Kucha, Khotan, Loulan, Turfan, and Dun-huang. The first translators of Buddhist texts into Chinese were not Indians but Parthians, Sogdians, and Kushans from Central Asia.

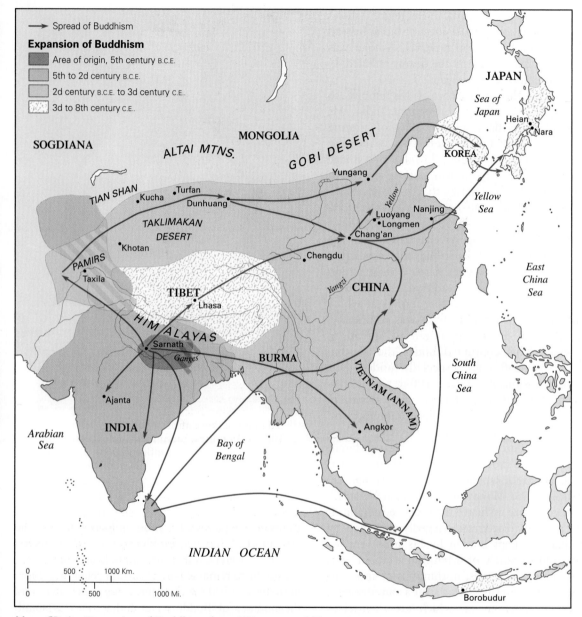

Map C2.1   **Expansion of Buddhism from 500 B.C.E. to 800 C.E.**

Central Asia in the centuries in which Buddhism was spreading east was ethnically and linguistically diverse, though various Indian and Persian languages were commonly used for administrative purposes. The economy of these city-states was dependent on the East-West trade. In Han times, the Chinese had become the overlords in the area, wanting both access to the fabled horses of Ferghana and to keep the area out of the hands of its foes, such as the Xiongnu. After the fall of the Han, most of these cities became independent and trade continued un-

abated. Buddhism thus reached China first as a religion of foreign merchants. Missionaries soon followed, however, and the hugely complex process of translating Buddhist sutras from Sanskrit or other Indian languages into classical Chinese was accomplished through the collaboration of Central Asian and Chinese monks.

Kumarajiva (350–413 C.E.) was one of the most important of these translators. His father, from a high-ranking family in India, had moved to the Silk Road oasis city of Kucha, attracted by the quality of

Yungang Cave Temples. Beginning about 460 C.E. the Northern Wei rulers constructed a series of caves at Yungang, not far from their capital. The Buddha on the left, shown here in a lotus meditation posture, is the largest at the site, 45 feet (13.7 meters) tall. The buddha in the next cave to the right is seated on a chair. Originally, each would have been protected from the elements by wooden structures, making each cave a separate chapel. *(Photo by Patricia Ebrey)*

the Buddhist scholarship there, and he married the younger sister of the king of Kucha. At this time, Kucha reportedly had a population of one hundred thousand, of whom ten thousand were monks. Already in this period, spectacular cave temples were being constructed in the nearby small town of Kizil. At home, Kumarajiva spoke Tokharian, an Indo-European language. He may also have learned some Chinese from merchants who came regularly to Kucha. From age seven, he studied Buddhist texts in Sanskrit as part of his Buddhist training. By age twenty, he had established himself as a brilliant Buddhist scholar, and the ruler of a small state in the modern Chinese province of Gansu sent a general to abduct him. He stayed in Gansu seventeen years, becoming fluent in Chinese. In 401, he was able to move to Chang'an, where another ruler gave financial support to his plan to translate Buddhist sutras into Chinese. Kumarajiva recruited a large group of learned monks and set up a systematic procedure for checking draft translations. Rather than borrowing terms from Daoism, which often proved misleading, Sanskrit terms were retained, represented by Chinese words borrowed for their sound. About thirty-five sutras were translated, including some of the most famous and popular, such as the *Lotus Sutra* and the *Vimalakirti Sutra*. An exponent of Mahayana, Kumarajiva also translated treatises by Nagarjuna and lectured on their content.

The translation of Buddhist texts into Chinese helped Buddhism spread throughout East Asia. Not only did these texts come to circulate throughout China (discussed in Chapters 4 and 5), but they also became the basis for Korean and Japanese schools of Buddhism. The Buddhism that reached Japan, for instance, was filtered through Central Asian, Chinese, and Korean lenses.

CHAPTER FOUR

Political Division in China and the Spread of Buddhism (200–580)

China's four centuries of unification under the Han Dynasty were followed by four centuries when division prevailed. This Period of Division began with a stalemate among the rivals to succeed the Han, resulting in the Three Kingdoms. In 280, China was reunited by the (Western) Jin Dynasty, but peace was short-lived. After 300, Jin degenerated into civil war. For the next two and a half centuries, north China was ruled by non-Chinese dynasties (the Northern Dynasties), while the south was ruled by a sequence of four short-lived Chinese dynasties, all of which were centered in the area of the present-day city of Nanjing (the Southern Dynasties). Although Buddhism gained a remarkable hold in both north and south, the two regions developed in different directions in other ways. In the north, despite frequent ethnic conflict, a hybrid culture emerged that drew from Chinese traditions of government administration and the military traditions of the non-Chinese rulers. In the south, although military men repeatedly seized the throne, high culture, especially the literary and visual arts, thrived among the émigré aristocrats.

The Northern Dynasties mark the first period in Chinese history when a large part of China proper was ruled by non-Chinese. Thus, scholars of this period have been particularly interested in issues of ethnicity and sinification (the process of absorbing Chinese culture). In what contexts did the Xianbei rulers promote or discourage adoption of Chinese ways? How was conflict between Chinese and Xianbei handled? How did these experiences shape Chinese notions of cultural and ethnic identity? One by-product of warfare in this period was enormous movements of peoples, voluntary and involuntary. What was the impact of these movements on Chinese civilization? Did they promote cultural integration, countering the effects of political division? In both north and south, birth meant more in this period than it had in the Han. Did the decline in the power of the central government foster growth in hereditary status? Another central issue in the understanding of this period is the success of Buddhism. If earlier philosophies laid the foundation for Chinese government and society, what was the effect of the spread of fundamentally different ideas?

THE THREE KINGDOMS (220–265) AND THE WESTERN JIN DYNASTY (265–316)

The Han Dynasty began to fall apart in 184 C.E. when the followers of a Daoist religious cult called the Way of Great Peace staged a major insurrection. In their efforts to seize power, hundreds of thousands of followers across the country simultaneously attacked local government offices. Although the original uprising was suppressed within a year, other groups preaching similar doctrines rose up elsewhere in the country. To respond to these uprisings, the Han court gave generals and local officials considerable autonomy to raise their own armies. In these unsettled conditions, they found no shortage of willing recruits from among refugees and the destitute. Larger armies were formed by absorbing smaller armies and their leaders. The top generals, once they no longer had rebels to suppress, turned to fighting each other, ushering in several decades of civil war. In 189, the warlord who gained control of the capital slaughtered more than two thousand eunuchs and took the emperor prisoner. Luoyang was sacked and burned, destroying the government libraries and archives.

By 205, Cao Cao had made himself the dominant figure in north China, even though he retained the Han emperor as a puppet. After Cao Cao's death in 220, his son Cao Pei forced the last Han emperor to abdicate and proclaimed the Wei Dynasty. The old Han capital of Luoyang was retained as the Wei capital.

Cao Cao and Cao Pei wanted to reconstruct an empire comparable to the Han but never gained control over all the territory the Han had once held. In the central and lower Yangzi valley and farther south, the brothers Sun Ce and Sun Quan established the state of Wu. A third kingdom, Shu, was established in the west, in Sichuan province, by a distant member of the Han imperial clan named Liu Bei (see Map 4.1). Although Liu Bei's resources could not compare to those controlled by Cao Pei in the north, he was aided by one of China's most famous military strategists, Zhuge Liang.

Wei was the largest and strongest of these three kingdoms, and several of the institutional measures Wei adopted remained important for the next several centuries. Wei made the status of soldier hereditary: when a commander or a soldier was killed or unable to fight any longer, a son or brother would take his place. Soldiers' families were classified as "military households" and treated as a group separate from ordinary commoners. Their families were assigned land to farm, and their children were required to marry into other military households. These farmers-turned-professional soldiers made good infantrymen, but Wei also needed cavalry. For that purpose, like the Han before them, they recruited Xiongnu in large numbers and settled them in southern Shanxi. To raise revenues to supply his armies, Cao Cao carved out huge state farms from land laid waste by war. He settled defeated rebels and landless poor as tenants on these farms, and had them pay their rent directly to state coffers. In other words, rather than trying to raise revenues by increasing tax collection on local magnates, who had many ways to resist tax collection, he made the state itself an enormous landlord.

Wei also introduced a new system of civil service recruitment known as the Nine Rank System. Although intended to select men with local reputations for talent and character, this system rapidly degenerated into a means for leading families to secure the best posts. Men whose families were ranked high did not have to start at the bottom of the bureaucratic ladder, making it considerably more likely that they would eventually rise to the highest posts.

Because Wei had more than twice the population of Shu or Wu, it was able to field a much larger army and eventually prevailed. The Wei general Sima Zhao defeated Shu in 263. Two years later, however, the general's son Sima Yan forced the Wei emperor to abdicate in his favor, and he established the Jin Dynasty. This was the first of many dynastic transitions in this period that began with a military coup. In 279, the Jin government sent a fleet of ships down the Yangzi River from Sichuan to overwhelm Wu forces and reunify China.

Hope that Jin would be able to restore the glories of the Han Dynasty did not last long. Although Jin held almost all the territory Han had, it did not have the Han government's administrative reach. The census of 280 recorded only 16 million people, evidence that many of those who had fled war, famine, or poverty had not been registered where they settled.

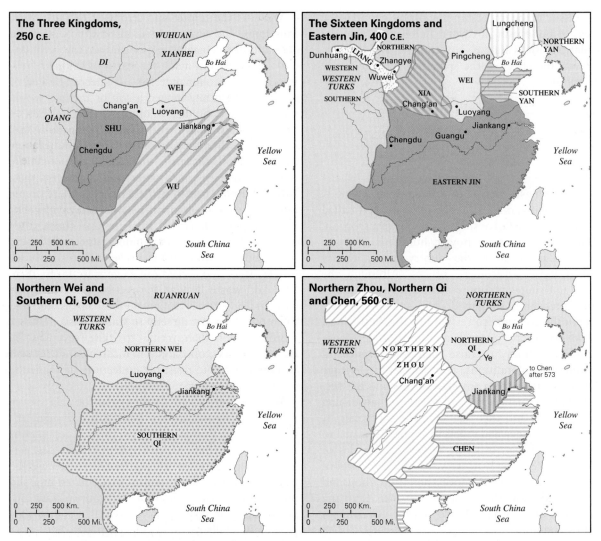

Map 4.1   **Rise and Fall of States During the Period of Division**

In Luoyang, the Jin Dynasty suffered from strife among the families of empresses. The powerful Jia family was suspected of arranging the assassination of an empress and more than one potential heir to the throne. Another threat came from princes of the Sima family. The Jin founder, wanting to make sure that no general could overthrow his dynasty the way he had overthrown Wei, parceled out the armies and enormous tracts of land to his own relatives. By the time he died in 290, more than half the regional armies were controlled by eight princes. Before long, their bloody struggles for dominance degenerated into general civil war. In 300, one prince marched his army to Luoyang, deposed the emperor, and took his place. One prince after another controlled the capital, but only as long as his army was able to

withstand the armies of his opponents. By the end of 304, governors leading locally raised militia forces had been drawn into the fray. By this point, the princes with fiefs in the north were incorporating more and more non-Chinese into their armies. When an army of Xianbei warriors took Chang'an in 306, they pillaged the city, reportedly slaughtering twenty thousand residents. By 307, only one of the original princes still survived, and little was left of the state. With the collapse of control from the center, people everywhere began building fortifications, taking up arms to defend themselves, or fleeing in search of safer places to live. With banditry endemic, both disease and famine spread.

These decades of warfare shaped the intellectual outlook of the educated elite. The late Han had

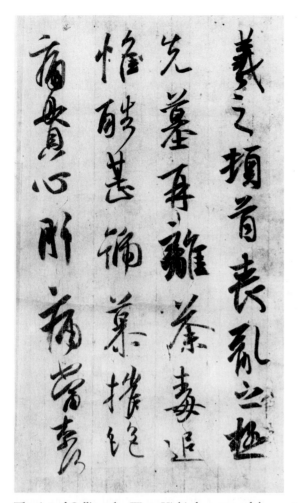

The Art of Calligraphy. Wang Xizhi, from one of the most eminent aristocratic families of the eastern Jin dynasty, came to be considered the greatest of Chinese calligraphers. His writing was admired for its grace, forcefulness, and subtle modulations. *(Imperial Collection, Japan)*

marked a high point in political activism, when many risked their lives and careers to oppose the domination of the court by eunuchs or consort families. When politics took a turn for the worse after 184, many educated men gave up the effort to participate in government.

The philosophically inclined turned to Daoist-inspired "Study of the Mysterious," which concerned such topics as the meaning of "being" and its relation to "nonbeing," subjects they discussed in new commentaries on the *Book of Changes, Laozi,* or *Zhuangzi.* Witty repartee, especially apt characterizations of prominent individuals, was much admired. Sophisticated aesthetes espoused "naturalness" and "spontaneity" and expressed disdain for mastery of established forms. In this environment, poetry flourished. Cao Cao and his two sons, Cao Pei and Cao Zhi, were all gifted poets. Another group of poets, known as the Seven Sages of the Bamboo Grove, gained fame for shocking their contemporaries. When someone rebuked Ruan Ji for talking to his sister-in-law, he replied, "Surely you do not mean to suggest that the rules of propriety apply to me?"

NON-CHINESE DOMINANCE IN THE NORTH

After the breakdown of Jin, non-Chinese seized power in north China. Why did this happen? One answer is military technology. The invention of the stirrup in about 300 C.E. made cavalry more crucial in warfare. The stirrup gave heavily armored riders

Seven Sages of the Bamboo Grove. Several tombs near the Eastern Jin capital at modern Nanjing have pictures of the eccentric "seven sages" depicted in the brick walls. In the example shown here, each of the figures is labeled and shown drinking, writing, or playing a musical instrument. *(Nanjing Museum, Jiangsu, China)*

greater stability and freedom of motion. From this time on, horses and their riders began wearing heavy armor, giving them more striking power and the ability to engage in shock combat. By the fourth century, sources mention the capture of thousands of armored horses in a single battle.

Another reason is that Xiongnu and other northern auxiliary troops had been settled within China proper ever since Han times. Most of these groups retained their tribal social structures and pastoral way of life, but settled into specific territories. After Cao Cao defeated the Wuhuan in 207, he moved many of them to interior counties and incorporated many of their men into his armies. Jin followed similar policies, in 284–285, moving about 130,000 surrendered Xiongnu to the interior. The non-Chinese soldiers were often dissatisfied with their conditions, and ethnic friction was not uncommon. In some areas of north China, the non-Chinese came to outnumber the Han Chinese. One Chinese writer claimed that in the region around Chang'an, the Chinese had become the minority.

Although many of these ethnic groups had been part of the Xiongnu confederation, they reasserted their distinct identities (such as Wuhuan, Xianbei, and Di) after it collapsed. But these identities continued to be flexible. Xiongnu who settled among the Xianbei, for instance, would in time call themselves Xianbei. As disorder worsened in the first years of the fourth century, uprisings of Xiongnu, Di, and Qiang occurred in scattered sites. The most threatening of these was the uprising of the Xiongnu chieftain Liu Yuan in 304. Liu Yuan was literate in Chinese and had spent part of his youth at the court in Luoyang. His familiarity with Chinese culture only made him resent Chinese policies toward the Xiongnu more strongly. When a prince sought his help in the civil war, Liu declared himself king of Han and made a bid for the throne as an heir to the Han Dynasty (from which his ancestors had received the Han imperial surname). On his campaigns, he incorporated bands of bandits, including both Chinese and non-Chinese. His armies, plundering as they went, moved south through Shanxi to the gates of Luoyang in 308–309.

Another important non-Chinese leader in this period was a much less sinified Jie tribesman named Shi Le. Shi Le had been sold into slavery by a Jin official. After gaining his freedom, he led a group of mounted brigands made up of escaped slaves and others on the margins of society, some of whom were Chinese. Early in these wars, Shi Le allied with Liu Yuan, and it was Shi Le's troops who captured and plundered Luoyang in 311. In 319, Shi Le broke with the Liu family and proclaimed himself king of Zhao. Within a decade, he had destroyed the Liu forces.

The regimes set up in the fourth century by various non-Chinese contenders did not have the institutional infrastructure to administer large territories. When they defeated a Chinese fortress, they normally gave the local strongman the title of governor and claimed him as part of their government. This was a fragile system, since the recently incorporated governor could easily change sides again.

The regimes established by Liu Yuan and Shi Le drew sharp distinctions between Chinese and non-Chinese. In essence, the non-Chinese were the rulers and the soldiers, while the Chinese were the subjects, who were expected to grow grain, pay taxes, and provide labor service. Enemy generals who surrendered were incorporated into the tribally organized military structure, still leading their old troops. Chinese soldiers were often incorporated into these armies, but usually as porters or infantry, not cavalry. Because much of north China had been depopulated, securing labor was more important than gaining land. Many campaigns were essentially slave raids, with those captured sent back to the victor's capital. Not surprising, most of the Chinese population saw none of these regimes as legitimate. Ethnic conflict flared from time to time. Different groups of refugees on the roads often robbed and murdered each other. When an adopted son succeeded to the Shi line in 350, he reverted to his Chinese identity and called for the slaughter of non-Chinese, which his Chinese subjects carried out with a vengeance.

During these decades, Chinese in the north faced a leadership crisis. Some scholars estimate that 60 percent of the elite of government officials and landowners fled south between 311 and 325, most of them taking relatives, retainers, and neighbors with them. Those who did not move south often took their followers to nearby hilltops, which they fortified in order to defend against marauders.

The Northern Wei and Hybrid Xianbei-Chinese Culture

By 400, the rising power in the north was the Northern Wei state founded by the Tuoba clan of the Xianbei. From its base in northern Shanxi, Northern Wei established dominance on the steppe to the

Color Plate 1
Bronze Mask. Larger than life size, this bronze mask from Sanxingdui in Sichuan is 60 centimeters wide and weighs 13.4 kilograms. Note the prominent eyes and wide mouth, found on all of the masks.
(Cultural Relics Publishing House)

Color Plate 2
Fighting from Horseback. This depiction of a warrior fighting a leopard is from an inlaid bronze mirror of Warring States date.
(Gugong Yuekan)

Color Plate 3
Lacquer Coffin from Chu. This coffin, the innermost of three
nested coffins, is a fine example of fourth century B.C.E. lacquer
art. The top and sides are decorated with seventy-two interlaced
serpentine dragons and an equal number of mythical birds.
(Hubei Provincial Museum, Wuhan/Cultural Relics Publishing House)

Color Plate 4
Galloping Horse.
Appreciation for fine
horses is evident in this
13.5 inch tall bronze
horse, found in a
second century C.E.
tomb in Gansu
province.
(Robert Harding)

Color Plate 5
Interior of Cave 285 at Dunhuang. Completed in 539, Cave 285 shows
the Buddha surrounded by other deities, meditating monks, and donors.
On the ceiling are celestial musicians and other flying spirits.
(Cultural Relics Publishing House)

Color Plate 6
Women Musicians. Note the range of instruments played by the women on this tenth
century tomb wall. Note also that the Tang appreciation of full-figured women has
continued into the subsequent Five Dynasties period.
(Hebei Provincial Cultural Relics Institute, Shijiazhang/Cultural Relics Publishing House)

Color Plate 7
An Elegant Party. A Song court artist, perhaps copying an earlier Tang painting, depicts an elegant gathering of literary men, hosted by the emperor. Note the array of dishes and cups on the table.

(National Palace Museum, Taipei/The Art Archive)

north, which gave it the advantage of access to the horses and horsemen of the steppe. Gradually Wei defeated the other states set up by other Xianbei clans and, in 439, reunified north China after more than a century of constant conflict.

Like their rivals, the Xianbei sent raiding parties to seize captives, horses, cattle, and sheep from other tribes or from Chinese settlements. Wei forced the relocation of thousands of Chinese to populate their capital and bring deserted land into cultivation. To avoid being overwhelmed by the numerically dominant Chinese, the early Wei rulers kept their capital at Pingcheng in north Shanxi. Xianbei warriors were settled nearby and made their living as herdsmen rather than as farmers. The army remained a north Asian preserve, with Chinese usually playing only support roles.

As the fifth century progressed, the Xianbei learned how to draw wealth from Chinese farmers. To collect taxes, the Xianbei rulers turned to educated Chinese, whom they employed as officials. They put into place the institutions these Chinese advisers proposed based on Chinese experience. In the late fifth century, the Northern Wei rulers adopted an "equal-field" system to distribute land to farmers and increase production. The state claimed exclusive right to distribute land.

Allotments were made to families based primarily on their labor power, with extra for officials and nobles based on rank.

The policy of keeping Chinese and Xianbei separate was abandoned by Emperor Xiaowen (r. 471–499). Born to a Chinese mother, Xiaowen wanted to unite the Chinese and Xianbei elites, and beginning in 493, he initiated a radical program of sinification. He banned the wearing of Xianbei clothes at court, required all Xianbei officials below the age of thirty to speak Chinese at court, and encouraged intermarriage between the highest-ranking families of the Chinese and Xianbei elites. He gave Xianbei new single-character surnames, which made them sound less foreign. The imperial house itself took the name *Yuan* ("primal").

The court itself was moved three hundred miles south to the site of the Han and Jin capital of Luoyang. This transfer was accomplished by subterfuge. Emperor Xiaowen mobilized his army for an invasion of the south, but he halted at Luoyang and announced the plan to build his capital there. By 495, about 150,000 Xianbei and other northern warriors had been moved south to fill the ranks of the imperial guards in Luoyang. Xiaowen also welcomed refugees or defectors from the south, such as

Filial Grandson Yuan Gu. This scene, from an incised Northern Wei stone sarcophagus, depicts the story of a boy who saved his grandfather from being abandoned in the woods. Note the depiction of landscape—rocks, trees, water, wind, and mountains. *(The Nelson-Atkins Museum of Art, Kansas City, Missouri [Purchase: Nelson Trust] 33-1543/1)*

Wang Su of the aristocratic Langye Wang family, who was put to work on the reorganization of the bureaucracy. To make southerners feel at home, they were served tea, newly popular in the south, at the palace rather than the yogurt-like drinks consumed in the north.

Within twenty-five years, Luoyang became a magnificent city again, with a half-million residents, vast palaces, elegant mansions, and more than a thousand Buddhist temples. It had a district where foreign traders lived and another occupied by rich merchants and craftsmen. Many members of the Xianbei nobility became culturally dual, fully proficient in Chinese cultural traditions and comfortable interacting with the leading Chinese families. So many southerners had been welcomed at Luoyang that there was a district known as Wu quarter, where more than three thousand families lived, complete with their own fish and turtle market.

The Revolt of the Garrisons and the Division of the North

This period of prosperity was cut short in 523, only a generation after the relocation, when the Xianbei who remained in the north rebelled. In the wars that ensued, hostility based on ethnicity repeatedly added to the violence. With the transfer of the Xianbei elite to Luoyang, the garrison forces saw their status plummet to hardly better than that of hereditary military households. When a shortage of food at the garrisons sparked rebellion, the government moved two hundred thousand surrendered garrison rebels to Hebei, where food supplies were more plentiful. This course of action proved to be a colossal mistake. In 526–527, a former garrison officer organized the displaced rebels into a much more potent force.

The Wei court then turned to one of its generals to deal with the new uprising, but he soon turned on the court. The thousand-plus officials who came out of the city to tender their submission were slaughtered by this general, who had the empress dowager and her new child emperor thrown in the Yellow River. He then installed his own puppet Wei emperor.

Struggles of this sort continued for years. In the east, power was seized by Gao Huan. Gao's grandfather was a Han Chinese official who had been exiled to the northern garrisons, and Gao had grown up in poverty, not even owning a horse until he married into a Xianbei family. He was one of the

two hundred thousand frontiersmen relocated to Hebei because of the famine, and he took charge of this group in 531. Because of his dual background, he could appeal to both Chinese and Xianbei.

Luoyang soon fell to Gao Huan, but the region of Chang'an was in the hands of rival forces. The central figure there was Yuwen Tai, not yet thirty years old. Yuwen Tai too came from the garrisons, but his father had organized a loyalist militia to resist the rebels. The struggle between Gao Huan and Yuwen Tai and their successors lasted forty years: neither could dislodge the other, even though they set off with armies of one hundred thousand or more troops. The Gao regime maintained a Tuoba prince on the throne until 550 (thus leading to the dynastic name Eastern Wei, 534–550), then declared a new dynasty, known as the Northern Qi (551–577). The Yuwen regime kept a Wei prince a little longer (Western Wei, 535–556), but eventually declared itself the founders of a new dynasty, called the Northern Zhou (557–580).

Gao Huan tried to convince both Chinese and Xianbei that it made sense for the Xianbei to do the fighting and the Chinese the farming. To the Xianbei he would say, "The Han are your slaves. The men till for you; the women weave for you. They provide you with grain and silk so that you are warm and well fed. For what reason do you bully them?" To Han Chinese he would say, "The Xianbei are your retainers. For a single measure of your grain and a single length of your silk they attack the bandits so that you are safe. For what reason do you regard them as a scourge?"[1] Ethnic strife continued, however, and there were several bloody purges of Chinese officials.

In the west, the Xianbei were not so numerous, and Yuwen Tai had to find ways to incorporate Chinese into his armies and his government. He encouraged intermarriage and bestowed Xianbei surnames on his leading Chinese officials, making them honorary Xianbei. The Chinese who joined him were mostly men of action who loved to hunt and take the lead in military ventures.

It was in this environment that the multiethnic militia system called the divisional militia (*fubing*) was created. The households of the soldiers enrolled

---

1. From Sima Guang's *Zizhi tongjian*, cited in David A. Graff, *Medieval Chinese Warfare, 300–900* (London: Routledge, 2002), p. 107.

in it were removed from the regular tax registers and put on the army registers. Such registration carried honorable status. Soldiers of these armies served in rotation as guards at the imperial palace, helping them identify with the dynasty.

With this army, Northern Zhou began expanding, taking Sichuan away from the south in 553 and parts of the middle Yangzi about the same time. In 577, this army defeated Northern Qi, reunifying the north.

THE SOUTHERN DYNASTIES AND ARISTOCRATIC CULTURE

Among those who fled the confusion that followed the sacking of Luoyang in 311 and Chang'an in 316 were members of the Jin royal house and its high officials. At Nanjing (then called Jiankang), these refugees created a government in exile after putting a Jin prince on the throne. Because Nanjing is east of Luoyang, the second phase of the Jin Dynasty is called the Eastern Jin (317–420), reminiscent of the Western and Eastern Zhou and the Western and Eastern Han. It was followed by four short dynasties that ruled from Nanjing (the Song, Qi, Liang, and Chen, collectively termed the Southern Dynasties, 420–589). The Yangzi River was the great battlefield of the south, with flotillas of ships sailing from the middle Yangzi to attack forces holding Nanjing, or vice versa. None of the successive Southern Dynasties was fully able to keep its military commanders under control, even when they were imperial relatives. One dynasty after another was founded when a general seized the capital and installed himself as emperor. These generals were strong enough to hold their governments together during their lifetimes but were not able to concentrate power in ways that would ensure successful transfers of power to their heirs.

Maintaining an adequate supply of soldiers was a constant challenge for the Southern Dynasties. The Jin tried to continue its earlier practice of designating certain households as military households, but the status of military households fell precipitously until they were looked on as little better than state slaves, making desertion a constant problem. Generals sometimes resorted to campaigns against the southern non-Chinese to capture men to make into soldiers (analogous to the slave raids of the north, this time with the Chinese as the raiders).

The south experienced considerable economic development during the Southern Dynasties, as new lands were opened and trade networks extended. Trade with countries in the South Seas expanded, especially Funan and Champa (in today's Cambodia and Vietnam), where Chinese came into contact with merchants from India and even farther west.

Social cleavages were pronounced in the south, with deep divisions between the northern émigrés and the local elite; between the aristocrats, who preferred to stay at court, and the generals given the task of defending against the north and maintaining the peace; and between Han Chinese, living in the river valleys, and various indigenous peoples, who largely retreated to upland areas. The aristocracy dominated the upper ranks of officialdom. These families saw themselves as maintaining the high culture of the Han but judged themselves and others on the basis of their ancestors. They married only with families of equivalent pedigree and compiled lists and genealogies of the most eminent families. At court they often looked down on the emperors of the successive dynasties as military upstarts. They dominated the Nine Rank System and used it to appoint men from their families to government service. One of the sharpest critics of the southern aristocrats was Yan Zhitui (see **Biography: Yan Zhitui**). As he saw it, because life was easy for the southern aristocrats, they saw no need to study. When important affairs were discussed, "they sit with foolish looks and widely-opened mouths as if sitting in a cloud or fog." When conversation turned to history or they were asked to compose poems, "they silently hang their heads, yawning and stretching, unable to say anything."[2] Members of the Liang royal family were even worse, he charged, perfuming their garments, shaving their faces, using powder and rouge, sitting on cushions and leaning on soft silk bolsters, and getting others to compose their poems for them. Once their dynasty fell, they had no skills to fall back on.

The most outstanding emperor in the south was Emperor Wu of Liang (r. 502–549). He was not only a major patron of Buddhism but also a patron of literature and the arts. A prolific poet himself, he summoned learned men to court and would order his

2. Ssu-yu Teng, trans., *Family Instructions of the Yen Clan* (Leiden: Brill, 1968), pp. 52–53.

BIOGRAPHY   Yan Zhitui (531–591+)

Many people were dislocated during the Period of Division, but few as many times as Yan Zhitui. The Yan family was one of the émigré families that had left north China in 317, and thereafter it continuously supplied officials for the Southern Dynasties. Yan's grandfather, out of loyalty to the Qi Dynasty, starved himself to death when Emperor Wu of Liang usurped the throne in 502. Yan's father, however, served at Emperor Wu's court. When he died, Yan Zhitui was only nine, so his elder brother was responsible for much of his education. In his teens Yan himself became a court attendant of one of the Liang princes. When Yan was eighteen years old, the rebel Hou Jing captured him and the prince he served, and they narrowly escaped execution.

In 552, Yan went with this prince to Jiangling in Hubei, where the prince set up a rival court. In 554, however, the northern state of Western Wei captured Jiangling, and Yan, at age twenty-four, was one of the one hundred thousand people enslaved and brought north to Chang'an. Two years later, he and his family managed to escape and make their way east, hoping to return to Liang. By this point, however, Liang had been overthrown. Unwilling to serve the successor state of Chen, Yan Zhitui stayed in the northeast, where the Northern Qi rulers gave him court appointments for the next two decades. In 577, Northern Qi was defeated by the Northern Zhou, and Yan, now forty-six years old, was again forced to move, this time back to Chang'an. He apparently did not serve at court for the next couple of years and seems to have faced poverty in this period. After the Sui Dynasty was founded in 581, Yan was given scholarly posts, working on a new dictionary and related projects.

In the twenty-chapter book of advice Yan wrote for his sons, he frequently commented on his experiences. He said his elder brother had not been strict enough with him, letting him develop bad habits that took years to overcome. He stressed to his sons the importance of a solid literary education; it was because he had skills that he had gained court posts under the Northern Qi. Less literate men who had faced the same dislocations had ended up working on farms or tending horses, even though their ancestors had been officials for centuries.

Yan Zhitui also recommended mastering calligraphy, painting, and lute playing, though he warned that those who became too good might be humiliated by being forced by those of higher rank to produce on demand. He said he had spent many hours copying model pieces of calligraphy, including the ten scrolls in his family's collection done by the fourth-century masters Wang Xizhi and his son Wang Xianzhi.

Although Yan Zhitui's advice to his sons shows him committed to the study of the Confucian classics and the Confucian ideal of service to the ruler, he also had strong faith in Buddhism and included a chapter defending Buddhism against its critics. He wanted Buddhist services after his death and told his sons to omit meat from the traditional ancestral offerings. Since he expected his sons to marry and have children, he did not urge them to become monks, but he did encourage them to "attend to the chanting and reading of the sacred books and thereby provide for passage to your future state of existence. Incarnation as a human is difficult to attain. Do not pass through yours in vain!"[3]

---

3. Ssu-yu Teng, trans., *Family Instructions of the Yen Clan* (Leiden: Brill, 1968), p. 148.

courtiers to compose and recite poems, rewarding the most successful with gifts of gold or silk. His sons were also ardent patrons, several establishing literary salons of their own. The eldest son, Xiao Tong, was an avid book collector and compiled an anthology of 761 great writings organized by genre, the *Selections of Literature (Wen xuan)*.

Not long after Emperor Wu's death, the southern court was hard hit by the rebellion of Hou Jing, a would-be warlord from the north who had gathered a huge army and set siege to Nanjing. The siege lasted four months, by which time many members of the great families had starved to death in their mansions. A general declared a new dynasty, Chen, but he could do little more than confirm local strongmen as his governors.

Poetry, Calligraphy, and Painting as Arts of Men of Letters

During the Period of Division, men of letters developed poetry, calligraphy, and painting into arts through which they could express their thoughts and feelings. Poets came to play a distinctive cultural role as exemplars of the complex individual, moved by conflicting but powerful emotions. Cao Cao's son Cao Zhi (192–232) was one of the first poets to create such a persona. Chafing at the restrictions his brother the emperor placed on him, he poured out his feelings into his verse.

Another poet whose persona is as important as his poems is Tao Qian (or Tao Yuanming, 365–427). At times Tao expressed high ambitions, at other times the desire to be left alone. Once when holding a minor post, he quit rather than entertain a visiting inspector, explaining, "How could I bend my waist to this village buffoon for five pecks of rice!" Many of Tao's poems express Daoist sentiments such as "excessive thinking harms life" or "propriety and conventions, what folly to follow them too earnestly." By the age of forty, Tao gave up office altogether and supported himself by farming. He was not a hermit, however, and continued to enjoy friends and family. His poems often express his enjoyment of wine, books, and music:

I try a cup and all my concerns become remote.
Another cup and suddenly I forget even
  Heaven.
But is Heaven really far from this state?
Nothing is better than to trust your true self.[4]

In the somewhat rarefied atmosphere of the aristocracy in Nanjing, calligraphy came to be recognized as an art almost on a par with poetry. Because calligraphy was believed to reflect the writer's character and mood, the calligraphy of men of refinement and edu-

cation was assumed to be superior to that of technically proficient clerks. Calligraphy was written with a highly pliable hairbrush, and the strength, balance, and flow of the strokes were believed to convey the writer's inner self. To attain a good hand took discipline, since one had to copy works by established masters for years before even thinking of developing a distinctive style. Pieces of calligraphy by former masters thus came to be treasured as works of art. With collecting also came forgeries and debates about authenticity. Works by Wang Xizhi (307–365) were highly prized even in his own day. Admirers would borrow pieces of his calligraphy to make tracing copies, so before long, copies were much more numerous than original products of his hand.

Once calligraphy came to be considered an appropriate art for the educated class, painting gained a similar status. Paintings came to be associated with known, named painters whose talents were compared and ranked. The most famous of these painters was Gu Kaizhi (344–406), who painted portraits of many of the notable men of his day. It was also in this period that works that criticized and ranked individual poets, calligraphers, and painters began to appear.

THE BUDDHIST CONQUEST OF CHINA

Why did Buddhism find so many adherents in China during the three centuries after the fall of the Han Dynasty in 220? There were no forced conversions. China's initial contact with Central Asia in Western Han times did not lead to significant spread of earlier religions of the region such as Zoroastrianism. Moreover, several basic Buddhist teachings ran up against long-established Chinese customs. In particular, becoming a monk involved giving up one's surname and the chance to have descendants, thus cutting oneself off from the ancestral cult.

On the positive side, Buddhism benefited from the dedication of missionaries who traveled east from Central Asia along the Silk Road (see **Connections: Buddhism in India and Its Spread Along the Silk Road**). Buddhism also had something to offer almost everyone. It offered learned Chinese the intellectual stimulus of subtle cosmologies, and rulers a source of magical power and a political tool to unite Chinese and non-Chinese. In a rough and tumultuous age,

---

4. From "Drinking Alone in the Rainy Season," in William H. Nienhauser, Jr., ed., *The Indiana Companion to Traditional Chinese Literature* (Bloomington: Indiana University Press, 1986), p. 768.

Buddhism offered everyone an appealing emphasis on kindness, charity, the preservation of life, and the prospect of salvation.

The monastic establishment grew rapidly after 300, with generous patronage by rulers, their relatives, and other members of the elite. By 477 there were said to be 6,478 Buddhist temples and 77,258 monks and nuns in the north. Some decades later, south China had 2,846 temples and 82,700 clerics. Those not ready to become monks or nuns could pursue Buddhist goals as pious laypeople by performing devotional acts and making contributions toward the construction or beautification of temples. Devotional groups were often organized around particular scriptures, such as the *Lotus Sutra*, the *Pure Land Sutra*, or the *Holy Teachings of Vimalakirti*. Maitreya, the Buddha of the Future, was frequently a central image in Buddhist temples.

In China, women turned to Buddhism as readily as men did. Although incarnation as a female was considered lower than incarnation as a male, it was also viewed as temporary, and women were encouraged to pursue salvation on terms nearly equal to men. Joining a nunnery became an alternative for women who did not want to marry or did not want to stay with their husband's families in widowhood. In 516, the first set of biographies of Buddhist nuns was compiled. Most of the nuns described in it came from upper-class families, but they entered the convent for varied reasons. Huiyao, who entered the convent as a child, had herself immolated as an offering to the Three Treasures (the Buddha, the sanga or body of monks and nuns, and the teachings). Miaoxiang, with her father's approval, left her unfilial husband to enter a convent. Tanhui, after study with a foreign meditation master beginning at age eleven, threatened suicide if forced to marry her fiancé. After her fiancé tried to abduct her, the foreign meditation master solicited funds to compensate him. The nun Xuanzao entered the convent after a miraculous cure at age ten. A monk had told her father that the illness was probably caused by deeds done in a former life, making medicine useless. They should instead single-mindedly turn to the bodhisattva Guanyin. After seven days of devotions, she had a vision of a golden image and then recovered.

Buddhism had an enormous impact on the visual arts in China, especially sculpture and painting. Earlier Chinese had rarely depicted gods in human form, but now Buddhist temples were furnished with a profusion of images. The great cave temples at Yungang, sponsored by the Northern Wei rulers in the fifth century, contain huge Buddha figures in stone, the tallest a standing Buddha about seventy feet high. Further west, in Dunhuang, the original painted plaster of Buddhist caves has often survived, giving testimony to the great accomplishment of artists (see **Material Culture: Cave 285 at Dunhuang**).

None of the great Buddhist temples in the capitals survive, but texts describe them as large and lavishly decorated (see **Documents: The Monastery of Eternal Tranquility**). These temples became sites of dazzling ceremonies. For the Great Blessing ceremony held in Luoyang on the seventh day of the fourth month, all the Buddhist statues in the city, more than a thousand altogether, were brought to the largest monastery, where music and incense filled the air and entertainers performed to amuse the crowds.

Buddhism also provided the Chinese with a new reason to travel. Chinese monks made pilgrimages to India to see the holy places of Buddhism and seek out learned teachers. The first pilgrim to leave a record of his journey is Faxian, who left Chang'an in 399, when he was already over sixty years old. His trip west was overland, through Kucha, Khotan, and Kashgar, into the Indus Valley and then the cities of the Ganges valley. On his return, he took ship in the Bay of Bengal and stopped in Sri Lanka and then in Sumatra, reaching Guangzhou in 412. By 414 he was back in Nanjing, where he set to work translating the sutras he had carried back with him.

One of the greatest royal patrons of Buddhism in this period was Emperor Wu of Liang (r. 502–549). Although he had studied Daoism as a young man, in 504 he urged his family and officials to give it up. Out of Buddhist faith he banished meat and wine from palace banquets. He also found a new way to divert court funds to Buddhism: in 527 he entered a monastery and refused to return to the throne until his officials paid a large "ransom" to the monastery. Two years later, Emperor Wu repeated this pious act, hoping that it would help save his people from a deadly plague then spreading.

Not everyone was won over by Buddhist teachings. Its critics labeled it immoral because it severed family ties and posed a threat to the state since monastery land was not taxed and monks performed neither labor service nor military duty. Twice in the north, orders were issued to close monasteries and force monks and nuns to return to lay life, but these suppressions did not last long, and no attempt was made to suppress Buddhist belief.

MATERIAL CULTURE

Cave 285 at Dunhuang

In 523, Prince Dongyang, a member of the Northern Wei royal house, was sent to Dunhuang to serve as its governor. During his fifteen-year tenure, he and a group of wealthy local families commissioned a new cave to be dug and decorated at the temple complex outside town, where the Buddhist faithful had been constructing and decorating caves along a cliff face for a century.

The cave the prince sponsored, cave 285, has as its central figure a statue of the historical Buddha seated (see Color Plate 5). He is flanked by figures of crossed-legged meditating monks who wear traditional monks' robes made of patchwork, symbolizing their indifference to material goods. Other monks are depicted on the walls. Temple guardians fill the lower reaches of the walls, heavenly beings the upper reaches.

Meditating Monk. On either side of the main image is a side niche with a statue of a cross-legged monk. *(Lois Conner, 1995. Courtesy of the Dunhuang Academy)*

DAOIST RELIGION

At the same time that Buddhism was gaining converts, the Daoist religion was undergoing extraordinary growth. This religion had many roots: popular religious movements; the elite pursuit of immortality; and, after the third century, the model of Buddhism with its sacred scriptures and celibate clergy. Although some Daoist masters became influential at court, most governments maintained a cautious reserve toward the Daoist religion, aware of the connection between Daoism and uprisings at the end of the Han. Daoism thus was never the recipient of government patronage on the lavish scale of Buddhism.

The Daoism of elite devotees was generally an individual practice aimed at bodily immortality in a kind of indestructible "astral body." One strove for this through dietary control, gymnastics, good deeds, mystic self-identification with the all-embracing Dao,

and visualization of the innumerable gods and spirits that dwelled inside the microcosm of the body. Many of the most famous men of letters of the period were devoted to such practices. Ge Hong (283–343), for instance, tried to convince his readers that immortality could be achieved and wrote on alchemy, breathing and meditation exercises, exorcism, sexual hygiene, herbalism, and talismanic charms. Ge gave a recipe for an elixir called gold cinnabar and described methods for walking on water and raising the dead.

The fall of Luoyang and the retreat of so many members of the northern elite to the south had a major impact on the development of Daoism. Priests from the north came into contact with local traditions of esoteric learning in the south. A series of revelations led to the writing down of a large number of scriptures. These texts formed the core first of the Supreme Purity sect and later of the rival Numinous Treasure sect. By the end of the Period of Division,

DOCUMENTS

The Monastery of Eternal Tranquility

After the Northern Wei moved their capital to Luoyang in 493, the city grew rapidly. Within twenty years, about a half million people had moved there and some thousand Buddhist temples had been built. The political fortunes of the dynasty went into decline beginning in 524, and in 534 the capital was moved to a safer place, leading to the rapid decline of Luoyang. In 547, Yang Xuanzhi, on a visit to it, was so moved by his memories of its former glories that he wrote a five-chapter book on the city and its famous monasteries. He began his account with the Monastery of Eternal Tranquility, just south of the palace.

The Monastery of Eternal Tranquility was built by Empress Dowager Hu in 516 about a *li* (one-third of a mile) south of the palace's Changhe gate, on the west side of the Imperial Road. . . . Within its walls was a nine-story wooden pagoda 900 feet tall; with the metal spire above it, its top was 1,000 feet above the ground. The pagoda could be seen from 100 *li* away. When the foundations were dug, thirty metal statues were found, which the Empress Dowager took as a response to her faith in Buddhism and used as a reason to build the monastery on such an immoderate scale.

On the top of the spire was a jewel-studded metal jar, large enough to hold twenty-five bushels. Under it were thirty metal plates for catching dew, which had metal bells hanging from them. Iron chains stretched from the pole to the four corners of the pagoda. Metal bells as big as bushel measures hung from the chains. Bells also hung from the corners of each of the nine stories, adding up to 120 bells in all.

The pagoda was four-sided, with three doors and six windows on each side. The doors were painted red and embellished with five rows of metal studs on each of the twelve doors' twenty-four leaves, for a total of 5,400 studs. There were also metal rings as knockers. The quality of the construction, the skill of the design, and the marvels of the Buddhist art were all beyond comprehension. The painted pillars and metal knockers captivated the viewer. At night when the wind was strong, the music of the bells could be heard more than ten *li* away.

North of the pagoda was the Buddha Hall, similar in design to the palace's Hall of the Great Ultimate. In it was an 18-foot tall

metal statue, ten life-sized metal statues, three statues embellished with pearls, five made of wire, and two of jade, all exceptionally finely made, the best of the age. The other buildings, including the monks' quarters, came to more than a thousand room-units. They were decorated with carved beams and painted walls; their doors and windows were painted blue; it was beautiful beyond description. Touching the eaves were junipers, cypresses, pine, and cedar trees; near the steps were fragrant herbs. . . .

When the decoration of the monastery was completed, Emperor Ming and the Empress Dowager ascended the pagoda. They looked down at the palace, which seemed small enough to fit in their palms. The whole capital seemed no bigger than a courtyard. People were prohibited from climbing the pagoda because from it one could see into the palace. . . .

In 528, [the general] Erzhu Rong quartered his troops and horses in the monastery. . . . In 530, the rebel Erzhu Zhao imprisoned Emperor Zhuang in the monastery. . . . In the second month of 534, the pagoda was destroyed by fire. . . . The fire started in the eighth story. By dawn the next day the building was ablaze. At the time, thunder and lightning pierced the darkness, and there was hail and snow. Everyone, monks and lay people, came out to watch the blaze, their sobs shaking the city. Three monks threw themselves into the fire and died. It took more than three months for the fire to burn out.

Translated from Yang Xuanzhi, *Luoyang qielan ji jiaozhu* (Shanghai: Shanghai guji chubanshe, 1958), 1–12, by Patricia Ebrey.

Daoism had its own canons of scriptures, much influenced by Buddhist models but constituting an independent religious tradition.

At the local level, popular collective forms of Daoism continued to thrive. Local masters would organize communal ceremonies for their parishioners. Incantations, music, fasting, and the display of penance and remorse would bring about the collective elimination of sins, which were seen as the main cause of sickness and premature death. According to the indignant reports of their Buddhist adversaries, Daoist ceremonies lasted days and nights and were ecstatic, sometimes even orgiastic. The participation of both men and women may explain the common allegation of sexual excesses at these ceremonies.

In the early centuries, Daoist priests usually married, and the office of Daoist master was hereditary. With the great success of Buddhism, some Daoist leaders introduced celibacy and monastic life in the sixth century. Daoist monasteries, however, never acquired the economic power of Buddhist ones.

Daoist borrowings from Buddhism did not lead to reconciliation of the two religions. To the contrary, each engaged in bitter polemics against the other throughout this period. Moreover, Daoist masters helped instigate some of the anti-Buddhist persecutions. As an answer to Buddhist claims of superiority, Daoist masters asserted that the Buddha had been merely a manifestation of Laozi, who had preached to the Indians a debased form of Daoism, which naturally China did not need to reimport.

SUMMARY

How did China change from the third to the early seventh centuries? China did not become more populous or larger, but it changed in other fundamental ways. Buddhism gained wide acceptance among people of all social levels and was transforming the landscape with its temples and monuments. Because of the popularity of Buddhism, Chinese civilization became much more closely tied to other parts of Asia. Daoism responded to Buddhism's challenge and acquired a large body of texts and monastic institutions. Although warfare disrupted many people's lives, this was an era marked in many ways by advances. The capacity of poetry, calligraphy, and painting to express personal feelings was expanded by a series of highly creative masters. The great migrations from north to south also meant that more and more land in the south was cultivated by Han Chinese farmers, putting pressure on non-Han indigenous peoples to withdraw or assimilate. The north absorbed a huge influx of non-Chinese peoples, leading to both sporadic ethnic conflict and more complicated notions of Chinese identity. Non-Chinese rule did not dim the memory of the greatness of the Han Dynasty, but it showed that non-Chinese rulers could build strong states.

5

The Cosmopolitan Empires of Sui and Tang China (581–960)

North and south China were politically reunited in 589 when the Sui Dynasty (581–618) defeated the last of the Southern Dynasties. After only two generations, the Sui was itself replaced by the Tang Dynasty (618–907), but progress toward cultural, economic, and political reunification continued, especially under three forceful rulers, Taizong, Empress Wu, and Xuanzong. The capital cities of Chang'an and Luoyang attracted people not only from all parts of China but also from all parts of Asia. The arts, and above all poetry, thrived in this environment. After the massive rebellion of General An Lushan wracked China in the mid-eighth century, many of the centralizing features of the government were abandoned, and power fell more and more to regional military governors. Yet late Tang should not be viewed simply in terms of dynastic decline, as art and culture continued to flourish.

Historians of the Sui-Tang period have devoted much of their energy to understanding the processes of unification and the military, political, and cultural strength of the early Tang. How did the Tang solve the problems that had kept dynasties short for the preceding four centuries? Did the strength of the early Tang government owe anything to the mixed ethnic background of its founders? What happened to the aristocracies of the north and south? To understand the changes from early to late Tang, scholars have addressed other questions: Why did trade thrive as the government withdrew from active involvement in managing the economy? What were the connections between China's changing military posture and cultural trends? Were late Tang trends in literature, Buddhism, Confucian learning, and other fields of culture linked to each other?

THE NORTHWEST MILITARY ARISTOCRACY AND THE SUI REUNIFICATION OF CHINA

That reunification came about from the north is not surprising, since by the fifth century the south had largely abandoned hope of reconquering the north. Reunification was delayed, however, by the civil war in the north after 523. Then in 577, when the Northern Zhou Dynasty defeated the Northern Qi, its battle-hardened armies were freed up to take on the south.

The rulers of the Northern Zhou were non-Chinese, like the rulers of the Northern Wei before them, though in this period ethnicity was fluid and intermarriage among ethnic groups common. Generally ethnicity was considered to be passed down with family names on the father's side, but family names could be changed. Yang Jian, the founder of the Sui Dynasty, offers a good example. He claimed descent from Han Chinese, but since *Yang* was one of the names given to Xianbei in the late fifth century, his ancestors may well have been Xianbei. His wife had the non-Chinese surname Dugu, but her mother was Chinese. Yang Jian's daughter married into the non-Chinese Yuwen family, the Northern Zhou royal house.

Yang Jian usurped the throne from his daughter's young son and proclaimed himself emperor of the Sui Dynasty. He quickly eliminated the possibility of Zhou Dynasty loyalists' ousting him in return by killing fifty-nine princes of the Zhou royal house. Nevertheless, he is known as Wendi, the "Cultured Emperor" (r. 581–604).

Wendi presided over the reunification of China. He built thousands of boats to compete for control of the Yangzi River. The largest of these had five decks, could hold eight hundred men, and was outfitted with six 50-foot-long booms that could be swung to damage an enemy vessel or pin it down. Some of these ships were manned by aborigines from southeastern Sichuan, which had recently been conquered by the Sui. By late in 588, Sui had 518,000 troops deployed along the north bank of the Yangzi River from Sichuan to the ocean. Within three months, Sui had captured Nanjing, and the rest of the south soon submitted.

After capturing Nanjing, the Sui commanders had it razed and forced the nobles and officials resident there to move to the new Sui capital at Chang'an. This influx of southerners into the northern capital stimulated fascination with things southern on the part of the old Northwest aristocracy.

Wendi and his empress were both pious Buddhists and drew on Buddhism to legitimate the Sui Dynasty. Wendi presented himself as a Cakravartin king, a Buddhist monarch who uses military force to defend the Buddhist faith. In 601, in imitation of the Indian king Ashoka, he had relics of the Buddha distributed to temples throughout the country and issued an edict expressing his goal that "all the people within the four seas may, without exception, develop enlightenment and together cultivate fortunate karma, bringing it to pass that present existences will lead to happy future lives, that the sustained creation of good causation will carry us one and all up to wondrous enlightenment."[1]

Both Wendi and his successor, Yangdi (r. 604–617), had grand ambitions to rebuild an empire comparable to the Han. The Sui tried to strengthen central control of the government by denying local officials the power to appoint their own subordinates. They abolished the system of recruitment used during the Age of Division, the Nine Rank System, and returned to the Han practice of each prefecture's nominating a few men for office based on their character and talents. Once in the capital, these nominees were given written examinations, an important step in the development of the civil service examination system.

The Sui helped tie north and south China together by a major feat of construction: the Grand Canal. Built by conscripted laborers, the canal linked the Yellow and Yangzi rivers. (In later dynasties, the canal was extended to the northeast as far as modern Beijing and to the south as far as Hangzhou.) The Sui canal was 130 feet wide and had a road running alongside it, with occasional relay posts and granaries. Water transport made it much easier to ship tax grain from the south to the centers of political and military power in north China.

Both Sui emperors viewed their empire building as incomplete because they had not recovered the parts of modern Korea and Vietnam that the Han Dynasty had held. The Hanoi area was easily recovered from the local ruler in 602, and a few years later the Sui army pushed farther south. When the army was

---

1. Arthur F. Wright, "The Sui Dynasty (581–617)," in *The Cambridge History of China* vol. 3, ed. Denis Twitchett (Cambridge: Cambridge University Press, 1979), p. 77.

attacked by troops on war elephants from Champa (in southern Vietnam), Sui feigned retreat and dug pits to trap the elephants. The Sui army lured the Champan troops to attack, then used crossbows against the elephants, causing them to turn around and trample their own army. Although Sui troops were victorious, many succumbed to disease, as northern soldiers did not have immunity to tropical diseases such as malaria.

Recovering northern Korea proved an elusive goal. The Korean state of Koguryŏ had its capital near modern Pyongyang and also held southern Manchuria as far as the Liao River. When in 598 Koguryŏ troops joined a raid into Sui territory, Wendi ordered three hundred thousand troops to retaliate (see Chapter 6 and Map 6.3). However, the Sui army had to turn back when food supplies ran short. Sui then sent a fleet from Shandong, but it lost many of its vessels in storms and accomplished nothing. Another attempt was made in 611. Three hundred sea-going ships were built in Shandong, manned by ten thousand sailors and carrying thirty thousand crossbowmen and thirty thousand javelin men. Yangdi himself traveled to the region of modern Beijing to oversee preparations. Fifty thousand carts were built to carry clothing, armor, and tents. Reportedly, six hundred thousand men were conscripted to transport supplies in wheelbarrows. The *History of the Sui Dynasty* gives the undoubtedly inflated figure of 1,133,800 combat troops summoned for the expedition. Some went overland, weighed down with shields, armor, clothing, tents, and one hundred days' supply of grain. Because the ships failed to resupply them, they had to turn back, hungry and exhausted. The vast majority of the soldiers sent across the Yalu River did not make it back to China.

The cost to the Sui Dynasty of this military debacle was enormous. When floods, droughts, and epidemics reached areas that had been hard pressed by mobilization for war, bandits were joined by deserters. Nevertheless, Yangdi was determined to try a third time to take Korea. The 613 expedition crossed the Liao River and set siege to Koguryŏ strongholds, but the campaign was cut short when word reached the emperor of a major rebellion in central China. Still, in 614, Yangdi ordered the Korea campaign continued. This time the naval force made enough progress that the Koguryŏ king sued for peace and Yangdi could claim victory. When the Koguryŏ king failed to appear at the Sui court as he had been commanded, Yangdi began mobilizing for a fourth

campaign in 615. Unrest was growing so serious, however, that nothing came of it. Yangdi, by leading the Korean campaigns himself, was personally humiliated by their failures. The imperial dreams of the Sui emperors had resulted in exhaustion and unrest.

THE FOUNDING OF THE TANG DYNASTY (618–907)

With the Sui government unraveling, power was seized at the local level by several kinds of actors: bandit leaders, local officials trying to defend against them, and local elites trying to organize defense on their own. The contenders who eventually founded the Tang Dynasty were Li Yuan, the Sui governor of Taiyuan, and his general son, Li Shimin, known respectively as Gaozu (r. 618–626) and Taizong (r. 626–649). Their family belonged to the same northwest military aristocracy as the Sui emperors (Yangdi's and Taizong's mothers were in fact sisters, making them first cousins). *Li* was a Chinese name, and the Tang imperial family presented themselves as Chinese by descent, much as the Sui imperial family had.

Taizong was commanding troops from the age of eighteen and proved a highly talented general. Skilled with bow, sword, and lance, he enjoyed the rough-and-tumble of combat and placed himself at the head of crucial cavalry charges. He later claimed to have killed over a thousand men by his own hand. Taizong was also an astute strategist, able to outmaneuver his opponents. As he defeated one opponent after another from 618 to 621, he began to look like the probable winner, which led local leaders to join him in order to end up on the winning side.

In 626, Taizong ambushed two of his brothers, one of whom was the heir apparent. (He later had the histories record that he was forced to take this step because they were plotting against him.) Taizong then saw to the execution of all ten of their sons and demanded that his father abdicate in his favor. Despite these violent beginnings, Taizong proved a capable monarch who selected wise advisers and listened to their advice. He issued a new legal code and ordered it to be regularly revised. This code, the earliest to survive, had great influence on the codes adopted not only by later Chinese dynasties but also by neighboring countries, including Vietnam, Korea, and Japan.

In the early Tang period, the Xianbei presence rapidly faded as Xianbei assimilated and their language fell out of use. Many men of Xianbei descent used the Chinese surnames that had been given to them at the end of the fifth century and served as civil rather than military officials.

Although the Sui and Tang founders evoked the memory of the Han Dynasty, they relied on the groundwork laid by the Northern Dynasties. The Sui and Tang governments retained the Northern Zhou divisional militia (*fubing*). Its volunteer farmer-soldiers served in rotation in armies at the capital or on the frontier in return for their allocations of farmland. Both Sui and Tang also retained modified forms of the equal-field system introduced by the Northern Wei and regularly redistributed land. They set the taxes in grain and cloth on each household relatively low, making it easier to enroll households on the tax registers. In the census of 609, the registered population reached about 9 million households (for a total population of about 46 million people). Even if considerable numbers of people escaped tax registration, it seems that the population of China had not grown since Han times (when the high point in 2 C.E. was about 59 million).

Both Sui and Tang turned away from the military culture of the Northern Dynasties and sought officials steeped in Confucian learning. Government schools were founded to prepare the sons of officials and other young men for service in the government. Recruitment through examinations grew in importance. In the mature Tang system, there were two principal examinations. One tested knowledge of the Confucian classics (the *mingjing*, or illuminating the classics examination). The other (the *jinshi*, or presented scholar examination) required less memorization of the classics but more literary skill. It tested the ability to compose formal styles of poetry as well as essays on political questions. Preparation for the *jinshi* examination was more demanding, but passing it brought more prestige. Even sons of officials who could have entered the government by grace of their father's rank often would attempt the *jinshi* examinations.

During the sixth century, a new ethnic group, the Turks (Tujue in Chinese), emerged as the dominant group on the Inner Asian frontier. To keep them in check, Sui and Tang governments used all the old diplomatic and military strategies. They repaired fortifications, received trade and tribute missions, sent princesses as brides, instigated conflict between different ethnic groups, and recruited non-Chinese into their armies. In 630, the Tang wrested northern

Soldier and Horse. Taizong, a successful military commander, had his tomb decorated with bas-reliefs of soldiers and horses. Notice the elaborate saddle and the stirrups, which made it easier for soldiers to rise in the saddle to shoot arrows or attack with lances. *(University Museum, University of Pennsylvania)*

Shaanxi and southern Mongolia from the Turks, winning for Taizong the title of Great Khan of the Turks. For the next half-century, Tang China dominated the steppe. Turks were settled in the Ordos region (as the Xiongnu had been in Han times), and several thousand families of Turks came to live in Chang'an. Joint Chinese-Turkish campaigns into the cities of Central Asia in the 640s and 650s resulted in China's regaining overlordship in the region much as it had during the Han Dynasty. (See Map 5.1.)

The early Tang rulers also embraced Sui ambitions with respect to Koguryŏ. In 644, Taizong began preparations for an invasion. A fleet of five hundred ships was built to transport forty thousand soldiers to the Korean coast, while an army of sixty thousand prepared to march. Despite impressive early victories, this army too had to retreat, and the retreat again proved an ordeal. It would not be until 668, when China allied itself with the southern Korean state of Silla, that Koguryŏ was finally subjugated (see Chapter 6). Eight years later, however, it was Silla, not Tang China, that controlled the area, and China had little to show for the effort put in over the course of eight decades to regain the borders staked out by the Han Dynasty so many centuries earlier.

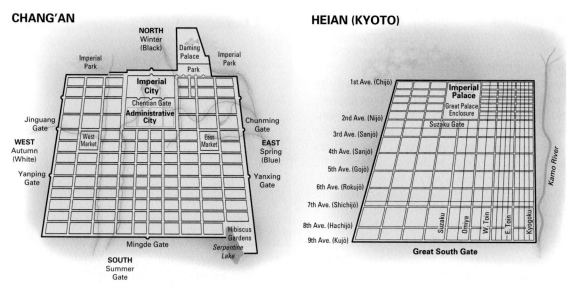

Figure 5.1   Layout of Chang'an and One of the Cities Modeled on It Outside China

THE TANG AT ITS HEIGHT

The Tang capital, Chang'an, was built by the Sui Dynasty near the site of the Han capital of the same name. It was the largest capital yet seen, nearly six miles east-west and more than five miles north-south. In the center against the north wall was the walled palace city, with the residence halls to the north and administrative offices to the south. From the south gate of the palace city stretched a wide avenue leading to the main south gate of the city wall. The rest of the city was divided by eleven north-south streets and fourteen east-west ones, making 108 rectangular walled wards, each with four gates. Two of the wards were government-supervised markets. Prime space was also reserved for temples.

Tang retained this city as its capital and made Luoyang a secondary capital. Both cities became great metropolises, with Chang'an and its suburbs growing to more than 2 million inhabitants. At these cosmopolitan cities, knowledge of the outside world was stimulated by the presence of envoys, merchants, and pilgrims from Central Asia, Japan, Korea, Vietnam, and Tibet, among other places. (See **Connections: Cultural Contact Across Eurasia (600–900)** and **Material Culture: Tea.**) Because of the presence of foreign merchants, many religions were practiced, including Nestorian Christianity, Manichaeism, Zoroastrianism, Judaism, and Islam,

although none of them spread into the Chinese population the way Buddhism had a few centuries earlier. Foreign fashions in hair and clothing were often copied, however, and foreign amusements such as polo found followings among the well-to-do. The introduction of new instruments and tunes from India, Iran, and Central Asia brought about a major transformation in Chinese music. (See Color Plate 6.)

In Tang times, Buddhism fully penetrated Chinese daily life. In 628, Taizong held a Buddhist memorial service for all of those who had died in the wars, and the next year he had monasteries built at the site of major battles so that monks could pray for the fallen of both sides. Buddhist monasteries ran schools for children, provided lodging for travelers, and offered scholars and officials places to gather for social occasions such as going-away parties. The wealthy often donated money or land to monasteries, and many monasteries became large landlords. Merchants entrusted their money and wares to monasteries for safekeeping, in effect transforming the monasteries into banks and warehouses.

In the Tang period, stories of Buddhist origin were spread by monks who would show pictures and tell stories to illiterate audiences. One of the best loved of these stories concerned a man named Mulian who journeyed to the netherworld to save his mother from her suffering there. The popularity of this story gave rise to the ghost festival on the fifteenth day of the seventh month. On that day, Buddhists and non-

MATERIAL CULTURE

Tea

Tea is made from the young leaves and leaf buds of *Camellia sinensis*, a plant native to the hills of southwest China. By Han times, tea was already being grown and drunk in the southwest, and for the next several centuries it was looked on as a local product with useful pharmacological properties, such as countering the effects of wine and preventing drowsiness.

Tea was common enough in Tang life that poets often mentioned it in their poems (see Color Plate 7). Perhaps the most famous tea poem was by the eighth-century author of a treatise on the art of drinking tea, Lu Yu. Written to express his thanks for a gift of freshly picked tea, it reads in part:

> To honour the tea, I shut my brushwood
> gate,
> Lest common folk intrude,
> And donned my gauze cap
> To brew and taste it on my own.
> The first bowl sleekly moistened throat and
> lips;
> The second banished all my loneliness;
> The third expelled the dullness from my
> mind,
> Sharpening inspiration gained from all the
> books I've read.
> The fourth brought forth light perspiration,
> Dispersing a lifetime's troubles through my
> pores.
> The fifth bowl cleansed ev'ry atom of my
> being.
> The sixth has made me kin to the
> Immortals;
> This seventh is the utmost I can drink—
> A light breeze issues from my armpits.[1]

By Tang times, tea had become a major commercial crop, especially in the southeast. The most intensive time for tea production was the harvest season, since young leaves were of much more value than mature ones.

Women, mobilized for about a month each year, would come out to help pick tea. Not only were tea

Tea Jar. The spread of tea drinking served as a stimulus to the ceramic industry, as tea aficionados carefully selected the containers for storing tea leaves and mixing, steeping, or drinking tea. This tea jar, made in south China in the fourteenth century, was exported to Japan, where it came to be treasured as an art object, eventually coming into the possession of the Tokugawa shoguns. *(The Tokugawa Art Museum)*

merchants among the wealthiest merchants, but from the late eighth century on, taxes on tea became a major item of government revenue.

Tea reached Korea and Japan as a part of Buddhist culture, as a drink appreciated by Buddhist monks, since it helped them stay awake during long hours of recitation or meditation. The Japanese priest Saichō, patriarch of Tendai Buddhism, visited China in 802–803 and reportedly brought back tea seeds.

---

1. John Blofeld, *The Chinese Art of Tea* (Boston: Shambhala, 1985), p. 12.

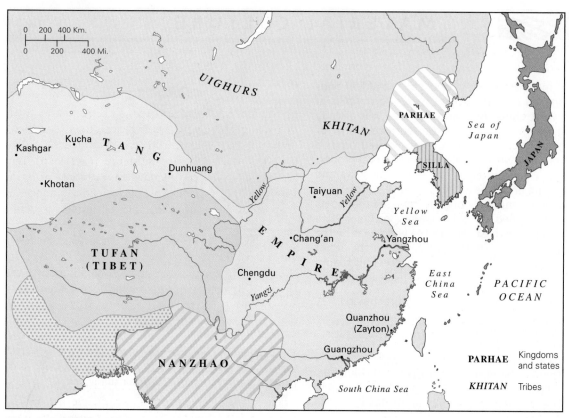

Map 5.1   **Tang China**

Buddhists alike would put out food to feed hungry ghosts suffering in purgatory. Popular elaborations of the Mulian story emphasized the centrality of filial devotion and reinforced the Buddhists' message that the truly filial draw on Buddhism to aid their deceased parents. During the Tang period, a new sacred geography for East Asia developed, with a network of pilgrimage sites in China. The manifestation of the bodhisattva Manjusri on Mount Wutai became so renowned that it attracted pilgrims from India. The Japanese Buddhist monk Ennin, who spent the years 838 to 847 in China, set his sights on a visit to Mount Wutai.

At the intellectual level, Buddhism was developing in distinctly Chinese directions. New sutras were written, "apocryphal" ones that masked their Chinese authorship by purporting to be translations of Indian works. Some of these texts were incorporated into the Buddhist canon; others were suppressed by the state or the Buddhist establishment as subversive. Among the educated elite the Chan school (known in Japan as Zen) gained popularity. Chan

teachings reject the authority of the sutras and extol mind-to-mind transmission of Buddhist truths. Chan claimed as its First Patriarch the Indian monk Bodhidharma, said to have come to China in the early sixth century C.E. The Sixth Patriarch, Huineng, was just as important to Chan traditions. The illiteracy of Huineng at the time of his enlightenment was taken as proof that enlightenment could be achieved suddenly through insight into one's own Buddha nature and did not require study of sutras. The "northern" tradition of Chan emphasized meditation and monastic discipline. The "southern" tradition was even more iconoclastic, holding that enlightenment could be achieved suddenly through a flash of insight, even without prolonged meditation.

In the late Tang period, opposition to Buddhism resurfaced, in large part because its tax-exempt status aggravated the state's fiscal problems. In 845, a Tang emperor ordered more than 4,600 monasteries and 40,000 temples and shrines closed and more than 260,000 Buddhist monks and nuns returned to secular life. Although this ban was lifted after a few years, the monastic establishment never fully recovered. Buddhism retained a strong hold among laypeople, and basic Buddhist ideas like karma and reincarnation had become ingrained, but Buddhism was never again as central to Chinese life as it was in Tang times.

The Tang Elite

The aristocracies of the Northern and Southern Dynasties suffered several blows with the reunification of China. The Sui abolished the Nine Rank System for recruiting men for office, ending nearly automatic access to office and its benefits for men from aristocratic families. Moreover, many of the highest-ranking families in the south were devastated by the wars of the sixth century, especially the rebellion of Hou Jing, which resulted in the death of thousands of members of elite families living in Nanjing. Nevertheless, throughout the Tang period, men from the thirty or so most famous families held an amazingly high share of the most prominent positions in the government. Moreover, the Tang elite remained avidly interested in questions of birth and relative family ranking.

Why did old families remain so prominent? One reason seems to be that their pretensions annoyed the early Tang rulers. In the early Tang, the new ruling house and its closest allies (largely from the northwest military aristocracy) resented continued admiration for old families from the east and south whose scions often held only midlevel positions in the Tang government and who, even in earlier eras, had never been associated with a dynasty as glorious as the Tang. The aristocratic families further annoyed the court by preferring to marry within their own circle, scorning proposals from the imperial house and its close allies. Taizong retaliated in 632 by ordering a thorough investigation of the genealogies of leading families and the compilation of a new genealogical compendium. When the work was completed, Taizong found that his own researchers supported the claims to eminence of the aristocratic families, and he demanded a revision to give more weight to official position under the Tang. Twenty years later Gaozong ordered yet another genealogical compendium, again wanting more emphasis on current offices. When it was completed, Gaozong went so far as to prohibit intermarriage by members of the seven old families whose pretensions rankled him most. The effect of this ban was to greatly add to the prestige of the seven named family lines, who from then on knew exactly whom they should marry.

At the same time, an unplanned accommodation was being worked out between the old families and the Tang court. Members of aristocratic families used their many resources to prepare carefully for office, and the government allowed them to occupy a disproportionate share of ministerial posts. With the greatness of the Tang established, the court stopped worrying about whether people also admired the old aristocratic families, who, after all, posed no military threat.

During the Tang, many of the old aristocratic families moved permanently to the region of Luoyang or Chang'an, the better to concentrate on political careers. By the eighth century, they were justifying their marital exclusiveness not by reference to the glory of their ancestors, but to their superiority in education, manners, and family morality. By bringing attention to characteristics that were largely a product of upbringing, it was easy for the old families to exclude outsiders and retain a common identity. Even if the examinations were becoming an avenue for people from modest backgrounds to rise, a surprising proportion of those who passed in Tang times came from eminent families. Moreover, when it was time for assignments to be made, candidates were judged on their deportment, appearance, speech, and calligraphy, all of which were subjective criteria, making it easy for the responsible officials to favor young men from families like their own. Certainly the elite became broader during the Tang, but at no time did the presence of new families pose much of a threat to the continued eminence of the old ones.

If the Tang elite is compared to the elite of the Han period, several differences stand out. Within the broad elite of those with the education that could qualify them for official appointment, three levels are clearly distinguishable: a very small elite of famous old families who were conspicuous in high office, below them a broader group of families that had produced officials since before Sui times, and below them families considered eminent in their own prefecture. Those in the two highest levels spent more time in the capitals than their Han counterparts did. Much more than in Han times, they took pride in their ancestry and discussed the ancestry of their peers and marriage prospects. At the same time, the

Tang elite was, if anything, better educated than the Han elite, and its members did not disdain competing in the examinations.

Empress Wu

The mid-Tang Dynasty saw several women rise to positions of great political power through their hold on rulers, the first of whom, Empress Wu (ca. 625–705), went so far as to take the throne herself. How could a woman become ruler? Historians of the time, who viewed her as an evil seductress and usurper, attributed her success to her lack of scruples and her skill at manipulation. A brief review of her career shows that luck and political acumen also played a role.

Although Wu entered Gaozong's palace in 651 as a lesser consort, within a few years she convinced him to demote his empress and promote her. The histories record a chilling story of how Wu accomplished this. One day after the empress had been playing with Wu's baby girl, Wu came in and smothered the baby. When Gaozong later found the baby dead, Wu became hysterical, saying the empress must have killed her. Gaozong's top officials could not calm his rage or keep him from deposing the empress. Wu was made empress and her son heir apparent.

Four years later, Gaozong suffered a stroke, and Empress Wu began to make decisions in his place. She followed the customary propriety of "ruling from behind a screen," and the councilors could not see her when they talked to her. Wu nevertheless proved a hard-working ruler. In 665, she and Gaozong traveled with a large entourage of princes and high officials to Mount Tai in Shandong province to perform the sacred *feng* and *shan* sacrifices to heaven and earth, not performed since Western Han times. She argued that while it was appropriate for the emperor to perform the sacrifice to heaven at the top of the mountain, since it was a yang sacrifice, she and her palace ladies should perform the sacrifice to earth at the bottom of the mountain, since it was a yin sacrifice, thus demonstrating the true complementarity of yin and yang.

By the 670s, Empress Wu's oldest son, the heir apparent, was beginning to take stands on issues, even sometimes opposing his mother's ideas. When he died in 675, many suspected that she had poisoned him. The next heir, not surprisingly, kept a lower profile. However, in 680, Wu accused him of plotting a rebellion; he was banished and later forced to commit suicide.

One of the ways Empress Wu was able to keep the government operating smoothly despite her questionable standing was by bringing new people to court through the civil service examinations. Many of those who had felt left out during the early Tang, when the court was dominated by the northwest aristocracy, were happy to take advantage of new opportunities to become officials.

After more than twenty years as an invalid, Gaozong finally died in 683. The seventeen-year-old heir apparent, posthumously known as Zhongzong, took the throne. After six weeks, Empress Wu had him deposed because he tried to appoint his wife's father as chancellor. Another one of her sons, known as Ruizong, was then placed on the throne, but he was kept in a separate palace and rarely consulted. Now nearly sixty years old, Empress Wu no longer concealed herself behind a screen, and she began using the Chinese term for the royal "we." She even ordered the construction of imperial-style ancestral temples for her own Wu ancestors.

In 684, a group of Tang princes and their allies staged a rebellion against Empress Wu. They captured the major city of Yangzhou and issued a proclamation detailing her crimes, ranging from killing her own children to favoring sycophants. The army remained loyal to Empress Wu, however, and within two months had suppressed the rebellion. Wu now was even more confident of her position and moved rapidly to rid herself of opponents. On the advice of new favorites, she undertook another Confucian ritual project based on the classics, the construction of a Bright Hall for the performance of key rituals. Her Bright Hall was huge — about 300 feet square and 300 feet tall. It had three stories, the bottom two square and the top one round. When the Tang princes outside the capital refused to attend ceremonies marking the hall's completion, Wu used it as a pretext to eliminate much of the Tang imperial clan.

Until 690, Empress Wu had been content to be the power behind the throne. That year, however, when she was about sixty-five years old, she accepted her son's abdication and declared herself emperor of a new dynasty, the Zhou Dynasty. She became China's first and only female emperor.

Although Empress Wu employed Confucian language and diligently performed Confucian state rituals, she was personally deeply drawn to Buddhism. She was the major patron for the great cave temples

Great Buddha at Longmen. In 672, Empress Wu donated twenty thousand strings of cash for the construction of this cave at Longmen outside the secondary capital of Luoyang. Excavating a "cave" 98 feet high and 130 feet long out of the limestone cliff and carving the five figures in high relief probably took twenty or more years. *(Marie Mathelin/Roger Viollet/Getty Images)*

carved at Longmen outside Luoyang. She found support for her political position in the *Great Cloud Sutra*, which prophesied that the Maitreya Buddha would be reincarnated as a female monarch and bring about an age free of illness, worry, and disaster. One of Wu's followers wrote a commentary to the sutra in 689 pointing out that the female monarch must be Empress Wu. When Empress Wu declared her own dynasty the next year, she had this sutra circulated throughout the country and ordered every prefecture to establish a Great Cloud temple.

When Wu made herself emperor, she did not designate an heir, apparently unsure whether she should let one of her own sons succeed her or have succession go to a member of her natal Wu family. In 697, when she was over seventy, she had her eldest surviving son, Zhongzong, brought back from exile and made heir apparent. Still, all through her seventies she retained power. It was not until 705, when she was about eighty and too ill to get out of bed, that the high officials successfully pressured her to abdicate.

Emperor Xuanzong

The removal of Empress Wu did not end the influence of women at court. Zhongzong was dominated by his wife, Empress Wei, who wanted their daughter to be made heir apparent. Her main rival was Zhongzong's sister, the Taiping Princess. After Empress Wei poisoned her husband, Zhongzong, in 710, she put his last remaining son, a boy of fifteen, on the throne. Two weeks later, probably with the encouragement of the Taiping Princess, another grandson of Empress Wu, the future emperor Xuanzong (r. 713–756), entered the palace with a few followers and slew Empress Wei and her daughter as well as other members of their faction. He installed his father, Ruizong, as emperor, but the Taiping Princess acted as the power behind the throne.

It was over the protests of the Taiping Princess that in 712, Ruizong abdicated in favor of Xuanzong. The princess's attempted coup failed, and she was permitted to commit suicide, ending more than a half-century of women dominating court politics.

Xuanzong, still in his twenties, began his reign as an activist. He curbed the power of monasteries, which had gained strength under Empress Wu. He ordered a new census to shore up the equal-field system. As a result of population growth, individual allotment holders in many areas received only a fraction of the land they were due but still had to pay the standard per household tax. Their only recourse was to flee, which reduced government revenue further. To deal with the threats of the Turks, Uighurs, and Tibetans, Xuanzong set up a ring of military provinces along the frontier from Manchuria to Sichuan. The military governors, often non-Chinese, were given great authority to deal with crises without waiting for central authorization. Their armies were professional ones, manned by costly long-service veterans rather than inexpensive part-time farmer-soldiers like the divisional militia.

Xuanzong appreciated poetry, painting, and music and presided over a brilliant court. The great horse painter Han Gan served at his court, as did the poet Li Bai. Although many of his leading officials had been selected for office through the examination system, family pedigree was still a great asset. He commissioned a two-hundred-chapter genealogical work that provided him with up-to-date assessments of the relative ranking of the elite families of his realm. After 736, Xuanzong allowed Li Linfu (d. 752), an aristocrat proud of his family background, to run the government as his chancellor.

Xuanzong took an interest in both Daoism and Buddhism and invited clerics of both religions to his court. Laozi, as the putative ancestor of the Tang imperial family (both had the family name Li), was granted grand titles. Xuanzong wrote a commentary on the *Laozi* and set up a special school to prepare candidates for a new examination on Daoist scriptures. Among Buddhist teachings, he was especially attracted to the newly introduced Tantric school, which made much use of magical spells and incantations. In 726, Xuanzong called on the Javanese monk Vajrabodhi to perform Tantric rites to avert drought. In 742, he held the incense burner while the Ceylonese Amoghavajra recited mystical incantations to secure the victory of Tang forces.

Some have blamed Xuanzong's growing interest in Daoism and Tantric Buddhism for his declining interest in administrative matters. He was also growing older and wearier. By 742, he was fifty-seven and had spent thirty years on the throne. More and more of his time he spent with his beloved

consort Yang Guifei, a full-figured beauty in an age that admired rounded proportions. To keep her happy, Xuanzong allowed her to place friends and relatives in important positions in the government. One of her favorites was the able general An Lushan, who spent more and more time at court. Eventually An got into a quarrel with Yang's cousin over control of the government, which led to open warfare.

THE REBELLION OF AN LUSHAN (755–763) AND ITS AFTERMATH

An Lushan had commanded the frontier army in northern Hebei since 744. Half Sogdian (Central Asian) and half Turk, he was a professional soldier from a family of soldiers, with experience fighting the Khitans, the dominant group in northern Manchuria at the time. When An rebelled, he had an army of more than a hundred thousand veteran troops. They struck southward, headed toward Luoyang. The court, on getting news of the advance, began raising an army, but the newly recruited troops were no match for the veterans. With the fall of the capital imminent, the heir apparent left to raise troops in western Shaanxi, and Xuanzong fled west toward Sichuan. The troops accompanying Xuanzong mutinied and would not continue until Yang Guifei and her relatives had been killed. The heir apparent, in the meantime, was convinced by his followers to enthrone himself, which Xuanzong did not contest.

How did the Tang Dynasty manage to recover from this disaster? The rulers had to make many compromises. To recover the capital, the Tang called on the Uighurs, a Turkish people allied with the Tang. After the Uighurs took Chang'an from the rebels, they looted it and would not leave until they were paid off with huge quantities of silk. Thereafter, to keep the Uighurs from raiding, the Tang had to trade them silk for horses at extortionate rates.

To get rebel leaders to submit, the Tang offered pardons and even appointed many as military governors of the regions they held. In key areas, military governors acted like warlords, paying no taxes to the central government and appointing their own subordinates. They even passed down their positions to their heirs. Posts that once had been held by civil officials were increasingly filled with military men, often non-Chinese or semi-sinified.

The Uighurs were only one of China's troublesome neighbors in this period. Antagonistic states were consolidating themselves all along Tang's borders, from Parhae on the northeast (see Chapter 6), to Tibet on the west, and Nanzhao on the southwest (Yunnan area). When Tang had to withdraw troops from the western frontier to fight An Lushan's forces, the Tibetans took advantage of the opportunity to claim overlordship of the Silk Road cities themselves. Although the Tibetan empire collapsed in 842 and the Uighur empire broke up soon after, the Tang court no longer had the ambition to dominate Central Asia. Tang did respond when Nanzhao attacked the Tang prefectures in northern Vietnam, and though Tang sent an army to reassert control, the Vietnamese declared their independence in the tenth century.

Because the central government no longer had the local infrastructure needed to enforce the equal-field system, the system was finally abandoned, and people were once more allowed to buy and sell land. In place of a one-tax-fits-all system, taxes were based on actual landholding and paid in semiannual installments. Each region was assigned a quota of taxes to submit to the central government and given leeway on how to fill it. With the return of free buying and selling of land, the poor who fell into debt sold their land to the rich, leading to the proliferation of great estates.

Besides reforming land taxes, the late Tang central government learned how to raise revenue through control of the production and distribution of salt, returning to a policy of the Han government. By adding a surcharge to the salt it sold to licensed salt merchants, the government was able to collect taxes indirectly, even from regions where it had minimal authority. By 779, over half the central government revenue came from the salt monopoly. The Salt Commission became a powerful agency run by officials who specialized in finance.

Although control of salt production and distribution could be seen as a major intervention into the economy, on balance the post-rebellion government was withdrawing from attempts to control the economy. Not only did it give up control of land, it gave up supervision of urban markets and the prices charged for goods. This retreat from government management of the economy had the unintended effect of stimulating trade. Markets were opened in more and more towns, and the provincial capitals became new centers of trade. By the ninth century, a new economic hierarchy of markets, towns, and cities had begun to emerge parallel to the government's administrative hierarchy of counties and prefectures. Merchants, no longer as burdened by government regulation, found ways to solve the perennial problem of shortages of copper coins by circulating silver bullion and notes of exchange, allowing trade to proceed without the use of coins.

The economic advances of the late eighth and ninth centuries were particularly evident in the south. During the rebellion, refugees from hard-hit areas sought safety and new opportunities in the south, much as they had in the fourth century. The late Tang was a time of prosperity for the cities of the Jiangnan region, such as Yangzhou, Suzhou, and Hangzhou, and many of those who came to these cities on official assignments or business decided to stay permanently.

Post-rebellion officials and emperors did not give up the goal of strong central control. They created a palace army to counter the power of the regional commanders. Unfortunately, the palace eunuchs placed in charge of this army soon became as troublesome as the regional commanders. In the early ninth century, eunuchs dominated court affairs, much as they had in late Han times. High officials had to ally with one faction of eunuchs or another to have any hope of influencing policy. After 820, factions of officials and eunuchs plotted and counterplotted to enthrone, manipulate, or murder one emperor after another. In 835, the emperor plotted with a group of officials to purge the eunuchs, but when their plan was discovered, the eunuchs ordered the slaughter of over a thousand officials. Three chancellors and their families were publicly executed in Chang'an's western marketplace.

THE ACHIEVEMENTS OF TANG MEN OF LETTERS

The Tang Dynasty was the great age of Chinese poetry—the *Complete Tang Poems* includes more than forty-eight thousand poems by some twenty-two hundred poets. Men who wanted to be recognized as members of the educated elite had to be able to recognize lines quoted from earlier poets' works and write technically proficient poems at social occasions. Skill in composing poetry was so highly respected that it was tested in the civil service examinations. The greatness of Tang poetry, however, lies not in its ubiquity but in the achievements of a handful of great poets who brought the art of poetry to new heights.

Prolific Tang Poets	
	number of poems
Bai Juyi	2,972
Du Fu	1,500
Li Bo	1,120
Liu Yuxi	884
Yuan Zhen	856
Li Shangyin	628
Meng Jiao	559
Wang Wei	426

In Tang poems, the pain of parting, the joys of nature, and the pleasures of wine and friendship were all common topics. Subtlety, ambiguity, and allusion were used to good effect. Wang Wei (701–761), a successful official strongly drawn to Buddhism, is known especially for his poetic evocations of nature. His "Villa on Zhongnan Mountain" uses simple, natural language:

In my middle years I came to love the Way.
And late made my home by South Mountain's
    edge.
When the mood comes upon me, I go off alone,
And have glorious moments to myself.
I walk to the point where a stream ends,
Then sit and watch when the clouds rise.
By chance I meet old men in the woods.
We laugh and chat, no fixed time to turn home.[2]

Wang Wei's contemporary Li Bai (701–762) had a brief but brilliant career at the court of Emperor Xuanzong. One of his most famous poems describes an evening of drinking with only the moon and his shadow for company:

Beneath the blossoms with a pot of wine,
No friends at hand, so I poured alone;
I raised my cup to invite the moon,
Turned to my shadow, and we become three.
Now the moon has never learned about my
    drinking,
And my shadow had merely followed my form,

But I quickly made friends with the moon and
    my shadow;
To find pleasure in life, make the most of the
    spring.
Whenever I sang, the moon swayed with me;
Whenever I danced, my shadow went wild.
Drinking, we shared our enjoyment together;
Drunk, then each went off on his own.
But forever agreed on dispassionate revels,
We promised to meet in the far Milky Way.[3]

The forms of poetry favored in the Tang were eight-line stanzas of five or seven characters per line. This form, called *regulated verse*, had fixed patterns of tones and required that the second and third couplets be antithetical. The strict antithesis is often lost in translation, but can be seen when lines are translated word for word. For instance, in the first stanza of Li Bai's poem in the previous paragraph, the antithetical couplets read word for word: "Lift cup, invite bright moon/Face shadow, become three men," and "Moon since not understand drinking/Shadow only follow my body."

Du Fu, a younger contemporary of Li Bai, is often paired with him, the two representing the two sides of Tang poetry: its more light-hearted side and its more solemn side (see **Biography: Du Fu (712–770), Confucian Poet**). In the next generation, Bai Juyi (772–846) encompassed both sides. When sent out to regional posts, he took his responsibilities seriously and sympathized with the people whom he governed. At times he worried about whether he was doing his job justly and well:

From my high castle I look at the town below
Where the natives of Ba cluster like a swarm of
    flies.
How can I govern these people and lead them
    aright?
I cannot even understand what they say.
But at least I am glad, now that the taxes are in,
To learn that in my province there is no
    discontent.[4]

---

2. Stephen Owen, *An Anthology of Chinese Literature* (New York: Norton, 1996), p. 390.

3. Trans. by Elling Eide in Victor Mair, ed., *The Columbia Anthology of Traditional Chinese Literature* (New York: Columbia University Press, 1994), p. 203.

4. Arthur Waley, trans., *More Translations from the Chinese* (New York: Knopf, 1919), p. 71.

BIOGRAPHY

Du Fu (712–777), Confucian Poet

Although the civil service examinations in Tang times tested candidates on their ability to write poetry, the man widely considered the greatest of all Chinese poets repeatedly failed the examinations. Du Fu wanted to follow in the path of his grandfather, who had passed the *jinshi* examination in 670 and held prestigious posts in the capital. Instead, he spent much of his adult life wandering through China, returning from time to time to the capital to try once more for a political career. In 751 he even tried presenting some of his literary works to the emperor directly. Emperor Xuanzong had a special examination set for him, and he was passed. Still, he spent the next two years waiting for an appointment. Just when it seemed Du Fu would get his chance, one catastrophe after another befell him. In 754 Du Fu had to move his family because of a famine brought on by floods, and not long afterward he had to move them again during the disorder caused by the An Lushan rebellion.

Nearly fifteen hundred of Du Fu's poems, some quite long, have come down to us. Du Fu's greatness as a poet lies in his poetic inventiveness and creation of the voice of the moral man protesting injustice. In a long poem written in 755, Du Fu began by making fun of his grand ambitions, none of them fulfilled, then described the sights he saw on his journey from the capital. As he approached the place where his family was staying, he heard wailing, which he soon learned was in response to the death of his youngest child. Rather than dwell on his own family's sorrows, however, he turned his thoughts to others:

> All my life I've been exempt from taxes,
> And my name is not registered for
>   conscription.
> Brooding on what I have lived through, if even
>   I know such suffering,

The common man must surely be rattled by
>   the winds;
> Then thoughts silently turn to those who have
>   lost all livelihood
> And to the troops in far garrisons.
> Sorrow's source is as huge as South Mountain,
> A formless, whirling chaos that the hand
>   cannot grasp.[1]

After the rebellion, Du Fu gave up hopes of an official career and devoted himself entirely to his poetry. In 760 he arrived in Chengdu (Sichuan) and for the next few years lived happily in a thatched hut outside the city. As Du Fu grew older, his poetry became richer and more complex. His eight "Autumn Meditation" poems, considered among the masterpieces of Chinese poetry, ponder the forces of order and disorder in both the natural and human worlds. One reads:

> I have been told that Changan looks like a
>   chessboard.
> A hundred years, a lifetime's troubles, grief
>   beyond enduring.
> Mansions of counts and princes all have new
>   masters,
> The civil and army uniforms differ from olden
>   times.
> Straight north past the fortified mountains
>   kettledrums are thundering
> From wagon and horse on the western
>   campaign winged dispatches rush.
> Fish and dragons grow silent now, autumn
>   rivers grow cold.
> The life I used to have at home is the longing
>   in my heart.[2]

---

1. Stephen Owen, *The Great Age of Chinese Poetry: The High T'ang* (New Haven: Yale University Press, 1981), p. 196.
2. Stephen Owen, *An Anthology of Chinese Literature* (New York: Norton, 1996), p. 436.

DOCUMENTS

Poking Fun

Among the texts surviving from the Tang is a set of four hundred sayings grouped under forty-two headings, a small part of which is given below. By making fun of situations and types of people, these witty sayings provide an amusing glimpse of Tang social life. They have traditionally been attributed to the late Tang poet Li Shangyin (ca. 813–858), but they are not included in his collected works and may well have been written by someone else.

INCONGRUITIES

1. A poor Persian.
2. A sick physician.
3. A (Buddhist) disciple not addicted to drink.
4. Keepers of granaries coming to blows.
5. A great fat bride.
6. An illiterate teacher.
7. A pork-butcher reciting sutras.
8. A village elder riding in an open chair.
9. A grandfather visiting courtesans.

RELUCTANT

1. A new wife to see strangers.
2. A poor devil to contribute to a feast.
3. A poor family to make marriages.
4. To visit retired officials.
5. A pregnant woman to go afoot.

VEXATIONS

1. Happening upon a tasty dish when one's liver is out of order.
2. Making a night of it and the drinks giving out.
3. For one's back to itch when calling upon a superior.
4. For the lights to fail just when the luck begins to favor one at cards.
5. Inability to get rid of a worthless poor relation.
6. A man cleaning out a well who has to go to the toilet in a hurry.

AMBIGUITY

1. Only of a poor gift does one say, "Can it be repaid?"
2. Only of an ugly bride does one say, "She is my fate."

Besides producing a huge volume of poetry, Tang writers wrote in many other genres, some humorous (see **Documents: Poking Fun**). They greatly advanced the art of fiction. Tang tales were short and written in the classical language (in contrast to the longer vernacular-language fiction and drama that became important in later periods). Bai Juyi's brother Bai Xingjian (775–826) wrote a story about an examination candidate who on arrival in Chang'an fell instantly in love with the beautiful prostitute Li Wa. Over the course of the next year, Li Wa and her owner gradually squeezed him of all his money and then disappeared. Bewildered and desperate, the young man was reduced to supporting himself as a funeral singer. When his father discovered this, he beat him nearly to death. Reduced further to begging, he was in the end saved by Li Wa, who took pity on him, nursed him back to health, and convinced him to resume his studies. When he passed the examinations and obtained an official post, his father accepted Li Wa as his daughter-in-law.

Popular stories like these circulated widely and sometimes became the basis for later dramas. The most successful story in terms of its later incarnations was *The Story of Yingying* by the eminent man of letters Yuan Zhen (779–831). In this case, the examination candidate, surnamed Zhang, fell in love with a woman of his own class, a distant cousin named Cui Yingying. She is first introduced to him by her mother, who wishes to thank him for coming to their aid during a bandit attack. Yingying is reluctant to greet him and refuses to be drawn into conversation. Zhang, however, is overwhelmed by her beauty and attracted by her shyness. He turns to Yingying's maid for ad-

3. Only of a nobody does one say, "Tai Gong met King Wen at eighty."[1]

4. Only of a poor appointment does one say, "It's a place to make a living."

5. Only to be rude to a guest does one say, "Make yourself at home."

6. Only of a poor dwelling does one say, "It's quite all right to live in."

7. Only those incapable of making a living for themselves rail at their ancestors.

BAD FORM

1. To wrangle with one's fellow guests.

2. To fall from one's polo pony.

3. To smoke in the presence of superiors.

4. Priests and nuns lately returned to ordinary life.

5. To shout orders at a banquet.

6. To cut into the conversation.

7. To fall asleep in somebody's bed with one's boots on.

8. To preface remarks with a giggle.

9. To kick over the table when a guest.

10. To sing love songs in the presence of one's father- or mother-in-law.

11. To reject distasteful food and put it back on the dish.

12. To lay chopsticks across a soup-bowl.

LAPSES

1. Talking to people with one's hat off.

2. Scolding another's servants.

3. Boring a hole in the wall to spy upon neighbors.

4. Entering a house without knocking.

5. Being careless about dripping snot or spitting on the mat.

6. Going into the room and sitting down uninvited.

7. Opening other people's boxes and letters.

8. Lifting chopsticks before the host's signal.

9. Laying down chopsticks before all have finished eating.

10. Stretching across the table to reach things.

---

1. It was not until he was eighty years old that King Wen invited Tai Gong to be his chief adviser.

Source: From E. D. Edwards, *Chinese Prose Literature of the T'ang Period, A.D. 618–906* (London: Probsthain, 1937–1938), pp. 128–144, slightly modified.

vice, and she suggests that he propose marriage. He counters that the pain of separation from her is so great that he could not wait for a proper engagement. The maid then tells him to try to win her over by sending her poems. Although Yingying at first rebukes Zhang for making advances, eventually she decides to go to his room one night. Although taking the initiative, she still appears weak, leaning on her maid's arm. The ensuing affair is interrupted when Zhang has to go to the capital to take the examinations. When Zhang does not return, Yingying writes him a long letter protesting his faithlessness. Unlike most other love stories, this one does not end happily in a marriage. Zhang decides that beautiful women spell disaster for men and lets his parents arrange a marriage for him to someone else. Yingying, too, in the end marries someone chosen by her mother.

Tang men of letters kept Confucian learning alive in an age when the pull of Buddhism and Daoism was strong. Confucian scholars worked out the ritual programs of the early Tang emperors, served as teachers in the state schools, and wrote commentaries to the classics. State support for Confucian activities coexisted with state patronage of Buddhism and Daoism and with private commitment to either religion on the part of many Confucian officials. Neither the state nor the scholarly community felt compelled to sustain exclusive positions.

With the restructuring of the Tang state after the rebellion of An Lushan, the state agencies that had provided the focus for Confucian scholarly activities deteriorated, forcing the scholarly community to reappraise its political and cultural responsibilities. A small group of scholars turned away from an emphasis on preserving inherited traditions in favor of looking directly to the classics to find the "Way of the Sages."

Han Yu (768–824) was perhaps the most important of these politically engaged writers and thinkers. Even though he passed the *jinshi* examinations (on his fourth try), Han Yu found political advancement frustratingly difficult. He was a strong supporter of efforts to strengthen the central government's control over the provinces, and he deplored the political and cultural fragmentation that had been tolerated in order to hold together the Tang state. He offended the emperor when he wrote "On the Buddha Bone," a memorial intimating that the emperor was risking his own life by letting something so inauspicious as the bone of a dead person into the palace. As a writer, Han Yu advocated the use of a plainer prose style, labeled "ancient style" as it aimed for the ancient virtues of clarity and concision. This style, he contended, offered the best way to convey the truths of the Confucian tradition. In an essay on the origin of the Confucian Way, Han Yu argued that the Confucian tradition had been passed down in a single line of transmission from the duke of Zhou to Confucius and Mencius, but that the transmission had afterward been disrupted. He proposed that to revive the Way of the Sages, scholars had to go back to the *Analects* and *Mencius*.

THE DUNHUANG DOCUMENTS

The historical sources historians can use to reconstruct what life was like in the Tang period are richer than for earlier periods. There are fuller sources on the workings of the government, including the first surviving legal code, the first surviving court ritual code, and several compendiums of government documents. Much more survives from writers' collected works by way of personal letters, epitaphs for friends and relatives, prefaces to poems, and the like, from which historians can reconstruct social circles, trace marriage patterns, and infer attitudes toward marriage, children, friendship, and other nonpolitical subjects. There is also a substantial body of short fiction, which provides scenes of life in the cities among merchants, beggars, and shop owners in addition to the elite.

An even greater boon to recovering everyday social and economic relations was the discovery of thousands of original documents sealed in a Buddhist cave temple at Dunhuang, at the far northwestern corner of China proper, about 700 miles from Chang'an. The cave was sealed up soon after 1000 C.E., when the region was threatened by invasion, and was not discovered again until 1900, when a Daoist monk living there investigated a gap in the plaster. In 1907 and 1908, he sold the bulk of the 13,500 paper scrolls to the British explorer Aurel Stein (1862–1943) and the French sinologist Paul Pelliot (1878–1945). The majority of the scrolls were Buddhist sutras, including numerous copies of the same texts, but there were also everyday documents such as bills of sale and contracts for services; calendars; primers for beginning students; sample forms for arranging divorce, adoption, and family division; circulars for lay religious societies; lists of eminent families; and government documents of all sorts.

From these documents, we can see that through the early eighth century, local officials kept the detailed registers of each household needed for the equal-field system. Although there was not enough land available to give everyone his or her full quota, the government did make reassignments every three years, as required by the law. Tenancy was also very common. Some people who found it inconvenient to work the land allotted to them by the government rented it to tenants while working as tenants themselves on other people's land. Monasteries were among the largest landowners, and monastery tenants had serf-like status, unfree to move elsewhere or marry outside their group. They could, however, hire others to help them work their land, as well as purchase their own land.

Among the more interesting documents found at Dunhuang were fifty or so charters for lay associations. Usually a literate Buddhist monk helped the group organize Buddhist devotional activities, such as meals for monks or offerings for ceremonies. Wealthier groups might sponsor the construction or decoration of a new cave. Other groups were more concerned with sudden large expenses, such as funerals, with each member making small monthly contributions to what was, in effect, an insurance pool. One association was limited to women, who promised to contribute oil, wine, and flour for a monthly meal.

Many of those who belonged to these associations were illiterate and drew marks beside their names instead of signing their names. Temples did their best to reduce illiteracy by offering elementary education. Numerous primers have survived, as well as multiplication tables, vocabulary lists, and etiquette books with rules on the language to use when addressing superiors, peers, and inferiors and the steps to follow for weddings and funerals.

Some of China's earliest printed works were found among the Dunhuang documents, including a calendar for the year 877 and a copy of the *Diamond Sutra* dated 868, widely considered the world's oldest printed book. It is not surprising that the Chinese discovered how to print so early, since China had a long history of mass production by use of molds. Moreover, people were familiar with ways to reproduce words on paper through the use of seals or rubbings taken from inscribed bronze or stone. The method of printing developed in Tang times involved craftsmen carving words and pictures into wooden blocks, inking them, and then pressing paper onto the blocks. Each block had an entire page of text carved on it.

THE TANG DYNASTY'S FINAL DECADES AND THE FIVE DYNASTIES

After the rebellion of An Lushan, the Tang central government shared political and military power with the military governors. After 860, this system no longer worked to maintain order. Bandit gangs, some as large as small armies, roamed the countryside and set siege to walled cities. These gangs smuggled illicit salt, ambushed merchants and tax convoys, and went on wild rampages through the countryside. Huang Chao, the leader of the most successful of these bands, was a failed examination candidate who had become a salt merchant. His army crossed the country several times. In 879, it took Guangzhou and slaughtered thousands of foreign merchants. Just two years later, his army captured Chang'an and set up a government. When someone posted a poem that ridiculed the new regime on a government building, the order was given to kill all those able to compose poems. Three thousand people are said to have died as a result.

During the century from 860 to 960 (when the Song Dynasty was founded), political and military power devolved to the local level. Any local strongman able to organize defense against rebels and bandits could declare himself king or even emperor. Many of these local rulers rose from very humble origins; one had started as a merchant's slave. In the south, no self-proclaimed king ever consolidated much more than the equivalent of one or two modern provinces (a situation labeled the Ten Kingdoms). Political fragmentation did not impair the economy of the south. In fact, in their eagerness to expand their tax bases, rulers of the southern kingdoms did their best to promote trade and tax it.

In the north, the effects of political fragmentation were less benign. Many of the regional warlords were not Chinese, but Turks from the old garrison armies. Both Chang'an and Luoyang had been devastated by the fighting of the late Tang period, and Kaifeng, located in Henan province at the mouth of the Grand Canal, became the leading city in north China. None of the Five Dynasties that in succession held Kaifeng was able to build a stable government before being ousted by rivals.

SUMMARY

How did China change over the course of the three centuries of Sui and Tang rule? The late Tang did not dominate East Asia the way the early Tang had, as all along its borders powerful states had established themselves. Nor was the late Tang as eager to adopt music, craft, and art styles from distant lands. Although military men held much of the power in both periods, China had not returned to the hybrid Xianbei-Chinese military culture of the Northern Dynasties. The late Tang official elite was oriented toward the civil arts, and more and more welcomed into its midst men of literary talent from undistinguished families. During Tang times, the Chinese economy grew much larger, first stimulated by the reunification of north and south and later by the abandonment of the equal-field system. The government found new ways to raise revenue, notably through control of salt production and distribution. In both the sixth and the ninth centuries, Buddhism was a major force within China, but much had changed about China's engagement with Buddhism. By late Tang, foreign monks were much less of a presence and Chan and Tantric monks much more of one. Confucianism was stronger at the end of the Tang, thanks to the intellectual flowering of the ninth century.

The Emergence of East Asian Civilization

Cultural Contact Across Eurasia (600–900)

IN 735, WHEN TAJIHINO MABITO HIRONARI returned to Japan after completing his mission to the Tang court at Chang'an, he was accompanied by a Chinese Buddhist monk, an Indian Brahman, a Persian musician, and another musician from Champa (southern Vietnam). This was an era when Korea and Japan turned to China as a model for everything from architecture to ceramics, music, and medicine. But the China they turned to was a cosmopolitan one that had absorbed much from the rest of Asia. (See Map C3.1.)

During the seventh, eighth, and ninth centuries, the major countries of Asia exchanged ideas, music, technology, art, and commodities. The Chinese avidly adopted Persian musical instruments and the game of polo. The Abbasid caliphs were connoisseurs of Chinese silk and ceramics. Persian seamen carried goods on ships that stopped at India, Sri Lanka, Malaysia, and China. Buddhist monks from India and Java performed ceremonies at the Chinese court. Chang'an hosted as many as twenty-five thousand foreigners, the majority of whom had arrived by the overland route through Central Asia. In Guangzhou there were even more foreigners active in the seaborne trade. In the eighth century, a monk described the port as full of "uncountable" Indians, Persians, and Malays who brought aromatics, drugs, precious stones, and other goods. A century later, in 878, the Persian Abu Zayd was willing to put a number on the foreign community of Muslims, Christians, Jews, and Zoroastrians in the city, but his number—120,000—is too high to be believable.

Although many more merchants than monks traveled the trade routes of Asia, most surviving records of journeys were written by monks. The monk Xuanzang, who left Chang'an in 629, took the northern arm of the Silk Road. His account testifies to the strictness of Chinese checkpoints, where travel permits were examined, and to the hardship of crossing the deserts. He stopped at the oasis towns of Turfan and Kucha. Next he had to climb the Tianshan Mountains where, he wrote, glaciers "rise mingling with the clouds." One-third of those in his party died crossing these passes. At Tolmak he was entertained by a Turkish khan, and from there he went to Samarkand, which he described as a rich entrepôt. He stopped at Balk and Bamiyan before turning south toward India. On his return trip fifteen years later, after Samarkand, Xuanzang took the southern route through the city-state of Khotan. Then, however, he had to pass the Taklamakan desert, where drifting sands obscured the path, and travelers were advised to look for bones of those who had not survived to find their way. More than once on his trip, his group was attacked by bandits.

The stories of those who crossed the deserts and mountains of Central Asia by foot and camel are full of romance and adventure. More goods and more people, however, went by the easier sea route. Ships regularly sailed from the Persian Gulf to India and from India to Southeast Asia and China, following the monsoons. A full round trip of the entire route would take about a year and a half. Traders would leave Persia or Mesopotamia in September to catch the northeast monsoon that would take them to the southern tip of India. After trading there, they would sail in December with the southwest monsoon across the Bay of Bengal, through the Straits of Malacca, reaching Guangzhou in south China by April or May. They would spend several months there, buying Chinese goods, before beginning the return trip in the fall. Among the objects that traders transported across Asia were glass cups, bowls, and beads made in Syria or Persia. Imported glass has been found in tombs in China, Korea, and Japan.

China, Japan, and Korea in these centuries were part of a larger world that encompassed all of Asia from Persia east. These were the regions of Asia where Buddhism had spread. These parts of the world were themselves undergoing major changes in this period

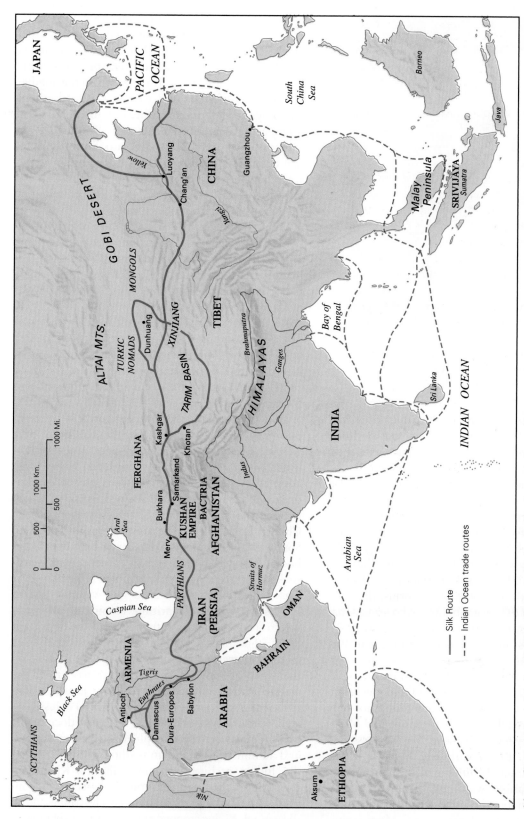

Map C3.1 Map of Asian Trade and Communication Routes in the Sixth–Tenth Centuries

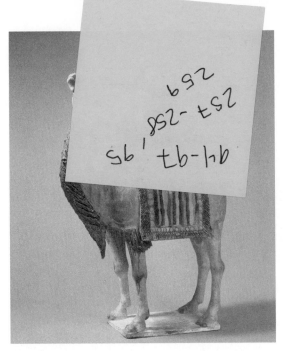

Musicians on a Camel. This Tang ceramic figurine, 23 inches tall, depicts Persian or Central Asian entertainers, a popular part of life in Tang cities. *(National Museum of China/Cultural Relics Publishing House)*

and looked quite different in 900 than they had in 600. In 600, Turks were dominant on the Inner Asian steppe. The major oasis cities, such as Kotan, Kucha, and Turfan, were largely autonomous and devotedly Buddhist. Sogdians dominated the region of Samarkand and Bukhara, and in Persia the Sassainian dynasty ruled. In Persia Zoroastrianism was the state-supported religion, but Manichaeism also had a substantial following, as it did in Sogdia as well. Christianity was to be found in both these regions, but it was Nestorian Christianity, an offshoot originating with the teachings of Nestorius, the fifth-century patriarch of Constantinople, who argued that Jesus had two distinct natures, human and divine.

By far the most momentous development in Persia and Sogdia during the Tang period was the coming of Islam. By the time Muhammad died in 632, his followers had formed a highly disciplined community in Arabia, and within a generation not only had they conquered the Arabian peninsula and Mesopotamia, but they had also taken over the Sassanian empire in Persia. By the early eighth century, they had added Bukara and Samarkand in Central Asia. Although populations were not forced to convert, political and economic incentives steadily led to more and more conversions. Zoroastrians, Manicheans,

and Nestorians who did not want to convert often chose to move, creating substantial diasporas, especially in India and China. Even before the arrival of Islam, Manicheanism had been spreading to the Uighur Turks of Chinese Turkestan, and the Sogdian Manicheans often moved east to the lands dominated by the Uighurs or farther east to China. Quite a few Manichean texts survived at Dunhuang. The influx of Nestorian Christians into Tang China began before Islam came to Central Asia but probably was stimulated by it. Zoroastrians, by contrast, mostly moved to India, where they were able to maintain their traditions into modern times.

India in these centuries was a land of petty kingdoms where regional cultures flourished. By this point, Hinduism was in the ascendancy and had more adherents than Buddhism, but there were still many major Buddhist monasteries. Tantric Buddhism was particularly popular and was spreading to Tibet. In these centuries, India came into contact with Islam. The northwest part of India, the Sind, was conquered in 711 by the Ummayad governor of Iraq, who sent a force with six thousand horses and six thousand camels, but Islam did not spread much beyond this foothold until several centuries later.

Tang China maintained sway in northern Vietnam, but elsewhere in Southeast Asia, traders from India were establishing a significant presence. Traders established many coastal settlements. Local rulers often adopted Indian customs and values, embraced Hinduism and Buddhism, and learned Sanskrit, which became the lingua franca of the region, much like Chinese in East Asia. The most important mainland Southeast Asian state was the Khmer Empire of Cambodia, founded in 802. Indian influence was pervasive; the impressive temple complex at Angkor Wat was dedicated to the Hindu god Vishnu. Just as impressive was the maritime empire of Srivijaya, which from the sixth century on held the important Strait of Malacca, through which most of the sea traffic between China and India passed. Based on the island of Sumatra, the Srivijayan navy ruled the waters around Sumatra, Borneo, and Java and controlled the southern part of the Malay Peninsula as well. Sanskrit was used for government documents, and Indians were often employed as priests, scribes, and administrators. Indian mythology took hold, as did Indian architecture and sculpture. Kings and their courts, the first to embrace Indian culture, consciously spread it to their subjects. The Chinese Buddhist monk Yixing stopped at Shrivijaya for six months

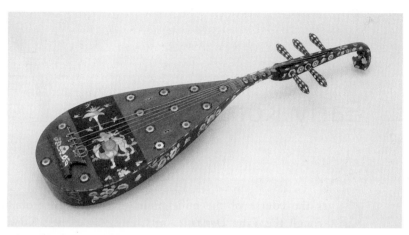

Five-Stringed Pipa/Biwa. This musical instrument, decorated with fine wooden marquetry, was probably presented by the Tang court to a Japanese envoy. It was among the objects placed in the Shōsōin. *(Shosoin Treasure House/DNPArchives.com)*

in 671 on his way to India and for four years on his return journey. He found a thousand Buddhist monks there, some of whom helped him translate Sanskrit texts. Borobudur, a stone monument depicting the ten tiers of Buddhist cosmology, was begun around 780.

Music and dance offers one of the most interesting cases of East Asia's adopting elements of culture from other parts of Asia. In Tang times, no tavern in Chang'an could compete without a troop of foreign musicians and a Western dancing or singing girl. Popular tunes included "South India," "The Three Platforms of the Turks," and "Watching the Moon in Brahman Land." One set of dancing girls from Sogdia who won the favor of Emperor Xuanzong (r. 712–756) were known as the Western Twirling Girls. They wore crimson robes with brocaded sleeves, green pants, and red deerskin boots, and they skipped and twirled on top of balls rolling around the dance floor. The poet Bai Juyi wrote about the dances of girls from modern Tashkent who began their act by emerging from artificial lotuses and ended it by pulling down their blouses to show their shoulders. Countries throughout Asia sent musicians as part of their tribute to Xuanzong's court. Court music was categorized into ten regional styles, including those of Samarkand, Bukhara, Kashgar, Kucha, India, and Korea. Among the instruments that entered the Chinese repertoire in this period is the pear-shaped plucked lute, originally of West Asian origins. From Kucha came oboes and flutes and a small lacquered drum. Percussion instruments from India, including gongs and cymbals, are often illustrated in Buddhist paintings of celestial orchestras. These instruments were adopted by orchestras not only in China but also in Korea and Japan.

Imported musical instruments were among the treasures the Japanese Empress Kōmyō placed in the Shōsōin repository at the Buddhist temple Tōdaiji in Nara in 756. These instruments included both four- and five-string *pipa/biwa* of Chinese manufacture. There also was a harp (*konghou/kugo*), another instrument that originated in West Asia. These instruments were greatly outnumbered by the 171 masks for use in dance performances. Masked dances were very popular in the Central Asian city of Kucha, and Kuchan dancers probably helped them gain popularity in China, Korea, and Japan. One mask is for a comic drama, *Drunken Persians*, about a Persian king and his attendant. "As the languid dance, punctuated with slow leaps, picked up tempo, the actors shed their inhibitions and behaved in a thoroughly uproarious manner, probably drawing enthusiastic cheers from the delighted spectators."[1] Central Asia thus provided not only some of the material trappings of this performance, but also its content.

1. Ryoichi Hayashi, *The Silk Road and the Shoso-in*, trans. Robert Ricketts (New York: Weatherhill, 1975), p. 102.

Early Korea to 935

6

Over the course of the millennium that stretched from the Han through the Tang Dynasties in China, the earliest Korean states appeared. These states, in the Korean peninsula and adjacent parts of Manchuria, were in frequent contact with the peoples and polities in Inner Asia, China, and Japan. In 108 B.C.E. the Chinese Han Dynasty expanded to incorporate the northwestern part of the peninsula, which led to increasing contact with Chinese culture and technology. After the Chinese outpost fell in the early fourth century, three main states emerged in the Korean region. Competition among these Three Kingdoms to expand their territories culminated in Silla's unification of much of the peninsula in 668. During these centuries, Korean elites successfully resisted determined efforts by the Sui and Tang governments to subjugate them, but they did not reject all things Chinese. They readily adopted ideas and practices from outside, including Buddhism, the Chinese writing system, and Confucian ideas about government.

Scholars who study early Korea have been particularly interested in questions of Korea's ethnic and cultural origins and connections to other parts of Asia. How do we reconstruct Korea's early history when most of the written sources are Chinese? How should we interpret the references in Chinese sources to the many "states" in the region? Do the textual and archaeological sources tell the same story? How close were the cultures of the Korean peninsula and Manchuria? What were the reasons for Silla's eventual victory over its rivals? How did the adopted religion of Buddhism interact with native religious beliefs? What led Silla's elites to borrow extensively from Tang China? How were they nevertheless able to maintain and develop Korea's cultural distinctiveness?

GEOGRAPHICAL SETTING

Korea is about 600 miles long and about 150 miles across at its widest point. Its area, about 85,000 square miles, is much smaller than China's (about one-fiftieth based on current borders) but is more than half the size of Japan and just slightly smaller than Great Britain. Most of the land is hilly, with major mountains in the north that cut off the penin-

Map **6.1**   **Korea, 200** B.C.E.–**100** B.C.E.

sula from Manchuria. The Taedong River in the north and the Han River in the center were the most important rivers, but they did not play the central role of the Yellow and Yangzi Rivers in China. The Yalu River (Amnok in Korean) and the Tumen (Tuman) River, the current boundary between North Korea and China, did not function as a state boundary until the fifteenth century.

The climate of Korea is shaped by its location. In winter the weather is cold, with heavy snowfall in the north because of cold continental air flowing south from Siberia. In summer it is hot and humid with monsoon winds depositing torrential rains in

July and August. Most of the best arable land is located in the south, where wet field rice is common and double cropping possible. Hill land can be terraced for rice cultivation, but most upland areas were traditionally cultivated in dry crops like barley, millet, ramie, and later cotton.

Human habitation in the Korean peninsula began about thirty thousand years ago. (See **Connections: The Prehistory of East Asia.**) From about 6000 B.C.E., a distinctive type of "comb-marked" earthenware was made. By about 1300 B.C.E., bronze artifacts such as knives were in use, but their use did not lead to such Bronze Age developments as cities, writing, or complex states as they did in Shang China. Rather, the distinctive narrow and broad swords, knives, and tools found in Korea belong to the Northern Zone culture found across the steppe from Scythia to Siberia.

Although today there are no significant ethnic minorities in Korea, in early times many different groups lived in the peninsula. The main flow of migration into the Korean peninsula came from Inner Asia, Mongolia, and Siberia through Manchuria, and migration also continued across the Tsushima Strait to the islands of Japan. The ancestors of the Koreans spoke languages that modern linguists call the Ural-Altaic language group; the languages were unrelated to Chinese. Verbs are placed at the ends of sentences, and relative clauses precede the nouns they modify. *Tungusic* is the term that has been assigned to the subgroup of languages of the prehistoric inhabitants of Manchuria and Korea.

A story in the early Zhou Dynasty *Book of Documents* tells of a Chinese nobleman and sage, Kija (Qizi in Chinese), who advised King Wen of the Zhou Dynasty (ca. 1000 B.C.E.) and was rewarded by the grant of a fief called Chosŏn (Chaoxian in Chinese), a term used in the Han Dynasty to refer to southern Manchuria and northern Korea. Koreans in later times pointed to this tale to claim that Kija brought the "Korean people" up to the advanced level of early Zhou civilization, but archaeological evidence provides no support for such early involvement with the Chinese heartland.

THE EARLY HISTORICAL PERIOD (200 B.C.E.–313 C.E.)

In addition to archaeological evidence, several sorts of written records help us reconstruct early Korean history. The early Chinese histories have passages about the various small polities in what later became Manchuria and Korea. Naturally, Chinese historians wrote from a Chinese perspective, reporting raids on Chinese territory or other military conflicts, the arrival of envoys, and what Chinese envoys, traders, or migrants reported back after their own travels. The earliest extant source written in Korea is an inscription dated 414 C.E. The earliest surviving histories written in Korea were compiled much later, in 1145 and 1279, respectively. They are commonly used as sources for much earlier periods on the

assumption that they made use of earlier records now lost, but naturally they were written from the perspectives of the victors in the successive struggles for supremacy, not the losers.

From these written sources, we know that during the Han Dynasty, the Korean peninsula was home to many different tribes, tribal confederations, or other types of small polities. In this period, there was no sharp break between lands dominated by the Xiongnu and Korea, and after the Xiongnu confederation broke down, the number of groups identifying themselves as distinct peoples only increased. Ethnicity was fluid as tribes vanquished each other, incorporating those subjugated as members of the tribe or as its slaves.

The North: Chosŏn, Puyŏ, Koguryŏ, and the Chinese Commanderies

Sima Qian's *Historical Records*, written around 100 B.C.E., records that in 195 B.C.E., when the king of the Han Dynasty state of Yan (in the region of modern Beijing) rebelled, one of his lieutenants named Weiman (Wiman in Korean) fled east to Chosŏn (Chaoxian in Chinese) with a thousand followers. The Chosŏn king put him in charge of guarding the frontier, but Weiman seized control of the country and set himself up as king. His descendants ruled until 108 B.C.E., much the way Chao Tuo/Trieu Da did in south China and Vietnam (see Chapter 3). The site of Weiman's capital is uncertain; Pyongyang, south of the Yalu River, is the most likely place, but recently Korean scholars have argued that it lay farther west near the Liao River in Manchuria (see Map 6.1).

In 108 B.C.E., Emperor Wu of the Han Dynasty, in his efforts to outflank the Xiongnu, invaded Chosŏn and incorporated its territory from the Liao River in southwestern Manchuria almost to present-day Seoul. This territory was divided into four commanderies and was administered like other commanderies by officials assigned from the Chinese capital. Lelang commandery, with its seat in modern Pyongyang, was the most important of the four. This part of Korea remained under Chinese control to 313 C.E., leading to increased trade and cultural contact between societies on the Korean peninsula and Han China. Excavations of Lelang have revealed brick-paved lanes, covered drainage culverts, and rows of foundation stones for pillared buildings thought to be government buildings because of finds of Han coins and government seals. Nearly fifteen hundred mounded tombs in the area show that Han officials assigned to Lelang brought Chinese burial practices and art styles with them. Luxury goods from all over the Chinese empire were transported to this distant outpost, including a famous lacquerware basket with images of Confucian worthies painted around the sides, thought to have been brought all the way from Sichuan in western China (see page 51).

From Chinese sources, it seems that the rest of Korea in this era was controlled by tribal chieftains or petty kings. The general picture that emerges is of mounted warriors claiming aristocratic origins who would lead a few hundred warrior followers to promising locations where they could extract resources by dominating the local farming and fishing families, their chiefdoms not much more than city-states. Chinese population estimates of these tribal polities ranged from several hundred to fifty thousand. Often councils of chiefs advised and limited the power of petty kings. Society was organized hierarchically with an elite class of what Chinese sources called "great families," who dominated "lower households," which probably included slaves. In these regards, the chiefdoms were much like other tribal societies in Manchuria, such as the Xianbei, who played important roles in China in the Period of Division. Warfare was conducted with bows and arrows, swords, and halberds, and each family had to supply its own weapons. Punishment included execution and reduction to slavery of the family members of criminals. Like the Xiongnu, some of these societies practiced the levirate (marriage to a brother's widow). See **Documents: The Widow of King Kogukch'ŏn.**

Puyŏ, located in central Manchuria around the Sungari River, and Koguryŏ, which straddled the Yalu River, were the most advanced of these polities. One of the main tasks of the Han commanderies was to attempt to suppress raids by Koguryŏ warriors. The Han officials often turned to Puyŏ to help them fight their common enemy, Koguryŏ. From 49 C.E. on, Puyŏ sent regular embassies to China. Both Puyŏ and Koguryŏ had adopted some marks of Chinese civilization, such as the use of ceremonial wine cups, status distinctions, New Year ceremonies, and sacrifices to Heaven. They enjoyed drinking, eating, singing, and dancing and preferred wearing white clothes. By contrast, the Okchŏ and Eastern Ye people in northeastern Korea were small and less advanced politically and culturally. They retained elements of Siberian customs, fought mostly on foot, and were famous for their bows and archery skills.

After 184 C.E., central control lapsed in China, and warlords seized power many places. The Chinese Gongsun family took over the Liaodong commandery in southern Manchuria, then tried to expand to the east. The Gongsun attacked the Koguryŏ capital, took over the Lelang commandery, and in 205 established the new Daifang commandery south of Lelang. Within a few decades, in 244 during the Three Kingdoms period in China, the Chinese state of Wei invaded Koguryŏ territory, captured the Koguryŏ capital, and forced the king to take refuge in Okchŏ. Koguryŏ recovered when Wei shifted its attention south to take over Lelang and Daifang. In 286, after Wei was replaced by the Jin Dynasty, the Murong branch of the Xianbei people attacked Puyŏ and took thousands of captives.

Early in the fourth century, in 313 and 314, when north China fell into the hands of Xianbei and other non-Chinese rulers, Koguryŏ seized Lelang and Daifang. Despite four hundred years of Chinese presence in those commanderies, the area quickly declined in importance. The educated elite either moved south to the Samhan confederation or were absorbed by Koguryŏ. Puyŏ also declined as Koguryŏ encroached on it, fully absorbing it in 494.

The South: The Three Han (Samhan)

In the southern half of the Korean peninsula, never under Chinese administration, early Chinese sources mention much smaller polities organized into three confederations of the Han (this "Han" is written with a different Han character than is the one for the Han Dynasty in China; this Han in time became an ethnic term for Korean). Mahan was in the southwest, Chinhan in the southeast, and Pyŏnhan between the other two on the southern coast (see Map 6.1). According to Chinese sources, Mahan comprised fifty chiefdoms and had a population of about five hundred thousand people in the third century; Chinhan and Pyŏnhan had a dozen chiefdoms each and about two hundred thousand people. All three were stratified societies with aristocratic elites that selected their chiefs and lorded it over not only commoners but also "low" households and slaves. The climate of the south favored growing rice and other grains, which were supplemented by hunting, gathering, fishing, sericulture, and the weaving of ramie cloth. In Chinhan, iron was produced.

Chinese sources paid less attention to these southern societies because they were not contiguous with

DOCUMENTS

The Widow of King Kogukch'ŏn

Like the Xiongnu, Mongols, and other Inner Asian peoples, early Korean ruling groups practiced the levirate. That is, a younger brother would marry the widow of his elder brother. According to the History of the Three Kingdoms, *written in 1145 but based on earlier records, when the Koguryŏ king died in 197, the choice of his successor largely fell to his widow, who picked which of his younger brothers she wished to marry.*

Upon the death of King Kogukch'ŏn, his queen, formerly named U, kept his death secret and at night went to the house of Palgi, the king's younger brother, and said, "The king has no heir; you should succeed him." Not knowing of the king's death, Palgi said, "Heaven dispenses its favors as it will. Moreover it is indecorous for a lady to travel about at night."

Ashamed, the queen went to Yŏnu, Palgi's younger brother. Yŏnu rose, put on his cap and gown, received the queen at the gate, and gave a banquet in her honor. The queen said, "Now that the king is dead and there is no heir, Palgi should succeed him; but instead he insolently accuses me of treason. That is why I have come."

Thereupon Yŏnu showed more respect and cut his finger while carving the meat. The queen undid her belt and wrapped his injured finger. Before returning to the palace, she said, "The night is dark, and I am fearful. Please take me home." Yŏnu complied. The queen then took Yŏnu's hand and drew him into the palace. The following morning at dawn, the queen lied to the officials and convinced them that the late king had wished Yŏnu to succeed him.

Palgi was furious when he heard the news. He surrounded the palace with soldiers and shouted, "It is not proper for a younger brother to succeed an elder brother. You have upset the proper order and usurped the throne. This is a grave crime. Come out at once. If not, your wife and children will be put to death."

Yŏnu closed the palace gate for three days, and none of the people followed Palgi. Anticipating a disaster, Palgi, together with his wife and children, took refuge in Liaodong and reported to the Governor Gongsun Du, "I am the brother of Nammu, king of Koguryŏ. Nammu died leaving no heir, but my younger brother Yŏnu has plotted with his sister-in-law and ascended the throne. This is a transgression of the eternal ways of man. In my anger I have come to you. I beg you to give me a troop of thirty thousand to attack and suppress the rebel." Gongsun Du complied.

Yŏnu had his younger brother Kyesu lead the defending army, and Kyesu routed the Chinese troops. When Kyesu personally led the van and pursued the fleeing enemy, Palgi asked, "Are you trying to kill your older brother?"

Kyesu was not so heartless as to kill his brother. He said, "It is not just for Yŏnu to have accepted the throne, but are you trying to destroy your own state in a fit of temper? How can you face your own father in the underworld?" Ashamed and remorseful, Palgi fled to Paech'ŏn, where he cut his own throat. Kyesu wept bitterly, gave the corpse a hasty burial, and returned.

———
Source: Peter H. Lee and Wm. Theodore de Bary, ed. *Sources of Korean Tradition Vol. 1: From Early Times through the Sixteenth Century* (New York: Columbia University Press, 1997), 30–31.

Chinese territories and posed no military threat. They reported that dwellings in the south had thatched roofs and earthen floors and that the people did not understand the value of precious metals like gold and silver or appreciate fine silks. Some of the men tattooed their bodies, and the men living in the islands of offshore Mahan wore their hair like the Xianbei and ran about half-naked. None of their towns were surrounded by walls as in China. In Chinhan and Pyŏnhan, the people flattened the heads of their babies and tattooed their bodies like the Wa people in Japan. Warriors fought on foot because there were no horses.

Early Chinese accounts claimed that the Wa (usually interpreted as a name for the Japanese) also lived along the southern coast. Other sources, too, suggest that groups crossed frequently between Korea and Japan in these early centuries, with ethnic and linguistic distinctions between them evolving only slowly.

THE THREE KINGDOMS: KOGURYŎ, PAEKCHE, AND SILLA (313–668)

During the fourth century, the welter of peoples, polities, and Chinese garrisons began to evolve into three distinct territorial states—Koguryŏ, Paekche, and Silla—all still very much ruled by warrior elites. Both the decline in Chinese power and a diaspora of Chinese fleeing turmoil contributed to the state-building process, which involved borrowing Chinese political practices as ways to strengthen the monarchy and central control. The kings were still military leaders, however, and regularly led their armies into battle. In archaeological terms, the Three Kingdoms period was the era of large, mounded tombs found throughout the area and into western Japan. They provide strong evidence that elites now controlled extensive resources and labor power. The scores of mountain fortresses built in the period similarly offer evidence of the military conflicts of the period.

The northernmost of these states, Koguryŏ, had slowly gained strength for centuries. It was centered in southern Manchuria, and its rulers claimed to be a branch of the Puyŏ ruling house. In the fourth century, Koguryŏ got caught up in the wars among the different Xianbei tribes in north China and southern Manchuria. Despite some serious setbacks, Koguryŏ was expanding by the late fourth century. In this period, the Koguryŏ king Kwanggaet'o ("the king who expands the territory," r. 391—413) was making advances against the Khitan tribes in Manchuria

and other tribes in the present-day Russian Maritime Province to the east, and by 410 controlled large territories in both places (see Map 6.2). He also began pushing southward down the Korean peninsula, in part because of pressure from the Xianbei states to the west. In 399 he sent an expeditionary force to help Silla drive out invading Paekche and Wa forces. He then enrolled King Namul of Silla as his vassal. In 406 he ended his long campaign against the Later Yan state (whose rulers were Murong branch of the Xianbei). The peace agreement required him to provide military aid against the powerful Northern Wei state in north China ruled by the Tuoba clan of the Xianbei. In 414, the year after he died, his successor erected a stone slab inscribed with a record of all his exploits, the earliest extant Korean document (written, though, in Chinese). It described his first victory in 395 as a defeat of three tribes of six hundred to seven hundred tents and the capture of uncountable numbers of cattle, sheep, and horses, clearly showing that this region should be considered part of Inner Asia in this period. From this time to about 450, Koguryŏ culture also had an increased influence on Japan (see Chapter 7).

Some of the best evidence of material culture in the Three Kingdoms period is found in murals in royal and aristocratic Koguryŏ tombs (see Color Plate 8). These murals are reminiscent of Han China's tomb murals in their depictions of the earthly life of the tomb occupant along with depictions of dancers and other entertainers, seemingly there to amuse the tomb occupant. Some tomb murals depict royal palaces with elaborate multicolored decorations on beams and rafters, the women living there garbed in elaborate and colorful clothing and served by slaves and servants. Some murals show mounted warriors out hunting, shooting arrows while at full gallop. Others depict kings conducting colorful processions with a full panoply of mounted guards and chariots with military banners waving in the breeze. Entertainers depicted on tomb walls include men wrestling and women dancing, wearing robes with elongated sleeves that they waved in circles in the air. The upper parts of the tombs were often decorated with images of the Heavens, including magnificent examples of phoenixes and intertwined snakes and turtles that were symbolic of the four points of the compass associated with the five phases (*wuxing*) theory of Chinese cosmology.

It was not until the late fourth century that Paekche and Silla were mentioned in Chinese records, suggesting that they did not become important powers until

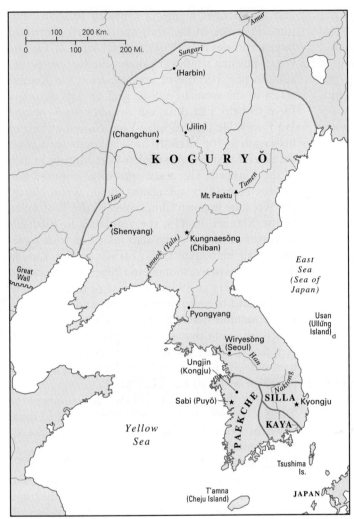

Map 6.2   **Koguryŏ at Its Largest Extent, Late Fifth Century** C.E.

that time. Like the Koguryŏ rulers, Paekche's rulers claimed descent from a Puyŏ prince. Paekche began with a base just west of the Liao River in southwest Manchuria. In 369, Paekche attacked and defeated its erstwhile Mahan overlord and soon absorbed much of the rest of Mahan territory, thus giving it control of the southwestern part of the peninsula.

In the late fourth century, Paekche society was dominated by five aristocratic lineages, of which the Chin and Hae were the most influential. To strengthen royal control, Paekche kings established the post of chief minister and set up a system of sixteen official ranks. They promoted Confucian ideas and ordered the compilation of historical records. In this era, Paekche was a maritime power. It developed a triangular trading, cultural, and military relationship with

China and Japan. It transmitted Chinese culture and Buddhism to Japan and sought weapons and military support from Japan.

As Paekche expanded, it came into conflict with Koguryŏ and Silla. In the mid-fifth century, it lost its base in Manchuria and suffered a Koguryŏ blockade of its ports. After defeat by Koguryŏ in 475, Paekche withdrew south of the Han River. Plagued by internal rivalry between the aristocratic Hae and Chin families, Paekche then forged an alliance with Silla against Koguryŏ in 493, which protected both states for over half a century.

In the sixth century, Paekche worked to strengthen central control by increasing the number of local magistrates assigned from the capital and registering commoners for labor service and tax collection. Paekche's

Women Dancers. Women dancers performing before an audience on the wall of the Dancing Tomb at Tongkou near the Koguryo capital of Kungnae, sixth century. *(Kim Wonyong, ed. Han'guk misul chonjip [the complete collection of Korean Art] vol. 4 Pyokhwa [wall paintings].* Seoul: Tonghwa ch'ulp'an kongsa, 1974, plate 55, p. 76)

effort to expand eastward was stymied when Silla took over the Kaya confederation in 562. By the time of its final defeat in 660–663, Paekche boasted two hundred cities and 760,000 households.

The third of the Three Kingdoms, Silla, started as the weakest but emerged victorious in the end. Silla began as a confederation of six tribes controlled by a council of tribal leaders, under the larger Chinhan confederation. The first chiefs came from the Pak family, and after that line ran out, from the Sŏk and Kim families. They were assisted by a shaman or spiritual chief. Like the rulers of Paekche and Koguryŏ, Silla's kings took steps to institutionalize their governments. They set up a ministry of war, issued a Chinese-style law code, made Buddhism a state-sponsored religion, and collected taxes on agriculture. When Silla conquered the chiefdom of Kŭmgwan in the Kaya confederation in 532, it incorporated its ruling family into the Silla aristocracy at a low rank. With further campaigns, Silla gained access to the Yellow Sea

and direct maritime contact with China, laying the groundwork for a decisive alliance with China a century later. By the 570s, Silla was replacing military lords with commissioners dispatched from the capital.

Besides the three main rival kingdoms, a loose confederation on the southern coast known collectively as Kaya was especially active in trade and iron production and had strong ties to Japan. Excavation of the royal Kaya tombs shows a prosperous society and rulers who could command considerable labor and resources. Too small to resist the expansion of their neighbors, Kaya fell bit by bit, the last part absorbed by Silla in 562.

The Introduction of Buddhism

Our knowledge of religion in Korea before Buddhism is fragmentary. The early migrating hunters and gatherers who lived in Manchuria and Korea had animistic belief in the spirits of mountains and large trees, and they probably used shamans to communicate with spirits of the dead in order to avert harm to the living, traditions that remain alive today. In wartime, the Puyŏ held a sacrifice to Heaven and then examined the hooves of a sacrificial ox to divine the outcome of upcoming battles. The Mahan conducted planting and harvest rituals in the fifth and tenth lunar months, and each chiefdom had a religious specialist called the Lord of Heaven who offered sacrifices to the spirit of Heaven. The Mahan also had a special holy place that functioned as a safe refuge for people fleeing punishment.

These earlier traditions came to be obscured by the great influence on Buddhism, which spread to Korea during the Three Kingdoms period (see **Connections: Buddhism in India and Its Spread Along the Silk Road**). Buddhism was introduced to Koguryŏ and Paekche in the 360s and 370s. Fu Jian, one of the non-Chinese rulers in North China, was an active patron of Buddhism and dispatched two monks to Koguryŏ. A monk from the Chinese Eastern Jin state came by sea to Paekche to introduce Buddhism. In the late fourth century, Paekche in turn sent Buddhist monks and two specialists in Confucian learning to Japan with the *Analects* and the *Thousand Character Classic*. It took another 150 years before Buddhism spread to Silla.

Even though Koguryŏ and Paekche kings sponsored Buddhism to gain a political edge over the dominant aristocratic families, Buddhism quickly became much more than a political weapon. Learned monks could read and write Chinese and helped spread Chinese learning and Confucian ethics. Buddhist temples and monasteries located in the mountains provided refuge from strife. The art and architecture of Buddhist temples were a source of inspiration open to all.

Unification by Silla (581–668)

In 589 the Sui Dynasty reunified China after centuries of division, changing the political and military balance in northeast Asia. The main foreign threat to Sui was the Turks, but Koguryŏ, because it sought an alliance with the Turks, was also a source of worry. In 598, Koguryŏ attacked Sui territory, and Sui responded by invading Koguryŏ by land and sea. The Sui campaign failed, but Sui did not abandon its ambitions. Another invasion in 612 was foiled by a brilliant naval victory at the Sal River. Three more unsuccessful invasions followed in 613, 614, and

Pottery Figure of a Silla Mounted Warrior, Fifth–Sixth Century C.E. *(National Museum of Korea)*

617. Uprisings soon toppled the Sui Dynasty, its loss of support in no small part the result of the enormous toll of its repeated attempts to regain the Lelang area.

The next Chinese dynasty, Tang, also aspired to match the Han Dynasty at its height, so it had its eyes on Koguryŏ from the start. For its first thirty years, its armies were busy reducing the Turks in the north and west and opening China to trade and contact with Central Asia. In 642 the powerful Koguryŏ aristocrat Yŏn Kaesomun seized power, creating a virtual dictatorship that allowed him to prepare the kingdom for the coming crisis with China.

Paekche and Silla understood the principle that "the enemy of my enemy is my friend." Sometimes they allied with each other against Koguryŏ; sometimes they tried to line up outsiders, including Tang China, to help them. Queen Sŏndŏk of Silla (r. 632–647) asked the Tang emperor Taizong to pressure Koguryŏ to cease its attacks on Silla. Taizong responded by launching a campaign against Koguryŏ in 644. It, too, failed. Still convinced that he could defeat Koguryŏ, Taizong dispatched two more expeditions against it in 647 and 648, neither of them successful.

After Tang failed once again to defeat Koguryŏ in 658, the Tang emperor Gaozong finally agreed to join Silla's forces to subjugate Paekche in 660. This was the first Chinese victory in Korea since Han times. With victory, Gaozong set up five military commands to administer Paekche territory rather than turning the area over to Silla, an insult Silla swallowed toward the greater goal of eliminating Koguryŏ. Fate turned in Silla's favor when the king of Koguryŏ died in 666 and a succession struggle broke out among his sons. Weakened by internal strife, Koguryŏ finally fell to the invading Tang and Silla forces in 668.

Why was Silla victorious? Koguryŏ was the largest and most militant of the Three Kingdoms. Yet in the mid-seventh century, Silla's diplomacy trumped Koguryŏ's militancy as the way for a small country to survive in the face of a huge and powerful neighbor. After the destruction of Koguryŏ, however, Silla was ready to turn on Tang. King Munmu organized a coalition of forces, including soldiers from the defeated armies from Paekche and Koguryŏ, to help drive the Chinese from the peninsula by 676.

Silla did not gain control over all of former Koguryŏ territory: Tang held the Liaodong peninsula, and Parhae gained most of the land north of the Taedong River (see Map 6.3), but it unified more of the Korean peninsula than had any earlier state. Relations with Tang were severed until the beginning of the eighth century, but after that time Silla and Tang established very strong relations. By that point, Tang's strategic interests had shifted, and it allied with Silla against their common foe, Parhae (see below). Silla, protected from foreign invasion by the Tang Empire, was able to reduce its military expenditures.

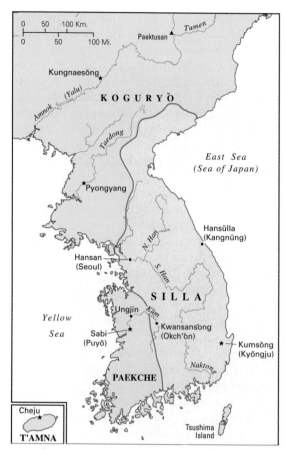

Map 6.3 **Silla After Conquest of Han River Region in 552 C.E.**

UNIFIED SILLA (668–892)

After Silla drove out Tang forces in 676, the government concentrated on consolidating its control and overcoming resistance. To win over aristocrats, privileges were granted to war heroes and important civil and military officials. Borrowing from the Tang bureaucratic model, post stations were set up, complete with horses, to speed the transportation of officials and communication of official messages. The government also created a board of academicians to promote Confucian learning, and it appointed specialists in medicine, law, mathematics or calculations, astronomy, and water clocks and agencies in charge of Buddhist temples and monasteries.

The Silla capital at Kyŏngju was laid out in checkerboard fashion like a miniature of the Tang capital at Chang'an. In 685, King Sinmun divided the country into administrative units modeled on Chinese practice, creating nine prefectures that were subdivided into two hundred superior districts and over three hundred ordinary districts. Magistrates selected from among the aristocrats were dispatched from the capital to govern the districts. Reluctant to move the capital to a more central area because of the resistance of the Kyŏngju aristocrats, by 680 the government established five small capitals in addition to the main one at Kyŏngju and sent members of the aristocracy to live at them and spread Silla culture throughout the conquered territories. The small capitals, however, did not flourish as expected because of the extraordinary attachment of the Silla elite to life at Kyŏngju. Silla also required powerful local clerks (*hyangni*) to send family members to the capital as hostages to guarantee their loyalty, a method that would not have been necessary had Silla been able to establish control through officials dispatched from the capital.

Silla military was less influenced by Tang models and resembled more closely the armies of northern powers. The army consisted of nine units called "oath banners," only three of which were staffed by Silla soldiers. Among the other banners were one for Paekche men, one for Paekche rebels against the Tang, one for Koguryŏ troops, and two separate ones for the followers of a Koguryŏ prince. The military seems to have declined in influence, however, as a strong army was no longer necessary under the umbrella of Tang military force.

Beginning in 780, political stability steadily spiraled downward as the aristocrats turned against the royal family in a series of murders, attempted coups d'état, and usurpations. A succession of four rebellions led by aristocrats known as True Bones broke out in the 760s and 770s. Finally the chairman of the Council of Notables took over the throne himself in defiance of the will of the council. The throne had become a football for any aristocrat with the will and fortitude to grab it.

The weakness of central control was made manifest when a local prefect rebelled in 822, proclaimed a new dynasty, and seized four of the nine prefectures and three of the five small capitals before he was defeated. The security afforded Silla by Tang power declined after the An Lushan rebellion of 756 in China. In 819, Silla's relations with Parhae were disrupted when King Hŏndŏk responded to a Tang request to dispatch thirty thousand troops to attack Parhae. In 826, after the expedition failed, he had to build a long wall along the border in the northeast. In 828 the court appointed an outsider, Chang Pogo, to take charge of a new naval garrison at Ch'ŏnghae (on Wando, or Wan Island) to suppress piracy. Chang was a commoner merchant prince who became the virtual commander of the seas for Silla, dominating the trade and transportation routes between Japan, Korea, and China. He made the mistake of incensing the capital aristocrats in 845 when he proposed that his daughter marry the king. Seeing their reaction, Chang rebelled and was quickly killed. Once his base at Ch'ŏnghae was destroyed in 851, Silla lost its maritime predominance.

In the late ninth century, when the Tang Dynasty was brought to collapse by the Huang Chao rebellion, Silla too fell into disorder as warlords competed for power. The period from 889 to 935, the interregnum between Silla and the next long dynasty, Koryŏ, is referred to as the Later Three Kingdoms, since warlords claimed to be reviving and continuing the old rival kingdoms.

SOCIETY AND CULTURE

Despite the strong influence of Tang culture, Silla society was fundamentally different from China's. The main reason why kings adopted elements of Chinese statecraft was to strengthen their own positions vis-à-vis the deeply entrenched nobility. The True Bone aristocrats who traced their ancestry to earlier kings did not think the king outranked them. As early as the third century, Silla had a council of chieftains that exerted a check on the development of royal power, which seems to have been the origin of the Council of Notables (*hwabaek*). The chairman of the Council of Notables was selected by the aristocrats in the council, and he held his position for the life of the king.

Although Tang China is considered a particularly aristocratic period in Chinese history, Silla was much more aristocratic than Tang. In China the examination system that tested knowledge of the Chinese classics had been established in the Sui Dynasty and was carried over into Tang times to provide an impersonal method of recruiting officials that allowed occasional "new men" to rise in office. Although Silla introduced examinations based on the Confucian classics in 788, it allowed only aristocrats to take them.

With Silla's victory over its rivals, its system of aristocratic ranks was applied to the entire society, but the highest rank was reserved for Silla's own nobility. In the Silla bone rank system, the descendants of its three royal clans were referred to as the True Bones (*chin'gol*), and they married only members of other True Bone families. No member of the True Bones could drop to commoner status, except as punishment for criminal action, and most members lived in the capital, Kyŏngju. The True Bones monopolized the top five of the nine grades of offices. This bone rank system of inherited status resembles the *kabane* of early Japan (see Chapter 7), both of which had similar roots in Inner Asian social organization.

Young men in the True Bones families participated in age groups called "flower youth" groups. These groups of aristocrat-warriors just coming of age practiced military skills together and later also engaged in such cultural activities as poetry-writing. The leaders of the Silla armies often had strong bonds to each other that originated in these age groups. Lower reaches of society included both commoners and slaves. Some of the True Bone aristocrats in the capital at Kyŏngju possessed several thousand slaves thanks to prisoners of war captured in Silla's victories over rivals. Nevertheless, the few extant village registers indicate that slaves made up only about 5 percent of the village population (their numbers would grow during the next dynasty). Silla also had special districts populated by people of inferior social status below that of commoners but above that of slaves.

Marriage was central to Silla kingship. The first eight kings (the dating of their reigns is unreliable) came from the Pak lineage, and all queens from the Kim lineage, and the next eight kings to 356 C.E. came from the Sŏk family with queens supplied mostly by the Kim family and some from the Pak. From 356 to 654, all kings were members of the Kim lineage, and all the queens came from the Pak family. This marriage practice has been labeled the double-descent system (and is similar to the marriage practices of the Khitan Liao dynasty, discussed in Chapter 8).

Since King Chinp'yŏng had no sons, one of his daughters succeeded as Queen Sŏndŏk (r. 632–647), and the next ruler was her cousin, Queen Chindŏk (r. 647–654). Her successor, King Muryŏl (r. 654–661), the man responsible for the conquest of Paekche, was another cousin of these two queens. These two women became queens not just because they had no brothers, but also because of the high status of the matrilineal line of descent among the wives and daughters of the Kim family kings. Thereafter, royal succession largely followed the patrilineal descent pattern in the Kim family. When a king died without an heir, there were occasions when a son-in-law or the son of a princess was chosen to be king, a sign of the high status shown to elite women in Silla.

Sometime in the ninth century, the bone rank system was expanded in Silla by instituting new ranks as a sop to lower aristocrats. However, the new ranks did not allow lower aristocrats to hold higher office, so the reform did not reduce their discontent, and they continued to serve as scribes and clerks (see **Biography: Kangsu the Scribe**). Resentful lower aristocrats were quick to move to the new Koryŏ Dynasty capital in Kaesŏng after Silla's collapse in 935 to seek higher posts in the new regime.

During the Three Kingdoms period, the use of the Chinese writing system had spread to Korea. Sometimes people simply wrote in Chinese; other times they used Chinese characters to write Korean, using some for their meaning and some for their pronunciation. To ease comprehension, *idu* were Chinese characters used for their pronunciation rather than their meaning; *idu* words were inserted among the ideographs to indicate particles and conjugations of verbs in Korean. *Idu* was continued by clerks through the Chosŏn Dynasty as a convenient writing system (similar to Japanese with its Chinese characters and *kana*).

The alliance between Tang and Silla facilitated travel between the two countries. Silla sent annual embassies to the Tang capitals and received many in return. Two or three hundred people might be part of these embassies. Much as China was open to art forms and other influence from Persia and India in Tang times, Korea in the same period was open to what China had to offer. Several Tang cities had "Sillan wards" where merchants and students from Silla lived. The Japanese pilgrim Ennin encountered Sillan boats not only traversing the Yellow Sea but also carrying cargoes of charcoal within China. Some ninety Sillan subjects passed the Chinese civil service examinations in the ninth century alone. Silla monks studied in China, Silla military officers enrolled in Tang armies, and Silla scholars competed successfully in the Tang examination system and were appointed to civil office in China. For instance, Ch'oe Ch'iwŏn, who was sent to China by his father at age twelve to study, passed the guest tribute examination for foreigners at eighteen and was assigned to a county-level office. He gradually rose in office for thirteen years before he announced that he wanted to return to Korea. Yet when Ch'oe and others like him returned home, they found it difficult to crack the upper ranks of the Silla government, dominated by True Bones aristocrats.

Buddhist monks who went to China brought back up-to-date Buddhist teachings. Among them the most popular was the Hwaŏm (Huayan in Chinese) sect based on the *Avatamsaka* or *Flower Garland Sutra*, brought back by the monk Ŭisang (625–702). Ŭisang had studied in China and wrote a famous exposition of the creed in 661 that became the foundation for the textual wing of Buddhism in Korea. Hwaŏm's main doctrine was that all noumena (dharmas, or ideas in the mind) and all phenomena (objects of sense experience) were mutually interrelated and yet transitory and unreal. If one could only realize this, it would be possible to free oneself from the desire for wealth, power, and sex that kept one bound to the world of suffering.

Ŭisang's contemporary, the monk Wŏnhyo (617–686), founded the Dharma-nature (Pŏpsŏng) sect. He traveled to Tang in 650 and influenced the Tang monk Fazang and the Chinese Flower Garland sect. He struggled to bring all sects together in ecumenical unity to avoid the divisiveness that had developed in

BIOGRAPHY   Kangsu, the Scribe

In the seventh century, True Bone aristocrats were more likely to be warriors than scholars, and knowledge of the Chinese classics was still a rare and valuable skill, in strong demand by the government for both interstate relations and internal administration. Men like Kangsu (d. 692) responded to this need and acquired facility in Chinese. Kangsu was born into a family of lower aristocratic rank (that is, not True Bones). According to his biography, once he learned to read, his father asked him whether he would study the way of the Buddha or that of Confucius, and he replied. "I have heard that Buddhism is a teaching that does not concern this world. Since I am a man of this world, how could I study Buddhism's path? I wish to study the way of Confucius."

Kangsu took seriously the Confucian principles he read about. When at twenty his parents wanted to marry him to the daughter of a respected local family, he refused on the grounds that he was already married, having had a child by a woman from a local metalworking family. His father was shocked at the idea of marrying someone of such low birth, but Kangsu cited Confucian principles of fidelity and indifference to wealth and rank. (He did not seem to worry, however, about Confucian teachings not to marry without parental approval or the services of a go-between.)

Kangsu's abilities to read and write Chinese helped him secure employment at court as a scribe. When an envoy from Tang China arrived with an edict that had passages no one else could explicate, the king called on Kangsu to try, and he was able to explain it on the spot. His performance was so impressive that the king also had him write the reply. The next king gave him credit for preserving friendly relations with neighboring states through his correspondence. When Kangsu died, the king paid his funeral expenses. His widow refused offers of government assistance, we are told, and returned to her native place.

China. Wŏnhyo spread the Buddhist message to the people of the lowest status to alleviate their suffering. Even if they did not have the means to pursue esoteric knowledge and meditation, they could appeal to the panoply of Buddhist images for solace and support against the hardships of life.

Some Silla monks journeyed beyond China. Kyech'o (ca. 700–ca. 780) wrote an account of his pilgrimage to India. He began his journey by sea from south China in 723, crossed India from east to west, visiting major Buddhist pilgrimage sites, then traveled north through Kashmir to return to China via Central Asian cities such as Kucha. After he reached Chang'an in early 728, he studied with the Indian missionary and Tantric master Vajrabodhi.

The Sŏn or meditation sect of Buddhism (Chan in Chinese, Zen in Japanese) is said to have been introduced by the monk Pŏmnang after his return from China in the mid-seventh century. The sect downplayed textual or scriptural learning and stressed gaining insight through meditation. By the ninth century, nine mountain sects of Sŏn had been established. The Silla Sŏn sect followed the gradual enlightenment approach of the Chinese Northern school until the monk Toŭi introduced the sudden enlightenment doctrine of the Chinese Southern school. Despite the division into competing schools, Buddhism was a unifying force in Korean culture. It contributed to self-effacing and tolerant ideals that transcended the national narrowness.

Buddhist teachings also inspired much of the painting and sculpture of this period. (See **Material Culture: Sŏkkuran Temple**.) Other evidence of the wealth and luxury of the Silla elite is found in tombs, which include magnificent crowns, earrings, necklaces, bracelets, belts, and other gold paraphernalia. The dazzling gold crowns of Silla kings were one sign of the splendor of the capital (and remarkably similar to objects found in Xianbei sites in north China). (See Color Plate 10.)

Poetry was a favorite pastime of the Silla elite from early times. Two of the few early poems remaining were addressed to a turtle, perhaps a spirit or totem, warning it to remain hidden. In other poems, an author laments the neglect of his master, a cuckolded husband is shocked when he returns home to

MATERIAL CULTURE

Sŏkkuram Buddhist Temple

The rock-cut temple of Sŏkkuram near Kyŏngju is one of the greatest monuments of Buddhist art in East Asia. It was built in the late eighth century on a hilltop overlooking the Sea of Japan. One of its purposes was to protect the area from marauding pirates.

Although inspired by the cave temples of Central Asia and China, this temple was not carved from a rock face, but rather constructed much like a stone-lined tomb. One enters through a corridor leading into a circular main hall. In the center is a seated Sakyamuni Buddha carved from a solid block of granite. On the surrounding walls are larger-than-life bas-reliefs of arhats (disciples of the Buddha) and bodhisattvas. Above them in niches are seated Buddhas. All the carvings are refined examples of the sculptor's art.

This spatial organization with a freestanding central figure was connected to Buddhist ritual practice. The Buddhist devotee would walk around the statue of Sakyamuni from left to right as part of his devotion.

Diagram of the Layout of the Sŏkkuram Buddhist Temple.

Central Image. The buddha seated on a lotus pedestal, carved from a single block of granite, is about eleven feet tall. *(Stock Connection/Fotosearch)*

find two pairs of legs in his bed, and a monk prays to the Amida Buddha that he might be reborn in the Pure Land. In the poem below, Master Wŏlmyŏng laments the end of autumn (written ca. 763 c.e.):

> We know not where we go,
> Leaves blown, scattered,
> Though fallen from the same tree,
> By the first winds of autumn.[2]

---

2. Peter Lee, *Korean Literature: Topics and Themes*, p. 9.

PARHAE (698–926)

Unified Silla's neighbor to the north and main rival was the state of Parhae (Bohai in Chinese), which proudly proclaimed itself heir to the Koguryŏ state. After the fall of Koguryŏ, one of its generals, Tae Choyŏng, described as a Malgal, led a group of Malgal back to a thinly inhabited area in central Manchuria where they lived along with several other ethnic groups. After he defeated pursuing Tang forces and

Bronze Statue of the Maitreya Buddha. Made in the early seventh century, this gilt bronze figure, 93 centimeters tall, portrays the buddha of the future as serene and graceful. *(National Museum of Korea, Seoul, Korea)*

moved his people eastward to near the modern Russian Maritime Province in Siberia, Tae established a state with about four hundred thousand people. Parhae territory extended south of the Sungari River and included the present Maritime Province in Siberia and about the northern third of the Korean peninsula. The southernmost of its five capitals was in the territory of modern Korea.

Should Parhae be viewed as Korean, since its founder and many of its subjects had been subjects of Koguryŏ? Or should it be viewed as an Inner Asian state, more like the Xianbei, Khitan, Jurchen, and later the Manchus who expanded from bases in southern Manchuria, since its founder was a Malgal? The Malgal people seem to have been a seminomadic group widely dispersed across Manchuria, northeast Korea, and southeast Siberia. Ethnicity in this region had long been fluid as tribes defeated each other, made alliances, or forced others into slavery. Many of Koguryŏ's subjects scattered with its fall, some south to Paekche or Silla, others west to Tang territory. Moreover, there is no reason to think that Koguryŏ's subjects were all of a single ethnic group (and that group indisputably "Korean"). Still, Parhae is part of Korean history in two distinct ways: it was the main enemy of Silla, which was indisputably Korean, and it ruled over land that today is part of Korea. Treating it as part of Korean history is much like treating the Xiongnu and Mongols as part of Chinese history.

About half of the 211 Parhae leaders known to history were members of the Tae family, and most of the rest were from the Ko (Gao in Chinese) family, which meant they could have been relatives of the Koguryŏ royal house, Chinese, or another ethnic group such as Xianbei. Other ethnic groups in the population were Wuji, Khitan, and Turks. Parhae's culture owed much to both Koguryŏ and Tang, not to mention Inner Asian traditions. Its capital in northern Manchuria (modern Heilongjiang province), like that of Silla (and Nara and Heian in Japan), was laid out in a grid on the model of Tang Chang'an. The structure of its government was also indebted to Tang models. The cultural artifacts and wall paintings of Parhae tombs indicate a continuation of Koguryŏ styles in some regards, but most pictures of formal dress appear closer to Tang styles.

The Tang court adopted a conciliatory policy toward Parhae in 705 to prevent it from allying with the Turks, but did not want Parhae to become so strong that it threatened Tang. Parhae relations with Tang turned sour in 719 when it abandoned the Tang calendar. When Emperor Xuanzong of Tang challenged Parhae in 726 by granting a title to the chief of the Amur River Malgal, a tribe that resisted Parhae rule, the Parhae king concluded a defensive alliance with Japan and in 732 attacked Tang territory on the Shandong peninsula. Silla assisted the Chinese by attacking Parhae territory in northeast

Korea in 733, but that expedition failed miserably and fouled Silla's relations with Parhae for three decades. Parhae and Japan maintained strong relations, however, and exchanged several dozen diplomatic missions. At the same time, Parhae sent many students to Chang'an to study. The Tang instituted parity between Silla and Parhae in the numbers of students allowed to take the guest examinations.

For two centuries, Parhae, although often at odds with Silla, also served as a buffer for it, separating it from Tang China and also from Inner Asian nomadic forces such as the Turks. Parhae was eventually undermined by rebellions of the Khitans, who captured its last capital in 926. The Manchuria region continued to be multiethnic, and some evidence suggests that the Jurchens, who overthrew the Khitans two centuries later, may have been descended from the Malgal tribes.

SUMMARY

How different was Korea in the early tenth century compared to the beginning of the historical period? Warrior aristocracies still could check the power of kings, but change was dramatic in many other regards. For many centuries, the Korean peninsula had been connected to Manchuria by tribes or states that straddled the Yalu River. With the fall of Parhae in 926, this phase of Korean history was brought to an end. At the same time, in the Korean peninsula itself, many different groups had been melded into a much more unified state with a stronger cultural identity. The aristocracies of many different polities had been amalgamated and if anything strengthened. Buddhism had gained tremendously in importance. Monasteries had become important institutions, and monks were among the most learned in society. With Buddhism had come many other elements of Chinese culture, including the use of the Chinese script, Confucian and Daoist teachings, and Chinese secular learning and literature. Histories had been written, giving Korea a story of its past, complete with heroes and villains. Korea had learned how to coexist with both strong and weak states in China as well as strong and weak Inner Asian powers in Manchuria. Korea had resisted repeated Sui and Tang attempts at conquest, but was ready to learn from Tang and benefit from allying with it. Because all writing was done in Chinese and education involved reading many Chinese books, higher culture had become closely linked to Chinese culture. Place names and family names were adapted to Chinese convention—the single syllable names Kim, Pak, Yi, Ch'oe, Wang, and so on—undoubtedly reflecting adaptation to writing in Chinese.

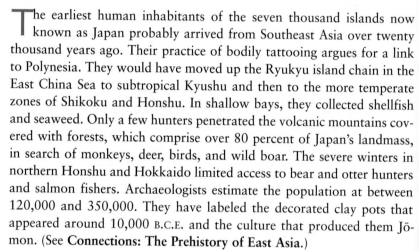

Early State and Society in Japan (to 794)

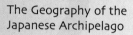

The earliest human inhabitants of the seven thousand islands now known as Japan probably arrived from Southeast Asia over twenty thousand years ago. Their practice of bodily tattooing argues for a link to Polynesia. They would have moved up the Ryukyu island chain in the East China Sea to subtropical Kyushu and then to the more temperate zones of Shikoku and Honshu. In shallow bays, they collected shellfish and seaweed. Only a few hunters penetrated the volcanic mountains covered with forests, which comprise over 80 percent of Japan's landmass, in search of monkeys, deer, birds, and wild boar. The severe winters in northern Honshu and Hokkaido limited access to bear and otter hunters and salmon fishers. Archaeologists estimate the population at between 120,000 and 350,000. They have labeled the decorated clay pots that appeared around 10,000 B.C.E. and the culture that produced them Jōmon. (See **Connections: The Prehistory of East Asia**.)

Archaeologists once differentiated between Jōmon hunter-gatherers and the agriculturally based Yayoi, but recently excavated evidence suggests that rice growing may have begun as early as 900 B.C.E. Starting around 500 B.C.E., the Jōmon had to compete with new arrivals from northeast Asia who settled in communities to grow rice and brought new techniques of metallurgy. Jōmon people disappeared from western Honshu around 200 B.C.E., replaced by Yayoi culture that maintained prolonged contact with the continent. By the end of the Yayoi era in approximately 300 C.E., the population had risen to between 1.5 and 4.5 million. Settled agriculture demanded complex social organization and generated a surplus that could be used to differentiate soldiers, rulers, artisans, and priests from full-time cultivators. Role specialization led to hereditary social classes and inequality.

Archaeologists and historians debate the stages in the process of state formation. What role did connections from the continent play? Where were the early states located, what kind of leadership did they have, and how did they expand and coalesce? What kind of impact did Chinese civilization have on elite life, and how did the introduction of Buddhism change religious beliefs and practices?

THE GEOGRAPHY OF THE JAPANESE ARCHIPELAGO

Geographic features shaped the development of Japanese civilization. The earliest centers of human habitation arose on the fertile plains of southwestern Japan, bordering on the relatively placid Inland Sea that later facilitated communications and trade. Protected by a spine of mountains, the Inland Sea basin usually enjoys mild winters, monsoon rains at the height of the growing season, and hot, humid days before the harvests. Later in the fall, typhoons provide moisture for winter crops. Occasionally the monsoon does not arrive, or typhoons come too early and devastate nearly ripe crops.

Other regions suffer more extreme conditions. Winter winds from Siberia blow across the Japan Sea, depositing snow 6 feet or deeper on the plains and mountains that face it. Melted snow cascades down short, fast-flowing streams. Although alluvial deltas acquired the fine soil necessary for agriculture, floods carry rocks and other debris down the mountains to damage fields. Rapids make navigating rivers treacherous, and only a few could support rafts and small boats for any distance. River mouths and innumerable small bays provide harbor for coastal vessels manned by fishers, smugglers, or pirates. Even whalers tended to stick close to shore.

The islands of what is now called Japan lost their land bridge to the Asian continent some fifteen thousand years ago, but the sea continued to permit access. Although visitors from across the vast Pacific had to wait until the sixteenth century, contact with Asia came via the Tsushima Strait, across the Japan Sea, and down the Kamchatka Peninsula, the Kurile islands, and Sakhalin to Hokkaido. Each route had its own character. The northern route brought pelts and marine products; the Tsushima Straits provided a bridge for agriculture and civilization. (See Map 7.1.)

EARLY KINGSHIP IN LATE YAYOI (ca. 100–350)

The earliest written records of rule are found in Chinese sources. The Han court received emissaries from small kingdoms, probably in Kyushu, in 57 and 107 C.E.. In 239, a queen called Himiko sent a tribute mission to the kingdom of Wei. She dominated an alliance of thirty chieftains and lived in a palace fortified by walls with watchtowers and guardhouses. She rarely appeared in public; instead, her brother, the only person to see her except for servants, conveyed her commands and prophecies to the people outside the gates. Her subjects trembled before her because they believed she had the power to communicate directly with the gods. When she died, over one hundred attendants of both sexes were buried with her in a giant tomb. Archaeologists debate whether her kingdom of Yamatai existed in Kyushu or in western Japan near present-day Kyoto. Equally problematic is the relationship between brother and sister. Should Himiko be seen not as a queen but as a priestess or shaman whose brother did the work of rule?

During this time, rulers frequently came in male-female pairs. As on the Korean peninsula, kinship was reckoned bilaterally. Important men had four or five wives. Children stayed with their mothers for an indefinite period before moving in with their fathers, and they relied on both their mothers' and fathers' kin for aid and support. Husbands and wives maintained their own establishments, held property separately, and decided how to divide it among their heirs independently. The lack of clear-cut rules governing inheritance and the privileges accruing to the family head made succession disputes inevitable.

Chinese sources note that warfare was endemic. We can suppose that Himiko sent her tribute mission to China to acquire advanced military technology and the prestige of validation by the Wei court. After her death, the chieftains who had supported her fought among themselves until they agreed on a young girl to become queen. The remains of fortified hamlets perched high above agricultural plains, and the discovery of a formidable array of weaponry indicates that the struggle for paramountcy was more military than political. There must have been several confederacies of chieftains, of whom the Chinese knew but one.

Map 7.1   **Islands of Japan**

Pseudo-kinship relations structured hamlet life. Each had a chieftain in charge of communication with the gods and relations with the outside world. Members of the chieftain's extended family all claimed descent from a common ancestor, no matter how distant. Their economic foundation rested on dependents who performed the work of cultivation, weaving, pottery, and fishing. When one hamlet fought another, warriors seized goods and turned the vanquished into slaves. Slaves could be traded between houses as a form of currency; tribute missions sometimes carried slaves to China.

The first Japanese historians writing five centuries later struggled to fit early Japanese rulers such as Himiko into a single patrilineage. They claimed that Japan had but one ruling family descended from the sun goddess, Amaterasu, who decreed that her descendant Jimmu was to rule over the land. Aided by his divine ancestress, Jimmu led an expedition eastward to Yamato on the Kinai plain. The histories incorporate a number of myth cycles, suggesting that in addition to the Yamato line that claimed the sun goddess as its tutelary deity, other lineages had deities who at one time had rivaled Amaterasu in importance. Historians today have identified at least four breaks in the Yamato line. When the current emperor recently acknowledged a special feeling of closeness with the Korean people because the mother of his ancestor Kanmu (736–806) was Korean, he alluded to a connection with the Korean peninsula that modern historians have only recently appreciated.

The Korea Connection

Twentieth-century Japanese nationalists preferred to stress the sinitic origins of the cultural artifacts from agriculture to written language that came from the Asian continent, rather than the role by people on the Korean peninsula who modified and transmitted them. Chinese military expansion pushed refugees into the peninsula now known as Korea. Conflicts between polities there, some of which allied with polities in Japan, sent migrants across the Tsushima Strait in three waves that began in the early fifth century and ended in the seventh. Seafarers plied the coasts of Korea and Japan, sometimes launching pirate raids into the interior. The immigrants first settled along the western coast of Honshu and the northern end of Kyushu, then accepted the Yamato ruler's invitation to colonize the Kinai heartland. Historians debate whether the immigrants became assimilated into the indigenous population or whether they took over.

The immigrants brought an Altaic language from northeast Asia that is the ancestor of modern Japanese. In addition to rice, they brought bronze bells, swords, and halberds for rituals as well as wheel-thrown, kiln-fired pottery and stoves. The crossbow and iron used for swords, armor, helmets, and plows originated on the Korean peninsula. Site of the capital from 710 to 784, Nara is a Korean word meaning "country." The Jōmon people had used horses as beasts of burden; the immigrants had bridles, saddles, and stirrups for warriors to ride them into battle. Immigrants irrigated their fields and brought stone-fitting technology used to build walls and burial chambers in tombs. Goldsmiths crafted crowns and jewelry for rulers; metal casters worked bronze. The first scribes and accountants came from the peninsula before 400. The Hata lineage settled in what is now a western suburb of Kyoto. It introduced sericulture and silk weaving; it founded a number of temples, among them Kōryūji, which still treasures a sixth-century statue of Maitreya, the Buddha of the future. Items that originated in China but were imported through the peninsula included bronze mirrors, ornaments, and coins.

The immigrants brought techniques of rule that contributed to the process of state building in the Japanese islands. The first system of court titles bore a striking similarity to the Silla bone rank system. Chieftains acquired surnames that they could then use to denote aristocratic status. Territorial divisions from the district (Korean in origin) to the province (Chinese in origin) achieved an administrative cast. Peninsular burial mounds and their murals provided the model for the giant tumuli that characterized the fifth to seventh centuries. The peninsular experience with Chinese-style civil and criminal law codes foreshadowed the Japanese adoption in the seventh century. Buddhism as taught in Paekche and Silla had a lasting impact on Japanese society and politics.

Ancient Religion

In Himiko's time, religious beliefs held society together. One of her tasks was to perform rituals that propitiated the deities, leading to the argument that politics and religion in ancient Japan were one and the same. When chieftains had to make decisions, they baked deer bones in a fire and examined the cracks to determine what the future might bring. They supervised the agricultural calendar, performed fertility rites, and prayed for victory in war. Female shamans warded off misfortune and communicated with the deities. Because rituals had to be performed by men and women together, priestesses were idealized as sisters helped by brothers. Women and men held secular and sacred authority.

Early Japanese believed that important people became gods, and the gods ordered the conditions for their existence. Gods had created the natural world; gods vitalized mountains and rocks; gods constituted the energy that made rice grow. Human reproduction recapitulated and stimulated the deeds of the creator deities that brought life to the world. This kind of belief system is called animism because it assumes that spiritual forces animate even inanimate objects. The gods abhorred pollution, especially the pollution of death. The death of a chieftain required the destruction of his residence. By the late fourth century C.E., large tombs filled with ritual objects pacified an otherwise threatening departed spirit; moats and clay figurines (*haniwa*) marked the periphery. (See **Material Culture: Haniwa**.) Sacred texts from the seventh and eighth centuries connected gods and mortals, celebrated sex and procreation, and venerated the natural world. Myths propagated by the Yamato court personified the spiritual forces, giving them names, associating them with local lineages, and ranking them in a hierarchy of kinship with the sun goddess at the top. This system of beliefs is now called Shinto, a term created out of Chinese characters that means "the way of the gods."

Excavations of hamlet burial grounds and giant tumuli show that the early Japanese honored the dead by burying them with items they had used in life. Clothing, cosmetics, and pottery can be found with pots holding human bones. Equal numbers of men and women were buried one to a tomb that contained armor, swords, and arrowheads, considered valuable because they came from Korea. Since the heavy iron swords forged in Japan with ore from abroad were used less for fighting than for ceremony, they suggest a stratified society in which funeral practices reflected disparities in ranks. Between 425 and 500, the number of iron items buried in tombs multiplied, and the objects themselves became more standardized as political authority became increasingly centered in the Kinai region.

THE FORMATION OF A CENTERED POLITY (350–794)

Beginning about 350 C.E., rulers in the Yamato basin of the Kinai region began to consolidate their power. By the fifth century, they had organized the manufacture of iron implements and had taken control of their distribution. Warriors on horseback improved the speed at which armies could travel and the distances they could cover. Five kings sent tribute missions to China to gain Chinese confirmation of their hegemony and acquire the accouterments of kingship with which to entice the chieftains of other lineages into alliance. They provided military support to their ally Paekche against Koguryŏ. When Paekche fell, many of its best-educated and highly skilled supporters fled to Yamato. They brought with them political and administrative talents that the local rulers put to good use.

Yūryaku (late fifth century), the most notable of these early monarchs, placed immigrant and indigenous chieftains into a ranking system. Each chieftain was deemed a lineage head and received lavish gifts, such as mirrors from China, and permission to build grand tombs. The lineage received a hereditary title derived from Korean nomenclature that defined its position in a new court hierarchy. The chieftains claimed descent from a lineage deity or from a person who had a special relationship with the lineage deity. They acknowledged Yūryaku's suzerainty with tribute and family members sent to serve at his court in return for the right to administer and tax the territories he allotted them, often those they already controlled. Occupational groups that took responsibility for goods and services were also organized into lineages. One provided weapons and the men to use them; another supplied Yūryaku's kitchens; others performed the ritual work that earlier rulers such as Himiko had done themselves. As Yūryaku expanded his dominion, he balanced the territories bestowed on titled lineages with those reserved for the crown. Men appointed to administer crown lands did not have the hereditary powers of the lineage chieftains; they were dependent on the court.

Yūryaku also used marital alliances to bolster his legitimacy and extend his power. His senior consort came from the lineage of an earlier king. Chieftains contributed other consorts to gain status as royal relatives and to exert influence at court. Combined with the court ranking system and gift giving, these connections placed the king above his mightiest supporters in a hierarchy of wealth and privilege that served to distinguish them from untitled, unconnected commoners.

Yūryaku's successors built on and fought over the state he had created in southwestern Honshu and northern Kyushu. Within twenty-five years of his death, his line had been replaced following power struggles between royal relatives aided and abetted by disgruntled chieftains. Rulers in the sixth century defined the royal regalia as mirror, sword, and jewel and selected a princess to serve the royal family's tutelary deity at the sun goddess's shrine at Ise. By the middle of the 500s, the immigrant Soga lineage had entrenched itself as principal consort givers. In 592 a Soga niece named Suiko became head of the Yamato house on the death of her husband, her half-brother, and ruled until 628, the longest reign for the next twelve centuries. Her capital at Asuka is famous for Japan's first flowering of Buddhist art.

The China Connection

Between 592 and 756, the Yamato kings, male and female, transformed themselves from chieftains of confederacies into Chinese-style monarchs. The efforts to expand the functions and reach of the state arose in part in reaction to the resurgence of the Chinese empire under the Sui and Tang Dynasties. Kings also saw the need to overcome the violent factional and succession disputes that had weakened ties between center and periphery and led to regicide and the assassination of chief ministers. Suiko and Prince Shōtoku (574–622), her nephew and adviser, opened

MATERIAL CULTURE

Haniwa

Clay figurines from the fifth to seventh centuries illustrate how people lived in ancient Japan. Shamanesses wear swirling headdresses; shamans hold mirrors; a falconer lifts his hawk; warriors ride horses and carry bows and arrows; one musician plucks a zither, and another strikes a drum; a cultivator carries a hoe. Women balance jugs on their heads with babies on their backs. Sheep, deer, birds, monkeys, dogs, and rabbits abound. Trading ships carry goods between Japan and the continent. Figurines provide evidence that chieftains sat on chairs and slept in beds, customs that later died out.

Clay figurines and cylinders are called *haniwa*—literally "clay rings"—because the vast majority are hollow tubes standing 3 to 5 feet high. They are found outside the giant tumuli that dot the Japanese landscape from Kyushu to northern Japan, with most clustered in the Kinai region near Osaka and Nara. Why *haniwa* were placed outside rather than inside the tomb is a matter for speculation. According to *Nihon shoki*, they substituted for the chieftain's attendants. Archaeologists debate whether they served to demarcate the sacred space of the tomb and to protect the deceased, much like the stone sculptures of the twelve animal signs that encircled Silla Dynasty burial mounds, or whether they guarded the living against the dangerously powerful spirit of a deceased chieftain.

Haniwa. Haniwa stand 3 to 5 feet tall. The photo on the left depicts a female shaman with flat hat and necklace. As a priestess, she would have presided over the funeral of the tomb's inhabitant. The photo on the right shows a warrior with helmet, side curls, and armor. *(Left: Brooklyn Museum of Art, New York, USA/Gift of Mr. and Mrs. Stanley Marcus/The Bridgeman Art Library; Right: Christie's/Corbis)*

relations with the Sui Dynasty in China, paving the way for later study missions and the immersion of elite Japanese men in Chinese culture. They promoted Buddhism as much for its magical efficacy as for its religious teachings. They reorganized the court by instituting a ladder of twelve official ranks bestowed on individuals to correspond to Sui rather than Silla practice.

In the Seventeen Injunctions promulgated in 604, Prince Shōtoku announced a new ideology of rule based on Confucian and Buddhist thought. He put a new distance between the ruling Yamato line and all other lineages by proclaiming, "The Lord is Heaven, the vassal is earth." This relationship was to be expressed in ritual and governed by propriety: "Harmony is to be valued and an avoidance of wanton opposition to be honored." Ministers were to put public duties, their duty to the throne, above the private interests of lineage and self. Only the ruler was to levy taxes because "in a country there are not two lords; the people have not two masters."[1] Suiko and Shōtoku's successors continued these efforts to distinguish the monarch from his ministers and the court from commoners by drawing on the rituals and regulations of Chinese kingship.

The reform of 645, later heralded as marking the start of monarchical rule, incorporated continental culture in the midst of conflict. It followed a bloody coup in which Nakatomi no Kamatari, founder of the Fujiwara lineage, destroyed the Soga and purged Koreans from government. The court appointed provincial governors and abolished private land ownership. It instituted a population census, a centralized tax system, a legal code, and a civil service examination. It tried to curtail the ability of local magnates to harass the people and protected the right of women to remarry. It provided a municipal government for the capital. It inaugurated the use of Chinese-style era names, and as in China at the time, the names worked magic. Just as people changed their names to change their luck, so did era names change when they had lost their potency to ward off disaster. The Great Reform era called *Taika* (645–650) did so little to mitigate factional strife that it was changed to *Hakuchi* (White Pheasant, a lucky omen; 650–654). Monarchs had to rely on powerful lineages in implementing these reforms. The Fujiwara consolidated

Prince Shōtoku. Prince Shōtoku is the subject of innumerable posthumous portraits. Painted in the eighteenth century, the one shown here features him dressed in the courtly attire of eighth-century China. *(Private Collection, Paris/Dagli Orti/The Art Archive)*

their position by giving their daughters to rulers, a tradition they had some success in maintaining down to 1924.

The Fujiwara supported monarchs in promoting Chinese models for administration. Following the Jinshin civil war (671–672), Tenmu and his wife, Jitō, daughter of the previous monarch, eliminated collateral claimants to the throne in order to preserve it for their descendants. Tenmu reorganized the bureaucracy and filled it with men he had appointed rather than the former chieftains, now titled aristocrats. In 685 he prohibited the private possession of weapons. Through the creation of a conscript army based on Chinese models, the state was to have a monopoly on the use of force. Tenmu tried to abolish the aristocrats' private economic basis by experimenting with the state allocation of land. He enticed the new aristocrats to court to participate in grand ceremonies of state that drew on Buddhist and Chinese models; he also sent envoys to coordinate worship at the regional shrines for lineage tutelary deities. Jitō claimed the sun goddess as Tenmu's ancestor, thereby

1. W. G. Aston, trans., *Nihongi: Chronicles of Japan from the Earliest Times to A.D. 697* (London: Kegan, Paul, Trench, Trübner, 1896), 2:129–133.

projecting his dynasty into the mythic past and asserting divine status for the ruling family. When she became ruler, she was styled *tennō*, a combination of two Chinese characters meaning "heaven" and "monarch." This title fell into abeyance in the tenth century as monarchical power declined relative to that of ministers. Rulers were called "lord" (*shujō*) in life and "temple" (*in*) in death. Revived in 1841, *tennō* was officially translated into English as "emperor" in 1868.

Fixing the Capital at Nara

Jitō and her successors oversaw notable advances in state formation. Tenmu started construction on a Chinese-style palace and capital city at Fujiwara, which Jitō occupied in 694. It marked a decision to use architecture in bolstering the ruler's authority. No longer would palaces be destroyed on the death of a monarch or would the ruler's consorts enjoy separate residences. Three generations of rulers lived at Fujiwara before the capital moved to the more central location of Nara in 710, where it remained until 794. (See Map 7.2.) The eighth century is now called the Nara period. Modeled on the Tang capital at Chang'an (see Figure 5.1), Fujiwara and Nara were laid out on a grid with the palace centered at the north and facing south, because in Chinese cosmology, the ruler's place was fixed like the pole star. By dominating the capital, the ruler brought heaven to earth. The central boulevard divided the city into symmetrical halves just as the Chinese-style bureaucratic structure balanced the minister of the left with the minister of the right lest either one monopolize power that rightfully belonged to the ruler. The physical layout mirrored social relations. Ministers in the Chinese-style bureaucracy took up residence in the capital on assigned building lots in accordance with their rank. Aristocrats and rulers vied in building Buddhist temples. District officials were encouraged to use coins for traveling expenses and land sales. In line with Chinese models and to learn about the realm in order to control it, monarchs had provincial gazetteers compiled that described local customs, places and their deities, specialties, and resources.

During Jitō's reign, officials started to compile official histories and create a set of written administrative statutes and law codes. Modified and expanded during successive reigns, this system became known as the regime of codes. The penal code set out punishments for rebels and robbers as well as for

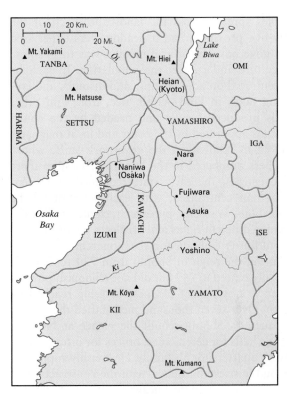

Map 7.2   **Kinai Area of Japan**

breaching the taboos that conferred sacral status on the king. The administrative code specified relations between the ruler and aristocrats in an effort to freeze the status quo and brought the ruler's jurisdiction down to the level of district magnates. It established political and religious hierarchies of public offices, temples, and shrines that reached from the center to the provinces. Just as district offices fell under the jurisdiction of administrators at the capital, so too were provincial temples subordinated to temple headquarters. The Yamato line's shrines at Ise and Nara ranked above lineage shrines in the provinces. Chief priests appointed by the ruler supervised the conduct of monks and nuns and coordinated ritual, while ministers of state ran the bureaucracy.

The codes also dealt extensively with land rights. All land belonged to the ruler, to be allotted to cultivators, except in the case of new fields. Opening them to cultivation was such an expensive undertaking that the person responsible, whether an individual or a temple, received permanent ownership.

The promulgation of these codes had long-lasting effects. Even chieftains resident in the provinces competed for official appointments and titles as local magnates. County, district, and provincial offices and temples spread across the landscape. Each of the sixty-five provinces had a headquarters supervised by a governor. His official mission was to promote agriculture and register the population. In fact, he concentrated on adjudicating land disputes and collecting taxes in kind—cloth, rice, iron, and other goods produced locally and needed by the court. Officials appointed by the court and local magnates worked in tandem on the governor's staff, whose members numbered in the hundreds. Despite these achievements, the early state remained more centered than centralized, with each segment of the population—aristocrat, bureaucrat, cleric, cultivator—claiming different rights and privileges relative to central authority embodied in the monarch.

During the reign of Shōmu from 724 to 756 (he officially retired in 749 but did not relinquish power), the ancient system of Japanese kingship reached its zenith. Over seven thousand men staffed the central bureaucracy. Shōmu rebuilt the palace at Nara to include halls for ceremonies, offices for officials, and private quarters for his family. He lavishly supported the Buddhist establishment with the construction of Tōdaiji as the Yamato lineage temple. It contained the world's largest bronze Buddhist statue. Monks came from China and Champa (Vietnam) for the inauguration ceremony. Shōmu sent armies to expand his sway across the Japanese islands and used diplomatic ritual to assert Japan's precedence over Korea.

Shōmu's successors had to deal with the consequences of his success. As power became more centered at the court, struggles for status and influence intensified. Except for a few families that enjoyed adequate access to economic resources, most aristocrats lived precariously close to poverty. Restive local magnates disobeyed directives and rebelled against the center, as did cultivators unhappy at tax collection efforts. Officials at the county and district levels tried to preserve their autonomy while accepting court rank and office. Despite a history of female monarchs, the spread of Confucian philosophy justified the aristocrats' resentment at being ruled by a woman—Shōmu's daughter, who reigned twice, first as Kōken (r. 749–758) and then as Shōtoku (r. 764–770). Deposed in a palace coup, Shōtoku was the last female monarch until 1630. Conflict between the ruler and the aristocratic bureaucracy was repeated in the 780s when two retired monarchs sponsored factional intrigue. Buddhist priests, collateral lines of Fujiwara, and other lineages competed for influence, while disgruntled members of the ruling family plotted against

their chief. A decrease in tax revenues forced rulers to scale back building projects and reduce the size of ceremonies. In 794, frustrated at the endless demands for favor that bedeviled him in Nara, the ruler Kanmu moved the capital to Heiankyō. There it was to remain until 1868.

The Conquest of Emishi and Hayato

In the early eighth century, aristocrats developed a sense of a Japanese ethnic identity that excluded people beyond the court's control. Many inhabitants in the northeast still practiced late Jōmon-style slash-and-burn agriculture. Since being Japanese was associated with rice-based settled communities, they were deemed barbarians (*Emishi*). The court encouraged the spread of settlements ever farther north, sent emissaries to set up district offices and collect taxes, and dispatched military expeditions to remove or enslave the *Emishi*. By 725, the first year of Shōmu's reign, these expeditions had pacified the region up to today's Sendai. Subsequent waves of soldiers and settlers spread agricultural settlements as far as Morioka.

Shōmu also expanded Yamato rule in Kyushu. In 740 the exiled Fujiwara Hirotsugu raised an army of ten thousand conscript troops against the throne. He gained the support of some district chiefs and members of the Hayato minority from southern Kyushu who, like the *Emishi*, resisted the civilization offered by the Yamato rulers. He even made overtures to Silla in search of allies. According to the official history, *Nihon shoki*, Shōmu dispatched an army of seventeen thousand, the largest royal army raised in the eighth century. Within two months, it had scattered the rebel army and executed Hirotsugu. The Hayato had no choice but to submit. The immigration of people from the Korean peninsula and the development of a stratified state in the Kinai basin divided the Japanese islands into three cultural and ethnic zones. By the end of Shōmu's reign, the central zone centered on Nara had squeezed the southern zone onto the Ryukyu island chain, while the northern zone, which extended up through Hokkaido, was shrinking on Honshu.

The Introduction of Buddhism

Buddhism played a major role in the development of the early Japanese state. First sponsored by the Soga and other immigrants from Paekche, it had to overcome opposition by Shinto ritualists before receiving official government support in 587. Enhanced by scribes, metallurgists, painters, and other artisans, it became the faith of rulers in a symbiotic relationship that strengthened both. Buddhism had a rich textual tradition; its monks paraded in majestic processions and held thunderous sutra recitations. From Paekche rulers the Japanese learned that worshipping the Buddha would bring their realm the protection of the Four Guardian Kings of the Buddhist law. In the Seventeen Injunctions, Prince Shōtoku urged the court to revere the Buddha, Buddhist law, and the monastic order. Tenmu and Jitō recognized the value of Buddhism in providing faith in a universal deity at the same time that they sent offerings to the Ise shrine of the sun goddess and regional shrines and read omens to divine heaven's will. By asserting their leadership in all dimensions of the religious realm, they sought to bolster their authority in secular affairs.

Tenmu and Jitō used Buddhism's resources to spread their rule across Japan. They built temples in the capital and provinces and used them as storehouses for population and tax records. They oversaw the copying of sutras, held Buddhist ceremonies, and performed Buddhist purificatory rituals. By restricting hunting, fishing, and the eating of meat, they promoted Buddhist beliefs that valued the lives of all sentient beings. The number of monks and nuns increased, their behavior minutely regulated. During Tenmu and Jitō's reigns, Buddhism became a core component of courtly life and practice.

Shōmu did even more to promote Buddhism and harness its power to the court. In line with the ideology of his day that deemed the natural order a reflection of the social order, he saw in natural disasters and rebellion his own lack of virtue. To compensate, he ordered sutra readings at temples, austerities such as cold-water baths at Shinto shrines, and the construction of new buildings. Following the Hayato rebellion in 741, he ordered each province to build a seven-storied pagoda, a guardian temple, and a nunnery and to provide adequate rice land to support the monks and nuns. In a thanksgiving service for his victory, he presented brocade, prayers, and Buddhist sutra readings to the shrine for Hachiman, the god of war. The giant Buddhist statue at Tōdaiji was cast in the image of Vairocana, the cosmic Buddha who encompasses the thousands of Buddhas and millions of enlightened beings just as Shōmu saw himself as ruling over all aristocrats and commoners. It was enshrined in a hall larger than the royal palace. The

temple complex contained Japan's first ordination platform as well as libraries and schools. There, monks translated texts and sutras for the so-called Six Sects. Rather than go to Tang China or Silla Korea, Japanese monks could now study and receive licenses at Tōdaiji under kingly sponsorship and supervision. After Shōmu passed the throne to his daughter, he established the precedent for abdicated rulers to enter the Buddhist priesthood.

Shōmu saw Buddhism primarily as a state religion, leaving it to monks and nuns such as Gyōki to proselytize among the populace. Through his sermons, Gyōki, the descendant of an immigrant Confucian scholar, propagated the Buddhist notions of causality and retribution and the humanistic promise that following the way of the universal Buddha can bring enlightenment to any person at any time or place. His followers built irrigation works, roads, bridges, and inns for commoners delivering tax payments to the capital, a material demonstration that the Buddhist law can benefit everyone, not just kings and aristocrats. In 717 the government accused Gyōki of violating the regulations that restricted nuns and monks to monasteries, of collecting an inordinate amount in alms, and of confusing the masses by claiming the power to heal, cast spells, and tell fortunes. Gyōki ignored the accusations, and other monks and nuns followed his example of good works and public preaching. The government then tried to co-opt his appeal. In 741, Gyōki received an official appointment to supervise the building of a bridge near the capital. In this way, the government acknowledged that he was indeed the bodhisattva his followers claimed him to be and brought belief in the saving power of the Buddha into line with official policy.

By the eighth century, Buddhism had become so naturalized in Japan that it had started to blend with native beliefs. Mountain ascetics joined the ancient belief in the sacrality of mountains with esoteric forms of Buddhism that emphasized occult practices. They promised to heal the sick and performed rituals to eliminate pollution and evil. The Mahayana Buddhism that entered Japan offered numerous paths to salvation through the pantheon of Buddhas and bodhisattvas (see **Connections: Buddhism in India and Its Spread Along the Silk Road**). Because the Buddha appeared in so many guises, perhaps he had also appeared as local deities. In what would later be known as Ryōbu Shintō, the deities received Buddhist names. Although an edict from 764 placed Buddhism above Shinto, the reverse was often the case.

DOCUMENTS
Poems from *Nihon shoki* and *Man'yōshū*

Compiled in the early eighth century, these documents include poems first composed centuries before. Here we see depicted fifth- to seventh-century rulers in the process of consolidating power by performing rituals to take possession of the land through viewing and naming, building magnificent palaces, making excursions, and planning for eternity. Even poems expressing personal feelings had a public dimension because the poet's hope for political advancement explains the poem's creation.

6th year [462 C.E.], Spring, 2nd month, 4th day. The ruler [Yūryaku] made an excursion to the small moor of Hatsuse. There, viewing the aspect of the hills and moors, in an outburst of feeling, he made a song, saying:

> The mountain of Hatsuse
> Of the hidden country
> Is a mountain
> Standing beautifully,
> Is a mountain
> Projecting beautifully
> The mountain of Hatsuse
> Of the hidden country
> Is truly lovely,
> Is truly lovely.

Thereupon he gave a name to the small moor, and called it Michi no Ono.

Poems by Kakinomoto Hitomaro at the time of the procession [by the divine monarch Jitō] to the palace at Yoshino.

> Many are the lands under heaven
> And the sway of our Lord,
> Sovereign of the earth's eight corners,
> But among them her heart

Finds Yoshino good
For its crystal riverland
Among the mountains,
And on the blossom-strewn
Fields of Akitsu
She drives the firm pillars of her palace
And so the courtiers of the great palace,
Its ramparts thick with stone,
Line their boats
To cross the morning river,
Race their boats
Across the evening river.
Like this river
Never ending,
Like these mountains
Commanding ever greater heights,
The palace by the surging rapids—
Though I gaze on it, I do not tire.

Envoy
Like the eternal moss
Slick by the Yoshino river
On which I do not tire to gaze,
May I never cease to return
And gaze on it again.

Our lord
Who rules in peace,

In the countryside, the style of worshipping the Buddha reflected beliefs associated with Shinto regarding the importance of fertility and worldly benefits rather than eliminating worldly attachments to achieve enlightenment. In place of large tombs surrounded by *haniwa*, provincial chieftains built Buddhist temples to hold memorial services for the dead and replicate the benefits they hoped to acquire when propitiating the deities: good harvests, health, prosperity, and progeny. People learned that deities and Buddhas supported each other, and both needed festivals and ceremonies. Important Shinto shrines acquired Buddhist temples so that the deities might hear sutra recitations, and deities protected Buddhist temples. In this way, particular deities (*kami*) and the universal Buddha entered into an enduring symbiotic relationship.

Elite Culture

The Yamato court attracted followers with its access to Chinese elite culture, including a written language, Daoism, Confucianism, the literary arts, sculpture

A very god,
Manifests her divine will
And raises towering halls
Above the Yoshino riverland
Where waters surge,
And climbs to the top
To view the land.
On the mountains
Folding upward around her
Like a sheer hedge of green
The mountain gods present their
    offerings.

They bring her blossoms in springtime
To decorate her hair
And, when autumn comes,
They garland her with yellow leaves
And the gods of the river
That runs alongside the mountains
Make offerings for her royal feast.

They send cormorants forth
Over the upper shoals,
They cast dipper nets
Across the lower shoals,
Mountain and river
Draw together to serve her—
A god's reign indeed!

A very god
Whom mountain and river
Draw together to serve,
She sets her boat to sail
Over pools where waters surge.

At Cape Kara
On the sea of Iwami,
Where the vines
Crawl on the rocks,
Rockweed of the deep
Grows on the reefs
And sleek seaweed
Grows on the desolate shore.
As deeply do I
Think of my wife
Who swayed toward me in sleep
Like the lithe seaweed.
Yet few were the nights
We had slept together
Before we parted
Like crawling vines uncurled.
And so I look back,
Still thinking of her
With painful heart,
This clench of inner flesh,
But in the storm
Of fallen scarlet leaves
On Mount Watari,
Crossed as on
A great ship,
I cannot make out the sleeves
She waves in farewell. . . .
And even I
Who thought I was a brave man
Find the sleeves of my well-worn robe
Drenched with tears.

Poem by Kakinomoto Hitomaro when he parted from his wife in the land of Iwami and came up to the capital.

Source: Gary L. Ebersole, *Ritual Poetry and the Politics of Death in Early Japan* (Princeton, N.J.: Princeton University Press, 1989), pp. 27, 30–32, 50–52, modified.

(particularly Buddhist icons), painting, and music. The Chinese writing system arrived in Japan at the end of the Yayoi period, in the late fourth century, brought by immigrants from the Korean peninsula who served as a closed occupational group of scribes for the Yamato court. They left traces of their work in sword inscriptions. Not until the unification of China under the Sui and the introduction of Buddhism did Japanese rulers realize the importance of literacy. Pilgrims to China brought back quantities of Buddhist sutras and Chinese books. In addition to

his Seventeen Injunctions of 604, Prince Shōtoku sponsored the writing of a history of Japan based on Chinese models. It later disappeared. The earliest examples of Japanese writing Chinese come from over 150,000 wooden tablets similar to those found in Korea, the vast majority dating from the seventh and eighth centuries. Inscribed on the tablets were official documents, including directives to and reports by local officials, summonses, transit passes, and labels attached to tax goods. They prove that women joined men as conscripts on public works projects.

After the wooden tablets came Japan's earliest extant histories. The *Kojiki* (Record of Ancient Matters) of 712 and *Nihon shoki* (Chronicles of Japan) completed in 720 relate histories of Japan from the creation of the cosmos to the establishment of the centered state in the seventh century. *Kojiki*, which details the age of the gods, can be read as an attempt by the Yamato court to justify its preeminence over other lineages. *Nihon shoki* opens with a passage that draws on Chinese yin-yang theory and cosmology. It narrates the history of the Yamato rulers in a straight line of descent from the sun goddess. Both histories exaggerate the antiquity of the early Japanese state and its control over local political arrangements.

Poetry had magical properties in the eyes of ancient Japanese. It both summoned and soothed the gods, and the words had spirits of their own. The earliest extant poetry collection, the *Kaifūsō* (Fond Recollections of Poetry), compiled in 751, contains the biographies of Japanese poets who wrote in Chinese. It is overshadowed by the *Man'yōshū* (Collection of Ten Thousand Leaves) compiled in 759, the first anthology of Japanese verse. (See **Documents: Poems from *Nihon shoki* and *Man'yōshū*.**) Its poems attested to the process of state building. They expressed the emotions of courtiers and frontier guards who forsook family and homeland to serve their monarch. They lamented the death of lovers as well as rulers in an intersection of personal feeling and the public realm.

Etiquette, ceremony, dance, and music introduced from China transformed provincial chieftains into court aristocrats. Played on flutes and stringed instruments punctuated by gongs and drums, continental music is said to have entered Japan when the king of Silla sent eighty musicians to attend funeral services for King Ingyō in 453. Stately dance performed by men wearing masks came from Silla in 612. The Court Music Bureau established in 702 and staffed chiefly by immigrants had charge of performing a repertoire of Chinese and Korean music and dance called elegant music (*gagaku*) at court ceremonies. Gagaku incorporated indigenous songs that retold tales of victory in battle, accompanied offerings from remote and hence quaint outposts, pleaded for aid from the gods, and celebrated the sexual union of men and women in fertility rites. The court thus appropriated elements of popular culture into an elite culture characterized by massive infusions from the continent. Viewing and participating in music and dance and learning the correct codes for conduct in ceremonies set ever higher standards for civilized behavior.

A Stagnant Agrarian Base

The spread of rice cultivation in the Yayoi period that had transformed western agricultural regions from slash and burn to settled farming soon reached its ecological limit. In contrast to the intensive agriculture that boosted yields in later centuries, cultivators during the eighth century continued to use extensive methods. In continuous cycles of cultivation and abandonment, they cleared fields and planted crops for a few years, and then repeated the process when a lack of proper irrigation and fertilizer depleted the soil. Although an edict from 723 noted that a recent increase in population had led to rural overcrowding, the eighth-century regime of codes made much more elaborate provision for returning fallow fields to cultivation than it did for opening new fields. Fragments of census surveys suggest that a population of from 3 to 5.5 million in 700 had grown little by 800. Population gains at the turn of the century were wiped out by an epidemic of smallpox or some similar disease in 733–737 that killed approximately 25 to 35 percent of the population. It was followed by repeated famines and epidemics later in the century. The state's demand for revenue to fund building projects and ceremonies was not matched by an increase in population or an enlarged economic base.

Rural villages tended to be large in area but small in population. Because depleted fields had to lie fallow for years before they could be returned to production, the earlier pattern of fortified hilltop hamlets gave way to dispersed dwellings, each containing a large household of extended family members along with servants and slaves. Each cultivator received an official allotment of land in return for paying taxes, but it did not suffice for survival. To make up the difference, cultivators planted fields hidden from the tax collector, worked as tenants, or foraged for supplies. To the dismay of officials, cultivators felt little connection to their land. Many simply absconded when times were bad, swelling the population of vagrants and weakening the tax base. Infant mortality was so high that a plan to give each child an allotment of land at birth had to be changed to allotments at age five, raised to age twelve in the case of a slave. The average life expectancy at birth was twenty-eight to thirty-three years, approximately the same as in Europe at that time.

Quarrelling Worker. Scribbled on the margin of a record regarding sutra copying in 740, this sketch of a quarrelling worker shows the hat and robes worn by commoners. *(Shosoin Treasure House/DNP Archives.com)*

In addition to paying taxes for the use of state land, cultivators had to meet service requirements and participate in the state's military adventures. In 713, for example, "For the first time Yamashiro-no-kuni was ordered to establish fifty households in charge of milking cows."[2] In this type of corvée (required labor) system, the cultivators' obligation to provide services did not mean they would be paid for the services. The corvée built the enormous tombs demanded by fifth-century rulers; it built the capitals, palaces, and temples of the later centuries. The court fielded conscript armies and marched them from Kyushu to Tohoku. Many men caught in this system could expect to be ill treated, malnourished, and abandoned once the project for which they had been pressed into service was completed. Although the centered monarchical structure created through the regime of codes provided relief from marauders and bandits as well as some security of landholding, its benefits for cultivators were decidedly mixed.

SUMMARY

How did Japan at the end of the eighth century differ from the Japan mentioned in first-century Chinese chronicles? Instead of confederacies of chieftains, a single monarch had corralled an aristocracy, built a bureaucracy, and issued legal codes. Rulers had become male by definition, although they claimed descent from a sun goddess. Successive waves of immigrants from the continent brought metallurgy, sericulture, Buddhism, literacy, and accounting techniques, though the extent to which these signs of civilization benefited the vast majority of the population eking out a living on depleted soil is debatable. The power holders who had imbibed Chinese culture defined themselves and the people over whom they ruled as the Yamato race. A centered state spread over Shikoku, Kyushu, and most of Honshu, gradually becoming attenuated as it reached the frontiers. Although historians disagree on the extent to which it enforced its decrees, it became a model for kingly rule for centuries to come.

2. Robert Karl Reischauer, *Early Japanese History (c. 40 B.C.–A.D. 1167)* (Gloucester, Mass.: Peter Smith, 1967), p. 173.

China Among Equals: Song, Liao, Xia, and Jin

The Song Dynasty did not dominate East Asia the way the Tang Dynasty had, or even rule all areas occupied largely by Chinese speakers. Northern Vietnam defended its independence. The Khitan Liao Dynasty held territory in the northeast down to modern Datong and Beijing, and the Tangut Xia Dynasty held a smaller territory in the northwest. In the twelfth and the thirteenth centuries, Song had new northern rivals, the Jurchens and then the Mongols, who took even larger parts of China proper. The Song period is, as a result, conventionally divided into the Northern Song (960–1127), when the Song capital was in Kaifeng and Liao was its chief rival, and the Southern Song (1127–1276), when the capital had been moved to Hangzhou and it confronted Jin on its northern border.

Modern historians have been fascinated by the evidence that Song China was the most advanced society in the world in its day, and many have drawn attention to all that seems progressive in this period: the introduction of paper money, the spread of printing and increases in literacy, the growth of cities, the expansion of the examination system, the decline of aristocratic attitudes, and so on. These successes naturally raise questions. Why couldn't Song China turn its economic might into military might? How did the increasing importance of the examination system in elite lives affect the operation of the bureaucracy? Why was factionalism such a problem. Because printing led to many more works surviving from the Song than had been the case for earlier periods, historians have also been able to ask questions they could not ask for earlier periods because of lack of sources. What can we learn of daily life among different groups—elite and commoner, men and women, peasants and townsmen? How does Song society, economy, or culture look from the local level?

THE FOUNDING OF THE SONG DYNASTY

The founder of the Song Dynasty, Zhao Kuangyin, was a general whose troops put him on the throne when their previous ruler was succeeded by a child. Known as Taizu (r. 960–976), he set himself the task of making sure that no army would ever again be in a position to oust the rightful heir. He retired or rotated his own generals and assigned civil officials to supervise them, thus subordinating the armed forces to the civil bureaucracy.

Curbing generals ended warlordism but did not solve the problem of defending against the Khitans' Liao Dynasty to the north. During the Five Dynasties, Liao was able to gain control of a strip of land in north China (the northern parts of Shanxi and Hebei) that had long been considered part of China proper (and was referred to by Song as the Sixteen Prefectures). Taizu and his younger brother Taizong made every effort to defeat Liao. They wanted to reclaim the Sixteen Prefectures because this area included the line of the Great Wall, the mountains and mountain passes that had been central to Chinese defense against northerners since before the Han Dynasty. However, although the Liao ruled over a population tiny by Chinese standards, their horsemen were more than a match for the Chinese armies. After a Liao invasion of 1004 came within a hundred miles of Kaifeng, the Song settled with Liao, agreeing to pay tribute to Liao in exchange for Liao's maintaining the peace. Each year Song was to send Liao 100,000 ounces of silver and 200,000 bolts of silk. In 1042 this sum was increased to 500,000 units.

The payments to the Liao and Xia probably did not damage the overall Chinese economy. Even after the tribute to Liao was raised to 500,000 units, it did not result in an increase in Liao's bullion holdings since Song exports to Liao normally exceeded imports by a large margin, which meant that the silver sent to Liao found its way back into China as payment for Chinese goods, a little like foreign aid today. At the time, however, the pro-war irredentists felt humiliated by these treaties and thought it only common sense that payments to Liao and Xia helped them and harmed Song.

The pro-peace accommodationists, however, could justly point out that tribute was much less costly than war. During the reigns of the first three emperors, the size of the armed forces increased rapidly to almost 1 million by 1022. By that time, the military was consuming three-quarters of the tax revenues. By contrast, even counting the expenses of the exchange of embassies, the cost of maintaining peaceful relations with the Liao consumed no more than 2 or 3 percent of the state's annual revenues. Just as Silla was able to prosper under the Tang peace, Northern Song was able to prosper under the peace of its agreements with Liao.

SONG'S RIVALS: LIAO AND XIA

The Khitan were a proto-Mongol people originally from the eastern slopes of the mountains that separate Mongolia and Manchuria. There they raised cattle and horses, moving their herds in nomadic fashion. They had been in regular contact with the Tang and with other sedentary societies, such as the multiethnic kingdom of Parhae (Bohai) in southern Manchuria. They knew of the wealth of cities to the south and the strategies used by the Uighurs and others to extract some of it by exerting military pressure.

In the early tenth century, Abaoji (d. 926), of the Yelü clan, united eight to ten Khitan tribes into a federation and secured control of the steppe. The political institutions he set up drew on both Chinese traditions and tribal customs. Abaoji set aside the traditional Khitan practice of tribal councils' electing chiefs for limited terms and in its place instituted hereditary succession on the Chinese model to ensure that his son would succeed him. The ruling Yelü clan married exclusively with the Xiao clan, and these two clans dominated the higher reaches of the government. In 926, Abaoji advanced southward toward Hebei and destroyed the kingdom of Parhae (see Chapter 6).

The Liao administered their Chinese territories differently from their Khitan territories. The southern section was governed on the basis of Chinese traditions, using a civil bureaucracy modeled on the Tang, complete with a civil service examination system. In contrast to the Tang, however, counties and even prefectures were granted to Khitan imperial relatives and high-ranking officials as fiefs over which they had full jurisdiction. The central city of the southern region was the Southern Capital, Yanjing, located at modern Beijing, thus beginning the history of that city as a capital. (See Map 8.1.) The southern section generated the bulk of Liao tax revenue.

Map **8.1**   Northern Song, Liao, and Xia, ca. 1050

The northern section of Liao was huge but sparsely settled. The government there was mobile, with the ruler and his chief officials moving from place to place in different seasons. To keep records in the Khitan language, a script was created with characters resembling Chinese characters (a language still not deciphered). This dual form of administration allowed the Khitans to maintain their tribal organization and resist sinification. Although the ruling elite became culturally dual, adept in both Khitan and Chinese languages and customs, ordinary Khitans in the north maintained their traditional social and military organization.

To the west of the Liao territories another non-Chinese state established itself in this period: the Xia, or Xi-Xia (Western Xia). It was founded by Tanguts, who spoke a language related to Tibetan. In Tang times, under pressure from the expanding Tibetan kingdom, the Tanguts had moved north and east from the Qingtang region into northern Shaanxi and Gansu. In 881 the Tang court appointed a Tangut chief as military governor of the region, and this office became essentially hereditary. By the end of the ninth century, after the collapse of the Tibetan and Uighur empires,

the Tanguts gained control of the important trade in horses with the Chinese.

During the tenth century, the Tanguts were largely outside the struggle for power in north China and were able to consolidate their state. Under Yuanhao (r. 1032–1048), a script was adopted for writing the Tangut language, and the dynastic name Xia was adopted. When Yuanhao demanded that the Song Dynasty recognize Xia as a sovereign state, the Chinese sent an army. The fighting went poorly for the Chinese, however, and in 1044 a treaty was reached in which the Song agreed to make payments to Xia much as it did to Liao, though in lesser amounts (200,000 units altogether).

The political institutions of Xia drew on Tang, Song, Liao, Tibetan, and Uighur models. There was a perennial tension between the imperial clan and the ministerial-consort clans, who often were able to dominate the court. Elements of Confucian statecraft were adopted, but Buddhism was firmly entrenched as the state religion. Xia was sometimes at war with Liao but also concluded treaties with it, recognizing Liao as the superior party.

A NEW ERA

The pace of change was rapid from the late Tang into the early Song period, and by the mid-eleventh century, China in many ways was a much more modern society, with cities and commerce transforming its economy and printing and examinations transforming elite culture.

The Medieval Chinese Economic Revolution

In 742, China's population was approximately 50 million, a little lower than it had been in 2 C.E. Over the next three centuries, with the expansion of rice cultivation in central and south China, the country's food supply steadily increased, and so did its population. Song population reached about 100 million in 1102. China was certainly the largest country in the world at the time; its population undoubtedly exceeded that of all of Europe (as it has ever since).

How did China's economy sustain such growth? Agricultural prosperity and denser settlement patterns fostered commercialization of the economy. In many regions, farmers found that producing for the market made possible a better life, and therefore they no longer aimed at self-sufficiency. Peasants in more densely populated regions with numerous markets sold their surpluses and bought charcoal, tea, oil, and wine. In many places, farmers purchased grain and grew commercial crops, such as sugar, oranges, cotton, silk, and tea. The need to transport these products stimulated the inland and coastal shipping industries, creating jobs for shipbuilders and sailors. Marco Polo, the Venetian merchant who wrote of his visit to China in the late thirteenth century, was astounded at the boat traffic on the Yangzi River. He claimed to have seen no fewer than fifteen thousand vessels docked at a single city on the river.

As more goods were bought and sold, demand for money grew enormously, leading eventually to the creation of the world's first paper money. The late Tang government had abandoned the use of bolts of silk as supplementary currency, which increased the demand for copper coins. By 1085 the output of currency had increased tenfold since Tang times to more than 6 billion coins a year. To avoid the weight and bulk of coins for large transactions, local merchants in late Tang times started trading receipts from deposit shops where they had left money or goods. The early Song authorities awarded a small set of shops a monopoly on the issuance of these certificates of deposit, and in the 1120s the government took over the system, producing the world's first government-issued paper money.

With the intensification of trade, merchants became progressively more specialized and organized. They set up partnerships and joint stock companies, with a separation of owners (shareholders) and managers. In the large cities, merchants were organized into guilds according to the type of product sold; they periodically set prices and arranged sales from wholesalers to shop owners. When the government requisitioned goods or assessed taxes, it dealt with the guild heads.

The Song also witnessed many advances in industrial techniques. Papermaking flourished with the demand for paper for books, documents, money, and wrapping paper. Heavy industry, especially iron, grew at an astounding pace. With advances in metallurgy, iron production reached around 125,000 tons per year in 1078, a sixfold increase over the output in 800. At first, charcoal was used in the production process, leading to deforestation of parts of north China. By the end of the eleventh century, however, bituminous coke had largely taken the place of charcoal.

Much of this iron was put to military purposes. Mass-production methods were used to make iron armor in small, medium, and large sizes. High-quality steel for swords was made through high-temperature metallurgy. Huge bellows, often driven by water wheels, were used to superheat the molten ore. The needs of the army also brought Chinese engineers to experiment with the use of gunpowder. In the wars against the Jurchens in the twelfth century, those defending a besieged city used gunpowder to propel projectiles at the enemy.

The quickening of the economy fueled the growth of great cities, especially the two capitals, Kaifeng and Hangzhou. The Song broke all earlier precedents and did not select either Chang'an or Luoyang as its capital, but a city that had prospered because of its location near the northern end of the Grand Canal. The Tang capital, Chang'an, had been a planned city, laid out on a rectangular grid with the walls built far out to allow expansion. Kaifeng, by contrast, grew over time as its economy developed. The city did not have the clearly demarcated wards of the Tang capital, and officials found themselves in frequent contact with ordinary city residents. The curfew was abolished in 1063, and from then on, many businesses in the entertainment quarters stayed open all night.

Knick-knack peddler. Song court painters sometimes portrayed life among ordinary people, as in this scene of a woman with several children eager to buy toys from the itinerant peddler who carries hundreds of items on a shoulder pole. *(National Palace Museum, Taipei, ROC)*

The medieval economic revolution shifted the economic center of China south to the Yangzi River drainage area. Rice, which grew there, provides more calories per unit of land than wheat or millet does and therefore allows denser settlements. Moreover, the milder temperatures of the south often allowed two crops to be grown on the same plot of land. The abundance of rivers and streams in the south facilitated shipping, which reduced the cost of transportation and thus made regional specialization economically more feasible.

International Trade

During the tenth through thirteenth centuries, trade connected all the states we now classify under China (Song, Liao, Xia, Jin), the less politically important Dali state in the region of modern Yunnan, the oasis city-states of Central Asia, and the other major countries of East Asia, notably Korea and Japan. Maritime trade routes also connected all these places to Southeast Asia and the societies of the Indian Ocean.

Trade between Song and its northern neighbors was stimulated by the indemnities Song paid to them. These states were given the means to buy Song products, and the Song set up supervised markets along the border to encourage trade. The Song government collected tariffs on this trade, and the trade itself helped sustain Song China's economic growth. Chinese goods that flowed north in large quantities included tea, silk, copper coin (widely used as a currency outside China), paper and printed books, porcelain, lacquerware, jewelry, rice and other grains, and ginger and other spices. The return flow included some of the silver that had originated with the Song and the horses that Song desperately needed for its armies, but also other animals such as camels and sheep, as well as goods that had traveled across the Silk Road, including fine Indian and Persian cotton cloth, precious gems, incense, and perfumes.

During Song times, maritime trade for the first time exceeded overland foreign trade. The Song government sent missions to Southeast Asian countries to encourage their traders to come to China. Chinese junks were seen throughout the Indian Ocean and began to displace Indian and Arab merchants in the South Seas. Shards of Song Chinese porcelain have been found as far away as East Africa. Chinese junks were larger than the ships of most of their competitors, such as the Indians and Arabs, and had many technical advances, including waterproofing with tung oil, watertight bulkheads, sounding lines to determine depth, and stern-mounted rudders for improved steering. Some of these ships were powered by both oars and sails and were large enough to hold several hundred men. Also important to oceangoing transport was the perfection of the compass. The way a magnetic needle would point north had been known for centuries, but in Song times, the needle was reduced in size and attached to a fixed stem (rather than floating in water). Sometimes it was put in a small protective case with a glass top, making it suitable for navigation at sea. The first reports of a compass used this way date to 1119. An early twelfth-century Chinese writer gave two reasons that the ships engaged in maritime trade had to be large and carry several hundred sailors. First, they had to be ready to fight off pirates. Second, high volume was needed so that there would still be a profit after giving substantial "gifts" to the authorities at every port they visited. The most common product carried by the ships, this author reported, was Chinese ceramics.

In 1225 the superintendent of customs at the port city of Quanzhou, named Zhao Rukua, wrote an account of the countries with which Chinese merchants traded and the goods they offered for sale. It includes sketches of major trading cities from Srivijaya (modern Indonesia) to Malabar, Cairo, and Baghdad. Pearls were said to come from the Persian Gulf, ivory from Aden, myrrh from Somalia, pepper from Java and Sumatra, cotton from the various kingdoms of India, and so on. Marco Polo a few decades later wrote glowingly of the Chinese pepper trade, saying that for each load of pepper sent to Christendom, a hundred were sent to China. On his own travels home via the

sea route, he reported seeing many merchants from southern China plying a thriving trade.

Much money could be made from the sea trade, but there were also great risks, so investors usually divided their investment among many ships, and each ship had many investors behind it. One observer thought eagerness to invest in overseas trade was leading to an outflow of copper cash. He wrote, "People along the coast are on intimate terms with the merchants who engage in overseas trade, either because they are fellow-countrymen or personal acquaintances. . . . [They give the merchants] money to take with them on their ships for the purchase and return conveyance of foreign goods. They invest from ten to a hundred strings of cash, and regularly make profits of several hundred per cent."[1]

In 1973 a Song ship that had been shipwrecked in 1277 was excavated off the south China coast. It was 78 feet long and 29 feet wide and had twelve bulkheads. Inside them were the luxury objects that the Song imported: over 5,000 pounds of fragrant wood from Southeast Asia, pepper, betel nut, cowries, tortoiseshell, cinnabar, and ambergris from Somalia.

The Song Scholar-Official Class

The Song period saw the full flowering of one of the most distinctive features of Chinese civilization: the scholar-official class certified through highly competitive civil service examinations. Compared to its Tang counterpart, the Song Chinese scholar-official class was larger, better educated, and less aristocratic in its habits. The legitimacy of the power of this class was enhanced by its Confucian commitment to public service and by the ostensibly fair and objective ways through which its members gained access to ranks and honors.

The spread of printing aided the expansion of the educated class. In China, as in Europe centuries later, the introduction of printing dramatically lowered the price of books. Song scholars could afford to buy many more books than could their counterparts in earlier dynasties. Song publishers printed the classics in huge editions. Works on philosophy, science, and medicine were avidly consumed, as were Buddhist texts. Han and Tang poetry and historical works were used as models by Song writers.

1. Cited in Shiba Yoshinobu, *Commerce and Society in Sung China*, trans. Mark Elvin (Ann Arbor: Center for Chinese Studies, University of Michigan, 1970), p. 33.

The Scholarly Life. This detail of a long hand-scroll by the court painter Ma Yuan (active 1189–1225) depicts a scholar writing a poem as others watch. Behind him is a monk; nearby are female attendants and a few children. *(The Nelson-Atkins Museum of Art, Kansas City, Missouri [Purchase: Nelson Trust], 63–19)*

The demand for books was fueled in part by eagerness to compete in the civil service examinations. From the point of view of the early Song emperors, the purpose of written examinations was to identify capable men. So long as the successful candidates were literate, intelligent, and willing to work hard and obey the rules, the rulers had reason to be satisfied with the results, even if some able man were overlooked. From the point of view of those aspiring to office, however, issues of equity loomed large. Was everyone given an equal chance? Did examiners favor those they knew? Why should skill in poetry be tested when officials did not have to compose poems as part of their jobs? To increase confidence in the objectivity of the examiners, the names of the test takers were replaced with numbers, and clerks recopied each exam so that the handwriting could not be recognized.

The Song examination system recruited four to five times more *jinshi* ("presented scholars," holders of the highest examination degree) per year than the Tang system had. Yet increasing the number of *jinshi* did not lower the prestige of the degree. Rather, it encouraged more men to enter the competition. Early in the eleventh century, fewer than thirty thousand men took the prefectural exams, which increased to nearly eighty thousand by the end of that century and to about four hundred thousand by the dynasty's end. Because the number of available posts did not change, each candidate's chances of passing plummeted, reaching as low as 1 in 333 in some prefectures. Men often took the examinations several times and were on average a little over thirty years old when they succeeded.

Young men whose fathers or grandfathers had risen to high rank in the government did not have to take the examinations to get government posts; they could instead take advantage of the privilege higher officials had of nominating sons and grandsons for civil service appointment. Around 40 percent or more of posts in Song times were filled this way. Men who started their careers through privilege usually had to begin at the very bottom, serving as sheriffs in remote places, and they might well spend their entire careers in county-level posts, never rising above magistrate. They may have spent much of their careers collecting taxes and hearing legal cases. It is no wonder, then, that most sons of officials were willing to at least try the civil service examinations.

In the 1950s and 1960s, Western historians stressed the meritocratic side of the Chinese examination system and the social mobility it fostered. Lists of examination graduates showed that only about half had fathers, grandfathers, or great-grandfathers who had served as officials. In recent decades, it has been more common to stress the advantages official families had in placing their sons in government posts and that even those who did not have recent patrilineal ancestors who had served in office might have an uncle or a maternal grandfather who had done so. If the comparison is to other premodern societies, including Korea and Japan, Song China was exceptional in the opportunities it offered to intelligent, hard-working young men without powerful relatives. However, no one should assume that mobility through education occurred with the frequency it does in modern society.

Families able to educate their sons were generally landholders. When the Song elite is looked at from the perspective of the local community, families prominent for generations are more striking than new men. In a county with twenty thousand households, a dozen or so family lines might account for nearly all those who gained national notice. Still, because property had to be divided among sons every generation, downward social mobility was always a possibility if nothing was done to add to the family's income or property every generation. Yuan Cai, writing in the late twelfth century, stressed the importance of finding ways to increase the family's holdings. When one brother had private funds from office, he should not convert it into gold and silver in order to hide it, but should invest it so that it would grow:

> *For instance, if he had 100,000 strings worth of gold and silver and used this money to buy productive property, in a year he would gain 10,000 strings; after ten years or so, he would have regained the 100,000 strings and what would be divided among the family would be interest. If it were invested in a pawn broking business, in three years the interest would equal the capital. He would still have the 100,000 strings, and the rest, being interest, could be divided. Moreover, it could be doubled again in another three years, ad infinitum.*[2]

Members of the Song scholar-official class would rarely have spent their entire lives in their home counties or prefectures. Many traveled considerable distances to study with well-known teachers. If they succeeded in the first stage of the examinations, they had to travel to the capital for the next stage, held every three years. A large proportion of those who succeeded began their careers in county or prefectural posts, and over the next ten or twenty years they might crisscross the empire several times, returning to the capital between assignments. Travel to a new post might take a month or more, during which time the official would call on his colleagues in the places he passed. When Lu You left his home county in 1170 to take up an assignment in Sichuan, he spent 157 days on the road and called on dozens of officials, retired officials, and Buddhist and Daoist clergy along the way. He also had the chance to visit many sites made famous by earlier visitors who had written poems or essays about them.

Many Song men of letters were adept at a wide range of arts and sciences. One of the most versatile was Shen Gua, who tried his hand at everything from mathematics, geography, economics, engineering, medicine, divination, and archaeology to military strategy and diplomacy. On an assignment to inspect the frontier, he made a relief map of wood and glue-soaked sawdust to show the mountains, roads, rivers, and passes. He once computed the total number of possible situations on a game board and another time the longest possible military campaign given the limits of human carriers who had to carry their own food as well as food for the soldiers. Interest in the natural world, of the sort Shen Gua displayed, was not as common among the educated elite in Song times as interest in art and art collecting. The remarkable poet and statesman Su Shi wrote glowingly of paintings done by scholars, who could imbue their paintings with ideas, making them much better than paintings that merely conveyed outward appearance, the sort of paintings that professional painters made. His friend Mi Fu, a passionate collector, would call on collectors to view and discuss their treasures. Often he would borrow pieces to study and copy. When he came across something that excited him, he made every effort to acquire it, generally by offering a trade.

Reformers and Anti-Reformers

How was the operation of the Song government affected by recruiting a large proportion of its staff through the examination system? Such men entered government service at older ages and after longer periods of study than men who entered other ways. Did the preponderance of such men alter the dynamics of political life?

One might have thought that *jinshi*, having been through much the same experience, would demonstrate remarkable solidarity with each other. But this did not happen. Exam graduates did not defend one another's qualifications or insist that every *jinshi* was fully qualified to practice government. The examination system did not lead to scholar-officials thinking alike or looking out for each other's interests. To the contrary, they seem to have fought among themselves more viciously than the officials of earlier dynasties.

One explanation for their divisiveness might be that even after passing the examinations, competition continued unabated. Promotions in responsibility, honor, and

---

2. Patricia Buckley Ebrey, trans., *Family and Property in Sung China: Yuan Ts'ai's Precepts for Social Life* (Princeton, N.J.: Princeton University Press, 1984), pp. 199–200.

pay did not come automatically. There were more men qualified for office than posts, so often after finishing one assignment, officials had to wait months or even years before getting their next one. Moreover, to get choice assignments, they often needed high officials to recommend them, adding to the uncertainty they faced.

What did officials fight about? Ostensibly, at least, they fought about how best to run the government. It was very common for younger officials, especially those who had done well in the examinations, to be disappointed in the performance of the average official, whom they viewed as morally lazy, unwilling to make any exertion for the dynasty or the common people. Idealistic officials criticized the examination system for selecting such mediocre men. Other areas of tension were military and fiscal policy. If one wanted to push the Khitan out of the Sixteen Prefectures, as many did, one had to be willing to raise revenue somehow, but no one liked to see new taxes.

Those with proposals to make had to find a way to get the emperor's ear and convince other officials to support their ideas. This meant lining up allies and maligning opponents. From the emperor's point of view, such activities were obstructionist. Rather, officials should speak candidly to the emperor about the realms of government they knew. It should be up to the emperor and his chancellors to weigh advice from diverse perspectives.

During the first phase of factional strife in the 1040s, a reform program was initiated by Fan Zhongyan, an idealistic Confucian best known for describing the duty of the Confucian scholar-official as "to be first in worrying about the world's troubles and last in enjoying its pleasures." Fan was an experienced official who had served as prefect of Kaifeng and had managed a successful military assignment against the Tanguts. Once appointed chancellor, he submitted a ten-point memorial calling for reforms of the recruitment system, higher pay for local officials to discourage corruption, more use of sponsorship to base promotions more on competence and character, and the like. His proposals evoked strong resistance from those who were comfortable with the existing system and did not want to see the rules changed in the middle of their careers. Within a year, the program was canceled and Fan replaced as chancellor. Fan's example, however, inspired many idealistic officials who hoped to take up where he had left off.

The one who managed to accomplish this was Wang Anshi (1021–1086). After a career largely in the provinces, he submitted a long memorial criticizing the exam-

ination system and the state schools. Shenzong, who had just succeeded to the throne at the age of nineteen, made Wang a chancellor and supported his program, called the New Policies.

Wang Anshi was intelligent and hard-working and had original ideas. Realizing that government income was ultimately linked to the prosperity of farming families, he instituted measures he thought would help them, such as low-cost loans and replacing labor service with a tax. To raise revenues, he expanded state monopolies on tea, salt, and wine. He also had land resurveyed to make land taxes more equitable. He introduced a local militia to reduce the cost of maintaining a large standing army. To speed up introduction of reforms, a Finance Planning Commission was established to bypass the existing bureaucracy. The poetry component of the civil service examination was dropped in the hope of recruiting men with a more practical bent. Wang Anshi's own commentaries on the classics became required reading for candidates hoping to do well on the examinations.

The resistance these reforms evoked has led historians to suspect that interests were at stake. Wang and many of the reformers came from the south, but the split was not a simple north-south one or an old elite versus a newly rising one. Personal antagonisms certainly played a role, as did philosophical differences. In the vocabulary of the time, however, the struggle was portrayed as one between men of principle motivated by concern for the common good and misguided or nefarious inferior men who could not or would not see the larger picture. Each side, of course, considered themselves the men of principle and their opponents the inferior men.

From the perspective of Wang Anshi and Shenzong, opposition amounted to obstruction. To put their program into place, they wanted officials who supported it, not ones dead set against it. Yet dismissing all critics would make it difficult for the emperor to learn of unforeseen problems. Usually officials deemed obstructive were assigned offices outside the capital, but when the court wanted to be particularly harsh, it could send them to the far south, the regions where malaria and other tropical diseases were sometimes fatal to officials from the north.

The reform program came to an abrupt halt when Shenzong died in his mid-thirties in 1085. His heir, Zhezong, was only ten years old, so his grandmother served as regent. She had never approved the reforms and quickly set about bringing to court opponents of them, led by the senior statesman Sima Guang. Once the anti-reformers were in power, they quickly made sure that the reformers suffered the same treatment they had, sending them out of the capital as prefectural officials or worse. The New Policies were canceled wholesale, even measures that many had appreciated, such as the substitution of a tax for often onerous labor service.

When his grandmother died in 1093, Zhezong began ruling on his own. He reversed his grandmother's policies and brought the reformers back to power. The cycles of revenge and retaliation continued as the reformers banished the anti-reformers. Zhezong succumbed to an illness while still in his twenties and was succeeded by his younger brother Huizong (r. 1100–1125), who also sided with the reformers. His government banned the writings of key opponents of reform including Sima Guang and Su Shi and elevated Wang Anshi. A statue of Wang Anshi was placed in the Confucian temple next to Mencius, and pictures of him were distributed throughout the country.

THE FALL OF THE NORTHERN SONG AND THE JIN DYNASTY

Huizong's interests extended well beyond the reform program. Committed to the cultural side of rulership, he collected paintings, calligraphies, and antiquities on a huge scale and had catalogues compiled of his collections. He took a personal interest in the training of court artists and instituted examinations for their selection. He wrote poetry as well as treatises on medicine and Daoism. He initiated an ambitious reform of court music and court rituals. He took a personal interest in architecture and garden design, created his own distinctive calligraphy style, and produced exquisite paintings.

While Huizong was busy with these projects, the balance of power among Song, Liao, and Xia was radically altered by the rise of a new tribal group in the northeast, the Jurchens. The Jurchens, just one of many tribal groups subordinate to the Liao, lived in villages and small walled towns in the forests and river valleys of the Liao and Sungari rivers, their economy based on fishing, hunting, animal husbandry, and some farming. Jurchens who lived near Chinese, Khitan, or Koryŏ cities adopted practices and technologies from these neighbors, leading to a distinction between the "civilized" Jurchens and their "wild" counterparts in more remote areas. The lands the Jurchens occupied were ideal for horse raising, and by the mid-eleventh century, the Jurchens were selling the

Khitans about ten thousand horses per year. During the mid- to late eleventh century, the Wanyan clan gradually gained the dominant position among the Jurchens. In the early twelfth century, under the leadership of Wanyan Aguda (1068–1123), the Jurchens began challenging Liao authority. In 1115 their repudiation of Liao overlordship was made explicit by the proclamation of their own dynasty, the Jin (Golden).

States North of Song

Dynasty name	Ethnic group
Liao	Khitan
Xia	Tangut
Jin	Jurchen
Yuan	Mongol

The Song heard rumors of what was happening from Chinese defectors from Liao. Huizong's leading general, Tong Guan (1054–1126), by then a member of the Council of State (see **Biography: Tong Guan, Eunuch General**), urged making a secret alliance with Jin. After a series of envoys had been exchanged, it was decided that Jin and Song would cooperate to defeat Liao, then divide its territory, with Song promised the recovery of the Sixteen Prefectures.

In the process of defeating Liao, Jin discovered that Song was not much of a military threat and attacked it next. Kaifeng was besieged, an enormous ransom paid to escape slaughter, and thousands taken captive, including Huizong, the imperial clan, craftsmen, and female entertainers. Jin went on to establish a stable government in north China and Manchuria. In the beginning, Jin continued the dual government of Liao and employed former Liao officials, both Chinese and Khitan. Jin ruled a much larger Chinese population than Liao had and had to distribute Jurchens throughout north China to maintain control. Gradually more and more Chinese political institutions were adopted and more Chinese officials employed. Jin moved its capital from central Manchuria to Beijing in 1153 and to Kaifeng in 1161. Like other non-Chinese rulers before them, the Jurchens found that Chinese political institutions such as hereditary succession were a potent weapon in their competition with their own nobles. The Jurchen rulers did not adopt Chinese traditions of respect for the dignity of

BIOGRAPHY   Tong Guan, Eunuch General

The eunuch Tong Guan (1054–1126) was the favorite general of the Song emperor, Huizong (r. 1100–1125). In Song times, it was not unusual to have eunuchs serve as military commanders, and Tong Guan began his military career as a protégé of the leading eunuch general of the 1080s.

According to contemporaries, Tong Guan was a striking-looking man, with a strong body, penetrating stare, and more beard than the typical eunuch. Soon after Huizong took the throne, he sent Tong Guan to Hangzhou to acquire old books and paintings for the palace. Not long afterward, Tong Guan was given a military assignment on the northwestern border, where he had a string of victories and developed a reputation as an excellent commander. In 1111 he accompanied a mission to Liao, and from then on his rank and influence steadily increased. In 1112 he reached the top of the military command structure, and in 1116 he became the first eunuch in Song times to be a member of the highest policy-forming organ in the government.

Huizong treated Tong Guan much as he would have a high civil official, to the annoyance of other high officials. In 1104, after Tong Guan achieved his first notable victory, Huizong conferred on him a piece of his calligraphy in his own distinctive "Slender Gold" style. Accounts of parties Huizong organized for his top officials in 1113 and 1119 list Tong Guan as a guest. When Huizong had the catalogue of his painting collection compiled, Tong Guan was one of ten palace eunuchs given biographies as talented painters. In it he is described as solemn and slow to show his feelings.

In 1118, Tong Guan proposed allying with the Jurchens against Liao as a way to recover the Sixteen Prefectures. Although many officials opposed this plan, Huizong approved it, and Tong Guan played a leading role in negotiations with envoys from Jin. In 1112, by then sixty-six years old, Tong Guan was sent out with his army to attack the Liao southern capital, Yanjing, But when he got his troops in place, he was ordered to turn his army around and march several hundred miles south to Zhejiang province, where the Fang La rebellion had broken out. He quelled the rebellion in a matter of months, then returned to the northern border. There his army was routed. The Jurchens took the city, looted it, and turned it over to Song in exchange for substantial payments. When Tong Guan returned to Kaifeng, he was forced to retire. Yet, in 1124 at age seventy-one, Tong Guan was recalled and sent back to the northern border. Huizong apparently had no other general he trusted as much as Tong Guan.

It was Tong Guan himself who arrived in Kaifeng in the last month of 1125 to tell Huizong that the Jurchens had invaded. Tong Guan took charge of the bodyguards who accompanied Huizong on his flight from the capital after abdicating. Once out of Kaifeng, Tong Guan, like Huizong's other top officials, had calumny heaped on him for his part in the military disaster, and before long Huizong's successor had him executed. Perhaps that was a better fate for a military man than to have remained with Huizong and been carried into captivity by the Jurchens.

officials, however. Jin emperors had high officials flogged in open court, a brutal violation of the Confucian dictum that officials are to be treated according to ritual and not subjected to corporal punishments.

Because they lived surrounded by Chinese, many Jurchens adopted Chinese customs in language, dress, and rituals. Jurchen generals opposed to sinification assassinated the Jin emperor in 1161, and the succeeding emperor did his best to raise the prestige of Jurchen as a written language. He ordered Jurchens to attend special Jurchen-language schools, had Chinese texts translated into Jurchen, and instituted Jurchen-language civil service examinations. Later Jin emperors largely accepted sinification, viewing the Chinese classics, for instance, as universal texts, not exclusively Chinese ones. In 1191 an emperor even outlawed referring to the Jurchens as "border people," a relatively polite Chinese term, seeing no reason that their country should not be viewed as the Central Kingdom (the common Chinese term for China).

HANGZHOU AND THE SOUTHERN SONG (1127–1276)

One of Huizong's sons was out of Kaifeng when the Jurchens occupied Kaifeng, and after his father and brothers were transported north, Song forces rallied around him and had him installed as emperor (Gaozong, r. 1127–1162). The south had never been held by forces from the steppe, and Gaozong wisely retreated to that region. Still, the military situation remained precarious: the Jurchens not only pursued Gaozong across the Yangzi River, but even out into the sea. To get far from the Jurchens, the Song ended up making its capital Hangzhou, a beautiful city well south of the Yangzi River (see Map 8.2).

Gaozong disavowed the New Policies reform program, but this did not end factional strife, as other issues emerged around which officials divided, above all how aggressively to pursue recovery of the north. Efforts to drive the Jurchens out of north China were largely abandoned in 1141, when a peace treaty was concluded with Jin. Song agreed to heavy payments of silk and silver to Jin, much as the Northern Song had made payments to Liao.

Because the economic center of the country had already shifted south, loss of the north did not ruin the Song economy. Sixty percent of the population was still under Song control, along with much of the most productive agricultural land. The government still had to devote a large part of its revenues to defense, but it was able to raise much of its revenue through taxes on commerce. The government's monetary policies in time, however, produced rampant inflation.

Hangzhou itself grew to 1 million or more residents. At the southern end of the Grand Canal, it was a natural center for trade. Fortunetellers, acrobats, puppeteers, storytellers, tea houses, and restaurants were all to be found in the entertainment quarters. There were brokers who had girls and young women available for purchase or hire as rough or refined maids, concubines, singers, or prostitutes. Schools were found throughout the city, which also had many Buddhist and Daoist temples. For banquets and other parties, there were catering companies that provided all the food, tents, tables, chairs, and even decorations. To combat fire, the government stationed two thousand soldiers at fourteen fire stations within the city and more outside it. Poverty was more of a problem in crowded cities than in the countryside, and the government not only distributed alms but operated public clinics and old-age homes as well as paupers' graveyards. The better-off residents in the city often formed clubs; a text written in 1235 mentions the West Lake Poetry Club, the Buddhist Tea Society, the Physical Fitness Club, the Anglers' Club, the Occult Club, the Young Girls' Chorus, the Exotic Foods Club, the Plants and Fruits Club, the Antique Collectors' Club, the Horse-Lovers' Club, and the Refined Music Society.

SONG CULTURE AND SOCIETY

The Song period was one of advances in many facets of culture, ranging from scientific discoveries to landscape paintings. In addition, because of the spread of printing, more books and more types of books survive from the Song than from earlier periods, providing more glimpses of ordinary people's lives.

The Revival of Confucianism and the Learning of the Way

The scholar-statesmen of the eleventh century, such as Fan Zhongyan, Wang Anshi, Sima Guang, and Su Shi, believed that they were pursuing Confucian agendas of advising the ruler and aiding the common people. Other influential Confucian teachers of the period, notably the Cheng brothers, Cheng Hao and Cheng Yi, were more interested in metaphysics and ethics and argued that moral self-cultivation was more fundamental than service to the ruler. Their explanations of the workings of principle (*li*) and vital energy (*qi*) can be seen as a response to the sophisticated metaphysics of Buddhism. The principle for something could be moral or physical; for example, the principle for wives is essentially moral in nature, that for trees, physical. For either to exist, however, there must also be the energy and substance that constitute things. The theory of principle and vital energy allowed Song thinkers to validate Mencius's claim of the goodness of human nature and still explain human wrongdoing: principle underlying human beings is good, but their endowment of vital energy is more or less impure, giving rise to selfish impulses. Followers of the Cheng brothers referred to their school as the Learning of the Way (Daoxue). In English this movement is often termed neo-Confucianism to stress how different it was from early Confucianism.

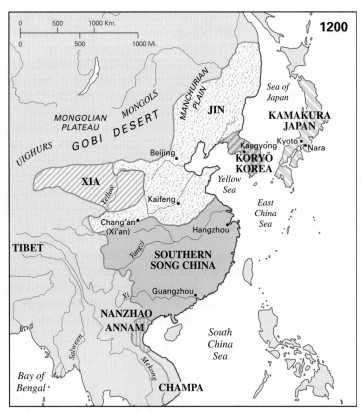

Map 8.2   Southern Song, Jin, and Xia, ca. 1200

After the loss of the north to the Jurchens, the elite lost confidence in the possibility of reform from above and began proposing ways to build a more ideal society by starting from the bottom, reforming families and local communities, establishing schools and academies, and spreading their message by publishing works for diverse audiences. The greatest of these Southern Song Confucian masters was Zhu Xi (1130–1200). Although he passed the *jinshi* examination at the young age of eighteen, he spent very little of the next fifty-two years in government service. (The government in essence supported his teaching career by regularly appointing him to sinecures with few or no duties.) Zhu Xi taught groups of disciples and led the way in establishing private academies as the institutional basis for the revived Confucianism. These gathering places for teachers and their disciples were often located on mountains, the way monasteries were, and like monasteries allowed a retreat from the world.

Zhu Xi extended the Cheng brothers' ideas in many directions. Confucius and Mencius had just said to be good, apparently assuming that anyone who desired to be good could do so. Zhu Xi's letters and

conversations show that many of his contemporaries wanted a path toward goodness, with steps to follow and ways to judge their progress. He encouraged his students to master the Four Books—the *Analects, Mencius, Doctrine of the Mean,* and the *Great Learning.* The last two, each a chapter in the canonical *Book of Rites,* stress that improvement of the world starts by improvement of the mind. As the *Great Learning* puts it:

> *Those in antiquity who wished to illuminate luminous virtue throughout the world would first govern their states; wishing to govern their states, they would first bring order to their families; wishing to bring order to their families they would first cultivate their own persons; wishing to cultivate their own persons, they would first rectify their minds; wishing to rectify their minds, they would first make their thoughts sincere; wishing to make their thoughts sincere, they would first extend their knowledge. The extension of knowledge lies in the investigation of things.*[3]

3. William Theodore de Bary and Irene Bloom, eds., *Sources of Chinese Tradition,* rev. ed. (New York: Columbia University Press, 1999), pp. 330–331.

Zhu Xi and his disciples frequently discussed what was entailed in this "investigation of things." Study, Zhu argued, should be intensive rather than extensive:

> *Zhengchun said, "I'd like to survey a great many books."*
>
> *"Don't do that," Zhu Xi said. "Read one book thoroughly, then read another one. If you confusedly try to advance on several fronts, you will end up with difficulties. It's like archery. If you are strong enough for a five-pint bow, use a four-pint one. You will be able to draw it all the way and still have strength left over. Students today do not measure their own strength when reading books. I worry that we cannot manage what we already have set ourselves."* [4]

Even if he urged his disciples to focus their energies, Zhu Xi's own interests were very broad. He discussed with his disciples everything from geomancy to the nature of fossils, the political events of the past century, and perplexing passages in the classics.

However much his disciples admired him, many of Zhu Xi's contemporaries found him offensively self-righteous. Near the end of his life, his teachings were condemned as "spurious learning," and candidates for the examinations were forbidden to cite them. Yet, within decades of his death, this judgment was reversed. In 1241 an emperor credited Zhu Xi with "illuminating the Way," and government students had to study his commentaries to the Four Books.

Gender Roles and Family Life

By Song times, sources are diverse enough to see that the old principles that men belong outside the house and women in it, or that men plow and women weave, should not be taken too literally. Song stories, documents, and legal cases show women participating in a wide range of activities never prescribed in Confucian didactic texts. There were widows who ran inns, midwives who delivered babies, pious women who spent their days chanting sutras, nuns who called on such women to explain Buddhist doctrine, girls who learned to read with their brothers, farmers' daughters who made money by weaving mats, childless widows who accused their nephews of seizing their property,

wives who were jealous of the concubines their husbands brought home, and women who drew from their dowries to help their husbands' sisters marry well.

Families who could afford it tried to keep their wives and daughters at home, where there was plenty for them to do. Not only was there the work of tending children and preparing meals, but spinning, weaving, and sewing took a great deal of time. Women in silk-producing families were very busy during the silkworm-growing period. Women had to coddle the worms, feeding them chopped mulberry tree leaves and keeping them warm, in order to get them to spin their cocoons.

Women tended to marry between the ages of sixteen and twenty. Their husbands were, on average, a couple of years older than they were. The marriages were arranged by their parents, who called on professional matchmakers (usually older women) or turned to friends or relatives for suggestions. Before a wedding took place, written agreements were exchanged that listed the prospective bride's and groom's birth dates, parents' and grandparents' names, and the gifts that would be exchanged, as well as the dowry the bride would bring. The idea was to match families of approximately equal status, but a young man who had just passed the civil service exams would be considered a good prospect even if his family had little wealth or rank.

A few days before the wedding, the bride's family sent her dowry, which at a minimum contained boxes full of clothes and bedding. In better-off families, it also included items of substantial value, such as gold jewelry or deeds for land. On the day of the wedding, the groom and some of his friends and relatives went to the bride's home to fetch her. Dressed in elaborate finery, she tearfully bid farewell to everyone in her family and then stepped into the fancy sedan chair that carried her to her new home. Musicians were an important part of the procession, alerting everyone on the street that a wedding was taking place. Meanwhile, the groom's family's friends and relatives gathered at his home so they would be there to greet the bridal party. The bride knelt and bowed to her new parents-in-law and later to the tablets representing the family's ancestors. Her husband, whom she was meeting for the first time, shared a cup of wine with her, a classical ritual still in practice. Later the young bride and groom were shown to their new bedroom, where the bride's dowry had already been placed, and people would toss beans or rice on the bed, symbolizing the desired fertility. After teasing the couple,

---

4. Patricia Buckley Ebrey, ed., *Chinese Civilization: A Sourcebook* (New York: The Free Press, 1993), p. 173.

the guests would finally leave them alone and go out to the courtyard for the wedding feast.

After the guests had all departed, the young bride's first priority was to try to win over her mother-in-law, since everyone knew that mothers-in-law were hard to please. (See Color Plate 11.) One way to do this was to bear a son for the family quickly. Within the patrilineal system, a woman fully secured her position in the family only by becoming the mother of one of the men.

Every community had older women skilled in midwifery who could be called to help when a woman went into labor. In a well-to-do family, a wet nurse might be brought in to help the woman take care of the newborn, though some Song scholars disapproved of depriving another child of milk for the sake of one's own child.

Families frequently had four, five, or six children, but likely one or more would die in infancy or early childhood. Within the home, women generally had considerable voice and took an active interest in issues such as the selection of marriage partners for their children. If a son reached adulthood and married before his mother was widowed, she was considered fortunate, for she would always have had an adult man who could take care of business for her—first her husband, then her grown son. But in the days when infectious diseases killed many people in their twenties and thirties, it was not uncommon for a woman to be widowed before her children were grown. If her husband had brothers and they had not yet divided their households, she would stay with them, assuming they were not so poor that they could not afford a few more mouths to feed. Otherwise she could return to her natal family. Taking another husband was also a possibility, though it was considered an inferior alternative from a moral point of view.

Women with healthy and prosperous husbands faced another challenge in middle age: the husband could bring home a concubine (or more than one, if the family was rich enough). Moralists insisted that it was wrong for a wife to be jealous of her husband's concubines, but many women could not get used to their husband's paying attention to another woman. Wives outranked concubines and could give them orders in the house, but concubines had their own ways of getting back, especially when the concubine was twenty and the wife was forty and no longer as attractive. The children born to a concubine were considered just as much children of the family as the wife's children, and if the wife had no sons, she would often raise a concubine's sons herself, since she would be dependent on them in her old age.

As a woman's children grew up, she would start thinking of suitable marriage partners for them. Women whose sons and daughters were all married could take it easy: they had daughters-in-law to do the cooking and cleaning and could enjoy their grandchildren and help with their education. Many found more time for religious devotions at this stage of their lives. Their sons, still living with them, were often devoted to them and did their best to make their late years comfortable.

The social and economic changes associated with the Tang-Song transition brought changes to gender roles. With the expansion of the educated class, more women learned to read. In the scholar-official class, many women were literate enough to serve as their children's first teachers. One of the most accomplished poets of Song times, Li Qingzhao (1084–ca. 1151), was a woman from a scholar-official family. After her husband's death, she wrote of the evenings she and he had spent poring over his recent purchases of paintings, calligraphy, or ancient bronze vessels. Many of her poems have been interpreted as expressions of her longing for him when he was away or her sorrow at his loss:

> Lovely in my inner chamber.
> My tender heart, a wisp; my sorrow tangled in
>   a thousand skeins.
> I'm fond of spring, but spring is gone,
> And rain urges the petals to fall.
> I lean on the balustrade;
> Only loose ends left, and no feeling.
> Where is he?
> Withered grasses stretch to the heavens;
> I can't make out the path that leads him home
>   to me.[5]

The Learning of the Way is sometimes blamed for a decline in the status of women in Song times, largely because Cheng Yi once told a follower that it would be better for a widow to die of starvation than

---

5. Trans. by Eugene Eoyang in Kang-i Sun Chang and Haun Saussy, eds., *Women Writers of Traditional China: An Anthology of Poetry and Criticism* (Stanford, Calif.: Stanford University Press, 1999), pp. 95–96.

MATERIAL CULTURE

Huang Sheng's Clothing

In 1242, at the age of fourteen or fifteen, Huang Sheng married an imperial clansman distantly related to the throne. Her father was a high-ranking official who had earlier served as superintendent of foreign trade in the major seaport of Quanzhou. Her husband's grandfather had recently been administrator of the imperial clan in Quanzhou. Both families hailed from Fuzhou. Fujian and her father and her husband's grandfather had become acquainted when they both were studying with a disciple of Zhu Xi.

The year after her marriage, Huang Sheng died, possibly in childbirth. Buried with her was a pro-

fusion of items that must have constituted her splendid and costly dowry. Altogether there were 201 pieces of women's clothing and 153 lengths of cloth, all finely made. Among the objects were several sets of shoes for bound feet. There were also long robes, jackets, vests, wraparound skirts, and various sorts of underwear. Patterned gauzes were very common, perhaps because of the warm climate of Fuzhou. From these items we cannot only imagine how elegantly upper-class women dressed, but also see how families passed property to their daughters.

Gauze Vest. The lightweight, transparent silk gauze of this vest has a woven-in decoration of peonies. *(Cultural Relics Publishing House)*

Floral Patterns. Many of Huang Sheng's garments were trimmed with ribbons decorated with floral designs, four of which are illustrated here.

to lose her virtue by remarrying. In later centuries, this saying was often quoted to justify pressuring a widow, even a very young one, to stay with her husband's family and not marry someone else. In Song times, however, widows commonly remarried.

It is true that foot binding began during the Song Dynasty, but it was not recommended by Confucian teachers; rather, it was associated with the pleasure quarters and with women's efforts to beautify them-

selves. Mothers bound the feet of girls aged five to eight, using long strips of cloth. The goal was to keep their feet from growing and to bend the four smaller toes under to make the foot narrow and arched. Women with feet shaped this way were considered beautiful. Foot binding spread gradually during Song times but probably remained largely an elite practice. (See **Material Culture: Huang Sheng's Clothing** for an upper-class woman who had bound

DOCUMENTS

Tales of Retribution

One of the most common themes in Chinese stories concerns the retribution inflicted on those who commit evil deeds. In these stories, unfilial sons may be struck by lightning, and those who have committed murder often suffer at the hands of the ghosts of those they have killed. In the twelfth century, Hong Mai (1123–1202) published hundreds of stories of this sort that he had been told on his travels around the country. In these stories, both men and women are depicted as wrongdoers, as the two stories below reveal.

Retribution for Miss Liu

Gao Junzhi, from Fuzhou, attained the *jinshi* degree and married a daughter of the Tan family. They had a son who when grown married a Miss Liu of the same prefecture. Before her husband died, Miss Liu bore two sons and a daughter. Gao Junzhi himself died after reaching the rank of Gentleman for Closing Court. His eldest grandson was dimwitted and the younger one was still young, so they lived with their grandmother Miss Tan and their mother Miss Liu.

Miss Liu was still young and rather than adhere to her duties as wife, she committed adultery with a monk in her home. When her mother-in-law discovered this, she reprimanded her, infuriating Liu.

Sometime later when her mother-in-law got sick, Miss Liu did not give her medicine, preferring to see her die. She poisoned her mother-in-law's two maids, then before her mother-in-law had taken her last breath, had her encoffined and cremated.

A few months later Liu got sick and every day called the names of the maids she had killed, pleading with them, "My head is extremely painful. Stop pulling my hair!" or "You've already beaten me a lot. Couldn't you forgive me a little?" When her family questioned her, she said, "Mom and the two maids are beating me." Ten days later she died.

Her son gained an office on the basis of his grandfather's rank, but did not do well. Today their house is desolate.

Liang Little Two

Liang Little Two, a commoner of Chixi village in Anyi county, Jie prefecture, came

---

feet in the late Song.) In later centuries, foot binding became extremely common in north and central China, eventually spreading to all classes. Women with bound feet were less mobile than women with natural feet, but only those who could afford servants bound their feet so tight that walking was difficult.

Religion in Song Life

The religious activities of laypeople are much better known for the Song than for earlier periods. The text that has attracted the most attention from historians of the Song is *The Record of the Listener*, a huge book of more than two hundred chapters written by Hong Mai (1123–1202). Hong came from a promi-

nent official family in the south (Jiangxi), and his book recorded events that he learned about firsthand or from friends, relatives, and colleagues. Many of these anecdotes dealt in one way or another with the spirit realm and people's interaction with it. (See **Documents: Tales of Retribution.**)

How did people conceive of the spirit realm? They understood that both blessings and misfortunes could be caused by all sorts of gods and spirits. The gods included the nationally recognized gods of Buddhism and Daoism as well as gods and demons particular to their locality. As was true in much earlier times, dissatisfied ancestors were seen as possible causes of illness in their descendants. Like ancestors, gods and demons were thought to feel the same sorts of emotions as people. Demons and other malevo-

from a family that for generations had been humble but honest and hard-working farmers. Liang was the first scoundrel. He treated his widowed mother very cruelly. His wife, Miss Wang, was quiet by nature and served her mother-in-law diligently.

During the Huangtung period [1141–1144] of the northern bandits [that is, the Jin Dynasty], there was a famine in Hedong and epidemics spread, so that refugees filled the roads. Liang took his mother, wife, and young child to Dongling in Gushan, where he begged for food for his child. Miss Wang, knowing that her mother-in-law had not eaten in a long time, gave her half the food. Liang got furious when he saw this, so falsely sent his wife ahead carrying the child while he stayed behind with his mother. When the distance between them was about a hundred paces, he dropped his mother on the ground, dragged her to the side of the road, stuffed mud and sand into her mouth, and left.

When he met up with his wife a little bit ahead, she asked where his mother was, and he said, "Old people walk slowly. We should go ahead to beg food from a great house, then wait for her to catch up." When she had not appeared after a long time, the wife suspected that her husband had hurt her, so went back to search for her. She found the body already stiff. She embraced her, cried mournfully, and tried to force a drink down her, but her vital spirit was already gone and she did not revive.

Miss Wang then quickly went to report to the local constable, who seized Liang to take him to the county government. On the road a storm arose. The sky became so dark that people were not visible. Thunder clapped, ghosts and spirits flew around, and weird forms appeared and disappeared. Everyone was so frightened that no one paid attention to where Liang was.

When the sky cleared up a little later, Liang was found lying in a pit. His eyes was burned by the lightning but the rest of his body was unaffected. He could not recognize people or things but he could drink, eat, and talk as before.

Liang regularly told people, "There are three ghosts in charge of me. At each meal I must first make offerings to them before daring to eat." The officials had pity for his wife and child and gave them grain. A few years later Liang was still alive.

———

Hong Mai, *Yijian zhi* (Beijing: Zhonghua shuju, 1981), 41, 784–785; translated by Patricia Ebrey.

lent spirits might extort offerings, acting much like local bullies. Gods were seen as parts of complex hierarchies, much like those in the human world. Some were seen as the rulers of small territories—local kings and lords. Others were seen as part of an otherworldly government, where gods held specific offices and transmitted paperwork from those below them to those above. Gods were not conceived of as omnipotent, and a god might inform a petitioner that he would have to seek the approval of a higher god.

One way people learned whether particular spirits were responsible for their problems was through divination. Another was through dreams or visions. Once they understood the source of the problem, there were steps they could take themselves, such as trying to gain spirits' favor by making offerings or beseeching them in prayers. But people also often turned to religious experts ranging from ordained Buddhist and Daoist clerics and unordained practitioners of these traditions, to professional fortunetellers, and to the wardens of temples to local gods who acted as spirit mediums or exorcists. In one instance, a man pestered by a ghost first employed a local exorcist. When that failed to solve his problem, he called on a visiting Daoist priest to perform an offering ceremony. He then called on Buddhist monks from the local monastery to recite incantations and conduct an exorcism, which finally brought results.

When medical doctors failed to cure them, people regularly called on religious experts. (See Color Plate 12.) Mediums could induce spirits to descend into the body of a boy, who would then speak in the voice of the spirit. In one such case, the voice of a maid who had died a few years earlier blamed her mistress for her accidental death. After the boy awakened, the medium wrote out a dispatch to send to the City God, who in turn had the spirit of the dead maid sent to purgatory. In this instance, the City God acted much like a government official in the human world, receiving and dispatching orders.

Sometimes educated men are portrayed by Hong Mai as skeptics. When Liu Zai (1166–1239) served in a low county post, we are told, he was the only official there to ignore a prominent local shrine. In fact, he raised his sleeve every time he went by in order to avoid having to look at the shrine. Before he had been there long, his wife's younger brother died. Then his pregnant wife had an ominous dream: the enshrined god told her that he had taken her brother because of her husband's impudence and would take her next if Liu did not repent. When she too died, Liu went to the shrine to beg forgiveness.

The Song state claimed the power to approve and disapprove local shrines. Occasionally the court ordered the destruction of illicit or excessive shrines, such as shrines whose divinities made extortionate demands on people. Much more common was the government's bestowal of titles on local gods. Local supporters of shrines regularly petitioned the government to confer titles of king, duke, or lord on their gods because of the miracles the god had performed.

SUMMARY

In what ways was the China of the late thirteenth century different from the China of the mid-tenth century? Its population had nearly doubled. More of the population lived in the south, which had become the undisputed economic center of China. China had become a more commercialized society, with a higher proportion of its farmers engaged in producing for the market. The scholar-official elite of the late Song was very different from the elite of the Five Dynasties or early Song. With the expansion of education, the size of the educated class had grown much larger, and *jinshi* examinations had become a defining element in its culture. The Confucian revival was shifting the focus of literati learning from literature toward the Four Books and Zhu Xi's commentaries on the classics. The Song Dynasty began with a powerful neighbor to the north, but over the course of the next three centuries, the balance of power continued to shift in favor of the north. Jin held more of China proper than Liao had, and the Mongols were a more formidable foe in the mid-thirteenth century than the Jurchens had been in the mid-twelfth. The concept of the Mandate of Heaven—that heaven recognizes a single Son of Heaven ruling over the civilized world—was more and more difficult to sustain. During Song times more than one ruler called himself "Son of Heaven."

Heian Japan
(794–ca. 1180)

When Kanmu moved the court to Heian-kyō ("capital of peace and stability," now called Kyoto) in 794, he modeled his city on the Chinese imperial layout just as the Nara rulers had. For the next century, the regime of codes continued to provide the basic framework for a bureaucratic-style government. The period from approximately 900 to 1050 marks the apogee of classical refinement during the golden age of the Fujiwara. Rebellions in the provinces suggest that its benefits did not accrue to all. During both periods, political life at the capital remained largely free from violence. The final phase, from 1050 to 1180, saw retired monarchs wrest political power from the Fujiwara while trying to take advantage of the private landholding system. Beginning in the 900s, an outpouring of literary texts ranged in writing styles from royally commissioned poetry anthologies to diaries, memoirs, and the novel *Tale of Genji*. Buddhist thought pervaded the way aristocrats saw the world; Buddhist institutions became a powerful political and economic force.

Scholars debate issues concerning the degree of central control, the naturalization of Chinese civilization, and gender. What changed in relations between state, periphery, and the continent? Why was this age so important for poetry and fiction by women? What kind of impact did the state have on commoners' lives?

THE AGE OF KINGLY RULE (ca. 794–900)

Kanmu continued the bureaucratic and ceremonial practices that had been instituted while the court was at Nara. Men qualified by birth and talent climbed administrative ladders. Commanders of imperial guards rose to become generals leading armies against the Emishi in the northeast. Kanmu relied on officials on the Board of Divination to interpret heavenly portents and omens in line with Daoist teachings. Following a factional dispute after his enthronement in 781, he ordered the era name changed to *Enryaku* (prolonged succession) to ensure a long and prosperous reign. Despite assassinations, pestilence, and famine, it remained until his death. Codifying the annual round of celebrations and ceremonies conducted by the Board of Divination began in 823, but the procedures had been in place for over a century.

Despite continuing the fascination with Chinese culture that had characterized the Nara period, Kanmu intended moving the capital to be a break with the past. Perhaps he wanted to free his administration from political interference by Buddhist clergy whose temples encircled Nara. Although he forbade Nara clergy to follow him to Heian-kyō, the court continued to support them financially and send representatives to ceremonies. Kanmu tried to control what was to become the great temple complex of Enryakuji that had opened on Mount Hiei northeast of Heian-kyō in 785 by appointing its abbots and restricting monks to monasteries. Another reason for the move may have been political. Taking advantage of a momentary decline in Fujiwara influence, Kanmu abandoned what had become their stronghold. Finally there was the question of prognostics. Violent factional and succession disputes had tainted Nara. If Kanmu was to launch a new initiative in righteous governance, he needed a fresh venue, one that the diviners promised would be auspicious.

Kanmu retained the formal structure of government defined in the regime of codes, but he also bypassed it in the interest of bureaucratic efficiency. Rather than rely on the large and unwieldy Council of State, he chose a small group of court councilors to advise him. As a necessary retrenchment measure given the limits to government revenues, he and his successors eliminated offices and reduced the number of officials. The Fujiwara having made a comeback, this left fewer positions for other lineages. In 792, Kanmu ended the Chinese-style system of conscripting commoners for the provincial militia. Cultivators made ineffective fighting men; militia commanders had abused their power by ordering conscripts to labor on private projects; and depopulation caused by repeated famines and epidemics threatened the manpower and tax base. Instead of conscripts, the court relied on hired warriors to resist piracy and push back the frontier. To guard the palace and prosecute crimes in the capital, the Office of Police assumed military and juridical responsibilities. In 894 the court ceased formal relations with China, although private trade and religious traffic continued.

The court gradually relinquished direct supervision over the countryside. It set tax quotas by province and appointed inspectors to audit provincial accounts and prevent provincial governors from returning to the capital until all taxes had been paid. Appointed to four-year terms, the governors selected their own assistants, but they delegated tax collection and ongoing administrative responsibilities to registered lineages of local magnates who staffed the district and county offices. The governors essentially became tax farmers because they kept any revenues collected beyond their quotas. Below the officials were the cultivators, hardly an undifferentiated mass. The "rich and powerful" (*fugō*) acted as middlemen in collecting taxes. They too overcollected so as to keep a share for themselves. They owned livestock and slaves whom they employed on large plots of land. Most cultivators barely scraped by on what they could squeeze from marginal plots and work for others. When harvests failed and provincial governors became too rapacious, they abandoned their fields to try their luck in another location.

Commoners in the countryside managed their own affairs. At most, the Office of Police might attack an army of bandits that terrorized a community near Heian-kyō. To handle ordinary thieves, the cultivators defined crimes and meted out punishments. In their eyes, the most heinous crime was theft of their food supply. Anyone caught stealing it was killed. In eastern Japan, people supplemented agriculture with hunting and fishing, woodcutting and charcoal burning, and horse breeding. They too punished theft of their livelihood with death. Cultivators also devised trials to determine whether a suspect was telling the truth; placing the suspect's hand in boiling water was a typical ploy. Whereas the Heian court exiled criminals in line with Buddhist teachings forbidding the taking of life, cultivators had no such scruples.

The rebellion by Taira no Masakado from 935 to 940 in the Kanto region of eastern Japan dramatizes the connection between court politics and local issues. Under the regime of codes, the ruler's descendants not in the direct line to rule received family names and gradually fell in rank for six generations. Losing royal status allowed them to fill civilian or military positions in the state bureaucracy closed to members of the royal family. Some chose the clerical route and became temple abbots. Since branches of the Fujiwara lineage monopolized the highest central offices, most royal scions went to the provinces, where their exalted lineage gave them prestige unobtainable in Heian-kyō. Kanmu's descendants took the name Taira. By the early tenth century, they and cadet branches of powerful aristocratic lineages dominated provincial headquarters staffs as clients of the governors.

Masakado's rebellion began as a family quarrel with his uncle that expanded into an attack on provincial headquarters. The court also had to contend with another revolt closer to Heian-kyō when Fujiwara no Sumitomo (?–941), an erstwhile official in Iyo province on Shikoku and the leader of a pirate band, began attacking granaries and administrative offices. By deputizing rivals of these rebels to fight in its name, the court managed to have both suppressed. Following his death, Masakado became a hero to the cultivators in the Kanto because he had sided with them against the provincial governor's staff. (His uncle had been vice governor.) They erected a shrine to his spirit in what later became Tokyo that still receives offerings today.

Masakado's attack on his uncle and other relatives exemplifies the rivalry that divided kin and undermined the state adapted from Tang models. Because relatives had the same progenitor, they vied for the same slots in the social and administrative hierarchy. Rival branches challenged the titled chieftain's authority to control the lineage's temples and shrines, educational institutions for the lineage's youth, and appointments for lineage members at court. Like the Fujiwara, the Taira became too unwieldy to function as an effective power bloc. Instead, the heads of houses (*ie*) based on residence locations competed among themselves for court honors and position regardless of who happened to be the chieftain. In eastern Japan, the connection between the ie and location was especially strong. There, family compounds (*yashiki*) tended to be dispersed. Each contained many members because, in the frontier setting, there was a chronic labor shortage. According to the convention of the time, when Masakado married his uncle's daughter, he should have gone to live in his uncle's compound and worked for him. When Masakado refused, he challenged his uncle's dominance in the lineage and threatened his economic base. This type of kin-based struggle over hierarchy and dominance far removed from the court and the treachery, arson, and pitched battles that ensued mark the beginning of a new stage in Japan's history of violence.

Early Heian Culture

Both luxury and privation characterized the Heian court. Aristocrats wore layer upon layer of beautifully dyed silks and Chinese brocades, especially in winter because they lacked any but primitive heating systems. They hosted elaborate banquets with drinking, dancing, and musical entertainment but kept to a meager diet. Their mansions overlooked landscaped gardens and contained almost nothing by way of furniture except for free-standing armrests, bedding, and screens.

Aristocrats refined their understanding of classical Chinese and took the literary arts in new directions. The monarchy sponsored three anthologies of Chinese poetry. The monk Kūkai, who had studied in China, and Sugawara no Michizane, the preeminent scholar of Chinese learning until the seventeenth century, penned some of the best Chinese poetry ever produced by Japanese. For centuries to come, intellectuals in Japan would employ Chinese categories of thought in the Chinese language. By the end of the ninth century, Japanese scribes had sufficiently modified Chinese characters that they had developed a syllabary (*kana*) in which to write Japanese poetry and prose. Such was the prestige of Chinese that men continued to use it for official documents and personal reflections. Being native to Japan and hence of less cultural value, the syllabary was largely though not entirely relegated to women.

Transformations in Religious Practice

In the early 800s, two monks, Kūkai and Saichō, returned from China with texts and practices that transformed the teachings of the earlier Nara sects and entrenched Buddhism ever more firmly in Japan's political, economic, and spiritual life. Kūkai's visit to China from 804 to 806 led him to esoteric rites, symbols, and scriptures. Challenging what he saw as an overdependence on Confucianism in political ideology, he developed rituals and wrote texts based on a philosophy of ideal leadership derived from the great cosmic Buddha Mahavairocana that was to be transmitted to the ruler through an esoteric initiation rite during enthronement ceremonies. In Kūkai's vision of the world, the ruler ranked below priests and nuns in the political hierarchy. Kūkai built a retreat for the Shingon (True Word) School on Mount Kōya, far from Heian-kyō, where he and his disciples prayed for protection of the state and prosperity for the people in rites that invoked the mystical power of prayer. His headquarters at Tōji in Heian-kyō put art to the service of religion. Rather than spend years studying sutras, aristocrats might find enlightenment in viewing the mandala (a stylized representation of Buddhist teachings) and achieve Buddhahood in their own bodies without having to die first.

Saichō is often contrasted with Kūkai, but they shared an interest in esoteric teachings and practice. Saichō performed the first officially sanctioned esoteric initiation rite in Japan because he believed it to be the fastest route to attain Buddhahood. He founded the eclectic Tendai school of Buddhism in Japan and

Gion Festival. By 1013 the Gion festival procession featured dancers, mounted musicians, and decorated floats pulled by oxen or carried by men. *(Private collection [Tanaka family]. Photo: Chuokoron-Shinsha, Inc./ DNP Archives.com)*

made the temple complex of Enryakuji on Mount Hiei its headquarters. From 804 to 805, he studied four schools of Buddhism in China, including Zen (Chan in Chinese; Son in Korean), and brought them back to Japan along with the Tendai sect's central text, the *Lotus Sutra* (see the sections on Buddhism in Chapters 5 and 6 for more detail on these schools). One of the most important Buddhist sutras, it contains a rich repository of stories and parables for explaining Buddhism to the uninitiated. It teaches that all Buddhist texts have merit because many are the ways that lead to enlightenment, and it promises that under extraordinary circumstances even women may attain Buddhahood.

The court's fascination with new Buddhist sects neither displaced the native deities nor eroded their assimilation to Buddhas. Daughters and sisters of rulers continued to serve as high priestesses at the family's Ise shrine. Geographic, not doctrinal, boundaries differentiated institutions and beliefs. Buddhist and Shinto deities brought prosperity; they also brought misfortune. In the ninth century, the belief was widespread that powerful spirits caused disease and epidemics. *Goryō*, either a cosmic force or the spirit of an aristocrat who had died unjustly, required cults to be appeased. The most famous cult originated at the Gion temple-shrine complex in 876. It climaxed in a midsummer festival performed when epidemics ran rampant. Angry spirits (*onryō*) resulted from an excess of strong emotion, usually after a well-born person had died unhappy. The conjunction of such a death with epidemics, earthquakes, and drought led the living to believe that the dead person's passion prevented his rebirth by trapping him in limbo. Pacifying his spirit required exorcism performed by mountain ascetics, whose knowledge of the realms of the dead and experiences of hell gave them powers unavailable to ordinary monks. The prayers of ritualists and ordinary people also proved efficacious in transforming angry spirits into guardian deities. *Onryō* cults culminated with Sugawara no Michizane in 947. (See **Biography: Sugawara no Michizane.**)

THE FUJIWARA ERA (900–1050)

The heyday for the Fujiwara lineage came between approximately 900 and 1050, idealized retrospectively as a peaceful golden age of court culture. During these years, a small number of aristocratic women and men produced what are universally deemed to be literary classics. They accomplished this feat despite a lack

BIOGRAPHY Sugawara no Michizane

Scholar and bureaucrat, Sugawara no Michizane (845–903) rose unsuitably high for a man of his modest birth, but he owes his fame to deeds done after he died.

A child prodigy, Michizane wrote his first poem in Chinese at age ten. In 867 he began his career at the junior sixth rank. He assisted in the reception of emissaries from the Manchurian kingdom of Parhae. When offered the post of ambassador to China, he recommended that missions to the Tang court be halted. He served a term as a provincial governor. He helped compile two histories of Japan and taught at the family school and the court university.

Michizane's reputation for scholarship and astute advice brought him to the attention of the monarch Uda, who ascended the throne in 887. Through Uda's patronage, he rose far beyond the rank normally permitted a man from a scholarly family. In 893 he became a court councilor. In 895 his daughter became one of Uda's consorts. Two years later, when Uda decided to abdicate and rule through his son Daigo, he had Michizane and the head of the Fujiwara lineage, Tokihira, share the highest positions in government. When Uda's son Tokiyo came of age in 898, he married yet another of Michizane's daughters, giving Michizane the intimate marital relations with the royal family customarily enjoyed by the Fujiwara. In 899, Michizane became Minister of the Right. Promotion to junior second rank soon followed. These promotions marked him as the retired monarch's favorite, whom everyone else despised. In 901, Tokihira found a man to accuse Michizane of plotting with Uda to force Daigo to abdicate and place Prince Tokiyo on the throne. Daigo promptly exiled Michizane and made Tokiyo a monk. Michizane died in exile, of grief, it was said, at having to leave his beloved plum trees, the urban amenities, and his cultivated friends for the wilds of Kyushu.

When men who had plotted Michizane's fall died in following years, people whispered that his angry spirit was responsible. Tokihira died mysteriously in 909. In 923 the crown prince, Tokihira's nephew, died. In an act of propitiation, the charges against Michizane were burned, the decree of exile was revoked, and he was restored to his previous court rank. In 930 a lightning bolt killed the man who had accused him of treason. Fearing that heaven had turned against him, Daigo died. Speaking through shamans, Michizane demanded that a shrine be built to transform him from a vengeful spirit to the protector of the nation. In 947 he and his literary works were enshrined at the Kitano shrine-temple complex north of Heian-kyō. Forty years later, he officially became a god when the ruler bestowed on him the title of Tenjin (heavenly deity). Over the centuries, he became identified as the god of literature. Today children pray to him for help in passing their school entrance examinations.

Source: Based on Robert Borgen, *Sugawara no Michizane and the Early Heian Court* (Cambridge, Mass.: Harvard University Press, 1985).

---

of growth in either the population or the economy. A population of perhaps 5 million in 700 grew by only five hundred thousand by 900, and it took another three centuries for it to reach at most 7 million in 1200. The lack of economic growth meant competition for scarce resources by ruler, aristocrats, and temples and a miserable existence for commoners.

The Fujiwara helped hollow out the institutions created by the regime of codes. Approximately twenty thousand men and women constituted the aristocracy, and by 900 they formed three distinct groups in a nine-rank system. The highest three ranks had great wealth derived from office lands and private estates, the prestige of the Fujiwara lineage, and the power to set policy. Approximately twenty houses qualified. Ranks four and five consisted of provincial governors and junior officials, who with the right background might advance to higher ranks. The people who filled ranks six through nine possessed specialized skills in scholarship, astronomy, medicine, and law. They had no hope of advancement and suffered under their inferior status. In 1030, for example, they were forbidden to roof their dwellings with cedar-bark shingles or surround them with earthen walls. As the functions of the court came to center increasingly on performing a yearly round of ceremonial observances, the task of everyday administration devolved to household officials.

High-ranked houses required large staffs to manage their economic, social, and legal affairs. Staff members served the house as private officials. They received appointments from the ruler at the behest of the house they served that came with court rank for which they were qualified by birth, normally the fourth through the sixth ranks. Even royal scions who had become military men in the provinces and former provincial governors of the fourth or fifth rank might take service in a Fujiwara household, and they too requested appointments for their servants. Reciprocal relations rather than office in a bureaucratic hierarchy mediated the bond between the head of a house and his court-ranked attendant. Household personnel granted fictive kin ties participated in important family ceremonies along with family members. They accompanied their patrons on outings to the family temples and shrines, to the palace, and on visits to other aristocrats. They served as messengers, prepared documents, and supervised the procurement of supplies. Reward came as protection in disputes and advancement in the court bureaucracy at the recommendation of their patron.

The state soon lost control over the extensive networks of patron-client relationships. Each aristocratic house had numerous helpers, military men as well as personal servants, all of whom were clients in that they worked for the house in the expectation that they would receive a benefit from the state. Even admission to an aristocratic house as a toilet cleaner freed a man and his family from conscript labor demanded by the state. Clientage tended to become hereditary and to continue for generations.

Marriage and Politics

Marriage bonds reinforced patron-client relations and integrated different levels of society. Because a man could use familial ties to advance, he continued the ancient pattern of visiting a wife in her father's household when the father was of higher rank and could serve as his patron. Since no one outranked the ruler, his women lived with him at court and returned to their natal families to give birth. Aristocratic women could inherit property from their parents. Not bearing an heir did not constitute grounds for divorce. A man might have additional wives of nondescript background who lived with him and managed his household. A man and a woman might also consider themselves to be husband and wife even if she lived alone and he visited her only on occasion. A fourth, less common practice was for the wife to move into her husband's parental household.

The Fujiwara used marriage politics as a skill at faction building and their illustrious lineage to dominate political life. During the peak of their influence, between 967 and 1068, eight rulers occupied the throne for average reigns of thirteen years. Politically, each functioned primarily as a spouse for Fujiwara women. As soon as a Fujiwara consort with a powerful father or brother bore a son to the ruler, the child was appointed crown prince. When he attained puberty, he received Fujiwara women as consorts. Once he had proven capable of siring sons, his father would be encouraged to abdicate, shave his head, and seek enlightenment. The average ruler ascended the throne at age eighteen and abdicated at age thirty-one. Some took the throne as toddlers and abdicated as teenagers. An underage ruler needed a regent to advise him, and who better than his maternal grandfather in whose house he had been born and raised? Even adult rulers needed regents to make policy decisions; they too were either Fujiwara grandfathers or fathers-in-law according to the precedent established in 884. Fujiwara no Michinaga made himself grandfather to two rulers and father-in-law to three. His son served as regent for three monarchs. The original Fujiwara lineage had already split into four branch houses when the court moved to Heian-kyō. In Michinaga's day, all but his house, the northern branch, disappeared in power struggles. By the middle of the eleventh century, Michinaga's descendants monopolized the positions of regent. They later split into five sublineages that competed for political power and forced the few remaining non-Fujiwara houses from the court.

Even during their days of greatest glory, the Fujiwara always had to contend with the possibility that a non-Fujiwara woman would bear the ruler a son. Women too received court rank, and the ruler's officially designated wife enjoyed a status far above that of concubines. Fujiwara women in the houses of high-ranking Fujiwara men started with significant advantages, but to maintain their position over the generations required a finely honed consciousness of status exclusivity. For the monarch, only a wife of the Fujiwara or royal lineage would do; for the Fujiwara, only a wife from another Fujiwara branch or the ruling family sufficed. Similar to practices in Silla Korea, monarchs and Fujiwara men married aunts, nieces, and first cousins. They continued to father children with concubines and serving women lest their official wives prove barren.

The Heyday of Aristocratic Culture

The florescence of female literary triumphs during the Fujiwara era is inseparable from political intrigue. When Fujiwara no Michinaga made his daughter Shōshi the monarch Ichijō's wife in 999, he selected a bevy of educated and engaging women to help her compete for Ichijō's attention. Guaranteeing her success in this regard was crucial because his rival and elder brother had a daughter who was already Ichijō's official wife. In Teishi's retinue was Sei Shonagon, famous for her brilliant wit and the author of *The Pillow Book*, a collection of essays on taste. "A preacher ought to be good-looking. For, if we are properly to understand his worthy sentiments, we must keep our eyes on him while he speaks." "A good lover will behave as elegantly at dawn as at any other time."[1] A consummate snob, Sei Shonagon hardly considered commoners to be the same species as herself. "Good people," by contrast, had impeccable lineage, taste, and spiritual virtue. Her contemporary and rival Murasaki Shikibu, who served in Shōshi's retinue, chided Sei Shonagon: "She thought herself so clever, and littered her writings with Chinese characters, but if you examined them closely, they left a great deal to be desired."[2] In addition to poetry and a diary, Murasaki Shikibu wrote *Tale of Genji*, a novel of court intrigue, life, and manners about a royal scion who exemplifies masculine perfection in physical appearance and behavior.

The tenth and eleventh centuries marked the pinnacle of classical women's literature. In the 970s, a woman known to us only as the mother of Fujiwara no Michitsuna wrote *Kagerō nikki*, a poetic memoir of her unhappy twenty-year marriage to a high-ranking court official who seldom visited her. *Izumi Shikibu Diary* is another memoir that recounts the life of a low-ranking court woman (also in Shōshi's service) who married a man of her own station, had affairs with two princes, and wrote poetry famous for its passion. *A Tale of Flowering Fortunes*, composed during the 1030s by Akazome Emon, Japan's first vernacular historian, begins in 887 and concludes with a triumphal biography of Michinaga. A daughter of Sugawara no Takasue wrote *Hamamatsu Chūnagon monogatari* (A Tale of Hamamatsu Chūnagon) around 1070, which

sets a love story in the travels of the eponymous hero who goes to China and returns. She also wrote *Sarashina nikki*, an autobiography notable for her recollections of her childhood with her father, who left eastern Japan to try his luck at court. Steeped in the aesthetic sensibility of their day, these women wrote in the Japanese syllabary. (See **Material Culture: Writing Japanese**.) Encapsulated in the phrase *mono no aware* (beauty, evanescence, and pathos), this sensibility derived from the Buddhist view that the material world is transitory.

Men, too, wrote in Japanese. The poet and aspiring bureaucrat Ki no Tsurayuki edited the first of the royally commissioned Japanese poetry collections, the *Kokinshū* (Collection of the Past and Present), in 905. Female and male poets contributed approximately eleven hundred poems to this anthology, famous for its polished, elegant, intellectual tone. "The seeds of Japanese poetry lie in the human heart," Tsurayuki claimed, and poetry "moves heaven and earth."[3] He also wrote *Tosa nikki*, an account of a two-month trip to the capital across the Inland Sea by the provincial governor and his retinue. In his Preface he pretended to be a woman so as to justify his use of the syllabary and enhance the pathos of having lost a child while away. Other men wrote anonymously in Japanese, compiling a history, *Ōkagami* (Great Mirror), to supplement and correct Akazome's portrait of Michinaga; the first military tales; a poetic tale titled *Tale of Ise*; and miscellanies of anecdotes and observations. Along with women, they also produced folding screens, wall panels, and handscrolls in what is known as *Yamato-e*, Japanese art. (See Color Plate 14.)

Men such as Ki no Tsurayuki wrote in both Japanese and Chinese, but until recently, modern scholars of Japan's national literature have slighted Chinese works and the activities they portrayed. *Tale of Genji* shows men with women or performing music, dance, and kickball at which women were spectators. But courtiers had another life apart from women. They practiced the martial arts of archery, hawking, and horseback riding. They compiled anthologies of Chinese poetry, copied examinations held in Chinese, made vows to the Buddha in Chinese, and wrote edicts, wills, petitions, and litigation settlements in Chinese.

1. Ivan Morris, trans., *The Pillow Book of Sei Shonagon* (New York: Columbia University Press, 1967), 1:29, 33.

2. Robert Bowring, trans. and ed., *Murasaki Shikibu: Her Diary and Poetic Memoirs* (Princeton, N.J.: Princeton University Press, 1982), p. 131.

3. Laurel Rasplica Rodd with Mary Catherine Henkenius, trans., *Kokinshū: A Collection of Poems Ancient and Modern* (Princeton, N.J.: Princeton University Press, 1984), p. 35.

MATERIAL CULTURE

Writing Japanese

When the Japanese first learned to read and write, they did so in Chinese, the only writing system available to them. Chinese is a tonal, mono-syllabic language. Japanese is polysyllabic with a different grammatical structure. Fortunately for the Japanese, the Chinese had already created a system for reproducing the sound of foreign words, primarily Buddhist terms, by using characters for their phonetic value alone. The author of *Kojiki* adopted this method for the names of places, gods, and people. The editor of *Man'yōū* also used characters for their phonetic value—twenty-nine of them for the sound *shi* alone. Thanks to the regularity of the poetic meter, it is usually clear when the editor expected characters to be sounded using their Japanese pronunciation—*uma* (horse) instead of *ma*, for example.

The introduction of calligraphy spurred the development of the Japanese syllabary. The so-called grass style brought from China by Kūkai became a favorite of poets. By the second half of the ninth century, it led writers to streamline commonly used characters, and by the eleventh century these streamlined characters were being used for their sound alone, although each syllable could be written in a number of ways. Called *kana* (borrowed names), the syllables continue to be used for grammatical markers and to soften the appearance of a text by writing out what might also be expressed in visually dense Chinese characters.

Two forms of the syllabary appeared. *Katakana*, angular *kana*, developed from pieces of characters. It was used to transcribe prayers and indicate the Japanese reading of Chinese texts. *Hiragana* has a smooth, round look. Known also as the woman's hand, it was used for poetry, essays,

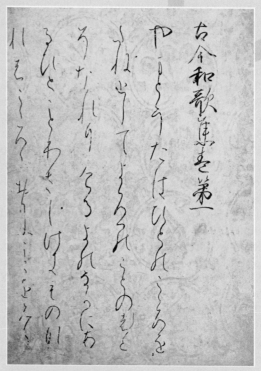

Preface to Kokinshū. *Kokinshū* was the first poetry anthology commissioned by the monarch in 905. Except for the title, the text is written in the cursive syllabary with calligraphy by Ki no Tsurayuki. *(Tokyo National Museum/DNPArchives.com)*

novels, and diaries. To show off the elegance of their hand, men and women linked individual *kana* in a cursive style that flowed down the page. The aim was to combine calligraphy, text, and paper into a harmonious and attractive whole.

Michinaga's diary records his activities to serve as precedents for his descendants. Like other male officials, he spent three-fourths of his time performing the annual cycle of ceremonial observances designed to arouse respect in subordinates and commoners while influencing supernatural powers to work on the court's behalf. He also fulfilled the duties associated with his position in the bureaucracy. Both ceremony and administration required knowledge of Chinese, from which women were excluded by virtue of their sex. In contrast to prehistoric rites and rituals in which men and women participated together, the Heian court differentiated between a man's world and a woman's. Because men could cross back and forth, whereas women could not, gender asymmetry characterized social relations and language.

For women from the middle to lower ranks of the aristocracy, an education in the arts and letters helped them advance at court without ensuring their future. Despite having written great works of literature, Sei Shonagon, Murasaki Shikibu, and Akazome Emon ended their lives in obscurity and probable poverty. Female attendants thronged the court and the mansions of the Fujiwara. When their patron died, they might, if they were lucky, be given a small stipend and be paid to recite Buddhist prayers for their master or mistress's salvation. Otherwise, lacking bequests from parents, they might join a group of mendicant nuns.

In the tenth century, female entertainers called players (*asobi*), who lived outside the court but made themselves available for casual relationships, posed a new threat to court women's monopoly over the male courtiers' attentions. They specialized in amusing travelers along the river and provided song and dance entertainment at banquets. A few *asobi* came from declining aristocratic families and possessed as much education and refinement as any court lady. Some became the consorts of courtiers or even monarchs. The gifts of rice and cloth they received for sexual favors differed only in scale from those received by women who enjoyed longer liaisons with a man, suggesting a continuum of male-female relationships from lifelong to a single evening. In the eleventh century, *asobi* who marketed their skills as entertainers and sex partners had become well established. By the twelfth, *asobi* had been joined by *shirabyōshi* (Masters of the White Clappers) who sang popular songs, danced in male clothing, and brandished swords. They too attracted the patronage of high officials and a retired monarch.

Buddhism and the Fujiwara

During the degenerate last days of the Buddhist law (*mappō*) said to begin in 1052, people had fallen so far from the true teachings of the Buddha that only reliance on the power of the Other could save them from hell. According to the Mahayana tradition, the merciful and compassionate Amida had vowed to take every person who believed in him to the Pure Land of the Western Paradise at death. There they would become buddhas and continue to enjoy their accustomed luxuries in a spiritual realm. Michinaga built an Amida Hall in 1020. In his diary, he recorded reciting from 110,000 to 170,000 invocations to Amida per day for five days. He died clutching a silk cord attached to nine statues of Amida who were to pull him to the Pure Land. In 1053 the Fujiwara regent built a graceful building called the *Hōōdō* (Phoenix

Hall) at his retirement villa of Byōdōin for the worship of Amida. At this and the ninety-five other Amida halls built before 1192, monks dressed as the Buddha and, wearing golden masks, ceremoniously welcomed high-ranking patrons to Amida's paradise.

Likewise popular in China and Korea, the Amida cult spread widely in the tenth to eleventh centuries. Scriptures describing the Pure Land in the Western Paradise had entered Japan during the Nara period, and monks on Mount Hiei had introduced the practice of chanting Amida's name in the ninth century. By 970, monks who had once spent twelve years studying the entire corpus of Tendai teachings spent ninety days in meditation during which they concentrated their thoughts on Amida, invoked his name, and circumambulated his statue. Holy men (*hijiri*) who shunned monasteries brought the promise of salvation through faith in Amida to the common people along with simple esoteric rites and devotion to the *Lotus Sutra* in one eclectic package. Kūya (903–972) spent his youth in the mountains, where he practiced spiritual exercises to eradicate bodily desires. He ordained himself and then walked all over Japan chanting the name of Amida with sutras and holy images carried on his back. He reached out to people through good works—building roads, burying corpses, and digging wells—because he believed that Buddhism had to be made available to everyone in terms they could understand. His message and that of other *hijiri* appealed to people who had to break the Buddhist precepts against the taking of life, in particular warriors, farmers, hunters, and fishermen.

Buddhist eclecticism coexisted with other teachings and beliefs. Aristocrats chanted Buddha's name, invoked the gods, and followed Daoist teachings regarding auspicious days, directions, and omens. Brushing teeth, washing hands, combing hair, and cutting fingernails and toenails had a ritual dimension that tied them to the worship of gods and Buddhas and protected the doer from malignant forces. Some doctrines preached that deity and Buddha existed as one body, others that deities manifested the essence of the Buddha. In the tenth century, a doctrine developed that whereas the Buddhas truly existed, deities did not; what appeared to be a deity was in reality the manifestation of a Buddha in deity form. This combination of Buddhism and native belief infused the edifying and didactic tales told to commoners, who learned that personal responsibility for their actions had to take into account the desires of the gods and the compassion of the Buddha. The search for salvation

DOCUMENTS

Sanbōe (The Three Jewels)

Sponsored by Princess Sonshi and written by Minamoto Tamenori, this was the first Buddhist instruction book to be written in Japan. The first volume explains the essential nature of the Buddha, the second contains biographies of Buddhist monks, and the third describes the monthly round of Buddhist services. The selection here illustrates the wondrous power of the Buddha and Buddhist teachings through stories about ordinary people.

A Woman of Yamato Province

There was a woman who lived in the village of Yamamura in Sōkami District in Yamato Province. Her name is unknown. This woman had a daughter who married and had two children. Her husband was appointed governor of another province. He took his wife and children with him and had been living in that province for two years when his wife's mother, back home in their native village, had an inauspicious dream about her daughter When she awoke, she was full of dread and grief. She wanted to sponsor readings of the sutras, but she was poor and had no property. She took off her own clothes and washed and purified them and gave them as a fee for the readings.

Her daughter lived in the governor's mansion with her husband. Her two children, who had been playing out in the courtyard, called inside to her: "There are seven monks on our roof, chanting sutras! Come out quickly and see!" Indeed, when she listened

for sounds from the roof, she could hear voices chanting, just like a crowd of droning bees. Incredulous, she went out into the yard to have a look. In the next instant, the house collapsed. Just as suddenly, the seven monks had disappeared. In fright and alarm, she thought to herself: "Heaven has come to my aid and kept me from being crushed to death beneath the falling house!"

Later her mother sent a courier who reported the inauspicious dream and how she had sponsored the sutra readings. Hearing this, her daughter's reverence for the Three Jewels [the Buddha, his teachings, and the clergy] was many times increased.

Thus it was known: the power generated by the chanting of the sutras brought her the protection of the Three Jewels.

A Miner of Mimasaka Province

In Agata District in Mimasaka Province there was a mine from which the government took ore. In the reign of Empress Kōken

and help in coping with the tribulations of disease and famine demanded pilgrimages to numerous temples and shrines in the hope that one might prove efficacious.

Men enjoyed a more diverse range of religious practices than did women. The Enryakuji monastery and the rituals it performed on behalf of the court were closed to women. Monks ordained men; they also ordained women and supervised the nunneries to ensure that nuns obeyed the precepts. Being prone to sin and to arousing sinful thoughts in men, women suffered greater obstacles and hindrances to achieving Buddhahood. In *The Three Jewels*, compiled in 984 for the edification of Princess Sonshi (?–985),

the scholar-bureaucrat who was its author set forth the teachings that promised to help her overcome these obstacles and described services held on Mount Hiei that she would never be allowed to see. (See **Documents:** *Sanbōe* [**The Three Jewels**].)

RULE BY RETIRED MONARCHS (1086–1180)

The last days of the Buddhist law coincided with political turmoil. In 1068 political and marital miscalculations on the part of the Fujiwara regent led to the enthronement of a ruler, GoSanjō, whose mother

[749–758] the governor of the province ordered ten men to go up to the mine and bring out some of the ore. While they were inside, the entrance suddenly crumbled and collapsed. The men were frightened, and they scrambled out. Nine of them managed to escape, but just as the tenth and last man was about to come out, the entrance caved in and was completely closed.

The governor of the province was terribly upset, and the man's wife and children grieved. Images of the Buddha were painted, sutras were copied, and a forty-nine-day period of memorial rites was observed.

The man inside the mine made a vow: "Long ago I planned to offer a copy of the *Lotus Sutra*, but I have not copied or presented it. If am saved, I swear that I will complete the project without delay."

Just then a crack about as wide as his finger opened between the rocks, and a tiny beam of sunlight shone through. A monk appeared and passed through the crack, gave him some food and said: "This was given to me by your wife and children. I have come to you because you are suffering." Then he disappeared through the crack.

Scarcely a moment after his departure, a crack opened immediately over the miner's head, through which he could see the sky. This opening was more than three feet wide and about five feet long.

Just then, thirty villagers had come to the mountain to cut vines. They happened to pass close to this opening. The man inside heard them draw near and shouted "Help!" The villagers heard him, though his voice seemed no louder than a mosquito's buzz. But the sound made them curious, so they tied a vine to a rock and lowered the end down through the opening, and the man inside pulled on it. Then they knew there was a man inside, so they tied vines together and made a basket, and they twisted more vines together to make a rope and lowered them through the opening. The man inside got into the basket, and the men above pulled him out.

They took him to his parents' house, and when his family saw him, there was no limit to their joy. The governor of the province was amazed, and when he made inquiry, the miner told him all about it. The miner, full of respect and awe, gathered together all the faithful of the province, and following his lead, they all contributed to the preparation of a copy of the *Lotus Sutra* and a grand offertory service.

He survived that which is difficult to survive. This was made possible through the power of his faith in the *Lotus Sutra*.

Source: Edward Kamens, *The Three Jewels, A Study and Translation of Minamoto Tamenori's Sanbōe* (Ann Arbor, Center for Japanese Studies, University of Michigan, 1988), pp. 220, 232–233, modified.

was not Fujiwara and who was already a mature adult. His chief advisers came from the Murakami Genji (the character for Gen can also be read as Minamoto) line of royal scions, and his youngest sons were born to Minamoto mothers. His son Shirakawa also exercised considerable authority by manipulating personnel practices in the bureaucracy to promote his supporters. Officials entrusted with provincial administration and tax collection on behalf of provincial governors paid Shirakawa kickbacks. Boys in their teens received appointment in provincial offices, and three or four members of one family served simultaneously. None actually ventured to the provinces; they too deputized tax collection. In 1086, Shirakawa abdicated in favor of his

son and became the dominant power at court. This initiated the rule by retired monarchs that added another institutional layer to the system already developed under the regime of codes and manipulated by the Fujiwara.

The retired monarchs had even more trouble than the Fujiwara in dealing with lawlessness. For years, the local magnate Taira no Tadatsune refused to pay taxes and attacked provincial offices in eastern Japan. When the court delegated a cousin and rival to subdue him, both sides engaged in scorched-earth tactics that left less than 1 percent of the arable land in Tadatsune's home province under cultivation. His revolt of 1031 preceded three major conflicts between

1051 and 1135: two wars in the northeast and piracy on the Inland Sea. In 1051, the court appointed Minamoto no Yoriyoshi to tackle the Abe family of Mutsu, tax evaders and chiefs of the Emishi. It took Yoriyoshi twelve years to subdue the Abe.

The next war, from 1083 to 1087, erupted when Yoriyoshi's son got drawn into an inheritance dispute involving his erstwhile allies, the Kiyowara family of Mutsu; also Emishi. Closer to Heian-kyō on the Inland Sea, provincial soldiers sent after pirates were often pirates themselves. In 1129 and again in 1135, the court dispatched Taira no Tadamori to suppress them. Royal scions figured prominently in all of these incidents, designated either lawbreakers or court-appointed commanders, and sometimes both.

The court also had to deal with obstreperous monks who wielded sacred symbols to gain political demands. Warrior monks from Tōdaiji launched the first violent confrontation when they marched on Heian-kyō in 949. The Fujiwara temple of Kōfukuji repeatedly terrorized the Fujiwara by dispatching monks armed with branches from the sacred sakaki tree prepared by the Kasuga shrine under its control. The monks from Mount Hiei expressed grievances by carrying portable shrines through the streets of Heian-kyō. It was popularly believed that any damage done to the shrines or to the monks who carried them would incur the wrath of the gods. An ongoing dispute between rival Tendai sects at Enryakuji and nearby Onjōji that began in 980 erupted into violence in 1039 when, furious at an ecclesiastical appointment that favored Onjōji, the Enryakuji monks set the regent's residence on fire. In 1075, they fought Onjōji's request for an ordination platform. In 1081, they burned the Onjōji temple complex, an act repeated in 1121, 1140, and 1163. These incidents and many others marked the militarization of the clergy. While abbots and their disciples continued to accept the precepts that forbade monks to carry weapons or take life, they allowed low-ranking and minimally educated monks to fight for them and summoned soldiers from temple estates to attack their enemies.

THE ESTATE SYSTEM

A backdrop to the wars and political turmoil of the eleventh century was a set of decrees by the monarch Go-Sanjō to regulate tax-exempt estates (*shōen*). Starting in 743, the court had decreed that temples and aristocrats who sponsored land reclamation projects would be allowed to hold the land in perpetuity, albeit subject to taxation. All other land belonged to the state. In this agrarian society, officials and holders of court rank received salaries in the form of land assignments that generated income. The same was provided for temple upkeep. In theory, these assignments changed when rank or office changed, but as offices became hereditary, land assignments tended to be seen not as the temporary and revocable grant of state land but as constituting a type of ownership. The labor force came largely from cultivators working state lands who rented the land grants on an annual basis. Occasionally, influential aristocrats and temples were able to get tax immunities for their land assignments that turned them into estates. What changed with Go-Sanjō's decree of 1068 and an earlier decree in 1045 was the recognition of a distinction between tax-exempt estates and government land (*kokugaryō*, literally, provincial land) that resulted in making the ownership hierarchy of estates more complicated and estates more permanent. Go-Sanjō tried to restrict the growth of estates by voiding estates created after 1045 and threatening to confiscate those created before if they were improperly documented. The bureau he set up for this purpose certified each proprietor's claims to income and gave him or her de facto legitimacy. Confiscated estates became not government land but monarchical land, its revenues destined for use by Go-Sanjō and his family. Go-Sanjō took this step because in the late tenth and early eleventh centuries, drought, armed conflict, and epidemics of killer diseases left too few cultivators to work the land and pay taxes. To bring land back into production, he gave institutions and individuals with political power incentive to sponsor land reclamation projects by permitting them to receive a guaranteed income from tax-exempt estates.

Although tax-exempt estates placed limits on the state's ability to tax and control landholdings, they did not replace government lands. Approximately 50 to 60 percent of the land remained subject to taxation by the state. This state land included ports, transportation routes on land and sea, and agricultural plots. Provincial governors or their deputies collected taxes on it, kept a portion for themselves and their staffs, and sent the rest to Heian-kyō.

Tax-exempt estates had political, social, and economic functions. In place of a unified bureaucratic framework, multiple quasi-independent centers of power—temples, high-ranking aristocrats, the retired

Heiji War. In the Heiji War of 1159, mounted warriors armed with bows and arrows attacked the retired monarch's residence and set it on fire. *(Museum of Fine Arts, Boston. Fenollosa-Weld Collection, 11.4000)*

monarchs, and the monarch—had the authority to levy taxes, conduct censuses, and police the inhabitants on their estates. Local magnates who had amassed extensive taxed holdings through clearance, purchase, or extortion in the tenth century petitioned the court for tax immunity through an aristocratic sponsor, who became the formal proprietor and received a share of the produce. That aristocrat in turn sought protection from temples or higher-ranking families. The local magnate remained in charge of the estate as its manager. The process of commendation from lower to higher levels increased the number and size of estates and complicated the levels of proprietorship without increasing the amount of land under cultivation. Each estate encompassed a broad, though not necessarily contiguous, territory divided into a welter of small holdings of cultivated wet and dry fields, fallow fields, mountains, forests, swamps, huts for the cultivators, and a residence-office block for the manager. The offices (*shiki*) for everyone from titled cultivators to the resident manager and his guards to the urban-based legal proprietor and protector all came with rights to income in recompense for fulfilling their documented responsibilities toward the estate. This income included food, clothing, and items of daily use. By the late Heian period, *shiki* became less associated with the duties of office than with income from and authority over estate residents.

SUMMARY

What changed in the course of the long Heian period? The flowering of aristocratic culture, in particular the literary masterpieces written in Chinese and Japanese, set the standard for cultivated expression. The last hundred years closely resemble the century that followed. Warrior monks, pirates, and confrontations in the northeast were the harbingers of military conflict that would bring warriors to new prominence. Political and factional strife at court took an increasingly militarized hue as aristocrats, monarchs, and retired monarchs called on warriors in the provinces to come to their aid or saw court nobles take to the profession of arms. The leaders of warrior bands, some of whom were royal scions, competed for the domination, not the elimination, of the court. Infected by the esoteric teachings that Kūkai and Saichō had brought back from China, the court performed ever more elaborate rituals that suffocated the monarch as a political player, while individuals both high and low sought salvation in the teachings of the *Lotus Sutra* or faith in Amida. The dual system of estate and provincial lands accommodated military, ecclesiastical, and aristocratic demands for income and power. These three power blocs were to dominate Japanese history for centuries to come.

The Mongols

BY THE THIRTEENTH CENTURY, CHINA AND Korea had accrued many centuries of experience with northern nomadic pastoralists who from time to time formed wide-ranging confederations that threatened and occasionally invaded their territory. To China and Korea, these neighbors may have seemed a local problem, but in fact settled societies across Eurasia had to cope with horse-riding herders skilled at warfare and raiding.

The grasslands that supported nomadic pastoralists stretched from eastern Europe to Mongolia and Manchuria. Twice before, confederations that rose in the East led to vast movement of peoples and armies across the grasslands. The rise of the Xiongnu in the East beginning in the third century B.C.E. caused rival groups to move west, indirectly precipitating the arrival of the Shakas and Kushans in Afghanistan and northern India and later the Huns in Europe. The Turks, after their heyday as a power in the East in the seventh century C.E., broke up into several rival groups, some of whom moved west into Persia and India. By the twelfth century, separate groups of Turks controlled much of Central Asia and the adjoining lands from Syria to northern India and into Chinese Turkestan, then occupied by Uighur Turks. It was not until the Mongols, however, that the military power of pastoralists created a unified empire linking most of Asia.

In Mongolia in the twelfth century, ambitious Mongols aspired not to match nomads who had migrated west but those who had stayed in the East and mastered ways to extract resources from China. In the tenth and eleventh centuries, the Khitans had accomplished this; in the twelfth century, the Jurchens had overthrown the Khitans and extended their reach even deeper into China. Both the Khitans and the Jurchens formed hybrid nomadic-urban states, with northern sections where tribesmen continued to live in the traditional way and southern sections politically controlled by the non-Chinese rulers but populated largely by Chinese. Both the Khitans and Jurchens had scripts created to record their languages, and both adopted many Chinese governing practices. They built cities in pastoral areas as centers of consumption and trade. In both cases, their elite became culturally dual, adept in Chinese ways as well as in their own traditions.

Chinese, Persian, and European observers have all left descriptions of the daily life of the Mongols in the thirteenth century, which they found strikingly different from their own. Before their great conquests, the Mongols did not have cities, towns, or villages. Rather, they moved with their animals between winter and summer pastures. To make them portable, their belongings had to be kept to a minimum. Mongols lived in tents (called yurts) about 12 to 15 feet in diameter, constructed of light wooden frames covered by layers of wool felt and greased to make them waterproof. A group of families traveling together would set up their yurts in a circle open to the south and draw up their wagons in a circle around the yurts for protection. The Mongols' herds provided both meat and milk, with the milk used to make butter, cheese, and fermented alcoholic drinks. Wood was scarce, so the common fuel for the cook fires was dried animal dung or grasses. Without granaries to store food for years of famine, the Mongols' survival was threatened whenever weather or diseases of their animals endangered their food supply.

Because of the intense cold of the grasslands in the winter, Mongols needed warm clothing. Both men and women usually wore undergarments made of silk obtained from China. Over them they wore robes of fur, for the very coldest times of the year, in two layers: an inner layer with the hair on the inside and an outer layer with the hair on the outside. Hats were of felt or fur, boots of felt or leather.

Mongol women had to be able to care for the animals when the men were away hunting or fighting. They normally drove the carts and set up and dismantled the yurts. They were also the ones who milked the sheep, goats, and cows and made the butter and cheese. In addition, they made the felt, prepared the skins, and sewed the clothes. Because water was scarce, clothes were not washed with water, nor were dishes. Women, like men, had to be expert riders, and many also learned to shoot. Women participated actively in family decisions, especially as wives and mothers. *The Secret History of the Mongols*, a book written in Mongolian a few decades after Chinggis's death, portrayed his mother and wife as actively involved in family affairs and frequently making impassioned speeches on the importance of family loyalty.

Mongol men made the carts and wagons and the frames for the yurts. They also made the harnesses for the horses and oxen, the leather saddles, and the equipment needed for hunting and war, such as bows and arrows. Men also had charge of the horses, and they, rather than the women, milked the mares. Young horses were allowed to run wild until it was time to break them. Catching them took great skill in the use of a long, springy pole with a noose at the end. One specialty occupation among the nomads was the blacksmith, who made stirrups, knives, and other metal tools. Another common specialist was shaman, a religious expert able to communicate with the gods. Some groups of Mongols, especially those closer to settled communities, converted to Buddhism, Nestorian Christianity, or Manichaeism.

Kinship underlay most social relationships among the Mongols. Normally each family occupied a yurt, and groups of families camping together were usually related along the male line (brothers, uncles and nephews, and so on). More distant patrilineal relatives were recognized as members of the same clan and could call on each other for aid. People from the same clan could not marry each other, so clans had to cooperate to provide brides for each other. A woman whose husband had died would be inherited by another male in the family, such as her husband's younger brother or his son by another woman.

Tribes were groups of clans, often distantly related. Both clans and tribes had recognized chiefs who would make decisions on where to graze and when to retaliate against another tribe that had stolen animals or people. Women were sometimes abducted for brides. When tribes stole men from each other, they normally made them into slaves, and the slaves were forced to do much of the heavy work. They would not necessarily remain slaves their entire lives, however, as their original tribe might be able to recapture them or make an exchange for them, or their masters might free them.

Although population was sparse in the regions where the Mongols lived, conflict over resources was endemic, and each camp had to be on the alert for attacks. Defending against attack and retaliating against raids were as much a part of the Mongols' daily life as were caring for their herds and trading with nearby settlements.

In the mid-twelfth century, the Mongols were just one of many tribes in the eastern grasslands, neither particularly numerous nor especially advanced. Their rise had much to do with the leadership of a single individual, the brilliant but utterly ruthless Temujin (ca. 1162–1227), later called Chinggis. Chinggis's early career was recounted in *The Secret History of the Mongols*. When Chinggis was young, the Mongol tribes were in competition with the Tatar tribes. Chinggis's father had built up a modest following and had arranged for Chinggis's future marriage to the daughter of a more powerful Mongol leader. When Chinggis's father was poisoned by a rival, his followers, not ready to follow a boy of twelve, drifted away, leaving Chinggis and his mother and brothers in a vulnerable position. In 1182, Chinggis himself was captured and carried to the camp of a rival in a cage. After a daring midnight escape, he led his followers to join a stronger chieftain who had once been aided by his father. With his help, Chinggis began avenging the insults he had received.

As he subdued the Tatars, Kereyids, Naimans, Merkids, and other Mongol and Turkic tribes, Chinggis built up an army of loyal followers. He mastered the art of winning allies through displays of personal courage in battle and generosity to his followers. He also proved willing to turn against former allies who proved troublesome. To those who opposed him, he could be merciless. He once asserted that nothing surpassed massacring one's enemies, seizing their horses and cattle, and ravishing their women. Sometimes Chinggis would kill all the men in a defeated tribe to prevent later vendettas. At other times, he would take them on as soldiers in his own armies. Courage impressed him. One of his leading generals, Jebe, had first attracted his attention when he held his ground against overwhelming opposition and shot Chinggis's horse out from under him.

In 1206 at a great gathering of tribal leaders, Chinggis was proclaimed the Great Khan. Chinggis decreed that Mongol, until then an unwritten language, be written down in the script used by the Uighur Turks. With this script, a record was made of Mongol laws and customs, ranging from the rules

Nomads' Portable Housing. This painting by a Chinese artist illustrates an event that took place in Han times, but it reflects the conditions on the grassland in Song times, when it was painted. *(The Metropolitan Museum of Art, Gift of the Dillon Fund, 1973 [1973.120.3])*

for the annual hunt to punishments of death for robbery and adultery. Another measure adopted at this assembly was a postal relay system to send messages rapidly by mounted couriers.

With the tribes of Mongolia united, the energies previously devoted to infighting and vendetta were redirected to exacting tribute from the settled populations nearby, starting with the Jurchen state that extended into north China (the Jin Dynasty). After Chinggis subjugated a city, he sent envoys to cities farther out to demand submission and threaten destruction. Those who opened their city gates and submitted without fighting could become allies and retain local power, but those who resisted faced the prospect of mass slaughter. Chinggis despised city dwellers and sometimes used them as living shields in the next battle. After the Mongol armies swept across north China in 1212–1213, ninety-odd cities lay in rubble. Beijing, captured in 1215, burned for more than a month. Not surprisingly, many governors of cities and rulers of small states hastened to offer submission when the Mongol armies approached.

Chinggis preferred conquest to administration and left ruling north China to subordinates while he turned his own attention westward to Afghanistan and Persia, then in the hands of Turks (see Map C4.1). In 1218, Chinggis proposed to the Khwarazm shah of Persia that he accept Mongol overlordship and estab-

lish trade relations. The shah, to show his determination to resist, ordered the envoy and the merchants who had accompanied him killed. The next year, Chinggis led an army of one hundred thousand soldiers west to retaliate. Mongol forces not only destroyed the shah's army but pursued the shah to an island in the Caspian Sea, where he died. To complete the conquest, Chinggis sacked one Persian city after another, demolishing buildings and massacring hundreds of thousands of people. The irrigation systems that were needed for agriculture in this dry region were destroyed.

On his return from Central Asia in 1226, Chinggis turned his attention to the Tanguts who ruled the Xia state in northwest China. They had earlier accepted vassal status, but Chinggis thought they had not lived up to their agreements. During the siege of their capital, Chinggis died of illness.

Before he died, Chinggis instructed his sons not to fall out among themselves but to divide the spoils. Although Mongol tribal leaders traditionally won their positions, after Chinggis died the empire was divided into four khanates, with one of the lines of his descendants taking charge of each. Chinggis's third son, Ögödei, became Great Khan, and he directed the next round of invasions.

In 1237 representatives of all four lines led 150,000 Mongol, Turkic, and Persian troops into Europe. During the next five years, they gained control of Moscow and Kievan Russia and looted cities in Poland and Hungary. They were poised to attack deeper into Europe when they learned of the death of Ögödei in 1241. In order to participate in the election of a new khan, the army returned to the Mongols' newly built capital city, Karakorum.

Once Ögödei's son was certified as his successor, the Mongols turned their attention to Persia and the Middle East. When the Abbasid capital of Baghdad fell in 1258, the last Abbasid caliph was murdered, and much of the population was put to the sword.

Under Chinggis's grandson Khubilai (r. 1260–1294), the Mongols completed their conquest of Korea and China. Not all campaigns succeeded, however. Perhaps because after the fall of the Song surrendered Chinese soldiers and sailors came to make up a large share of the invasion forces, the attempts to conquer Japan, Vietnam, and Java in the 1270s–1290s all failed.

Chinggis and His Descendants

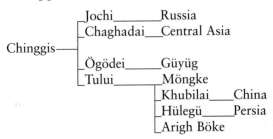

Why were the Mongols so successful against so many different types of enemies? Although their population was tiny compared to that of the large agricultural societies they conquered, their tactics, weapons, and organization all gave them advantages. Like nomadic herdsmen before them, they were superb horsemen and excellent archers. Their horses were short and stocky, almost like ponies, and able to endure long journeys and bitter cold. Even in the winter they survived by grazing, foraging beneath the snow. Their horses were extremely nimble, able to change direction quickly, enabling the Mongols to maneuver easily and ride through infantry forces armed with swords, lances, and javelins. On military campaigns, Mongol soldiers had to be able to ride for days without stopping to cook food; they would carry a supply of dried milk curd and cured meat, which could be supplemented by blood let from the neck of their horses. When time permitted, the soldiers would pause to hunt, adding to their food dogs, wolves, foxes, mice, and rats.

Marco Polo left a vivid description of the Mongol soldiers' endurance and military skill:

> They are brave in battle, almost to desperation, setting little value upon their lives, and exposing themselves without hesitation to all manner of danger. Their disposition is cruel. They are capable of supporting every kind of privation, and when there is a necessity for it, can live for a month on the milk of their mares, and upon such wild animals as they may chance to catch. The men are habituated to remain on horseback during two days and two nights, without dismounting, sleeping in that situation whilst their horses graze. No people on earth can surpass them in fortitude under difficulties, nor show greater patience under wants of every kind.[1]

The Mongols were also open to new military technologies and did not insist on fighting in their traditional ways. To attack walled cities, they learned how to make use of catapults and other engines of war. At first they used Chinese catapults, but when they learned that those used by the Turks in Afghanistan were more powerful, they quickly adopted the better model. The Mongols made use of exploding arrows and gunpowder projectiles developed by the Chinese. They made good use of intelligence and tried to exploit internal divisions in the countries they attacked. Thus, when attacking the Jurchens in north China, they reminded the Khitans of their bitter defeat by the Jurchens a century earlier. In Syria, they exploited the resentment of Christians against their Muslim rulers.

Because of his early experiences with intertribal feuding, Chinggis mistrusted traditional Mongol tribal loyalties, and as he fashioned a new army, he gave it a nontribal structure. Chinggis also created an elite bodyguard of ten thousand sons and brothers of commanders, which served directly under him. Chinggis allowed commanders to pass their posts to their sons, but he could remove them at will.

Since, in Mongol eyes, the purpose of warfare was to gain riches, they regularly looted the settlements they conquered, taking whatever they wanted, including the residents. Land would be granted to military commanders, nobles, and army units, to be governed and exploited as the recipients wished. Those who had worked on the land would be distributed as

---

1. *The Travels of Marco Polo, the Venetian,* ed. Manuel Komroff (New York: Boni and Liveright, 1926), p. 93.

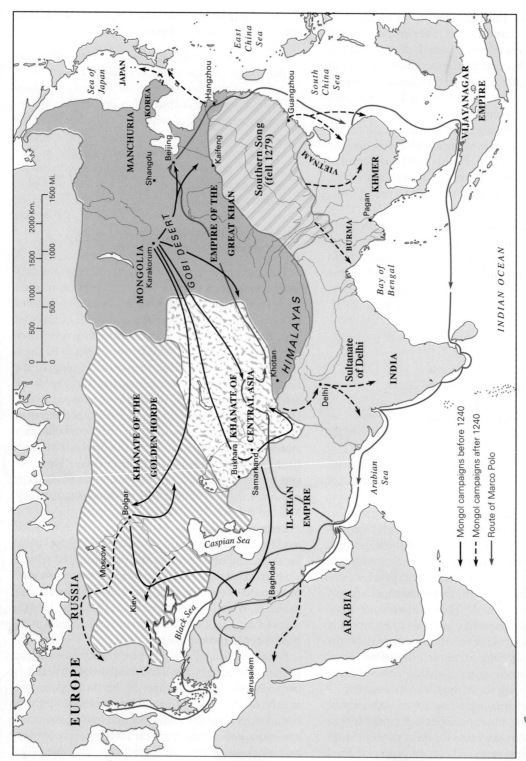

Map C4·1   Map of Mongol Conquests

Sea of Japan

JAPAN

KOREA

East China Sea

MANCHURIA

Shangdu

Beijing

Kaifeng

Hangzhou

Guangzhou

South China Sea

VIJAYANAGAR EMPIRE

EMPIRE OF THE GREAT KHAN

Southern Song (fell 1279)

VIETNAM

KHMER

MONGOLIA

Karakorum

GOBI DESERT

Pagan

BURMA

HIMALAYAS

INDIAN OCEAN

KHANATE OF THE GOLDEN HORDE

KHANATE OF CENTRAL ASIA

Khotan

Sultanate of Delhi

INDIA

Bay of Bengal

Bukhara

Samarkand

Delhi

IL-KHAN EMPIRE

Arabian Sea

Bolgar

Moscow

Kiev

Caspian Sea

Baghdad

Black Sea

ARABIA

EUROPE

RUSSIA

Jerusalem

1500 Mi.

2000 Km.

1500

1000

1000

500

500

0

0

→ Mongol campaigns before 1240

⇢ Mongol campaigns after 1240

→ Route of Marco Polo

serfs. To bring Karakorum up to the level of the cities the Mongols conquered, they transported skilled workers there. For instance, after Bukhara and Samarkand were captured, some thirty thousand artisans were seized and transported to Mongolia. Sometimes these slaves gradually improved their status. A French goldsmith working in Budapest named Guillame Boucher was captured by the Mongols in 1242 and taken to Karakorum, where he lived for at least the next fifteen years. He gradually won favor and was put in charge of fifty workers making gold and silver vessels for the Mongol court.

The way the Mongols ruled China and Korea is addressed in Chapters 10 and 12. In Central Asia, Persia, and Russia, the Mongols tended to merge with the Turkish nomads already there and converted to Islam. Russia in the thirteenth century was not a strongly centralized state, and the Mongols were satisfied to see Russian princes and lords continue to rule their territories as long as they paid adequate tribute. The city of Moscow became the center of Mongol tribute collection and grew in importance at the expense of Kiev. In the Middle East, the Mongol Ilkhans were more active as rulers, continuing the traditions of the caliphate.

Mongol control in each of the khanates lasted about a century. In the mid-fourteenth century, the Mongol dynasty in China deteriorated into civil war, and in the 1360s the Mongols withdrew back to Mongolia. There was a similar loss of Mongol power in Persia and Central Asia. Only on the south Russian steppe was the Golden Horde able to maintain its hold for another century.

The Mongol empire did more to encourage the movement of people and goods across Eurasia than had any earlier political entity. The Mongols had never looked down on merchants as the elites of many traditional states did, and they welcomed the arrival of merchants from distant lands. Even when different groups of Mongols were fighting among themselves, they usually allowed caravans to pass unharassed.

Once they had conquered a territory, the Mongols were willing to incorporate those they had conquered into their armies and governments. Chinese helped breach the walls of Baghdad in the 1250s, and Muslims operated the catapults that helped reduce Chinese cities in the 1270s. Chinese, Persians, and Arabs in the service of the Mongols were often sent far from home. Especially prominent were the Uighur Turks of Chinese Central Asia, whose familiarity with Chinese civilization and fluency in Turkish were extremely valuable in facilitating communication. Literate Uighurs provided many of the clerks and administrators running the Mongol administration.

One of the most interesting of those who served the Mongols was Rashid al-Din (ca. 1247–1318). A Jew from Persia, the son of an apothecary, Rashid al-Din converted to Islam at the age of thirty and entered the service of the Mongol khan of Persia as a physician. He rose in government service, traveling widely, and eventually became prime minister. Rashid al-Din became friends with the ambassador from China, and together they arranged for translations of Chinese works on medicine, agronomy, and statecraft. He had ideas on economic management that he communicated to Mongol officials in Central Asia and China. Aware of the great differences between cultures, he believed that the Mongols should try to rule in accord with the moral principles of the majority in each land. On that basis, he convinced the Mongol khan of Persia to convert to Islam. Rashid al-Din undertook to explain the great variety of cultures by writing a history of the world that was much more comprehensive than any previously written. The parts on Europe were based on information he obtained from European monks. The sections on China were based on Chinese informants and perhaps Chinese Buddhist narratives. This book was richly illustrated, with depictions of Europeans based on European paintings and depictions of Chinese based on Chinese paintings, leading to the spread of artistic styles as well. (See Color Plate 15.)

The Mongols were remarkably open to religious experts from all the lands they encountered. Khubilai, for instance, welcomed Buddhist, Daoist, Islamic, and Christian clergymen to his court and gave tax exemptions to clerics of all religions. More Europeans made their way as far as Mongolia and China in the Mongol period than ever before. This was the age of the Crusades, and European popes and kings sent envoys to the Mongol court in the hope of enlisting the Mongols on their side in their long-standing conflict with the Muslim forces over the Holy Land. These and other European visitors were especially interested in finding Christians who had been cut off from the West by the spread of Islam, and in fact there were considerable numbers of Nestorian Christians in Central Asia. Those who left written records of their trips often mention meeting other Europeans in China or Mongolia. There were enough Europeans in Beijing to build a cathedral and appoint a bishop.

The most famous European visitor to the Mongol lands was Marco Polo, who was enormously impressed with Khubilai and awed by the wealth and splendor of Chinese cities. There have always been skeptics who do not believe Marco Polo's tale, and some scholars think that he may have learned about China from Persian merchants he met in the Middle East. But most of what he wrote about China tallies well with Chinese sources. The great popularity of his book in Europe familiarized Europeans with the notion of Asia as a land of riches.

The more rapid transfer of people and goods across Central Asia in the thirteenth century spread more than ideas and inventions: it also spread diseases, the most deadly of which was a plague called the Black Death in Europe (long thought to be the modern bubonic plague, though some recent scholars have argued that it more closely resembles Ebola-like viral diseases). Europe had not had an outbreak of the plague since about 700 and the Middle East since 1200. There was a pocket of active plague in the southwestern mountains of modern Yunnan province in China, the area that had been the relatively isolated Nanzhao kingdom of Thai speakers. Once the Mongols established a garrison there, plague was carried to central China, then northwestern China, and from there to Central Asia and beyond. By the time the Mongols were assaulting the city of Kaffa in the Crimea in 1346, they themselves were infected by the plague and had to withdraw. But the disease did not retreat and was spread throughout the Mediterranean by ship. The Black Death of Europe thus was initiated through breaching the isolation of a remote region in southwestern China. The confusion of the mid-fourteenth century that led to the loss of Mongol power in China, Iran, and Central Asia probably owes something to the effect of the spread of this plague and other diseases.

Traditionally, the historians of each of the countries conquered by the Mongols portrayed them as a scourge. Russian historians, for instance, saw this as a period of bondage that set Russia back and cut it off from Western Europe. Today it is more common to celebrate the genius of the Mongol military machine and treat the spread of ideas and inventions as an obvious good, probably because we see global communication as a good in our own world. There is no reason to assume, however, that every person or every society benefited equally from the improved communications and the new political institutions of the Mongol era. Merchants involved in long-distance trade prospered, but those enslaved and transported hundreds or thousands of miles from home would have seen themselves as the most pitiable of victims, not the beneficiaries of opportunities to encounter cultures different from their own.

In terms of the spread of technological and scientific ideas, Europe seems to have been by far the main beneficiary of increased communication, largely because in 1200 it lagged far behind the other areas. Chinese inventions such as printing, gunpowder, and the compass and Persian expertise in astronomy and mathematics spread widely. In terms of the spread of religions, Islam probably gained the most. It spread into Chinese Central Asia, which had previously been Buddhist, and into Anatolia as Turks pushed out by the Mongols moved west, putting pressure on the Byzantine Empire.

Perhaps because it was not invaded itself, Europe also seems to have been energized by the Pax Mongolica in ways that the other major civilizations were not. The goods from the East brought to Europe whetted the appetites of Europeans for increased contact with the East, and the demand for Asian goods eventually culminated in the great age of European exploration and expansion. By comparison, in areas the Mongols had conquered, protecting their own civilization became a higher priority for elites than drawing from the outside to enrich or enlarge it.

Koryŏ Korea
(935–1392)

The Koryŏ Dynasty, founded in 935 by the military commander Wang
Kŏn, lasted four and a half centuries. China was no longer its main neighboring power; in this era Korea had to cope with strong non-Chinese
northern neighbors: the Khitans, Jurchens, and Mongols. Society continued to be highly stratified, with the *yangban* aristocracy at the top and a
large slave population at the bottom. Buddhism remained strong, but
Confucianism was also penetrating more deeply, especially among *yangban*. The spread of printing led to the survival of more books, among the
most important of which were histories of early Korea. The dynasty suffered a military takeover of the government in 1170. Still, during the period of Ch'oe family dominance, the Koryŏ royal line was maintained, as
it was during the subsequent era of Mongol supremacy from 1258 to 1351.
In the mid-fourteenth century, the ambitious King Kongmin restored the
authority of the throne and promoted Confucian learning.

Historians of the Koryŏ period have concentrated their attention on
the challenges the government faced because of unprecedented military
threats from the north. How successful was the Koryŏ military in defending the country against powers in Manchuria? Did Koryŏ make good use
of diplomacy in meeting foreign challenges? Why did civilian rule succumb to military takeover? Another important issue is assessing change.
In what ways did Koryŏ society differ from Silla society before it? What were
important continuities? Were there any long-term consequences of the period of Mongol domination? Did Korean culture develop in any new directions during this period?

EARLY KORYŎ GOVERNMENT (935–1170)

The last king of Silla abdicated in 935 to the military commander Wang
Kŏn, who had already declared himself king of the Koryŏ Dynasty (*Koryŏ*
derived from *Koguryŏ* and is the origin of the modern name "Korea").
Wang Kŏn came from a powerful merchant family. Known as King T'aejo
(r. 935–943), he moved the capital northwest to his hometown, renamed
Kaegyŏng (modern Kaesŏng), near the mouth of the Han River. T'aejo

consolidated his power not by centralizing the government, but by seeking alliances through intermarriage with local strongmen, whom he controlled by requiring them to send relatives to reside in the capital as hostages. The old Silla bone rank system became irrelevant, but a new aristocracy emerged. T'aejo chose men to staff his central government from a much wider range of families and regions than the True Bone aristocrats from Kyŏngju but did his best not to alienate the old aristocracy. He welcomed the Confucian-educated elite of Kyŏngju into the new Koryŏ elite, granted the last Silla king a prebend (that is, the right to collect taxes in the place of central government officials) over Kyŏngju, and paid respects to the Silla scholar Ch'oe Ch'iwŏn. Other ways T'aejo built support were by patronizing Buddhism and Confucianism. He built many Buddhist temples in the capital and worked for harmony among Buddhist sects. He continued the Silla Festival of Light every year on the fifteenth day of the first lunar month to celebrate the Buddha and pray for peace and prosperity for the state and royal house.

Further efforts to increase the power of the throne and the central government vis-à-vis the aristocracy were taken by the third king, Kwangjong (r. 949–975). In 956 he set up a commission to investigate slaves' origins so those who had been acquired illegally could be restored to commoner status and thus pay taxes and do labor service, an act that naturally enraged slave owners. In the same year, he had a Chinese refugee, Shuang Ji, design a Chinese-style civil service examination system to recruit officials on the basis of talent. Social mobility hardly increased, however, as the examinations were not held frequently enough to make a dent in the domination of hereditary aristocrats in officialdom. When a centralized school system was established in 992, admission to the best schools was restricted to families of high rank. Kwangjong also carried out a purge of his officer corps and began to favor civil over military officials in emulation of Song Dynasty policy.

To appease aristocrats, his successor initiated a land allotment system. Allotments of arable and wooded parcels of land of varying size were granted to men according to the level of their personal rank, not the rank of their office. These land grants were really prebends. Such prebends were also granted to men who served the state as magistrates or military officers. These prebendal grants, which began in 976 and continued to 1076, constituted income over and above any salaries aristocrats received as officials. Presumably if a prebend was granted on land that the recipient already owned, it meant that he was being granted a tax exemption on his own land. The state also made grants to Buddhist

monasteries, princes and princesses, foreign settlers, degree holders, state offices, schools, and military colonies. Although some historians have connected this fiscal system to the Tang equal-field system, it was in fact very different.

Koryŏ's centralizing measures were based on Tang and Song models, but Koryŏ never became as centralized as those Chinese states because officials from the center were dispatched to only a third of the three hundred or so districts. The other two-thirds were headed by magistrates recruited from local magnates, who later might move up the bureaucratic ladder and even into posts in the capital. Moreover, with so much of the land allotted as prebends, the tax basis of the state was weak, limiting what it could do. Enhancing tax collection would have been difficult not only because of the power of landholding aristocrats, but also because the economy was backward compared to Tang or Song China, with little use of money and very limited trade.

The tenth century ended with both domestic and foreign crises. Because King Mukchong (r. 997–1009) lacked an heir and could not enforce his choice of successor, he called on Kang Cho, the military commander for the Western Capital, to help him. Unfortunately for Mukchong, Kang Cho not only persuaded him to abdicate in favor of a prince, but Kang Cho also killed the king and the relatives of the rival candidate. Kang Cho's machinations provided the Khitan Liao state with a pretext for an invasion of Koryŏ (see below).

After 1020, Koryŏ politics was dominated by an oligarchy of powerful clans. Bloody succession struggles marred politics between 1095 and 1109. Still, Confucian culture gradually gained stronger hold. In the eleventh century, a number of officials traveled to Song China and learned of the development of the Song Confucian school called the Learning of the Way (*tohak*) (see Chapter 8). With time, the examination system slowly became more of a force in government. In the 1050s, on average only eleven candidates passed per year, but by 1120 the number had doubled to twenty-two. By then, besides state schools there were also private academies for educating the sons of the aristocracy.

The system of prebendal allotments began to break down as aristocrats treated prebends as private property. By the twelfth century, they were forming estates and inducing indebted peasants to commend their lands or become their private slaves to escape the depredations of the government tax collectors. This concentration of land and slaves increased the aristocrats' wealth and power significantly. The three most prominent aristocratic clans were the Kyŏngju Ch'oe, the Haeju Ch'oe, and the Kyŏngwŏn Yi. The Kyŏngwŏn Yi became the most prominent political family and solidified its power by supplying queens to the royal family and intermarrying with other leading clans. During the reign of King Ŭijong (r. 1146–1170), bureaucratic corruption, domestic rebellions, piracy, and the king's neglect of business created deepening problems for the government. The growth of slavery and private estates went unchecked. The king, we are told, ignored his responsibilities and enjoyed himself in making the rounds of his various palaces and immersing himself in spiritualism. King Ŭijong also antagonized the ascetic Sŏn meditation sect of Buddhism by favoring other sects that appealed more to ordinary people. Until 1158 he left business in the hands of Chŏng Ham, perhaps the most powerful eunuch in Korean history.

Maybe King Ŭijong could have weathered increasing resentment had it not been for the *yangban* officials' growing contempt for military officers. The arrogance of civil officials reached its limit when Kim Tonjung playfully set fire to the beard of a royal guard company commander, who tied up Kim and administered a tongue-lashing. Kim's high-ranking father demanded that the commander be tortured, but King Ŭijong refused, an act of toleration that he was soon to regret. Dynastic fortunes had reached a low ebb.

THE CHANGING INTERNATIONAL CONTEXT (943–1146)

Because of its alliance with Tang China, Silla had not needed to invest heavily in military forces after 700, but Koryŏ did not have that luxury. The Song Dynasty, as discussed in Chapter 8, did not dominate its neighbors militarily. Koryŏ had to face northern neighbors who had been strengthened by their ability to extract resources from Song China. In the case of the Khitan Liao, two decades of military confrontation ended in 1020 with a negotiated settlement to transfer Koryŏ's vassal status from the Song to the Liao. In the case of the Jurchen Jin, the court decided to transfer its tributary relationship from the Liao to Jin before serious violence broke out. In the case of the Mongol Yuan, the court and its military rulers took refuge on Kanghwa Island, while the Koryŏ military leadership refused to negotiate and suffered almost three decades of warfare that laid waste the country.

Korea became aware of the rise of the Khitans when the founder of its confederation, Abaoji, destroyed Parhae and refugees from Parhae poured into Korea. Abaoji next set his sights on China. In 938, when Abaoji was doing battle with one of the Five Dynasties in China, King T'aejo decided to help the Chinese side. Abaoji sent an envoy with a gift of fifty camels to T'aejo in 942 to seek an alliance, but T'aejo confined the envoy to an island and starved the camels to death, a rash act that caused much trouble for Koryŏ. After T'aejo's death, to prepare for an attack by the Khitans, King Chŏngjong (r. 945–949) built forts along the northern frontier, fortified the Western Capital, and created a new thirty-thousand-man Army of Light.

Liao demanded that Koryŏ enroll as its tributary even though Koryŏ had enrolled as a Song tributary in 963. Faced with such a military threat, Koryŏ had to abandon any notion of moral obligation to China and adopt a more pragmatic foreign policy based on a calculation of the relative power of the two neighboring states. These decisions were always opposed by Confucian moralists, who felt that Koryŏ belonged to the superior Chinese civilized world and disdained the horse-riding "barbarians."

In 985, Emperor Taizong of Song asked Koryŏ to join Song in an attack against Liao, but Liao forces blocked Koryŏ reinforcements and cut off Koryŏ's land contact with Song. King Sŏngjong of Koryŏ defied the Khitan by building forts along the south bank of the Yalu River in 991, but Liao forces invaded Koryŏ territory in 993. Instead of pushing for total victory, the Khitans negotiated a peace that forced Koryŏ to adopt the Liao calendar and end tributary relations with Song (a violation of King T'aejo's testamentary injunction never to make peace with the Khitan).

Once Liao settled with Song in 1005, the Khitan army was free to harass Koryŏ. In 1010, on the pretext that Kang Cho had deposed King Mukchong without seeking approval from the Liao court, the Khitan emperor personally led an attack. After defeating Kang Cho's army in battle, he had Kang Cho executed and had the Koryŏ capital set on fire. Several other confrontations followed until, in 1020, Koryŏ reaffirmed its tributary relationship to Liao. The final border between Liao and Koryŏ was farther north than the earlier border between Silla and Parhae (but not as far north as the modern border; see Map 10.1).

Although cut off from Song by land, Koryŏ continued trade and cultural exchange with Song by developing the sea route from the mouth of the Yesŏng River below Kaegyŏng to Zhejiang Province. Trade was spurred by Koryŏ enthusiasm for Song products like silks, ceramics, and books, which included printed copies of the Chinese classics and a 983 printed edition of the Buddhist Tripitika. Arab merchants attracted to China's coastal seaports also traveled on to trade with Koryŏ. Song cultural influence was important in painting styles,

Map 10.1   Koryŏ Dynasty After 1126

itary forces by adding a new cavalry unit and recruiting soldiers from all social statuses, including Buddhist monks and slaves. Koryŏ forces won a major victory against the Jurchen in 1107 but suffered a serious defeat in 1109.

Under Aguda, the Jurchen rebelled against Liao and in 1115 declared the Jin Dynasty. Soon Song secretly allied with Jin to oppose Liao, and Koryŏ consented to an elder brother–younger brother relationship with Jin. When Jin turned on Song and invaded north China, Jin also demanded that Koryŏ recognize its overlordship. Although most Koryŏ officials wanted to resist, pragmatists who argued that the Jin forces were too strong to resist prevailed, and Koryŏ enrolled as a Jin tributary (see Map 10.1). Among those who urged resisting the Jurchen was Myoch'ŏng, a Buddhist monk favored at court. Myoch'ŏng detested the Jurchen and insisted that King Injong declare his independence, assume the title of emperor, and launch a campaign against Jin. He knew that aristocrats surrounded and controlled the king in the capital and that the king's Confucian advisers, headed by Kim Pusik, preferred tributary subservience to an independent and assertive foreign policy. To get the king away from them, Myoch'ŏng urged him to move to the Western Capital, which he claimed had superior geomancy. Myoch'ŏng's enemies were quick to counterattack and soon brought him down. Although reviled by the Confucian scholars who wrote the *History of Koryŏ* (*Koryŏsa*) in 1454, Myoch'ŏng is adored by modern nationalists who have portrayed him as one of the rare heroes in an era when few resisted either Chinese culture or alien domination. Had Myoch'ŏng succeeded and attacked Jin, however, Koryŏ would have been conquered outright, as north China was. Because the Confucians held sway, peace with Jin was preserved for close to another century.

SOCIETY AND CULTURE IN THE KORYŎ PERIOD

Koryŏ society was as deeply stratified as Silla society before it. The Koryŏ founder may have tried to strengthen the central government at the expense of the aristocracy, but his own supporters quickly developed into a hereditary aristocracy as entrenched as Silla's. In the eleventh century, the new aristocracy came to be called the *yangban*, a term that referred to those qualified to participate in audiences with the king. Below them were commoners, most of whom were peasants, though smaller numbers were merchants or artisans. Although

particularly the monumental monochrome landscape paintings, and in ceramics, especially celadon, the most outstanding examples of which were produced in the Koryŏ period. (See **Material Culture: Celadon** and Color Plate 13.) Distinctly Korean arts also flourished, such as poetry in Korean (see **Documents: Popular Songs**).

In the early twelfth century, the Khitans were supplanted as the northern power by the Jurchen. As discussed in Chapter 8, the Jurchen were a Manchurian people who had been living as small, isolated tribes in the eastern part of Liao territory. Much of this region had earlier been part of the Parhae kingdom. The Jurchens made their first contacts with Koryŏ in the 980s and began to launch pirate raids on Koryŏ's east coast in 997, and there was sporadic friction in subsequent years. Koryŏ extended the long wall it had built in the northeast in the 1030s to block Jurchen raids but at the same time tried to conciliate Jurchen chiefs and get them to pay tribute to the Koryŏ court.

In the late eleventh century, the Wanyan branch of the Jurchen grew in power. They attacked Koryŏ territory in 1103 and defeated a Koryŏ army the next year. Koryŏ King Sukchong tried to build up his mil-

MATERIAL CULTURE

Celadon

Perhaps the greatest contribution of the Koryŏ Dynasty was the perfection of a type of pottery—the grayish green celadon—that has become known the world over. Similar pieces were produced in Song China, but in many cases the Koryŏ versions surpass the Chinese in incisions under the glaze, pieces with filled cavities, and designs. The variety of forms include flasks, vases, ewers, cauldrons, teapots, wine bowls, pitchers, bottles, jars, headrests, water pots, boxes, incense burners, bowls, cups, and plates. In addition to plain and undecorated pieces, the most impressive include bas-relief ornaments in the shape of clouds, lotus leaves, and waves, colors that are not found on Chinese pieces, and incised designs on the surface filled with white kaolin or black clay. Many pieces have the famous crackled surface achieved by interrupting the firing of the vessel. In late Koryŏ, designs were painted with ferro-manganese date-plum juice to produce dark brown or black lines or petals.

The main kilns that produce these pieces were located in the Kangjin area of modern South Chŏlla province, and they were shipped to Kaegyŏng for distribution by the famous merchants of the capital to the rest of the country and China in the Song and Yuan Dynasties. Original pieces are found in museums around the world, and kilns in Korea have been turning out hundreds of copies of Koryŏ archetypes, so proud have Koreans been for centuries of these magnificent pieces. Several shipwrecks discovered in recent years off the west coast of Korea have yielded thousands of pieces of celadon that were being transported from one site in Korea to another.

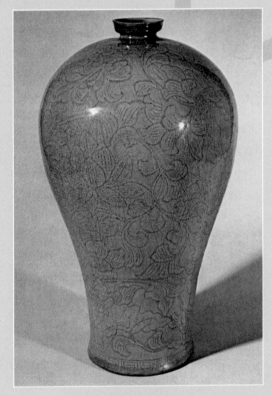

Celadon, Koryŏ Dynasty, Tenth–Fourteenth Centuries. See also Color Plate 13. *(Kansong Museum of Fine Arts, Seoul)*

"free" in contrast to the slaves, who were the private property of their masters, commoners were mostly "free" to pay taxes to the state and rent to landlords, perform uncompensated labor service for the state to build roads and palaces, or serve as soldiers. The wars of the transition from Sill to Koryŏ had enabled the *yangban* to add to their land and slave holdings. Although some of T'aejo's officials suggested that he manumit recently acquired slaves, he did not want to challenge the new elite's property interests.

T'aejo's failure to manumit captives turned slaves created the basis for hereditary slavery that distinguished Koryŏ from contemporary Chinese and Japanese states, where slavery was a much more minor element in society. Although no Koryŏ king ever ordered that slavery henceforth be hereditary, a decree issued in 1037 provided that the children of mixed marriages between commoners and slaves would inherit the social status of the mother. Obviously, if both parents were slaves, the children would automatically be slaves. Since the slave owners soon violated the new rule by taking over the offspring of all mixed marriages, hereditary slavery expanded rapidly and most likely reached at least 30 percent of the population by the eleventh or twelfth centuries, so high that some scholars call Koryŏ a slave society.

DOCUMENTS

Popular Songs

Among the earliest surviving poetry in Korean are love songs dating from the Koryŏ period. They probably originated among female entertainers, who transmitted them orally, but they also were popular at court. Commonly they include repeated refrains, often of meaningless syllables. Most have no known authors, but one of the three here, "The Turkish Bakery," is said to have been written in 1279 by a court official serving King Ch'ungyŏl (r. 1274–1308), who was very fond of this sort of entertainment.

The Turkish Bakery

I go to the Turkish shop, buy a bun,
An old Turk grasps me by the hand.
If this story is spread abroad,
You alone are to blame, little actor.
I will go, yes, go to his bower:
A narrow place, sultry and dark.

I go to the Samjang Temple, light the
  lantern,
A chief priest grasps me by the hand.
If this story is spread abroad,
You alone are to blame, little altar boy.
I will go, yes, go to his bower:
A narrow place, sultry and dark.

I go to the village well, draw the water,
A dragon within grasps me by the hand.
If this story is spread abroad,
You alone are to blame, O scooper.
I will go, yes, go to his bower:
A narrow place, sultry and dark.

I go to the tavern, buy the wine,
An innkeeper grasps me by the hand.
If this story is spread abroad,
You alone are to blame, O wine jug.
I will go, yes, go to his bower:
A narrow place, sultry and dark.

Song of Green Mountain

Let's live, let's live,
Let's live on the green mountain!
With wild grapes and thyme,
Let's live on the green mountain!
Yalli yalli yallasyŏng yallari yalla

Cry, cry, birds,
Cry after you wake.
I've more sorrow than you
And I've more sorrow than you
And cry after I wake.
Yalli yalli yallasyŏng yallari yalla

Family and Kinship

Enough is known of family and kinship organization among the Koryŏ elite to see that it differed markedly from the Chinese patrilineal and patrilocal system and was much closer to Heian Japan (see Chapter 9). In contrast to Chinese practice, the Koryŏ family traced its ancestry back through the female as well as the male line and mourned grandparents in both lines. Wives might move into the homes of their husbands, but husbands more frequently moved into the homes of their wives, and their children grew up among their mother's parents, uncles, and brothers. When the head of a family died, all siblings, including the sisters, shared equally in the inheritance of property. When a sister married, she retained ownership of her property. She could divorce her husband virtually at will and move back to her natal family or support herself on her inherited property. After divorce, she retained possession of her children.

For a man, eight lines of descent through fathers and mothers provided key relatives to whom he could turn for political allies. There were few restrictions on choice of marriage partners, and once married, a man's wife's relatives were as important to him as his own relatives. King T'aejo married twenty-nine consorts and had twenty sons and nine daughters. He made those alliances even more secure by marrying some of his daughters to their own half-brothers, a practice that was anathema to the Chinese. Marriage between cousins occurred not only within the royal family but among the aristocratic elite as well.

I see the bird passing, bird passing,
I see the passing bird beyond the waters.
With a mossy plow
I see the passing bird beyond the waters.
Yalli yalli yallasyŏng yallari yalla

I've spent the day
This way and that.
But where no man comes or goes,
How am I to pass the night?
Yalli yalli yallasyŏng yallari yalla

Where is this stone thrown?
At whom is this stone thrown?
Here no one to hate or love,
I am hit and I cry.
Yalli yalli yallasyŏng yallari yalla

Let's live, let's live,
Let's live by the sea!
With seaweed, oysters, and clams,
Let's live by the sea!
Yalli yalli yallasyŏng yallari yalla

I've listened as I went, went,
Turning an isolated kitchen I've listened.
I've listened to the stag fiddling
Perched on a bamboo pole.
Yalli yalli yallasyŏng yallari yalla

I have brewed strong wine
In a round-bellied jar.
A gourdlike leaven seizes me.

What shall I do now?
Yalli yalli yallasyŏng yallari yalla

Song of P'yŏngyang (Without Refrain)

Although P'yŏngyang is my capital,
Although I love the repaired city,
Instead of parting I'd rather stop
  spinning
If you love me I'll follow you with tears.

Were the pearls to fall on the rock,
Would the thread be broken
If I parted from you a thousand years,
Would my heart be changed?

Not knowing how wide the river is,
You pushed the boat off, boatman.
Not knowing how loose your wife is,
You had my love board the ferry,
  boatman.

The flower beyond the Taedong River,
When he has crossed the shore
When he has crossed he will pluck
  another flower!

Peter H. Lee, ed., *The Columbia Anthology of Traditional Korean Poetry* (New York: Columbia University Press, 2002), pp. 39–45.

Because succession in both the royal house and the aristocracy was not limited to descendants in the male line, brothers, cousins, and even relatives of wives could inherit the headship of a family. As in the Three Kingdoms and Silla periods, women could reign as queens.

Buddhism and Confucianism

During the Koryŏ period, Buddhism remained strong and developed more independently of Buddhism in other parts of East Asia. Leading Buddhist thinkers put effort into reconciling doctrinal differences among rival schools. Centuries earlier, the Buddhist monk and geomancer Tosŏn had traveled to China and returned with information on geomancy and occult teachings along with Buddhism. Koryŏ kings honored

him posthumously, and his teachings gained respect throughout the land. The monk Ŭich'ŏn (1055–1101), the fourth son of King Munjong (r. 1046–1083), returned from a year's visit to China and attempted to merge the meditative Sŏn sect with the textual Ch'ŏndae (Tiantai, Tendai) sect. The monk Chinul (b. 1158) devoted his life to reforming Buddhism. He was distressed because many monks had become too concerned with wealth and finery. He abandoned ties with established sects and in 1190 established a separate Sŏn Cultivation Community of monks and laypeople. Not only did he attempt to reconcile Sŏn with Hwaŏm (the Flower-Garland Sect), but he also tried to combine the gradual and sudden enlightenment approaches of the northern and southern Chan schools in China. He admired the Tang monk Zongmi, who had argued for gradual cultivation even after enlightenment to make sure that the individual would continue to cultivate the mind to distinguish good from evil and act accordingly in society.

Confucian scholars in the Koryŏ period concentrated on ethical governance and skill in literary composition rather than on the study of the classics, self-cultivation, or metaphysics. In poetry, Tang Dynasty styles were in fashion, but very little poetry has been preserved. In the twelfth century, some scholars were won over to the less ornate writing style then prevalent in China (the ancient style prose, *guwen*) and began to criticize the emphasis on ornate prose as detracting from the study of Confucian ethics and governance. As a result, in 1154 the civil service examinations were reformed to place priority on policy questions and essays rather than on poetry. When the military took power in 1170, however, that reform was reversed.

One of the most significant developments in late Koryŏ was the introduction of the Song Dynasty version of Confucianism, called the Learning of the Way (*tohak*). The Yuan Dynasty court had adopted Zhu Xi's commentaries on the Four Books for the civil service examinations in 1315, and several dozen Koryŏ men who studied them in China later returned to Korea. In 1344, the Four Books were established as a subject for study in Koryŏ. Eminent scholars like Yi Chehyŏn, Yi Saek, Chŏng Mongju, and Kwŏn Kŭn admired Zhu Xi's teachings because of its emphasis on the cultivation of virtue.

Printing came into wider use during the Koryŏ period and was adopted by both Confucian and Buddhist scholars to make their books more widely available. Korea led the world in inventing metal movable-type printing in 1234 (China had made movable type out of clay), but as in China most books continued to be printed by carving wooden blocks. A particularly notable printing project was undertaken from 1237 to 1251 as an act of piety to gain the aid of the cosmic Buddha in resisting the Mongol armies. It involved carving the entire Buddhist canon (*Tripitika*) onto woodblocks. Although the effort failed to stop the Mongols, it did result in the survival of many texts that otherwise would have been lost. The woodblocks have been preserved to this day in the Haeinsa monastery near Taegu.

History-Writing

History-writing also advanced in the Koryŏ period with the compilation in 1145 of the *History of the Three Kingdoms* (*Samguk sagi*) under the direction of the versatile Kim Pusik. Earlier histories, includ-

Woodblocks of Buddhist *Tripitaka* at Haeinsa. Carved 1237–1251, Koryo Dynasty. *(Korean Buddhism published by Korean Buddhist Chogye Order, 45, Kyonji-dong, Chongno-gu, Seoul, Korea, May 1996, p. 57; photos by Lee Hone Bae Slide Bank)*

ing ones used to compile this text, were subsequently destroyed or lost, making this the earliest extant history of Korea. Kim borrowed the format of Sima Qian's *Records of the Grand Historian* (see Chapter 3) and like him made explicit historian's comments. One of Kim Pusik's favorite themes was that despite the division of the Korean people into three kingdoms, they were all part of a single nation. In this spirit, he lauded Ulchi Mundŏk of Koguryŏ for his victory over Chinese invaders at the Sal River, and he praised all Three Kingdoms for having strong kings even though he was born into a Kyŏngju Kim family from the previous Silla Dynasty. At the same time, he defended the Silla conquests over Paekche and Koguryŏ because their rulers were cruel to their own people, and Silla provided stability to replace the confusion of the other states. Possibly because Silla's relations with Parhae were bad, he failed to take note of the Parhae kingdom, much less argue that it was part of Korean history, as many Korean scholars today insist.

The History of the Three Kingdoms was heavily influenced by Confucian values and traditions of didactic historiography. The biographies were designed to praise good and blame evil to guide future generations. Stress was placed on those who were loyal and subordinated their own interests to the public good, particularly those who died in battle in defense of their country. Kim Pusik also defended the tributary system as the proper way to conduct relations with powerful neighbors, in sharp contrast, for instance, to Myoch'ŏng's independent stance. Despite his belief in the universality of Confucian ethical standards, Kim Pusik justified the Silla practice of marriage between close relatives as a legitimate local custom. He also criticized Chinese stories of self-mutilation by filial sons to express their ultimate devotion to their parents as a rather poor substitute for the use of medicine.

MILITARY RULE AND THE MONGOL INVASIONS (1170–1259)

Koryŏ suffered a major blow in 1170. A group of military officers, claiming to be enraged by King Ŭijong's frequent pleasure trips, overnight poetry competitions, and drinking sessions with his refined aristocratic friends, carried out a coup d'état. They slaughtered numerous civil officials and eunuchs, deposed King Ŭijong and his crown prince, and put the king's younger brother on the throne (King Myŏngjong, r. 1170–1197). Ŭijong was assassinated shortly after by a general of slave origins, Yi Ŭimin. The coup leaders then appointed military officers to civil posts and made the supreme military council the highest council of state.

The military takeover of the civil government was a major turning point in Koryŏ history. For a decade, military commanders, civil officials, monks, pirates, and low-status communities attacked the authorities and each other. The most dangerous uprising lasted from 1174 to 1176 and was led by the minister of war and concurrent magistrate of the Western Capital, Cho Wich'ong. The leader of the original coup was killed by the son of a newly risen military officer of merchant background.

King Myŏngjong then recalled his father's assassin, Yi Ŭimin, to run the government. Yi Ŭimin, whose mother was a monastery slave and father a salt and liquor merchant, had worked his way up the ranks in the capital guards to the post of superior general, a prime example of the complete overturning of the social order that characterized the period of military rule. Because his rule was marked by extreme corruption, domination of the court by eunuchs, peasant unrest, and a Silla restoration uprising, it was no surprise when another commander, Ch'oe Ch'unghŏn, staged another coup in 1196 and executed Yi, his whole family, and thirty-six high civil officials and military commanders.

Ch'oe Family Dominance

Ch'oe Ch'unghŏn demanded that King Myŏngjong dismiss superfluous officials, confiscate illegally acquired land, carry out tax reform, and eliminate Buddhist influence and monastic moneylending. When the king failed to respond to his directives, Ch'oe replaced him with his younger brother, King Sinjong, who obediently did as he was told.

After his death in 1220, Choe was succeeded by his direct heirs for several decades. The Ch'oe family regime created a new structure to govern the country. The supreme agency was the military headquarters. Ch'oe I set up a personal guard with three thousand private retainers. The Directorate General of Policy Formulation handled security, and the Ch'oe family sent its own tax-collecting agents to the provinces. Ch'oe I's Government Chamber took charge of personnel appointments, and his Chamber of Scholarly Advisers was staffed by rotating civil officials.

The Ch'oe family maintained the civil service examinations for the *yangban*, many of whom intermarried with members of the Ch'oe family. Ch'oe Ch'unghŏn held writing and poetry contests. Still, some scholar-officials refused to serve under the Ch'oes, particularly the Seven Worthies of the Bamboo Grove (whose name was borrowed from the escapist literati of the Period of Division in China), who wrote escapist poems as an outlet for their frustrations.

Ch'oe rule had its share of turmoil. The Ch'oe family deposed two kings and enthroned four. During their rule, there were two slave uprisings, two popular revolts on the eastern coast, a Silla restoration revolt, a Koguryŏ restoration movement in the Western Capital in 1217, and the revolt of a Paekche pretender in 1237. All were put down successfully, securing Ch'oe family rule over Koryŏ for four generations to 1258, but after 1216 that security was limited by the Mongols. The Ch'oe regime resembled the Kamakara regime in Japan in 1185, except that it emerged from the capital guards rather than provincial forces (see Chapter 11).

The Mongols

It was during the period of Ch'oe rule that the Mongols appeared near Koryŏ's northern border (see **Connections: The Mongols**). The Mongols posed the greatest challenge to the survival of the Korean people that they had ever faced. In the 1210s, the Mongols gained control of Manchuria, pushing Jurchen Jin commanders to the area around the Tumen River in northeast Korea, where they established an independent state. At the same time, a Khitan army moved south across the Yalu River to the Korean peninsula in 1216 to evade Mongol forces. The local population in northern Koryŏ, who supported themselves by hunting, weaving willow baskets, and sending their daughters out to become female entertainers (*kisaeng*), cooperated with the Khitans. The Koryŏ government had never bothered to tax them or to register them for labor and military service, so when Ch'oe Ch'unghŏn imposed taxes on them for the first time, they decided to join forces with the Khitans. Ch'oe, meanwhile, overestimated the strength of his army and did not want to be bothered by reports of disturbances. We are told that he ordered the border commanders not to inform him of attacks unless at least two or three walled towns had been captured.

Not surprisingly, Koryŏ government forces were repeatedly defeated. Some Khitan forces made it to the gates of the capital, and other units raided deep into the south. In 1218, three years after the Mongols had taken over the Jin Central Capital, they sent units south across the Yalu River in pursuit of the Khitans. The local Koryŏ commander, Cho Ch'ung, joined in the Mongol operation in 1219 to mop up the Khitan force. The Mongol commander became friends with Cho and promised him that the Mongol-Koryŏ alliance was so firm that it would last forever. A Mongol envoy arrived at the Koryŏ court to request a peace agreement, but the court officials were offended by the envoy's arrogant attitude and wary of the Mongols' reputation for cruelty.

The Mongols severed relations with Koryŏ in 1225 after their envoy was murdered by bandits on his return from Kaegyŏng. The Mongols demanded that Koryŏ sign a peace treaty and pay immense tribute. When Ch'oe I, then military ruler of Koryŏ, failed to respond, Mongol forces invaded Koryŏ almost to Kaegyŏng in 1231 before Koryŏ sued for peace and agreed to disband its army, pay heavy tribute, and send five hundred young men and five hundred young women to the Mongols as hostages. The Mongols withdrew the next year but left military garrisons and governors behind. Because some of the Mongol governors were murdered later that year, Mongol forces again invaded Koryŏ. The king, Ch'oe I, and the court took refuge on Kanghwa Island, just off the coast near Kaegyŏng, where they remained for the next two decades.

A year after their final destruction of the Jin Dynasty in 1234, the Mongols again invaded Koryŏ. They wreaked tremendous destruction, but they were unable to capture Kanghwa Island. King Kojong did send hostages to them, but he encouraged individual commanders to conduct guerrilla warfare against the Mongols on their own. After Möngke became the Great Khan of the Mongols, he pressed King Kojong to leave Kanghwa Island, return to the old capital at Kaegyŏng, then proceed to the Mongol capital to offer obeisance. After Kojong stalled for two years, Möngke sent an army in 1253 to enforce his demand. After Mongol forces captured several mountain forts and slaughtered the inhabitants, Kojong was inclined to surrender, but the Ch'oe family head stopped him. Finally King Kojong crossed over to the mainland from Kanghwa Island in 1254 and sent his second son to pay court to Möngke. When he quickly returned to the island, the Mongols charged Kojong with duplicity. The Mongol commander, Jalayir, showed up with another army and over the next six years wreaked even more destruction. In 1254 alone, about 207,000 Koreans were taken captive, and the number of deaths reached new heights as starvation and famine spread throughout the country.

Ch'oe Hang was assassinated in 1257 by a cabal of military and civil officials and Ch'oe family slaves. When his successor, Ch'oe Ui, was also murdered the next year, Ch'oe family rule collapsed, and King Kojong sent the crown prince to the Mongol court as a hostage, tore down the fortifications on Kanghwa Island, and submitted to the Mongols.

KORYŎ UNDER MONGOL DOMINATION (1260–1351)

Khubilai, who became khan of the Mongols and emperor of China in 1260, did not impose direct rule over most of Koryŏ. Koryŏ Korea, in contrast to Song China, was treated more like an Inner Asian power. The dynasty was allowed to survive, and intermarriage with Mongols was encouraged, even with the Mongol imperial family, while the Song Dynasty was ended and marriage between Chinese and Mongols was strictly forbidden.

In 1260, Khubilai sent the crown prince back to Koryŏ to take the throne (as King Wŏnjong, r. 1260–1274) but required him to send the new crown prince to Beijing. In 1270, Khubilai took over the territory north of the Chabiryŏng pass (in Hwanghae province) in Korea, and it remained under direct Mongol control until 1290.

More devastation came when Khubilai decided to invade Japan (see Chapter 11). In 1274, he ordered

Color Plate 8
Hunting Scene. This image of a hunting scene appears on the wall of the Dancing Tomb at Tongkou near the Koguryŏ capital of Kungnae, north of the Yalu River, sixth century.

(Kim Wonyong, ed. *Han'guk misul chonjip [the complete collection of Korean Art] vol. 4, Pyokhwa [wall paintings].* Seoul: Tonghwa ch'ulp'an kongsa, 1974, plate 56, p. 68.)

Color Plate 9
Women Dancers. Women dancers performing before an audience on the wall of the Dancing Tomb at Tongkou near the Koguryŏ capital of Kungnae, sixth century.

(Kim Wonyong, ed. *Han'guk misul chonjip [the complete collection of Korean Art] vol. 4 Pyokhwa [wall paintings].* Seoul: Tonghwa ch'ulp'an kongsa, 1974, plate 55, p. 76)

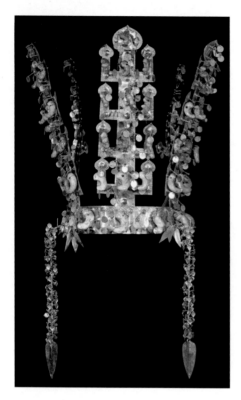

Color Plate 11
Respecting the Elders. This scene from the
handscroll *Women's Classic of Filial Piety
Illustrated* shows a man kneeling before
his parents as his wife and a maid wait for
orders.

(National Palace Museum, Taipei, Taiwan, Republic
of China)

Color Plate 10
Silla Gold Crown. This is the largest
example of Silla gold crowns from the
Tomb of the Heavenly Horse, early
sixth century.

(Kyongju National Museum, Kyongju)

Color Plate 12
Liao Sculpture of a Luohan. Buddhist art
flourished under the Liao, as can
be seen from this 30-inch tall ceramic
sculpture of one of the Buddha's leading
disciples.

(The Metropolitan Museum of Art, Frederick C.
Hewitt Fund, 1921 [21.76]. Photograph by Lynton
Gardiner. Photograph ©1989 The Metropolitan
Museum of Art.)

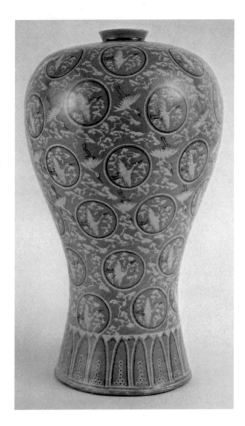

**Color Plate 13
Celadon vase with
inlaid cloud and cranes.**
This is an example of
the beautiful celadon
vases for which the
Koryŏ Dynasty is
known. It dates back to
the late twelfth century.

(National Treasure No. 68,
Kansong Museum of Fine Arts,
Seoul. Plate 87 on p. 83 of
Choi Sunu, *5000 Years of
Korean Art* [Soeul: Hyonam
Publishing Co., 1970].)

**Color Plate 14
The Tale of Genji.** This
picture scroll contains
text interspersed with
illustrations. Both men
and women blackened
their teeth and painted
eyebrows high on their
foreheads. Men wore
hats, women let their
hair trail down their
backs.

(Goshima Art Museum in
Tokyo/Corbis)

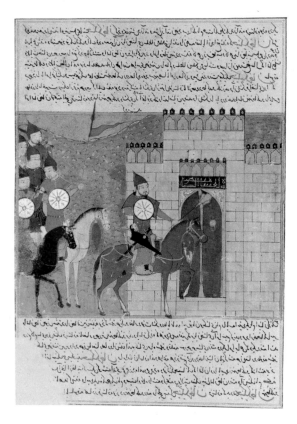

Color Plate 15 Persian View of the Mongols. This fourteenth-century illustration of Rashid ad-Din's *History of the World* shows the Mongols attacking Chengdu. Chinese sources report that the entire population of the city was slaughtered, something one would never guess from the Persian depiction.

(Bibliotheque Nationale, Paris/The Art Archive)

Color Plate 16 Receiving Medical Attention. The fourteenth century wall paintings at the Daoist temple Yongle gong survive in remarkably good condition. Depictions of the miracles performed by Daoist Perfected Ones often show scenes of daily life, such as this one of a woman receiving medical attention.

(Cultural Relics Publishing House)

twenty-five thousand Mongol and Chinese troops and another eight thousand Korean troops and sixty-seven hundred sailors to begin the invasion of Japan after meeting up with forces from China. Koreans were required to build about nine hundred ships and provide supplies for them. A huge typhoon the Japanese referred to as the "divine wind" (*kamikaze*) wrecked over half the ships at anchor off Kyushu and forced the return of the expedition.

King Wŏnjong's son, King Ch'ungnyŏl (r. 1274–1308), had married Khubilai's daughter in 1272, the first of seven marriages of a Korean crown prince to a Mongol princess. Korean kings were looked on as "sons-in-law" of the Mongol emperor (even when that was not the exact kinship relationship). Ch'unyŏl's queen acted like the Mongol woman she was, riding and hunting with her husband. From this time on, the Koryŏ royal house became more and more Mongol in its ways, to the dismay of many Korean *yangban*. Princes spent much of their time in the Mongol capital and with mothers and grandmothers who were Mongol, and they might well have more Mongol relatives than Korean ones. Many Koryŏ kings chose to abdicate early and retire to Beijing, bringing a large retinue of Korean officials. In Korea, Ch'ungnyŏl established the Falconry Office (*Ungbang*) in emulation of the Mongols' favorite sport and used it as a personal guard. He surrounded himself with interpreters of the Mongol language, eunuchs, inner palace functionaries, military officers with little education, scribes, petty clerks, and slaves. When Khubilai began preparations for his second invasion of Japan, Ch'ungnyŏl was much more cooperative than his father had been before the first invasion in 1274.

In 1279, Khubilai established ten branch secretariats throughout China as an intermediate level of Mongol military control over existing Chinese prefectures. He also established one in Koryŏ, called the branch secretariat for the chastisement of Japan, to manage the second invasion. By this point, the Southern Song had been conquered, and the Mongols had several hundred thousand Chinese troops to use on new campaigns. The second invasion force left Korea with forty thousand soldiers, of whom ten thousand were Koreans, in 1281. An additional eighteen thousand Korean sailors manned the ships. They were joined by forces from China, but the second expedition was as ill-fated as the first. After six weeks, a typhoon destroyed the ships and rendered the army vulnerable to Japanese counterattacks. About one hundred thousand Chinese and Mongol troops and seven thousand Korean soldiers were lost before the survivors were recalled.

After the failed invasion, Khubilai left the branch secretariat in place with authority to supervise the Mongol military colonies in southern Korea and manage defense in case of a Japanese counterattack. Mongol emperors deposed Koryŏ kings who failed to serve their interests in 1298, 1313, 1321, 1330, 1332, 1343, and 1351. Some kings were held in detention in Dadu (Beijing) to issue decrees in absentia. Insult was added to injury in 1343 when Mongol envoys arrested King Ch'unghye for initiating reforms detrimental to Mongol interests. They kicked him around, tied him up, and exiled him to China, but he died on the way, a blatant act of maltreatment that energized the anti-Yuan Dynasty group in Koryŏ.

As in China, once Mongol domination was firmly established, more and more people worked with the Mongols. Many Koreans vying for office and power gravitated to the Mongol capital at Dadu, where they established connections or passed the examinations to hold office in China. Contact between Koreans and those they met in the capital aided the spread of ideas and technology. It was during this period that Korea acquired from China knowledge of how to grow cotton and make gunpowder and from the Muslim world advanced mathematical and medical knowledge. The greatest impact, however, probably came from increased contact in Beijing with Chinese scholars. Korean scholars brought back with them new currents in Chinese painting, calligraphy, and literature, and above all the philosophy of the Cheng-Zhu school (Learning of the Way, *tohak*).

Reportedly there were also thousands of foreigners in Korea in this period, many of them Mongols. Some new families rose to power by gaining favor under the Mongols. For instance, the Ki family gained influence at the Koryŏ court after a woman from their family became the favored consort of the Mongol emperor Toghun Temür (r. 1332–1370).

An interesting cultural clash occurred in 1300 when the Mongol official Körgüz tried to get King Ch'ungnyŏl to reform the Koryŏ system of slavery to conform to Yuan Dynasty rules by making all children of mixed slave-commoner marriages commoners, presumably to increase the population under the state's control for taxation and labor service. King Ch'ungnyŏl objected that the Korean custom of hereditary slavery was so firmly entrenched that any attempt to change it could cause serious political resistance from *yangban* slave owners. The Mongols also objected

BIOGRAPHY

Lady Ki, Consort of the Mongol Emperor

During the period of Mongol domination, not only did Mongol princesses become Korean queens, but Korean young women were recruited for the harems of the Mongol emperors. The young woman who rose highest came from the *yangban* Ki family and was literate in Chinese. Her personal name is preserved in Mongolian only—Oljei Quduc.

From Lady Ki's early years in the palace, she allied herself with another Korean—a boy who had been taken to serve as a court eunuch. In his case, not even his Korean surname has been preserved—only the Mongol name transcribed into Chinese as either Pubuhua or Baobuha.

The Mongol emperor Toghun Temür came to the throne in 1332 at age thirteen. He was under the domination of the Mongol grandee Bayan, who had his daughter made empress. Toghun Temür did not particularly like her, much preferring the Korean woman who brought his food and tea, Lady Ki. She also bore him his first and only son in 1339. His first empress was killed when her father fell from power, and another Mongol woman was appointed empress to replace her, but the emperor was so attached to Lady Ki that he had her promoted to secondary empress.

Both Lady Ki and her eunuch ally Pubuhua are given credit in their dynastic history biographies for organizing the response to the great famine and epidemic of 1358–1360, when starving people streamed into the capital and corpses were piled on top of each other in the streets. Lady Ki asked Pubuhua to collect funds from the imperial family and others to pay for relief and burial. She must have given him many gifts, or encouraged the emperor to do so, as his personal contributions are said to have included a jade belt, a gold belt, and two silver ingots, as well as 34 bushels of rice and 6 of wheat. When all was done, they had arranged for the purchase of burial grounds and Buddhist funeral services for a total of two hundred thousand victims.

Toghun Temür may have been very fond of Lady Ki, but he was not a particularly good emperor, and he was certainly not up to stemming the rapid decline of the dynasty after 1350. Lady Ki gradually shifted her allegiance to her son. In 1356, the Koryŏ king had the temerity to slaughter Lady Ki's relatives, who had gained power at the Koryŏ court because of their connection to her. She clearly saw this as a personal affront and asked her son to avenge their deaths. He had an army of ten thousand soldiers sent across the Yalu to try to install a brother of Kongmin as king, but the army was badly defeated. By this time, the Yuan armies had lost control of much of the country to rebels and independent strongmen, so sending an army to Korea seemed perverse to leading generals, who forced the emperor to send Lady Ki out of the capital on the grounds that she was interfering in politics.

As the situation became more desperate, Lady Ki twice made use of Pubuhua to try to carry messages to leading officials, asking them to help her force the emperor to abdicate in favor of the crown prince. By that point, power was held mostly by two rival Mongol warlords. In 1364, the warlord Bolod Temür marched into the capital. The crown prince fled, Pubuhua was executed, and Lady Ki was impeached and confined to her quarters. The emperor did not turn against her, however, and when the fall of the dynasty was imminent, he took her with him on the retreat to Kharokotum in Mongolia. He died two years later; how long she lived is not recorded.

---

to Korean marriages to close kin, including first cousins on both sides and even stepsiblings with different mothers. King Ch'ongsŏn, whose mother and grandmother were both Mongol, spent much of his time in Beijing and decided in 1308 to prohibit marriages to people of the same surname, as well as marriages to matrilateral cousins, at least among the royal house and the *yangban*.

CONFUCIAN REVIVAL (1351–1392)

When King Kongmin ascended the Koryŏ throne in 1351, the Yuan emperor's favorite consort was a Korean (see **Biography: Lady Ki, Consort of the Mongol Emperor**). This might have benefited Koryŏ, but the power of the Mongols was rapidly deteriorating.

King Kongmin quickly set about asserting Korean independence and restoring civil agencies that had existed prior to military rule and the Mongol conquest.

King Kongmin's reform efforts were interrupted by frequent pirate attacks and by two major invasions by the Red Turban rebels from China between 1359 and 1361. Nahachu, a Yuan official who took advantage of Yuan weakness to try to establish his own satrapy in Manchuria, invaded next. During his occupation of the capital, his forces burned the national slave registers in the capital and the household registers of Kyŏnggi province, thus weakening the government's ability to levy taxes and labor service. After several months, Koryŏ forces under Northeast Army commander Yi Sŏnggye (who decades later established the Chosŏn Dynasty) drove out Nahachu's forces. King Kongmin returned to the capital, and he survived another coup in 1363 thanks to aid from a pro-Yuan commander, Ch'oe Yŏng. Ch'oe and Yi Sŏnggye also defeated a division-sized force dispatched from Mongol territory by Empress Ki in 1363 to unseat King Kongmin.

These military threats did not deter Kongmin from pushing for his reforms, even against the resistance of his military protectors and *yangban* officials. By the time the Mongols were losing influence, the Confucian establishment in Korea was a force to contend with. The new breed of scholars was not satisfied with the hitherto limited role of Confucianism in Korean life and wanted nothing less than the transformation of Korea into a morally perfect Confucian society. One of the scholars Kongmin recruited was Yi Chehyŏn (1287–1367), who had been traveling back and forth from Beijing for several decades in the service of earlier Koryŏ kings and was a staunch supporter of Zhu Xi's thought. With Yi Chehyŏn's help, Kongmin reformed the civil service. He set up new schools to train officials in *tohak*, increased the number of lower degree graduates in the civil service examinations, and appointed more degree holders to office, especially to posts in the censorate.

Not all those favored by the king were *tohak* scholars. Kongmin chose a Buddhist monk of slave origins, Sin Ton, to take charge of the monk registers, the office of yin yang and geomancy, the Royal Guards, and the personnel bureau. Since Sin Ton had no landed estates and no independent economic base, he was totally dependent on the king's favor. In 1366, Sin Ton was appointed director of the General Directorate for the Investigation of Land and Slaves to register everyone who had illegally been made a slave during the period of turmoil and all the land that the landlords had been hiding from the central government. These measures infuriated wealthy *yangban*.

When the Chinese rebel Zhu Yuanzhang founded the Ming Dynasty in China in 1368, the Mongols fled north to Mongolia. King Kongmin abandoned the Yuan year period and in 1370 accepted a patent of investiture as king of Koryŏ from the Ming founder. Meanwhile, the political tide in Koryŏ had turned against Sin Ton. When trumped-up charges were leveled against him in 1371, Kongmin withdrew his support, executed him, and purged about fifty officials. Sin Ton had been placed in the impossible situation of leading a frontal attack against the interests of the most powerful families without a political base of his own. Three years later, King Kongmin himself was assassinated. Although his reforms had failed, he had set in motion a process that reached fruition in the next dynasty.

SUMMARY

How different was Korea in the late fourteenth century than in the early tenth century, four and a half centuries earlier? After a period of extensive, active contact with Tang China, Korea had found itself separated from China by powerful Inner Asian states. In this period of close contact with Inner Asian powers, the more Inner Asian side of Korea seems to have been allowed room to flourish, as seen in the ascendance of the military, violent succession struggles, and the pervasive practice of slavery. China remained very important, but it was no longer the great power of the region. What we tend to think of as the great achievements of Song China, such as the burgeoning economy and high level of urbanization, seem to have had little impact on contemporary Koryŏ. China became the source of books and ideas, of Confucian culture and such associated arts as printing and history-writing. Perhaps this encouraged Koreans to be more selective in what they adopted from China and more willing to develop in new directions ideas that had been borrowed from China.

Kamakura Japan
(1180–1333)

The Kamakura period takes its name from the military government established in the seacoast town by that name. (See Map 11.1.) Located a week's journey northeast of Kyoto and tucked into the mountains of the Miura Peninsula, Kamakura had none of the capital's spacious grandeur. Instead it provided housing, offices, and places of worship for a military regime. The task of awing visitors was delegated to the colossal statue of Amida and the Tsurugaoka Hachiman shrine to the god of war, tutelary deity of the Minamoto. The Kamakura regime sought not to displace Kyoto but to keep the peace and dispense justice while the royal court continued to perform essential rituals and ceremonies.

During the Kamakura period, new forms of literature and religion began to supplement the courtly tradition. By the middle of the thirteenth century, improved agricultural technologies had overcome the stagnation of the previous centuries. Economic growth made the practice of partible inheritance feasible until the defense against the Mongol invasions of 1274 and 1281 exposed fault lines in warrior society. When they fissured some fifty years later, they brought down the regime.

Where did samurai come from, and what was the nature of the relationship between the Kyoto court and the military regime? What kind of roles did women play in samurai families, and how did Buddhism enhance its appeal?

RISE OF THE WARRIOR

The samurai plays such a central role in Japanese history from the twelfth to the nineteenth centuries that he appears almost timeless. Yet his connections with monarchy and court, and what it meant to be a samurai, changed from one age to the next. Where he came from is a matter of debate. Historians once thought that the aristocracy reneged on its responsibility for maintaining peace early in the Heian period when it stopped executing criminals, allowed the conscript army to deteriorate, and permitted provincial governors to hire deputies rather than forsake the

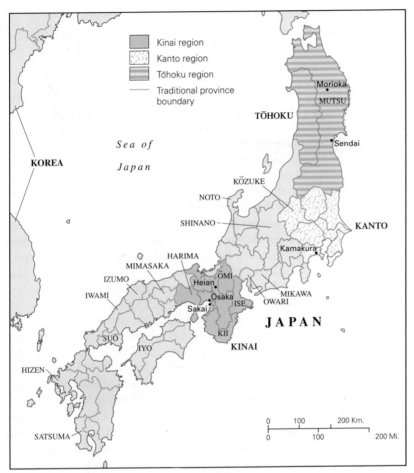

Map 11.1   Major Provinces, Regions, and Cities in Japan

capital. By the tenth century, the countryside had fallen into disorder. Men in the provinces active in land reclamation projects armed themselves in local disputes and turned to warfare to protect their interests. A substantial warrior class arose, and in the twelfth century it turned on an effete and ineffectual monarchy.

Historians today argue that the monarchy was a dynamic success, functional at least to the beginning of the fourteenth century and capable of manipulating the samurai for its own ends. According to one interpretation, the monarchy deliberately encouraged new forms of military organization after the killer epidemic of smallpox or a similar disease in 733–737. Rather than support a large, ill-trained army, it hired professional mercenaries for police work and military protection.[1] Another interpretation is more evolutionary: it claims that conscript armies never completely replaced Yayoi period fighters (300 B.C.E.–300 C.E.)

and that military men of later times were descendants of these professional warriors. Under the regime of codes, they found a niche in offices at provincial headquarters.[2] Even when it could not control how or when it would be used, the monarchy retained the right to sanction military force down to the end of World War II. The monarchy also kept the privilege of granting rank and office.

A third interpretation emphasizes the difference in culture and values between aristocrats and warriors.

---

1. See Karl F. Friday, *Hired Swords: The Rise of Private Warrior Power in Early Japan* (Stanford, Calif.: Stanford University Press, 1992).

2. See Wayne W. Farris, *Heavenly Warriors: The Evolution of Japan's Military, 500–1300* (Cambridge, Mass.: Harvard University Press, 1992).

Warriors originated as hunters in eastern Japan and seamen along the Inland Sea whose occupations and values contrasted with cultivators, who abhorred killing. Rather than initiate land reclamation, they appropriated fields opened by others through forged documentation or force. Instead of releasing captured animals in Buddhist rites that sought merit through freeing sentient beings, they hunted them for meat, for recreation, and to test their martial skills. In eastern Japan, they raised horses and practiced shamanism. They dressed in iron armor and animal skins rather than silk, and many were illiterate. In the eyes of the Kyoto aristocrats, they were rustic boors, hardly more civilized than the Emishi they were called on to fight.[3]

The verb *samurau* means "to serve"; the first samurai were warriors who held the sixth court rank along with scholars, scribes, and artisans. Other terms for fighting men did not carry the connotation of service to the court. By acquiring court rank and offices, such as guard at the left gate, samurai distinguished themselves from commoners. Warriors either sought rank themselves or accepted the leadership of someone who did. When royal scions or Fujiwara descendants moved to the provinces in search of careers that eluded them at court, their qualifications for rank based on their distinguished lineage helped them attract followers. In political terms, the need to have success at arms legitimized by court approbation, rank, and title always limited warrior autonomy.

Warriors fought with bows and arrows on horseback. Their preferred tactic was to catch the enemy off guard, often in night attacks. They violated promises and truces if that would gain them an advantage. Honor lay in winning. Being of lowly rank, samurai felt none of the compassion a superior exhibits toward inferiors. They did not hesitate to burn villages and kill or enslave the inhabitants. The fighting season lasted from the fall harvest to the spring planting, and men stayed with the army only so long as they received rewards. They fought for personal glory and social advancement. There was no point in engaging the enemy if the commander was not watching or in risking one's life against a lowly opponent. Samurai sanctioned by the court engaged not in conquest but in police actions. The goal was to eliminate rivals, not seize territory.

---

3. See Eiko Ikegami, *The Taming of the Samurai: Honorific Individualism and the Making of Modern Japan* (Cambridge, Mass.: Harvard University Press, 1995).

PRELUDE TO KAMAKURA RULE (1156–1185)

Competition between and within the Taira and Minamoto lineages epitomized political conflicts of the twelfth century. Royal scions with followers in provincial governors' offices used their military credentials to gain access to power holders at the center. The Minamoto became the retired monarch's clients by serving as the leader of his personal bodyguard, but rival claimants to this position fought each other so viciously in 1106 that they left an opening for Taira no Tadamori, victor against Inland Sea pirates, to replace them. Access to the throne enabled Tadamori to obtain lucrative positions in the provincial governors' offices in western Japan and to promote Taira interests at court. His son Kiyomori was to take the Taira to such preeminence that he rivaled the Fujiwara.

In the middle of the twelfth century, factional disputes in the Heian court merged with warfare, pitting family members against each other in the countryside. The death of the retired monarch in 1156 turned his sons against each other. The retired head of the Fujiwara house wanted his second son to succeed him as chieftain and regent, to the dismay of his first son, who already held these positions. The Minamoto too were divided between father and son. Only Taira no Kiyomori led a unified house. When rival claimants to the throne and the Fujiwara headship called on samurai to aid their cause, Kiyomori and the Minamoto obliged in the Hōgen Incident of 1156. Marked by patricide and fratricide, it brought warfare to the streets of Kyoto for the first time. Kiyomori won and received the fourth rank under the new ruler, Go-Shirakawa. In the 1159 Heiji Incident, provoked by renewed conflict within the Fujiwara house, Kiyomori eliminated his chief Minamoto rivals.

Kiyomori's rise from an obscure branch of the Taira family to the grandfather of a ruler, followed by the Taira's rapid collapse after his death, is the stuff of legend. Kiyomori intended to use his dominance in military affairs to replace the Fujiwara as the monarch's controller. In 1167 he became prime minister and the proud possessor of the first rank, an unprecedented achievement for a samurai. One daughter bore the monarch Antoku. The other daughters married Fujiwara. Kiyomori's kinsmen monopolized the bureaucracy, holding governorships for over thirty provinces, managing over five hundred tax-exempt estates, and amassing a fortune in trade with Koryŏ Korea and Song China. Even before Kiyomori's death, resentment at his usurpation of aristocratic privilege had brought his henchmen under attack.

In 1180, one of Go-Shirakawa's sons issued a proclamation ordering the samurai to punish Kiyomori. Although the hapless prince was immediately forced to commit suicide, this edict provided the justification for samurai and the warrior-monks of Kōfukuji to initiate a five-year struggle celebrated in legend as the Genpei War (1180–1185). Minamoto no Yoritomo amassed an army in the Kanto region of eastern Japan and proclaimed himself Minamoto chieftain at a shrine to Hachiman. Other aspiring Minamoto chieftains also revolted against the Taira. Following Kiyomori's death in 1181, the Taira still held the Kinai region around Kyoto and western Japan, but Minamoto forces dominated the Japan Sea coast and the east. Yoritomo's cousin and rival chased the Taira out of Kyoto and installed himself as what the court saw as the boorish leader of a band of hooligans. Go-Shirakawa appealed to Yoritomo for help. Yoritomo dispatched his brothers Noriyori and Yoshitsune to fight under Go-Shirakawa's banner while he stayed in the Kanto to consolidate his control.

Decisive battles in the Genpei War were few; most conflict erupted between kin in skirmishes that degenerated into endemic lawlessness. Weakened by years of drought in western Japan, the Taira forces melted away. When the first Minamoto forces ventured too far west and remained too long, they too ran out of supplies. Yoshitsune, by contrast, proved to be a brilliant tactician. He quickly defeated rival Minamoto troops and immediately marched west against the Taira who had reassembled around the child monarch Antoku. Yoshitsune's string of naval and land victories against the Taira climaxed at Dannoura at the lower end of the Inland Sea in 1185. The Taira chieftains were annihilated, and Antoku's nurse threw herself into the sea with the child clasped in her arms.

MILITARY GOVERNMENT AT KAMAKURA (1180–1333)

While Yoshitsune was fighting battles, Yoritomo was building a power base in the east. In 1180, he summoned housemen and supporters to his residence to witness his claim to jurisdiction over the east as lord of Kamakura by virtue of his distinguished lineage and the call to arms he had received from the now-deceased prince. Each then signed his name to an oath of allegiance under the scrutiny of the head of Yoritomo's Bureau of Samurai. In return, Yoritomo promised to protect each claim to land and office. This oath began the process of differentiating the samurai as a self-conscious class. The estates and offices confiscated from men who might be expected to oppose Yoritomo, in particular the provincial governors' deputies and Taira supporters, were used to reward achievements on Yoritomo's behalf. Although Yoritomo usurped the monarchy's authority to confirm landholdings and office, he did so only in terms of military personnel. Court officials and temples that had not sided with the Taira retained the rights to income they already enjoyed.

Yoritomo's nascent regime gained new legitimacy in the autumn of 1183. Years of poor harvests, a virtual blockade between eastern and western Japan, and refusals to fulfill financial obligations had reduced the revenue owed the government, aristocrats, and temples by provincial headquarters and private estates. After negotiation, Go-Shirakawa bestowed the fifth court rank on Yoritomo, and Yoritomo guaranteed the flow of income from eastern Japan. This official recognition of Yoritomo's de facto jurisdiction in the east proved the springboard for him to assert it across the country, but always as the monarchy's delegate.

Once Yoritomo received formal recognition of his control over eastern Japan, he exercised it in ways that amassed power to himself while benefiting Go-Shirakawa and the aristocracy. He intervened in land disputes, suppressed outlawry, and issued orders for payments to be made to Kyoto all across Japan, not just in the east. Several weeks after Yoshitsune's first major victory against the Taira in 1184, Yoritomo informed Go-Shirakawa that he was now the emergency protector for the entire country. He claimed the sole right to raise armies, giving him a hold over the entire warrior class. He forbade the monarchy to reward any Minamoto man without his approval. He urged it to restore virtuous rule and to be judicious in its appointments of provincial governors. To assist the operations of provincial headquarters, Yoritomo appointed military governors (*shugo*) who had the power to arrest bandits and pirates, punish traitors, and summon Minamoto housemen to serve their lord. He even dispatched deputies to western Japan to identify and recruit military men to accept his rule in return for confirmation of their holdings and rewards for defeating his enemies. The monarchy retained its prestige; Yoritomo ended up with a military regime.

Minamoto Yoritomo. This wooden sculpture of Minamoto Yoritomo depicts the warrior in the robes and hat of a court noble. Realistic portraits and sculptures of Buddhist deities characterize art of the Kamakura Age. *(Tokyo National Museum/DNPArchives.com)*

After the Taira had been defeated, Yoritomo found new ways to perpetuate his claim to govern Japan. The defeat had not brought an end to disorder; local warriors continued to raid tax-exempt estates and interfered with the collection of taxes by provincial headquarters. To rein in lawlessness and reward his followers, Yoritomo began to replace Taira supporters on estates by appointing estate stewards (*jitō*) and making them responsible for keeping the peace and continuing to forward the income owed Kyoto. Just as estate personnel remained administratively distinct from provincial governors, so did *jitō* remain independent of military governors. Each *jitō* received his own rights to income (*shiki*), and these *shiki*, guaranteed by Kamakura, not by Kyoto, became the means by which Yoritomo rewarded his followers and demonstrated the necessity for his rule. In 1189, he defeated a family calling itself Fujiwara that had ruled a semi-autonomous state in northern Honshu for a century. This victory enabled him to reward a substantial number of followers with the position of estate steward and its attendant rights to income and to infiltrate his men into the provincial government. Although aristocrats and temples continued to be the

protectors and proprietors of estates, the monarchy's sovereignty had been compromised. Yoritomo had taken over the policing of the entire country, and he had created a new office, the *jitō*, that under his control became the backbone for his military.

Family Politics

After the Taira defeat at Dannoura, Yoritomo's kin became his chief adversaries. By executing Yoritomo's elder brothers along with their father, Kiyomori had rid Yoritomo of senior rival claimants to the Minamoto chieftaincy. As architect of the Taira's military defeat, Yoshitsune lacked only birth to qualify to head the Minamoto lineage; Yoritomo's mother was the daughter of a shrine official, whereas Yoshitsune's was a menial. When Go-Shirakawa offered Yoshitsune the position of provincial governor and Yoshitsune accepted without waiting for Yoritomo's approval, Yoritomo hounded his brother to his death. Yoritomo dispatched his uncle and his uncle's children in 1186. He had his youngest brother, Noriyori, killed despite the latter's protestations of loyalty. After Yoritomo eliminated his kinsmen, nothing should have prevented his sons from succeeding him.

In the competition not to overthrow social superiors but to displace kin, a man's staunchest allies were his in-laws. Following his father's execution, Yoritomo had been placed as a hostage in the Hōjō family, followers of the Taira in eastern Japan. There he seduced his host's daughter, Masako. While Yoritomo was consolidating his power base, the Hōjō proved loyal supporters. His father-in-law even went to Kyoto in 1184 to get the court's permission for Yoritomo to appoint estate stewards.

As Yoritomo's wife, Masako exercised authority in his name, but she also promoted Hōjō interests. She drove away Yoritomo's mistresses, lest their relatives replace hers. After Yoritomo died, Masako held together the coalition of housemen and allies who had pledged loyalty to him. Their first son, Yoriie, succeeded Yoritomo. In less than five years, Yoriie so preferred his wife's family that Masako and her father killed them all and forced Yoriie to abdicate. He died a few months later. The second son, Sanetomo, then became lord of Kamakura with Masako's father as regent. In 1205 Masako had her father arrested because he favored the children born of his second wife over Masako's full brother. Masako and her brother made the Hōjō not only the dominant power in Kamakura, but also the wealthiest of the Minamoto supporters. When Yoriie's son killed Sanetomo in 1219 and was then summarily executed, Yoritomo's line became extinct. Only Masako provided continuity. As her husband's representative, she adopted a courtier infant to become titular head of the Kamakura regime. When the retired monarch Go-Toba declared Masako's brother an outlaw in 1221, Masako rallied Yoritomo's supporters by presenting herself as the incarnation of his ideals. Despite occasional attempts at coups d'état by the disgruntled descendants of Yoritomo's supporters, successive generations of Hōjō regents governed the samurai through children summoned from Kyoto. Although Masako preserved her husband's legacy, she did so in ways that enriched the Hōjō.

Masako's dual roles as wife and daughter suggest that women played a crucial role in military households. Marriage remained a private matter between a man and a woman, often marked with scant or no ceremony. The Kamakura regime never insisted that marriages be registered, nor did it try to prevent marriages across classes. Sanetomo married a princess. The property women received or inherited from their mothers and fathers remained theirs and continued to link them to their natal families; it went with them in marriage, left with them at divorce, and was theirs to bestow on their children. Like their brothers, daughters competed for shares in the family estate and frowned when the sibling set grew uncomfortably large. Given the ubiquity of sibling rivalry, people without heirs turned to adoption rather than enrich a brother or sister. Adoption needed no ratification by the state. When a husband died without heirs, his wife, not his siblings, arranged for his successor.

Kamakura Shogunate

The office of *sei-i-tai shōgun* meant little to Yoritomo because it designated a general with only temporary powers to raise troops and suppress barbarians. Yoritomo used it for three years following his investiture in 1192; thereafter, he accepted higher court office. The Hōjō acquired the title of shogun for the series of figureheads for whom they acted as regents and applied it retroactively to Yoritomo to legitimize their stratagem. Historians often use the term *bakufu* to designate the military regimes between 1180 and 1867, but it is a nineteenth-century anachronism that elides the substantial differences between them.

In 1221, the retired monarch Go-Toba misjudged samurai support for the Hōjō and tried to rally military men in western Japan to crush the Kamakura regime. Following his defeat and exile, the Hōjō extended their reach into western Japan. They confiscated estates belonging to Go-Toba's supporters and apportioned them to estate stewards who fought for Kamakura. They stationed two members of their family in Kyoto to oversee relations with the court and ensure that no future monarch followed Go-Toba's example. They followed the precedent set by Yoritomo in guaranteeing local land rights. Across Japan, estate managers proclaimed themselves loyal followers of Kamakura in order to attack proprietor land rights and appropriate the office of estate steward. As the leaders of the samurai, the Hōjō wanted to have samurai declare themselves for Kamakura. They also had to prevent the fighting that their new followers provoked to gain income. Although the Hōjō and their chief supporters became provincial governors, neither they nor the estate stewards tried to seize territory. Final authority over land rested with the monarchy, and the provincial headquarters continued to administer large portions of it. The hierarchical estate structure

DOCUMENTS

The Estate Stewards in Legal Documents

Underpinning the rise of the samurai was the office of estate steward (jitō shiki), a position central to understanding the nature of Kamakura rule. With it came rights to income that supported a martial lifestyle in return for loyal service. The documents here enumerate the estate steward's responsibilities, adjudicate lawsuits, recognize women's rights to hold office and receive income, and promote land reclamation. They provide glimpses of what this office entailed for the steward, his descendants, and previous estate personnel.

Ordered to the residents of paddy and up-land areas in Ryūzōji village, Ozu-Higashi Gō. Hizen Province that Fujiwara Sueie shall henceforth be *jitō*.

Concerning the aforesaid place, and owing to Fujiwara Sueie's hereditary claim, an order by the government-general for the island of Kyushu authorizing him to administer it was granted. However, a local chief of Kanzaki district, Shigezane, has reportedly been obstructive. Sueie did not join the Heike rebellion and served loyally, honoring imperial authority. Shigezane plotted rebellion as a Heike partisan, in itself a great crime. Worst of all, his failure to submit formally before the Kamakura lord is evidence of a continuing sympathy for the Heike rebels. The import of this is outrageous. Accordingly, Shigezane's disturbances are to cease permanently, and Sueie is to hold the *jitō shiki*. Regarding the stipulated taxes and annual rice levy, the orders of the proprietor are to be obeyed and duty discharged in accordance with precedence. It is commanded thus. Wherefore, this order.
1186, 8th month, 9th day.

The chancellery of the shogun's house orders to the residents of three districts—Iwamatsu, Shimo Imai, Tanaka—within Nitta estate, Kōzuke Province that in accord with the last will of the husband, Yoshikane, his widow shall forthwith be *jitō*.

The aforesaid person, in accordance with the will, is appointed to this *shiki*. As to the fixed annual tax and other services, these shall be paid in accordance with precedent. It is commanded thus. Wherefore, this order.
1215, 3rd month, 22nd day.

Concerning the estate manager *shiki* of Tarumi estate, Settsu province:

Regarding the above, the former estate manager Shigetsune had his lands confiscated because of his Heike affiliation [and bestowed on a *jitō*]. However, the palace woman Izumo-no-tsubone has stated: This estate is a land first opened by my ancestors with a estate managership that is hereditary. Given this original-holder status, we request that the *shiki* be reconferred. Since it is difficult to ignore a suit lodged by a court person, the reappointment will be

---

remained dominated by Kyoto and defended by Kamakura in a system of dual governance.

Neither Yoritomo nor the Hōjō instituted a government that would be considered fully fledged today. Yoritomo ruled through a chancellery similar to the administrative offices in provincial headquarters, aristocratic households, and temple complexes. In 1225, Masako's nephew Yasutoki established a thirteen-member council composed of the senior Hōjō and the heads of allied families. It made policy decisions and appointments and served as a court of last appeal. There was no public treasury. The thirteen councilors had their own sources of income as the stewards for numerous estates and as Kyoto-appointed officials holding court rank and office. Litigants paid court costs for the judicial system; the residents of Kamakura paid fees for city administration; Minamoto housemen provided the upkeep for the Tsurugaoka Hachiman shrine; and compensation for Yoritomo's followers came out of the revenues generated by the tax-exempt estates.

Legal disputes over land generated the most paperwork (see **Documents: The Estate Stewards in Legal Documents**). Conflict between siblings was common, and women as well as men brought suit. Newly ap-

made to this *shiki*. By command of the Kamakura lord it is decreed thus.
1204, 9th month, 6th day.

Ordered to the *jitō* headquarters of Fukunaga Myō in Matsuura estate in Hizen province that forthwith undeveloped areas shall be opened and taxes paid from them.

Regarding this, a petition from the *jitō* and others states: "this estate is populous, but has too few paddy and upland fields. Accordingly, new fields should be opened and taxes produced." In essence, the restoration of smoke from every house will mean prosperity for the village, and will also ensure the peace. You may open new land, as requested. During the first year of development, taxes will be waived. For the next year the rate will be one-half bushel per .294 acre of whatever the commodity being grown, with an increase of one-half bushel the following year, and ultimately a rate of one and one-half bushels. As regards the miscellaneous obligations, a similar exemption will be in force. Should the newly opened fields become a pretext for the desolation of established ones, payment quotas will conform to those of the old fields, even in newly cultivated areas. As for the stipulated regular taxes, these will be paid, without fail, into the estate warehouse. Also, the number of workers engaged in developing the new land is to be reported each year when the proprietor's agents conduct their annual survey. In response to the petition, it is so decreed.
1229, 2nd month, 21st day.

Concerning a dispute of Ōeda village, a holding of Kashima shrine, between the Kashima priest Tomochika and Nomoto Shirō Gyōshin.

Although both plaintiff and defense have submitted many details regarding the above, it is evident that the land of this village was divided in 1237 by mutual agreement. Nevertheless, Gyōshin now argues that because the 1237 compromise was effected through negotiations with an uninformed deputy *jitō*, the land should be totally controlled by the *jitō*, with rents paid to the shrine. Relative to the original compromise document, the statute of limitations has passed, with dual possession dating from 1237; it is thus very difficult to attempt to disrupt things now. Therefore, authority will be exercised in accordance with the 1237 document. By command of the Kamakura lord, it is so decreed.
1298 2nd month, 3rd day.

Source: Jeffrey P. Mass, *The Kamakura Bakufu: A Study in Documents* (Stanford, Calif.: Stanford University Press, 1976), pp. 41, 48, 55, 101, 151 (modified).

pointed estate stewards wanted clarity in the extent of their authority over the cultivators, their relations with the staff already in place, and the collection of rents. When a steward appropriated too much income for himself or interfered in the activities of the estate staff, the injured party in Kyoto appealed to Kamakura to restore its rights. For over 150 years, judges in Kamakura made a serious effort to maintain the status quo by adjudicating these cases more or less fairly.

The Hōjō soon realized that disciplining the stewards required clear guidelines. In 1232, Yasutoki published a new code, the *Goseibai shikimoku* (a list of rules for making judgments), the first step in the evolution of juridical procedures passed on contemporary norms. Steeped in the Chinese classics, Yasutoki believed that government had to be just in order to be legitimate. Stewards had to be held accountable for unlawful acts. A steward convicted of starting a brawl, for example, would lose his estates. Adultery and rape were to be punished by exiling the couple and confiscating their estates. Unlike previous codes based on Chinese models, this code was based on precedent:

the decisions made by Yoritomo and Masako cited in the text. When no precedent fit a particular situation, the judges were to rely on reason. In its provisions dealing with inheritance rights, the code made legal what had been customary, including women's legal prerogatives. Women had the right to inherit property and the office that went with it. A woman could become the family head, and a widow could become a steward. The code protected the rights of the monarchy to its income and added legal protection to the land grants made to stewards. The steward in effect owned his or her land rights and could do what he or she liked with them: buy, sell, or divide them among heirs.

Toward Intensive Agriculture and Economic Growth

As an unintended consequence of the tax-exempt estate system, farmers who held permanent title to cultivation rights as *myōshu* had an incentive to cultivate land more intensively. In Kyushu and western Japan, they tried growing two crops a year, rice and a lesser grain such as barley. Toward the end of the twelfth century, a hardier rice variety arrived from China that could be grown on previously marginal fields and that proved resistant to drought and cold weather. Cultivators expanded their acreage by using upland areas for dry fields and orchards, and they stopped allowing fields to lie fallow. To keep land in continuous production, they spread processed fertilizer—ashes, mulch, and manure. The dissemination and improvement in iron smelting technology to make armor and weapons also produced better plows and harrows. Pulled by draft animals, these tools allowed laborers to till more fields more thoroughly. Irrigation canals regulated the flow of water to paddy fields, and human-powered water wheels lifted water from streams to canals. The result was higher agricultural productivity that more than compensated for population growth.

Intensive agricultural practices did not spread uniformly. In the east, only the northern lowlands of the Kanto plain grew wet rice. Mulberry leaves raised on dry fields provided the fodder for silkworms. Alluvial terraces supplied pasturage for horses. The central Kanto plain sheltered deer, boars, and bandits. Areas separated from the core agricultural regions by mountains, such as southern Shikoku, southwestern Kyushu, and the regions along the Japan Sea, had lower populations and fewer cultivators.

Cultivators included *myōshu*, responsible for paying taxes to the state and rents to proprietors, and their dependents. Although squeezed by estate managers and stewards, the *myōshu's* cultivation rights made them wealthy. The dependents ranged from slaves to serfs to small holders. The Kamakura shogunate issued bans on trade in human beings several times in the thirteenth century, but professional slave traders continued to kidnap women and children, and people voluntarily sold themselves when they were destitute. Serfs called *shoju* (those who obey) had their own parcels of land and huts for their families. They were not free in that their masters disposed of them in wills and legal testaments as though they were property. Small holders leased fields from the *myōshu* and tilled dry field plots that they had cleared from marginal land. Since these were less likely to be taxed than rice-bearing paddies, they gave their cultivator a measure of independence and a tiny income.

Although regional crop failures owing to drought and unseasonable cold continued to cause famines, demographic crises had been relegated to the past. Major contagious diseases had become endemic, mostly killing children rather than adult workers. After 1189, warfare ceased to be a problem. A population of perhaps 7 million at the beginning of the Kamakura period had grown to roughly 8.2 million by its end and was more densely concentrated in western Japan than in other regions. The roads built by the state in the seventh and eighth centuries still centered on Kyoto.

In addition to aristocrats, clerics, warriors, and cultivators, there was a large unsettled population. It included entertainers, itinerant artisans and traders, traveling proselytizers, prostitutes, fishermen, pirates, hunters, bandits, and an amorphous category of outcasts deemed polluted or unclean for reasons of disease, work with dead animals, or ill fortune. Fishermen and people of the forest paid tribute to the court with fish, game, seaweed, and wild vegetables. Between the eleventh and thirteenth centuries, they received privileges from aristocrats, temples, shrines, and retired monarchs that authorized them to travel freely and avoid taxes. Artisans who traveled in search of raw materials and markets for their products also sought the court's protection. Female entertainers and prostitutes received licenses to travel and organized themselves into fictive kin groups under the control of influential female chiefs. Buddhist monks who castigated entertainers for leading men astray practiced same-sex relations to satisfy their sexual needs. Some didactic tales told of prostitutes who became nuns; in others they were depicted as bodhisattvas who led men to salvation. Most outcasts enjoyed the protection of religious establishments or the court. They performed police work

Shinran. The illustrated scroll of Shinran's life portrays him expounding on his teachings as he traveled around Japan. *(Bukkoji, Kyoto/DNP Archives.com)*

for warriors. They ran inns where they offered hot baths to travelers. Even beggars performed a useful function because they enabled the wealthy to perform acts of charity.

Buddhism

The six Nara sects, as well as the Tendai and Shingon sects, dominated mainstream Buddhism and religious life during the Kamakura period, and they attracted some of the greatest minds of the age. A cult grew up around Prince Shōtoku for having propagated Buddhism. Zenkōji in the mountains of central Japan had what was reputed to be a living icon that drew pilgrims from all walks of life, as did the bronze statue of Amida at Kamakura completed in 1252. Simplified practices and doctrines plus hope for salvation in the latter days of the Buddhist law contributed to Buddhism's mass appeal. In 1245, a group of aristocratic nuns received the precepts for novices at the Hokkeji nunnery in Nara, reviving an order that had died out in the ninth century. Ceremonies that pointed to the mysteries of esoteric Buddhism spread to provincial temples; their audience contained commoners as well as nobles. Aristocrats drew on esoteric ini-

tiation rites in formulating secret traditions for the transmission of poetic styles and explained the hidden meaning of poetry collections in terms of Tantric Buddhism. Samurai modeled themselves on aristocrats in patronizing and building shrines and temples. In the history titled *Gukanshō (Humble Interpretations)*, the Tendai priest Jien explained the court's lack of virtue and the warrior's rise to power in the context of the latter days of the Buddhist law. Temple-shrine complexes constituted one of the three power blocs, along with the Kyoto court and Kamakura regime. The relations between them were never stable, and the distinctions between aristocrats, warriors, and clerics easily blurred.

Outside the mainstream appeared teacher-monks who reformulated doctrines taught at the Tendai headquarters on Mount Hiei and instituted new practices. They criticized the established temples for their superficial ceremonies and monastic decadence. They reached out to new constituents, including women, and addressed female concerns, especially the issue of whether women could be reborn after death in the Buddhist paradise called the Pure Land.

Faith in Amida was already prevalent when Hōnen and Shinran started preaching. Hōnen told listeners that Buddhism was available to all through absolute faith in the saving power of Amida. The best way to achieve faith was not through pious deeds or religious study but by reciting "praise to Amida Buddha." In 1207, Hōnen was exiled when some of his disciples overstepped the bounds of propriety in taking his message to the ladies-in-waiting at Go-Toba's court. Following his death in 1212, his disciples created the Jōdo (Pure Land) sect. Shinran took Hōnen's teachings to low-ranking warriors, the poor, and criminals. He preached that Amida had vowed to save everyone—sinners, murderers, thieves, the humble, and evil alike—even people who did not know he would save them. All that was required was faith. "At the moment that faith is established, birth in the Pure Land is also established."[4] He rejected monasticism because cutting oneself off from the world in order to study and pray was meaningless. He married, begot children, and encouraged his disciples to do the same. He had not planned to start a new sect,

4. Quoted in Endō Hajime, "The Original Bōmori: Husband and Wife Congregations in Early Shin Buddhism," in *Engendering Faith: Women and Buddhism in Premodern Japan*, ed. B. Ruch (Ann Arbor: Center for Japanese Studies, University of Michigan, 2002), p. 513.

but after his death in 1262, his children and disciples founded *Jōdo shinshū* (True Pure Land sect).

Hōnen and Shinran taught people to rely on Amida for salvation; Zen taught reliance on the self. Its teachers had such close ties with China and knowledge of the Chinese language that the shogunate used them as envoys to the Yuan court. Following his training on Mount Hiei, Eisai went twice to China and then settled in Kamakura, where he founded the Rinzai school that uses riddles (*kōan*) to concentrate the mind during meditation. By exposing the limits to rational thought, riddles helped achieve enlightenment. Eisai became the shogunate's master of religious ceremonies when he developed close ties with Hōjō Masako that brought the Rinzai school wealth and power. Dōgen went to China for five years, where he studied Zen in what is now popular in Japan as the Sōtō school. Upon his return, he taught that the essence of Buddha is in everyone but is concealed under layers of desire. To remove these layers, the practitioner has to achieve an inner awakening through sitting meditation (*zazen*). Chanting sutras and reciting the Buddha's name were secondary. During his lifetime, Dōgen's austere quest for absolute truth attracted few disciples.

Nichiren opposed all forms of Buddhism that did not center on the *Lotus Sutra*. Only it offered the true way to salvation. He taught his followers to beat drums and chant, "Praise to the glorious teachings of the *Lotus Sutra*," because the sutra's title contained the essence of the sutra and the sutra contained the summation of Buddhist teaching. Performing the chant enabled the achievement of buddhahood in this very body or at least access to the Pure Land. Salvation came through faith, not doctrinal study or meditation. Calling on the *Lotus Sutra* could bring wealth and good luck for individuals and protection for the state. (See **Biography: Nichiren**.)

Literature and Popular Arts

Buddhist beliefs permeated Kamakura period literature and the visual arts. A section in the seventh royally commissioned poetry anthology, the *Shinkokinshū* (*New Collection of Ancient and Modern Poems*), completed in 1206, was devoted to Buddhist poetry. The court-poet-turned-priest Kamo no Chōmei wrote about his life as a recluse in *Hōjōki* (*An Account of My Hut*) that explored the tension between his pleasure in artistic pursuits and his desire to renounce the world to seek salvation. The realism of portrait sculptures took on meaning only in the context of Buddhist icons that

served as a focus for religious devotion. Picture scrolls (*emakimono*) depicted the battles that ushered in the Kamakura period and the Mongol invasions; they also brought to life the torments that await the unbeliever in hell. (See **Material Culture: The Mongol Scroll and Mongol Combat**.) The classic war story *Tale of the Heike* began with an evocation of the transience of existence expressed in the tolling of a temple bell. Didactic tales recounted miraculous stories of the Buddha's power. Even the chronicle *Azuma kagami* (*Mirror of the East*), a major source of information on the day-to-day affairs of the Kamakura regime, dwells on Yoritomo's and his successors' pilgrimages to and support for temples.

War tales recounted the course of major conflicts. *Tale of Masakado* (*Shōmonki*) contained imaginative reconstructions of battles and traced Taira no Masakado's defeat in 940 to arrogance. It reproduced historical documents supplemented by stories created decades after the event. Yoshitsune was a particular favorite of storytellers, from his youth in Kyoto where he challenged the Herculean warrior monk Benkei to his death in the mountains of northern Japan. Accounts of the Genpei War portrayed it as an epic struggle between the Taira and the Minamoto for control of Japan. Political intrigue and fierce battles filled these tales, as they did *Tale of the Heike*.

Tale of the Heike began as stories recited by blind storytellers to assuage the souls of the Taira who had fallen in battle. Accompanied by the lute, storytellers traveled across Japan to bring people to an understanding of the Buddha by crafting miraculous and edifying tales. Each generation of storytellers enriched the story, adding embellishments and anecdotes, before it was written down in the fourteenth century. Their accounts featured Kiyomori, entertainers, guards, widows, and a host of warriors. By speaking their names, the storyteller summoned the dead. By recounting their exploits, he pacified their spirits and sought to save them from hell. *Heike* is permeated with connections between humankind and unseen forces and the importance of karma in deciding one's fate.

Another category of tale is *setsuwa* (popular tales). The most famous, *Tales of Times Now Past*, compiled in the early twelfth century, contains more than a thousand short stories set in India, China, and Japan. The Japanese corpus encompasses Buddhist tales, stories about aristocratic and warrior families, and anecdotes, many humorous, about ordinary people such as artisans, criminals, unhappy wives, and abducted ladies, as well as about animals and the supernatural. A later collection contains stories that trace

BIOGRAPHY Nichiren

Born in a fishing village northeast of what is now Tokyo far from the traditional centers of power, Nichiren (1222–1282) became the most notorious figure in Japan's religious history. His life is so encrusted with legend and so ignored in contemporary documents that little is known of his early years. He received training at a local temple and at Kamakura before seeking higher education on Mount Hiei and Mount Kōya. There he became convinced that the *Lotus Sutra* embodied the ultimate truth. Any other teaching was not just delusional, but harmful.

In 1253 Nichiren carried his message back to eastern Japan where, thanks to his charismatic personality, he acquired congregations of devoted followers, men and women, commoners and samurai. In 1260 he wrote his most famous tract, *Risshō ankokuron* (On establishing the truth to bring peace to the nation), and submitted it to the retired but still powerful Hōjō regent. In it he blamed adherents to the Pure Land and Zen sects for the string of natural disasters that had afflicted Japan in previous years (the regent had retired to a Zen temple) and warned of worse calamities to come. In particular, he predicted that unless the government stamped out false teachings, Japan would suffer foreign invasion. Although the Hōjō ignored the treatise, its contents became known. When Nichiren's enemies tried to kill him, he attributed his narrow escape to the miraculous power of the *Lotus Sutra*. He continued proselytizing in Kamakura until the Hōjō had him exiled to Izu.

When the Mongols sent threatening letters to Japan, Nichiren took them as proof that he had been right. Returned from exile, he increased his attacks on other Buddhist sects and called on the government to create an ideal state based on the *Lotus Sutra*. He stirred up such controversy with his intolerant views that again he was exiled, this time to the island of Sado in the Japan Sea. Pardoned in 1274, he retired to Mount Minobu, where he established a temple for the clerics he had ordained himself. To unite the communities of believers, he issued pastoral letters, one telling a woman to continue reading and reciting the sutra even while menstruating because menstruation was not a source of pollution. He also taught his followers to welcome persecution because this proved that they were worthy of receiving the ultimate teaching reserved for those suffering through the Last Days of the Buddhist Law.

At the end of his life, Nichiren preached that he was the reincarnation of the bodhisattva to whom the original Buddha Sakyamuni had entrusted the *Lotus Sutra*. Buddhism had arisen in India, but it reached its ultimate moment of truth in Japan. In the name he chose for himself, the character for *nichi* represents the sun as in the Japanese word for Japan, *Nihon*, the origin of the sun. *Ren* means "lotus." Today a stele engraved with the chant he taught his followers is located in Washington, D.C., and a new religion based on his teachings has established Sōka University in southern California.

Source: Richard Bowring, *The Religious Traditions of Japan 500–1600* (Cambridge: Cambridge University Press, 2005), pp. 334–343.

the appearance of the supernatural in everyday life. *Kokonchomonjū* (*Stories Heard from Writers Old and New*), compiled in 1254, contains folk stories, stories about the gods, and stories illustrating the Buddha's teachings. There, Yoritomo's pilgrimage to the mountain temple of Zenkōji reveals that its central icon was alive.

War tales and popular tales brought new classes of people into literature, but they did not displace the aristocrats who continued to compile poetry collections, keep diaries, and write essays in the manner of their Heian forebears. Fujiwara no Teika set high standards for poetic diction and kept a diary of distinction. His niece wrote *Mumyōzōshi* (*Anonymous Writing*), which critiqued the classical literary tradition. In 1307, Lady Nijō wrote a memoir that illustrates how the court continued to model its ceremonies on the past, albeit with considerable attention to drinking and fornication. The Hōjō and their supporters at Kamakura avidly sought training in the civilizing arts. They hired teachers from Kyoto, studied poetry, and immersed themselves in Buddhist texts.

MATERIAL CULTURE

The Mongol Scroll and Mongol Combat

In 1293 or thereabouts, the samurai Takezaki Sue-naga commissioned scrolls of the Mongol invasions to commemorate his achievements. He had just succeeded in getting the Kamakura shogunate to recognize his merit in having been the first to engage the enemy in 1274. His aim in acquiring the scrolls may have been to buttress his claim for reward, to provide a pictorial record for his descendants, or to make an offering to the shrine of his tutelary deity in gratitude for having survived the conflict.

With a troop of five mounted men, Suenaga galloped into battle. The Mongols let fly a withering hail of arrows. Suenaga's standard-bearer fell when his horse was hit. Suenaga was hit in the left chest and left knee. His horse too was wounded, and a Mongol arrow made a direct hit on his helmet. At this critical juncture, a troop of mounted samurai arrived to rescue him.

The Mongols sent masses of cavalry into battle. They received orders via gongs that launched attacks and drums that signaled retreats. The Mongol infantry followed the cavalry lined up behind tall shields. They used crossbows that fired heavy arrows capable of piercing armor, and the arrows were tipped with poison. Their catapults hurled cannonballs filled with gunpowder that exploded with a roar and gushed fire. Samurai picked off Mongol soldiers with arrows fired from longbows.

Mongol Scroll. Commissioned by Takezaki Suenaga, the Mongol Scroll shows him in the vanguard of the attack, his horse frightened by an exploding shell. On the left stand the Mongols in long coats, their faces covered with whiskers. *(Laurie Platt Winfrey, Inc.)*

THE MONGOL INVASIONS (1271–1281)

Under threat of Mongol invasion, Kamakura summoned the samurai to defend Japan starting in 1271 after the fall of Korea. (See **Connections: The Mongols.**) Fierce fighting in 1274 proved that the Japanese enjoyed near military parity and numerical superiority. Unable to prevail, the Mongols retreated. The samurai strengthened their fortifications before the second onslaught in 1281. Stone walls on the landing beaches hedged in the Mongol troops, and ships harassed their fleet. Fighting raged for almost a month before an epidemic ravaged the tightly packed attacking forces and a typhoon sank Mongol ships. The samurai then killed the thirty thousand troops left stranded. In later centuries, the shrine-temple complexes that had prayed for supernatural intervention claimed that a divine wind (*kamikaze*) had destroyed the Mongols.

The invasions extended Kamakura's reach into Kyushu and made the shogunate a truly national government. It came at a cost. Preparations for the second invasion curtailed food production. The Hōjō made promises of rewards they could not keep and pressured temples for money. They appointed new provincial governors in the west, all of them from the Hōjō family or its allies. Many of the warriors from Kyushu who fought against the Mongols had not previously been subject to Kamakura rule. Their only recompense was confirmation of their rights to the income from estates they already held. For warriors from western Japan who joined the battle, Kamakura announced debt amnesties, a tactic it also used to placate the shrines and temples that had prayed for victory. Since warriors fought not for glory or love of country but for reward, these returns were paltry indeed.

FALL OF THE KAMAKURA REGIME (1293–1333)

The growing sophistication of the Hōjō underscored the gulf developing between them and the majority of provincial warriors. Every aristocratic or royal child brought to Kamakura to serve as the figurehead shogun had a retinue of cultivated female and male attendants. Yoritomo had emphasized austerity and simplicity; his successors led lives of luxury. They were also growing more despotic. In 1293, the Hōjō regent abolished the councilor form of government. He and his successors exiled opponents, seized governorships, and had their housemen fill positions in the shogunate. In 1297, the regent announced an "edict for virtuous government" aimed at restoring land to impoverished samurai, especially the stewards who had been forced to sell or mortgage their land over the preceding twenty years. It was based on the notion that the sale of land did not mean that the original owner lost all claim to it; rather, a family that had worked land for generations possessed it by inalienable right. Under this ruling, former owners retrieved ancestral land. Any satisfaction they obtained was only temporary, because it did not alleviate their poverty and made it more difficult to sell land in the future. The former buyers were naturally disgruntled. The result of the edict was to lose friends for the regime and narrow its support base.

Partible inheritance was a major cause of the stewards' impoverishment. When every child received a portion of the patrimony, the result was an expansion in the size of the warrior class without a concomitant growth in the income at its disposal. Bequeathed an inadequate inheritance, stewards fell into debt and had to mortgage their rights to income. Although the patrimony could be divided, the obligation to fulfill the duties of military service to Kamakura was not divisible. Even women had to field a warrior on horseback should the need arise.

Generations had passed since Yoritomo had rewarded followers by making them estate stewards. Diffused by time and space, the stewards' descendants stayed on their land save when a lawsuit called them to Kamakura. In 1285, the Hōjō regent decided that the shogunate would no longer intervene in disputes between its retainers and Kyoto aristocrats. Instead litigants had to seek redress from Kyoto, a move that heightened conflict between supporters of the two centers. This decision estranged Kamakura from its followers in the provinces. With Kamakura now reluctant to guarantee land rights, support for it weakened.

Challenges to the shogunate multiplied in the early fourteenth century. Stone-throwing brawls had long erupted in Kyoto on festival days, but in Kamakura in the early 1300s, they turned into gang warfare. Bands of mounted bandits ravaged the provinces of central Japan, sometimes in league with estate stewards who refused to send income to protectors and proprietors. Pirates ranged as far as Korea, attacking coastal settlements, carrying off goods, and enslaving the inhabitants. The swell of disorder suggested to people both high and low that they could act with impunity.

SUMMARY

How did Japan change in the Kamakura period? The conflict between the Taira and Minamoto over different strategies for translating military force into political power resulted in the establishment of a military regime separate from yet dependent on the Kyoto court for legitimization. Rewarding Kamakura's followers with the new offices of military governor and estate steward provided institutional niches for samurai in provincial offices and at the ground level. Measures for adjudicating disputes resulted in the creation of a new law code based more on local needs than on Chinese precedents. While aristocrats continued to write in the style of their Heian forbearers, anonymous storytellers recounted the deeds of warriors and ordinary people. The founders of new sects brought new practices to Buddhism, from austere Zen meditation to the promise of salvation for all, no matter how evil, in the Pure Land. Increases in agricultural production laid the foundation for an increase in trade and manufacturing. One practice that did not carry forward was the division of family assets among all children and female economic autonomy.

China Under Mongol Rule (1215–1368)

The Mongols conquered China in successive campaigns stretching over seven decades. Even the non-Chinese rulers of north China, the Tanguts and Jurchens, themselves horsemen proud of their reputations as fierce fighters, had to submit to the superior striking force of the Mongols. Although the Mongols brought massive destruction in their early campaigns, by the time of Khubilai (r. 1360–1394), they had become more sophisticated administrators. Since Mongols and people from elsewhere in Asia occupied a large share of administrative posts, the traditional elite of Confucian-educated men generally had to turn to other occupations.

Scholars of this period have devoted much of their energy to working out the political and military history of the period. How did Jin and Song officials organize resistance, and why did it fail? What policies did the Mongols put in place? Why did the Yuan Dynasty in China fail to last even two centuries? Another set of questions revolves around how Chinese coped with the Mongol presence. Did the experience of bitter defeat have any long-term effects on Chinese culture? What was going on in society at local levels, beyond the purview of Mongol rulers?

THE MONGOL CONQUEST OF THE JIN AND XIA DYNASTIES

North China fell to the Mongols early in Chinggis's campaigns. Chinggis had raided Jin territory in 1205 and 1209 and launched a major campaign in 1211. He led an army of about 50,000 bowmen, and his three sons led another of similar size. The Jin, with 150,000 cavalry, mostly Jurchen, and more than 300,000 Chinese infantrymen, thought they had the strongest army known to history. Yet Mongol tactics frustrated them. The Mongols would take a city, plunder it, and then withdraw, letting Jin take it back and deal with the food shortages and destruction. Both the Jin Western Capital (modern Datong) and their Central Capital (Beijing) were taken this way more than once.

Jin did not have stable leadership during this crisis. In 1213 a Jurchen general murdered the Jin emperor and put another on the throne, only to be murdered himself two months later. In 1214, Jin negotiated a humiliating peace with Chinggis, who then withdrew his armies from the Central Capital. The new Jin emperor decided that the Central Capital was too vulnerable, so he moved the court to the Southern Capital, Kaifeng, bringing thirty thousand carts of documents and treasures (reversing the journey north of 1126). Since Chinggis thought Jin had agreed to vassal status, he interpreted the transfer of the capital as revolt. When the Central Capital fell in 1215, it was sacked and burned. From then on, Jin controlled little more than a province-sized territory around Kaifeng.

The rump Jin state, hoping to expand to the south, attacked Song from 1216 to 1223. The next Jin emperor concentrated on defending against the Mongols, but in 1229, when the new khan, Ögödei, sent the main Mongol army to destroy Jin, Jin could barely slow their advance and succumbed by 1234.

As the Mongols captured Jin territory, Chinggis recruited more and more Chinese and Khitans into his armies, arguing that they had little reason to be loyal to the Jurchen. Chinese soldiers and generals were incorporated into Mongol armies, and literate Chinese were given clerical jobs. Chinese also were put to work as catapult operators during sieges. In 1218 the Mongol commander leading the north China campaigns recommended to Chinggis a well-educated and highly sinicized Khitan named Yelü Qucai. Chinggis is said to have addressed him, "Liao and Jin have been enemies for generations; I have taken revenge for you." Yelü had the courage to disagree: "My father and grandfather have both served Jin respectfully. How can I, as a subject and son, be so insincere in my heart as to consider my sovereign and my father as enemies?"[1] Chinggis, admiring his forthrightness, took him into his entourage. Yelü served the Mongols for the next twenty-five years, patiently trying to get them to see the benefits of ruling their Chinese subjects in Chinese ways.

The Tangut Xia Dynasty suffered much the same fate as Jin. Early on, in 1209, Xia submitted to Chinggis and agreed to help the Mongols attack Jin, but during the next dozen years also tried to secure alliances with Jin and Song. Chinggis eventually decided that Xia had failed to live up to the terms of its submission to the Mongols and personally led a large force into Xia territory in 1226. It only enraged Chinggis when Xia soldiers fought well; in response, he had his generals systematically destroy Xia city by city. Chinggis himself led the final siege of the capital, which valiantly held out for five months. Chinggis died during the siege, but his death was kept secret. When the Xia ruler offered to surrender, he was persuaded to walk out of the capital with a small entourage. Perhaps because he was held in some way responsible for Chinggis's death, he was promptly hacked to death, and the Mongol troops, on entering the city, did their best to slaughter every living being in it.

North China in this period suffered enormous destruction. Mongol armies did not try to control territory; they only plundered it. Sometimes they slaughtered the entire population of a town, and even when people were not slaughtered, they were frequently seized like their cattle and enslaved. The Mongols began by giving out large chunks of land as fiefs to generals, both Mongols and allies. This did not lead to orderly government, however, as the fief holders were generals on campaigns elsewhere. With no one maintaining order, farmers suffered the depredations not only of Mongol soldiers but also of bandits, rebels, and local defense forces.

Ögödei's Mongol advisers proposed turning much of north China into pastureland. Yelü Qucai offered the counterargument that the Mongols should leave the Chinese farmers in place because great wealth could be extracted from them through equitably collected taxation. He calculated that the Mongols could raise revenues of 500,000 ounces of silver, 80,000 bolts of silk, and over 20,000 tons of grain by direct taxation of subjects. He was given authorization to put his tax plan into effect, but before it had much chance to show its benefits, Yelü's rivals convinced Ögödei that an even more lucrative way to raise revenue was to let Central Asian Muslim merchants bid against each other for licenses to collect taxes. To the Chinese, these Central Asian tax farmers were even more oppressive than the Mongol lords.

Some Chinese who had served the Jurchen refused to serve the Mongols out of loyalty to the defeated dynasty. Yuan Haowen (1190–1257) passed the examinations in 1221 and served in Kaifeng during Jin's final struggle. When Kaifeng fell, he wrote a letter to Yelü Qucai, asking that fifty-four men of letters be spared by the Mongols. He himself was interned for

---

1. Igor de Rachelwiltz et al., eds., *In the Service of the Khan: Eminent Personalities of the Early Mongol-Yuan Period (1200–1300)* (Wiesbaden: Harrossowitz, 1993), p. xx.

two years and on his release devoted himself to collecting materials for a history of the Jin Dynasty. A poet, he also wrote poems on the fall of the Jin. He viewed continuing to write as a way to preserve Chinese civilization. The following poem, "Crossing the Yellow River, June 12," describes what he saw around the time Kaifeng fell:

> White bones scattered
> like tangled hemp,
> how soon before mulberry and catalpa
> turn to dragon-sands?
> I only know north of the river
> there is no life:
> crumbled houses, scattered chimney smoke
> from a few homes.[2]

Other Chinese subjects of the Jin took a different attitude. From experience with the Jin, they knew that the Chinese would fare better if Chinese were the administrators and could shield Chinese society from the most brutal effects of Mongol rule. Therefore, many Jin officials willingly served the Mongols. Some dedicated Confucian scholars such as Xu Heng devoted themselves to the task of teaching Mongol rulers the principles of Confucian government.

THE MONGOL CONQUEST OF THE SOUTHERN SONG

The Song Dynasty had plenty of time to get ready to fight the Mongols. They knew of the Mongols' conquests of both Xia and Jin. In the 1230s, the Mongols had also attacked Sichuan, under Song control, and refugees from Sichuan brought stories of the horror of the Mongol advance. Song knew it had to raise revenues and prepare its armies for a fearsome enemy. In a desperate attempt to raise revenues, an activist chancellor confiscated parts of the lands of the rich, leading to the disaffection of important segments of the population. But the attack did not come when expected in the 1240s or 1250s, a period when the Mongols were busy extending their conquests into

Central Asia, Persia, and Russia. Song therefore had more time to prepare and the Mongols more time to learn how to deal with south China.

Khubilai

The man behind the final conquest of the Song was Khubilai (b. 1215), a grandson of Chinggis, son of his youngest son, Tolui. In Khubilai's youth, his uncle Ögödei was Great Khan (r. 1229–1241), and succession went to Ögödei's descendants until 1251, when Khubilai's elder brother Möngke became Great Khan.

In the 1240s, Khubilai spent much of his time in Mongolia. One of the Chinese who came to call on him there was Liu Bingzhong (1216–1274), a believer in Three Teachings syncretism (which drew from Confucianism, Buddhism, and Daoism). Khubilai appointed Liu as a major adviser, and Liu in turn introduced Khubilai to many other Chinese, both generals and scholars. From them, Khubilai came to understand that the repeated plundering of north China had greatly reduced its worth and that letting Mongol lords make the residents of their lands slaves had impoverished the society and made it practically ungovernable.

In 1251, Khubilai was assigned control of all north China and put in place a much more Chinese style of government. Khubilai never learned to read Chinese and did not identify with Chinese culture, but he did come to appreciate that China could be exploited most effectively through Chinese methods. In 1254, Möngke sent Khubilai to lead a campaign south from Sichuan into Yunnan, where he defeated the independent country of Dali, incorporating this region into China for the first time. (See **Documents: The Luoluo.**) When Khubilai was enraged at the resistance of the king of Dali, a Chinese adviser convinced him not to slaughter the population for the faults of their ruler by reminding him of a passage in which Mencius asserted that only someone "who takes no pleasure in killing people" would be able to unify the realm (*Mencius* 1A6).

Möngke died in 1259 during a campaign against Song. His death brought the campaign to a close as the Mongols headed north to select a new khan. Before a full assembly met, however, Khubilai declared himself the successor. Elsewhere, his younger brother Arigh Böke did the same thing. It took a four-year civil war to end this dispute in Khubilai's favor. In 1264, Khubilai constructed a new capital at the site of the Liao and Jin capitals. This capital, Dadu (modern Beijing), became the main capital of the khanate of the Great Khan, which stretched from Mongolia

---

2. Translated by Stephen West in Wu-chi Liu and Irving Yucheng Lo, *Sunflower Splendor: Three Thousand Years of Chinese Poetry* (Garden City, N.Y.: Anchor Books, 1975), p. 407.

through north China and Korea. In the 1270s, Khubilai began more concerted efforts to gain legitimacy in the eyes of the Chinese. In 1271, he adopted the Chinese name Yuan ("primal") for the Mongols' state in China, casting it as a dynasty to the Chinese. He explained the choice of the word *yuan* by reference to a passage from the ancient *Book of Changes*. Although the Yuan retained the traditional Chinese county and prefectural governments, it added a new higher level, the province, which had the authority to handle much of government business on its own, without seeking approval from the central government.

Crossing the Yangzi River

Many non-Chinese groups had gained control of north China in the past, from the Xianbei of the Northern Wei to the recent Khitans and Jurchens. None of them, however, had been able to secure control of any territory south of the Yangzi River, in no small part because cavalry were of little advantage in a land crisscrossed with streams and canals. Moreover, controlling the Yangzi required a navy. When Jin had conquered Shu in the third century and Sui had conquered the last of the Southern Dynasties in the sixth century, the first step to conquest of the south had been the construction of a fleet of ships large enough to contest control of the Yangzi River. By the 1260s, the Mongols had plenty of Chinese advisers to explain this to them. They soon put Chinese shipbuilders to work building a fleet. Khubilai also sent envoys to Song to urge them to surrender (see **Biography: Hao Jing, Imprisoned Envoy**).

In 1268, the Mongols set siege to Xiangyang, a major city on a northern tributary leading into the Yangzi River. Both sides saw this city as the key to control of the river, and as a consequence the siege lasted five years. Each side had thousands of boats and tens of thousands of troops. The Mongols' force was multiethnic, with Chinese, Uighur, Persian, Jurchen, and Korean experts in siege warfare and naval tactics. Muslim engineers demonstrated their superior catapults, which could throw rocks weighing up to a hundred pounds each. To keep the residents of the city from starving, the Chinese fleet regularly ran the blockade to ferry food supplies into the city.

Once Xiangyang fell to the Mongols in 1273, the Mongol general Bayan (1237–1295) was put in charge of the invasion of the south. He led an army of 200,000, mainly Chinese. Victory was often achieved without fighting: generals who had already gone over

to the Mongols were sent ahead to persuade Song commanders of the wisdom of surrender. At one point, the Song chancellor, Jia Sidao, personally led an army of 130,000 and a navy of twenty-five hundred ships to keep the Mongols from entering the lower Yangzi region. The Mongols, landing their cavalry on both sides of the river and using catapults to destroy Song ships, still prevailed. Jia was dismissed from office and soon killed by angry local officials.

Although by the 1260s many Chinese in the north were working for the Mongols, Song officials and the educated class more generally tended to see in the Mongols the greatest threat Chinese civilization had ever faced. As Song officials readied themselves for the inevitable onslaught, many committed themselves to an all-out effort. That China had survived rule by non-Chinese before did not allay their fears. The Mongols seemed more savage and less likely to protect key features of Chinese culture and tradition than any previous foe.

Although Song had generals willing to resist to the bitter end, it lacked adequate leadership. The emperor at the time was a child, and the advisers to the empress dowager spent much of their energy opposing each other's plans. By the time the Mongol armies crossed the Yangzi in 1275, the empress dowager was reduced to calling on the people to rise up and fight the invading barbarians. Although some two hundred thousand recruits responded to the call, they were no match for the battle-hardened Mongols. The Mongols also had the advantage of scare tactics. To frighten Hangzhou into submitting without a fight, on the way there the Mongols ordered the total slaughter of the city of Changzhou. The ploy worked. The empress dowager, wanting to spare the people of the capital, surrendered. She, the child emperor, and other members of the Song imperial family were taken north to Beijing as hostages. Song loyalists, however, held out for three more years, placing young children from the Song imperial family on the throne. The final battle occurred off the coast of Guangdong province. Many Chinese fled into Vietnam, which the Mongols soon unsuccessfully attacked with an army of recently defeated Chinese soldiers.

Prominent among the Song loyalists was Wen Tianxiang, a poet and official who took up arms. Long after there was any real chance of driving the Mongols out, Wen kept fighting, withdrawing farther and farther south. Even after he was captured, he resisted all inducements to serve in the Yuan government, preferring execution to serving the Mongols.

DOCUMENTS

The Luoluo

The region of modern Yunnan province in southwest China became part of China for the first time during the Yuan period, after the Mongols conquered it in the mid-thirteenth century. During Tang and Song times, this region was ruled by the independent kingdoms of Nanzhao and Dali. In 1301 the Chinese official Li Jing was given the post of deputy pacification commissioner for the northwest corner of Yunnan and neighboring Guizhou. After two years there, he wrote a treatise on the many different ethnic groups of the area, with particular attention to where they stood on a continuum from "raw" to "cooked"— that is, how civilized they were. In this passage, he describes the Luoluo. Also called the Yi, the Luoluo remain a major ethnic group in the area.

The Luoluo [Yi] are also known as the Wu Man or Black Barbarians.

The men put their hair up in a coil and pluck their facial hair or shave their heads. They carry two knives, one at each side, and enjoy fighting and killing. When a disagreement arises among fathers and sons and among brothers, they are known to attack each other with military weapons. Killing is taken lightly, and they consider it a sign of valor. They prize horses with cropped tails, their saddles have no trappings, and their stirrups are carved from wood in the shape of a fish's mouth to accommodate the toes.

The women wear their hair down and wear cotton clothing, and the wealthy wear jewelry and embroidered clothes; the humble are garbed in sheepskin. They ride horses side-saddle. Unmarried girls wear large earrings and cut their hair level with their eyebrows, and their skirts do not even cover their knees. Men and women, rich and poor, all wear felt wraps and go barefoot, and they can go as long as one year without washing face or hands.

It is the custom of husbands and wives not to see each other during the day, but only to sleep together at night. Children as old as ten *sui* most likely have never seen their father. Wives and concubines are not jealous of each other. Even the well-to-do do not use padding on their beds, but just spread pine needles on the ground with only a layer of felt and mat. Marriages are arranged with the maternal uncle's family, but if a suitable partner cannot be found, they can look elsewhere for a match. When someone falls ill, they do not use medicine, but

LIFE IN CHINA UNDER THE MONGOLS

Life in China under the Mongols was much like life in China under earlier alien rulers. Once order was restored, people did their best to get on with their lives. Some suffered real hardship. Many farmers had their lands expropriated; others were forced into slavery or serfdom, perhaps transported to a distant city, never to see their family again. Yet people still spoke Chinese, followed Chinese customary practices in arranging their children's marriages or dividing their family property, made offerings at local temples, celebrated New Year and other customary festivals, and turned to local landowners when in need. Teachers still taught students the classics; scholars continued to write books; and books continued to be printed. (See Color Plate 16.)

The Mongols, like the Khitans and Jurchens before them, did not see anything particularly desirable in the openness of Chinese society, with opportunities for people to rise in status through hard work or education. They aimed instead at stability and placed people in hereditary occupational categories: farmer, Confucian scholar, physician, astrologer, soldier, artisan, salt producer, miner, Buddhist monk, and others. Many occupational groups had to provide unpaid services according to a rotational schedule and earn their liv-

instead call in a male shaman, who is known as the *daxipo*. He uses chicken bones to divine good and evil fortunes. The tribal leader always has the shaman at his side, and he must consult the shaman to make a final decision in all matters great and small.

A woman who is about to get married must first have relations with the shaman, and then "dance" with all the groom's brothers. This custom is known as "making harmony." Only after that can she be married to her husband. If any one of the brothers refuses to go along with this custom, he will be regarded as unrighteous and everyone will be disgusted with him.

The first wife is known as the *naide*, and it is only her children who can inherit their father's position. If the *naide* has a son who dies before marrying, she will go ahead and arrange a wife for him anyway. Anyone can then have relations with the deceased son's wife, and any child born is considered the child of the deceased. If the tribal leader does not leave a male heir, his wife's [the *naide*'s] daughter then becomes the leader. However, she then has no female attendants—only ten or more young male attendants, with whom she can have relations.

When the tribal leader dies, they wrap his body in a leopard skin, cremate him, and then bury his bones on a mountain at a location known only to his closest relatives. After the burial they take images of the Seven Precious Things and place them on a high platform. They then go steal the head of a neighboring nobleman and offer it as a sacrifice. If they are not able to obtain one, they cannot make the sacrifice. At the time of the sacrificial ceremony all the relatives arrive, and they sacrifice more than a thousand cattle and sheep, or at least several hundred. Every year when they celebrate the spring festival during the twelfth month, they take a long vertical pole and a horizontal piece of wood, [and arranging a seesaw] with one person on each side, they go up and down together playing.

They support many soldiers, who are called *juke*, and they generously provide for them. When they go off to battle, they view death as "returning home." They expertly craft armor and swords that are worth dozens of horses. On their javelins and crossbow arrow tips they put a poison that kills instantly.

They are found in Shunyuan [near Guiyang, Guizhou], Qujing, Wumeng [Zhao-tong], Wusa [near Weining, Guizhou], and Yuexi [north of Xichang, Sichuan].

———
Source: Translated by Jacqueline M Armijo-Hussein, in *Under Confucian Eyes: Writings on Gender in Chinese History*, ed. Susan Mann and Yu-yin Cheng (Berkeley: University of California Press, 2001), pp. 91–92.

ing the rest of the year. Often the only alternative for those whose obligations threatened to bankrupt them was to abscond.

Besides these occupational categories, the Mongols classified the population into four grades, apparently as a way to keep the Chinese from using their numbers to gain a dominant position. Not surprisingly, the Mongols put themselves in the top grade. Next came various non-Chinese, such as the Uighurs and Central Asians. Below them were the former subjects of Jin, called the Han. And at the bottom were the former subjects of the Song, called southerners. These classifications affected methods of taxation, the judicial process, and appointment to office. The Han, for instance, were taxed by household according to Jin practice, whereas the southerners were taxed by acreage following Song precedent. In legal cases, each group was tried and sentenced according to its own legal tradition, which meant, for instance, that Chinese were the only ones tattooed if convicted of theft.

The reason for codifying ethnic differences in this way was to preserve the Mongols' privileges as conquerors. Chinese were not allowed to take Mongol names, and great efforts were made to keep them from passing as Mongols. Intermarriage was discouraged, though it did occur. Many of the differences in how Chinese were treated, however, came from Mongol fear that they would rebel or attempt sabotage. Chinese

BIOGRAPHY   Hao Jing, Imprisoned Envoy

Hao Jing was born in north China in 1223, while his family was fleeing the Mongols and his father was eking out a modest living as a teacher. Because of the chaotic conditions, during his childhood, his family moved ten times. In 1238, when he was fifteen, Hao Jing started taking on tutoring jobs himself. Once he spent five years as the children's tutor in the home of an official who owned a large library, which enabled him not only to continue study himself, but also to get to know some prominent literary men.

In 1253, Hao visited the ruins of the former Jin capital (at modern Bejing), largely destroyed by the Mongols in 1215. In 1255 he traveled through Shandong and visited Qufu, the birthplace of Confucius and Mount Tai, the sacred mountain. When Hao Jing was thirty-three, he was recommended to Khubilai, then in charge of China proper and gathering around him a group of Chinese advisers. The histories report that Khubilai engaged him in dialogue on how best to govern "from morning to night" for several days. Hao largely argued the Confucian position that virtuous rule is the most effective.

Hao Jing had to return home when his father became very ill, but after his father died, Hao Jing rejoined Khubilai and participated in the assault on Song in 1259. Because Hao Jing gave good advice, Khubilai assigned him a military post. When victory was not immediate, Hao Jing recommended to Khubilai that he send an envoy to Song to propose a peace treaty of the sort Song had had with Liao and Jin, involving yearly tribute.

Khubilai abandoned his campaign against Song when his elder brother, the Khan Möngke, died, and he needed to go north to compete for the khanship. One of his first acts on becoming khan was to appoint Hao Jing special envoy to the Song emperor. When someone warned Hao Jing that his assignment might be dangerous, he supposedly answered, "I have read about the Way and studied it for thirty years, yet I have not yet accomplished any real good in the world. Now the North and the South are courting disaster, a situation which has reached calamitous proportions. If I can stop the armies from fighting, calm the disturbances, and save the lives of millions of peo-

ple who are now living under the shadow of war, my learning will finally be of some use."[3]

Before Hao Jing departed, Khubilai asked him to submit an assessment on his views of the current situation. Hao Jing responded with a long essay begging the khan to take as his model not only the Tang and Song Dynasties, but also the Liao and Jin Dynasties, which had drawn on Chinese officials and Chinese institutions.

Hao Jing set off on his mission with a retinue of about forty, all of them Chinese, since Khubilai said this was a mission for properly trained Chinese, not Mongols. After nearly four months on the road, Hao Jing and his party entered Song territory. They were allowed to proceed for another month, then were taken to a fort outside Yangzhou. Because there had been a recent attack by a rebellious warlord, the Song court suspected Hao's mission might be a ruse and kept him there for what turned out to be sixteen years. Hao wrote to the local officials, to Khubilai, and to the Song emperor, but it is unclear which, if any, of his messages got through. For a long time the guards tried to get Hao Jing to defect to Song, but he remained firmly loyal to the Mongol rulers.

Hao Jing did his best to keep the other members of his retinue from going stir-crazy. The better educated he taught about Confucian scholarship; the illiterate he tried to teach to read. To pass his time he wrote poetry and commentaries on the classics. After six years, the soldiers in his retinue got into a brawl, with the result that several were killed. Hao Jing and six others then constructed a separate shelter in the compound to separate themselves. After ten years, Hao was able to borrow some of the dynastic histories and set to compiling books on inconsistencies in them.

Not until 1275, when the Mongols had crossed the Yangzi River and Hao Jing's younger brother was sent as an envoy to Hangzhou, did Song agree to release Hao Jing and his party. On his return to the north, he was treated like a hero, but unfortunately by the time he got to Dadu and his audience with Khubilai, he was quite ill, and he died within a few months.

---

3. Igor de Rachewiltz et al., *In the Service of the Khan: Eminent Personalities of the Early Mongol-Yuan Period (1200–1300)* (Wiesbaden: Harrossowitz, 1993), pp. 358–359.

were forbidden to own weapons or congregate in public. Khubilai even prohibited Chinese from dealing in bamboo because it could be used to make bows and arrows. Chinese were subject to severe penalties if they fought back when attacked by a Mongol. Mongols, however, merely had to pay a fine if found guilty of murdering a Chinese.

Since the Mongols wanted to extract wealth from China, they had every incentive to develop the economy. They encouraged trade both within China and beyond its borders. The Mongols allowed the conversion of Song paper money into Yuan currency and tried to keep paper money in circulation. They repaired the Grand Canal, which had been ruined during the initial conquest of north China. Chinese industries with strong foreign markets, such as porcelain, thrived during the Yuan period. A recently excavated vessel headed from Ningbo to Japan that was wrecked off the coast of Korea in 1323 contained about seventeen thousand pieces of ceramics, such as bowls and cups. More than half were green celadon from a kiln complex not far from Ningbo; the next largest group came from the Jingdezhen kilns in Jiangxi. In Yuan times, these kilns invented a new style of decoration using underglaze blue drawing that was widely exported throughout Asia (see **Material Culture: Blue-and-White Porcelain**).

Despite Mongol desire to see China rich, the economy of north China, in particular, was hard hit by the Mongols and began a downward spiral that took centuries to reverse. First came the devastation of the initial conquest. Restoring production was impeded by widespread scattering of the population, much of it forced by the conquerors. Taxation, once it was in the hands of tax farmers, was often ruinous. The Mongols had difficulty regulating the paper currency, and by the fourteenth century inflation was rampant.

After the death of Khubilai in 1294, Mongol administration began to decline. Cliques of Mongol nobles fought over the place of China within the khanate of the Great Khan. Should traditional steppe strategies of expansion remain central to the Mongol state, or was there too much to be gained from exploiting China that they should give up steppe-based expansion? Unlike the Jurchen, who had largely moved into north China, most of the Mongols remained in Mongolia. Renzong, who came to the throne in 1311, was the first Mongol emperor able to both read and speak Chinese, and he shifted the emphasis toward China. In 1313 he reestablished a limited civil service exam system. His son Yingzong succeeded him in 1320, but when he continued the China-centered policies, he was

assassinated by opposing factions. Civil wars and factional violence marred the next several reigns. The last Mongol emperor, who came to the throne in 1333 at age thirteen, was bright and well educated in Chinese but not a strong ruler. By his reign, the central government was failing to keep order in China or even maintain a stable currency. A colder than average climate and the spread of deadly diseases added to the hardship. Power devolved to the local level, to anyone who could organize an area well enough to suppress banditry.

The Chinese Educated Elite During the Mongol Era

Government service, which had long been central to the identity and income of the educated elite in China, was not as widely available during the Yuan Dynasty. Since the Mongols employed Mongols, Tibetans, Uighurs, Persians, Jurchens, and others in their government in China, there were fewer positions for the Chinese educated elite than there had been under either Jin or Song. Moreover, the large majority of Chinese who gained government positions came from clerk, not from scholar-official, families. The Mongols had no interest in doing their own paperwork and employed clerks to keep the records that made government possible. Clerks without classical educations had always been looked down on by Chinese scholars. To the Mongols, however, they seemed perfectly suited to doing their bidding.

The Mongols reinstituted the civil service examinations in 1315, but opportunities for scholars were still very limited. There were quotas to ensure that no more than a quarter of those who passed would be southerners, no more than a quarter would be Han, and half would be Mongols and other non-Chinese. In addition, there were regional quotas, which had the effect of limiting opportunities for those from the southeast, where educational traditions were strongest. On top of that, only about 2 percent of the positions in the bureaucracy were filled through the examination system anyway.

In the south, the generation that had devoted itself to resisting the Mongols rarely also served them, but that generation's sons, growing up under Mongol rule, frequently did. The Mongols were tolerant of all religions but tended to favor Buddhists over Confucians. Khubilai gave the Tibetan cleric Yang Lianjianjia wide powers in postwar Hangzhou. He not only converted the Song palaces to Buddhist temples but also excavated

MATERIAL CULTURE

Blue-and-White Porcelain

Porcelain is distinguished from other types of ceramics by its smoothness, whiteness, and translucence. Only certain types of clays can be used to make porcelain, and the wares must be fired at very high temperatures (1280–1400°C, 2336–2552°F). During Song times, Jingdezhen in Jiangxi became a major center for making porcelain.

The development of the highly popular blue-and-white style of porcelain owes much to the circumstances created by the Mongol Empire. The Yuan rulers established an official agency to supervise ceramic production at Jingdezhen. Artists at these kilns invented a new style of decoration, with underglaze-painted decoration using cobalt blue. West Asia was the best source for cobalt, so Chinese production depended on stable trade relations across Asia. Moreover, the designs of this type of porcelain seem to have been stimulated by Arab clients who wanted ceramics that would be more durable and refined than the ones they were used to but with designs of the sort common in their region. Some Yuan-period blue-and-white wares exported to the Middle East are kept today in the Topkapi Museum in Istanbul. They have dense, busy designs reminiscent of the textiles and carpets of the region.

Blue-and-White Dish. This fourteenth-century dish eventually entered the Ottoman collection and is today in the Topkapi Museum in Istanbul. Note how it combines Chinese imagery, such as the auspicious, imaginary *qilin* in the center, with dense floral patterns highly appreciated in the Islamic world. *(Hadlye Cangokce/Topkapi Saray Museum, Istanbul)*

the Song imperial tombs to extract valuables from them to cover the cost of building more Buddhist temples. Defeated Song loyalists gave meaning to their survival by secretly searching for the bones of the Song emperors and respectfully reburying them.

Zhao Mengfu (1254–1322) is a good example of a southern literatus who decided to serve the Mongols. Descended from the first Song emperor, Zhao had grown up as a member of the privileged imperial clan. He had enrolled in the imperial academy in Hangzhou before the fall of the Southern Song, but he had not yet held office. For the first five years after the Song surrender, he kept to his circle of friends interested in poetry, painting, and calligraphy. Several of them had lost their property during the wars and were dependent on patrons to survive. This group looked on painting in archaic styles as a way to express longing for the past and dissatisfaction with the present.

Wintry Landscape. Ni Zan (1301–1374) was known for his sketchy monochrome landscapes. In his inscribed poem, he states that he did this painting as a present for a friend who was departing to take up an official post, to remind him of the joys of peaceful retirement. *(Palace Museum, Beijing)*

When Khubilai in 1286 dispatched a southerner to recruit prominent southern literati to serve the Mongols, Zhao Mengfu decided to accept the call. Not all of his friends and relatives approved; some refused to speak to him after they learned of his decision. Once in the north, Zhao used Khubilai's favor to work for Chinese interests. He pressed for better treatment of officials, arguing that literati should be exempt from corporal punishment. He proposed major currency reforms and did his best to cause the downfall of the notoriously corrupt Tibetan chancellor Sangha. By 1316, he had risen to president of the Hanlin Academy, the prestigious government organ that supplied literary men to assist the emperor.

Southern literati who did not serve the Mongols found other ways to support themselves. Some could live off the income from their lands; others worked as physicians, fortunetellers, children's teachers, Daoist priests, publishers, booksellers, or playwrights. Many took on leadership roles at the local level, such as founding academies for Confucian learning, organizing their kinsmen into lineages, and promoting local charitable ventures. Through such activities, scholars out of office could assert the importance of civil over military values and see themselves as trustees of the Confucian tradition.

One art that benefited from the political frustrations of Chinese literati in the Yuan period was painting.

Scholars like Su Shi in the Northern Song period had written of the superiority of paintings done by scholars who imbued their paintings with ideas. Still, through the Southern Song period, court painters and professional painters were at the center of stylistic developments, and even of marrying painting and poetry. During the Yuan period, however, men of letters were in the forefront. Some of these painters, like Zhao Mengfu, held office. Others, like Huang Gongwang and Wu Zhen, supported themselves as clerks or diviners. Ni Can had enough family wealth to live comfortably without working. All of them painted for a restricted audience of like-minded individuals and often used the allusive side of paintings to make political statements.

Drama

The literary art of drama was given a boost in Yuan times by literati who wrote for the theater. Performing arts had flourished in earlier eras, with plays and performing styles passed down orally from master to disciple among hereditary groups of singers and actors, who were treated as a demeaned caste. Plays generally alternated prose passages and songs. Because women who performed in public were looked on as little better than prostitutes, female roles were often taken by boys or young men impersonating women. The presence of female impersonators, however, only added to the association of the theater with sexual laxity.

With the diminished career prospects of educated men in Yuan times, some talented writers began writing scripts for impresarios, and their scripts began to circulate as texts. About 160 Yuan plays survive, some of which can be read as covert protest against the Mongols. The best known of the Yuan dramatists is Guan Hanqing (ca. 1240–ca. 1320), author of sixty plays, fifteen of which survive complete. The leading characters of most of his plays were virtuous women who act forcefully in a wide variety of social situations, such as a courtesan who befriends a poor examination candidate, a widow who protects her husband's honor, a daughter-in-law who lets herself be executed to spare her mother-in-law from judicial torture, and a mother who is so strict in her education of her sons that all three place first in the civil service examinations in successive years.

There is even a Yuan play in which writing plays is treated as superior to studying the classics. Set in the Jin period Kaifeng, *Grandee's Son Takes the Wrong Career* has as its protagonist the son of a Jurchen official who has fallen in love with a girl whose parents are itinerant performers. When she chides him for studying too much, he distracts her by reading a recent collection of plays, and the two learn the songs in them. The play ends with the young man giving up his studies and joining the troupe. When her father hears of his proposal, he responds, "The only man I want for my son-in-law is a writer of play books."[4] Only after the young man has shown that he can write speeches and will carry their costumes does the father consent to the marriage.

SUMMARY

How different was China in the 1360s than it had been before the Mongols took control? The more destructive side of this period helped reinforce in China a preference for things Chinese and a wariness about things from outside. Some innovations can be attributed to this period, most notably the province as a political unit with a full array of administrative functions. The elite were given even more incentives than they had in Song times to find ways to maintain their standing without participation in the government. Population had declined, but population records are not good enough to be certain by how much. The gap between north and south China had been reinforced, though it also had very deep roots, leaving the north farther behind economically.

---

4. William Dolby, *Eight Chinese Plays from the Thirteenth Century to the Present* (New York: Columbia University Press, 1978), p. 48.

Meeting New Challenges (1300–1800)

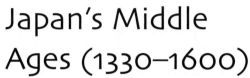

CHAPTER THIRTEEN

Japan's Middle Ages (1330–1600)

New Political Alignments
(1338–1573)

Biography: Hino Meishi

Civil War (1467–1600)

Material Culture: Nō

Documents: *The Journal of Sōchō*

H istorians today see the fourteenth century as marking a decisive break between ancient Japan and its middle ages. Political power became increasingly fragmented among contending military configurations, the court, ecclesiastical establishments, urban residents, and cultivator leagues. International and domestic trade networks expanded, carrying a greater variety of goods over longer distances than ever before, while urban markets supplied the needs of social and political elites as well as of ordinary residents. Women exchanged economic autonomy for domestic authority. Samurai became moralists and poets. The fourteenth century began with conflict between samurai and the court. The fifteenth and sixteenth centuries saw civil war. Europeans brought new weapons and a new religion in the middle of the sixteenth century. At its end, the world turned upside down: a commoner ruled Japan and sent his armies to invade Korea.

Historians disagree over who were significant political actors, the losers such as Go-Daigo, the religious establishment, and commoner leagues, or the winners among the samurai. Much of the dynamism in this period came from its unsettled margins. What impact did they have on the center? How did men and women protect their interests? How did the arts manage to flourish in the midst of unrest?

NEW POLITICAL ALIGNMENTS (1338–1573)

The monarch Go-Daigo's plan to restore power to the monarchy provided the catalyst for the Kamakura shogunate's fall. In 1321, Go-Daigo got his father to renounce the political power held by the retired monarch. Go-Daigo revived the monarchical records office and attracted able administrators who reasserted the royal prerogative of adjudicating lawsuits. Three years later, the shogunate learned of his plots against it and arrested his accomplices. Go-Daigo continued to insist on monarchical privilege. When the shogunate tried to force him to abdicate in favor of his cousin's line in 1331, he called on loyalists across Japan to revolt.

Although the shogunate exiled Go-Daigo to the remote island of Oki, men rallied to his cause. Some believed in it; others saw an opportunity to gain wealth and power. Ashikaga Takauji first led Kamakura's legions against Kyoto and then switched sides. In 1333 his forces set fire to Kamakura. The Hōjō family and its retainers, over eight hundred men, women, and children, committed suicide. Takauji brought Go-Daigo back from exile, only to turn on him when forced to share spoils of war with members of the aristocracy. Having overcome a string of reversals, Takauji drove Go-Daigo out of Kyoto and placed his cousin on the throne. Takauji built his headquarters in the Muromachi section of Kyoto, where he could supervise the new monarch and oversee his followers. Claiming descent from Minamoto Yoritomo to legitimize his rule, he had himself named shogun in 1338. Despite this title, the administrative structure that he and his successors pieced together over the next sixty years owed nothing to the Kamakura regime and everything to the exigencies of the moment.

Takauji's victories over Go-Daigo did not bring peace to an increasingly militarized Japan. Go-Daigo's sons established a rival southern court in the mountains of Yoshino that held out until 1392. The coexistence of two courts, northern and southern, allowed men to fight in the name of rival claimants to the throne, depending on which suited their interests. Takauji's grandson Yoshimitsu brought an end to rival courts by promising to alternate rule between their descendants. He later broke this promise. He brought recalcitrant fighters in Kyushu under his control, but he had less success with military leaders under a rival Ashikaga branch in eastern Japan. In 1402 he received the title "king of Japan" from the Ming emperor (a title not previously used in Japan, although analogous to the Yi Dynasty's ruler being titled "king of Korea") and appeared poised to replace the monarchy with his son. His reign marked the high point of Ashikaga power, although the shogunate remained in Ashikaga hands to 1573.

The Ashikaga shoguns tried to rule Japan through a combination of family ties and marriage politics. As a gesture at institutional continuity with the Kamakura shogunate, they used the title of shugo (military governor). The shugo appropriated the administrative functions of the provincial governors appointed by the court. By the end of the fourteenth century, they had also taken over the responsibilities and the income of the estate stewards (jitō). Fourteen shugo were branches of the Ashikaga family; the remaining

seven, such as the Shimazu of Satsuma in Kyushu, lived far from Kyoto and supported the Ashikaga in return for a free hand at home. Shugo served as high officials, military governors, and the Ashikaga's chief retainers. Takauji and his heirs exchanged women with shugo to maintain their allegiance and solidify alliances. Each ruled large, unwieldy territories defined in patents of appointment made by the shogun. The Ashikaga shoguns were the chief of the shugo and derived some of their income from being shugo of two provinces. They also controlled some sixty estates scattered across Japan.

The most important office under the shogun was the deputy shogun (kanrei), a position normally filled by the Shiba, Hatakeyama, and Hosokawa. They had prestige as the shogun's close relatives, governing Japan's richest provinces as shugo made them wealthy, and their office gave them authority. By combining these three constituents of power, they formed an inner bastion of support for the shogun. When they acted together on his behalf, they made it possible for him to dominate the other shugo and his retainers. When they quarreled, they tore the country apart.

The shugo normally supported the shogun because they also had weaknesses. Although they had jurisdictional authority over entire provinces, they did not control land. Even when a military man had managed to expropriate the aristocrats' claims to income from estates, he still had to contend with temples, other shugo, or even the shogun. Not all military families within a shugo's province were his direct retainers. With increasing frequency, rustic warriors (kokujin) accepted no one as their overlord. The longer the shugo resided in Kyoto, the more they relied on deputies to manage provincial administration. To intimidate their underlings, they needed the prestige bestowed by the shogun. The problem left unsolved by both the Kamakura and Ashikaga regimes was how to maintain the connection between center and periphery. Unlike China, where a bureaucracy marinated in a common ideology was first gathered to the center, then dispatched to the provinces, Japan remained in danger of fragmentation.

Apologists for the Ashikaga wrote the history of the Kamakura regime in such a way as to provide precedents for the new relationship between the Ashikaga shoguns, the shugo, and the monarch. The shugo had much broader power than any single office at Kamakura. The monarchy had lost so much of its income and autonomy that one ruler had to put off his enthronement ceremony for twenty years because the shogun refused to fund it. The Kamakura regime had subsisted on a relatively small income generated from land. The Ashikaga shoguns cast their net more broadly, collecting fees to license both foreign and domestic trade, demanding kickbacks from temples, dunning the populace in the name of the monarch, and erecting toll barriers to tax commerce. Whereas during Kamakura times, monarch and shogun had ruled Japan together, if not to the same ends, during the Muromachi period, neither can be said to have exercised effective governance.

Changes in Roles for Women

Nothing better marks the break between ancient and medieval Japan than changes in the relationships between men and women, especially at the higher reaches of society. Even before the Mongol invasions, it had become clear that dividing property among all children, men and women alike, seriously weakened a family's viability. At the same time, the fluidity in marriage arrangements that had characterized the Heian period largely disappeared. Women increasingly moved to their husband's residence. If they took property with them, less was left for their brothers. Loath to bestow property on daughters or too many sons, powerful families selected a single heir. With women and their husbands out of the picture, brothers and cousins competed to inherit the family estate. Property rights in cultivator households evolved differently. Increases in agricultural productivity plus new commercial opportunities left more income in cultivator hands. Women as well as men traded in land and other goods. A woman continued to manage her own property even when she moved into her husband's household.

Marriages became more durable and of greater consequence. When seen as a way to ally two families, the exchange of betrothal gifts and the bride's entry into her husband's residence became ceremonies. Once ensconced in her new home, the bride served her parents-in-law as well as her husband. Her trousseau supplied her with what she needed for daily life, but she lost the autonomy that had come from owning real property. She became her husband's property. No legal distinction was made between adultery and rape because both constituted crimes against the husband. On the other hand, the woman's position as wife became much more secure. The marriage ceremony's public character meant that only compelling political reasons justified divorce. If a man fathered children by a concubine, his wife became their official mother. A wife became the person primarily responsible for domestic affairs.

When her husband went to war, she managed the household economy and dispatched his supplies. A mark of her responsibilities was her title: *midaidokoro* (the lady of the kitchen).

Women at the Kyoto court had always participated in public ceremonies; during the medieval period, they assumed administrative functions as the circle around the monarch shrank. (See **Biography: Hino Meishi.**) Only the highest-ranking aristocrats managed to survive the turmoil of the age; others rusticated to keep close to their sources of income. Women replaced them in running the monarch's household, a transformation in female function seen especially in their writing. Earlier women's diaries and memoirs had been subjective and recorded their lives and thoughts. Those from the fourteenth century and later recorded men's deeds. Women also served as secretaries, writing letters and transmitting orders on behalf of monarch, regent, and shogun.

Trade in Town and Country

The fourteenth century saw a series of transformations in rural Japan. The conversion of dry fields to paddy, the growing of two crops per year, and the extensive use of irrigation made possible by water wheels brought increased yields, population growth, and commercial expansion. Estates split into corporate villages. On estates, each cultivator manager (*myōshu*) had his own legal relationship with multiple overlords. In villages, former *myōshu*, who might also be warriors, plus smallholders dealt with overlords as a unit. They presented petitions for reductions in taxes and corvée labor, and they asserted corporate control over common land and irrigation systems. This process was hastened by the development of self-governing organizations encouraged by overlords as a way to replace the Kamakura-sanctioned estate stewards. Land rights became transferable commodities rather than being associated with office and status. During times of endemic social disorder when overlords were far away, cultivators banded together in nucleated villages, constructed walls and moats, and defended themselves. They met in committee to handle village administration—irrigation procedures and tax payments, for example—and deal with judicial issues. In central Japan these village assemblies took the form of shrine associations that discriminated among members according to status and gender. Many of today's hamlets trace their names back to this century, suggesting the creation of a village identity that excluded outsiders and regulated the behavior of insiders.

BIOGRAPHY Hino Meishi

Aristocrat, official, mother, and writer, Hino Meishi (?–1358) lived through a time of political intrigue and learned what it meant to be a wife while the family structure was in transition.

Meishi was the daughter of Hino Sukena, who served the monarch Kōgon (r. 1331–1333). When she was about ten years old, she became a maid to Kōgon's mother, Kōgimonin. Meishi developed expertise in court ceremonies at Kōgon's coming-of-age ceremony. When he was enthroned as a replacement for Go-Daigo, she stood directly behind the new monarch.

Sometime before 1331, while Meishi was fulfilling official public functions, she started a romance with Kōgimonin's nephew, Kinmune, from the powerful Saionji branch of the Fujiwara lineage. They continued to see each other while Kyoto was thrown into turmoil by Go-Daigo's return, Kōgon's dethronement, and her father's involuntary decision to shave his head and become a monk. For a while they met at hideaways far from the eyes of their parents and their employers. In 1333, Meishi became Kinmune's recognized consort when he wrote her a poem pledging his fidelity. He then visited her publicly at her father's home and stayed the night. A few months later, the Saionji family summoned Meishi to its main residence at Kitayama as Kinmune's official wife in a move that united two aristocratic opponents to Go-Daigo's rule.

In 1335 Kinmune and Sukena were both arrested for having plotted against Go-Daigo. The night before Kinmune was to be exiled to Izumo, Meishi visited him at the mansion where he had been confined. They exchanged a tearful farewell, and Kinmune handed over several mementos. Before Meishi left, a messenger arrived with the news that Kinmune was to be transferred to another residence. As he was bending down to enter a palanquin, the messenger cut off his head. The pregnant Meishi fled to the Saionji mansion, where she gave birth to her son, Sanetoshi. A messenger from Go-Daigo's court arrived with an offer to find a wet nurse for the child. Kinmune's mother told him that Meishi had miscarried to protect her grandson from his enemies. When the northern court was restored in 1337, Meishi used her connection with the now retired monarch Kōgen to promote her son and restore the Saionji family to its former glory.

Meishi wrote a two-volume memoir. The first volume covers the period of her romance with Kinmune from 1329 to 1333; the second takes up the restoration of the northern court in 1337 and the revival of the Saionji family fortunes. She thus omitted the years of turmoil that exposed the political calculations behind her marriage.

Source: Based on Hitomi Tonomura, "Re-Envisioning Women in the Post Kamakura Age," in *The Origins of Japan's Medieval World: Courtiers, Clerics, Warriors, and Peasants in the Fourteenth Century*, ed. Jeffrey P. Mass (Stanford, Calif.: Stanford University Press, 1997).

Trade had spread in Kamakura times, but the early fourteenth century saw new developments. First was the monetization of commerce by relying on coins imported from Ming China. Although cultivators continued to present taxes in kind and barter never disappeared, large and small transactions came to be denominated in cash. Second, commercial centers evolved out of places where people congregated: at toll barriers, river crossings, harbors, post houses, and the entrances to shrines and temples. Men and women from nearby villages brought their wares for sale, primarily vegetables, but also processed food such as bricks of tofu. As in earlier ages, proselytizers followed the crowds; some used pictures to teach faith in Amida or to warn of the torments of hell. Nuns solicited donations for the Kumano temple complex. The authorities tried to keep people tied to a specific place and required that travelers carry a passport. Markets received a dispensation from such regulation, making them a zone where people could mingle and exchange goods and information.

The third development centered on the spread of guilds (*za*). They first appeared in the twelfth century and reached their peak in the fourteenth to fifteenth centuries. The idea behind a guild was that the traders or artisans dealing in a specific product would pay a fee to a patron (court noble, religious establishment, shogun) and receive two privileges in exchange: a monopoly on the sale or production of their product and the right to travel in pursuit of trade. Comb makers, sesame oil producers, metal casters, and potters all joined guilds. Many of them lived in the countryside, where they were listed in land records as *hyakushō* (the hundred names). Although this term came to specify cultivators in the seventeenth century, in the fourteenth century it simply meant anyone who was not an aristocrat or warrior. It thus included fishermen and salt makers. Horse traders from central Japan relied for centuries on a monarchical decree that gave them exclusive rights to trade in horses. They expanded their monopoly to everything carried by horses from the Pacific to the Japan Sea. Not until modern times did researchers discover that the decree was a forgery.

Kyoto functioned as both the political and economic center of Japan. The court, shogunate, and religious establishments competed as well as cooperated to control and tax commoners in cross-cutting systems of overlord authority that made for interdependence, exploitation, and tax evasion. During the Kamakura period, low-ranking monks from Enryakuji on Mount Hiei had begun to brew and sell sake and lend money. By the fourteenth century, wealthy moneylenders provided cash loans to aristocrats, warriors, townspeople, and cultivators at annual interest rates of up to 300 percent. Enryakuji issued business licenses and ran a protection racket, fending off attempts by other overlords to tax the moneylenders and helping to collect debts. As lobbyist for its clients, Enryakuji paid stipends to shogunal officials to protect their interests, and moneylenders bribed them to grant tax exemptions. The shoguns made prominent moneylenders their storehouse keepers and later their tax agents in return for 10 percent of the take and the prestige of an official appointment, although the relationship was more ad hoc than bureaucratic. The shogunate's income shrank while individual officials grew rich.

The shogunate strove to control and profit from the maritime trade that flourished regardless of political boundaries. Seafarers of mixed ethnicities pursued trade and piracy with equal aplomb, ravaging the Korean, Japanese, and Chinese coasts. Communities of foreign traders thrived in all the port cities of East Asia, including Japan. The Ming Dynasty closed China to foreign commerce after 1368, with the only exception being official trade carried on between states under the rubric of tribute. In 1402, the Chinese em-

Female Moneylender. This segment from a twelfth- or thirteenth-century scroll of diseases (*yamai no sōshi*) depicts a female moneylender so suffering from obesity brought on by her wealth that she needs help to walk. *(Fukuoka Art Museum)*

peror agreed to provide two ships a year with the official seal that allowed them to trade in China. By 1465, two *shugo* had taken over this tally trade, although the shogunate continued to assess a fee of 10 percent on private merchandise. Late-fourteenth-century state formation in the Ryukyu Islands led three principalities to merge into one under King Sho Hashi in 1429. The Ryukyuans sent tribute missions to China and received official permission to pursue trade. As a maritime nation, they sailed their ships from Southeast Asia to Japan and Korea. Through piracy, smuggling, and legitimate trade, Japan participated in economic networks stretching across the East Asia seas. Japanese seafarers established a community in Vietnam's Hoi An. In the sixteenth century, these networks brought Europeans in search of trade and Christian converts. (See **Connections: Europe Enters the Scene**.)

Life on the Margins

Trade did not alleviate the disruptions caused by crop failures. Famines forced desperate people to sell themselves into bondage, a form of slavery that could last for generations. Disease was another scourge. Leprosy terrorized people in Japan as it did in Europe. The afflicted suffered increasing disfigurement as their flesh rotted away. How could it be other than punishment for evil committed in a previous life? Lest they contaminate the healthy, lepers had to leave their families and join groups of paupers, the infirm, and entertainers, referred to as the people of the riverbank (*kawaramono*).

The *kawaramono* were outcasts. They included people whose occupations brought them into contact with things deemed to be polluting, death in particular. Tanners, butchers, policemen, and undertakers were excluded from ordinary society. For them, the only fit habitation was on untaxed land that nobody wanted. Occasionally, riverbank people were hired to cleanse a shrine after it had been desecrated by fire or by the loss of life in a fight. Purifying the shrine involved the dirty work of removing dead bodies, but such rites also suggest a social imagination in which two negatives become a positive and the power to purify lies with the impure.

Other people used marginal spaces carved out of ordinary life as temporary refuges. Markets, river crossings, the entrances to temples and shrines, and graveyards offered sanctuary to unfree people fleeing bondage. Mountains provided shelter for entire villages that absconded to protest unjust taxes or forced labor. Another form of protest was for groups of warriors or cultivators to dress in the persimmon-colored robes reserved for lepers. It was a desperate measure because it cut them off from normal human interaction. It worked because spaces set apart from ordinary life were protected by deities and Buddhas.

Changes in Religious Practice

An important characteristic of Japan's Middle Ages was the power of the Buddhist establishment. Although Ashikaga shoguns dominated the court, they had to conciliate the temples that largely controlled the urban economy and had their own police force as well as deep roots in the lives of Japanese people. The major temples that had received support from the Heian court continued to flourish; the popular sects that originated in the Kamakura period attracted sometimes vehement converts. Zen Buddhism made major contributions to Japanese aesthetics and played an important political role.

Rather than patronize the temples already entrenched in the Kyoto court, Ashikaga shoguns preferred the Rinzai Zen sect. At the suggestion of a Zen monk, Takauji and his son set up official temples named Ankokuji (temples for national peace) in each province to console Go-Daigo's spirit and raise the shogun's prestige. They also had pagodas built in the precincts of temples belonging to other sects for the same purpose.

Later shoguns promoted and ranked Zen temples in Kyoto and Kamakura in loose accord with the system already developed for Zen (Chan) temples in China. Priests jockeying for position and shogunal preference meant that rankings could shift. By 1410, ten temples enjoyed the top rank of "five mountains" (*gozan*), and all the Kyoto temples ranked above their Kamakura counterparts. Next in importance were the sixty-odd "ten temples" (*jissetsu*). At the bottom were the "multitude of temples" patronized by powerful provincial families. Many had originally been temples of other sects that changed their affiliation to Zen to become part of this ranking system that bestowed prestige and connections to the center on its affiliates.

The Ashikaga established a hierarchy of priests that aligned the Rinzai sect even more closely with its fortunes. When Yoshimitsu built Shōkokuji next to his palace on Muromachi Street in 1382, he had the chief Rinzai priest reside there. This priest decided appointments to the heads of the Rinzai temples, recommended promotions, and determined ceremonial procedures. Owing to his prowess in the Chinese language, he prepared documents related to maritime trade and foreign affairs. In the fifteenth century, the shogunate appointed men from aristocratic families to this position, with the result that the chief priest often had little interest in routine administration or religious observances.

As the Rinzai school became increasingly associated with the dominant power structure, its teachings and practice moved farther from what is conventionally associated with Zen. Instead of seeking the path to enlightenment through meditation, Rinzai became syncretic. It absorbed secret teachings and incantations from esoteric Buddhism that had proved popular with the aristocracy. Even in provincial temples, question-and-answer sessions between master and disciple took a fixed form based on oral tradition handed down in secret. In Kyoto the chief priests participated with the military and civilian aristocracy in literary and artistic pursuits.

Yoshida Shinto (also called Yuiitsu Shinto—"one and only") opposed Zen Buddhism and Buddhist-Shinto syncretism by insisting on the worship of deities only as deities rather than as bodhisattvas. Justified by his claim to a tradition stretching back to the creation of Japan through his Urabe lineage of court diviners, Yoshida Kanetomo (1435–1511) invented Shinto rituals, some of which had an open, exoteric dimension accessible to ordinary worshipers. Secret esoteric rituals for initiates surprisingly similar to Buddhist rites drew on Buddhist hand gestures called *mudras* and used quotations from *Nihon shoki* in place of mantras. Yoshida Shinto dogma and practice reasserted the centrality of the monarch in indigenous terms and rescued Shinto from complete submersion in Buddhism.

Muromachi Culture

The cult of sensibility (*aware*) from the Heian period and the Kamakura aesthetic characterized by austerity were combined in the fifteenth century into a notion of beauty and elegance modified by stern simplicity. The key term was *yūgen*, used to describe the profound, the remote, the mysterious—a term taken from Nō, the quintessential dramatic form of the day. (See **Material Culture: Nō**.) In Nō every gesture must be refined, the dance graceful, and the language elevated. The most meaningful moments are those when the actor's unspoken, unmoving spiritual presence allows the audience a glimpse of the inexpressible. The same search for the presence behind the form can be seen in monochrome ink brush painting wherein the spaces left blank give shape to the composition, in flower arranging based on the asymmetrical placement of a blossom or two, and in the tea ceremony.

Zen permeated the arts and architecture of the time. Natural settings depicted in ink brush paintings became allegories of doctrinal points just as did the late-fifteenth-century rock garden at Ryōanji. Raked white sand surrounds fifteen rocks, only fourteen of which are visible from any one perspective. It takes the experience of enlightenment to grasp all fifteen at once. Partly inspired by Song Dynasty architecture, the Golden Pavilion (Kinkakuji) and its pond built in 1398 were designed to model paradise. Ashikaga Yoshimasa built the Silver Pavilion (Ginkakuji), a more modestly refined building, seventy-five years later. A truncated cone of white sand designed to reflect moonlight on the pavilion dominates its Zen garden.

Literary arts also reflected Buddhist influence. Between 1310 and 1331, the poet and recluse Yoshida Kenkō wrote *Essays in Idleness*, a collection of reflections on his time, didactic statements, and meditations, all suffused with longing for the past. In the late fourteenth century, stories about the conflict between the northern and southern courts coalesced in *Taiheiki* (*Records of Great Pacification*). Castigating Ashikaga Takauji as a traitor and emphasizing the legitimacy of the southern court, this late military history became a favorite of storytellers. Ghost stories, didactic tales, folktales, testimonials to the saving power of the Buddha, and sermons were sold in booklets later called *otogi zōshi* (chapbooks).

The tea ceremony, from which women were excluded, assimilated warriors and priests to aristocratic standards of taste. In the first century of Ashikaga rule, imbibing bitter green tea provided the occasion for parties at which the host displayed his finest art treasures in a beautifully appointed sitting room overlooking a garden. With the coming of warfare in the late fifteenth century, this florid style gave way to a simpler, more ritualized and disciplined ceremony performed in a hut. Instead of richly decorated Chinese vessels, the emphasis shifted to plain, often misshapen pots because the aesthetic of the time expressed in the combination of *wabi* and *sabi* (elegant simplicity) celebrated the beauty of imperfect objects. The practitioners included provincial samurai and merchants from Kyoto and Sakai, who found the tea ceremony an excellent excuse to mingle with aristocrats. Linked verse (*renga*), a collaborative form of poetry writing, provided a venue for the talented but lowborn to attract attention. Traveling priests such as Sōchō carried the practices of poetry and tea to provincial strongmen across Japan. (See **Documents: *The Journal of Sōchō*.**)

In contrast to the Zen-influenced arts of earlier times, exuberant color characterized the Momoyama period at the end of the sixteenth century. Epitomized in Toyotomi Hideyoshi's golden tearoom, parvenu extravagance marked lacquer boxes dusted with gold and wall paintings with gold leaf background. Vividly painted screens depicted European traders and missionaries and celebrated local customs. (See Color Plate 17.) Artistic triumphs based on technological innovation led to elaborate textile designs and towering castle keeps.

CIVIL WAR (1467–1600)

The hundred years of civil war that began with the Ōnin conflict of 1467–1477 diffused elite cultural practices across the country. The breakdown of unified public authority spurred innovations from military organization to village life. Estates vanished. Buddhist temples lost power and income when they were not simply destroyed. Without their protection, the Kyoto moneylenders and other guild organizations disappeared. Territorial units of domains and villages replaced the former patchwork of competing jurisdictions.

MATERIAL CULTURE

Nō

Combining music, dance, and narrative, Nō drew on rural dances that appealed to the gods for good harvests, comical skits, popular songs, and tales told by jongleurs. The early spectacles were vulgar and exuberant, attracting crowds of people from all walks of life. At a performance in 1349, monks solicited donations, princes and the Fujiwara regent were among the spectators, and thieves tried to steal the actors' costumes.

Protégé and lover of Ashikaga Yoshimitsu, Zeami transformed Nō into art. In some plays he took themes from *The Tale of Genji*, and in others he used the elevated diction of the court to recast *The Tale of the Heike*. He crafted stories about ghosts condemned by jealous passion or murderous deed to wander the netherworld between death and salvation. Not content to remain spectators, shoguns and daimyo performed Nō and made it a state ceremony.

The accouterments of Nō are simple yet elegant. The wooden stage is bare, with a pine tree painted across the backdrop. The musicians and chorus perform on drums and flute for one or two performers. Men in black arrange costumes and provide the occasional prop. One performer wears a mask denoting men and women of various ages, gods, the possessed, and demons. Subtle movements of the head combined with skillful carving lend these masks great expressive power. In contrast to the stern simplicity of the set, the robes are of brilliant brocade, their glitter designed to gleam in torchlight. (See Color Plate 20.)

Nō Performance. One detail on a folding screen showing scenes in and around Kyoto depicts the audience for a Nō performance in the early sixteenth century. Men and women, old and young, commoners, monks, and nobles all found it absorbing. *(National Museum of Japanese History/DNPArchives.com)*

DOCUMENTS

The Journal of Sōchō

Written by Saiokuken Sōchō, an acclaimed master of linked verse and a Zen monk, these entries show how the poet received commissions to write poetry from a high shogunal official amid the ravages of civil war. During his travels around central Japan in search of patrons and poetic inspiration, Sōchō turned a critical eye on his society in describing people on the margins, merchants, sake brewers, impoverished samurai, and lazy priests.

1522: We crossed to Ōminato harbor in Ise and proceeded to Yamada, where we visited Ise shrine. The matter had been raised earlier of a thousand-verse sequence to be presented to the shrine, and I had invited the priest Sōseki down for that purpose. He arrived near the end of the seventh month, and we began composing the sequence soon thereafter, on the fourth of the eighth month. Two hundred verses a day for five days. The work was commissioned as a votive sequence by the present shogunal deputy, Hosokawa Takakuni, when he returned to the capital from Ōmi. His opening verse (*hokku*) for the first hundred verses was sent from Kyoto:

> Everywhere aglow
> in the morning sunlight—
> the haze!
> > Takakuni
> Plum trees blossom,
> willows bend, and even
> the wind abates!
> > Sōchō

Sōseki then left for Owari. Knowing it was likely to snow before long, I decided to set out for the north on the sixteenth. There has been fighting in this province beyond Kumozu river and Anonotsu, making it difficult to get from place to place.

Anonotsu has been desolate for more than ten years, and nothing but ruins remains of its four or five thousand villages and temples. Stands of reeds and mugwort, no chickens or dogs, rare even to hear the cawing of a crow.

1525: *Item.* There is nothing like going into business for profit. People who do so never speak of gods or Buddhas, give no thought to the world's prosperity or decline, know nothing of the elegant pursuits of snow, moon, and blossoms, grow distant from friends, reject appeals from their near and dear, and spend every waking moment thinking of making money. But that is how to get on in the world. Note, though, that those with even nominal lands, and monks with temple properties, should not take an interest in business. But note too that the sake dealers in the capital, Sakai, the Southern Capital, Sakamoto, and also in this part of the country do very well.

Item. Consider the low-ranking samurai, starving with no land to call his own. There is no help for him. He obviously cannot part from his wife and children. Their food runs out, and the woman must draw water and the man must gather brushwood. Their children are taken away before their eyes to slave for others. Their bowing and scraping is pitiful. Driven to that pass, those with

Succession disputes provided the pretext for retainers and overlords to push their own interests. In the Hatakeyama case, the aging *shugo* first appointed a nephew to be his heir, but when a son was born to his concubine, he tried to have his decision reversed. In the 1450s, powerful retainers and the shogunal deputy backed the nephew and got the shogun to censure the son. Son and nephew fought on the political front, each being censured three times and forgiven three times, and on the military front where their retainers demanded rewards after each battle. This conflict foreshadowed the dispute in the Ashikaga house when Yoshimasa appointed his younger brother his successor, only to be forced to change his mind

self-respect may even do away with themselves. Someone said that to such unfortunates one should give a little something. That is the essence of charity. Of course one must give as well to those who beg by the roadside and wait by houses and gates.

Item. Lion dancers, monkey trainers, bell ringers, bowl beaters, and the like have something they can do for a living. People somehow provide for them, though their need is no greater than that of those I have just mentioned. It is the latter, for whom there is no help at all, who are the world's true unfortunates, even more than lepers and beggars. They are truly wretched.

Item. People who pursue the study of Zen are embarked on a difficult and estimable course. But those who are perfunctory in their Zen practice, even highly placed samurai in the capital and provinces, easily fall into error.

Item. Where today can one find an inspirational teacher of the doctrines of "separate transmission outside the teachings" and "nonverbalization"? Some call today's Zen practitioners a pack of devils, of the lowest guttersnipe sort. Abbots, monks, and novices these days consort with the high and mighty, curry donations from provincial gentry, pursue their austerities only when it suits them, run hither and yon all day, and dally with other practitioners. But who are the masters they practice with themselves? Some say it is far better to repeat the Holy Name [of Amida]. I am more attracted to those who follow a simple and ignorant practice, as I do.

Item. Acquiring bows, horses, and armor and maintaining good retainers—that is the way of the samurai. But there is no need to run out and buy things for which one has no specific purpose. Constant spending and extravagance must be avoided, I am told.

1526, fourth month: We crossed the Mountain of Meeting and entered the capital at Awataguchi without meeting a soul. This route used to be filled with horses and palanquins, everyone bumping shoulders and tilting hats to squeeze by. As I looked out over the city, I saw not one in ten of the houses that had been there formerly, either rich or poor. The sight of tilled fields around farmhouses, with the Imperial Palace in the midst of summer barley, was too much for words.

1527: On the fourth of the third month I left Yashima. A village called Minakuchi [Water's mouth] in Kōga continued for about ten chō, and I recalled the old palace built here once for an imperial pilgrimage to Ise. There are many toll gates in these parts, and as we went along people would shout "Stop! Toll!" at every one., whereupon I composed the following:

> I must have appeared
> at the water's mouth,
> for at every gate
> "Stop! Toll!" is what
> they cry together.

Source: H. Mack Horton, trans. and anno., *The Journal of Sōchō* (Stanford, Calif.: Stanford University Press, 2002), pp. 15–16, 84–86, 104, 143.

when his wife, Hino Tomiko, gave birth to Yoshihisa in 1465. Her dedication to her son's future shows how family loyalties had changed from Hōjō Masako's day. Already at odds over the Hatakeyama dispute, the two chief *shugo* each picked a rival claimant.

The *shugo* fought their first battles in and around Kyoto in 1467. Their chief weapon was arson, used to punish and exorcise enemies. Temples, aristocratic mansions, and the treasures of the ages burned. Commanders marched armies through the streets to intimidate their opponents. When they fought, they did so during the day, and seldom did they pursue a fleeing adversary. In the early years, a defeated opponent might be sent into exile or allowed to retire to a monastery. Later, a demand for retribution led to the slaughter of hostages and prisoners, the mutilation of corpses, the lacquering of an enemy's skull for use as a drinking cup. By the end of the Ōnin war, Kyoto's palaces had become fields; the *shugo* had become pawns of their erstwhile retainers when they had not disappeared; and Yoshihisa had inherited an empty office. He died in 1489 while trying to subdue a recalcitrant retainer who had organized rustic warriors in Ōmi to expropriate estates that paid tithes to nobles and temples.

The shogunate became irrelevant to power struggles that rent Japan. *Shugo* families split in fratricidal disputes over titles and the power to control landholdings that they conferred. Retainers manufactured factional disputes or betrayed one lord for another. Believing their honor to be at stake in every encounter, they fought deadly duels over imagined slights. Fortunately for the residents of Kyoto, even before the Ōnin war drew to an inconclusive close in 1477, battlefields had shifted to the provinces, closer to the spoils of war.

Local Leagues

The power vacuum at the top provided an opportunity for locally based leagues (*ikki*—literally, "union of minds") to escape from the vertical hierarchies that had tied them to aristocratic, ecclesiastical, and military patrons. In 1487 rustic warriors in Yamashiro united province-wide to resist the incursions of overlords. Theirs was a horizontal alliance of self-reliant men of no particular pedigree. They organized mass demonstrations village by village. On occasion they looted, burned, and killed. Between 1428 and 1526, twenty-four *ikki* demanding debt amnesty from moneylenders erupted in Kyoto and its environs. Many were at least partially successful; indeed they ceased to be a threat only when moneylenders mobilized Kyoto townspeople to go on the offensive in 1536. They took the lead in consolidating the cityscape into two defensible sectors and in building fortifications. (See Map 13.1.) They had already organized neighborhood associations for crime prevention, mutual protection, and firefighting. When the shogun proved unable to defend the city, the associations hired mercenaries. Many moneylenders helped build the temple fortresses belonging to the Lotus sect that dominated the commoners' religious life.

The Lotus League (*hokke ikki*) attracted adherents in urban areas with its exclusive faith in the saving power of the *Lotus Sutra*. In teaching that this world can be the Buddhist paradise, it encouraged worldly success. It provided institutional support independent of traditional elites, thus making it feasible for moneylenders to end their subordination to Enryakuji. It supported a paramilitary organization useful in times of disorder. With the shogun on the run after 1521, believers in the *Lotus Sutra* massed in tens of thousands not only to defend the city but also to attack military commanders and adherents of different Buddhist sects. They withheld rents, collected taxes, and settled disputes, in effect setting up a commoner-run city government, though the merchants in Sakai went farther in developing the instruments of self-rule. Enryakuji was the first to organize opposition to the league, soon joined by a military commander in Ōmi. In eight days of fighting in 1536, the attackers destroyed all the Lotus temples, burned the entire lower city and one-third of the upper, and slaughtered men, women, and children suspected of being true believers. Kyoto suffered worse damage than it had during the Ōnin war. From a military point of view, suppression had to be brutal because the Hokke teachings placed commoners on the same level as their masters.

The most radical renunciation of allegiance to overlords came in the One-Mind Leagues (*Ikkō ikki*) that flourished in central Japan after the Ōnin war. Adherents to the True Pure Land school of Buddhism believed that Amida offered salvation to all who accepted his gift of faith. Since everyone was equal in Amida's eyes, the One-Mind Leagues rejected both religious and secular hierarchies. Although their adherents lived in largely autonomous communities organized around a lay teacher and temple, they were linked to a nationwide organization through the sect's headquarters situated in the fortified temple complex called Ishiyama Honganji built in Osaka in 1532. The most militant and long lasting of the One-Mind Leagues on the Noto peninsula held out against warlords from 1488 to 1578.

Rise of Warlords

Out of the same crucible of disorder that produced *ikki* appeared military men determined to create a new vertical hierarchy. Unlike the *shugo*, who depended on the shogun for patents of rule, the new leaders, called *daimyo*, relied on nothing other than military force. Daimyo constructed domains from the inside out. They ignored provincial boundaries in favor of natural defenses—rivers, mountains, and seas. Their

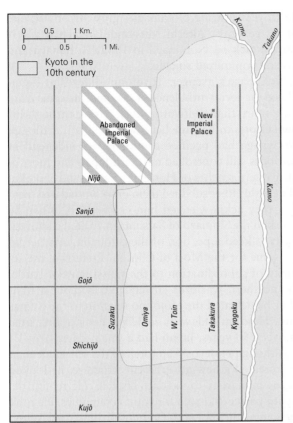

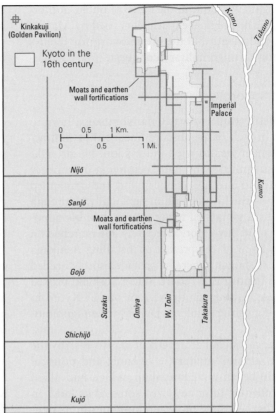

Map 13.1   Kyoto in the Tenth–Eleventh Centuries and Its Transformation in the Sixteenth Century

domains were smaller than those held by the former *shugo*, but they were more secure. To the impoverishment of the Kyoto aristocrats and temples, they tolerated no absentee proprietors. In order to survive, monarch and court sold themselves as arbiters of taste and erected toll barriers to tax goods in transit.

Warlords acquired territory through conquest, alliance, or marriage. Territory came with fighting men, the samurai, and cultivators, often one and the same. Samurai were incorporated into the warlord's retainer band through an oath of loyalty in return for land or perhaps a stipend. Sometimes this meant confirming a samurai's hold over the land he brought with him, though when possible warlords preferred to move retainers to a different area, often with the promise of a raise, in order to break their ties with former supporters. Even village headmen swore allegiance to a warlord in return for protection. They were expected to fight in time of war in addition to cultivating their land, maintaining order, and collecting taxes.

Warlords tried to mold their territories and retainer bands into a cohesive unit. They surveyed land to find

out how much it produced and who was responsible for its taxes. They promoted irrigation works to open new land. They forbade cultivators to move away. They relaxed restrictions on commerce. They issued laws to maintain order and tame the samurai. They suppressed private feuds by announcing that in cases of quarrels, both sides would be judged equally guilty and punished accordingly. They wrote house codes that warned against fomenting factions or indulging in luxury. Income and responsibility rewarded dedication to duty, loyalty, and obedience. In this way, warlords created competing power blocs centered on castle towns.

The most notable warlords of the sixteenth century were self-made men who rose from obscurity to become mighty conquerors, a process summarized in the term *gekokujō* (the overthrow of those above by those below). Maeda Toshiie of Kaga started his career as a low-ranking retainer. He initiated land surveys and reorganized his retainer band to reduce its autonomy. Takeda Shingen fought nearly constantly from age twenty to his death. Realizing that military force legitimizes nothing, he claimed that his quest for personal gain was done in the name of public authority (*kōgi*). The political experiments tried by Maeda, Takeda, and others laid the groundwork for Japan's unification through military conquest.

The Conquerors

The earliest conqueror was Oda Nobunaga, born to a junior branch of an obscure lineage. His first accomplishment was to wipe out his kin. He brought masterless samurai who had been living by robbery and extortion into his retainer band and demanded that they swear loyalty to him personally. Although Nobunaga commanded fewer troops than his opponents, he used them more effectively. He marched on Kyoto in 1568 on the pretext of installing Ashikaga Yoshiaki as shogun. There he provided sorely needed aid to the impoverished court. When Yoshiaki proved recalcitrant, Nobunaga drove him out of Kyoto in 1573, bringing the Ashikaga Dynasty to an ignominious end.

Nobunaga's signal achievement was to destroy the Buddhist temples' military, economic, and political power. He began with Enryakuji, which had allied with his enemies after he seized some of its land. In 1571 he burned three thousand buildings in its temple complex on Mount Hiei and massacred the monks. By threat or force, he expropriated the holdings of several other monasteries and ordered them to reduce their personnel. Between 1570 and 1580, he waged war against the *Ikkō ikki*, showing no mercy to its adherents and slaughtering tens of thousands. To destroy the fortified headquarters at Ishiyama Honganji, he may have outfitted ships with cannon. As a result of his efforts, the power of the Buddhist establishment, which had characterized Japan's Middle Ages, was permanently eliminated.

As befit a man who aspired to bring the entire realm under one military regime, Nobunaga designed new economic and social policies. He freed merchants from having to seek the protection of guilds in return for monetary contributions called "thank-you money." He eliminated toll barriers within the areas he controlled. He tried to stabilize the exchange rates between different types of coins. He collected tax registers to gauge how much his land was worth and assert his authority over its disposal. In this way, he could argue that his retainers held their ancestral lands only at his pleasure. They had to be willing to move from place to place as he deemed fit; otherwise they would be marked as traitors and

destroyed. Fearing Nobunaga's growing power, one of his generals, Akechi Mitsuhide, launched a surprise attack on Nobunaga in 1562. Nobunaga and his son committed suicide.

Nobunaga's avenger, Toyotomi Hideyoshi, exemplified the social turbulence of the time. He came from little more than cultivator stock, rising through his own efforts to become hegemon of Japan. Although Nobunaga had pacified central Japan, independent warlords still controlled northern Japan and most of the western reaches of Honshu, Kyushu, and Shikoku. Hideyoshi either subdued them or so intimidated them that they acknowledged him as overlord. When he defeated the Shimazu of Satsuma in 1586, he allowed them to keep a portion of their domain, and he did the same for the Mōri of Chōshū. Preferring the security of subordination to the vicissitudes of battle, the northern warlords surrendered without a fight after he defeated the Hōjō (no relation to the Kamakura Hōjō) at Odawara in 1590. For the first time in over 250 years, Japan had a single ruler.

Although Hideyoshi epitomized the self-made man and created a new government structure, he looked to the monarchy to validate his rule. He rebuilt the Kyoto palace and paid for court ceremonies. He took the name Fujiwara and had himself appointed retired regent (*taikō*). He allowed his chief supporters and even his rivals to remain as daimyo of domains, though he carefully interspersed them to prevent collusion. He rewarded his faithful supporter Tokugawa Ieyasu with the eight Kantō provinces after the defeat of the Hōjō in a move that shifted Ieyasu from his homeland in Mikawa to an unfamiliar region swarming with rustic warriors. Hideyoshi commanded enormous resources through the land he controlled and his taxes on commerce in Osaka and Sakai. He minted huge gold coins, the first time since 958 that a Japanese government had issued currency. Rather than spend his own money, he had the daimyo pay for construction projects and provide military service on demand. He created an ideological basis for his rule by claiming descent from the sun god who had entered his mother's womb, a drama he enacted on the Nō stage for the benefit of aristocrats, daimyo, and foreign visitors.

Desiring order and stability above all, Hideyoshi tried to ensure that no one would be able to rise as he had. Building on the work of his rivals, he instituted a nationwide land survey to determine the extent of arable land and to fix a name to every plot. Hideyoshi's land survey marked the beginning of

Korean Invasion. Japanese landing at Pusan, 1592. *(National Treasure 391, Cultural Heritage Administration, Seoul, South Korea)*

efforts to quantify landholdings and estimate tax revenues. By eliminating intermediary claims to landed income, the land survey marked the end of the largely defunct estates. He ordered subsidiary castles torn down and destroyed the remaining fortified neighborhoods in Kyoto. In 1588, he also tried to insist on a rigid status distinction between samurai and commoners by forbidding all but samurai from wearing two swords, one long and one short. Thereafter, commoners might own swords, but they could not put them on display. Hideyoshi issued a series of decrees prohibiting samurai from leaving their lord's service to become merchants or cultivators and preventing farmers from deserting their fields to become city folk. Although it proved impossible to make clear distinctions between various statuses and some domains such as Satsuma or Tosa continued to recognize rustic samurai (*gōshi*), Hideyoshi's intent remained the law of the land until 1871.

In 1592, Hideyoshi turned his attention to an invasion of Korea. (For Chinese and Korean perspectives, see Chapters 14 and 15.) He mobilized 158,000 samurai supported by 9,200 sailors and kept 100,000 men as a backup force, one indication of how heavily militarized Japanese society had become. In his most grandiloquent pronouncements, Hideyoshi promised to conquer both Korea and China and to put the Japanese monarch on the Chinese throne with Hideyoshi's adopted heir as regent. (He later withdrew the adoption when his concubine bore a son.) The first invasion plundered as far as Pyongyang. The troops were forced to retreat when supplies ran low, the Ming came to Korean aid, and the Korea admiral Yi Sunsin attacked Japanese ships with armor-plated ships and cannon. Hideyoshi tried again in 1597. When he died the next year, the Japanese troops in Korea decamped to participate in the succession dispute to come.

Hideyoshi had hoped to pass his dominion to his son by establishing a balance of power in the five-man advisory council created shortly before his death. Its most powerful member was Tokugawa Ieyasu who, like Nobunaga and Hideyoshi, came from an obscure background in central Japan. Ieyasu strengthened his retainers' devotion and loyalty by making them completely dependent on him for their rewards. Rather than kill his kin, he left them with the original Matsudaira name when he took the Tokugawa name in 1566. He honored them as his relatives while he relied on men he had made to be his advisers and generals. Upon moving from central Japan to the Kantō plain, he turned the village of Edo into his castle town and started to build an administrative and personnel system based on the initiatives of his peers. He fought only those battles he knew he could win. By the time the advisory council fell apart in 1600, he had neutralized, compromised, or won over most of his rivals.

The battle of Sekigahara in 1600 brought the civil wars to a close. Although Hideyoshi's son remained ensconced in Osaka castle, his supporters were samurai who had lost their masters (*rōnin*) and other warriors who found that peace left little outlet for their talents. When Ieyasu decided to move against the castle in two campaigns in 1615 and 1616, the resistance was fierce but futile. Another threat to peace was the Shimabara Christian rebellion of 1637 in Kyushu, the last of the religiously based *ikki*. Like its predecessors, it was suppressed with the slaughter of approximately ten thousand men, women, and children. Its end marked the last military conflict Japan was to suffer for over two hundred years.

SUMMARY

What changed during Japan's middle ages? Warfare destroyed the estate system and forged new political institutions from the village to the domain. The shaved pate for men originated during the Onin war because it made wearing helmets less hot. Warlords instituted land surveys and sword hunts to consolidate their rule. Shifting patterns in marriage and the spread of primogeniture affirmed patriarchal authority in the ruling class. Despite, or perhaps because of, the disruptions caused by war, domestic trade based on increased agricultural productivity led to new occupations, while international trade linked Japan with Korea, China, and Southeast Asia, although not always in channels approved by rulers. Some social experiments, such as vertically organized warrior bands, endured into subsequent centuries. Others—the religiously based horizontally constructed leagues—became historical dead ends. Religious institutions lost economic and political power, but religious beliefs informed cultural values. Arts inspired by Zen such as ink brush painting and rock gardens came to define what people often think is the quintessential Japanese aesthetic. The popularity of the tea ceremony among merchants prefigured the spread of popular culture centered on townspeople.

The Ming Empire in China (1368–1644)

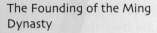

The Ming Dynasty was founded by a man who lived through the disorder of the late Yuan and knew poverty firsthand. His efforts to impose order on Chinese society sometimes took draconian forms, but his thirty-year reign brought China peace and stability. Although he and some of his successors treated officials cruelly, in time competition to join officaldom surpassed Song levels. Literati culture was especially vibrant in the economically well-developed Jiangnan region, south of the lower Yangzi River. As population increased, both rural and urban areas took on distinctive traits. Rural areas differed greatly by region, with powerful lineages, tenantry, and absentee landlords much more common in some areas than in others. The merchant-centered culture of cities found expression in vernacular fiction and drama, published in increasing quantity and accessible even to those with rudimentary educations.

Since the Ming Dynasty was succeeded by a non-Chinese conquest dynasty (the Qing Dynasty of the Manchus, 1644–1911), the Ming was the last of the native dynasties. Historians have therefore often turned to it for a baseline against which modern change has been judged. How did China compare to Western Europe in the fifteenth and sixteenth centuries? Had China already begun to fall behind Western Europe in technology, standard of living, or pace of change? At the local level, were communities becoming more integrated into the realm as standardizing policies and economic linkages spread? Or were they becoming more diverse as the economy developed in different directions in different places? A related set of questions concerns the government and the educated elite. How effective and how adaptable was the government? Why did educated men continue to seek office when the government so often treated them poorly? What was the impact on the educated class of the changes in the examination system and the explosion of printing?

THE FOUNDING OF THE MING DYNASTY

The founder of the Ming Dynasty, Zhu Yuanzhang (1328–1398), started life at the bottom of society. His parents often moved to look for work or evade rent collectors. His home region in Anhui province was hit by drought and then plague in the 1340s, and when he was only sixteen years old, his father, oldest brother, and brother's wife all died, leaving two penniless boys with three bodies to bury. A neighbor let them bury them in his field, but they had no way to provide coffins or anything to eat. With no relatives to turn to, Zhu Yuanzhang asked a monastery to take him on as a novice. The monastery was short of funds itself, as its tenants could not pay their rent, and in less than two months, Zhu was sent out to beg for food. For the next three to four years, he traveled widely through central China. Not until he returned to the monastery did he learn to read.

A few years later, in 1351, a millenarian sect known as the Red Turbans rose in rebellion. The Red Turbans were affiliated with the White Lotus Society, whose teachings drew on two distinct traditions. One was Manichaeism and its idea of the incompatibility of the forces of good and evil. The other was the cult of the Maitreya Buddha, who would in the future bring his paradise to earth to relieve human suffering. The Red Turbans met with considerable success, even defeating Mongol cavalry. In the course of fighting the rebels, the Yuan government troops burned down Zhu Yuanzhang's temple. Zhu, then twenty-four, joined the rebels. The leaders of the Red Turbans were men of modest origins, and Zhu Yuanzhang rose quickly among them. One of the commanders let Zhu marry his daughter. Within a couple of years, Zhu had between twenty thousand and thirty thousand men fighting under him.

At this time there were strongmen all over China—some rebels, some loyal to the Yuan, but all trying to maintain control of a local base. Zhu quickly attracted literati advisers who thought he had a chance to be the final victor and hoped to help shape his government. They encouraged him to gradually distance himself from the Red Turbans, whose millenarian beliefs did not appeal to the educated elite. In 1356, Zhu took Nanjing, made it his base, and tried to win over the local population by disciplining his soldiers.

Many of Zhu's followers developed into brilliant generals, and gradually they defeated one rival after another. In 1368 his armies took the Yuan capital (which the Yuan emperor and his closest followers had vacated just days before). Then forty years old, Zhu Yuanzhang declared himself emperor of the Ming Dynasty. The word *ming*, meaning "bright," resonated with the Manichaean strain in Red Turban ideology. His first reign period he called Hongwu ("abundantly martial"), and since he did not introduce a new reign period for the rest of his thirty-year reign, he is often referred to as the Hongwu emperor. It became the custom from this point on for emperors not to change their reign period names. Zhu Yuanzhang's posthumous temple name (the name used in the sacrifices to him after his death) is Taizu, so he is also called Ming Taizu.

Ming Taizu, the Hongwu Emperor

In the milieu in which Taizu grew up, the deities in Daoist temples labeled "emperors," such as the Yellow Emperor and the Emperor of the Eastern Peak, provided a folk image of imperial rule. The Hongwu emperor seems to have taken these divine autocrats as his model and did everything he could to elevate the position of emperor to their level. He required his officials to kneel when addressing him, and he did not hesitate to have them beaten in open court. He issued instructions to be read aloud to villagers, telling them to be filial to their parents, live in harmony with their neighbors, work contentedly at their occupations, and refrain from evil.

Taizu wanted a world in which people obeyed their superiors, and those who committed evil acts were promptly punished. In order to lighten the weight of government exactions on the poor, he ordered a full-scale registration of cultivated land and population so that labor service and tax obligations could be assessed more fairly. Taizu called for the drafting of a new law code and took it through five revisions. He had legal experts compare every statute in it to the Tang code in his presence, but he made the final decisions.

Some Yuan practices Taizu retained. One was the strengthening of the provinces as the administrative layer between the central government and the prefectures. The creation of provinces should not be viewed as a decentralization of power, but instead as a way for the central government to increase its supervision of the prefectures and counties. Another Yuan practice that the Hongwu emperor retained was use of hereditary service obligations for artisan households that had to supply the palace or government as their tax obligation. The army too made use of hereditary households. Centuries earlier, during the Northern and Southern Dynasties, armies composed of men with inherited obligations to serve had been common. Among the non-Chinese in the north, the status was an honorable one, but in the south, the status became despised. In the Tang, the divisional militia, with its hereditary obligations, had worked well for a half-century, but then it was supplanted by recruited professional armies, a practice the Song retained. The Mongols, however, made military service a hereditary obligation as they did so much else, and the Ming took over this practice.

Under the Hongwu emperor, the Ming army reached 1 million soldiers, drawn from the armies that had fought for control of China as well as some conscripts and some convicts. Once a family had been classed as a military household, it was responsible for supplying one soldier in succession, replacing soldiers who were injured, who died, or who deserted. Garrisons were concentrated along the northern border and near the capital; each garrison allocated a tract of land that the soldiers took turns cultivating to supply their own food, a system that had been repeatedly tried since the Han Dynasty. Although in theory this system should have supplied the Ming with a large but inexpensive army, the reality was less satisfactory. Just as in earlier dynasties, garrisons were rarely self-sufficient, men compelled to become soldiers did not necessarily make good fighting men, and desertion was difficult to prevent.

Many of the soldiers in the Ming army were Mongols in Mongol units. Although anti-Mongol sentiment was strong among the rebels, Taizu recognized that the Yuan Dynasty had had the Mandate of Heaven and told Mongols that they would be welcome in his dynasty: "Those Mongols and Inner Asians who live on our land also are our children, and those among them who possess talent and ability also shall be selected and appointed to office by us."[1] Taizu did not try to conquer the Mongols, and Ming China did not extend into modern Inner Mongolia or Central Asia. Where it did expand was to the southwest. In the 1380s, Ming took control of modern Yunnan and created the new province of Guizhou east of it.

Taizu had twenty-six sons, several in their teens by the time he became emperor, and he took measures to see that they and their descendants would not interfere in the government. The princes were sent out of the capital to fiefs, and Taizu issued rules that they and their descendants were not to take examinations, serve in office, or follow any sort of career other than specified military assignments. They were to live outside the capital, supported by government stipends.

Taizu had deeply ambivalent feelings about men of education and sometimes brutally humiliated them in open court. His behavior was so erratic that most likely he suffered from some form of mental illness. In 1376, Taizu had thousands of officials killed because they were found to have taken a shortcut in their handling of paperwork related to the grain tax. In 1380, Taizu concluded that his chancellor, Hu Weiyong, was plotting to assassinate him. Anyone remotely connected to Hu was executed, the investigations taking nearly a decade, with as many as fifteen thousand people losing their lives. From 1380 on, the Hongwu emperor acted as his own chancellor, dealing directly with the heads of departments and ministries.

As Taizu became more literate, he realized that scholars could criticize him in covert ways, using phrases that had double meanings or that sounded like words for "bandit," "monk," or the like. Even poems in private circulation could be used as evidence of subversive intent. When literary men began to avoid official life, Taizu made it illegal to turn down appointments or resign from office. He began falling into rages that only his wife, Empress Ma, could stop. After her death in 1382, no one could calm him.

Chengzu, the Yongle Emperor

Taizu lived a long life, to seventy-one *sui*, outliving his eldest son, who had been his heir apparent. He made that son's eldest son the next heir, and this grandson succeeded to the throne at the age of twenty-one. (He is known as Huidi, or the Jianwen emperor.) Almost immediately, however, the eldest of Taizu's surviving sons by the empress, a man known then as the Prince of Yan, launched a military campaign to take the throne himself. After a three-year civil war, he prevailed. He is known as Chengzu, or the Yongle emperor (r. 1403–1425).

Chengzu was a military man like his father, and he was married to the daughter of a leading general,

---

1. Cited in F. W. Mote, *Imperial China, 900–1800* (Cambridge, Mass.: Harvard University Press, 1999), p. 560.

who encouraged his military interests. He directed the civil war himself and often led troops into battle, leading to victories over the Mongols. In 1406 he authorized a major expedition into Vietnam, which had been independent for over four centuries. Although the campaign was a success, the region was held only two decades. Also like his father, Chengzu was willing to use terror to keep government officials in line. Quite a few officials serving Huidi resisted his usurpation. When the leading Confucian scholar, Fang Xiaoru, refused to draft the proclamation of his accession, Chengzu not only had him executed by dismemberment, but had his relatives and associates to the tenth degree executed as well, including all those who had been passed when he conducted the civil service examinations. Tens of thousands were killed.

Yet the Yongle emperor also had impressive accomplishments. He put two thousand scholars to work making a fifty-million-word (22,938-chapter) compendium of knowledge drawn from seven thousand books (the *Yongle Encyclopedia*). To assist those studying for the civil service examinations, he had a selection of texts from the Cheng-Zhu school of Confucianism compiled. He expanded and regularized the court diplomatic system.

Early in his reign, Chengzu decided to move the capital from Nanjing to Beijing, which had been his own base as a prince as well as the capital during Yuan times. Construction employed hundreds of thousands of workers and lasted from 1407 to 1420. Although little of the original city walls and gates survives today, the palace complex remains, its layout and architecture still reflecting the fifteenth-century design. The city was a planned city, like Chang'an in Sui-Tang times, built near the site of the Yuan capital, but starting afresh. Like Chang'an, it was built on a north-south axis and consisted of boxes within boxes. The main outer walls were forty feet high and nearly fifteen miles around, pierced by nine gates. Inside it was the Imperial City, with government offices, and within that the Forbidden City, the palace itself, with close to ten thousand rooms. The main audience halls were arranged along the central axis, with vast courtyards between them where attending officials would stand or kneel. The design, as intended, awes all who enter.

The areas surrounding Beijing were not nearly as agriculturally productive as those around Nanjing. To supply Beijing with grain, the Grand Canal was extensively renovated, broadening and deepening it and supplying it with more locks and dams. The fifteen thousand boats and 160,000 soldiers of the transport army, who pulled loaded barges from the tow paths along the canal, became the lifeline of the capital.

Weaknesses of the Imperial Institution

Ming Taizu had decreed that succession should go to the eldest son of the empress, or the latter's eldest son if he predeceased his father, the system generally, but not inflexibly, followed by earlier dynasties. In Ming times, the flaws in this system became apparent as one mediocre, obtuse, or erratic emperor followed another. Yingzong (r. 1436–1450), who came to the throne at age eight, liked to play soldier; with the encouragement of his favorite eunuch, he led an army against the Mongols when he was twenty-one years old, resulting in the destruction of his fifty-thousand-man army and his own capture. The Mongols found him so useless that they returned him the next year, after his brother had been enthroned. Xianzong (r. 1465–1488), after coming to the throne at age sixteen, let himself be manipulated by a palace lady almost twenty years his senior; she had his children born to other women systematically killed. Wuzong (r. 1505–1521) willfully defied established practices and spent much of his time drunk. Shizong (r. 1522–1567) refused to treat his predecessor as his adoptive father. Subject to fits of rage, he was so cruel to his palace ladies that a group of them tried to murder him in 1542. In 1565 the brave official Hai Rui submitted a memorial saying that the emperor had failed as a man, a father, and a ruler and had been a disaster for the country. Shenzong, the Wanli emperor (r. 1573–1620), was intelligent but refused to hold court for years at a time and allowed memorials to pile up unopened and vacancies to go unfilled.

Because Ming Taizu had abolished the position of chancellor, the emperor had to turn to members of the inner court to help him. At first, relatively junior men in the Hanlin Academy served as secretaries, a practice that became regularized as a kind of cabinet of grand secretaries. Although they were given concurrent titles as vice ministers to enhance their standing, their lack of actual administrative experience hampered their dealings with the outer court. Added to this, they had to work with the eunuchs to manage the flow of paperwork, and some of the stigma attached to eunuchs spilled over to them.

Eunuchs became as serious a problem in Ming times as they had in late Han and late Tang. From the time of Ming Taizu on, eunuchs were employed in the palace, their numbers gradually growing. As in earlier dynasties, emperors often preferred the always compliant eunuchs to high-minded, moralizing civil service officials. A eunuch bureaucracy developed, headed by the director of ceremonial, who was responsible for seeing that the emperor was attended at all times, that security was maintained, and that documents were properly handled. When the emperor allowed it, the director of ceremonial became a kind of chief of staff who could impose his will on the civil service. In 1420, Chengzu set up the Eastern Depot, headed by a eunuch, which acted as a secret service and investigated cases of suspected corruption and sedition. During the late fifteenth century, the eunuch bureaucracy grew as large as the civil service, each with roughly twelve thousand positions. After 1500, the eunuch bureaucracy grew much more rapidly, and by the mid-sixteenth century, seventy thousand eunuchs were in service throughout the country, with ten thousand in the capital. Eunuch control over vital government processes, such as appointments, was especially a problem during the long reign of the derelict Shenzong (1573–1620).

Confucian writers generally vilified eunuchs, as though they were by nature evil, and rarely showed sympathy for their unfortunate circumstances. Eunuchs were essentially slaves. Many were acquired by dubious means as children, often from non-Chinese areas in the south, and once they were castrated, they had no option but to serve the imperial family. Zheng He, for instance, was taken from Yunnan as a boy of ten by a Ming general assigned the task of securing boys to be castrated. Society considered eunuchs the basest of servants and heaped scorn on them.

What was a conscientious official to do, given the flaws in the Ming government? Officials serving in local posts could do their best to make the government work, even when they knew that needed reforms would not be made. Some, discouraged, left office after a few years. If they had enough property to live on, they could enjoy the status of retired official and concentrate on matters more within their control, such as writing local histories or collecting works of calligraphy.

Although the educated public complained about the performance of emperors, no one proposed or even imagined alternatives to imperial rule. High officials were forced to find ways to work around uncooperative emperors but were not able to put in place institutions that would limit the damage an emperor could do. They came to prefer weak emperors who let them take care of the government, knowing that strong emperors often acted erratically. Probably one of the reasons so many Ming emperors resisted their officials' efforts to manage them was that the officials were indeed trying to keep emperors engaged in tasks where they could do relatively little harm.

Many officials did in fact risk their careers, and sometimes their lives, trying to admonish emperors. The tradition of protesting against evil officials, harmful policies, and wrong-headed imperial decisions was strong throughout the Ming, though it rarely led to the results the protesters sought. In 1376, when Taizu asked for criticism, Ye Boju submitted a memorial objecting to harsh punishment of officials for minor lapses. In it he noted that many officials considered themselves fortunate to be out of office. Taizu, incensed, had Ye brought to the capital in chains and let him starve to death in prison. A few decades later, many of Huidi's top officials protested Chengzu's usurpation, with dire consequences to themselves and their families. In 1519, when Emperor Wuzong announced plans to make a tour to the southern provinces, he was flooded with memorials objecting to his decision. Over a hundred officials staged a protest by kneeling in front of the palace. Wuzong was outraged and ordered the officials to remain kneeling for three days, after which he had them flogged; eleven died. A few years later, in 1524, during the crisis over Shizong's refusal to treat the previous emperor as his adopted father, hundreds of officials again gathered at the palace gate. The emperor had 134 of them imprisoned, and 16 died of the floggings they received. The Confucian tradition celebrated these acts of political protest as heroic. Rarely, however, did they succeed in moving an emperor to change his mind; more often they exacerbated factional tensions within the government.

DIPLOMACY AND DEFENSE

The Ming government faced both new and old challenges along its borders. Until 1600 and the rise of the Manchus, the Ming looked on the Mongols as their primary military threat. The seacoast at this time was presenting new challenges. Ming China was being drawn more deeply into maritime trading networks, which brought both piracy and new sources of wealth.

Early in the Ming, the government expanded and regularized the court diplomatic system, trying to make it conform to the idealized view of how it had functioned in the Han and Tang Dynasties, when China had dominated East Asia, rather than in Song times, when a multistate system had operated and Song had paid tribute to its northern neighbors. To the Ming court, the arrival of envoys from dozens of countries, bringing their strange or valuable goods with them, served to confirm China's moral centrality. As in earlier dynasties, countries that sent missions had their own agendas and were as eager to benefit from the trade that the missions made possible as to stay on China's good side. Vietnam, for instance, regularly sent missions to the Ming court after it expelled the Ming invaders.

Zheng He's Voyages

In order to invite more countries to send missions, the Yongle emperor Chengzu authorized an extraordinary series of voyages to the Indian Ocean under the command of his trusted eunuch Zheng He (1371–1433).

Zheng He was from a Muslim family in Yunnan and may have learned Arabic in his youth (both his father and grandfather had made the Hajj to Mecca). When about ten, however, during the Ming conquest of Yunnan, he was taken along with other boys to be castrated and to serve in the palace as eunuchs. Zheng He was assigned to the prince who later became the Yongle emperor and gained extensive military experience in battles with the Mongols and later the wars that secured Yongle's succession.

Within three years of seizing the throne, Yongle put Zheng He in charge of a series of unprecedented naval expeditions. The first of the seven voyages was made by a fleet of 317 ships, of which 62 were huge "treasure ships," reportedly 440 feet long. Each expedition involved from twenty thousand to thirty-two thousand men, including sailors, soldiers, navigators, doctors, and laborers. Some of the ships were water tankers, carrying about a month's supply of fresh water. Others carried food. The design of the ships took full advantage of the many advances in nautical technology since Song times that had enabled Chinese mariners to become a dominant presence in maritime trade. Assembling so large a fleet and sending it so far from home testified to the power of the Ming Dynasty. Suppressing piracy was another goal. During the first voyage in 1405, Zheng destroyed the fleet of a powerful Chinese pirate who had for

years been harassing ships passing through the Straits of Malacca.

The ships followed well-established trading routes. The first three voyages (1405–1411) stopped in Vietnam, Malaysia, the islands of Indonesia, Sri Lanka, and India. The fourth (1413–1415) went to the Persian Gulf and Arabia. The last three (1416–1422 and 1430–1433) reached east Africa (see Map 14.1). At each stop, Zheng He would go ashore to visit rulers, transmit messages of China's peaceful intentions, and bestow lavish gifts. Beginning with the third voyage, rulers invited to come to China or send envoys were offered passage.

Besides envoys, Zheng He brought back exotic animals and goods likely to delight the emperor, including giraffes and lions from Africa, fine cotton cloth from India, and gems and spices from Southeast Asia. Another Muslim who accompanied him on three of his voyages, Ma Huan, wrote a book-length account of the places they visited that gave details about their geography, politics, climate, economy, and local customs.

Why were these voyages abandoned? One likely reason is that they did not bring much of a return. Officials complained of the cost of the expeditions, which they saw as wasteful. Another possibility is that they had special appeal to the Yongle emperor, who died in 1424 after the sixth expedition. The next two emperors had other priorities, including dealing with the rising power of the Mongols. Zheng He did get to make one final journey after his patron's death, in 1430–1433, but he died during it. Thereafter the boats sat in harbor. Four decades later, in 1474, all the remaining ships with three or more masts were broken up and used for lumber.

Not long after the destruction of Zheng He's fleet, the more modest expeditions of Vasco da Gama and Christopher Columbus changed the course of world history.

The Mongols and the Great Wall

The early Ming emperors held Mongol fighting men in awe and saw in them the potential for another great military machine of the sort Chinggis had put together. Both Taizu and Chengzu were determined to avoid the fate of the Song Dynasty, which had to pay off its powerful northern neighbors. Both emperors personally led armies into Mongolia. Chengzu, in fact, died on his fifth campaign in 1424, at age sixty-four.

As it turned out, the Mongols in Ming times never formed the sort of federation that could have seriously threatened China. After the last Yuan emperor retreated to Mongolia, he did not find it easy to keep the Mongols united under his leadership, since his loss of China discredited him. Ensuing Mongol civil wars weakened Mongolia and led to division. Through much of the Ming, the 3 million or so Mongols were loosely divided into six groups, located in today's Inner Mongolia, Manchuria, and Mongolia, or north of those areas. Under Taizu and Chengzu, the Ming sent large and well-provisioned armies into Mongol territory, with as many as 250,000 troops. Such campaigns were extremely expensive and did not accomplish much, given the Mongols' mobility. Later in the dynasty, the Ming was less inclined to send armies into Mongolia and concentrated on defending its borders against attack.

Although in Ming times, the Mongols were never united in a pan-Mongol federation, groups of Mongols could and did raid, and twice they threatened the dynasty: in 1449, when Esen, the khan of the Western Mongols, captured the emperor, and in 1550, when Beijing was surrounded by the forces of Altan Khan, khan of the Mongols in Inner Mongolia. The Ming was very reluctant to grant any privileges to Mongol leaders, such as trading posts along the borders, and wanted the different groups of Mongols to trade only through the envoy system. Repeatedly Mongol envoys said friction could be reduced if regularized trade could be introduced, but until 1570, when an agreement was reached with Altan Khan, the Ming court refused.

Two important developments shaped later Ming-Mongol relations: the building of the Great Wall and the Mongols' forging of close ties with Tibetan Buddhism. Work on the wall began by the mid-fifteenth century, when administrators of the western sections of the border began connecting principal garrison points and had some successes in trapping contingents of Mongol cavalry. Extending the wall was later seen as a solution to the deadlock between officials who argued that the Mongols could be managed by allowing more trade and those who insisted that no concessions be made to them.

Much of the Ming Great Wall survives today. It is about 1,500 miles long, from northeast of Beijing into Gansu province. In the eastern 500 miles, the walls average about 35 feet high and 20 feet across, with towers every half-mile for lookouts. The wall itself is faced with brick much of the way, giving it an imposing appearance that greatly impressed the first westerners who saw it.

Although there was considerable trade between Tibet and China through Sichuan and Yunnan, Ming China did not have close diplomatic ties to Tibet, then largely ruled by the major monasteries. When Tibetan monasteries needed military assistance, they called for help from competing Mongol leaders, and many struggles were decided by Mongol military intervention. Tsong-kha-pa (1357–1419) founded the Yellow Hat or Gelug-pa sect, whose heads later became known as the Dalai Lamas. In 1577 the third Dalai Lama accepted the invitation of Altan Khan to visit Mongolia, and the khan declared Tibetan Buddhism to be the official religion of all the Mongols. The Dalai Lama gave the khan the title "King of Religion," and the khan swore that the Mongols would renounce blood sacrifice. When the third Dalai Lama's reincarnation was found to be the great-grandson of Altan Khan, the ties between Tibet and the Mongols, not surprisingly, became even stronger.

Trade and Piracy Along China's Coasts

The Ming court's obsession with defending against the Mongols was not because its other borders posed no problems. The court wanted trade subordinated to diplomacy and stipulated that envoys from the Philippines were supposed to enter only through the port of Fuzhou, those from Japan only through Ningbo, those from Indonesia only through Guangzhou, and so on. Moreover, the size and frequency of missions was restricted; Japanese embassies, for instance, were not to call more than once in ten years or bring more than two ships with three hundred men. In the sixteenth century, this formal system proved unable to contain the emergence of an international East Asian maritime trading community composed of Japanese, Portuguese, Spanish, Dutch, and Chinese merchants and adventurers. Because the profits to be had from maritime trade were high, both open and clandestine trade took place all along the coast.

Boats leaving China carried silk and porcelains; those entering it brought silver from Peruvian and Mexican mines, transported via Manila, to pay for the Chinese goods. Boats laden with goods attracted pirates. Pirates grew so strong that they took to raiding the coast from Shandong to Guangzhou. Instead of trying to suppress the pirates by expanding its navy, the Ming government forced people to move away from the coast, hoping to starve out the pirates.

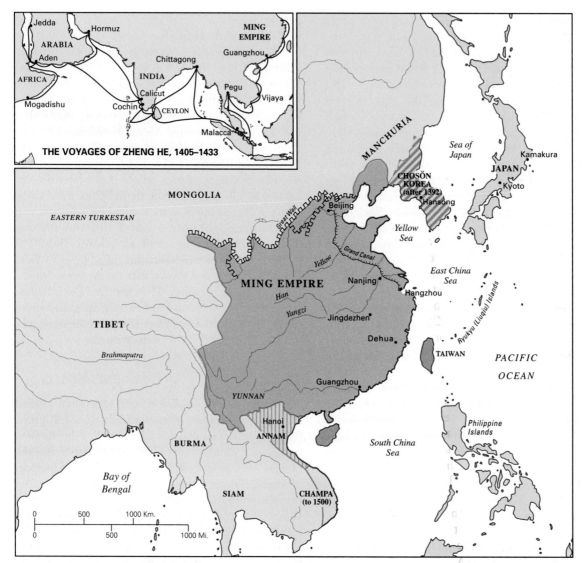

Map 14.1   **Ming Empire**

Anti-pirate efforts did not have much success until maritime trade restrictions were eased in the late sixteenth century. Under the new policies, Portugal was permitted to set up a trading base at Macao in 1557, which it held until 1999.

Besides stimulating the Ming economy, the expansion of maritime trade brought New World crops to China. Sweet potatoes, maize, peanuts, tomatoes, chili peppers, tobacco, and other crops were quickly introduced into China. Sweet potatoes and maize in particular facilitated population growth because they could be grown on land that had not been cultivated because it was too sandy or too steep. Spanish and Portuguese ships also began to bring missionaries

with radically different sets of ideas about the nature of the world (see **Connections: Europe Enters the Scene**).

SOCIAL AND CULTURAL TRENDS

During the first half of the Ming, as China recovered from the wars and dislocations of the Yuan period, attempts were made to stabilize society. By the sixteenth century, however, Chinese society and culture were breaking free of many of the restraints that the early Ming government had tried to impose on them, and social and cultural change sped up.

The Educated Class and the Examination Life

Despite the harsh and arbitrary ways in which Ming emperors treated their civil servants, educated men were as eager to enter the bureaucracy as in earlier ages. As discussed in Chapter 12, civil service examinations played only a very small part in the recruitment of officials during the Yuan period. In Ming times, the examinations more than regained their significance as the most prestigious way to enter government service. To a greater degree than in Tang or Song times, the Ming examination system created a nationwide culture for all those who participated. All had to learn to write in the approved "eight-legged" style, which emphasized reasoning by analogy and pairing statements. The orthodoxy of Zhu Xi's teachings was an integral part of the Ming system. All had to study the Four Books and Zhu Xi's interpretations of them. Since Zhu Xi considered writing poetry of no value to moral cultivation, the poetic composition component of the examinations was dropped.

Another new feature of the Ming examination system was a screening test taken at the province level, adding to the number of tests a successful candidate would eventually have to pass. There were thus three principal degrees: the *shengyuan*, at the county or prefectural level; the *juren*, at the province level; and the *jinshi*, those selected at the capital examination and confirmed at the palace examination. Fewer men made it to the top in Ming times than in Song times. In contrast to the 135 *jinshi* per year in Southern Song plus the 149 per year given at the same time by the Jin, the Ming average was only 89 per year.

Another difference between the Song and Ming systems was that the Ming made a more concerted effort to ensure that the wealthy and cultured Jiangnan area did not dominate the examination results. Quotas were established for the number of candidates each province could send on to the capital. In 1397 all of those passed at the palace examination were southerners, leading Taizu to execute two of the examiners. Taizu retested everyone and passed only northerners. Thereafter, the examiners considered regional origin and tried for a balance. After 1427, northern candidates were ensured 35 percent of the places.

The lowest degree holders, the *shengyuan*, had to pass tests periodically to retain their status and compete for the privilege of traveling to the provincial capital to take the *juren* examination. By 1500, there were about thirty thousand *shengyuan* in the country (about one in three thousand people, counting women and children). Since only a small number of the *shengyuan* became *juren* in each triennial exam, taking exams became a way of life for most degree holders.

Preparation for the examinations required, in essence, learning a different language—the classical written language, which was quite different from everyday spoken language. Education thus was best started young. Moreover, the young are usually more adept at memorizing long texts, a necessary part of examination preparation. Calligraphy counted at this level, since tests were not recopied by clerks until the provincial level. Literati families who started to teach their sons at age four or five had a significant advantage.

As in earlier periods, well-off families hired tutors for their boys, but schools became more and more available in Ming times. Families that for generations

Ming Examination Degrees				
Degree	How Attained	Benefits	Likely Age	Likely Percentage Passed
Shengyuan	Pass test to enter county or prefecture school	Exempt from labor service; may take test to qualify for provincial exams; need to recertify regularly	17–30	Highly variable
Juren	Pass provincial examinations	Permanently qualified to take capital examinations; may receive less desired appointments	20–30	2–4%
Jinshi	Pass capital and palace examinations	Qualified for entry-level official appointment	30–40	7–9%

Figure 14.1 Examination Cells. The spare cells that candidates occupied during the three days of the examination were furnished only with two boards, which could be arranged to make a bed or a desk and seat. *(As seen in Benjamin Elman,* A Cultural History of Civil Examinations in Late Imperial China, *University of California Press, 2000, p. 184.)*

had pursued other careers, such as physician or merchant, had more opportunities than ever before to attain success through the exams (see **Biography: Tan Yunxian, Woman Doctor**). Lineages were especially active in setting up and sometimes endowing schools for their members. Because the lineage as a whole would enjoy the prestige that came with examination success, lineage leaders were willing to invest in the education of any talented boy in the lineage.

The provincial and capital examinations had three sessions spread out over a week and involved a series of essays. In the first session, the essays were on passages from the Four Books and the classic of the candidate's choice. In the second and third sessions, candidates had to write essays on practical policy issues and a passage from the *Classic of Filial Piety*. In addition, they had to show that they could draft state papers such as edicts, decrees, and judicial rulings. Reading the dynastic histories was the best way to prepare for the policy issue and state paper questions.

Examinations themselves were major events not only for the candidates but also for the officials serving in the locality and for nearby residents. At the county or prefectural level, the tests lasted a day and drew hundreds or thousands of candidates. The government compound was taken over to give all candi-

dates a place to sit and write. Outside were stalls selling supplies, friends and relatives pressing gifts on those entering, and curious people eager to watch the examiners and the candidates file in.

Even more elaborate were the weeklong affairs of the provincial examinations. From five thousand to ten thousand candidates descended on the city and filled up its hostels. Candidates would show up a week in advance to present their credentials and gather the needed paper, ink, brushes, candles, blankets, and food they would need to survive in their small exam cells. Each cell was open in the front, to allow guards to watch the candidate, and was bare except for two shelves, which could be arranged together to make a bed, or at different levels to form a seat and a table to write on.

Candidates were searched before being admitted, as no written material could be taken into the cells. Anyone caught wearing a cheat-sheet (an inner gown covered with the classics in minuscule script) was thrown out of the exams and banned from the next session; he might also lose his status as *shengyuan*. Each exam had three two-day sessions. Clerks used horns and gongs to begin and end each session. Candidates had time to write rough drafts of their essays, correct them, then copy final versions in neat, regular script. Tension was high. Sometimes rumors that

BIOGRAPHY   Tan Yunxian, Woman Doctor

The grandmother of Tan Yunxian (1461–1554) was the daughter of a physician, and her husband had married into her home to learn medicine himself. At least two of their sons—including Tan Yunxian's father—passed the *jinshi* examination and became officials, raising the standing of the family considerably. The grandparents found Yunxian very bright and therefore decided to pass on their medical knowledge to her.

Tan Yunxian married and raised four children but also practiced medicine, confining her practice to women. At age fifty she wrote an autobiographical account, *Sayings of a Female Doctor*. In the preface she described how, under her grandmother's tutelage, she had first memorized the *Canon of Problems* and *Canon of the Pulse*. Then, when her grandmother had time, she asked her granddaughter to explain particular passages in these classic medical treatises.

Tan Yunxian began the practice of medicine by treating her own children, asking her grandmother to check her diagnoses. When her grandmother was old and ill, she gave Yunxian her notebook of prescriptions and her equipment for making medicines, telling her to study them carefully. Later, Yunxian became seriously ill herself and dreamed of her grandmother telling her on what page of which book to find the prescription that would cure her. When she recovered, she began her medical career in earnest.

Tan's book records the cases of thirty-one patients she treated. She treated only women, and mostly women with chronic complaints rather than critical illnesses. Many of the women had what the Chinese classed as women's complaints, such as menstrual irregularities, repeated miscarriages, barrenness, and postpartum fatigue. Others had

ailments men could also suffer, such as coughs, nausea, insomnia, diarrhea, rashes, and swellings. Like other literati physicians, she regularly prescribed herbal medications. She also practiced moxibustion. The theory behind burning moxa (dried artemisia) at specified points on the body was similar to the theory behind acupuncture: it stimulated the circulation of *qi*. Because the physician applying the moxa has to touch the patient, it was not something male physicians could perform on women.

Tan's patients included working women, and she seems to have often thought that their problems sprang from overwork. One woman came to her because she had had vaginal bleeding for three years. When questioned, the woman told her that she worked all day with her husband at their kiln making bricks and tiles. Tan Yunxian's diagnosis was overwork, and she gave her pills to replenish her yin. When a boatman's wife came to her complaining of numbness in her hands, Tan found out on questioning that the woman worked in the wind and rain plying the boat and advised a respite. Tan Yunxian explained to a servant girl that she had gone back to work too quickly after suffering a wind damage fever. By contrast, when her patient came from an upper-class family, Tan saw negative emotions as the root of her problems, particularly if she reported that her mother-in-law had scolded her or that her husband had recently brought a concubine home. Two women who had miscarried were told that they had hidden their anger, causing fire to turn inward and destabilize the fetus.

Tan Yunxian herself lived a long life, dying at the age of ninety-three.

Source: Based on Charlotte Furth, *A Flourishing Yin. Gender in China's Medical History, 960–1665* (Berkeley and Los Angeles. University of California Press, 1999), pp. 285–295.

the examiners had been bribed to leak the questions led to riots in the exam quarters, and knocked-over candles occasionally caused fires.

After the papers were handed in, clerks recopied them and assigned them numbers to preserve anonymity. Proofreaders checked the copying before hand-

ing them on to the assembled examiners, who divided them up to read. The grading generally took about twenty days. Most candidates stayed in the provincial capital to await the results. Those few who became the new *juren* would be invited to the governor's compound for a celebration. By the time they reached home, most of their friends, neighbors, and relatives would have already heard their good news.

Wang Yangming's Challenge to Confucian Orthodoxy

One might have thought that the intellectual conformity encouraged by the examination system would stifle thought or channel it narrowly. But the government's ability to channel the intellectual and literary pursuits of the elite should not be overestimated. Members of the educated class did not lose their love of poetry, even though it was no longer tested, and examiners were not immune to new intellectual trends. Moreover, although the government continued to use Zhu Xi's teachings as the standard for the civil service examinations, during the sixteenth century Confucian thought developed in new directions, with a remarkable official and teacher, Wang Yangming, leading the way.

Wang Yangming (1472–1529) grew up in the Jiangnan region in a literati family that had not had an official in a century. When he was ten, however, his father passed the examinations in first place, guaranteeing him a prominent career in the capital. Wang Yangming went with him to Beijing, where as a youth he met court officials, poets, writers, and thinkers and pursued interests in military strategy, horsemanship, and archery. Like so many others, he failed the *jinshi* examinations the first two times he took them, but he passed in 1499. During his first term in office, he fell ill and had to return to Zhejiang, where he became more interested in philosophy. After he returned to the capital in 1504, he fell afoul of the eunuch dictator Liu Jin by defending two officials who had submitted memorials condemning Liu. Wang was arrested, sent to the eunuch-controlled secret service prison, and severely beaten. On his release, he was assigned a banishment post in an aboriginal region of Guizhou province in the far southwest. He took this post seriously, however, doing his best to understand the problems of the Miao tribesmen. It was in Guizhou that he had his spiritual and intellectual breakthrough.

Wang had been struggling with Zhu Xi's concept of "the extension of knowledge"—that is, gaining understanding through careful and rational investigation of things and events, usually through study of the classics and other books. Wang came to realize that universal principles existed in every person's mind. People could discover them by clearing their minds

Portrait of an Official. The man depicted here in official dress, Jiang Shunfu, lived from 1453 to 1504. The front of his robe had a panel with the two cranes, a "rank badge" that indicated he was a civil official of the first rank. *(Nanjing Museum)*

of obstructions such as selfish desires and allowing their inborn knowledge to surface. The teachings of others, even those of Confucius and Mencius, are mere aids; they are not the source of truth. According to Wang, "If words are examined in the mind and found to be wrong, although they have come from the mouth of Confucius, I dare not accept them as correct."[2] Since everyone has a mind with similar capacity, common people have just as much potential to become sages as those who have pored over the classics their entire lives. Wang also argued against distinguishing knowledge and action. Moral action results spontaneously from true understanding. One does not truly understand filial piety if one does not practice it, any more than one understands taste, smell, or pain without experiencing them. True knowledge compels action.

Wang believed firmly that people could pursue sagehood in the midst of everyday activities. When

---

2. Wing-tsit Chan, trans., *Instructions for Practical Living and Other Neo-Confucian Writings* (New York. Columbia University Press, 1963), p. 81.

an official told him that his official duties left him no time to study, Wang urged him not to abandon his work: "Real learning can be found in every aspect of record-keeping and legal cases. What is empty is study that is detached from things."[3] Wang wanted his followers to concentrate on the basic moral truths that everyone could understand. He once asserted that what was truly heterodox was not Buddhism but ideas incomprehensible to average people. Critics of Wang, however, saw his teachings as dangerously contaminated with Chan Buddhist ideas.

Wang Yangming lived up to his own ideals. Even after he attracted dozens of disciples, he did not give up his official career. After the eunuch Liu Jin was executed in 1510, Wang accepted high-ranking appointments in Nanjing and Beijing while still lecturing to his growing circle of disciples. Conservative officials, disturbed by his message, got him out of the capital by arranging an assignment as governor of a special military district in southern Jiangxi, an area with many non-Chinese ethnic groups. Once there, he had to lead the regional armies into battle and set up a governing structure for the local people. He was a successful military commander, and when a prince rebelled nearby, it was Wang who led troops to capture him. On Wang Yangming's way back to the capital, his father died, which necessitated his retiring from office to mourn him. In 1527 he was called out of retirement because of uprisings among the non-Chinese in Guangxi. He spent a year there, directing campaigns, winning victories, and negotiating surrenders, but his health was failing, and he died on his way home in 1529.

In the century after Wang Yangming's death, his followers extended his ideas in many directions. Some took a new interest in both Daoism and Buddhism. Some questioned the traditional social hierarchy, such as the elevation of the scholar above the farmer. One of Wang's most enthusiastic followers, Wang Gen, came from a plebeian family of salt workers. He gave lectures to crowds of ordinary people, focusing on issues important in their lives and encouraging them to pursue education to improve their lots. In the next generation, He Xinyin was more radical in that he challenged the age-old elevation of the family. To He, the family was a restrictive, selfish, and exclusive institution, and loyalty to family was inferior to loyalty to friends. His contemporary Li Zhi championed the validity of feelings and passion and ridiculed conforming to conventional patterns of behavior. He contended that women were the intellectual equals of men and should be given fuller educations. Li Zhi also reinterpreted history to present some of the great villains as heroes.

Only a small minority of late Ming literati were ready to hear these messages. Both He Xinyin and Li Zhi died in prison, having been arrested on charges of spreading dangerous ideas.

Local Society

As best historians can reconstruct, China's population more than doubled over the course of the Ming Dynasty, from between 60 and 80 million to between 150 and 200 million. Small market towns appeared all over the country. Regional specialization increased as communities took advantage of the availability of cheap water transport to take up cash cropping. By the end of the sixteenth century, the Yangzi River delta area had become a center of cotton and silk production; coastal Fujian was known for tobacco and sugar cane; and porcelain manufacture at Jingdezhen in Jiangxi had achieved unprecedented levels of output. All of this occurred despite continued government suspicion of those who pursued profit.

The Ming founder Taizu had grown up in a family that lived in fear of rapacious tax collectors, and he redesigned tax collection at the village level in the hope that future families would not have to suffer as his had. In each village, the better-off families were identified and assigned the obligation to perform low-level judicial, police, and tax-collecting services without pay as part of what was called the *lijia* system. In other words, villagers themselves, not underlings of the magistrate, would be responsible for assessing, collecting, and transporting taxes, paid mostly in grain.

Taizu's efforts to organize his government around unpaid service created many headaches for later Ming administrators. Local officials found that legal sources of revenue were so limited that they had no choice but to levy extralegal ones to continue basic services, leading to just the sort of abuses Taizu had wanted to prevent. Ordinary households, for their part, often were devastated by the burden of uncompensated responsibility for delivering taxes or maintaining local hostels for government travelers. Reforms that converted most obligations into a monetary tax eventually had to be introduced.

3. Patricia Buckley, ed., *Chinese Civilization: A Sourcebook*, rev. ed. (New York: Simon & Schuster, 1993), p. 258.

The *lijia* system and subsequent tax reforms were supposed to be enforced uniformly around the country. Much of local social organization, however, was highly variable from place to place, depending on the crops grown, whether there were significant non-Han populations, when migrants had arrived, and the like.

During the Ming Dynasty, voluntary associations that included both educated men and ordinary villagers became a common feature of local society. Religious associations were formed to support a temple and its ceremonies. Lineages were formed to promote cooperation among relatives descended from a common ancestor. Often the lineage held land in common to support joint ancestral rites. When income was sufficient, a lineage might also build an ancestral temple or school. Generally lineages were more common in the south than in the north, perhaps a reflection of migration patterns. In Fujian, large lineages were evident in Song times and continued to play prominent roles through the Ming. In Huizhou in Anhui province, lineages were flourishing in the mid-Ming, their strength owing much to the wealth of local merchant families. In Taichang in Jiangxi province, most of the lineages were deliberately formed in the early Ming by educated men to enhance their own status at a time of intense competition for social prestige. In Guangdong, by contrast, most of the major lineages date back only to the seventeenth century or later. In some areas, lineages seem to have been initiated by members of the educated class; in other places, by ordinary people who saw advantages in banding together.

By the mid-Ming, lineages in some parts of the country were setting up systems to discipline and control members, complete with long lists of rules and ways to handle disputes. In this they resembled community compacts, a form of local organization Zhu Xi had praised, believing it could promote moral renewal. Members of the compact had to agree to correct each other's faults, offer assistance to those in need, and expel those who failed to cooperate. Wang Yangming used the term *community compact* for the organizations he set up as part of a rebel pacification program. His followers made even broader use of the plan, urging villagers to form compacts in which they all encouraged each other to strive for goodness.

One reason Confucian scholars encouraged this form of voluntary social organization was the common fear that the moral fabric of society was unraveling. Many complained that the rich and poor no longer helped each other but looked on each other as enemies. Some educated men turned to charitable works as a way to try to lessen social tensions. At the end of the sixteenth century, for instance, one man set up the Society for Sharing Goodness, whose members paid monthly dues to support projects such as repairing roads and bridges or offering assistance to families unable to cover funeral expenses.

Urban Culture

Many literati, especially those with ample means, lived in cities where they could pursue the elegant life (see **Material Culture: Gardens of Suzhou**). But literati were not the only cultural force in the cities. As cities grew and the commercial economy thrived, a distinctive urban culture emerged, a culture of those with money to spend in the cities, centered on entertainment of many sorts.

Books accessible to the urban middle classes were now published in large numbers, including reference books of all sorts and popular religious tracts, such as ledgers for calculating the moral value of one's good deeds and subtracting the demerits from bad ones. To make their books attractive in the marketplace, entrepreneurial book publishers commissioned artists to illustrate them. By the sixteenth century, more and more books were being published in the vernacular language, the language people spoke. Writing in the vernacular had begun on a small scale in Tang and Song times, when it was used to record the oral teachings of Buddhist and Confucian teachers. By mid-Ming it was widely used for short stories, novels, and plays. Ming short stories written in the vernacular depicted a world much like that of their readers, full of shop clerks and merchants, monks and prostitutes, students and matchmakers.

It was during the Ming period that the full-length novel appeared. The plots of the early novels were heavily indebted to story cycles developed by oral storytellers over the course of several centuries. *Water Margin* is an episodic story of a band of bandits set at the end of the Northern Song period. *The Romance of the Three Kingdoms* is a work of historical fiction based on the exploits of the generals and statesmen contending for power at the end of the Han Dynasty. *The Journey to the West* is a fantastic account of the Tang monk Xuanzang's travels to India; in this book he is accompanied by a monkey with supernatural powers as well as a pig. *Plum in the Golden Vase* is a novel of manners about a lustful merchant with a wife and five concubines, full of details of daily life

MATERIAL CULTURE

Gardens of Suzhou

Well-to-do families in the Jiangnan region often constructed gardens within the walls enclosing their homes. The gardens of Suzhou became particularly famous for their sophisticated beauty. These gardens were places to entertain friends and pass leisure hours. They were considered works of art in progress. Like landscape painters, garden designers tried to capture essential features of nature and made use of objects laden with metaphorical meaning, such as bamboo, gnarled pine trees, and craggy rocks.

Architecture was integral to garden design, and Suzhou gardens had walkways, pavilions, bridges over ponds, and other features. Views were appreciated, but they were intimate in scale, not broad vistas. The spaces within a garden were often visually linked by views glimpsed through open doorways and lattice windows.

About twenty Ming gardens still survive in Suzhou. (See Color Plate 18.)

Garden of the Humble Administrator. The pathways and small pavilions invite strolling and pausing to view the water and plants. *(AA World Travel Library/Alamy)*

as well as the quarrels and scheming of the women. In none of these cases is much known about the author. Competing publishers brought out their own editions, sometimes adding new illustrations or commentaries.

Musical drama was also a major element in Ming urban culture. The Jesuit missionary Matteo Ricci, who lived in China from 1583 to 1610, described resident troupes in large cities and traveling troupes that "journey everywhere throughout the length and breadth of the country" putting on operas. The leaders of the troupes would purchase young children and train them to sing and perform. Ricci thought too many people were addicted to these performances:

These groups of actors are employed at all imposing banquets, and when they are called they come prepared to enact any of the ordinary plays. The host at the banquet is usually presented with a volume of

DOCUMENTS

Scene from *The Peony Pavilion*

The Peony Pavilion, written in 1598, is probably Tang Xianzu's best-loved play. Its main characters are a young woman from an official family who falls in love with a young man she encounters in a dream, then pines away for him. Before she dies, she buries a portrait of herself in the garden. Her family moves; the young man moves into the garden, discovers the portrait, and falls in love with her from her picture. His love is so strong it revives her.

With fifty-five scenes, this play was rarely performed in its entirety, but people knew the play and would ask for specific scenes. Minor characters provide much of the humor of the play. In the early scene here, the young woman's maid, Fragrance, talks to herself and then with the recently hired tutor.

The parts that are sung are here indented.

Scene 9. Sweeping the Garden
FRAGRANCE:

> Little Spring Fragrance
> favored among the servants,
> used to pampered ways within the
>   painted chambers
> waiting on the young mistress,
> I mix her powder, match her rouge,
> set her feather adornments, arrange
>   her flowers,
> ever waiting beside the boudoir mirror
> ready to smoothe the brocaded quilt,
> ready to light the fragrant nighttime
>   incense,
> urged on by Madam's stick on my puny
>   shoulders.
> Bondmaid with petaled cheeks just
>   into my teens,
> sweet and charming, wide awake to
>   the spring's arrival.
> A real "passion flower" is what we need
>   now
> to follow our every step with admiring
>   glances.

Day and night you will find me, Fragrance, by the side of my mistress. She, though she might win fame above all others for her beauty, is more concerned with jealous guarding of the family reputation. Maiden modesty composes her gentle features, and it is her nature to be serious and reverent. The master having engaged a tutor to instruct her, she commenced the study of the *Book of Songs*; but, when she reached the lines "So delicate the virtuous maiden, a fit mate for our Prince," she quietly put the book down and sighed, "Here we may observe the full extent of love to the true sage. As men felt in ancient times, so they feel today, and how should it be other than this?" So then I suggested, "Miss, you are tired from your studies, why don't you think of some way to amuse yourself?" She hesitated and thought for a moment. Then she got to her feet. "And how would you have me amuse myself, Fragrance?" she asked me. So I said, "Why, miss, nothing special, just to take a walk in that garden behind the house." "Stupid creature," says the young mistress, "what would happen if my father found out?" But I said, "His Honor has been out visiting the country districts for several days now." Then for ages the young mistress walked up and down thinking, not saying a word, until at last she began to consult the calendar. She said tomorrow was a bad day, and the day after not very good, but the day after that is a propitious day because the God of Pleasure Trips is on duty for the day. I was to tell the gardener to sweep the paths to ready for her visit. I said I would. I'm scared of Madam's finding out, but there's nothing we can do about that. So let me go give the gardener his instructions. Hello, there's Tutor Chen at the end of the verandah. Truly,

> on every side the glory of the spring
>   and what does this old fool see?—
>   Not a thing.

TUTOR CHEN (*enters*).

> Aging book lover
> now for a while "within the green
>   gauze tent"
> where once the learned Ma Rong gave
>   instruction
> curtain flaps against hook in warmth
>   of sun.
> Ha, there on the verandah
> young girl with hair in double coil
> seeming to speak, but wordless, closer
>   now, who can it be?
> Oh, it's Fragrance. Tell me,
> where is your gracious lord
> and where his lady?
> And why is my pupil absent from her
>   lessons?

FRAGRANCE: Oh, it's you, Tutor Chen. I'm afraid the young mistress has not had time for classes these last few days.
CHEN: And why is that?
FRAGRANCE: I'll tell you.

> Spring in its splendor
> cruel to a sensitive nature
> —everything's gone wrong?

CHEN: Why, what has gone wrong?
FRAGRANCE: Ah, you've no idea how angry the governor is going to be with you.
CHEN: For what reason?

FRAGRANCE: Why, that *Book of Songs* of yours, you've been singing a bit too sweetly, my poor young mistress—

> your classical exegesis
> has torn her heart to pieces.

CHEN: All I did was explicate the "*Guanguan cry the ospreys.*"
FRAGRANCE: That was the one. *Guan means* "shut in," doesn't it? My young mistress said, "Even though the ospreys were shut in, they still had the freedom of the island: why should a human being be treated worse than a bird?"

> In books the head must be buried,
> but it lifts itself to gaze on a scene of
>   beauty.

Now she has ordered me to take her in a day or two to stroll in the garden behind the house.
CHEN: What will be the purpose of this stroll?
FRAGRANCE.

> Unsuspected the spring has struck
> and before it hastens
> past she must cast off there in the
>   garden
> spring's disquiet.

CHEN: She should not do this.

> When woman walks abroad
> lest eyes should light upon her
> at every step she should be screened
> from view.

Fragrance, by the grace of Heaven I, your tutor, have enjoyed some sixty years of life, yet never have I felt such thing as "spring-struck," nor have I ever strolled in any garden.

——

Source: From Tang Xianzu, *The Peony Pavilion*, trans. Cyril Birch (Bloomington: Indiana University Press, 1980), pp. 38–40.

plays and he selects the one or several he may like. The guests, between eating and drinking, follow the plays with so much satisfaction that the banquet at times may last for ten hours.[4]

People not only enjoyed watching and listening to plays; they also avidly read the scripts. Perhaps because so much of a dramatic script was composed of poetry, authors of plays were less likely to conceal their identity than the authors of novels. The greatest of the Ming playwrights was Tang Xianzu, whose love stories and social satires were very popular. His *Dream of Han Tan* tells the story of a young man who falls asleep while his meal is cooking. In his dream he sees his whole life: He comes in first in the *jinshi* examinations, rises to high office, is unfairly slandered and condemned to death, then cleared and promoted. At the point of death, he wakes up and sees that his dinner is nearly done. He then realizes that life passes as quickly as a dream. (For a passage from Tang's most popular play, a love story, see **Documents: Scene from The Peony Pavilion**.)

Fiction and plays were so avidly consumed in Ming times that the values and attitudes expressed in them began to have an impact on the culture of the literati. Educated men and women often seem to have judged themselves and others on the standards of purity of feelings that they had come to expect in literary characters. Headstrong attachments—verging on obsessions—came to be admired. Courtesan culture flourished in this environment, and writers wrote of the romantic liaisons between well-known writers and famous courtesans. Because they associated courtesans with high aspirations and disappointed hopes, writers saw parallels between the frustrated official and the talented but powerless woman waiting for her lover to appreciate her full worth.

DYNASTIC DECLINE

After 1600 the Ming government was beset by fiscal, military, and political problems. The government was nearly bankrupt. It had spent heavily to help defend Korea against a Japanese invasion (see Chapters 13

and 15), had to support an ever-increasing imperial clan, and now was called on to provide relief for a series of natural disasters.

The bureaucracy did not pull together to meet these challenges. Officials diagnosed the problems confronting the dynasty in moral terms and saw removing the immoral from power as the solution, which led to fierce factionalism. Accusations and counter-accusations crossed so often that emperors wearied of officials and their infighting. Frustrated former officials who gathered at the Donglin Academy in Jiangsu province called for a revival of orthodox Confucian ethics. They blamed Wang Yangming for urging people to follow their innate knowledge, which seemed to the critics equivalent to urging them to pursue their personal advantage.

At this time a "little ice age" brought a drop in average temperatures that shortened the growing season and reduced harvests. When food shortages became critical in northern Shaanxi in 1627–1628, army deserters and laid-off soldiers began forming gangs and scouring the countryside in search of food. By 1632 they had moved east and south into the central regions of Shanxi, Hebei, Henan, and Anhui provinces. Once the gangs had stolen all their grain, hard-pressed farmers joined them just to survive. Li Zicheng, a former shepherd and postal relay worker, became the paramount rebel leader in the north. The ex-soldier Zhang Xianzhong became the main leader in the central region between the Yellow and Yangzi Rivers. The Ming government had little choice but to try to increase taxes to deal with these threats, but the last thing people needed was heavier exactions. Floods, droughts, locusts, and epidemics ravaged one region after another. In the Jiangnan area, tenants rose up against landlords, and urban workers rioted. Meanwhile, the two main rebel leaders were in a race to see which of them could topple the Ming and found a new dynasty.

Part of the reason people rioted over rents was that real rents had risen due to deflation, itself brought on by a sudden drop in the supply of silver. In 1639 the Japanese authorities refused to let traders from Macao into Nagasaki, disrupting trade that had brought large quantities of silver to China. Another major source of silver was cut off a few months later when Chinese trade with the Spanish in the Philippines came to a standstill after a slaughter of Chinese residents there. For China the drop in silver imports led to hoarding of both silver and grain, creating artificial shortages.

---

4. Louis J. Gallagher, trans., *China in the Sixteenth Century. The Journals of Matthew Ricci: 1583–1610* (New York: Random House, 1953), p. 23.

In 1642 a group of rebels cut the dikes on the Yellow River, leading to massive flooding. A smallpox epidemic soon added to the death toll. In 1644, Li Zicheng moved through Hebei into Beijing, where the last Ming emperor, in despair, took his own life. Zhang Xianzhong had moved in the opposite direction into Sichuan, where his attacks on Chongqing and Chengdu led to widespread slaughter. Both Li and Zhang announced that they had founded new dynasties, and they appointed officials and minted coins. Neither, however, succeeded in pacifying a sizable region or ending looting and violence. That would await the arrival of the Manchus (see Chapter 16).

SUMMARY

How different was China in the early seventeenth century than in 1368? China was more populous, with a population in the vicinity of 175 million by 1600. Some of this increase was made possible by pushing deeper into the southwest, but much of it occurred in long-occupied areas that became more densely populated with more towns and larger cities. Many more books were in circulation, and more of these books were aimed at an audience looking to be entertained rather than educated. Regional disparities may well have increased, as the Jiangnan area stayed several steps ahead of other regions. At the intellectual level, China was much more lively in 1600, with writers and thinkers offering much more sustained critiques of inherited ideas. The fear of the Mongols had largely abated, but those fears had left their trace in the Great Wall. The civil service was discouraged by failures of leadership at the top, but with the expansion of education, the number of those aspiring for civil service careers was much larger in 1600 than it had been in the first generation of the Ming.

Painting a Self-Portrait. Popular editions of Ming novels and plays were frequently illustrated with wood block prints. In the scene shown here the heroine of *The Peony Pavilion* uses a mirror to paint a self-portrait. *(Beijing Library)*

Chosŏn Korea (1392–1800)

The Chosŏn Dynasty was founded in 1392 by Yi Sŏnggye. The next four centuries were marked by extensive Confucianization. Chinese statecraft and the examination system were copied more closely. The hereditary *yangban*, who now had to devote themselves to education to gain office, could provide a powerful check on the power of kings but often fell into extreme factionalism. Confucianization reached the level of the family; the paterfamilias became recognized as the owner of family property, and women's rights to inherit were largely lost. The dynasty survived serious crises, including invasions by the Japanese and the Manchus. Yet, by the eighteenth century, there were increasing signs of economic growth, social change, and new cultural openness.

Historians of the Chosŏn period have looked closely at its elite and government. Was the founding of the dynasty the result of a social revolution? Why was factionalism so bitter and so bloody? Did the emphasis on Confucian orthodoxy make factionalism worse? Would Chosŏn have been stronger if its kings had been able to control their *yangban* officials more effectively? Or did the power of the officials—imbued with Confucian ideas—save the country from tyranny? Given the flaws in the government system and the many crises, why did the dynasty last so long? Chosŏn's international situation has also been a subject of close scrutiny. Was the tributary relationship with Ming China beneficial or detrimental? Why was Chosŏn unable to repel Hideyoshi's invasion? How did Korea respond to its first encounter with Christianity? Scholars today are also asking basic questions about social and economic change. How large was the population? Why did commercialization lag behind China and Japan? Why was so much labor unfree?

YI SŎNGGYE'S RISE TO POWER

In the mid-fourteenth century, the Koryŏ dynasty was revived after the period of Mongol domination. As discussed in Chapter 10, King Kongmin took steps to strengthen royal power; he strengthened the military,

Vowel pairs	ㅏ a ㅑ ya, ㅓ ŏ ㅕ yŏ, ㅗ o ㅛ yo, ㅜ u ㅠ yu, ― ŭ ㅣ i.			
Some consonant pairs	ㄱ k ㅋ k', ㄷ t ㅌ t', ㅂ p ㅍ p', ㅈ ch ㅊ ch'.			
Some other consonants	ㅅ s, ㄴ n, ㅁ m, ㅇ ng.			

Syllables*	Chosŏn	조선	Taedong	대동
	ch'ŏnmin	천민	T'aejong	태종
	Puyŏ	부여	*yangban*	양반
	Pyongyang	평양		

K, t, p, and *ch* are voiced (*g, d, b,* and *j*) when occurring between vowels. The symbol ㅇ is used both for a final *ng* and to indicate the absence of an initial consonant. *Ae* is written ㅐ (*ai*).

Figure 15.1   Han'gul Chart

expanded tax revenue, and promoted Confucianism. After his reign ended with his assassination, Confucian reformers allied themselves with a powerful general, Yi Sŏnggye, who became the force behind the throne. Steps were taken to reclaim authority over prebendal grants, cancel tax-free exemptions to favored *yangban*, and carry out a national land survey. In 1389, Yi eliminated his principal rival, paving the way to declare a new dynasty in 1392. As its first emperor, he is known as T'aejo (r. 1392–1398). In essence a coup from within, this was a relatively bloodless dynastic transition. Most of the great families of Koryŏ survived to play leading roles during Chosŏn.

Among T'aejo's successors were three of the most successful kings in Korean history—T'aejong, Sejong, and Sejo—noted for their achievements in culture, science, and military theory. King T'aejong twice called up one hundred thousand corvée laborers to build a new capital at Hanyang (Seoul), not far from the Koryŏ capital. He strengthened the armed forces, confiscated Buddhist temple and monastery property, and created a sound fiscal base for the state. His son, King Sejong (r. 1418–1450), established a record of accomplishment that far outshone any of his successors. He improved both the army and navy, defeated the Wakō pirates on Tsushima Island, and extended Chosŏn's territory north to the Yalu and Tumen Rivers. To secure control of those areas, until then settled by Jurchens and other Manchurian groups, he dispatched thousands of Koreans from the south as colonists. He revised the land registration system to make it more equitable. He published books on agriculture and sericulture to promote better yields. He reinstituted state-sponsored grain loans to peasants to tide them over the spring planting season and famine periods. His legal reforms prohibited cruel punishments, allowed appeals in death penalty cases, and added penalties for masters who beat their slaves without first obtaining official permission. He tried (unsuccessfully) to introduce metallic and paper currency.

One of Sejong's most important achievements was the establishment of the Hall of Worthies (*Chiphyŏnjŏn*) in 1420, where scholars collected documents and published books. Sejong put this agency in charge of inventing an alphabet in 1443—the first and only one of its kind in East Asia. Sejong's goal was to spread learning beyond the elite *yangban*, who recognized that its use would break their stranglehold on knowledge and therefore opposed it (see Figure 15.1). Among the books Sejong sponsored were *Episodes from the Life of the Buddha (Sŏkpo sangjŏl)*, eulogies of his ancestors, *The Songs of the Flying Dragons (Yongbi*

Courtyard of a Sixteenth-Century Confucian Academy. A half century after the death of the teacher Yi Onjŏk, the academy where he had taught was dedicated as a shrine to his memory.

ŏch'ŏnga), and *Illustrated Guide to the Three Moral Relationships (Samgang haengsil)*, as well as works on science, medicine, and astronomy. Scientific accomplishments of his reign included sundials, an astronomical chart, a new type of water clock, and a rain gauge invented in 1442 (two centuries before Europe's first).

Despite the great accomplishments of King Sejong, he was unable to bequeath political stability to his heirs. His successor died early, and his twelve-year-old grandson, King Tanjong, was robbed of his throne by his uncle, King Sejo (r. 1455–1468), an act that sowed the seeds of political discord for the rest of the century.

Sejo was devoted to military strategy and published three treatises on it. He authorized attacks against the Jurchens in 1460 and 1467, established military colonies to support troop units, and established the Five Guards Command in 1466 to function as a supreme national defense council. He adopted the famous Chinese ever-normal granaries to stabilize the price of grain by buying or selling grain on the market, and he tried, but failed, to put iron cash into circulation to promote commerce. He also ordered the compilation of a major law code, the *Grand Institutes for Governing the State (Kyŏngguk taejŏn)*.

Sejo antagonized the Confucian officials by patronizing Buddhism and finding ways to circumvent Confucian critics. He neglected the state council, ordered the six ministries to send all their communications directly to him, and abolished the Hall of Worthies. Thus, despite Sejo's accomplishments, his reputation was tarnished, making it easier for Confucian officials to regain their power under subsequent kings.

KINGS AND *YANGBAN* CONFUCIAN OFFICIALS

The early Chosŏn period saw the culmination of what might have seemed contradictory trends. Kings consolidated their authority through extension of central control. Committed neo-Confucians, as critics of power, circumscribed both the authority of the king and the authority of military men and aristocrats. And *yangban* aristocrats maintained their political and social predominance.

Although for centuries Korean kings had been adopting elements of Chinese statecraft, it was not until the early Chosŏn period that centralization reached the point where magistrates in all of the three-hundred-odd local districts were appointed by the central government. It was also in this period that the civil service examinations became the main route to high office. As in China, government service became the goal of the elite. The exams were used to select men with literary educations and inclinations to be put in charge of the government apparatus. Birth alone was no longer enough. To advance to high office, passing the examinations became necessary.

Nevertheless, the vast majority of officials in the Chosŏn Dynasty came from long-established *yangban* families. They were the ones who could best afford education. There was no attempt by any of the early Chosŏn kings to manumit slaves and challenge the property rights of the *yangban* aristocrats. As competition for government posts increased, the *yangban* found ways to give themselves advantages. They banned the Koryŏ practice of allowing *hyangni* (local clerks) to be promoted to the central bureaucracy. They further narrowed the pool of candidates by barring sons of concubines from taking the examinations.

The majority of *tohak* Confucian scholars supported the overthrow of the Koryŏ Dynasty. They inherited Chinese scholars' arguments against Buddhism, such as the claim that the Buddhist emphasis on the individual attainment of enlightenment interfered with the Confucian obligation of filial piety. As a result of their campaigns, many Buddhist monasteries were disbanded and stripped of their land, and eighty thousand of their slaves were converted to government slaves.

Chosŏn Confucians recognized Ming China as a mature example of a Confucian society, but they did not see Confucian civilization as uniquely Chinese or the Chinese manifestation of it as intrinsically superior. Zealous Korean Confucians aspired to create a more perfect Confucian society, one that adhered more closely to the classics than Ming China did.

Confucian emphasis on filial piety and loyalty to the ruler was useful to the Chosŏn kings in gaining conformity to their authority. On the other hand, as in China, Confucian scholars viewed themselves as responsible for guiding the ruler toward moral perfection, and they insisted that the ruler should listen to their counsel, even if it tended to hamstring the king's authority and protect their *yangban* class interests.

Did the moral authority of the *yangban* Confucian scholars keep Chosŏn Korea from becoming a despotism like Ming China? Chosŏn kings found it difficult to exercise their theoretically absolute power because of the obstruction and remonstrance of the

Map 15.1   Chosŏn Dynasty, 1392–1910

civil officials, almost all of whom came from *yangban* families with longer histories and more prestige than the Yi royal family. One of Sejo's successors, Yŏnsan'gun, took a strong stand against the Confucian establishment. He acted in ever more arbitrary fashion against real and supposed insults to his authority, ordering the execution of people for minor offenses. His critics saw themselves as waging a moral crusade against a usurper and his political appointees, but he thought he was defending his rights as an absolute monarch. He carried out a purge of the literati in 1504, canceled the royal lectures because the lecturers were aggressive in criticizing his actions, and neglected the National Academy. He became so paranoid that a cabal of high officials deposed him in 1506.

Under Yŏnsan'gun's successor, King Chungjong, the political tide turned in the opposite direction.

The *Yangban* Confucians serving as censors gained the upper hand by criticizing the men the king had rewarded for putting him on the throne. These censors were led by Cho Kwangjo, who styled himself a moral man with better qualifications than the new political appointees at the top of the government. He persuaded King Chungjong to allow a new "recommendation" examination to provide opportunities for neglected but outstanding scholars. When the examination was held in 1515, however, it turned out that Cho's friends and supporters passed the examinations and immediately joined in his efforts to topple those they labeled unworthy political appointees. By 1519, Chungjong had lost patience with his critics; he purged the young censors and executed Cho. To students of the National Academy, Cho Kwangjo became a martyr to the cause of ethically pure Confucian government. Cho and his associates can also be viewed, however, as skillful politicians playing the moral card to gain political advantage.

By the late sixteenth century, many scholars with high reputations for virtue were holding high office, and they debated the ethical and metaphysical arguments of Zhu Xi. Zhu Xi and his predecessors had argued that everything in the cosmos consists of two inseparable factors: pattern (or principle, *i; li* in Chinese) and psychophysical force (*ki; qi* in Chinese). A debate began over which of the two elements was primary. Yi T'oegye held that the nonphysical pattern in the mind took priority because it contained all the elements of pure virtue, while the younger Yi Yulgok took the view that psychophysical force was prior because without it, the mind would not exist at all. Zhu Xi himself had allowed space for different interpretations, and the debate was carried on without rancor at the time. The followers of these two men became political rivals, however.

In China at that time, the main challenge to Zhu Xi's orthodoxy came from Wang Yangming and his followers. Wang challenged Zhu Xi's stress on the need for textual study and emphasized the capacity of everyone to decide what is morally right by looking within himself. Yi T'oegye defended Zhu Xi's formula and condemned Wang as a heterodox thinker who relegated the judgment of Confucian virtue to the whims of the imperfect vagaries of the emotions beclouded by *ki*. T'oegye's rejection of Wang Yangming set the tone for Korean Confucianism for the rest of the Chosŏn Dynasty. T'oegye's reputation was so powerful at the time that those attracted to Wang Yangming's ideas had to keep their views secret.

The *yangban* preserved their elite position through the Chosŏn period and kept a near monopoly on access to high office (see Material Culture: *Yangban Children's Board Games*). At the same time, the *yangban* stratum grew in size and began to separate into two levels. The percentage of successful examination passers from the top two dozen *yangban* families gradually increased, as they became the elite among the *yangban*. Since an average of only thirty men per year passed the examinations, many *yangban* who studied for the examinations had no chance for office and were left in the countryside to make their way there. Some were able to form single-family villages and further strengthen their local power. In other villages, *yangban* power declined because of reforms in tax collection. In order to alleviate the tax burden, village associations called *tonggye* were formed of all households regardless of status to divide the tax burden equitably among all families. Thus many *yangban* in the countryside became indistinguishable from ordinary farmers in the ways they lived (though legally they were still distinct).

In the Chosŏn period, *chung'in*, or middle people, formed a new hereditary class. The *chung'in* were clerks, legal specialists, accountants, interpreters, and the like who had lost any hope of rising to regular office but at the same time wanted to save these positions for themselves.

DYNASTIC DECLINE AND THE JAPANESE INVASION

The decline of Chosŏn institutions contributed to the inability of the government to withstand the Japanese invasion in the late sixteenth century. Over the course of the fifteenth and sixteenth centuries, rich landlords expanded their holdings by legal and illegal means at the expense of small-holding commoner peasants. *Yangban* landlords lent money to small holders, then foreclosed when they could not repay. Indebted poor peasants often commended their land to *yangban* and became their slaves to escape both the tax collector and military service. The state failed to remedy this situation by conducting timely cadastral surveys to record landownership and maintain the tax base. It also failed to provide relief loans to small holders in distress.

There was a strong trend for *yangban* without office and even rich commoners to escape military ser-

MATERIAL CULTURE

Yangban *Children's Board Games*

Boys in *yangban* families were under a lot of pressure to gain facility in classical Chinese—a written language unrelated to the language they spoke. To be able to recognize people's names and place names, they had to know hundreds of Chinese characters, and if they hoped to take the civil service examinations, they not only had to know several thousand characters but also be able to recognize passages from the Confucian classics and terms used for government offices and policies.

Games could make this learning more fun. Shown here are two board games. In both, the goal is to be the first to complete the route, moves determined by the roll of the dice. On the circular board, each circle names a scenic place in Korea. Landing on certain spots can bring favorable winds that speed the journey or obstacles like battlefields that slow it. On the rectangular board, the boxes are the names of government posts, arranged to show career paths. When the player lands on certain spaces, he can be cashiered or even poisoned. Promotion games had been popular in China since the Tang dynasty and helped teach not only the names of offices but also the role of chance in advancement in office.

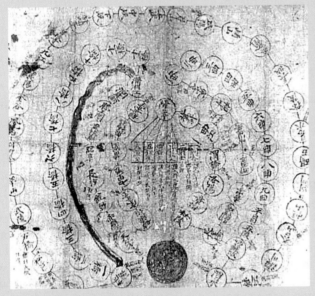

Geography Game.

Promotion Game.

vice by bribing clerks to register them falsely as students to qualify them for exemptions from military duty and the military cloth tax. Local commanders conspired with them by letting them off actual duty in return for bribes or military cloth tax payments. As a result, there was a serious decline in the number of troops on duty in the army and the local garrisons. Although a new national security agency, the Border Defense Command, had been created in 1522 to deal specifically with defense against Japanese pirate raids, the government failed to stem the hollowing out of the military. In 1582, Yi Yulgok recommended the creation of an armed force of one hundred thousand men to be assigned around the country in anticipation of military threats. Other officials called for the establishment of naval bases on strategic islands

BIOGRAPHY Admiral Yi Sunsin

One of the greatest military heroes of Korean history was Admiral Yi Sunsin (1545–1598), who successfully led his small fleet against Hideyoshi's forces between 1592 and 1598. In the first phase of the war (1592–1593), he won a major contest with a fleet of a dozen ships. His command ship, in the shape of a turtle with a dragon's head at the bow, was unprecedented in its use of iron cladding. Ten oars on each side of the ship allowed it to escape enemy pursuit. The surface had long iron spikes camouflaged with straw mats to prevent enemy sailors from jumping on board. The ship had a lower deck with six gun ports and an upper deck with twenty-two gun ports on each side. The cannons inside shot shells of gunpowder and iron splinters.

The ships were first used at the battle of Sach'ŏn on July 7, 1592. From August through October, Yi won major battles at Yulp'o, Hansan Island, and Angolp'o and destroyed an additional four hundred Japanese ships in ten battles in December alone, preventing Japanese forces from entering the Chŏlla province area in the southeast. In the battle at Angolp'o, the Japanese beached their ships rather than challenge the turtle boat.

After a brief imprisonment on false charges in 1597, during which Yi Sunsin's replacement, Wŏn Kyun, suffered the loss of all but twelve Korean ships, Yi was recalled to service. He won one of his greatest victories at Myŏngnyang on October 26, 1597, where he defeated three hundred Japanese ships with those dozen ships. He won victories in seventeen of the eighteen naval battles he fought. Tragically, he died in his last battle in 1598, but he ordered his aides to keep his impending death secret and maintain the attack against the enemy.

off the coast and a major army base at Pusan to block any attack from Japan. The court of King Sŏnjo, however, failed to act on any of those suggestions, leaving three walled towns—Pusan, Tongnae, and Kimhae—as the only defense against invasion. The exacerbation of factionalism among the *yangban* officials also weakened defense. A struggle began in 1575 over two men competing for appointment to a key post in the ministry of personnel. They and their followers became known as Easterners and Westerners, terms related to the location of their homes in the capital, not to different parts of the country. To be sure, personal relations based on blood ties, marriage alliances, schoolboy friendships, and master-disciple relations had shaped political group formation for centuries, but no permanent factional groups had been created until 1575. After 1575, factions became hereditary, and frequent purges prevented unity even in times of crisis.

Although factionalism was disesteemed traditionally because it kept the king from getting impartial advice, Korean officials justified their factions in the same way Chinese officials had in the Song period: moral men had to join forces against the immoral. King Sŏnjo (r. 1567–1608) disliked the factions but failed to eliminate them. Instead, he made the situation worse by shifting his favor from one faction to another repeatedly.

When a rebellion broke out in the southwest in 1589, King Sŏnjo accepted the unreasonable charge of the Westerners that the rebellion was an Easterner plot, and he executed over seventy Easterner officials. He then sent a delegation to Japan in 1591 to assess the intentions of the Japanese leader, Toyotomi Hideyoshi. On the delegation's return, Sŏnjo rejected the warning of the Westerner ambassador that Hideyoshi was preparing an invasion of Korea and took no action to prepare the country for war.

Japan, by contrast, had been engaged in almost constant internal warfare among powerful warlords (daimyo) since the outbreak of the Ōnin War in 1467. The victor in that long struggle was Toyotomi Hideyoshi, an uneducated peasant who had risen from the ranks and now could mobilize the mounted samurai warriors and archers and the commoner foot soldiers from all domains of Japan (see Chapter 13). In addition, his armies were equipped with muskets and cannon, which had been introduced into Japan in the sixteenth century by the Portuguese but that Korea lacked. In 1592, Hideyoshi asked King Sŏnjo for free passage through Korea so that he could attack Ming China. When Sŏnjo refused, Hideyoshi sent his army to invade Korea and overwhelmed the Korean defenders. Hideyoshii's forces occupied Seoul in three weeks and Pyongyang in two months, then settled in for the winter. The only major military success of Chosŏn forces was naval: Admiral Yi Sunsin blocked Japanese ships from landing men off Chŏlla province on Korea's west coast (see **Biography: Admiral Yi Sunsin**).

Under the tributary system, the Ming emperor had a moral obligation to send forces to defend Chosŏn, but the Ming government was at that time plagued by the raids of Mongol tribesmen, internal conflict between powerful eunuchs and Confucian reformers, fiscal shortages, and a decline in the number and quality of soldiers. Still, seven months after the Japanese invasion, Ming forces began to arrive. Although they succeeded in defeating Japanese forces at Pyongyang in February 1593, they suffered a stunning defeat just north of Seoul at the battle of Pyŏkchegwan later that month. Ming generals became much more cautious after that and later that year negotiated a truce with the Japanese commander, Katō Kiyomasa, that lasted until 1597.

Hideyoshi renewed the fighting in 1597 because he was angered by the terms that the Chinese offered. This time, Japanese ground forces were blocked by the Ming army and forced to retreat to the southern littoral, while Yi Sunsin's naval forces won major victories against enormous odds. When Hideyoshi died in 1598, Japanese forces withdrew from the peninsula. Ming military intervention had saved Chosŏn from destruction, but Korea was left devastated. About 2 million lives had been lost, and agricultural production was so disrupted that it took a century to reach pre-1592 levels.

RELATIONS WITH THE MANCHUS

Korea severed all relations with Japan after the invasion. Hideyoshi's successor, Tokugawa Ieyasu, had no interest in invading Korea, however, and Korea reestablished relations in a 1609 treaty. The treaty restricted trade to Tongnae, near Pusan, where a Japanese office was established behind a palisade fence, and the Japanese were left to administer the enclave. Trade with Japan was regulated through tallies that were issued to the head of the Japanese Sō family on Tsushima Island and then distributed to various

daimyo throughout Japan. Trade was limited specific number of ships per year.

Just as stable relations with Japan were being established, Korea found itself embroiled in a conflict between the declining Ming Dynasty and the rising Jurchen tribes in Manchuria. In the 1590s, the Jurchens, previously divided into a number of independent small units, were united by Nurhaci, who changed their name from Jurchen to Manchu. Korea soon found itself in a difficult spot between the two rivals, both of whom wanted its aid. The Chosŏn king, Kwanghaegun, tried to maintain neutrality, but the vast majority of his own officials wanted him to support the Ming, whose armies had saved Chosŏn from Hideyoshi.

Factional strife complicated foreign relations in this period. Kwanghaegun was the son of one of King Sŏnjo's concubines and was elected crown prince by the king during the Japanese invasion. Once Sŏnjo's second queen gave birth to a son, called Great Lord Yŏngch'ang, however, many officials of the small Northerner, Southerner, and Westerner factions wanted to depose Kwanghaegun on the grounds that the son of a queen took ritual precedence over the son of a concubine. With the support of the Great Northern faction, Kwanghaegun had Grand Prince Yŏngch'ang and his younger brother assassinated for plotting against him.

In 1623 the Westerner faction led a coup to depose Kwanghaegun. They replaced him with King Sŏnjo's grandson, known posthumously as King Injo. All the Northerners who had supported Kwanghaegun were executed or banished, and they remained out of high office for the next two centuries. Upon seizing power, the Westerners reversed Kwanghaegun's controversial foreign policy and supported the Ming against the Manchus.

Injo prepared for war with the Manchus but kept much of his army near the capital to guard against potential rebels. When the Manchus invaded Korea in 1627 with a force of 30,000, they overran Korean resistance and imposed a peace treaty on King Injo. When the king stubbornly refused Manchu demands, they sent an invasion force of 120,000 men. Because the Chosŏn border commander failed to transmit the war beacon signals to the capital on time, King Injo received word of the invasion only two days before Manchu troops arrived at Seoul. Surrounded, he was forced to submit to the Qing demand that he sever relations with the Ming Dynasty and enroll as a Qing tributary. This was seven years before the Manchus conquered China in 1644.

Landscape of the Diamond Mountains (Kŭmgangsan).
This painting by Chŏng Sŏn (1676–1759) depicts the
landscape of the Diamond Mountains (Kŭmgangsan)
with a touch of animistic spirits in the swaying
mountains. Chosŏn Dynasty. (*Hoam Museum of Fine
Arts, Yong'in; Koreana: Korean Cultural Heritage,
Volume 1, Fine Arts Korea Foundation, 1994, p. 56*)

To help pay for its expansion, the Manchus levied
heavy tribute demands on Chosŏn. Not until the end
of the seventeenth century did Chosŏn kings abandon anti-Qing policies and the Qing court lighten its
tribute demands. Most Korean *yangban*, however,
still held the Manchus in contempt and remained loyal
to the memory of the Ming.

Why did the Manchus leave Korea independent
but fully conquer China? Like the Mongols before
them, the Manchus apparently did not see Korea as
much of a prize. Early on, they were satisfied to extract tribute from Chosŏn to help them in their campaigns into China. After the conquest of the Ming,
they had so much territory to administer that adding
to it was not a high priority. The Qing did later add
territories when security was at stake, but Chosŏn
proved a nonthreatening vassal that could safely be
allowed to remain autonomous.

INTERNAL POLITICS IN THE SEVENTEENTH AND EIGHTEENTH CENTURIES

The poor showing of the Chosŏn army during the
Japanese and Manchu invasions made reorganization of the armed forces necessary, but that ran up
against strict Manchu surveillance. Everyone recognized that military weakness had been caused by evasion of military service, and so attention was turned
to requiring military duty from slaves. Nevertheless,
evasion by the *yangban* persisted.

Factional disputes subsided after 1623 as officials
were consumed primarily with recovery from devastation. Factionalism reemerged when what seemed a
minor ritual issue led to a series of major purges and
executions. It began in 1659 when Song Siyŏl of the
Westerner faction insisted that a member of the royal
family should perform a lesser degree of mourning
for the deceased King Hyojong because he was the
second son of King Injo. The Southerner faction, led
by Yun Hyu, accused Song Siyŏl and the Westerners
of impugning the legitimacy of King Hyojong and
his heirs. The Southerners eventually persuaded King
Hyojong to adopt their position and dismiss Song.
Westerners led by Yun Ch'ung, who disliked Song's
uncompromising and arrogant leadership of the Westerner faction, also split to form their own Disciples
faction, leaving Song and his supporters to form
their own Patriarchs faction. King Sukchong (r. 1674–
1720) contributed to the conflict by switching his
support almost whimsically. He replaced Patriarchs
and Disciples with Southerners in 1689 because they
opposed his decision to replace his first queen with
a palace concubine and then turned around and purged
the Southerners in 1694 after he lost interest in her.
When the Patriarchs regained power, they excluded
the descendants of Southerners from office until the
late eighteenth century.

The Patriarchs and Disciples factions then turned
against each other over the choice between two of
King Sukchong's sons for crown prince: the Disciples favored Yi Kyun, and the Patriarchs favored
Lord Yŏnning. King Sukchong chose the childless
and sickly Yi Kyun, but he appointed Lord Yŏnning
as crown prince. When Yi Kyun became King Kyŏngjong in 1724, his Disciple supporters persuaded him
to execute the four leading Patriarchs for supporting
Lord Yŏnning, but Yŏnning remained crown prince.
King Kyŏngjong died an early death in 1727, at which

time Lord Yŏnning became King Yŏngjo, and his Patriarch supporters exacted revenge on the Disciples. King Yŏngjo, however, decided that the time had come to put an end to factional strife. He appointed moderate members of both the Disciples and Patriarchs' factions and excluded not only vengeful members of those two factions but Northerners and Southerners as well. The radical Disciples, however, rose up in rebellion under Yi Injwa in 1728 in Ch'ungch'ŏng province. King Yŏngjo put the rebellion down and maintained his coalition cabinet, but the rebellion alerted King Yŏngjo to serious danger in the future if he endangered *yangban* interests.

Despite King Yŏngjo's efforts to end factionalism, he made politics more complicated in 1762 when he decided to lock Crown Prince Sado in a small rice box in the palace courtyard and left him to starve to death; the crown prince died eight days later. In 1749, Yŏngjo had given fifteen-year-old Sado responsibility as prince regent to take over many of the king's tasks, but Sado's fear of his father's ridicule pushed him over the edge of sanity. He released his pent-up frustrations in paroxysms of rage in which he murdered palace ladies who offended him. (See **Documents: Lady Hyegyŏng's Memoirs.**) King Yŏngjo reportedly decided to commit filicide when it was reported to him that Prince Sado was overheard praying for his father's death. This action immediately split the government into those (mostly Patriarchs) who agreed with Yŏngjo's decision and those (mostly Southerners) who sympathized with the deceased crown prince, laying the groundwork for another round of purges. Years later in 1776 when the son of the deceased Sado came to the throne as King Chŏngjo, he ardently desired a way to honor his father, restore his reputation, and take revenge on the factions against him. In 1795 he led a procession of six thousand men to Hwasŏng (Suwŏn) with his mother, Princess Hyegyŏng, ostensibly to honor her seventieth birthday, but the underlying goal was to honor his father, who was buried there.

Chŏngjo wanted to be a model king like the ancient Chinese sage kings but was hampered by the factionalism of his officials. Chŏngjo chastised his officials for their devotion to their own private interests and their failure to master the moral teachings of the Chinese classics. To rectify this problem, he ordered the importation of Chinese classical texts for the new Royal Library and turned the library staff into his own private cabinet for advising him on state affairs. Nevertheless, he banned the free importation

Procession for Crown Prince Sado. Procession returning from a visit to Hwasŏng (modern Suwon) to Seoul in 1795 led by King Chongjo with his mother, Lady Hyegyŏng, to honor the sixtieth birthday of his father, Crown Prince Sado, who had been murdered by his own father, King Yŏngjo, in 1762. *(Han Yong'u,* Tasi ch'annuin uri yoksa *[Our History, Rediscovered], p. 11 left)*

DOCUMENTS

Lady Hyegyŏng's Memoirs

One of the most outstanding literary works of the Chosŏn period is Memoirs of Lady Hyegyŏng (Hanjungnok or Records Written in Silence), *written in han'gul by the wife of Crown Prince Sado, who was starved to death by his father, King Yŏngjo, in 1762. The book consists of four separate accounts written in 1795, 1801, 1802, and 1805. No other source provides a better introduction to the vicissitudes of palace life, particularly at a time when the slightest slip could mean death. In fact, her uncle and younger brother were executed in 1776 and 1801, respectively. Probably the most interesting of her narratives was in her* Memoir *of 1805, in which she relates Sado's psychosis to the deficiencies of King Yŏngjo as a father.*

His Majesty's [King Yŏngjo] sagacious heart became irritated with small things at the Prince's quarters, mostly imperceptible and of an unspecified nature. Consequently, without really knowing why, he visited his son less frequently. This happened just as the Prince began to grow; that is just when a child, suffering some inattention or relaxation of control, might easily fall under other influences. As the Prince was often left to himself at this stage, he began to get into trouble. . . .

In his study sessions with tutors, however, Prince Sado was a serious and attentive student. . . . Thus it is all the more sad that, in his father's presence, the prince grew inarticulate and hesitant out of fear and nervousness. His Majesty became more and more exasperated with him during these encounters in which the Prince was hopelessly tongue-tied. He was alternately angry and concerned about his son. Nonetheless, he never sought a closer relationship with his son, never sought to spend more time with him or to teach him himself. He continued to keep the Prince at a distance, hoping that his son would become on his own the heir he dreamed of. How could this not lead to trouble? . . .

Sometime around the ŭlch'uk year (1745) [when he was ten], the Prince's behavior became strange indeed. It was not just the behavior of a child playing excitedly or loudly. Something was definitely wrong with him. The ladies-in-waiting became quite concerned,

---

of books from China because he saw many as subversive, including works by Wang Yangming, popular novels, and treatises on Christian theology. Chŏngjo's efforts to be a model king did not bring about the moral transformation of society that Confucian theory predicted; to the contrary, plotters tried to have him assassinated seven times.

ECONOMIC GROWTH AND THE DECLINE OF SLAVERY

During the Chosŏn period, the Korean economy was not as advanced as that of China or Japan, but it was beginning to develop along similar lines of commercialization. During the early Chosŏn period, the economy was predominantly agrarian with limited commercial activity. All taxes were paid in kind or by physical labor. Most artisans were slaves who served the needs of the *yangban* and the royal house. Commerce in the capital was restricted to monopoly merchants and in the countryside to itinerant peddlers and fifth-day markets. Commercial towns and permanent shops were rare. National defense was based on military service for all adult males except for merchants, slaves, and men in official schools; sons of *yangban* with official rank (not necessarily office) were allowed to serve in special guard units set aside for them.

Many government fiscal policies were in need of reform, especially the tribute tax on local products, the maldistribution of the land tax burden, and the military conscription system. The local products tribute tax originated as a fixed and unchanging assessment

whispering to each other of their fears. In the ninth month of that year, the Prince fell gravely ill, often losing consciousness. . . .

[In 1749, when Sado was fifteen, King Yŏngjo appointed him Prince-Regent to sit in court and conduct business.] There was nothing that the Prince-Regent did that His Majesty found satisfactory. He was constantly discontented and angry with his son. It reached a point where the occurrence of cold spells, droughts, poor harvests, strange natural omens, or calamities caused His Majesty to denounce "the Prince-Regent's insufficient virtue" and to reproach the Prince most severely. . . .

In the sixth month of chŏngch'uk (1757) . . . Prince Sado began to kill. The first person he killed was Kim Hanch'ae, the eunuch who happened to be on duty that day. The Prince came in with the severed head and displayed it to the ladies-in-waiting. The bloody head, the first I ever saw, was simply a horrifying sight. As if he had to kill to release his rage, the Prince harmed many ladies-in-waiting. . . .

In the ninth month of that year, Prince Sado took in Pingae, a lady-in-waiting. . . . Before this, he had been intimate with many ladies-in-waiting. Whoever resisted him in any way he beat until he rent her flesh and consummated the act afterwards.

Needless to say, no one welcomed his advances. Despite the many women he had been intimate with, he neither cared for anyone for long nor showed any particular fondness while it lasted. This was true even of the secondary consort who had borne him children. It was different with Pingae [Prince Sado's concubine who bore him two children]. He was mad about her. . . . His Majesty learned of Pingae. He was highly provoked. He summoned the Prince to question him, "How dare you do that?"

By this time [1761], whenever he was seized by his illness the Prince invariably hurt people. For some time now, Pingae had been the only one to attend the prince when he dressed. Hopelessly in the grip of the disease, he grew oblivious even of his beloved. One day, for one of his outings incognito, he was suddenly overwhelmed by a fit of rage and beat her senseless. No sooner had he left than Pingae drew her last breath there where he left her. How pitiful her end was! . . . Upon his return, Prince Sado heard of what had happened, but he said nothing. He was not in his senses.

Source: JaHyon Kim Haboush, trans., *The Memoirs of Lady Hyegyŏng* (Berkeley: University of California Press, 1996), pp. 247, 250–251, 252, 258, 283–285, 301.

on local villages that specialized in the production of certain goods, but when many villages ceased producing those products, they had to pay fees to so-called tribute merchants to procure those products elsewhere. This practice of tribute contracting was regarded by the authorities as illegal, and those caught doing it were subject to punishment and fines, but there was no other way for villagers to meet their tribute tax quotas. Yet although tribute contracting was illegal, it contributed to the expansion of commercial activities by private merchants in the countryside.

After the invasions, the Chosŏn government extended military service to private slaves for the first time. It also replaced local product payments in kind by imposing an extra land tax in grain, which it used to purchase the special goods it needed. The new tax was adopted gradually, but by 1708 the new system covered the whole country and more than doubled the tax burden on landowners. The law stimulated increased commercial activity, particularly among private, unlicensed merchants.

In 1650, the official Kim Yuk returned from a trip to China with large amounts of cash he had purchased with funds saved from his expenses. He received King Hyojong's approval to put it into circulation, and in 1654 he persuaded the king to order that the cash be accepted in payment of the tax. This marked the first use of cash in about a hundred years.

The Chosŏn population grew to 14 million by the year 1810, a 40 percent increase over 1650. Connected to this growth were increases in agricultural productivity, allowing farmers to abandon the fallow system, under which land was left fallow for a year or two to recover fertility. The conversion of dry fields

.d ones also increased productivity, as ~~.ion~~ of transplanting rice seedlings (in ~~ing~~ seeds directly in the field). Yet even as la~~ ~~)00, average production per acre in Korea was about 15 bushels, about the same as China in 1400 and about one-third less than production in Japan and China around 1880.

The eighteenth century witnessed expanded commercial activity. Although the number of commercial towns remained small, the number of periodic five-day markets increased. Seoul was the largest city, with about two hundred thousand people. Market growth was slowed when King Sukchong decided to stop minting cash in 1697 because of inflation from excessive minting. That policy continued for thirty-three years and produced deflation. King Yŏngjo reluctantly agreed to mint more cash in 1731, and minting continued for the rest of the dynasty. Private, unlicensed merchants began to compete with the licensed merchants in the capital. In the 1740s the government capitulated and stopped prosecuting merchants who traded in monopoly goods without licenses. In 1791 the court adopted a compromise solution, the joint-sales policy, which protected monopoly privileges for only six shops in Seoul and allowed private merchants to manufacture or sell all other products.

In the early Chosŏn period, both private and government slavery were pervasive. State slaves alone in the late fifteenth century numbered about 350,000, and government efforts to limit private slaveholding never got far. Yet, as the economy became more commercialized in the eighteenth century, slavery declined. Between 1750 and 1790, there was a sharp reduction in the slave population from about 30 percent to less than 10 percent of the population. King Yŏngjo contributed a little to this reduction when in 1730 he approved readopting the matrilineal rule governing the inheritance of slave status by offspring of mixed slave-commoner marriages. The main cause of the decline, however, was the increase in the number of runaway slaves. Instead of paying the cost of chasing after them, *yangban* and rich landlords took advantage of the recent increase in landless peasants to whom they could rent their land. Escaped slaves did not necessarily see a rise in income and standards of living because now they had to pay rents to landlords, interest on grain loans from the state or private lenders, and the commoner military cloth tax. Another factor in the decline in the slave population was that the government had begun to replace official slaves with hired commoner labor. The number of official slaves dropped from 350,000 in 1590 to 60,000 by 1801.

CULTURAL DEVELOPMENTS

The social and economic changes of the seventeenth and eighteenth centuries were accompanied by a new openness to cultural variety and innovative thinking.

Literature

Literary activity burgeoned in the seventeenth and eighteenth centuries. Poetry remained a favorite pastime of both men (in Chinese) and women (in *han'gŭl*). The favorite forms in this period were the short *sijo* poems, their longer versions (*sasŏl sijo*), and the still longer lyrical *kasa*. Poems in Korean (unlike those in Chinese) did not use rhymes; poetic language instead depended on alliteration and cadence.

Hundreds of short tales and long novels were also written in this period, either by men in classical Chinese or by women in the *han'gŭl* alphabet. Many of the stories deal with women. Some portray women defending their womanly virtues, but suffering is a common theme. In some tales, courtesans exert their independence despite their low status by demanding or stealing their lovers' money or humiliating them in public. The most popular of all tales concerned a woman named Ch'unhyang. It was both a didactic tale of the triumph of womanly virtue over evil and a romantic tale about the son of a *yangban* official who fell in love with the daughter of a courtesan who did not want to continue in her mother's occupation. In defiance of convention, the two wed secretly at the age of fifteen. The husband then left for Seoul to prepare for the civil service examinations, which he passed in first place. Meanwhile, a cruel governor arrived in Ch'unhyang's town and demanded that the young woman become his concubine. When she refused, he ordered her beaten unmercifully and threw her in jail to die. The husband then returned as a secret inspector to cashier the governor, and the two lived happily ever after. The story contains many dream sequences, constant reminders of unexpected dangers, and Buddhist awareness of karma, life after death, and resignation to fate. The erotic description of the two lovers affirms the priority of love over stifling convention, undoubtedly one reason that the story has remained so popular.

One of the great classic novels, *Nine Cloud Dream*, was written by Kim Manjung (1637–1692), a high official and member of the Patriarch faction who was twice dismissed in purges of the Patriarchs. Set in Tang China, the novel's main message is Buddhist.

A monk dreams that he is reborn and sees his life unfold—the glories of a Confucian education, promotion to high office, and unrestricted access to sex with two wives and seven concubines. But then he wakes up and sees the emptiness of it all. In this story, the wives and concubines are all independent, resourceful women who stand out as more vivid characters than the supposed hero.

Two other famous literary works of the period are more political in nature. *The True History of Queen Inhyŏn (Inhyŏn wanghujŏn)*, written by an unknown member of the Patriarch faction, was a biased account aimed at defending Queen Inhyŏn of the Min family, who was deposed by King Sukchong in 1689 and then later reinstated. The other was Lady Hyegyŏng's brilliant memoirs of her life in the palace married to the mad Prince Sado (see **Documents: Lady Hyegyŏng's Memoirs**).

Popular oral literature also flourished. *P'ansori* was an oral song tradition that became popular in the countryside in the eighteenth century. It was performed by the singer as a chant, usually in a guttural tone accompanied by a drummer who varied the tempo according to the mood of each segment. Famous singers could improvise. Many of the songs mocked the *yangban*, but as time passed, classical Chinese phrases were inserted into the songs to appeal to *yangban* as well as commoners. There were also rural dances and local masked plays that were biting in their satire.

Northern Learning

For much of the Chosŏn period, *tohak* Confucianism was intellectually rigid. This too changed in the eighteenth century as scholarly circles became more open to new ideas. One important group, dubbed the Northern Learning group, challenged the conventional prejudice against the Manchus. They urged that Korea learn from the Qing Dynasty to improve the economy and the material aspects of life. Most came from the minority Southerner or Northerner factions.

Hong Taeyong was attracted to the statecraft writings of Yi Yulgok and Yu Hyŏngwŏn. When he accompanied his uncle on a mission to the Qing capital in 1765, he became interested in Western astronomy and mathematics. He rejected the idea that China was either at the center of the earth or the only enlightened country on earth, and he criticized his fellow *yangban* for focusing only on China and neglecting the history and culture of their own country. He also criticized *yangban* disdain for manual labor and the backwardness and poverty of the Chosŏn economy.

Pak Chiwŏn, one of Hong's disciples, left a detailed record of his travels as a member of a tribute mission to China in 1780. He attacked the *yangban* monopoly of the examination system and satirized them in stories like *Master Hŏ* and *The Yangban*. He demanded an end to discrimination against sons of concubines, the manumission of official slaves, and adoption of a land-limitation scheme. He encouraged everyone to engage in commerce and industry and recommended improving transportation by copying the superior carts and boats used in Qing China.

Pak Chega was a Southerner who studied with Pak Chiwŏn. In 1786 he proposed that the king invite Christian missionaries in China to come to Korea to teach Western astronomy and mathematics. In his 1788 book entitled *Northern Learning*, he expanded on themes introduced by Hong Taeyong and Pak Chiwŏn and urged the king to appoint the best merchants to office and expand trade with Qing China.

Northern Learning represented a liberalization of intellectual thought, but it had a very limited effect on government policy because anti-Manchu prejudice and the Confucian bias against merchants were too deeply entrenched.

Christianity and Western Learning

After the Jesuit Francis Xavier arrived in Japan in 1549, many Japanese were converted to Christianity (see **Connections: Europe Enters the Scene**). Some Korean captives who were taken to Japan during Hideyoshi's invasions converted, but they had a negligible effect on Korea. Many of Matteo Ricci's works in Chinese on Catholic theology and Western mathematics, astronomy, and geography were brought into Korea from China in the early seventeenth century, and they had more impact. The Koreans lumped Christian theology and Western science together in a single term, *Western Learning (Sŏhak)*. Koreans were won over to Western astronomical ideas and adopted the Western calendar in 1653, nine years after the Qing Dynasty did.

Scholars who looked into Christianity in the 1720s often rejected its basic premises. Although Yi Ik was greatly impressed by *Seven Victories (Jige)* by Diego Pontoja (1571–1618) because it praised self-denial, frugality, and other virtues compatible with Confucianism, he rejected the overall claims of Christian theology. Yi Imyŏng in 1720 rejected the Catholic notion of heaven and hell, and Yi Ik's disciple, Sin

Hudam, in 1724 condemned Christianity for its resemblance to Buddhism in its selfish emphasis on individual salvation and its concern with life after death. Much Jesuit philosophical argument passed over the heads of Confucian scholars, who were interested primarily in whether Catholic doctrines would aid or hinder adherence to Confucian social morality. What did attract Korean attention was the pope's 1715 condemnation of Chinese ancestral rites as idolatry and the Yongzheng emperor's subsequent ban against Christian proselytization.

In 1784 the student Yi Sŭnghun traveled to China to be baptized, only to be refused by the Catholic missionaries because of his inadequate knowledge of Catholic doctrine. Still, he brought back Christian texts to proselytize among acquaintances. Several dozen men formed the first Christian congregation and worshipped at the home of the *chung'in* Kim Pŏm'u, who became Korea's first Christian martyr.

In 1788 two high officials asked the king to ban European books. The Southerner Councilor of the Right, who had many Catholic relatives, pleaded with King Chŏngjo not to punish the Christians for their ignorance. Chŏngjo agreed, but he also ordered the destruction of all Christian books. In 1791, after being reminded of the pope's ruling on ancestral rites, two Catholics who were also Southerners, Paul Yun Chich'ung and his cousin, James Kwŏn Sangyŏn, burned the ancestral tablets for Yun's mother. When they refused to recant, King Chŏngjo ordered their decapitation and forced their associates to commit apostasy.

The first Christian missionary to Korea, the Chinese Zhou Wenmo, was discovered in 1794. King Chŏngjo executed him and demoted or exiled Southerners suspected of being sympathetic. King Chŏngjo's attempt at toleration had backfired, and he adopted a hard line against both Southerners and Christians.

THE FAMILY AND WOMEN IN THE CONFUCIAN AGE

Chosŏn Confucianists were zealous in their efforts to reshape Korea into a model Confucian society. Korea's original family system was quite different from China's, so making Koreans conform to the strictures in the Chinese classics required much more radical change in Korea than it ever had in China.

In Koryŏ times, the Korean family was neither patriarchal nor patrilineal. Sons-in-law usually lived with their wives' families for several years before setting up their own homes. Oldest daughters often stayed permanently in their parents' home, and continuing a family through a daughter was an accepted practice. Women inherited equal shares of their parents' property and could take their property into marriage and maintain control of it; if they had no children to inherit the property, it was returned to their natal family. Both men and women remarried if widowed. Men could have several wives who were treated equally. Ancestor worship was not common, and funerals were largely Buddhist affairs. Rather than bury the dead in coffins, families followed the Buddhist practice of cremation. Mourning, too, followed Buddhist customs and was generally limited to one hundred days.

To the early Chosŏn *tohak* scholars, all these practices needed to be reformed, and yangban should set the example for the rest of society. Some reforms were accepted relatively quickly. By the end of the fifteenth century, *yangban* were observing Confucian mourning prescriptions. This is seen in Ch'oe Pu's accounts of his travels in China after he was shipwrecked there in 1488. At the time he was in mourning for his father and made every effort to follow all the rules. By the late fifteenth century, *yangban* were also more often adopting nephews and other close patrilineal relatives when they had no sons, rather than letting a daughter inherit the family property. Remarriage of widows also declined markedly, perhaps in part due to a law issued in 1474 that barred sons of remarried widows from taking the civil service examinations. By the eighteenth century, Confucian ancestor worship had completely replaced Buddhist ceremonies for the deceased, and the Confucian pattern of patriarchal domination of the family reached its zenith. It took about three hundred years before Buddhist burial practices and beliefs were replaced at the lowest level of society.

Confucian promotion of patrilineal kinship led to the compilation of genealogies. At the beginning of the dynasty, women were listed in the family genealogy along with their brothers in the order of birth. By the eighteenth century, however, women were all listed after their brothers, and when they married, their names were expunged and were listed instead in their husband's genealogy as the daughter of their father. Their personal names were not even recorded.

One reason practices of this sort spread is that the lower levels of *yangban* society, whose members had no hopes of official careers, saw meticulous observance of Confucian family practices as a way to show their

MAKING COMPARISONS   Women's Situations

How similar were the situations of women in premodern China, Korea, and Japan? In broad terms, if East Asia and Europe in 1700 or 1800 are compared, women in each of the three countries of East Asia were probably more like each other than like women in England or France. In China, Korea, and Japan, men could take concubines and could divorce their wives relatively easily, but women could not divorce their husbands, and wives were expected to act deferentially in the presence of men. Girls did not go to schools with boys, and male literacy was substantially higher than female literacy. In all three countries, female entertainers were also a prominent part of social life; they associated with men of high rank but did not have high social standing themselves. In all three countries, too, there has been a tendency to see women's situations as declining over time, with the high point in the period between 650 and 1050.

Despite these broad similarities, the history of women's positions and gender ideology in China, Korea, and Japan differ in many significant ways. The Chinese family was patrilineal and patriarchal from as far back as historians can trace, but in Korea in the Silla and Koryŏ periods and Japan in the Nara and Heian periods, people traced kinship through both men and women, and it was more common for a newly married couple to live with the wife's family than the husband's. Over time, however, the family systems of both Korea and Japan moved in patrilineal and patriarchal directions. One reason for these shifts might be the influence of Chinese law codes, used as models in both Korea and Japan. Beyond that, in the case of medieval Japan, scholars have pointed to the shift in the structure of elite. In samurai families, property came to be transmitted to a single heir, marriages became more durable, and wives moved into their husbands' families. In the case of Korea, scholars have given more weight to the commitment of *yangban* to Confucianism and the conscious efforts made to instill such Confucian virtues as filial piety and wifely deference. Still, neither Korea nor Japan went as far as China in the patrilineal direction. In Korea, maternal kinship mattered, and the son of a *yangban* father and a lowborn mother could not take the civil service examinations.

The issue of women's literacy and writing is less tied to Confucianism and more to writing sys-

tems. With the development of the *kana* syllabary in the ninth century, it became much easier to write in Japanese. Japanese women were quick to make use of the new way to write, and Heian women wrote an astonishing number of books. The script is not the full story, however, as it continued to be available in later centuries, but women writers attracted less attention after the Heian period. In Korea, the invention of *han'gul* in the fifteenth century similarly made it possible to write in Korean. As in Japan, women predominated among earlier users of the script, and many more writings by women survive after the development of *han'gul* than before. In the Chinese case, by contrast, women stuck with the more literary way to write after writing in the vernacular became established. By Qing times, there were more women who published poetry than in any earlier period. By this time, ways to write that reflected speech more closely had been developed and were used to write fiction and drama, but women rarely wrote in these vernacular forms. Instead, they chose to use the more elegant classical language.

In the case of China, the impression that women's situations deteriorated is based above all on the spread of footbinding and growing pressure on widows not to remarry. Both footbinding and condemnation of widow remarriage can be traced back to the Song period, but it penetrated more deeply through society in later centuries. Footbinding was not copied by Korea or Japan, or even by most non-Han ethnic groups within China. Widow chastity, however, did become the ideal in Korea as Confucianism gained strength in the Chosŏn period. The government went so far as to ban the sons of remarried widows from taking the civil service examinations.

For all three countries, there is a large discrepancy between what didactic texts say women should do, how they are portrayed in fiction and anecdotes, and what their writings suggest. Before concluding that women were submissive in late traditional East Asia, it is useful to think of the highly varied women portrayed in literature, such as resourceful servants and overbearing mothers-in-law, not to mention malicious schemers, and the opportunities they seized to craft their own lives.

yangban credentials. But Confucians thought that these practices should be observed by all, and they encouraged moral tracts written in *han'gul* to spread them to those with less education.

Because Korean reformers were copying the system described in the Chinese classics, not the family system of China in their day, many differences between the two family systems persisted. Perhaps most significant, whereas in China distinctions in status between brothers had been greatly reduced from Han times on and by law all brothers were to receive equal shares of property, Korea adhered to the classical rules that discriminated against younger sons and, even more so, sons of concubines. To preserve their narrow notion of the purity of the male blood line in the family, Chosŏn Confucian purists relegated the sons of concubines to inferior status and banned them from taking the examinations.

How were women' lives affected by these changes in law and ideology? Women in *yangban* families were affected most, because their behavior impinged on the social standing of the family, putting them under more pressure to conform to such ideals as avoiding contact with men who were not relatives. Certainly women could still have considerable power within the family, especially older women who chose spouses for their children and had daughters-in-law subordinate to them.

Moreover, we should not assume that women always bought into the dominant ideology. Even in families where the men were Confucians, the women continued to engage in religious practices usually frowned on by men. They prayed to mountains, trees, and household gods. They regarded their dreams as predictive of the sex and capacity of a new child, and they had to take care to defend the family against bad omens around the home. A special ceremony might be held for cutting the umbilical cord, and unusual burials were practiced for women who died in labor or committed suicide to prevent their spirits from plaguing surviving members of the family. Women also attended religious festivals, such as the Tano Festival (see Color Plate 22).

In popular religion, women were active agents. They hired shamans, usually female ones (*mudang*), to go into a trance and communicate with the angry spirits of a woman's own dead parents and grandparents, who were believed to cause sickness and other problems among family members. Women, as well as many men, continued to believe in Buddhist ideas despite Confucian condemnation, particularly transmigration, karma, and punishment in Buddhist hell, especially when facing illness or impending death. Literature of the Chosŏn period as just discussed often depicts women as independent-minded and articulate.

SUMMARY

How different was Korea in 1800 than in 1392? Much, of course, had not changed. Korea was still unified under kings of the same dynasty who competed for power with the entrenched *yangban* elite. But in other regards, life in Korea had changed dramatically. Buddhism had been pushed to the sidelines as aggressive Confucianization prevailed. Although Korean food, houses, and clothing remained distinct, many other features of Korean life were strongly affected by the Confucianization campaigns, which changed such basic social practices as where people lived after marriage and how family property was transmitted. The economy had evolved from one rooted in control over land and people with very little use of money to one where coins circulated, trade was more prevalent, and slavery had declined substantially. By 1800 it was rare for *yangban* aristocrats to have military skills. The *yangban* stratum had steadily grown and gradually divided into a national elite who held office and local *yangban* with much less power. The national *yangban* elite in turn were divided into largely hereditary factions who competed for control of the court. In culture, while the most learned continued to acquire knowledge from China, it had become more common for intellectual leaders to develop ideas in original ways. Of particular significance in this regard was the development of a new script for writing Korean, making possible the development of literature in the vernacular language, which could be written and read by those who know no Chinese, including women.

CONNECTIONS

Europe Enters the Scene

TRADE ROUTES FLOURISHED BETWEEN NORTH-east and Southeast Asia long before European merchants and Catholic missionaries entered the South China Sea. Lured by Asian silks, ceramics, and spices, ships under the Portuguese flag were the first to risk the voyage in the early sixteenth century. The Spanish, British, and Dutch followed. In early seventeenth-century Japan, early eighteenth-century China, and early nineteenth-century Korea, rulers put a stop to missionary activities, albeit for different reasons. Trade between Europe and East Asia continued, but it was confined to Guangzhou in China and Nagasaki in Japan.

Hemmed in by Spain, Portugal relied on trade to fill royal coffers. At the beginning of the fifteenth century, Portuguese ships started exploring the west coast of Africa in search of gold. African gold then financed a voyage around the Cape of Good Hope in 1488. From there, the Portuguese established a colony at Goa on the west coast of India and followed Muslim and Indian trade routes to the Spice Islands of Indonesia. Once Queen Isabella and her husband, Ferdinand, captured Grenada, the last Muslim emirate in Spain, in 1492, they funded Christopher Columbus's voyage across the Atlantic in hopes of finding an alternative route to China. In 1494, the pope divided the world beyond Europe between Spain and Portugal. Spain's sphere included most of the Western Hemisphere except Brazil; Portugal went east.

China's contact with Portugal began in 1511 when Admiral Alfonso de Albuquerque captured the Chinese entrepôt of Malacca near the tip of the Malay Peninsula. With this as a base, the first official Portuguese embassy followed traders to China in 1517. The embassy behaved badly by refusing to conform to Chinese customs. Ship captains acted more like pirates than traders. Few Portuguese were willing to risk the long voyage in tiny ships around the Horn of Africa, across the wide expanse of the Indian Ocean, and through the Strait of Malacca to Macao. Most were neither officials dispatched from the Portuguese court nor explorers seeking glory and territory. What they had in limited resources and manpower had to go toward making a profit in competition with local traders (see Map C5.1).

Periodic prohibitions on maritime travel by Ming emperors at Beijing did not stop the Portuguese or seafaring people on the south China coast who made little distinction between trade, smuggling, and piracy. In 1521, the Ming tried to ban Portuguese from China. Two years later, an expeditionary force commissioned by the Portuguese king and charged with negotiating a friendship treaty defeated its mission by firing on Chinese warships near Guangzhou. In 1557, without informing Beijing, local Chinese officials decided that the way to regulate trade was to allow the Portuguese to build a trading post on uninhabited land near the mouth of the Pearl River. This the Portuguese called Macao. It became the first destination for all Europeans going to China until the nineteenth century, and it remained a Portuguese settlement until 1999.

The only significant products Portuguese traders brought to networks that had already developed in East Asia were firearms and New World crops such as corn, sweet potatoes, chili peppers, and tobacco. They reached Japan by accident in 1543 when a typhoon blew a ship with a mixed crew of Southeast Asians to a small island called Tanegashima. Among the goods exchanged for Japanese silver was the matchlock, a type of musket. The island's ruler ordered his retainers to study its operation and manufacture and distributed samples to more powerful mainland warlords. In 1570, Japanese troops deployed the Tanegashima matchlock in battle. In the meantime, Portuguese traders profited from the Ming ban on Japanese ships because they had raided the coast. The Portuguese carried 20 metric tons of Japanese silver a year to China in exchange for silk, sugar, medicine, and dye.

Trade between China and Europe increased in the late sixteenth century through an economic conjuncture that included the Americas following the discovery by Andrés de Urdaneta of a return route to Mexico. China needed foreign silver because its monetary system depended on it and domestic production had declined after 1430. China bought Japanese silver carried on Portuguese ships. China also absorbed 50 percent of silver mined in Mexico and Bolivia and carried in Spanish ships to Manila, founded in 1571 when Spain made the Philippines a colony. Disruptions in the flow of silver from Japan and the Western Hemisphere in 1639 contributed to the fall of the Ming. Spanish silver bought manufactured goods—Chinese silk, porcelain, and lacquer—that dominated the luxury trade in Europe and funded Spain's wars against multiple enemies for generations.

Portuguese merchants seeking profits in East Asia faced competition from their government when the Portuguese viceroy at Goa made the Japan trade a royal monopoly in 1550. The Ming approved because their officials also wanted to see trade regularized. Each year, a captain major appointed by the crown sent ships to Japan, where warlords competed to attract the ships to their ports. (See Color Plate 19.) The governor of Macao forbade the sending of goods to Japan on private ships via third-party countries, especially the Philippines. His directives were futile; Portuguese and Spanish traders with crews drawn from all over East and Southeast Asia found Manila too convenient to abandon.

Catholic missionaries seeking converts who followed the traders hoped to keep the religious wars that undermined the pope's spiritual hegemony secret from Asia. The first were Jesuits, from the order founded by Ignatius Loyola in 1534 to promote Catholic scholarship and combat the Protestant Reformation initiated by Martin Luther in 1517. Jesuits insisted that Christianizing China and Japan was not to be done with the intent to conquer, as had been the case in the Western Hemisphere. As individuals, they displayed a rare sensitivity to other cultures. They were willing to find universal principles of belief outside a European context, but they served an institution that refused to compromise with indigenous beliefs and practices. Despite the efforts of charismatic missionaries, the Catholic Church never gained the ascendancy in East Asia enjoyed by that other foreign religion, Buddhism.

The Jesuit priest Francis Xavier had worked in India and the Indies before China and Japan attracted his attention. After many misadventures, he landed on Satsuma in 1549. The Satsuma lord hoped that by treating Xavier well, he would attract the official Portuguese trading ships the next year. When the ships went instead to the island of Hirado, the lord expelled Xavier's party. Xavier traveled throughout western Japan as far as Kyoto, proselytizing wherever warlords gave permission. Asked why the Chinese knew nothing of Christianity if it was indeed an ancient and true religion, Xavier decided that Japan would become Christian only if China led the way. His efforts to enter China ended when he died on an island off the China coast in December 1552.

Jesuits and Dominicans soon joined the missionaries and converts Xavier left behind in Japan. In 1565, Louis Frois met Oda Nobunaga, who befriended the Jesuits to discomfort his Buddhist enemies. In 1580, Jesuits acquired Nagasaki from a warlord interested in promoting trade with Portuguese ships. In 1582, four young Kyushu samurai left Nagasaki for Lisbon and Rome, where they helped Jesuits get a papal bull that put Japan off limits to other orders. It proved to be ineffective, and quarrels between the Catholic orders over how best to present Christianity to East Asia damaged the missionaries' credibility in the eyes of Asian rulers.

Warlords trying to unite Japan under secular authority became increasingly suspicious of Christianity. If an absolute god demanded absolute loyalty, where did that leave the bonds between lord and retainer? Repression began in 1587 and intensified nine years later when the pilot of a ship wrecked on the Japanese coast allegedly pointed out that soldiers had followed Spanish missionaries to the Philippines. In 1614, Tokugawa Ieyasu decided that missionaries undermined the social order and were not essential to foreign trade. He ordered them expelled under threat of execution. He also tortured and killed Christian converts who refused to apostatize. Among the martyrs were Koreans who had been brought to Japan as slaves during Toyotomi Hideyoshi's invasions in the 1590s. The shogunate broke off relations with Catholic countries in 1624. The remaining Christians practiced their religion in secret by crafting statues of the Virgin Mary in the guise of Kannon, the Buddhist goddess of mercy.

Christianity arrived later in China. Not until 1583 did the Jesuit Matteo Ricci receive permission to move farther inland than Macao. Once he had educated himself in the style of Chinese literati, he set himself up in Nanjing. In 1601, he received tacit imperial permission to reside in Beijing. From him the Chi-

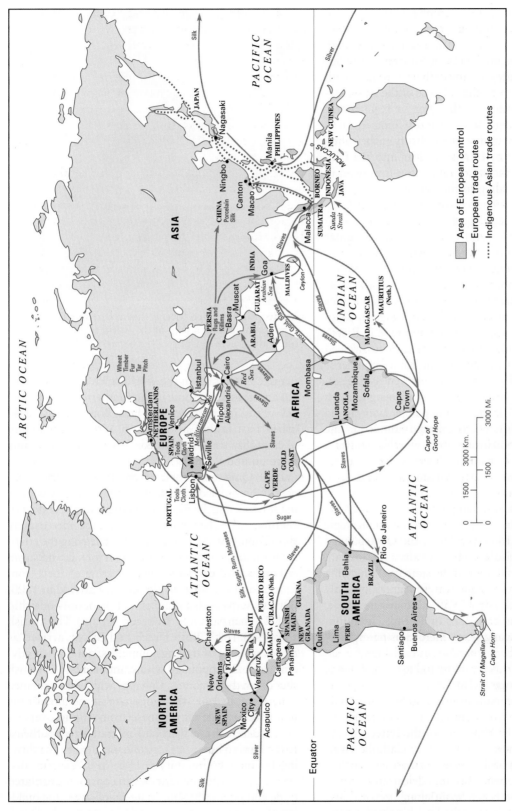

Map C5.1 Seaborne Trading Empires in the Sixteenth and Seventeenth Centuries

nese learned Western-style geography, astronomy, and Euclidean mathematics. In the years after Ricci's death in 1611, Jesuits regulated the Chinese lunar calendar. They suffered occasional harassment from xenophobic officials, but they retained their standing with Chinese literati through the collapse of the Ming Dynasty and the founding of the Qing in 1644. Catholic mendicant orders allowed into China in 1633 criticized Jesuits for aiming their efforts at the ruling class and trying to fit Christian ideas into the Chinese worldview rather than remaining European in approach and appealing to the masses.

Ricci and his Jesuit successors believed that Confucianism as a philosophy could be assimilated to monotheism. Confucianists and Christians shared similar concerns for morality and virtue. Rites of filial piety performed for the ancestors did not constitute a form of worship, which made them compatible with Christianity. Mendicant orders disagreed. In 1715, religious and political quarrels in Europe exacerbated by longstanding antagonism to the Jesuits resulted in Ricci's accommodation with Chinese practices being deemed heretical. Angry at this insult, the Kangxi emperor forbade all Christian missionary work in China, although he allowed Jesuits to remain in Beijing to assist with the calendar. A Jesuit portrait painter later proved popular at the courts of his son and grandson. The outcome of the controversy over whether converts should be allowed to maintain ancestral altars, exacerbated by accusations that missionaries had meddled in the imperial succession, led the Qing to view all Europeans with suspicion.

China's rulers also tried to limit trade for strategic reasons. Between 1655 and 1675, the Qing banned maritime trade to isolate Ming loyalists on Taiwan. In addition to official trade at the state level, the Qing permitted merchants to trade with foreigners, but only under tight control. After 1759, all maritime trade, whether with Southeast Asia or Europe, was confined to Canton (Guangzhou). Merchants put up with burdensome restrictions because in exchange for silver, China provided luxury items and tea, a bulk ware, introduced to Europe in 1607.

The profits to be made in East and Southeast Asia lured traders from Protestant countries following the religious wars of the latter half of the sixteenth century. Determined not to allow their Catholic rivals to dominate the world, Protestant nations sent explorers across the oceans. Britain's defeat of the Spanish Armada in 1588 began Spain's long decline. Early in the seventeenth century, the Dutch gained a com-

Matteo Ricci. Matteo Ricci is shown here in a French lithograph holding a map of the world to which he offers the crucified Christ. *(The Granger Collection)*

petitive advantage in the world spice trade by opening a faster sailing route in the southern Indian Ocean before turning northward to Java. Both nations established East India Companies in 1600 whose ability to capitalize trade far exceeded that of the merchants of Spain and Portugal.

Like Qing emperors, seventeenth-century Japanese shoguns tried to regulate foreign trade by confining it to specific harbors. In contrast to the sixteenth century, they also tried to prevent the increasingly short supply of precious metals from leaving the country by practicing import substitution for silk and sugar. A Dutch ship carrying a mixed crew of men from Europe and the Western Hemisphere arrived in 1600. (Of five ships with a crew of 461 men, only one ship and 25 men survived to reach Japan.) The British arrived in 1613. Both Dutch and British arrived as representatives of trading companies, not of their governments. Disappointed with scant profits, the British shut down their quarters. Unhappy with what it deemed smuggling, in 1635 the shogunate issued a maritime ban that forbade all Japanese from sailing overseas and ordered those who had migrated to Southeast Asia to return home or face permanent exile. The thriving Japanese community at Hoi An in Vietnam disappeared. In a further attempt to control unregulated trade and piracy, the shogunate later banned the building of oceangoing ships. In 1641, it ordered the Dutch to move to the artificial island called Dejima in Nagasaki bay originally constructed for the Portuguese. The annual visits by Dutch ships allowed an exchange of information, continued Japan's connections with Southeast Asia, and opened the door to Western science and medicine.

Korea proved inhospitable to merchants and missionaries alike. In the seventeenth century, British and Dutch traders made several attempts to insert their goods into the trade route between Korea and Japan that later developed into a triangular trade carrying Japanese copper, Korean ginseng, and Chinese silver. Memories of piracy, fear of unregulated trade that smacked of smuggling, and suspicion of European intentions led the government to reject them. Korean scholars in residence at the Chinese court read the Jesuits' religious, scientific, and mathematical treatises and took them back to Korea, where they attracted a small following for Catholic Christianity. The converts soon became embroiled in the factional infighting that characterized politics in eighteenth-century Korea and suffered severe persecution starting in 1791. No European missionary or merchant tried to visit Korea until three French priests landed illegally in 1836–1837. The Korean court had them and their converts executed in 1839 for spreading the "evil teaching" that ran counter to the dictates of filial piety.

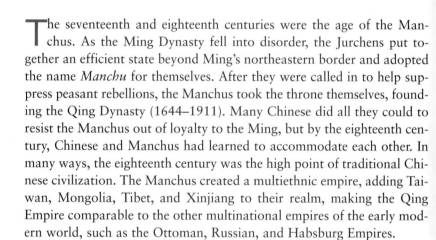

The Creation of the Manchu Empire (1600–1800)

The seventeenth and eighteenth centuries were the age of the Manchus. As the Ming Dynasty fell into disorder, the Jurchens put together an efficient state beyond Ming's northeastern border and adopted the name *Manchu* for themselves. After they were called in to help suppress peasant rebellions, the Manchus took the throne themselves, founding the Qing Dynasty (1644–1911). Many Chinese did all they could to resist the Manchus out of loyalty to the Ming, but by the eighteenth century, Chinese and Manchus had learned to accommodate each other. In many ways, the eighteenth century was the high point of traditional Chinese civilization. The Manchus created a multiethnic empire, adding Taiwan, Mongolia, Tibet, and Xinjiang to their realm, making the Qing Empire comparable to the other multinational empires of the early modern world, such as the Ottoman, Russian, and Habsburg Empires.

Many historians have been attracted to research on the seventeenth and eighteenth centuries because it provides a baseline of traditional China before the rapid changes of the modern era. Besides the usual questions of why the Ming fell and the Qing succeeded, scholars have recently been asking questions about the Manchus themselves. Who were they, and how did their history shape the way they ruled China? How did they compel the allegiance of peoples of different backgrounds? How did they manage to give traditional Chinese political forms a new lease on life? Other historians have focused more on what was going on among the Chinese during these two crucial centuries. Was population growth a sign of prosperity? Or was it beginning to cause problems? How did scholars respond to Manchu rule?

THE MANCHUS

The Manchus were descended from the Jurchens, who had ruled north China during the Jin Dynasty (1127–1234). Although they had not maintained the written language that the Jin had created, they had maintained their hairstyle. A Manchu man shaved the front of his head and wore the rest of his hair in a long braid (called a queue). The language the Manchus spoke belongs to the Tungus family, making it close to some of the languages spoken in nearby Siberia and distantly related to Korean and Japanese.

During the Ming Dynasty, the Manchus had lived in dispersed communities in what is loosely called Manchuria (the modern provinces of Liaoning, Jilin, and Heilongjiang). In the more densely populated southern part of Manchuria, Manchus lived in close contact with Mongols, Koreans, and Chinese, the latter especially in the Ming prefecture of Liaodong (see Map 16.1). The Manchus were not nomads but rather hunters, fishers, and farmers. Like the Mongols, they had a tribal social structure and were excellent horsemen and archers. Also like the Mongols, their society was strongly hierarchical, with elites and slaves. Slaves, often Korean or Chinese, were generally acquired through capture. From the Mongols, the Manchus had adopted Lamaist Buddhism, originally from Tibet, and it coexisted with their native shamanistic religion. Manchu shamans were men or women who had experienced a spiritual death and rebirth and as a consequence could travel to and influence the world of the spirits.

Both the Chosŏn Dynasty in Korea and the Ming Dynasty in China welcomed diplomatic missions from Manchu chieftains, seeing them as a counterbalance to the Mongols. Written communication was frequently in Mongolian, the lingua franca of the region. Along the border with the Ming were officially approved markets where Manchus brought horses, furs, honey, and ginseng to exchange for Chinese tea, cotton, silk, rice, salt, and tools. By the 1580s, there were five such markets that convened monthly, and unofficial trade occurred as well.

The Manchus credited their own rise to Nurhaci (1559–1626), who in 1583 at age twenty-four became the leader of one group of Manchus. Over the next few decades, he was able to expand his territories, in the process not only uniting the Manchus but also creating a social-political-military organization that brought together Manchus, Mongols, and Chinese.

When the Korean Sin Chung-il traveled to Nurhaci's headquarters in 1595–1596, he encountered many small Jurchen settlements, most no larger than twenty households, supported by fishing, hunting for pelts, collecting pine nuts or ginseng, or growing crops such as wheat, millet, and barley. Villages were often at odds with each other over resources, and men did not leave their villages without arming themselves with bows and arrows or swords. Interspersed among these Manchu settlements were groups of nomadic Mongols who lived in yurts in open areas. Sin observed that Nurhaci had in his employ men from the Ming territory of Liaodong who could speak both Chinese and Manchu and could write in Chinese. Nurhaci's knowledge of China and Chinese ways was not entirely secondhand, however. In 1590, he had led an embassy to Beijing, and the next year he offered to join the Ming effort to repel the Japanese invasion of Korea. Nurhaci and his children married Mongols as well as Manchus, and these marriages cemented alliances.

Early Manchu Rulers and Their Reign Periods	
Nurhaci (Tianming)	1616–1626
Hong Taiji (Tiancong)	1627–1635
(Chongde)	1636–1643
Fulin (Shunzhi)	1644–1661
Xuanye (Kangxi)	1662–1722
Yinzhen (Yongzheng)	1723–1735
Hongli (Qianlong)	1736–1795

Like Chinggis, who had reorganized his armies to reduce the importance of tribal affiliations, Nurhaci created a new social basis for his armies in units called *banners*. Each banner was made up of a set of military companies but included the families and slaves of the soldiers as well. Each company had a captain whose position was hereditary. Many of the commanding officers were drawn from Nurhaci's own lineage. Over time new companies and new banners were formed, and by 1644 there were twenty-four banners (eight each Manchu, Mongol, and Chinese banners). When new groups of Manchus were defeated, they were distributed among several banners to lessen their potential for subversion.

In 1616, Nurhaci declared war on the Ming Empire by calling himself khan of the revived Jin Dynasty and listing his grievances against the Ming. In 1621 his forces overran Liaodong and incorporated it into

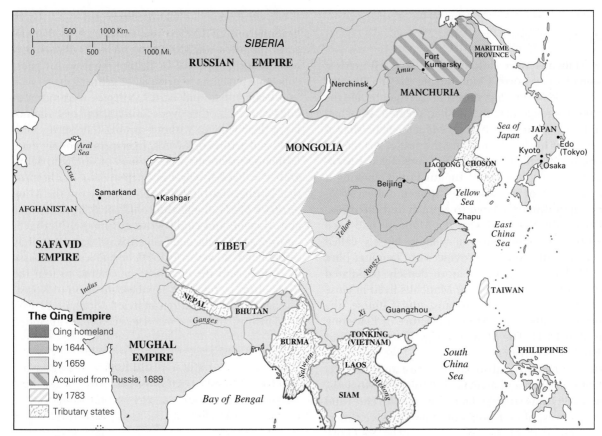

Map 16.1   **Manchu Empire at Its Height**

his state. After Nurhaci died in 1626, his son Hong Taiji succeeded him. In consolidating the Jin state, then centered on Mukden, Hong Taiji grudgingly made use of Chinese bureaucrats, but his goal was to replace them with a multiethnic elite equally competent in warfare and documents. In 1636, Hong Taiji renamed his state Qing ("pure"). When he died in 1643 at age forty-six, his brother Dorgon was made regent for his five-year-old son, Fulin, the Shunzhi emperor (r. 1643–1661).

The distinguished Ming general Wu Sangui (1612–1678), a native of Liaodong, was near the eastern end of the Great Wall when he heard that the rebel Li Zicheng had captured Beijing. Dorgon proposed to Wu that they join forces and liberate Beijing. Wu opened the gates of the Great Wall to let the Manchus in, and within a couple of weeks they had occupied Beijing. When the Manchus made clear that they intended to conquer the rest of the country and take the throne themselves, Wu joined forces with them, as did many other Chinese generals.

MING LOYALISM

When word of the fall of Beijing to the Manchus reached the Yangzi valley, Ming officials selected a Ming prince to succeed to the throne and shifted the capital to Nanjing, the Ming secondary capital. They were thus following the strategy that had allowed the Song Dynasty to continue to flourish after it had lost the north in 1126. The Ming court offered to buy off the Manchus, just as the Song had bought off the Jurchens. Dorgon, however, saw no need to check his ambitions. He sent Wu Sangui and several Manchu generals to pursue the rebel forces across north China. Li Zicheng was eliminated in 1645, Zhang Xianzhong in 1647.

At the same time, Qing forces set about trying to defeat the Ming forces in the south. Quite a few able officials joined the Ming cause, but leadership was not well coordinated. Shi Kefa, a scholar-official who had risen to minister of war in Nanjing, took charge of defense and stationed his army at Yangzhou. Many other generals, however, defected to the Manchu side, and their soldiers were incorporated into the Qing armies. As the Qing forces moved south, many local officials opened the gates of their cities and surrendered. Shi Kefa refused to surrender Yangzhou, and a five-day battle ensued. The Manchu general was so angered at Shi's resistance that he unleashed his army to take revenge on the city, slaughtering hundreds of thousands. As cities in the south fell, large numbers of Ming loyalists committed suicide, their wives, mothers, and daughters frequently joining them.

In the summer of 1645, the Manchu command ordered all Chinese serving in its armies to shave the front of their heads in the Manchu fashion, presumably to make it easier to recognize which side they were on. Soon this order was extended to all Chinese men, a measure that aroused deep resentment and made it easier for the Ming loyalists to organize resistance. When those newly conquered by the Qing refused to shave their hair, Manchu commanders felt justified in ordering the slaughter of defiant cities such as Jiading, Changshu, and Jiangyin. Still, Ming loyalist resistance continued long after little hope remained. The Manchus did not defeat the two main camps until 1661–1662, and even then Zheng Chenggong (Koxinga) was able to hold out in Taiwan until 1683.

Ming loyalism also took less militant forms. Several leading thinkers of this period had time to think and write because they refused to serve the Qing. Their critiques of the Ming and its failings led to searching inquiries into China's heritage of dynastic rule. Huang Zongxi (1610–1695) served the Ming resistance court at Nanjing and followed it when it had to retreat, but after 1649 he lived in retirement at his home in Zhejiang province. The Manchu conquest was so traumatic an event that he reconsidered many of the basic tenets of Chinese political order. He came to the conclusion that the Ming's problems were not minor ones like inadequate supervision of eunuchs but much more major ones, such as the imperial institution itself.

Gu Yanwu (1613–1682) participated in the defense of his native city, then watched his mother starve herself rather than live under Manchu rule. He traveled across north China in search of a better understanding of Ming weaknesses, looking into economic topics Confucian scholars had rarely studied in depth, such as banking, mining, and farming. He had only disdain for scholars who wasted their time on empty speculation or literary elegance when there were so many practical problems awaiting solution. He thought that the Ming had suffered from overcentralization and advocated greater local autonomy.

A third example is Wang Fuzhi (1619–1692). He had passed the provincial exams under the Ming, but marauding rebels made it impossible for him to get to Beijing to take the *jinshi* exams in 1642. After Beijing fell to the Manchus two years later, Wang joined the resistance. He raised troops in his native Hunan province and held a minor post at the court of the Ming pretender for a while, but he fell victim to factional strife and in 1650 withdrew to live as a retired scholar. Wang saw an urgent need not only to return Confucianism to its roots, but also to protect Chinese civilization from the "barbarians." He insisted that it was as important to distinguish Chinese from barbarians as it was to distinguish superior men from petty men. It is natural for rulers to protect their followers from intruders: "Now even the ants have rulers who preside over the territory of their nests, and when red ants or flying white ants penetrate their gates, the ruler organizes all his own kind into troops to bite and kill the intruders, drive them far away from the anthill, and prevent foreign interference."[1] The Ming rulers had failed in this basic responsibility.

THE QING AT ITS HEIGHT

For more than a century, China was ruled by just three rulers, each of whom was hard working, talented, and committed to making the Qing Dynasty a success. The policies and institutions they put in place gave China a respite from war and disorder, and the Chinese population seems to have nearly doubled during this period, from between 150 and 175 million to between 300 and 325 million. Population growth during the course of the eighteenth century has been attributed to many factors: global warming that extended the growing season; expanded use of New World crops; slowing of the spread of new diseases that had accompanied the sixteenth-century expansion of global traffic; and the efficiency of the

---

1. W. Theodore de Bary and Richard Lufrano, *Sources of Chinese Tradition from 1600 Through the Twentieth Century* (New York: Columbia University Press, 2000), p. 35.

Dinnerware. China turned out enormous quantities of plates, cups, and other dishes for export to Western countries. This set, made in the 1780s, includes cups for both tea and coffee. The design on the dishes would have been specially ordered by the importer. *(Metropolitan Museum of Art, Bequest of James Woodward, 1910. Photograph © 2002 The Metropolitan Museum of Art.)*

Qing government in providing relief in times of famine. Some scholars have recently argued that China's overall standard of living in the mid-eighteenth century was comparable to Europe's and that the standards of China's most developed regions, such as the Jiangnan region, compared favorably to the most developed regions of Europe at the time, such as England and the Netherlands. Life expectancy, food consumption, and even facilities for transportation were at similar levels (see **Biography: Jiang Chun, Salt Merchant**).

Kangxi

After the Shunzhi emperor died of smallpox (which struck many Manchus after they settled in Beijing), one of his sons who had already survived the disease was selected to succeed him. Known as the Kangxi emperor (r. 1661–1722), he lived to see the Qing Empire firmly established.

The Kangxi emperor proved adept at meeting the expectations of both the Chinese and Manchu elites. At age fourteen, he announced that he would begin ruling on his own and had his regent imprisoned. He could speak, read, and write Chinese and appreciated the value of persuading educated Chinese that the Manchus had a legitimate claim to the Mandate of Heaven. Most of the political institutions of the Ming Dynasty had been taken over relatively unchanged, including the examination system, and the Kangxi emperor worked to attract Ming loyalists who had been unwilling to serve the Qing. He undertook a series of tours of the south, where resistance had been strongest, and held a special exam to select men to compile the official history of the Ming Dynasty.

The main military challenge the Kangxi emperor faced was the revolt of Wu Sangui and two other Chinese generals who in the early years of the conquest had been given vast tracts of land in the south as rewards for joining the Qing. Wu was made, in effect, satrap of Yunnan and Guizhou, and it was his armies that had pursued the last Ming pretender into Burma. When the Qing began to curb the power of these generals in 1673, Wu declared himself the ruler of an independent state, and the other two "feudatories" joined him. The south was not yet fully reconciled to Qing rule, but Wu, as a turncoat himself, did not attract a large following. Although it took eight years, the military structure that the Qing had put together proved strong enough to defeat this challenge. At the conclusion of these campaigns, Taiwan, where the last of the Ming loyalists had held out, was made part of Fujian province, fully incorporating it into China proper.

By annexing Mongolia, the Kangxi emperor made sure the Qing Dynasty would not have the northern border problems the Ming had faced (see Map 16.1). In 1696 he led an army of eighty thousand men into Mongolia, and within a few years Manchu supremacy was accepted there. Qing forces were equipped with cannons and muskets, giving them military superiority over the Mongols, who were armed with bows and arrows only. They thus could dominate the steppe cheaply, effectively ending two thousand years of northern border defense problems.

The Qing also asserted its presence in Tibet. This came about after a group of Western Mongols tried to find a new place for themselves in Tibet. The army the Qing sent after them occupied Lhasa in 1718. In the 1720s, the Qing presence in Tibet was made firm with the establishment of a permanent garrison of banner soldiers. By this time, the Qing Empire was coming into proximity of the expanding Russian

BIOGRAPHY Jiang Chun, Salt Merchant

Jiang Chun's (1725–1793) family originally came from Huizhou in Anhui, a place famous for its merchant families. His great-great-grandfather moved to Yangzhou to enter the salt trade centered there. Salt was a special commodity, as the government claimed a monopoly over it and licensed merchants to transport and sell it. Salt merchants could grow exceptionally rich; it has been estimated that the twenty to thirty head merchants could pocket 50,000 to 100,000 taels of silver a year from the salt business alone. Government connections made possible the great wealth of the salt merchants, and the government regularly called on them to contribute huge sums for disaster relief, repair of the waterworks, or visits of the emperor.

As the Jiang family grew rich, many of its men pursued scholarly or official careers (often gaining positions through purchase, a legal but less prestigious route). But in each generation one man, like Jiang Chun, served as one of the head salt merchants. Although there are several biographical sketches of Jiang Chun, they say little about him as a merchant. Rather they concentrate on his social life; his accomplishments in poetry, archery, and cricket-raising; and the honors he received.

A description of the great sites of Yangzhou written in 1795 provides an elaborate description of Jiang Chun's garden, naming its halls, ponds, towers, terraces, and so on. Besides discussing Jiang and his talented kinsmen, the author added notes on thirty-nine men of talent in his entourage, including scholars, painters, poets, calligraphers, physicians, musicians, connoisseurs able to authenticate antiquities, craftsmen-painters good at portraits, gardeners expert in pruning plum trees, and the architects who had designed the buildings in his garden. Some were relatives through marriage. Others had lived in different buildings of his estate for years, sometimes decades. Jiang is also said to have kept two opera troupes, one that specialized in Kunqu, the other in Huapu, which was performed in the local Yangzhou accent. His Kunqu troupe was said to be one of the "seven great troupes of Yangzhou." Jiang once organized an archery contest in his Garden of Pure Fragrance. The prominent courtesan Su Gaosen was among the guests and scored three bull's-eyes in a row, an event other guests celebrated in poems.

The Qianlong emperor made six visits to Yangzhou on his "southern tours of inspection" (1751, 1757, 1762, 1765, 1780, and 1784). Jiang met him every time, and during the last four visits, Jiang hosted the imperial party at one or both of his famous gardens. In fact, the name "Garden of Pure Fragrance" was chosen by Qianlong. The emperor wrote out the three characters of the name, which Jiang then had carved in stone and placed in a special pavilion. On one of his visits, Qianlong put Jiang's seven-year-old son on his lap, patted his head, and took off an ornamental purse and gave it to the boy, which Jiang's biographer Yuan Mei considered an exceptional honor. In 1765, Qianlong gave Jiang Chun four sable skin pelts and two ornamental silk pouches. Jiang Chun's thank you note has been preserved in the archives. Qianlong must have had some discussions of practical matters with Jiang Chun, as he once told the new director-general handling transport of tax grain to consult the experienced and knowledgeable Jiang Chun if he needed any advice.

In 1768 the top salt administration officials were accused of gross embezzlement and cashiered. Jiang Chun, like the other salt merchants, had to go to the capital to testify during the investigation. Qianlong, Yuan Mei tells us, was impressed by Jiang Chun's demeanor and made sure that the charges against him were dismissed. Nevertheless, by 1771, Jiang was out of money. Qianlong, we are told, personally lent him 500,000 taels as working capital (to be repaid with 10 percent annual interest).

None of Jiang Chun's boys or girls lived to adulthood. He adopted his brother's son, but that boy also died young. When Chun was on his deathbed at age sixty-nine, he selected another nephew to succeed him. After Jiang Chun died, on Qianlong's suggestion, the Yangzhou salt merchants purchased his famous garden to use as a clubhouse. The 50,000 taels they paid for the garden became his adopted son's main source of income.

Empire. In 1689 the Manchu and the Russian rulers approved a treaty—written in Russian, Manchu, Chinese, and Latin—defining their borders in Manchuria and regulating trade. Another treaty in 1727 allowed a Russian ecclesiastical mission to reside in Beijing and a caravan to make a trip from Russia to Beijing once every three years. The Russians were especially interested in securing a steady supply of tea.

The Kangxi emperor took a personal interest in the European Jesuit priests who served at court as astronomers and cartographers and translated many European works into Chinese. However, when the pope sided with the Dominican and Franciscan orders in China who opposed allowing converts to maintain ancestral altars (known as the "rites controversy"), he objected strongly to the pope's issuing directives about how Chinese should behave. He outlawed Christian missionaries, though he did allow Jesuit scientists and painters to remain in Beijing.

The Kangxi emperor's heir, Yinzheng, ruled for twelve years as the Yongzheng emperor (r. 1723–1735), taking the throne when he was forty-five years old. A hard-working ruler, he tightened central control over the government. He oversaw a rationalization of the tax structure, substituting new levies for a patchwork of taxes and fees.

Qianlong

The Yongzheng emperor's heir, Hongli, the Qianlong emperor (r. 1736–1795), benefited from his father's fiscal reforms, and during his reign, the Qing government regularly ran surpluses. It was during the Qianlong reign that the Qing Empire was expanded to its maximum extent, with the addition of Chinese Turkestan (the modern province of Xinjiang). Both the Han and Tang Dynasties had stationed troops in the region, exercising a loose suzerainty, but neither Song nor Ming had tried to control the area. The Qing won the region in the 1750s through a series of campaigns against Uighur and Dzungar Mongol forces. Like Tibet, loosely annexed a few decades earlier, this region was ruled lightly. The local population kept their own religious leaders and did not have to wear the queue.

The Qianlong emperor put much of his energy into impressing his subjects with his magnificence. He understood that the Qing capacity to hold the empire together rested on their ability to speak in the political and religious idioms of those they ruled. Besides Manchu and Chinese, he learned to converse in Mongolian, Uighur, Tibetan, and Tangut and ad-

dressed envoys in their own languages. He was as much a patron of Lamaist Buddhism as of Chinese Confucianism. He initiated a massive project to translate the Tibetan Buddhist canon into Mongolian and Manchu. He also had huge multilingual dictionaries compiled. He had the child Dalai Lamas raised and educated in Beijing. He made much of the Buddhist notion of the "wheel-turning king" (cakravartin), the ruler who through his conquests moves the world toward the next stage in universal salvation (see Color Plate 20).

To demonstrate to the Chinese scholar-official elite that he was a sage emperor, Qianlong worked on affairs of state from dawn until early afternoon, when he turned to reading, painting, and calligraphy. He took credit for writing over forty-two thousand poems and ninety-two books of prose. He inscribed his own poetry on hundreds of masterpieces of Chinese painting and calligraphy that he had gathered into the palace collections. He especially liked works of fine craftsmanship, and his taste influenced artistic styles of the day. The Qianlong emperor was ostentatiously devoted to his mother, visiting her daily and tending to her comfort with all the devotion of the most filial Chinese son. He took several tours down the Grand Canal to the Jiangnan area, in part to emulate his grandfather and in part to entertain his mother. Many of his gestures were costly. His southern tours cost ten times what the Kangxi emperor's had and included the construction of temporary palaces and triumphal arches.

For all of these displays of Chinese virtues, the Qianlong emperor still was not fully confident that the Chinese supported his rule, and he was quick to act on any suspicion of anti-Manchu thoughts or actions (see **Documents: Fang Bao's "Random Notes from Prison"**). After more than thirty years on the throne, when rumors reached the Qianlong emperor that sorcerers were "stealing souls" by clipping the ends of men's queues, he suspected a seditious plot and had his officials interrogate men under torture until they found more and more evidence of a nonexistent plot. A few years after that episode, the Qianlong emperor carried out a huge literary inquisition. During the compilation of the *Complete Books of the Four Treasuries*, an effort to catalogue nearly all books in China, he began to suspect that some governors were holding back books with seditious content. He ordered full searches for books with disparaging references to the Manchus or previous alien conquerors. Sometimes passages were omitted or rewritten, but when the entire book was offensive, it was destroyed. So thorough was the proscription that no copies survive of more than two thousand titles.

The Qianlong emperor lived into his eighties, but his political judgment began to decline in his sixties when he began to favor a handsome and intelligent young imperial bodyguard named Heshen. Heshen was rapidly promoted to posts normally held by experienced civil officials, including posts with power over revenue and civil service appointments. When the emperor did nothing to stop Heshen's blatant corruption, officials began to worry that he was becoming senile. By this time, uprisings in several parts of the country were proving difficult to suppress. Heshen supplied the Qianlong emperor with rosy reports of the progress in suppressing the rebellions, all the while pocketing much of the military appropriations himself.

The Qianlong emperor abdicated in 1795 in order not to rule longer than his grandfather, the Kangxi emperor, but he continued to dominate court until he died in 1799 at age eighty-nine.

The Banner System

The Kangxi, Yongzheng, and Qianlong emperors used the banner system to maintain military control and preserve the Manchus' privileges. In the first few decades of the Qing, as the country was pacified, banner forces were settled across China in garrisons, usually within the walls of a city. All the Chinese who lived in the northern half of Beijing were forced out to clear the area for bannermen, and Beijing became very much a Manchu city. In other major cities, such as Hangzhou, Nanjing, Xi'an, and Taiyuan, large sections were cleared for the banners' use. The bannermen became in a sense a hereditary occupational caste, ranked above others in society, whose members were expected to devote themselves to service to the state. They were also expected to live apart from nonbanner Chinese and were not allowed to intermarry with them.

Outside the cities, lands were expropriated to provide support for the garrisons, some 2 million acres altogether, with the densest area in the region around Beijing. In China proper, bannermen did not cultivate the fields (as they had in Manchuria) but rather lived off stipends from the rents, paid part in silver and part in grain. The dynasty supported banner soldiers and their families from cradle to grave, with special allocations for travel, weddings, and funerals. Once the conquest was complete, the banner popu-

Imperial Bodyguard Zhanyinbao. Dated 1760, this life-size portrait was done by a court artist in the European-influenced style favored by the Qianlong emperor. *(The Metropolitan Museum of Art, The Dillon Fund, 1986 [1986.206])*

lation grew faster than the need for soldiers, so within a couple of generations, there were not enough positions in the banner armies for all adult males in the banners. Yet bannermen were not allowed to pursue occupations other than soldier or official. As a consequence, many led lives of forced idleness, surviving on stipends paid to relatives. By the time of the Qianlong emperor, this had become enough of a problem that he had most of the Chinese bannermen removed from the banner system and reclassified as commoners, increasing the Manchu dominance of the banner population.

Bannermen had facilitated entry into government service. Special quotas for Manchus allowed them to gain more than 5 percent of the *jinshi* degrees, even though they never exceeded 1 percent of the population. Advancement was also easier for bannermen, since many posts, especially in Beijing, were reserved for them, including half of all the top posts. In the

DOCUMENTS

Fang Bao's "Random Notes from Prison"

As more and more varied types of sources survive, it becomes possible to get better glimpses of the less pleasant sides of life. The ordeal of judicial confinement was hardly new to the eighteenth century, but it was not until then that we have so vivid a depiction of it as that provided by Fang Bao (1668–1749). In 1711 he and his family members were arrested because he had written a preface for the collected works of one of his friends whose works had just been condemned for language implying support for revival of the Ming Dynasty. After Fang spent two years in prison, he was pardoned and went on to hold a series of literary posts. Despite this brush with imperial censorship, Fang was willing in his account of his time in prison to point to the inhumane way people not yet found guilty of a crime were treated and the corruption of prison personnel, who demanded cash in exchange for better treatment.

In the prison there were four old cells. Each cell had five rooms. The jail guards lived in the center with a window in the front of their quarters for light. At the end of this room there was another opening for ventilation. There were no such windows for the other four rooms and yet more than two hundred prisoners were always confined there. Each day toward dusk, the cells were locked and the odor of the urine and excrement would mingle with that of the food and drink. Moreover, in the coldest months of the winter, the poor prisoners had to sleep on the ground and when the spring breezes came everyone got sick. The established rule in the prison was that the door would be unlocked only at dawn. During the night, the living and the dead slept side by side with no room to turn their bodies and this is why so many people became infected. Even more terrible was that robbers, veteran criminals and murderers who were imprisoned for serious offenses had strong constitutions and only one or two out of ten would be infected and even so they would recover immediately. Those who died from the malady were all light offenders or sequestered witnesses who would not normally be subjected to legal penalties.

I said: "In the capital there are the metropolitan prefectural prison and the censorial prisons of the five wards. How is it then that the Board of Punishment's prison has so many prisoners?" [My fellow prisoner, the

middle and lower ranks of the Beijing bureaucracy, Manchus greatly outnumbered Chinese. One study suggests that about 70 percent of the metropolitan agencies' positions were reserved for bannermen and less then 20 percent for Chinese (the rest were unspecified). In the provinces, Manchus did not dominate in the same way, except at the top level of governors and governors-general, where they held about half the posts.

Bannermen had legal privileges as well. They fell under the jurisdiction of imperial commissioners, not the local magistrate or prefect. If both a Chinese and a Manchu were brought into court to testify, the Chinese was required to kneel before the magistrate, but the Manchu could stand. If each was found guilty of the same crime, the Manchu would receive a lighter punishment—for instance, wearing the cangue (a large wooden collar) for sixty days instead of being exiled for life.

Despite the many privileges given to Manchu bannermen, impoverishment of the banner population quickly became a problem. Although the government from time to time forgave all bannermen's debts, many went bankrupt. Company commanders sometimes sold off banner land to provide stipends, which made it more difficult to provide support thereafter. The Qianlong emperor also tried resettling Manchus back in Manchuria, but those used to urban life in China rarely were willing to return to farming, and most sneaked back as soon as possible.

magistrate] Mr. Du answered: ". . . The chiefs and deputy heads of the Fourteen Bureaus like to get new prisoners; the clerks, prison officials, and guards all benefit from having so many prisoners. If there is the slightest pretext or connection they use every method to trap new prisoners. Once someone is put into the prison his guilt or innocence does not matter. The prisoner's hands and feet are shackled and he is put in one of the old cells until he can bear the suffering no more. Then he is led to obtain bail and permitted to live outside the jail. His family's property is assessed to decide the payment and the officials and clerks all split it. Middling households and those just above exhaust their wealth to get bail. Those families somewhat less wealthy seek to have the shackles removed and to obtain lodging [for the prisoner relative] in the custody sheds outside the jail. This also costs tens of silver taels. As for the poorest prisoners or those with no one to rely on, their shackles are not loosened at all and they are used as examples to warn others. Sometimes cellmates guilty of serious crimes are bailed out but those guilty of small crimes and the innocent suffer the most poisonous abuse. They store up their anger and indignation, fail to eat or sleep normally, are not treated with medicine, and when they get sick they often die.

"I have humbly witnessed our Emperor's virtuous love for all beings which is as great as that of the sages of the past ages. Whenever he examines the documents related to a case, he tries to find life for those who should die. But now it has come to this [state of affairs] for the innocent. A virtuous gentleman might save many lives if he were to speak to the Emperor saying: 'Leaving aside those prisoners sentenced to death or exiled to border regions for great crimes, should not small offenders and those involved in a case but not convicted be placed in a separate place without chaining their hands and feet?'". . .

My cellmate Old Zhu, Young Yu, and a certain government official named Seng who all died of illness in prison should not have been heavily punished. There was also a certain person who accused his own son of unfiliality. The [father's] neighbors [involved in the case only as witnesses] were all chained and imprisoned in the old cells. They cried all night long. I was moved by this and so I made inquiries. Everyone corroborated this account and so I am writing this document.

Source: From Pei-kai Cheng, Michael Lestz, and Jonathon D. Spence, *The Search for Modern China: A Documentary Collection* (New York: Norton, 1999), pp. 55–58, slightly modified.

Within a generation of settling in China proper, the banner population were using the Chinese dialect of the Beijing area as their common language. The Qing emperors repeatedly called on the Manchus to study both spoken and written Manchu, but it became a second language learned at school rather than a primary language. Other features of Manchu culture were more easily preserved, such as the use of personal names alone to refer to people. (Manchus had names for families and clans but did not use them as part of their personal names.)

The elements of Manchu culture most important to the state were their martial traditions and their skill as horsemen and archers. Life in the cities and long stretches of peace took a toll on these skills, despite the best efforts of the emperors to inspire martial spirit. The Qianlong emperor himself was fully literate in Chinese, but he discouraged the Manchu bannermen from developing interests in Chinese culture. He knew the history of the Jin Dynasty and the problems the Jurchens had faced with soldiers living in China taking up Chinese ways, and he did everything he could think of to prevent this. Although the Qing court was as opulent as any other in Chinese history, the emperor tried to convince the bannermen that frugality was a Manchu characteristic, to be maintained if they were not to lose their ethnic identity.

Perhaps because they were favored in so many ways, the bannermen proved a very loyal service elite. Unlike their counterparts in other large empires, the banner armies never turned on the ruling house or used the resources that had been assigned to them to challenge central authority.

CONTACTS WITH EUROPE

The Qing regulated its relations with countries beyond its borders through a diplomatic system modeled on the Ming one. Countries like Korea, Ryukyu, Japan, Vietnam, and many of the other states of Southeast Asia sent envoys to the court at Beijing. Europeans were not full players in this system, but they had a marginal presence.

Trading contacts with Europe were concentrated at Guangzhou in the far south (see **Connection: Europe Enters the Scene**). Soon after 1600, the Dutch East India Company had largely dislodged the Spanish and Portuguese from the trade with China, Japan, and the East Indies. Before long, the British East India Company began to compete with the Dutch for the spice trade. In the seventeenth century, the British and Dutch sought primarily porcelains and silk, but in the eighteenth century, tea became the commodity in most demand. By the end of the century, tea made up 80 percent of Chinese exports to Europe.

In the early eighteenth century, China enjoyed a positive reputation among the educated in Europe. China was the source of prized luxuries: tea, silk, porcelain, cloisonné, wallpaper, and folding fans. The Manchu emperors were seen as wise and benevolent rulers. Voltaire wrote of the rationalism of Confucianism and saw advantages to the Chinese political system as rulers did not put up with parasitical aristocrats or hypocritical priests.

By the end of the eighteenth century, British merchants were dissatisfied with the restrictions imposed on trade by the Qing government. The Qing, like the Ming before it, specified where merchants of particular countries could trade, and the Europeans were to trade only in Guangzhou, even though tea was grown mostly in the Yangzi valley, adding the cost of transporting it south to the price the foreign merchants had to pay. The merchants in Guangzhou who dealt with Western merchants formed their own guild, and the Qing government made them guarantee that the European merchants obeyed Qing rules. In the system as it evolved, the Europeans had to pay cash for goods purchased and were forbidden to enter the walled city of Guangzhou, ride in sedan chairs, bring women or weapons into their quarters, and learn Chinese.

As British purchases of tea escalated, the balance of trade became more lopsided, but British merchants could not find goods Chinese merchants would buy from them. The British government also was dissatisfied. It was becoming suspicious of the British East India Company, which had made great fortunes from its trade with China, and wanted to open direct diplomatic relations with China in part as a way to curb the company. To accomplish all this, King George III sent Lord George Macartney, the former ambassador to Russia and former governor of Madras, to China. Macartney was instructed to secure a place for British traders near the tea-producing areas, negotiate a commercial treaty, create a desire for British products, arrange for diplomatic representation in Beijing, and open Japan and Southeast Asia to British commerce as well. He traveled with an entourage of eighty-four and six hundred cases packed with British goods that he hoped would impress the Chinese court and attract trade: clocks, telescopes, knives, globes, plate glass, Wedgwood pottery, landscape paintings, woolen cloth, and carpets. The only member of the British party able to speak Chinese, however, was a twelve-year-old boy who had learned some Chinese by talking with Chinese on the long voyage.

After Lord Macartney arrived in Guangzhou in 1793, he requested permission to see the emperor in order to present a letter to him from George III. Although the letter had been written in Chinese, its language was not appropriate for addressing an emperor. Still, the British party was eventually allowed to proceed to Beijing. Once there, another obstacle emerged: when instructed on how to behave on seeing the emperor, Macartney objected to having to perform the kowtow (kneeling on both knees and bowing his head to the ground).

Finally Macartney was permitted to meet more informally with the Qianlong emperor at his summer retreat. No negotiations followed this meeting, however, as the Qing court saw no merit in Macartney's requests. It was as interested in maintaining its existing system of regulated trade as Britain was interested in doing away with it.

Several members of the Macartney mission wrote books about China on their return. These books, often illustrated, contained descriptions of many elements of Chinese culture and social customs, less rosy than the reports of the Jesuits a century or two earlier. The official account of the embassy, prepared by George

Staunton, depicted Chinese women as subjugated: "Women, especially in the lower walks of life, are bred with little other principle than that of implicit obedience to their fathers or their husbands." Although the wives of the peasantry worked very hard at domestic tasks and did all the weaving in the country, they were treated badly: "Not withstanding all the merit of these helpmates to their husbands, the latter arrogate an extraordinary dominion over them, and hold them at such distance, as not always to allow them to sit at table, behind which, in such case, they attend as handmaids."[2] From books like these, Europeans began to see more of the complexity of China. The Chinese, by contrast, did not learn much about Europe or Britain from this encounter.

SOCIAL AND CULTURAL CROSSCURRENTS

During the late Ming, Chinese culture had been remarkably open and fluid. Especially in the cities of Jiangnan, new books of all sorts were being published; the theater flourished; and intellectuals took an interest in ideas of Buddhist, Daoist, or even European origin and, encouraged by Wang Yangming's teachings, pursued truth in individualistic ways.

The Conservative Turn

With the collapse of the social order in the early seventeenth century and the conquest by the Manchus, many Confucian scholars concluded that the Ming fell as a result of moral laxity. Wang Yangming and his followers, by validating emotion and spontaneity, had undermined commitment to duty and respect for authority. The solution, many thought, was to return to Zhu Xi's teachings, with their emphasis on objective standards outside the individual.

This conservative turn was manifested in several ways. Laws against homosexuality were made harsher. Because literati argued that drama and fiction were socially subversive, theaters were closed and novels banned. Qian Daxian, a highly learned scholar, went so far as to argue that the vernacular novel was the main threat to Confucian orthodoxy. The cult of widow

chastity reached new heights, with local histories recording more and more widows who refused to remarry, including those who lived their entire lives as the celibate "widows" of men to whom they had been engaged but who had died before they had even met.

The conservative turn in scholarship fostered a new interest in rigorous textual analysis. Some Confucian scholars turned back to the Han commentaries on the classics, hoping that they could free their understandings of the texts from the contamination of Buddhist and Daoist ideas that had infiltrated Tang and Song commentaries. Others wanted to rely solely on the classics themselves and to concentrate on verifiable facts. Yan Ruoju compiled a guide to the place names in the Four Books and proved that the "old text" version of the *Book of Documents* could not be genuine. Research of this sort required access to large libraries, and it thrived primarily in Jiangnan, with its high densities of both books and scholars.

There are always those who resist calls for decorum and strenuous moral effort, and in the eighteenth century, both the Manchu rulers and the Chinese intellectual elite provided room for the less conventional to contribute in creative ways. Exploration of the potential of ink painting for self-expression reached a high point in the eighteenth century with a closely affiliated group of painters known as the Eight Eccentrics of Yangzhou (see **Material Culture: Jin Nong's Inscribed Portrait of a Buddhist Monk**). These painters had no difficulty finding patrons, even among social and cultural conservatives. Similarly, Yuan Mei, on familiar terms with the great classicists and philologists of his day, was willing to risk their censure by taking on women as poetry students. One of his female poetry students, Luo Qilan, wrote in 1797 to defend him from charges of impropriety, arguing that if Confucius had believed in the principle that women's words spoken inside a chamber must stay indoors, he would have removed poems by women from the *Book of Poetry*.

The Dream of Red Mansions

Women with poetic talents figure prominently in an eighteenth-century novel, *The Dream of Red Mansions* (also called *Story of the Stone*), considered by many the most successful of all works of Chinese fiction. Concerned with the grand themes of love and desire, money and power, life and death, and truth and illusion, it is at the same time a psychologically sensitive novel of manners. The author of the first eighty chapters was Cao Xueqin (1715–1764). He

---

2. George Staunton, *An Authentic Account of an Embassy from the King of Great Britain to the Emperor of China* (London: W. Bulmer, 1798), 2:109.

MATERIAL CULTURE

Jin Nong's Inscribed Portrait of a Buddhist Monk

Chinese painters often combined words and images, sometimes inscribing poems or explanations of the occasions that gave rise to the paintings on the paintings themselves. The highly individualistic painters of the eighteenth century known as the Eight Eccentrics of Yangzhou sometimes carried this practice to the extreme, filling all the space on a painting with their writing. The painting shown here, by Jin Nong (1687–1764), is dated 1760. Writing in his highly distinctive calligraphy, Jin Nong fills the space around the Buddha with a history of the painting of images of Buddhas followed by personal remarks:

> I am now a man beyond seventy years of age who has no false ideas and desires. Though physically I am in the dusty world, I earnestly try to live cleanly. I wash my ten fingers, burn incense, and hold the brush to record the dignity and seriousness of humanity. What I do is not far from the ancient tradition. I offer good wishes to all men on earth.
>
> In the second lunar month, 1760, on the date when Buddha achieved enlightenment, I painted several Buddha images, four Bodhisattvas, sixteen Lohans, and distributed these sacred materials. These works are the product of my deep conviction, not in the style of famous masters of the Jin and Tang. My inspiration came from the Longmen caves that were carved a thousand years ago. When my priest friend, Defeng commented, "These paintings found [a new school] and will be followed by the coming generations," I roared with laughter.[3]

3. Tseng Yuho, trans., *A History of Chinese Calligraphy* (Hong Kong: University of Hong Kong Press, 1993), p. 94, slightly modified.

Portrait of a Monk. This hanging scroll, painted by Jin Nong in 1760 in ink and colors on paper, measures 133 by 62.5 cm. *(Collection of the Tianjin History Museum)*

died before the novel was completed, but another writer added forty chapters to complete it before it was published in 1791. Cao Xueqin came from a Chinese family that had risen with the Manchus. As bondservants of the ruling house, his family was in a position to gain great wealth and power managing enterprises for the rulers. In the eighteenth century, however, the family lost favor and went bankrupt.

The *Dream* portrays in magnificent detail the affairs of the comparably wealthy Jia family. The central characters of the novel are three adolescents: Jia Baoyu and his two female cousins of other surnames who come to live with his family. One of the cousins, Lin Daiyu, is sickly and difficult; the other, Xue Baochai, is capable and cheerful. A magnificent garden is built in the family compound in order to receive a visit from Baoyu's sister, who had become an imperial consort. After the visit, Baoyu, his cousins, and their personal servants move into the garden, an idyllic world of youth and beauty. This magical period comes to an end when Baoyu is tricked into marrying Baochai (thinking he is marrying Daiyu). While the wedding is taking place, Daiyu is on her sickbed, dying of consumption. The novel ends with Baoyu passing the *jinshi* examinations, only to leave his wife and family to pursue religious goals.

Much of the power of *Dream* comes from the many subplots and the host of minor characters from all walks of life—officials, aristocrats, monks and nuns, pageboys, gardeners, country relatives, princes, gamblers, prostitutes, actors, and innkeepers. The seamier side of political life is portrayed through memorable cases of abuse of power. The machinations of family politics are just as vividly captured through numerous incidents in which family members compete for advantage. The maids in the family are often unable to keep the lustful men away, in the process attracting the anger of the men's wives. A concubine of Baoyu's father plots demon possession against both Baoyu and his sister-in-law, the household manager Xifeng. One of Baoyu's mother's maids commits suicide after Baoyu flirts with her. This incident, coupled with Baoyu's dalliance with an actor, provokes his father into administering a severe beating.

At one point Baochai notices that Daiyu has unconsciously quoted a line from a play. She then confesses that since she was seven or eight, she and the other children in her family had read plays:

All of us younger people hated serious books but liked reading poetry and plays. The boys had got lots and lots of plays: The Western Chamber, The Lute-Player, A Hundred Yuan Plays—*just about everything you could think of. They used to read them behind our backs, and we girls used to read them behind theirs. Eventually the grown-ups got to know about it and then there were beatings and lectures and burnings of books—and that was the end of that.*[4]

---

4. Cao Xueqin, *The Story of the Stone*, vol. 2, trans. David Hawkes (New York: Penguin Books, 1977), p. 333.

THE LESS ADVANTAGED AND THE DISAFFECTED

The eighteenth century is considered one of the most prosperous periods in Chinese history, when the government frequently ran a surplus and the population grew rapidly. General prosperity, however, did not mean that everyone benefited equally or that conflict and strife disappeared.

Qing China was both huge and economically diverse. Regions varied in density of population, types of crops grown, extent of trade, and so on. The most advanced area, with the highest level of wealth and commercial development, is generally referred to as the Jiangnan ("south of the Yangzi River") region or sometimes just as "the south." In that region, cultivation was intensive, and farmers often sold much of what they grew. It was common for cultivators to rent land from absentee landlords for fixed cash amounts, agreed to in written contracts. In north China, in most places a majority of the farmers owned their own land, but their farms were often tiny, and they might well be no richer than tenant farmers in the south. There were also differences within regions between core areas centered on major cities and more peripheral areas, where population density was much lower because the land was harder to farm. During the course of the eighteenth century, as population grew, people pushed into these peripheral areas, clearing upland areas and moving to the frontiers, in the process often pushing out aboriginal peoples who had lived in the area for centuries. New World crops, such as sweet potatoes, white potatoes, peanuts, and tobacco, made possible exploitation of land previously rejected as too hilly or infertile.

Villages all across China were "open," not closed corporate villages like in Japan (see Chapter 17). That is, villages held no land in common and had little say in who could buy or sell land or houses there. Because small farmers could easily fall into debt and sell or mortgage all or part of their land, village families could vary markedly in wealth. Families whose land was not adequate for their support often put effort into sideline work—their women and children weaving mats and baskets, for instance. During the winter, when there was little work to be done in the fields, the men might go into nearby towns to look for temporary jobs.

In some parts of the country, single-surname villages were common, with all males descended from a common patrilineal ancestor who had settled in the area centuries earlier. In those cases, village organization and lineage organization would overlap, with the lineage ancestral hall serving as the center of village life. In villages or clusters of villages where families with several surnames lived, the temple to a local god often served as the focus for communal activities.

Villages were connected to each other through marriages and marketing. Villagers normally married people from another village, so their mother's brothers and sisters and their father's sisters would reside in other local villages. Men and boys made regular trips to market towns, sometimes several hours away by foot, in order to sell agricultural surplus and buy needed tools or foodstuffs such as salt and oil. Farmers also needed to cooperate across village lines in order to maintain water-control systems, whether the diking of rivers prone to flooding or the diverting of water into irrigation canals or reservoirs. For projects of this sort, the local village heads might get together, or each village might be represented by several of its larger landowners. Written agreements would be drawn up recording what the different parties had pledged to do. When one party thought another was diverting more water than agreed, a complaint could be taken to the county magistrate to adjudicate.

By Qing times, there was relatively little in the way of legal status distinctions among the rural population. Slavery was insignificant (a contrast with Korea), and there were no nationwide outcast groups (a contrast with Japan). But that does not mean that there was no discrimination. In certain localities, particular groups might be treated as lower than commoners—such as the so-called Boat People in Guangdong and the Duomin in Zhejiang who worked as musicians, funeral managers, and yamen runners. In addition, ethnic differences were a common basis for discrimination. Throughout the south, local indigenous peoples—called Miao, Yao, Zhuang, and many other names—were often exploited and treated with contempt.

The routine of village life was from time to time disrupted by calamity, most often in the form of too little or too much water—flooding or drought. North China was particularly subject to drought, though occasionally heavy rains led to breaks in the dikes along the Yellow River, leading to devastating floods. In the drainage area of the Yangzi River, floods were more common than droughts.

When lack of rain ruined a harvest, better-off farmers might be able to hold out till the next harvest, but those without much in the way of reserves would have to try other strategies—ranging from pawning their clothes, tools, and land, to foraging for edible plants in forests, to sending out able-bodied men to look for work in nearby towns, to the entire family's taking to the roads in search of food. When a drought lasted through two harvests or covered a large geographical areas, the numbers of refugees on the road would swell. Bands of hungry men might well seize the grain stores of the rich or crops in the field. Starving peasants would also descend on cities, expecting local officials to open soup kitchens and refugee camps. The lack of sanitation in these camps, coupled with the weakened condition of the refugees, made it all too easy for epidemics to spread, adding to the famine's death toll.

Bad harvests hurt townsfolk as well because they led to rapid escalation in the price of food. Understanding the law of supply and demand, townspeople would gather to prevent merchants from sending their grain to areas with severe shortages, fearing price rises. They would also protest officials who did not keep government granaries open long enough to bring down prices. Sometimes officials called on troops to quell food riots of these sorts.

The Qing government was remarkably successful in curbing the death toll of major famines by careful administration of granaries and provision of direct relief. Its success contributed to the rapid rise in population in the eighteenth century.

This population growth, coupled with the practice of partible inheritance, led to the proliferation of farms too small to support a family. In addition, many men could not marry because of a shortage of marriageable women—caused not only by the rich taking extra women as concubines but also by sex-selective infanticide practiced by poor families unwilling to rear another daughter. Men with little or no land and unable to marry commonly would leave their villages in search of work. Some would travel with their tools to do carpentry or farm work. Others found jobs pulling the boats that carried grain up the Grand Canal or working in cities as dock hands, sedan chair carriers, or night-soil collectors. When copper mines were opened in the southwest, unemployed men traveled long distances to get work as miners. Both the government and settled villagers were wary of these rootless men. They were quick to suspect strangers when crimes occurred.

Single men often found support in groups called brotherhoods or secret societies. The best known of these brotherhoods was called the Heaven and Earth

Society, but other names were also used, such as the Three Harmonies Society or the Three Dots Society. (In English they are often called the Triads.) To marginalized men, the attraction was security, mutual aid, and empowerment. Drawing on ideas from Daoism and popular religion, the groups promised access to supernatural powers through rituals and cultivation. Appearing first in the 1760s, the Heaven and Earth Society spread quickly through Taiwan, Fujian, Jiangxi, Guangdong, and Guangxi. Government functionaries and urban workers were among their members. The societies were explicitly antiestablishment in that they espoused a rhetoric of "overthrow the Qing and restore the Ming." Members away from home could get in touch with members elsewhere through secret signals or passwords. Lodge brothers helped each other with loans, funeral costs, and lawsuits. Lodges would arbitrate disputes between members and mete out punishments for cheating at gambling and other offenses. But their morality was not Confucian. Many lodges controlled gambling, narcotics, prostitution, and smuggling in their region. The first uprising led by the Heaven and Earth Society occurred in the 1780s in Taiwan, after which the Qing government tried without much success to suppress the society.

The Qing government was also wary of the White Lotus Society, which drew on folk Buddhist teachings that dated back to the Song period. This society had been an important element in the rebellions at the end of the Yuan Dynasty. It was not approved by regular Buddhist clergy because of its syncretic teachings, married clergy, and noncanonical scriptures. It incorporated millenarian doctrines derived from both Manichaeism and the Buddhist idea of the future Maitreya Buddha who would usher in an era of peace. Its central deity was the Eternal Mother, the original progenitor of all humankind. Grieving that her earthly children had lost their way, she wanted to bring them back to the Original Home, identified with nirvana. She sent Buddhas to earth to teach people the true way to salvation. When the end was near, floods, fires, and winds would destroy everyone who lacked faith in the Eternal Mother. Adherents were taught that repeating the mantra "Eternal Progenitor in Our Original Home in the World of True Emptiness" would bring blessings and protection from calamities. Martial arts exercises and breathing techniques that circulated *qi* were also taught as other ways to cure illnesses and promote health.

White Lotus teachings had particular appeal to women, who were welcomed as members on the same terms as men. When leaders were arrested or executed, often their wives took over. A Qing official whose city was seized by White Lotus forces described the woman who led the local group:

> When she emerges in a home, five or six young women will hold tobacco bags and towels for her, and she will be seated at the center of the hall. Both men and women make obeisance: the man puts the palm of his right hand on the back of his left hand and the woman, the palm of her left hand on the back of her right hand. They kowtow in reverence.[5]

The White Lotus sect survived repeated attempts by the government to suppress it, probably because local congregations did not depend on a central establishment. The sect was especially strong in the central provinces, from Sichuan and Shaanxi to Shandong. Itinerant prophets and teachers carried the message to new places. Leaders of these sects often combined talk of salvation with martial arts and herbal healing. In 1774 a White Lotus leader in Shandong convinced his followers that he was the Future Buddha and that his techniques would make them invulnerable, even though they were armed only with spears. They were able to capture several small towns before the Qing sent in massive armies to quell them.

Many White Lotus adherents were pious vegetarians who tried to live good lives. An offshoot of the White Lotus called the Luo sect established a mission to help canal boatmen far from their homes who normally had no means of support for several months in the winter. The sect set up hostels in Suzhou and Hangzhou where the boatmen could stay for free and could get meals on credit, to be repaid when they were paid in advance for the next year's work. Since many of these men were never able to marry, the hostels also served as retirement homes for elderly boatmen. The Qing government, however, was deeply suspicious and had all the hostels destroyed.

In 1793 the Qing government initiated a major investigation of White Lotus congregations, which soon had to take up arms to protect themselves from predatory elements in the local government. In 1796 open revolt began in Hubei and soon spread to Sichuan and Shaanxi. White Lotus forces held fortified

---

5. Cited in Kwang-ching Liu, "Religion and Politics in the White Lotus Rebellion of 1796 in Hubei," in *Heterodoxy in Late Imperial China*, ed. K. Liu and R. Shek (Honolulu: University of Hawaii Press, 2004), pp. 295–296.

villages and towns, and they used those bases to raid larger cities. Armed bands often joined them—martial arts groups and bandits alike. It took the government more than eight years to fully annihilate White Lotus forces.

Another segment of society that often felt aggrieved were non-Han ethnic groups. As the Han Chinese population swelled, more and settlers moved into Miao territories, often expropriating Miao land. The Miao aborigines put up fierce resistance beginning in the 1720s, and officials repeatedly tried to find ways to separate the Miao and the Han settlers, but with little progress. In 1795 there was a great revolt of Miao along the Hunan-Guizhou border, where a Han ethnic group called the Hakka had recently been moving in. The Qing government found the Miao uprisings to be as difficult to suppress as the concurrent White Lotus ones.

SUMMARY

How different was China in 1800 than it had been in 1600? China was part of a much larger empire—the largest since the Mongol Empire. For the first time, China was administered as part of the same polity as Tibet and Xinjiang. China was the most populous and economically dominant part of the empire, but politically the Manchus were in control. The Manchus depended on Chinese officials and soldiers to help administer their empire, but they perfected ways to ensure that the Manchus would maintain their dominance. The Manchu rulers were highly sensitive to ethnic slights, however, which may have made Chinese in high office especially cautious.

Although a large segment of the educated elite alive during the conquest did everything in its power to resist the Manchus in deep dread of another "barbarian" dynasty, the Manchus proved to be very different sorts of rulers than the Mongols had been, and by 1800, Chinese of all social levels had gotten used to Manchu rule. The Manchu rulers made a point to patronize Chinese culture, and many facets of Chinese culture thrived during this period, ranging from historical research to manufacturing technology. The standard of living in the mid-eighteenth century was high, and the population was growing. Benefits were not spread evenly, of course, and as in prior periods, those who were marginalized often also became disaffected.

CHAPTER SEVENTEEN

Edo Japan (1603–1800)

Tokugawa Settlement (Seventeenth Century)

Material Culture: Night Soil

Documents: Ihara Saikaku's "Sensible Advice on Domestic Economy"

Biography: Tadano Makuzu

Maturation and Decay (Eighteenth Century)

Making Comparisons: Neo-Confucianism

The social and political order imposed under the Tokugawa shoguns consolidated trends long in the making. The demarcation of villages as corporate communities, the separation of samurai from commoners, the creation of bounded domains, and the growth of and restrictions on commerce all had antecedents in the late sixteenth century. The structure of family life, in particular the emphasis on primogeniture and the custom of brides serving their husbands' families, continued practices already apparent in the fourteenth century. Yet peace also made possible economic developments that some historians deem proto-industrialization, unprecedented urbanization, and a flourishing of theater, fiction, poetry, and intellectual life.

What distinguished the Tokugawa shogunate from previous military regimes? What were the consequences of the political settlement for economic and demographic growth? To what extent did shogunal efforts to restrict foreign contact isolate Japan? What did samurai do without battles to fight? How did urban and rural commoners make their presence felt?

TOKUGAWA SETTLEMENT (SEVENTEENTH CENTURY)

Cadastral surveys and separation of warriors from the land were aimed at ordering society according to fixed criteria. The Tokugawa brought an end to the conflicts caused by sibling rivalry by insisting on primogeniture for the military ruling class and confiscating domains rived by succession disputes. As a result, a ruler's personality and level of competence mattered less than his office, and the retainers' loyalty focused on the position, not the individual. The monarch and his court lived, according to popular parlance, "above the clouds" in Kyoto. Samurai stood at the top of the official status order, followed by commoners in order of their contributions to society. In principle no one was to change residence or status, nor was marriage permitted across status lines. In reality, status boundaries were fluid. Since changing names changed identity, a commoner woman took an aristocratic name when serving a military household. Individual actors and prostitutes became celebrities, and the exclusive right to work with animal skins made some outcasts wealthy.

Tokugawa Social Hierarchy		
Core Social Statuses	Other Social Groups (Between Statuses)	Outcasts
Samurai	Priests	Blind Female
Cultivators	Doctors	Entertainers
Artisans	Monks	Beggars
Merchants		Prostitutes
		Actors
		Non-Humans *(Hinin)*
		Polluted Ones *(Kawata)*

This status order restricted rural communities to cultivators. In the seventeenth century, most villages had at least one dominant family, often descended from a rusticated warrior, which monopolized the position of headman. A council of elders comprising landholding cultivators known as *honbyakushō* provided a sounding board for matters pertaining to village affairs. The *honbyakushō* households included family members, house servants, and field workers. In central and eastern Japan, complex lineage systems with multiple branches defined relations within villages. Across Japan, social, economic, and political inequality structured village life. The men who claimed descent from village founders expected to be treated with deference; they claimed the largest and best fields, and they dominated village politics. Their wives shared their prestige; a male of lesser standing had to treat such women with respect.

Villages divided up the countryside. A village contained residential plots, rice paddies, and dry fields, each assigned to households. In some regions agricultural lands periodically rotated from family to family. These households cooperated in doing the heavy work of leveling rice paddies and building dikes, managing irrigation networks, and transplanting rice seedlings into the paddies. Women performed this last backbreaking task in a carryover of medieval religious beliefs that sanctified it as a fertility ritual (see Color Plate 17). Beyond this basic level, each household was on its own to prosper or to fail. Village boundaries also enclosed wastelands and forests, with access to their products carefully regulated by the village council. As a corporate entity embodied by the headman, the village was collectively responsible for paying taxes, both the yearly tribute measured in units of rice (*koku*—1 *koku* equals 5.1 bushels of rice, the amount needed to feed one man for a year) and various ancillary exactions—for example, fees for the privilege of exploiting forest resources.

Contiguous villages with definable boundaries constituted the building blocks of domains ruled by daimyo. The shogun had the largest domain concentrated chiefly in eastern and central Japan totaling approximately one-fourth of the total agricultural base. Vassal daimyo (*fudai*) were hereditary retainers. They governed domains; they also served as the shogun's chief advisers and his first line of defense against potential foes. According to a decree of 1634, only vassals whose domains contained over 10,000 *koku* enjoyed the status of daimyo. The shogun's retainers with smaller fiefs, often made up of parcels in several villages, were called *hatamoto* ("beneath the banner"). In addition, the shogun commanded the services of thousands of housemen who received stipends from the shogun's warehouses. Daimyo who had been shogun Tokugawa Ieyasu's rivals or peers were deemed outside lords (*tozama*). Fewer in number than the vassal daimyo, the mightiest controlled large domains that functioned almost as nations. Some of the shogun's collateral relatives also numbered among the daimyo. They were neither wealthy nor politically powerful, but they enjoyed great prestige. All daimyo, who numbered between 250 and 280, had retainer bands to be supported and employed.

Government

The government pieced together by the Tokugawa shoguns developed an elaborate bureaucratic structure (later called a *bakufu*—tent government). The senior councilors—four to five men who rotated on a monthly basis, each of them a vassal daimyo worth at least 30,000 *koku*—took responsibility for policy decisions, personnel matters, and supervising the daimyo. Their assistants, also vassal daimyo, handled matters relating to the shogun's retainers. The *hatamoto* staffed the administrative positions, beginning with the magistrates in charge of finances, cities, and temples and shrines. Finance magistrates supervised the intendants responsible for seeing that the villagers paid their taxes and general agrarian affairs. They also managed the increasingly futile task of balancing expenditures with income. Their staff, and those of the other magistrates, included an array of functionaries, guards, and servants. Although the shogun tried to reduce the size of his army in the seventeenth century, he was never able to provide more than part-time employment to his retainers; 42 percent of *hatamoto* (1,676 in 1829) served in the fatigue regiment, the default category for men without office. Each daimyo likewise had an overly abundant staff of advisers, accountants, liaison officers, attendants, tax collectors, doctors, teachers, guards, servants, and placeholders.

The shogunal and domainal governments developed the most complex, sophisticated, and coherent bureaucracies Japan had ever seen. Retainers learned to wield a brush as well as a sword, understand high finance, and accustom themselves to routinized office jobs. Administrative systems also retained non-modern elements. The shogun bestowed his former family name of Matsudaira on important *fudai* and *tozama* daimyo, both as an honor and as a reminder that rulers were kin. Opportunities for promotion depended on hereditary rank; men born of guards stayed guards. The senior councilors may have been policy experts, but they were also the shogun's vassals. Their duties included watching him perform ancestral rites, lecture on the Chinese classics, and dance in Nō. When he left the castle to go hawking or to visit one of their number, they and their subordinates had to attend him. The shogun maintained a large staff of palace women ordered in a female bureaucracy to serve him, his wife, and his mother in the great interior (*ōoku*). Their responsibilities included a yearly round of ceremonies and managing gift exchanges with the Kyoto court and daimyo families.

Although the daimyo ran their domains as they saw fit, the shogunate started to issue decrees to regulate their behavior in 1615. It limited the number of guns allowed per castle and restricted castle repairs. The daimyo were not to harbor criminals, collude against the shogun, or marry without the shogun's permission. All daimyo had the responsibility of contributing men and money to the shogun's building projects, and they could be relocated from one domain to another at the shogun's pleasure. Most important, the shogunate issued increasingly stringent guidelines governing the daimyo's attendance on the shogun. Known as *sankin kōtai* and formalized in 1635, this system stipulated that each daimyo spend half of his time in his domain and half in the shogun's capital at Edo. Each daimyo's wife and heir had to reside in Edo as hostages. Designed to keep the daimyo both loyal to the shogun and effective in local administration, the system bal-anced the centrifugal forces that had weakened the Kamakura regime and the centripetal tendencies that had destroyed the Ashikaga. *Sankin kōtai* also had the inadvertent consequence of stimulating trade, encouraging travel, and fostering cultural exchange.

The shogunate appropriated certain national responsibilities to itself. It refurbished the highway system with post stations and checkpoints to keep guns out of Edo and female hostages in. For its own defense, it forbade the building of bridges over major rivers. It oversaw the development of coastal shipping routes, took over the mines for precious metals, and minted copper, silver, and gold coins. It initiated an official handwriting style for documents. It forbade the practice of Christianity and set up a nationwide system of temple registration to ensure compliance. In 1635 it forbade Japanese to travel overseas and banned foreign books. In 1639 it regulated relations with the West by allowing only the Dutch to trade at Nagasaki. It delegated the oversight of trade and diplomacy with neighboring countries to three domains: Satsuma for the Ryukyus, Tsushima for Korea, and Matsumae for the Ainu and the north. The shogunate supervised trade with China that took place at Nagasaki; it had less control over Chinese goods that arrived indirectly through the Ryukyus and Hokkaido.

Under the Tokugawa regime, people inhabiting the Ryukyu Islands found themselves forced into much closer proximity to Japan. An independent kingdom with tributary ties to China as well as Japan in the sixteenth century, the Ryukyus suffered invasion by Satsuma in 1609. Although the king survived and trade with China continued, he had to surrender control over his islands' diplomatic and economic affairs, to the detriment of the islanders' well-being. Intellectuals in the Ryukyus tried to craft a new identity by claiming that although they were politically subservient to Japan, they achieved moral parity with both Japan and China by cultivating the way of the Confucian sage.

Relations with the Ainu in Hokkaido evolved differently. There the shogunate had the Matsumae family with long-standing ties to the region establish a domain on the island's southern tip. The Matsumae received the privilege of monopolizing trade with the Ainu in exchange for a pledge of loyalty. In 1669 conflict between Ainu tribes over access to game and fish escalated into a war to rid Hokkaido of the Japanese.

Following its vicious suppression, the Ainu and the Japanese solidified distinct ethnic identities that incorporated elements of the other—eagle feathers and otter pelts for the Japanese ruling class and ironware,

Ainu Feeding a Hawk. This mid-nineteenth-century drawing of an Ainu feeding a hawk depicts the bird as being almost as large as its captor. The Ainu is stereotypically hairy with full beard and heavy eyebrows. *(Brett Walker/Collection for Northern Studies, Hokkaido University Library)*

rice, and sake for the Ainu. Between 1590 and 1800, the Ainu became increasingly dependent on trade with Japan for their subsistence, while periodic epidemics brought by traders ravaged their population. Many ended up working as contract laborers in fisheries that shipped food and fertilizer to Japan.

The Tokugawa shogunate survived for over 250 years not simply because it dominated Japan militarily but because, like Oda Nobunaga and Toyotomi Hideyoshi, Ieyasu and his heirs recognized the importance of ideology in transforming power into authority. Nobunaga claimed that he acted on behalf of the realm (*tenka*), not his private, selfish interests. Governance of his domain became public administration (*kōgi*). He also built a shrine to himself. Hideyoshi actively promoted a cult to his own divinity.

Ieyasu's posthumous title apotheosized him as *Tōshō daigongen*—the Buddha incarnate as the sun god of the east. Enshrined at Nikkō, he protected the shogunate from malignant spirits and worked for the good of all people. (See Map 17.1.) The third shogun Iemitsu claimed that the shogunate manifested a just social order that followed the way of heaven (*tendō*). This way is natural, unchanging, eternal, and hierarchical. The ruler displays the benevolence of the Buddha, the warrior preserves the peace, and the

commoners are obedient. The fifth shogun, Tsunayoshi, tried to domesticate the warriors by codifying mourning rituals, lecturing on Confucian classics, and forbidding the killing of animals, especially dogs (used for target practice). His successor reversed the last stricture, and the eighth shogun, Yoshimune, sought to revive the martial arts. One aim of later reforms between 1787 and 1793 was to redress the balance between brush and sword, suggesting that, for samurai, how to follow the way of heaven was not self-evident.

Agricultural Transformations and the Commercial Revolution

Cultivators, merchants, artisans, and rulers quickly exploited the peace dividend. Large- and small-scale reclamation projects, often funded by merchants at a daimyo's behest, opened rice paddies and expanded arable land by 45 percent. Rivers were diked and new channels dug to bring irrigation water to fields. Countless building projects, partly to repair the ravages of war in Kyoto but mainly to build the plethora of daimyo mansions, shogunal palaces, and merchant quarters in the new capital at Edo and the castle towns, seriously depleted forests. By the end of the seventeenth century, floods sweeping down denuded mountains threatened hard-won fields. The shogunate tried to regulate the use of forestry products, but the agricultural base continued to press against ecological limits. (See **Material Culture: Night Soil.**)

The introduction of better seeds and new crops intensified the use of land and labor. The accumulation of small innovations based on observations of soil types and climatic conditions led to the development of rice varieties suited for specific local conditions. Fast-ripening rice spread cultivation into the marginal lands of the northeast. Farther south, it allowed the sowing of a second crop, often wheat, although some paddies in Kyushu supported two rice crops a year. As in China and Korea, corn, tobacco, and sweet potato, products of the Western Hemisphere, became dry field staples along with barley and millet. In a trend that continued throughout the Tokugawa period, seventeenth-century agronomy experts traveled Japan building social networks of like-minded experimenters, seeking the most advanced methods for increasing crop yields, and disseminating their findings in books.

Cultivators also grew cash crops and developed products based on Chinese technology. The spread of cotton growing in western Japan beginning in the

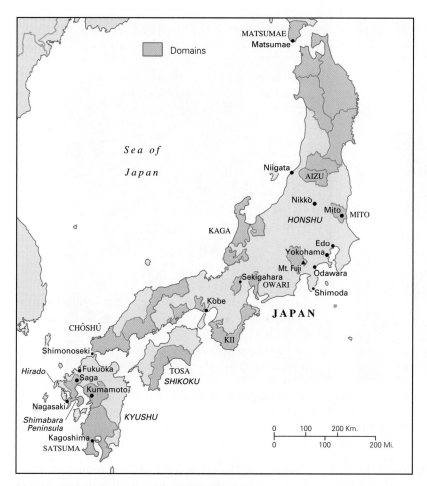

Map **17.1**   Tokugawa Japan, 1600–1868

sixteenth century reduced the hours women had to spend preparing cloth for their families while revolutionizing clothing and bedding. During the seventeenth century, Japan imported Chinese silk and sugar. By the 1730s for silk and the 1830s for sugar, domestic production provided substitutes. The daimyo competed in developing products for export to fund their mandated trips to Edo. They hired teachers to show cultivators how to harvest lacquer, make paper, and raise silkworms. They promoted distinctive styles of wooden combs, paper hair ties, and ceramics. Merchants supplied the capital, and cultivators supplied the labor, although a few rural entrepreneurs managed to profit from the distribution of raw materials and the transportation of goods. Lights fueled by rapeseed oil enabled work to continue after dark. Increases in agricultural productivity spurred demand for nonagricultural goods produced by rural households. The growth of cottage industries diversified income sources

and led to a virtuous cycle of interaction between agriculture and manufacturing. Neither entrepreneurs nor domains tried to set up large-scale production units. Instead they emphasized quality and variety, trying to beat the competition by producing regional specialties found nowhere else.

The agricultural and commercial revolutions meant higher per capita productivity and a trend toward smaller families. After almost a threefold increase in the seventeenth century, Japan's population remained surprisingly stagnant in contrast to the populations of China and Korea at the same time. In villages the extended families characteristic of earlier times broke down into main families and branches or landlords and tenants. Most households cultivated parcels just big enough to support a stem family of grandparents, parents, and children. There was not enough to bestow on more than one heir. Historians have supposed that cultivators practiced abortion and infanticide lest they

Artisans. Cottage industries relied on families. Both the pattern dyers depicted on the screen to the right and the weavers shown on the screen to the left employed men and women, children and grandparents. *(LEFT: Werner Forman/Corbis. RIGHT: Sakamoto Photo Research Laboratory/Corbis)*

have more children than they could afford. Even if the heir died, the ease of adoption meant that a family could usually find someone to carry on the family line. Other factors were also at work. Men often left their homes for months at a time to work in towns and cities, especially during the winter. The female age at marriage went up in central Japan because women increasingly worked to gain experience before settling down. Disease mattered: Smallpox can reduce male fertility by 50 percent. Syphilis struck urban populations. Periodic famines hit some regions harder than others. In the early nineteenth century, population decline in the impoverished northeast offset growth in the more commercially developed and prosperous west.

One characteristic of Japan's early modern growth was that while labor remained in the countryside, capital largely concentrated in cities. Not until the late eighteenth century did rural entrepreneurs amass significant amounts of capital, and they often depended on urban merchants for financial backing. Daimyo traveling on *sankin kōtai* marketed rice they collected in taxes to merchants in Osaka who advanced them

currency and letters of credit. These promissory notes, redeemable at the merchant's branch in Edo, served as Japan's first paper money. Domains later printed their own currency, modeled on religious talismans to gain users' trust. Merchants either advanced the money to make specialty products or bought them at a discount to sell to urban consumers. Some merchants acted as purveyors to daimyo and their women, stimulating the desire for high-quality labor-intensive goods. Others catered to the broader market by selling cotton cloth, lamp oil, and soy sauce. At the end of the seventeenth century, a few Osaka and Edo merchants had become extremely wealthy, and a number of daimyo found themselves deeply in debt.

Urban Life and Culture

Edo's spatial layout mirrored the shogun's strategic concerns. Taking advantage of technological advances in fortifications, the shogun's castle was enclosed behind multiple stone walls surrounded by moats. The shogunate drained the swamp on which the city was built through canals that provided transportation for

MATERIAL CULTURE

Night Soil

The Edo city government left waste disposal in the hands of individual landlords. Daimyo and *hatamoto* contracted with nearby villages to bring vegetables to their compounds and remove waste. Communal toilet facilities in each commoner ward also had to be cleaned.

In the eighteenth century, cultivators planted crops where they had once foraged for green fertilizer. The more intensive use of land forced them to look outside their communities for soil amendments. Vegetable farmers near Edo carted away night soil and other organic wastes to supplement the manure they produced themselves. Separated into solids and liquid and cooked in its own heat to kill harmful organisms, night soil became a valuable commodity.

In the late eighteenth century, townspeople expected cultivators to pay for the privilege of collecting night soil. Landlords insisted that tenants use their toilet facilities and tried to sell their product to the highest bidder. Transactions between subcontractors, wholesalers, and middlemen raised costs. Regional alliances of cultivators petitioned the shogunate to keep prices down.

The price placed on night soil reflected status inequality. Landlords segregated toilets by sex because men's excrement was valued more highly than women's. Samurai received more for their waste than did commoners. An eighteenth-century farmhouse had a toilet for samurai made of polished wood. The tenant farmers and family members used an open pit.

Toilets. The photo on the left depicts a toilet for the use of samurai officials next to the formal reception room at a village headman's house. On the opposite side behind the stable is the pit for family and servants (right). *(Photos courtesy of Anne Walthall)*

goods and people. Bridges over moats were faced with guardhouses, forcing the traveler to make a sharp turn, and no roads led directly to the castle. Vassal daimyo and the shogun's retainers lived in its immediate vicinity, providing another ring of protection. The wealthy *tozama* daimyo had large compounds containing barracks for their retainers, storehouses, mansions, and gardens. None was allowed moats and stone walls, and quarters for the vassal daimyo surrounded them. Each daimyo maintained multiple compounds; the total number was over one thousand. The ruling class took the salubrious highlands for itself, leaving the lowlands directly east and south of the castle for com-

moners. Scattered throughout the city were shrines and temples. Daimyo castle towns followed a similar pattern of segregating people according to status and occupation.

The seventeenth century saw an unprecedented increase in urban growth, from little more than 1 percent of Japan's population to almost 15 percent after 1700. In addition to the castle towns were three metropolises: Kyoto became a manufacturing center of luxury goods, Osaka served as Japan's chief market, and Edo's swollen population of daimyo and bureaucrats made it a consumption center. Urbanization stimulated the growth of commercial publishing

DOCUMENTS

Ihara Saikaku's "Sensible Advice on Domestic Economy"

Ihara Saikaku (1642–1693) is often considered Japan's first professional author because he lived by his pen, writing haiku, short stories, novels, and essays that described life in Osaka during the townspeople's heyday. Here he feeds the merchants' obsession with the making and saving of money by focusing on the details of daily life and the qualities desired in a wife.

"The immutable rule in regard to the division of family property at the time of marriage," said the experienced go-between from Kyoto, "is as follows: Let us suppose that a certain man is worth a thousand *kan*. To the eldest son at his marriage will go four hundred *kan*, together with the family residence. The second son's share will be three hundred *kan*, and he too is entitled to a house of his own. The third son will be adopted into another family, requiring a portion of one hundred *kan*. If there is a daughter, her dowry will be thirty *kan*, in addition to a bridal trousseau worth twenty *kan*. It is advisable to marry her off to the son of a family of lower financial status. Formerly it was not unusual to spend forty *kan* on the trousseau and allot ten *kan* for the dowry, but because people today are more interested in cash, it is now customary to give the daughter silver in the lacquered chest and copper in the extra one. Even if the girl is so ugly that she can't afford to sit near the candle at night, that dowry of thirty *kan* will make her bloom into a very flowery bride!"

"In matchmaking, money is a very important consideration. If thirty *kan* of silver is deposited with a trustworthy merchant at six-tenths percent interest per month, the income will total one hundred and eighty *momme* monthly, which will more than suffice to support four women: the bride, her personal maid, a second maid, and a seamstress. How unselfish must be the disposition of a bride who will not only look after the household faithfully, meantime taking care never to displease her husband's family, but also at the same time will actually pay for the food she eats! If you are looking merely for beauty, then go where women are made up solely to that end, to the licensed quarters. You are free to visit them any time of night you may wish, and thoroughly enjoy it, but next morning you will have to pay out seventy-one *momme*—which is not in the least enjoyable!"

"It is better on the whole to give up dissipation in good time, for a roué is seldom happy in later life. So even if life at home seems dry and tasteless, you'd better have patience with a supper of cold rice, potluck

---

that created and fed a reading public hungry for knowledge and entertainment. It provided space for exhibitions from religious icons to botanical specimens and for private salons where scholars, artists, and writers met patrons. Urban residents paid for services—hairdressing, amusements—that had once been provided by servants. They bought processed food and cloth that their ancestors had made themselves. Labor and leisure were oriented toward the market, and purchasing finished products saved time. This transformation stimulated a consumption revolution—the increased demand for a greater variety of goods, from durable luxury items such as elaborately carved transoms to drug foods such as sake and tobacco.

Unprecedented urban prosperity culminated in the Genroku era (1688–1704), the heyday of townsman (*chōnin*) culture, justly celebrated in art and literature. Ihara Saikaku wrote stories about the samurai passion for boys, but most of his works focused on the foibles of the townspeople in books such as *Five Women Who Loved Love* and *The Life of an Amorous Man*. He also wrote books on how to make and keep money. (See **Documents: Ihara Saikaku's "Sensible Advice on Domestic Economy."**) Matsuo Bashō raised the seventeen-syllable verse form known as

bean curd, and dried fish. You may lie down whenever you like, at perfect ease, and have a maid massage you down to the very tips of your toes. If you want tea, you may sip it while your wife holds the cup for you. A man in his own household is the commander supreme, whose authority none will dare to question, and there is none to condemn you. There's no need to seek further for genuine pleasure."

"Then, too, there are certain business advantages to staying home. Your clerks will stop their imprudent visits to the Yasaka quarters and their clandestine meetings at that rendezvous in Oike. And when in the shop, since they can't appear to be completely idle, maybe they'll look over those reports from the Edo branch office, or do some other work that they have been putting off doing—all to the profit of you, the master! The apprentice boys will diligently twist wastepaper into string, and in order to impress you, the master, sitting in the inner room, they will practice penmanship to their profit. Kyushichi, whose habit it is to retire early, will take the straw packing from around the yellowtail and make rope on which to string coins; while Take, in order to make things go more smoothly tomorrow, will prepare the vegetables for breakfast. The seamstress during the time you're at home will take off as many knots of Hino silk as she ordinarily does in a whole day. Even the cat keeps a wary watch in the kitchen and when she hears the least sound

in the vicinity of the fish hanger she will mew to scare away the rats. If such unmeasured profit as this results from the master's remaining at home just one night, think how vast will be the benefits that will accrue within the space of a whole year! So even if you are not entirely satisfied with your wife, you have to exercise discretion and realize that in the gay quarters all is but vanity. For a young master to be well aware of this is the secret of the successful running of his household."

Such was the counsel offered by the veteran go-between.

Be that as it may, let me say that the women of today, under the influence of the styles of the gay quarters, dress exactly like professional entertainers. Prominent drapers' wives, who in public are addressed as mesdames, are so attired as to be mistaken for high-class courtesans; while the wives of small shopkeepers, who once served as clerks of the drapers, look exactly like courtesans one grade lower. Again, the kimono worn by wives of tailors and embroiderers who live on the side streets bear a startling resemblance to those of the women employed in teahouses. It is fun to spot them in a crowd dressed in conformity with their respective degrees of fortune.

Source: Saikaku Ihara, *This Scheming World*, trans. Masanori Takatsuka and David C. Stubbs (Rutland, Vt.: Charles E. Tuttle Company, 1965), pp. 54–57 (modified).

---

haiku to a fine art, in the process making poetry accessible to commoners in town and country. Passing by a battlefield, he wrote: "A thicket of summer grass, all that remains of warriors' dreams."[1] Chikamatsu Monzaemon wrote librettos for the puppet theater that explored the complex interplay between social obligations and human feeling, as when a young man in love with a prostitute wants to buy the contract that indentures her to the brothel owner but lacks the resources to do so without causing irrepara-

ble harm to his family's business. Caught between love and duty, the couple resolves the dilemma by committing double suicide. Although Chikamatsu wrote for puppets, the literary artistry of his scripts endeared them to amateur performers and raised the quality of theatrical performances.

Two pleasure zones are associated with the Genroku era: the brothel district and the theaters, often located in proximity to each other on the margins of respectable society. These constituted the "floating world" (*ukiyo*) celebrated in woodblock prints of courtesans and actors along with pornography. In the early seventeenth century, entrepreneurs in the

1. Translated by Anne Walthall from *Oku no hosomichi* (*The Narrow Road to the Deep North*).

three metropolises petitioned the shogunate to establish districts for prostitution where it could be regulated and controlled. A moat and walls surrounded Edo's Yoshiwara with a main gate where guards noted the men who entered and prevented women from leaving. The earliest customers were daimyo and samurai. Merchants whose lavish spending brought them great renown soon eclipsed them. In this status-conscious society, courtesans too were ranked.

Kabuki began in the early seventeenth century on a riverbank in Kyoto where a prostitute erected a stage on which to sing and dance to attract customers. Fights over her charms led the shogunate to forbid women from appearing on stage in 1629. Boys then replaced them as actors and prostitutes. Again the shogunate stepped in to quell disorder, banning all but mature men from performing in public. To make up for a lack of sex appeal, actors developed the techniques of acting, singing, and dancing performed on elaborate and frequently changing sets that made kabuki the spectacle known today. It became enormously popular, with the highest acclaim reserved for the men who specialized in playing women. It staged reenactments of the scandals arising in townspeople's society, but it became best known for swashbuckling melodramas set in the past, for the shogunate forbade any discussion of its own affairs or those of contemporary samurai society.

Intellectual Trends

The Edo period saw an explosion in intellectual pursuits. Deprived of the opportunity to gain fame in battle, some samurai turned to scholarship and made serious efforts to understand society. In the seventeenth century, Hayashi Razan formulated the Tokugawa ideology in neo-Confucian terms that saw the social order as a reflection of the visible natural order in that both realized an underlying metaphysical principle. Among his students was Yamaga Sokō, famous for defining a way for samurai to survive during a time of peace: "The business of the samurai consists in reflecting on his own station in life, in discharging loyal service to his master, . . . in deepening his fidelity in associations with friends, and . . . in devoting himself to duty above all."[2] Kyoto scholar Itō Jinsai likewise began as a neo-Confucianist, only to reject the notion of metaphysical principle in favor of studying Confucius himself. For him, the purpose of

scholarship was to show how to put morality based on benevolence and love into practice, a goal achievable by commoners as well as samurai. Such was the cachet of Chinese philosophy that any man who had pretensions of becoming learned had to employ Chinese categories of thought. Women were not subject to this restriction, but for that reason, they had little access to scholarship beyond the study of Japanese poetry. (See **Biography: Tadano Makuzu**.)

Ogyū Sorai gained influence by attacking the neo-Confucian Hayashi school and Itō Jinsai. He argued that only the most ancient Chinese texts, those that predated Confucius, were worthy of study because they contained the teachings of the sage kings, the creators of civilization. The social order did not reflect the natural order of beasts; instead it was an artificial construct, made in history, and that was good. Men needed rules lest their passions run away with them. Japan was fortunate that its own sage king Ieyasu had created the shogunate, and his deeds were not for mere mortals to challenge. Sorai's rational bureaucratic view of government called on samurai to devote themselves to public duty. In 1703 forty-seven retainers from the Akō domain assassinated their dead lord's enemy (an incident dramatized as "The Treasury of Loyal Retainers," *Chūshingura*) because, they claimed, their honor as samurai left them no choice. Sorai applauded the deed but acceded to the official position that since they had broken the law against private vendettas, they had to atone by committing suicide. As long as people obeyed the law, government had no business interfering in their private lives.

The eighteenth century saw a proliferation of schools and thinkers. Dazai Shundai explored the ramifications of political economy. He urged daimyo to supplement flat revenues derived from an agrarian tax base by promoting the production of goods for export. Kaiho Seiryō took Shundai's ideas a step farther by arguing that all social relationships are predicated on the measured exchange of goods and services, a principle understood by merchants but not, unfortunately, by samurai. Andō Shōeki claimed that Sorai's sage kings were thieves and liars who created governments to deceive and cheat the cultivators. In his eyes, the samurai were no better than parasites.

Merchants pondered business ethics. Troubled by the excesses of the Genroku period when some financiers had gone bankrupt through lavish spending and making bad loans to daimyo, Ishida Baigan founded the Shingaku school (literally, study of the heart). He argued that merchants deserved to make a just profit

---

2. Ryusaku Tsunoda et al., eds., *Sources of the Japanese Tradition* (New York: Columbia University Press, 1959), 1:390.

Color Plate 17
Rice Planting. This sixteenth-century painting of *Rice Planting* depicts it as a fertility festival with men providing the music while women work.
(Tokyo National Museum/ DNP Archives.com)

Color Plate 18
The Garden of the Master of Nets. A large pond is the central feature of the *Garden of the Master of Nets* in Suzhou. Notice the use of plants, rocks, and walkways.
(Dennis Cox/ChinaStock. All Rights Reserved.)

Color Plate 19
Arrival of the Portuguese. This six-panel folding screen depicts the *Arrival of the Portuguese*—soldiers in short pants, merchants in balloon pants, and priests in black robes accompanied by African servants.

(Musee des Arts Asiatiques-Guimet, Paris, France/RMN/Art Resource, NY)

Color Plate 20
The Qianlong Emperor Receiving Tribute Horses. This detail from a 1757 painting by the Italian court painter Giuseppe Castiglione (1688–1768) shows the reception of envoys from the Kazakhs. Note how the envoy, presenting a pure white horse, is kneeling to the ground (performing the kowtow).

(Musee Guimet, Paris/The Art Archive)

**Color Plate 21
Dry Goods Store in
Surugacho.** In this
painting entitled *Dry
Goods Store in
Surugacho, Edo,*
customers take off their
shoes to enter the shop.
Male clerks serve female
customers while others
gather around the
manager. The owner is
at the back of the store.

(Corbis)

**Color Plate 22
Women at the Tano
Festival, by Sin Yunbok
(1758–?), Chosŏn
Dynasty.** This painting
captures the eroticism
that is frequently
associated with Sin
Yunbok's depiction of
women. Notice the two
boy monks stealing a
glance at the women
from behind the rocks.

(Kansong Museum of
Fine Arts, Seoul)

Color Plate 24
Noh Robe. Fabric and design signaled age, status, and gender as well as the presence of demons and other spirits. Featuring silk embroidery and gold leaf on satin, this eighteenth-century role signified the aristocracy.

(Photograph © 1981 The Metropolitan Museum of Art/Art Resource, NY)

Color Plate 23
Procession for Crown Prince Sado. Procession returning from a visit to Hwasŏng (modern Suwŏn) to Seoul in 1795 led by King Chŏngjo with his mother, Lady Hyegyŏng, to honor the 60th birthday of his father, Crown Prince Sado, who had been murdered by his own father, King Yŏngjo, in 1762.

(Han Yong'u, *Tasi ch'annuin uri yoksa [Our History, Rediscovered]*, p. 11 left)

BIOGRAPHY   Tadano Makuzu

Male intellectuals focused on morality, politics, and economics. Tadano Makuzu (1763–1825) drew on her observations and experience as a daughter of the samurai to analyze human relations.

Born Kudō Ayako, she grew up in a lively family of parents, her father's mother, and seven siblings. At age nine she insisted that her mother teach her classical Japanese poetry. Ayako enjoyed her grandmother's company because she was a cheerful and attractive woman who loved kabuki. To complete her education, at fifteen Ayako became an attendant to the lord of Sendai's daughter, a position she held for ten years.

Ayako's father, Heisuke, had many friends who shared his interests in medicine, botany, foreign trade, and Western countries. He hoped to arrange a good marriage for Ayako should his proposal for the colonization of Hokkaido and trade with Russia lead to a position with the shogunate. The fall of his patron in 1786 stymied his career and his plans for his daughter.

When Ayako left service, she was too old to make a good match. In 1789 she was married to a man so decrepit that she cried until she was returned to her parents. In 1797 her father found her a husband in a widower with three sons, Tadano Iga Tsurayoshi, a high-ranking Sendai retainer with an income four times that of the Kudō family. Marrying Iga meant that Ayako had to leave the city of her birth for Sendai, a move she likened to "the journey to hell." There she spent the remainder of her life, visited only occasionally by her husband, who remained on duty in Edo.

Signed with the pen name Makuzu, "Solitary Thoughts" (*Hitori kangae*) encapsulates Ayako's views on her society distilled during her years of isolation in Sendai. She bemoans her ignorance of Confucianism because her father thought it inappropriate knowledge for a woman. It was of little use even for men, she believed, because it was too clumsy to regulate the niceties of Japanese behavior. Like other intellectuals of her day, she pitied the samurai for not understanding the principle of money. Instead of a well-ordered harmonious society, she saw competition, hatred, and strife: "Each person in our country strives to enrich him or herself alone without thinking of the foreign threat or begrudging the cost to the country." Townspeople despised warriors: "They take secret delight in the warriors' descent into poverty, hating them like sworn enemies." Antagonism governed even relations between the sexes: "When men and women make love, they battle for superiority by rubbing their genitals together."

Source: Bettina Gramlich-Oka, *Thinking Like a Man: Tadano Makuzu* (1763–1825) (Leiden: Brill Academic Publishers, 2006).

because their profit was equivalent to the samurai's stipend. They should devote themselves to their enterprises with the same devotion a samurai owed his lord, and like the samurai they should strive for moral perfection. Texts and teachers could guide this quest, but it could be completed only through meditation and the practice of diligence, thrift, and fortitude. Baigan and his followers had no political agenda; the idea that merchants might have something to say to samurai was left to the merchant academy in Osaka, the Kaitokudō, founded in 1724. Its teachers denied that merchants caused famine and indebtedness through their pursuit of profit. Merchants, they argued, played a crucial role in society by facilitating the circulation of goods based on objective and accurate calculations. When they applied this principle to domain finances, their advice regarding fiscal policy ought to be followed. A number of them gained coveted positions as advisers to daimyo and shogun.

Other thinkers found inspiration in the Japanese past. The greatest was Motoori Norinaga, whose prodigious memory enabled him to decipher the patterns of Chinese characters used to write *Kojiki*, Japan's most ancient history. Through the study of history and literary classics, he affirmed Japan's unique position in the world as the sole country ruled by descendants of the sun goddess, and he celebrated the private world of the individual. Based as they were on the spontaneity of human feeling, Japanese values were superior to those of other peoples. "In foreign countries, they place logic first, even when it comes to revering the gods . . . all this is but shallow human reasoning." The Chinese had introduced rules that, while they might be necessary in China where people were naturally inclined toward error, were entirely unsuited to Japan, where people were intrinsically perfect in their possession of the "true heart" (*magokoro*).[3] Even when he was asked by a daimyo to comment on the conditions of his day, Norinaga remained apolitical, claiming that rulers should live in accordance with the way of the gods discernible in the study of history and poetry.

Official interest in Western studies began in 1720 when Shogun Yoshimune lifted the ban on Western books so long as they did not promote Christianity. Japanese doctors and scientists, attracted to what was called "Dutch studies," paid little attention to Western philosophy; their enthusiasm was for practical matters, in particular the study of human anatomy, astronomy, geography, and military science. Sugita Genpaku discovered that a Dutch human anatomy book provided names for body parts not found in Chinese medical texts. In 1771 he watched the dissection of a criminal's corpse, a fifty-year-old woman, performed by an outcast. Although this was not the first dissection performed in Japan, the evidence of his own eyes plus the Dutch text led him to invent Japanese terms for pancreas, nerve, and other body parts; these terms were later exported to China. The belief in empirical reason and the efficacy of experiment promoted by the Chinese "practical learning" school already constituted one strand of Japanese intellectual life; the opportunity to engage with Western scientific texts developed it further. Sugita spread his ideas through his writing and salons, whose members ranged from merchants to daimyo. Western instruments such as the telescope and microscope fascinated intellectuals. The insights they gained into the natural world percolated into popular culture when Utagawa Kunisada drew pictures of greatly magnified insects to illustrate a story about monsters.

MATURATION AND DECAY (EIGHTEENTH CENTURY)

Following the excesses of the Genroku period, shogunal and domainal officials fretted over the state of government finances and their retainers' morale. The miserly

Ieyasu had left stores of gold bullion, but his heirs spent them so freely that by the 1690s, the shogunate had to devalue the currency. Creeping inflation eroded the value of tax revenues and samurai stipends, while the growing availability of consumer products stimulated demand. Shogun Yoshimune responded by instituting reforms in the 1720s. To aid the samurai who received their stipends in rice, he supported rice prices even though urban consumers complained. He assessed a "voluntary contribution" from all daimyo of a rice donation in proportion to their domain's size in return for spending less time in Edo on *sankin kōtai*. Instead of basing taxes on each year's harvest, he tried to eliminate fluctuations in revenues by establishing a fixed tax rate. He allowed villages to open new fields in regions previously set aside to provide forage and fertilizer and encouraged the cultivation of cash crops. To reduce expenditures, he issued sumptuary legislation and cut the staff of palace women. He inaugurated a petition box, already tried in some domains, to allow commoners' suggestions to reach his ear. A famine caused by a plague of locusts in western Japan in 1732 brought the reform period to an end.

Popular Culture

In contrast to the ruling class, urban commoners generally enjoyed the benefits of the consumption revolution. By 1750, Edo's population had reached well over 1 million inhabitants, making it perhaps the largest city in the world at the time. A fish market dominated the hub of the city at Nihonbashi; the surrounding streets were lined with shops selling goods of every sort. Restaurants catered to people for whom dining out had become a pleasure. Innkeepers who specialized in accommodating plaintiffs became proto-lawyers in an increasingly litigious society. The draper Echigoya innovated a fixed price system for cash (see Color Plate 21). The world's first commodity futures market opened in Osaka. Kabuki actors incorporated advertisements into their routines starting in 1715. In 1774 a popular actor affixed his name to cosmetics sold in his store, mentioned his products on stage, and placed them in woodblock prints. Best-selling authors accepted money to praise products such as toothpaste and pipes.

The spread of commerce made education both possible and necessary. In thousands of villages across Japan, priests, village officials, and rural entrepreneurs opened schools to provide the rudiments of reading and mathematics. Coupled with private academies in castle towns and cities for samurai and merchants, their

---

3. Sey Nakamura, "The Way of the Gods: Motoori Norinaga's *Naobi no Mitama*," *Monumenta Nipponica* 46 (Spring 1991): 39.

Schoolchildren and Teacher. In this early-nineteenth-century cartoon by Hokusai, the teacher listens to three boys recite. Another student counts on his toes; roughhousing turns into a fight. *(Corbis)*

efforts led to impressive rates of literacy by the mid-nineteenth century: approximately 40 percent for men and between 10 and 15 percent for women. Students studied didactic texts; texts for women emphasized docility, modesty, and self-restraint lest the young working woman slip from seamstress to prostitute. Publishers printed one-page almanacs and Buddhist mandalas as well as pamphlets giving advice on agriculture and etiquette. Some students read well enough to enjoy multivolume works of historical fiction, but for many, the aim was more practical: to learn when to plant crops and how to calculate profit and loss.

The national road system designed to bring daimyo to Edo began to attract increasing numbers of commoners in the eighteenth century. Although the shogunate prohibited travel in the interests of preserving order, it allowed pilgrimages, visits to relatives, and trips to medicinal hot springs. With a passport issued by a local official giving name, physical description, and destination, travelers set off, usually on foot, always in groups, accompanied by neighbors to see them to the community border. Many traveled in confraternities that raised money to send a few members on pilgrimage each year. The most popular destination was Ise, with its outer shrine to the god of agriculture. Since few travelers were likely to repeat the pilgrimage experience, they were determined to see as much

as possible. They took enormous detours through temple circuits and stopped in Edo and Osaka for sightseeing and theater. Men traveled in the prime of life; women traveled either before they were married or after they had a daughter-in-law to raise the children and run the household. Rather than suffer the invasive inspection procedures required at checkpoints, women hired guides to show them byways. Men and women bought souvenirs to ship back home and distribute to those who had given them money before they left. They kept diaries of their trips; some were little more than expense accounts, and others were lengthy descriptions of things seen and heard.

Not every pilgrim was literate or had the permission of a local official. Fired, they said, with the imperative to make a pilgrimage to Ise or some other sacred spot, they escaped from parents or employers with nothing but the clothes on their backs. They depended on the charity of strangers who hoped to accrue some of the merit of making the pilgrimage by giving alms. They also fell prey to bandits and procurers. At approximately sixty-year intervals, thousands of people left towns and villages to make a thanksgiving pilgrimage (*okage mairi*) to the inner shrine of the sun goddess at Ise. Many never returned home. Instead they found their way to cities, where they joined a floating population of day laborers and prostitutes.

MAKING COMPARISONS   Neo-Confucianism

As a philosophical system and set of practices, what historians today call neo-Confucianism had a lasting impact on China, Korea, and Japan. It was distinguished by a search for a unifying explanation for the universe, the physical world, and human nature. Philosophers found this explanation in *li* (principle or pattern), an invisible metaphysical principle that informs everything. Plants, mountains, and people are what they are because of *li*, and *li* provides the link between them. Thus all things are fundamentally one, a view of the world with strong Buddhist overtones. At the same time, *li* is different in different objects—the principle in men is different from the principle in women. What gives things their physicality is *qi*—often translated as "ether," "physical force," or "matter." According to the great Song philosopher Zhu Xi (1130–1200), neither *li* nor *qi* could exist without the other.

Some philosophers believed that since human beings encapsulated *li* and *qi*, knowledge should be sought through meditation; others believed that it should be attained through studying books and examining the external world. What mediates between *li* and *qi* in human beings is *xin*—mind or heart. In its metaphysical form, *xin* is pure and flawless; in its physical form, it is clouded by desires (*yu*) and feelings (*qing*). Because desires and feelings can lead to evil, they have to be regulated.

Zhu Xi used precepts and rites centered on the virtues promoted in the Chinese classics to regulate individual behavior and family life in accordance with *li*. He warned that while food and procreation are necessary to sustain life, tasty food and too much contact with women stimulate desire. Men and women should lead separate lives, and the wife's position should differ from that of the concubines. To train people in the key virtue of filial piety, Zhu Xi detailed the appropriate rites for paying homage to ancestors. The household head and his wife played the central role, and the wife knew that, unlike concubines, she would join the ancestors on the family altar.

In Yuan, Ming, and Qing China, Zhu Xi's commentaries on the Confucian classics became required reading for all who hoped to pass the civil service examinations. The effects of this government-imposed orthodoxy were not as stultifying as one might expect, and in both Ming and Qing times it was not uncommon for neo-Confucian thinkers to reject Zhu Xi's understandings and propose radically different ideas.

In Korea, Chôson period *yangban* opposed to Buddhism seized on neo-Confucianism to order social relations and explore the nature of the universe. In the sixteenth century, scholars delved deeply into the relationship between *li* and *qi*, disputing which came first and trying to quantify their relative importance. In the eighteenth century, the positions staked out in this debate became aligned with different factions and justified purges.

Yangban incorporated separation of the sexes and filial piety into their daily lives. They reformed gender relations in the fifteenth century by diminishing women's status and property rights. As in China, they emphasized integrity, which for a widow meant that she must never remarry. The spatial arrangements for their houses separated male quarters at the front from female quarters at the back by walls and courtyard. Only sons by the primary wife could participate fully in *yangban* society, especially in taking civil service exams. The king had to venerate his father's wife in public rituals; if his mother had been a concubine, she received only private rites. When a man died, his eldest son moved to a grass hut beside the tomb where he performed elaborate rituals to feed and honor the departed.

In Tokugawa Japan, neo-Confucianism served the ideology of rule. The social hierarchy was deemed to reflect the natural order; by a sleight of hand, warriors turned into gentlemen. Even shoguns expounded on the classics praised by Zhu Xi and hired scholars to lecture on similarly suitable topics. While recognizing the centrality of filial piety and compiling records of filial children, samurai turned loyalty into an abstract, all-encompassing dictum for behavior. While some scholars investigated the external world, others evaluated desire and human feeling. A merchant philosopher taught meditation to clear the cloudy heart.

Living the neo-Confucian way was more problematic. Only wealthy members of the warrior class had the wherewithal to segregate their living space. They distinguished between wife and concubines as much for political as for moral reasons, although birth mothers received greater public acknowledgment than in Korea. Rather than waste a political asset, they forced their sisters and daughters to marry repeatedly. At the turn of the eighteenth century, the shogun codified mourning rituals that took into consideration the complex family relationships created by adoption, but Buddhist ritual specialists continued to mediate between the dead and the living. Even the most devoted follower of Zhu Xi's teachings could not bring himself to wail at his father's grave.

Hard Times and Peasant Uprisings

The underside to prosperity, continuing inequities, and injustice gave rise to thousands of incidents of rural protest. The corporate structure of the village meant that protest was organized collectively. When cultivators lodged complaints against unjust officials or pleas that the tax burden be reduced following a crop failure, they petitioned the lord to show compassion to the honorable cultivators because their hardships threatened their survival. As the village's representative, the headman was supposed to take the responsibility for seeking redress from samurai officials dealing with rural affairs. If officials deemed the matter worthy of consideration, they passed it up the chain of command. If at any point an official decided not to trouble his superiors, those below had no legal recourse. According to rural lore, in the seventeenth century a few brave headmen, epitomized by Sakura Sōgorō, made a direct appeal to the daimyo, or, in Sōgorō's case, to the shogun. Sōgorō paid for his audacity by suffering crucifixion along with his wife and saw his sons executed before his eyes. Although historians doubt his existence, he became Japan's most famous peasant martyr.

Few headmen in the eighteenth century were willing to risk their families to help their neighbors. Instead of an individual groveling before his superiors, cultivators marched together to assert their grievances en masse. They called their deeds *ikki*, harking back to the leagues that had bedeviled political authorities in the sixteenth century. In 1764, approximately two hundred thousand cultivators marched toward Edo to protest new demands for forced labor to transport officials and their goods on the national roads. Smaller outbursts roiled domains, peaking at times of economic hardship. Seldom did any district erupt more than once, and protestors wanted redress, not revolution. Yet fear that rural protest would expose such weaknesses in domainal administration that the shogun would transfer the daimyo or simply dispossess him limited efforts to expropriate the products of cultivators' labor.

The 1780s brought hard times to Japan. Mount Asama erupted in 1783, spewing ash that blocked sunlight all summer. Crop failures exacerbated by misguided governmental policies led to famine, a catastrophe repeated in 1787. It is said that the population declined by 920,000. In the eyes of many sufferers, the cause of their plight was not so much natural disaster as human failing. Unlike earlier rural protests that had demanded tax relief and government aid, the majority of incidents in the 1780s focused on commercial issues and the perfidy of merchants accused of hoarding grain while people starved. Commoners rioted for five days in Edo, punishing merchants by smashing their stores, trampling rice in the mud, and pouring sake in the street.

The famine exposed problems at all levels of society. The shogunate had struggled for years with an inadequate tax base and the increasing competition among daimyo, merchants, and cultivators for access to commercial income. Under the aegis of senior councilor Tanuma Okitsugu, it had proposed schemes to force merchants to buy shares in guilds granted a monopoly over trade in a specified item. The guild then paid regular fees in "thank you" money to the shogun. These monopolies angered those excluded, manufacturers forced to accept lower prices for their products, and daimyo who had their own schemes for profiting from trade. Following the Edo riot, the shogunate launched a second reform led by essayist, novelist, and staunch neo-Confucian Matsudaira Sadanobu to rectify finances and morals. He established new standards for bureaucratic conduct that endured to modern times. His "Edo first" policy ensured that the city remained quiescent for almost eighty years.

Sadanobu's reforms also had a darker side. A floating population of men without families or property worked as day laborers in fields and cities. Sadanobu had those in Edo rounded up and confined to an island in the bay. From there they were transported to the gold mine on Sado in the Japan Sea, where most of them died within two or three years. The harshness of this measure brought universal condemnation, and it was not repeated. Instead governments encouraged urban wards and rural villages to police themselves.

SUMMARY

What difference did two hundred years of peace make to Japan? Because the shogunate restricted foreign trade, historians once assumed that Japan stagnated. Such was not the case. Governments developed bureaucratic procedures that taught military men expertise in handling routine paperwork. Ideologues preached the virtue of the public performance of duty. Loyalty to one's lord became abstracted from individuals, a one-sided affair, and was no longer tied to reward. In economic terms, peace made possible an agricultural revolution based on a larger arable, better quality seeds, double cropping, and cash crops that forced people to work harder. Commerce boomed, and people let their pocketbooks regulate their behavior. To be sure, cultivators suffered under heavy taxes. Merchants had to accept arbitrary restrictions on commerce and pay ad hoc forced loans to meet the governments' endemic financial crises. *Sankin kōtai* kept the daimyo

coming to Edo to pay homage to the shogun and scheming to enhance their domain's prosperity. Many samurai could not afford the pleasure districts, nor did their offices keep them occupied. They retreated to the private world of intellectual stimulation and the pursuit of pleasure, where they joined townspeople and rural entrepreneurs in fostering a vibrant popular culture.

CREDITS

Chapter 1

p. 14: "Diagram Showing How Early Chinese Bronzes Were Formed," from *Treasures From the Bronze Age of China: An Exhibition From the People's Republic of China* (New York: Metropolitan Museum of Art, 1980). p. 17: Adapted from "The Announcement of Shao," translated by David S. Nivison in *Sources of Chinese Tradition,* 2nd Edition, compiled by Wm. Theodore de Bary and Irene Bloom (New York: Columbia University Press, 1999). Copyright © 1999 Columbia University Press. Reprinted with permission of the publisher. p. 19: Excerpt from *The Book of Poetry,* Ode 189, "A male child is born . . . ," translated in Paul Rakita Goldin, *The Culture of Sex in Ancient China* (Honolulu: University of Hawaii Press, 2002). p. 24: Reprinted by permission of University of Hawai'i Press.

Chapter 2

p. 25: Reprinted by permission of Oxford University Press, UK. p. 34: "The Yellow River's Earl" by Ch'u Yuan, translated by Stephen Owen, from *An Anthology of Chinese Literature: Beginnings to 1911* by Stephen Owen, editor and translator. Copyright © 1996 by Stephen Owen and The Council for Cultural Planning and Development of the Executive Yuan of the Republic of China. Used by permission of W.W. Norton & Company, Inc.

Chapter 3

p. 37: Figure, "Unifying Characters," excerpted from the *Book Journey into China's Antiquity,* Vol. 2, Morning Glory Publishers, Beijing, China. p. 45: Excerpted from the book *Journey into China's Antiquity,* Vol. 2, Morning Glory Publishers, Beijing, China.

Chapter 4

p. 69: Reprinted with the permission of Cambridge University Press.

Chapter 5

p. 79: Reprinted by permission of Harpercollins Publishers, Ltd. Copyright © 1985 by John Blofeld. p. 87: Stephen Owen, *The Great Age of Chinese Poetry: The High T'ang.* Copyright © 1981 by Yale University Press. Reprinted by permission of Yale University Press. p. 86: "Villa on Zhong-nan Mountain," translated by Stephen Owen, from *An Anthology of Chinese Literature: Beginnings to 1911* by Stephen Owen, editor and translator. Copyright © 1996 by Stephen Owen and The Council for Cultural Planning and Development of the Executive Yuan of the Republic of China. Used by permission of W.W. Norton & Company, Inc. p. 89: Excerpt adapted from E. D. Edwards, *Chinese Prose Literature of the T'ang Period, A.D. 618–906* (London: Probsthain, 1937–1938), pp. 128–144. Reprinted with permission.

Chapter 6

p. 133: Reprinted by permission of the Association for Asian Studies.

Chapter 7

p. 125: Ebersole, Gary L., *Ritual Poetry and the Politics of Death in Early Japan.* Copyright © 1989 Princeton University Press, 1992 paperback edition. Reprinted by permission of Princeton University Press.

Chapter 8

p. 142: Kang-I Sunb Chang and Haun Saussy, *Woman Writers of Traditional China: An Anthology of Poetry and Criticism.* Copyright © 1999 by the Board of Trustees of the Leland Stanford Jr. University.

Chapter 9

p. 156: Edward Kamens, *The Three Jewels: A Study and Translation of Minamoto Tamenori's Sanbōe* (Ann Arbor: Center for Japanese Studies, the University of Michigan, 1988), pp. 166–67, 220, 232–33. Used with permission of the publisher.

Chapter 10

p. 172: Adapted from "The Turkish Bakery," translated in Peter H. Lee, ed., *The Columbia Anthology of Traditional Korean Poetry* (New York: Columbia University Press, 2002). Copyright © 2002 Columbia University Press. Reprinted with permission of the publisher.

Chapter 11

p. 186: Excerpt from Mass, Jeffrey P., *The Kamakura Bakufu, A Study in Documents*. Copyright © 1976 by the Board of Trustees of the Leland Stanford Jr. University.

Chapter 12

p. 198: Li Jing, "Description of the Luoluo," translated by Jacqueline M. Armijo-Hussein, in *Under Confucian Eyes: Writings on Gender in Chinese History*, ed. Susan Mann and Yu-yin Cheng (Berkeley, CA: University of California Press, 2001), pp. 91–92 [ISBN: 0-52022274-1]. Reprinted by permission of The University of California Press.

Chapter 13

p. 214: Excerpt from Horton H. Mack, translator, *The Journal of Sōchō*. Copyright © 2002 by the Board of Trustees of the Leland Stanford Jr. University.

Chapter 14

p. 236: Excerpts from Tang Xianzu, *The Peony Pavilion*, translated by Cyril Birch (Bloomington: Indiana University Press, 1980), pp. 38–40. Reprinted by permission of Indiana University Press.

Chapter 15

p. 250: From JaHyon Kim Haboush, translation, *The Memoirs of Lady Hyegyóng* (University of California Press, 1996), p. 301 [ISBN: 0520200543]. Reprinted by permission of The University of California Press.

Chapter 16

p. 322: Fang Bao's "Random Notes from Prison," from *The Search for Modern China, A Documentary Collection* by Pei Kai Cheng, Michael Lestz, and Jonathan Spence. Copyright © 1999 by W.W. Norton & Company, Inc. Used by permission of W.W. Norton & Company, Inc.

Chapter 17

p. 286: Excerpt adapted from Saikaku Ihara, "Sensible Advice on Domestic Economy" from *The Scheming World*, translated by Masanori Takatsuka and David C. Stubbs (Rutland, Vermont: Charles E. Tuttle Company, 1965), pp. 54–57. Reprinted by permission of Tuttle Publishing.

Chapter 18

p. 318: J. Mason Gentzler, ed., *Changing China: Readings in the History of China from the Opium War to the Present*. Copyright © 1977 by Preager Publishing. Reproduced with permission of Greenwood Publishing Group, Inc., Westport, CT.

INDEX

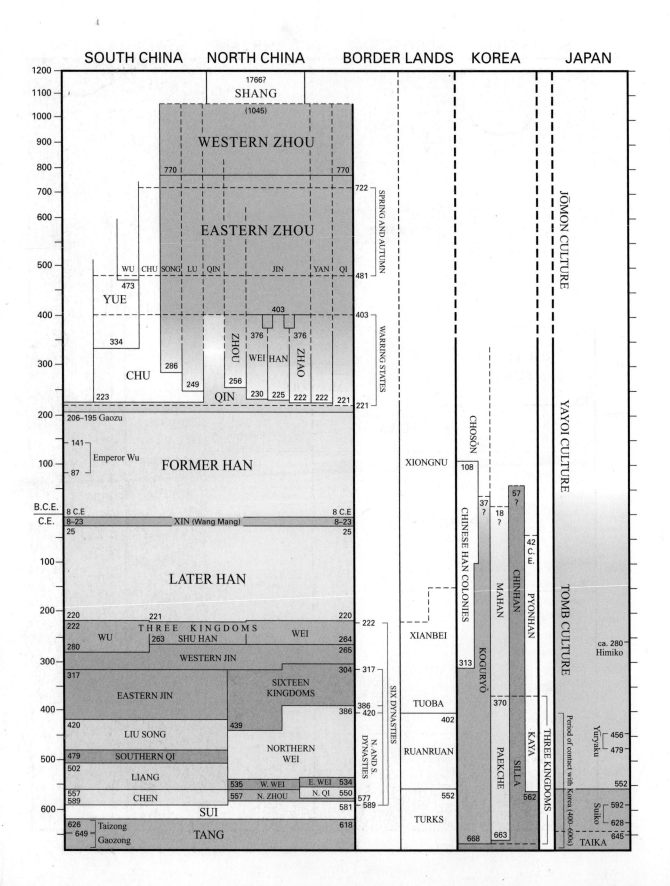